Cause and Consequence in American Politics

JOHN J. COLEMAN
University of Wisconsin-Madison

KENNETH M. GOLDSTEIN
University of Wisconsin-Madison

WILLIAM G. HOWELL
University of Chicago

PEARSON

Boston   Columbus   Indianapolis   New York   San Francisco   Upper Saddle River
Amsterdam   Cape Town   Dubai   London   Madrid   Milan   Munich   Paris   Montreal   Toronto
Delhi   Mexico City   Sao Paulo   Sydney   Hong Kong   Seoul   Singapore   Taipei   Tokyo

Executive Editor: Reid Hester
Director of Development: Eileen Calabro
Senior Development Editor: Lisa Sussman
Editorial Assistant: Nesin Osman
Executive Marketing Manager: Wendy Gordon
Associate Development Editor: Corey Kahn
Digital Editor: Lisa Dotson
Senior Digital Media Editor: Paul DeLuca
Production Manager: S.S. Kulig

Project Coordination, Editorial Services, and Text
    Design: Electronic Publishing Services Inc., NYC
Art Rendering and Electronic Page Makeup: Textech
Cover Designer/Manager: John Callahan
Cover Art: Olney Vasan/Getty Images,
    Sergey Kamshylin/Shutterstock
Manufacturing Manager: Mary Fischer
Printer/Binder: Quad/Graphics-Taunton
Cover Printer: Lehigh-Phoenix

For more information about the Penguin Academics series, please contact us by mail at Pearson Education, attn. Marketing Department, 51 Madison Avenue, 28th Floor, New York, NY 10010, or visit us online at www.pearsonhighered.com/polisci.

Credits and acknowledgments borrowed from other sources and reproduced, with permission, in this textbook appear on the appropriate page within text or on page 490.

Library of Congress Cataloging-in-Publication Data
Coleman, John J., 1959–
    Cause and consequence in American politics / John J. Coleman, Kenneth M. Goldstein, William G. Howell.
        p. cm.
    Includes bibliographical references and index.
    1. United States—Politics and government—Textbooks.   I. Goldstein, Kenneth M., 1965–   II. Howell,
William G. III. Title.
    JK276.C65 2011
    320.473—dc23

                                                                                            2011032797

10 9 8 7 6 5 4 3 2 1—QGT—14 13 12 11

www.pearsonhighered.com

ISBN 10: 0-205-74362-5
ISBN 13: 978-0-205-74362-9

JOHN J. COLEMAN is a professor and chair of the Political Science Department at the University of Wisconsin, Madison. Professor Coleman is the author or co-editor of six books, including *Party Decline in America: Policy, Politics, and the Fiscal State* (Princeton University Press, 1996). His articles on political parties, elections, public knowledge, Congress and the presidency, divided government, campaign finance, and American political development have appeared in the *American Political Science Review, American Journal of Political Science, Journal of Politics,* and *Studies in American Political Development,* among other journals. His current research includes projects on campaign finance and party accountability in elections.

KENNETH M. GOLDSTEIN is a professor of political science at the University of Wisconsin, Madison. He is the author of *Interest Groups, Lobbying, and Participation in America* (Cambridge University Press, 1999) and *Campaign Advertising and American Democracy* (Temple University Press, 2007) as well as over 30 refereed journal articles and book chapters on political communication, voter turnout, campaign finance, survey methodology, Israeli politics, presidential elections, and news coverage of health issues. Professor Goldstein is a consultant for the ABC News Elections Unit and a member of their election-night decision team. He has worked on network election-night coverage in every U.S. federal election since 1988.

WILLIAM G. HOWELL is the Sydney Stein Professor in American Politics at the University of Chicago. He holds appointments in the Harris School of Public Policy, the Department of Political Science, and the College. He has written widely on separation of powers issues and American political institutions, especially the presidency. His recent research examines the relationships between war and presidential power. He is the co-author (with Jon Pevehouse) of *While Dangers Gather: Congressional Checks on Presidential War Powers* (Princeton University Press, 2007), author of *Power Without Persuasion: The Politics of Direct Presidential Action* (Princeton University Press, 2003), co-author (with Paul Peterson) of *The Education Gap: Vouchers and Urban Schools* (Brookings Institution Press, 2002), co-editor (with George Edwards) of *The Oxford Handbook on the American Presidency* (Oxford University Press, 2009), and editor of *Besieged: School Boards and the Future of Education Politics* (Brookings Institution Press, 2005). His research has appeared in such journals as *International Organization, American Political Science Review, American Journal of Political Science,* and *Journal of Politics,* as well as in numerous edited volumes.

Brief Contents

4   Federalism   82

5   Civil Liberties and Civil Rights   114

6   Public Opinion and the Media   155

8 Political Parties 225

WHAT POLITICAL PARTIES DO 227

Parties fill gaps left by the Constitution. 227

Parties recruit candidates into the electoral process and nominate them for office. 228

9   Interest Groups   257

12   The Federal Court System   343

Preface

The talking heads populating cable news channels make numerous claims and predictions on a daily or even an hourly basis. Consider the discussion about the Tea Party movement during the 2010 mid-term elections. Some pundits claimed that Tea Party supporters were the driving force that enabled Republicans to take control of the U.S. House of Representatives in November 2010 and win important Senate victories in places like Wisconsin and Pennsylvania. Others thought that the Tea Party movement doomed GOP chances of winning the Senate because of the impact the movement had in nominating candidates like Christine O'Donnell, Sharron Angle, and Ken Buck—all of whom lost winnable races for the Republicans. Some pundits claimed that the Supreme Court's decision in *Citizens United v. FEC* allowed corporate money to buy the 2010 election for business interests, while others said the electoral forces strongly favored major Republican gains regardless of the *Citizens United* decision. Although plenty of pundits were able to "predict" the Republican victory in 2010 after it happened, or explain Barack Obama's march to the presidency in 2008 after he was elected, the fact of the matter is that the answers and predictions of the "chattering class" are often wrong.

Why? Because many of us—not just talking heads—often attempt to explain events in our political world by oversimplifying and making causal connections where there are none. Too often, explanations flow from our own political viewpoints or the need to explain something quickly. Although such answers make for good television debates and effective headlines, they fail to give us the understanding of the political world that we need to make informed decisions and demand real accountability from our political leaders.

Political scientists, on the other hand, see the world differently. We believe that there are rarely simple answers and that sorting out fact from fiction and the news from the noise can be a challenge. We gather and analyze evidence. We evaluate research and interpret arguments. We use the tools of political science to go beyond simplistic answers in a quest to explain and provide real understanding of politics and government.

We wrote *Cause and Consequence in American Politics* because it was our sense that political scientists are often wary of bringing to bear the full force of our research into our teaching. Our goal is to give students and those interested in politics the critical thinking tools that will empower them to make sense of the political world themselves. We are also "political junkies," and we pull the examples we use in this book right from the real world of politics to convey our own excitement about the political world that we hope readers will share.

What we attempt to do in the following pages is shake away any notions that "the book is closed" on American politics. Rather, we present the study of American politics and government as a dynamic field full of interesting questions, controversies, and puzzles, for which we provide the analytical tools and perspectives—*the ways of thinking*—needed to explore, evaluate, and solve. To that end, throughout the text, we emphasize the importance of understanding the causal factors behind political developments, and we help readers distinguish between correlation (when something is related to or associated with something else) and causation. In every chapter we cover the strategies that political scientists use—and the challenges they face—in answering political questions.

Thinking analytically not only helps in a variety of educational and professional settings, but it also produces thoughtful citizens who are interested in participating in politics. Plenty of civics classes and well-meaning organizations preach participation for the sake of participation, but we think that participation is more likely when people have the confidence to take part in American politics. Part of that confidence can come from knowing the basics of politics in America and how to argue and analyze. We hope those who read this book will come away being able to think and view their world critically, as social scientists do and as truly educated citizens must.

The starting point for this book is our introductory text, *Understanding American Politics and Government*. In *Cause and Consequence in American Politics*, however, we focus, on the most essential causal questions facing political scientists and the key tools that readers need to analyze American politics. As a result, the book is considerably shorter, and some of the themes, topics, and examples from *Understanding American Politics and Government* receive less emphasis here. In addition, *Cause and Consequence in American Politics* is written in a style designed to appeal to students and others who are interested in learning more about American politics without resorting to large, standard textbooks.

An Emphasis on Causal Questions

From the very first chapter, *Cause and Consequence in American Politics* trains students to distinguish between the concepts of **correlation** and **causation** as they examine political phenomena, helping them become better critical thinkers and more thoughtful citizens.

Each chapter opens with a **vignette** designed to draw readers into the chapter's subject matter. These stories will pique students' interest and begin to suggest some of the causal questions one might ask regarding the chapter's topic.

Marginal **Thinking Causally** icons are used throughout to highlight discussions in which particular causal questions are explored. The icons are accompanied by questions that prompt students to actively consider causal relationships.

Thinking Causally Why would a political party seem to downplay the concerns of some members of its coalition, when it knows it needs the votes of these coalition members to win?

The **How Do We Know?** feature in every chapter poses provocative political questions and then demonstrates the techniques political scientists use to answer them. Each box provides context for—and underscores the importance of—the question, highlights the means and challenges of answering it, includes Thinking Critically questions, and ends with a Bottom Line summary on what conclusions social scientists have reached.

HOW DO WE KNOW?

Is America Polarized?

The Question

In the eyes of many Americans, politics in the United States has become nasty, bitter, and rife with conflict. In 2008, presidential candidates Barack Obama and John McCain both criticized the nature of political debate in the United States, with Obama deriding it as "do-anything, say-anything, divisive politics" and McCain labeling it as "mindless, paralyzing rancor."[50] "Two Americas," the "50/50 nation," "red and blue America," and "culture war" are labels said to define current American politics.[56] Is America polarized? How do we know?

Why It Matters

Both for citizens and for politicians looking to influence the policy process, it matters whether Americans

are in two different worlds politically or have political differences that are modest in degree. If the country is polarized, then political success will depend on highly charged mobilization based on strong rhetoric. If the country is not, then success will depend more on mobilizing the support of those whose views are relatively moderate. Party differences might also influence one's appraisal of the health of American democracy. Some citizens might consider different viewpoints to be the lifeblood of a healthy democracy. Others might see high degrees of partisan conflict as an obstacle to solving problems and a blot on democracy.

Investigating the Answer

Television election result maps in 2000 and 2004 showing the country divided sharply into regions of Republican

(continues)

Cultural Perspectives

Chapter 2 sets the stage for the book's attention to how American **political culture**—the prizing of individualism, democracy, liberty, respect for property, and religious rights—influences our politics and government. Students will learn how these beliefs are balanced against each other, how they are defined and change, and how they compete and coexist with other beliefs. Values and beliefs motivate participants in the political process, and they also make some policy paths more likely than others in American politics. When people become involved in and passionate about politics, it is due in large part to their excitement and interest in competing ideas, values, and beliefs.

Case Study

Getting to Know Voters, One by One

One feature of the party machine praised by political scientists was its tight connection with voters. The machine was, in part, a social service or welfare agency. In exchange for providing help, the machine sought votes. It knew its voters.

Party organizations today also try to know their voters, but they do not have the deep personal connection with voters that the machine did. Nor do they provide social services. However, through microtargeting, they try to understand voters one by one to target messages to each. The hope is to persuade the undecided to support the party's candidate and to motivate the already decided to get out to vote.[34]

Microtargeting consists of building huge databases of information about voters. For each potential voter, party workers enter hundreds of bits of information, ranging from neighborhood characteristics available from the U.S. Census to consumer characteristics, such as purchasing habits, brand of car owned, television networks watched, magazine subscriptions, gun ownership, sports preferred, type of musical preference, and much more. Phone or direct contact from a party staffer or volunteer—known as party canvassing—might extract some additional information for the database. Canvassing is one of the main ways young people become involved in party activity.

Examining voter records and lists, which are readily available from states, provides information on a voter's turnout history, party registration, and possibly which party primary she or he voted in. Voter visits to the party's website or, for example, its Facebook profile, provide additional information.[35] Public opinion data are then merged into the file, allowing data analysts to unearth connections between demographic, consumer, and other information and views on public issues.

These data are then analyzed to produce a specific message tailored to a voter's key interests. The database helps generate sophisticated and narrowly targeted advertising, mailings, phone contact, personal contact, and get-out-the-vote drives on behalf of a range of party candidates.[36] Analysts compute scores for each individual to estimate his or her likelihood of supporting the party's

GETTING OUT THE VOTE Political parties engage in extensive get-out-the-vote (GOTV) activities. Urging individuals to vote on Election Day is the culmination of a long and often precisely targeted effort to appeal to voters' key concerns. Through microtargeting, parties appeal to voters on issues of specific interest to them. The parties consult massive databases to discern what an individual's key issues might be.

candidates, so the party can target its outreach efforts efficiently.[37]

Republicans in 2002 were the first to use microtargeting in a systematic way, and it was a prominent part of the party's campaign effort in 2004. The Republican National Committee, in coordination with the Bush campaign and Republican state and local party organizations, purchased commercial databases that held hordes of information on individuals. The party also purchased or received from

(continues)

Critical Thinking

The *Case Study* in each chapter tells an engaging story about recent major political events. These high-interest, in-depth examples apply the ideas developed in the book to the real world, bringing our political system to life and making abstract concepts concrete. Each Case Study concludes with Thinking Critically questions that help students understand, apply, and synthesize key points.

Resources in Print and Online

Name of Supplement	Print	Online	Available to	Description
MyClassPrep		✓	Instructor	This new resource provides a rich database of figures, photos, videos, simulations, activities, and much more that instructors can use to create their own lecture presentation. For more information visit www.mypoliscilab.com.
Instructor's Manual 0205864694		✓	Instructor	Offers chapter overviews, lecture outlines, teaching ideas, discussion topics, and research activities.
Test Bank 0205762549		✓	Instructor	Contains over 100 questions per in multiple-choice, true-false, short answer, and essay format. Questions are tied to text Learning Objectives.
MyTest 0205762980		✓	Instructor	All questions from the Test Bank can be accessed in this flexible, online test generating software.
PowerPoint Presentation 0205854850		✓	Instructor	Slides include a lecture outline of the text, graphics from the book, and quick-check questions for immediate feedback on student comprehension.
Pearson Political Science Video Program	✓		Instructor	Qualified adopters can peruse our list of videos for the American government classroom. Contact your local Pearson representative for more details.
Classroom Response System (CRS) 0205082289	✓		Instructor	A set of lecture questions, organized by American government topics, for use with "clickers" to garner student opinion and assess comprehension.
You Decide! Current Debates in American Politics, 2013 Edition 0205251749	✓		Student	This debate-style reader by John Rourke of the University of Connecticut examines provocative issues in American politics by presenting contrasting views of key topics.
Voices of Dissent: Critical Readings in American Politics, Ninth Edition 0205251714	✓		Student	This collection of critical essays assembled by William Grover of St. Michaels College and Joseph Peschek of Hamline University goes beyond the debate between mainstream liberalism and conservatism.
Diversity in Contemporary American Politics and Government 0205550363	✓		Student	Edited by David Dulio and John Klemanski of Oakland University and Erin E. O'Brien of Kent State University, this reader examines the significant role that demographic diversity plays in our political outcomes and policy processes.
Writing in Political Science, Fourth Edition 0205617360	✓		Student	This guide, written by Diane Schmidt of California State University, Chico, takes students step by step through all aspects of writing in political science.
Choices: An American Government Database Reader	✓		Student	This customizable reader allows instructors to choose from a database of over 300 readings to create a reader that exactly matches their course needs. For more information, go to www.pearsoncustom.com/database/choices.html.
Ten Things That Every American Government Student Should Read 020528969X	✓		Student	Edited by Karen O'Connor of American University. We asked American government instructors across the country to vote for the 10 things they believe every student should read. Available at no additional charge when packaged with the text.
American Government: Readings and Cases, Nineteenth Edition 0205116140	✓		Student	Edited by Peter Woll of Brandeis University, this longtime best-selling reader provides a strong, balanced blend of classic readings and cases that illustrate and amplify important concepts in American government. Available at a discount when packaged with this text.
Penguin-Longman Value Bundles	✓		Student	Longman offers 25 Penguin titles at more than a 60 percent discount when packaged with any Longman text. Go to www.pearsonhighered.com/penguin for more information.
Longman State	✓		Student	These primers on state and local government and political issues are available at no extra cost when shrink-wrapped with the text. Available for Texas, California, and Georgia.

*Instructor Resource Center available at **www.pearsonhighered.com/educator**

The moment you know. MyPoliSciLab®

Educators know it. Students know it. It's that inspired moment when something that was difficult to understand suddenly makes perfect sense. Our MyLab products have been designed and refined with a single purpose in mind—to help educators create that moment of understanding with their students.

The new MyPoliSciLab delivers **proven results** in helping individual students succeed. It provides **engaging experiences** that personalize, stimulate, and measure learning for each student. And, it comes from a **trusted partner** with educational expertise and a deep commitment to helping students, instructors, and departments achieve their goals.

MyPoliSciLab can be used by itself or linked to any learning management system. To learn more about how the new MyPoliSciLab combines proven learning applications with powerful assessment, read on!

MyPoliSciLab delivers **proven results** in helping individual students succeed.

▶ Pearson MyLabs are currently in use by millions of students each year across a variety of disciplines.

▶ In surveys of instructors and students over the last five years, more than 80% reported that they were satisfied with their MyPoliSciLab experience, over 87% agreed that it was easy to use, and 80% recommended MyPoliSciLab's continued use.

▶ MyPoliSciLab works—but don't take our word for it. Visit our MyLab/Mastering site to read white papers, case studies, and testimonials from instructors and students that consistently demonstrate the success of our MyLabs.

MyPoliSciLab provides **engaging experiences** that personalize, stimulate, and measure learning for each student.

▶ **Assessment** Track progress and get instant feedback on every chapter, video, and multimedia activity. With results feeding into a powerful gradebook, the assessment program identifies learning challenges early and suggests the best resources to help.

▶ **Personalized Study Plan** Follow a flexible learning path created by the assessment program and tailored to each student's unique needs. Organized by learning objectives, the study plan offers follow-up reading, video, and multimedia activities for further learning and practice.

▶ **Pearson eText** Just like the printed text, highlight and add notes to the eText online or download it to a tablet or iPad.

▶ **Flashcards** Learn key terms by word or definition.

▶ **Video** Analyze current events by watching streaming video from major news providers.

▶ **PoliSci News Review** Join the political conversation by following headlines in newsfeeds, reading analysis in the blog, taking weekly current events quizzes and polls, and more.

▶ **ClassPrep** Engage students with class presentation resources collected in one convenient online destination.

Unique for American Government courses:

▶ **Simulations** Engage the political process by experiencing how political actors make decisions.

▶ **Comparative Exercises** Think critically about how American politics compares with the politics of other countries.

▶ **Timelines** Get historical context by following issues that have influenced the evolution of American democracy.

▶ **Visual Literacy Exercises** Learn how to interpret political data in figures and tables.

▶ **MyPoliSciLibrary** Read full-text primary source documents from the nation's founding to the present.

▶ **Voter Registration** Voting is a right—and a responsibility.

▶ **Citizenship Test** See what it takes to become an American citizen.

MyPoliSciLab comes from a **trusted partner** with educational expertise and a deep commitment to helping students, instructors, and departments achieve their goals.

▶ Pearson supports instructors with workshops, training, and assistance from Pearson Faculty Advisors— so you get the help you need to make MyPoliSciLab work for your course.

▶ Pearson gathers feedback from instructors and students during the development of content and the feature enhancement of each release to ensure that our products meet your needs.

Acknowledgments

We are grateful to all of the reviewers and instructors who participated in the development of the first edition of *Understanding American Politics and Government*, and the following reviewers who contributed to the development of the second edition, as well as this text, *Cause and Consequence in American Politics:*

Perry Ballard, Daytona State College

Michael Brown, Emerson College

Jason Casellas, University of Texas at Austin

David Chadwick-Brown, Palomar College

Rodolfo Espino, Arizona State University

Jean-Gabriel Jolivet, Southwestern College

Stephanie Hallock, Harford

William Hatcher, Eastern Kentucky University

Sharon Jones, Columbia College (SC)

Sean Kelly, California State University, Channel Islands

Kenneth Kersch, Boston College

William Lester, Jacksonville State University

Seth Masket, University of Denver

Paul Manna, College of William and Mary

David C. W. Parker, Montana State University

Stacey Pelika, College of William and Mary

John Riley, Coastal Carolina University

Margaret Scranton, University of Arkansas, Little Rock

Kate Scheurer, University of North Dakota

Mark Shomaker, Binn College

Chris Soper, Pepperdine University

Patricia Strach, University at Albany

Martin Sweet, Northwestern University

Jonathan Wharton, Stevens Institute of Technology

Thinking About American Politics

PALIN FACES COURIC Many pundits blamed Sarah Palin—and her performance in interviews like this one with Katie Couric of CBS News—for Barack Obama's win over John McCain. There were, however, much larger and more fundamental forces that led to the big victory for Democrats in 2008.

CHAPTER LEARNING OBJECTIVES

After reading this chapter you will be able to:

1-1 Assess the challenges that researchers face when studying causal relationships within politics.

1-2 Analyze the purposes of government and explain why government is necessary.

1-3 Compare and contrast the U.S. government to other democratic systems, and identify core values and beliefs within American political culture.

On the night of September 3, 2008, the relatively unknown governor of Alaska saved the Republican National Convention for presidential candidate John McCain. With her charm, folksiness, and brisk frankness, vice presidential nominee Sarah Palin electrified the large gathering in St. Paul, Minnesota, along with millions of people watching across the country.

McCain, an Arizona senator who as a Navy pilot had made split-second, life-and-death decisions, appeared to have come up with a last-minute call that saved the ticket. With Palin as his running mate, he brought back the base of the party, who had doubted his conservative credentials. Perhaps even more important, Palin seemed to intrigue undecided voters as well as women who had supported former Democratic presidential candidate Hillary Clinton. The McCain–Palin ticket drew enormous and enthusiastic crowds as they traveled together after the Republican convention.

However, just two months later, the McCain–Palin ticket laid in ruins, swamped by an Obama–Biden tsunami that swept across the nation on election night. In the aftermath of such a defeat, when finger-pointing is often part of the political terrain, many of the fingers pointed to Sarah Palin and to John McCain for choosing her as his running mate. Late-night comedian Conan O'Brien summed up the conventional wisdom: "President-elect Barack Obama spent the day thanking the people who helped him win the election. . . . Yeah, and actually, Obama's first phone call was to Sarah Palin. He sent her flowers."

What happened in just two months—from September 3 to November 4— that would have caused this dramatic reversal from Republican savior to national joke? One popular criticism was that Palin was too inexperienced. Not ready for the Oval Office. No foreign policy expertise. Palin's handlers didn't help; they sequestered her from most of the press at the start, and when they finally allowed interviews they were with two of the biggest and most seasoned journalists, Charlie Gibson of ABC and Katie Couric of CBS. When the Alaska governor slipped up on foreign policy, those clips played over and over on network television and went viral on the Internet. Even more damage was done by comedian Tina Fey's satiric portrayal of Palin in skits on *Saturday Night Live,* earning that television show its highest ratings in decades. Added to the mix was "clothing-gate," in which it was discovered that the Republican National Committee had spent over $150,000 on clothes for Palin and her family. Palin had been reduced to a joke and became a drag on the ticket. But did Sarah Palin actually *cause* the defeat of the Republican ticket just 62 days after her electrifying convention speech?

As we will see in politics, rarely does one single factor decide a presidential election. The McCain–Palin ticket pulled even with Obama–Biden and was ahead in important battleground states up to September 15. But on that critical date, Lehman Brothers, one of the oldest and most venerable financial institutions on Wall Street, failed. For the first time since the Great Depression, Americans worried about the solvency of their bank accounts.

Sarah Palin did not cause this unprecedented financial crisis. Nor did she cause the significant dip in the approval rating of the sitting Republican president, George W. Bush. Palin did not cause Republican Party identification to fall 8 points in just four years. She did not send troops into Iraq looking for weapons of mass destruction that never materialized, and she was not the sole reason that Barack Obama put together the most astounding fundraising machine in modern times, allowing him to outspend McCain in some states by 5 to 1. Could she have had an impact on the race in other ways? Did she make it difficult for McCain to talk about experience? Did she cause Democrats to come home to their nominee? ■

Thinking About Politics

1-1   Assess the challenges that researchers face when studying causal relationships within politics.

Causal questions are concerned with "what causes what." Such questions address the roots or origins of particular events or behaviors. They attempt to explain which factor or factors made a particular outcome occur. You deal with causal questions every day: Did I get a "C" on that exam because I didn't study hard enough, or because I didn't study the right material? Which major gives me the best chance of getting into law school—political science or economics? Which will improve my job prospects more—taking extra classes during the summer, or working in an unpaid internship? In all of these cases, you are trying to understand an actual or potential outcome—getting a "C," getting into law school, getting a good job—in terms of factors that may bring it about. In this sense, you are always asking causal questions, and coming up with answers, as you seek to understand your world.

> **causal question** a question regarding the factors responsible for a particular outcome.

Answering causal questions in the realm of politics and government is what political science and this book are all about. The question of Sarah Palin and her impact on the outcome of the 2008 election is a particular causal question. However, before you address this sort of question and identify what factors determine different sorts of political behaviors or outcomes, you should first be able to describe and understand the basic characteristics and organization of American government and society. Furthermore, questions regarding a specific politician's impact on the outcome of a presidential election lead to larger questions about who and what forces influence election outcomes, policy decisions, and governing more generally. What factors combine for a successful campaign? How can politicians and groups influence voters? Who decides what goes on the policy agenda? How do politicians of different parties and ideologies govern together?

Public officials, political activists, journalists, and pundits often have simple answers to such questions. Sorting out fact from fiction in the hurly-burly of political debate can be difficult, however, and can make citizens wary about getting involved in political arguments or political activity. Although you do not need to run for office or get involved in every political campaign, knowing the fundamentals of your political system and the fundamentals of good thinking allows you to keep your leaders—not to mention your friends and family—accountable. How health care will be funded, what sorts of taxes you will pay, and the shape of your retirement are all major issues that will surely be debated in the coming years.

This book provides you with the tools to see through simplistic answers that are often put forward in political debates, cable talk shows, and dinner-table conversations, and to help you become a more informed and active citizen. Throughout this text, you will encounter political scientists' answers to important questions in American politics. As you study each topic, pay close attention to the different ways researchers gather and analyze evidence as they try to understand politics and political decisions. Whatever the topic, we encourage you to take a critical view of how these arguments are framed and made. This will not only enable you to make sense of class material but it will also give you the confidence to evaluate research and make arguments in other settings—academic, political, professional, or even social.

Examples of causal questions include

- Why do some people become Democrats, others Republicans, and others independents?
- Why does the United States have low rates of voter turnout compared with other countries?
- Do the major media in this country give preferential treatment to one political party over the other?
- Why are members of Congress reelected at such high rates?
- Why do views of the president fluctuate so much over the course of a term in office?

All of these questions have outcomes that political scientists try to explain: party attachments, voter turnout, media bias, congressional election outcomes, and presidential approval. In addressing these questions and explaining these outcomes, the first step for researchers is identifying which factors could influence or cause change in the specific outcome they are studying.

There are rarely simple solutions to political questions.

Whereas political scientists see a world in which more than one factor contributes to an outcome, journalists and politicians often focus on one major cause, even claiming it is the sole cause of something. If the economy is bad, it is because taxes are too high. If a candidate loses an election, it is because he or she ran a poor campaign. If the president suffers a legislative defeat, it is because the media covered his proposal in negative ways. If a political protest evolves into a riot, it is because the police failed to keep order. Simple answers make the journalist's job and the politician's job much easier.

Often these single-cause explanations flow from a particular viewpoint or partisan posture, or, in today's world, the need to explain something in a quick sound bite. Generally, they do not represent good theory or good social science research, or even the whole story. Political scientists see the world as complex, with most conditions having not just one but a variety of causes. One of our goals in this book is to help you get beyond the shouting matches in the news and give you the tools to make, interpret, and evaluate arguments on your own—and thus to be an informed and critical citizen who can question the world of sound bites and see the issues in more realistic, more complex terms.

Correlation does not equal causation.

Challenges arise when analysts conduct research on politics. One challenge occurs with such frequency that it needs special attention: correlation is not the same as causation. Consider a fairly silly example from outside the world of politics. Imagine that when ice cream sales went up, so did residential burglaries. Likewise, when ice cream sales went down, residential burglaries went down as well. What would you conclude from this? One conclusion would be that the increase in ice cream sales was somehow causing the rise in burglaries. Perhaps when criminals eat ice cream, they get a sudden rush of carbohydrate energy and break into the nearest house they can find. Or maybe it works the other way. Criminals who have just broken into a home have more money to spend. With more money to spend, they buy more of all the things they normally buy—including ice cream. Most likely, however, it is probably the case that during the summer, people buy more ice cream in order to cool down. Also during the summer, people tend to go on vacation, leaving their homes empty. These homes then become attractive targets for burglars.

Thus, ice cream sales and residential burglaries move up and down together; they are correlated and therefore are associated with one another. But, in this case, **correlation** does not necessarily mean **causation**; that is, increased ice cream sales do not cause increased burglary.

Consider another example. It is a fact that the more firefighters who respond to a fire, the worse the damage and the injuries. Are more firefighters getting in the way of each other and causing injuries? Not likely. A more likely explanation is that this is another case of two factors that occur together—they are related but their relationship is not causal. Political scientists call this a **spurious relationship**. The more serious the fire, the more firefighters that respond. Of course, the more serious the fire, the more likely it is that damage and injuries will occur. The same factor that is influencing the number of firefighters that are sent is also influencing the amount of damages and injuries that result.

correlation a relationship between factors such that change in one is accompanied by change in the other.

causation a relationship between variables such that change in the value of one is directly responsible for change in the value of the other.

spurious relationship a relationship between variables that reflects correlation but not causation.

FIGURE 1-1 Correlation Does Not Equal Causation.

When you hear people make causal arguments, make sure there is not some other factor at work. A small fire will probably cause less damage and fewer injuries, but not because there are fewer firefighters.

The concept of a relationship that is correlated but not causal is illustrated in the simple "inverted V" diagram in Figure 1-1. It illustrates how a third factor is influencing both of the other two outcomes. In this case, the seriousness of the fire influences both the number of firefighters who are called to the fire and the amount of damage from the fire.

Now, consider an example from the world of politics. Congressional studies show that politicians tend to vote in ways consistent with the preferences of the interest groups that contribute to their campaigns. Politicians who receive funds from the National Rifle Association (NRA), for example, reliably vote against gun control legislation and in support of an expansive interpretation of the Second Amendment to the Constitution, which guarantees citizens the right to bear arms.

You could conclude from this example that the NRA is buying votes—that the correlation between their campaign contributions and the votes of members of Congress is actually evidence of causation. This is precisely the sort of case, however, in which one must exercise caution. Maybe the NRA supports those candidates who vote in favor of its issue positions. Rather than the NRA buying votes with its contributions, maybe members of Congress are attracting NRA contributions with their votes. Again, what at first appears to be a case of correlation and causation is not so straightforward. There may be another more complex, more realistic explanation.

How do you sort through such issues? First, for a change in a particular factor or situation to cause a change in an outcome, the situation must precede the outcome. World War II could not have caused World War I. If you want to assert a causal relationship between two factors, make sure that any change in the value of the one precedes a change in the value of the other. Second, try to rule out the possibility of outside factors that may be responsible for the movement or change. For example, a researcher in France found a strong, positive correlation between young men who play sports and those who took

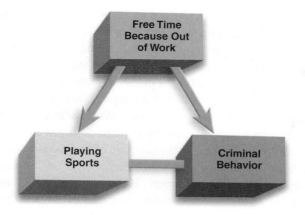

FIGURE 1-2 Playing Sports Does Not Lead to Criminal Behavior.

Riots among the youth in France began in the suburbs of Paris in October 2005. Although many of the rioters played sports, their criminal behavior was not caused by playing sports. Other factors may have caused both of these behaviors, such as not having jobs and thus having more time for both sports and criminal activity. Correlation does not equal causation.

part in riots in the suburbs of France's biggest cities. The argument was that playing sports made young men more aggressive and prone to violence. This finding seems surprising since conventional wisdom and the rationale behind the funding of many sports programs is that they instill discipline and keep kids off the streets—helping to decrease crime. The positive correlation between playing sports and violent behavior could be driven by a third factor. We know that those without jobs are more likely to engage in crime. Perhaps those without jobs also have more time to play sports (see Figure 1-2)?

This example reinforces an earlier point: the world is complex, and there is rarely a single cause for any observed effect. We should always be careful, therefore, to consider all variables that might be driving a relationship we have observed. Throughout this text, we will be examining causal relationships. Such discussions will be highlighted by a marginal causation flag like the one in the margin here.

Thinking Causally
Causality flags in subsequent chapters provide a question that highlights the causal question being explored.

How do we know that we are right?

How do political scientists arrive at answers that they can be confident are better than the simple, single-cause answers? What techniques do they use and what techniques can you use to be a more informed citizen and make better arguments? The explanations in this book are based on the findings of the most recent research in our field. But, instead of just presenting you with the results of that research and expecting you to accept it, we want to help you understand how such research is done and how you can employ good research and good thinking both in and out of the classroom. Hence, subsequent chapters contain a feature called "How Do We Know?"

The "How Do We Know?" features begin with an important research question, puzzle, or serious methodological challenge relevant to the material in the chapter and to being a good citizen. For example, when we study political participation, we will examine how we know how to calculate voter turnout.

And when we study elections, we will examine the challenges involved in determining the effect of campaign spending on election outcomes. We describe each question, puzzle, or challenge in some detail and tell you why political scientists consider it important. We then explain how scholars have tried to answer the question, solve the puzzle, or meet the challenge using the methods and principles discussed in this chapter. Through the "How Do We Know?" features, we hope you will see how political scientists approach their work, and will begin to use some of those methods as you observe the activities of American government and the coverage of those events in the media.

We also want you to see how many of the concepts we discuss in the book have tangible, real-world consequences. We study politics and tackle causal questions because we find issues revolving around elections, presidential power, congressional decisions, and public policy debates to be interesting and important. Accordingly, throughout this book, we will illustrate important concepts and arguments with up-to-date and exciting examples of politics and political decision making. Every chapter will begin with a short story that illustrates a key puzzle for the subject at hand. In addition, each chapter contains a Case Study section that examines in more depth how citizens or our leaders went about making political decisions or how a particular political event played itself out.

Government and Why It Is Necessary

1-2   Analyze the purposes of government and explain why government is necessary.

government the institutions that have the authority and capacity to create and enforce public policies (rules) for a specific territory and people.

When this book refers to **government**, it means the institutions that create and enforce rules for a specific territory and people. As we noted previously, there are many governments in the United States. Although this book focuses almost exclusively on the central or national government based in Washington, D.C., a citizen of the United States is also subject to the authority of many other governments. These include state government, county government, city and town councils, local school boards, and special entities that cross the boundaries of local governments such as water, tourism, and transportation authorities. All may have direct relevance to you and your family as they determine the amount of local taxes you pay, the quality of your schools, and the size of your community's police force.

Citizens in a democracy make a fundamental bargain with their government.

Government is different from other institutions in society in that it has a broad right to use force. To put the matter bluntly, government can make citizens do things they otherwise might not do (such as pay taxes, educate their children, carry car insurance, and pay for lost library books). If citizens refuse to do these things, or insist on doing things that are prohibited by law, government can take action against them—imposing financial or other penalties, including extreme penalties, such as life imprisonment or, in some states, death.

No other segment of society has such wide-ranging authority or ability to enforce its rules. Even corporations and wealthy individuals, which many Americans think of as very powerful, ultimately must use the court system—that is, the government—to get others to do what they want.

Why do people willingly grant government this monopoly on force and compulsion? Because, as people often say about getting older, it beats the alternative. The alternative to a government monopoly on force is a collection of individuals trying to impose their will on each other. Imagine, for example, that your neighbor was hungry, while you had abundant food. If you did not wish to share, your neighbor might attempt to steal some of your food in order to feed his family. Without government, the only way to stop this would be to take matters into your own hands. You would have to forcibly prevent your

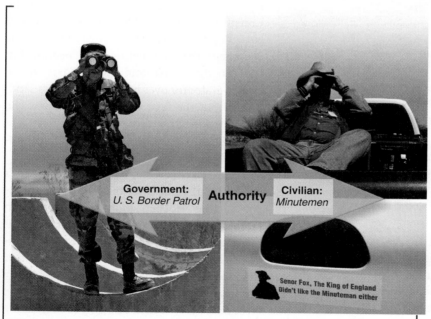

Government:
U. S. Border Patrol   **Authority**   **Civilian:**
Minutemen

Senor Fox, The King of England Didn't like the Minuteman either

WHOSE JOB IS IT?

One of the core definitions of government is that it has the sole authority to enforce laws. On the U.S.–Mexican border, some citizens and groups like the Minutemen are taking the law into their own hands to discourage illegal immigration. What should citizens do if they believe the government is not providing essential services?

neighbor from stealing. He, of course, would try to resist all of this. Now imagine this scenario multiplied tens of thousands of times per day, as men and women pursue their own self-interests without any restrictions, regulations, or protection provided by a governing authority. In the words of Thomas Hobbes, a famous political thinker writing during the English Civil War in the 1600s in his treatise *Leviathan*, it would soon lead to "a war of all against all," and a world in which life was "solitary, poor, nasty, brutish, and short."[1]

Governments arise or must arise because individuals do not wish to live in such a world. Accordingly, they enter into a **social contract** with one another to create, and give authority to, a governing body with a legal monopoly on power or force. Under this arrangement, individuals give up any claim to use force to get what they want. They give the instruments of compulsion—laws, courts, police, prosecutors, and prisons, for example—to the arms of government. In exchange for these, individuals get to enjoy life, liberty, and property without constant fear of outside interference. In the United States, the social contract is the Constitution. In Chapter 3, we will discuss in great depth the nature and logic behind this document that has defined the relationship between the people and their leaders in the United States for over two hundred years. And, throughout the text, we will discuss how the Constitution structures the institutions and the political decisions and debates that happen today.

The idea of government as a social contract was popularized by three major political thinkers—Thomas Hobbes, John Locke, and Jean Jacques Rousseau.[2] Among those Enlightenment philosophers who influenced the framers of the U.S. Constitution, few loomed larger than Locke. Writing in seventeenth-century Britain, Locke laid a logical foundation for the creation of government and civil society. Locke was primarily concerned with the protection of individual property, by which he meant each individual's "life, liberty, and estate." Locke shared Hobbes' concern that in the state of

social contract an agreement among members of a society to form and recognize the authority of a centralized government that is empowered to make and enforce laws governing the members of that society.

A WAR OF ALL AGAINST ALL
Thomas Hobbes's *Leviathan* popularized the idea of a social contract that people enter into with one another to create and give authority to government.

nature individual property was continually threatened. Individuals, then, logically surrendered some rights to a government so that their property might be protected.

Notice that in Locke's thinking, government receives its authority from the people. The people decide, through their contract with one another, which rights and authorities they will give over to government and which they will retain for themselves. Moreover, if the government breaks its side of the contract and engages in tyranny, the people retain the right to revolt. Indeed, for philosophers like Locke, revolution constituted the ultimate check on government tyranny.

Because in a democracy governmental authority rests on an agreement among the governed, that authority can be modified. In the United States, for example, the people can change government's authority by changing or amending the Constitution. Or if they wish, the people can revoke the authority of government altogether. This is one check against the possibility of government overstepping its bounds in the social contract agreement. In **authoritarian (or totalitarian) systems**, in which one person or group enjoys total power, there are no such checks.

Government provides public goods and services.

Government not only protects us from each other, it also provides us with **public goods**. Public goods are products or services that are enjoyed by all citizens and are unlikely to be provided by anyone other than government.

The best example of a public good is national defense. The United States currently spends more than $400 billion per year on various elements of its national defense. This kind of investment, year in and year out, is simply beyond the reach of any private-sector institution.

National defense is also difficult to exclude from those unwilling to pay for it. Imagine that U.S. national defense was provided by a private company, and that individual consumers could choose whether they wished to pay to be defended. If a missile were headed toward a state that had not paid for this service, there would be no way for the defense company to protect only those homeowners who had paid its services. Instead, the company would have to defend all of the state's residents.

Such a scenario is problematic in two respects. First, the company is providing a service and not being compensated by everyone benefiting from it. Second, homeowners who did pay for the service would quickly begin to think they were being taken advantage of. Why should they continue to pay for the service if others will receive the service for free?

Government overcomes such problems by providing the service itself and then compelling everyone to contribute by paying taxes. Any situation

authoritarian (or totalitarian) system a political system in which one person or group has absolute control over the apparatus of government, and in which popular input in government is minimal or nonexistent.

public goods goods (and services) that are enjoyed by all citizens and unlikely to be provided by any organization other than the government.

that has the characteristics of a public good will be a prime area for government involvement.

Although government's primary responsibilities are to keep order, protect individual rights, and provide public goods, in practice, government's activities extend well beyond these areas. One of the federal government's largest areas of responsibility, for example, is providing retirement security for workers and their families through the Social Security system. The government does this even though provision of Social Security is unrelated to ensuring public order or preserving individual rights. Furthermore, government provides Social Security even though it is not a public good.

Politics is about influencing decisions.

Of course, exactly which goods and services are public and how they are provided can vary significantly depending on who gets to decide this. In the context of this book, **politics** refers to individual and collective efforts to influence the workings of government. Engaging in politics, therefore, means trying to influence

politics individual and collective efforts to influence the workings of government.

- who will lead government,
- how government will operate and make decisions,
- what the nature and substance of government decisions will be, and
- how government enforces its decisions.

Often, politics is referred to in a negative manner: "it was all about politics," or so and so "was just playing politics." But there is nothing inherently negative in the definition of politics. Certainly, politics can in some ways be distasteful to people. But efforts to influence the workings of government can also be noble and high minded.

Furthermore, although we might cringe at times at the way politics is conducted, it is surely better than the alternative. Without politics, many differences would be settled violently, outside the accepted processes of government. Americans experienced that most clearly in the Civil War, when differences over slavery were settled on the battlefield and at the cost of hundreds of thousands of lives.

One of the differences Americans have with each other is over which issues are appropriate for government consideration. For example, is the content of movies, music, and video games a purely private matter, or is it a public concern? Should government have the right to require that movies, music, and video games come with a rating label?

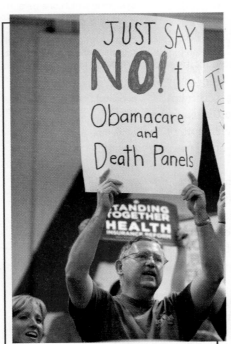

MAKING YOUR VOICE HEARD
Here, a man exercises his right to be heard by protesting against the Democratic health care reform plan at a town hall meeting in 2010.

One policy debate that resulted in legislation during the Obama administration was whether the federal government should provide every citizen with health insurance. The debate was really about whether health care was mostly a private concern or a public concern. Should health insurance coverage be a public matter decided by the government? Should it be a private matter, decided by individual citizens and their employers? Or does it fall somewhere in the middle?

Clearly, then, politics "starts" even before an issue makes it to the governmental agenda. As this book will frequently note, much of the substance of politics is devoted to the complex questions about which issues belong on that agenda in the first place.

Contexts for Studying American Government and Politics

1-3 Compare and contrast the U.S. government to other democratic systems, and identify core values and beliefs within American political culture.

Helping you begin to think logically and carefully in investigating important causal questions related to American government is a main goal of this book. We think that understanding how government and politics in America work is important and even exciting. Today, however, lots of partisan bickering and hyperbolic media coverage of politics can turn people off and make them cynical about their government. Pundits and politicians make causal claims at every turn, and it can be difficult to think about wading into these arguments and participating in politics. That said, for American democracy to survive and thrive, students must engage in politics and in political arguments. We believe that providing you with the tools to explore answers to political questions and make political arguments can make you more confident and give you the skills to be more thoughtful, critical, and empowered citizens.

The presidential system and rights are central to American government.

Democracy, a word derived from ancient Greek, means "rule by the many" (in contrast to its opposite, **autocracy**, which means "rule by a single person," such as a king or emperor). The defining principle in a democracy is that government is based on the consent of the governed. In other words, democratic government operates at the pleasure or will of the people.

Democracy in its purest form is known as **direct democracy**. In a direct democracy, the people vote directly on laws. Many U.S. states, such as California, have a form of direct democracy in which citizens can both

democracy a form of government in which the people rule. This can take place directly, through participation by the people in actual lawmaking, or indirectly, through free elections in which the people choose representatives to make laws on their behalf.

autocracy a form of government in which a single person rules with effectively unlimited power.

direct democracy a form of democracy in which the people themselves make the laws and set the policies adopted by the government.

initiate and vote on ballot measures to change state law. (Examples are the initiatives in a number of states to amend the state constitution to ban same-sex marriage.)

The U.S. federal government, however, has no such mechanism. It is organized entirely as a **representative democracy**. In a representative democracy, also known as a republic, people vote for their leaders through elections. But those leaders, not the people themselves, make the laws. Whether direct or representative, democracy implies more than just providing avenues for individuals to influence government. American democracy, for example, is also characterized by the following principles:

representative democracy a form of democracy in which the people, through free elections, select representatives to make laws on their behalf and set policies adopted by the government; also known as a republic.

- Political equality. All adult Americans (with some narrow exceptions) have the right to vote, and each American's vote counts equally. Furthermore, all adult Americans have an equal right to participate in politics at every level.

- Plurality rule and minority rights. Plurality rule means that whoever or whatever gets the most votes wins, and in American politics the will of the plurality of people usually prevails. However, pluralities may not use their dominant status to trample the rights of those in the minority. Specific minority rights are guaranteed in state and federal law, in state and federal constitutions, in state and federal court decisions, and in the operating rules at various levels of government. Thus, even if one group could muster a winning margin for the proposition that a smaller group be denied the right to vote, state and federal constitutions would prevent this from happening.

- Equality before the law. With only a few exceptions, every American has the same legal rights and obligations as do all other Americans. Every American is subject to the same laws and must be treated the same by the government. Of course, in reality, this is a principle or goal that has not been fully accomplished in American democracy.

constitutional democracy a form of democracy in which there is a foundational document (such as the U.S. Constitution) that describes the structure, powers, and limits of government.

America is a **constitutional democracy**. Thus, the U.S. Constitution is a document with the force of law that defines and constrains government's exercise of power. It expressly identifies, for example, the responsibilities of each branch of government, ensuring that the president, Congress, or the courts will not overreach. The Constitution also makes clear, through the Bill of Rights, that the government must do certain things and may not do certain things. For example, it must ensure that criminal defendants receive a speedy and fair trial. And it must not limit freedom of speech, religion, or assembly.

As we will discuss in Chapter 2 on political culture, people's attitudes toward their government, their role as citizens in a democracy, and their support for the freedoms that government is supposed to protect are highly important to the healthy functioning of a democratic government.

Politics in America is not the only model for politics or democracy.

America is one among a number of the world's democracies. It shares some common features with all of them, such as a commitment to majority rule through elections. It also differs from them in many respects. The U.S. Constitution, for example, is rightly seen as a limiting document, one intended by the founders as a bulwark against the possibility of governmental tyranny. Not all democracies set such limits on themselves at their founding. When Israel became a state, major political interests there were unable to agree on a constitution. In place of a single constitutional document, therefore, Israel has a series of "basic laws" and court decisions that have accumulated over the years. These define the contours of government responsibility. Similarly, the United Kingdom has no single, limiting document like the U.S. Constitution. Instead, it has an evolving set of laws, judicial decisions, customs, and practices that are the rough equivalent of American constitutional law.

American democracy also differs from others in that it is a federal system in which there is a national government with responsibility for the affairs of the nation as a whole, and 50 separate state governments, each with responsibility for affairs within state borders.

Federalism is not the only structure by which a democracy can be organized. France, Japan, and Uruguay, on the one hand, have only one layer of decision-making authority—at the national level. In these countries, there are no equivalents to American governors or state legislatures. Canada, Germany, and India, on the other hand, are organized as federal systems—with a national government and regional governments, just as in the United States.

Finally, the United States differs from most other democracies in being a **presidential system** rather than a parliamentary one. In a presidential system, the voters select separately their chief executive and their legislators. It is possible for a voter to cast one vote for a Republican presidential candidate and a separate vote for a Democratic senatorial candidate.

In a **parliamentary system**, this kind of "split-ticket" voting, in which one votes for one party for president and another for Congress, would be impossible. In fact, in the United Kingdom, voters do not cast a ballot for the chief executive at all. Instead, they vote for representatives to the national legislative assembly, the House of Commons. From among their ranks, the members of that body then choose the chief executive, the prime minister.

On occasion, this book will make these sorts of comparisons, contrasting American politics and government with the corresponding processes and institutions in other countries. These cross-national comparisons can also shed light on underlying causal processes here in the United States and help us make causal arguments about the roles of parties, elections, culture, and other aspects of American politics.

presidential system
a political system in which the head of the executive branch is selected by some form of popular vote and serves a fixed term of office. The United States has a presidential system.

parliamentary system
a political system in which the head of the executive branch is selected by members of the legislature rather than by popular vote.

Unique values and attitudes define politics in America.

American politics and government are continually shaped by the uniquely American **political culture**. Political culture refers to the orientation of citizens toward the political system and toward themselves as actors in it—the basic values, beliefs, attitudes, predispositions, and expectations that citizens bring to political life.

political culture the values and beliefs of citizens toward the political system and toward themselves as actors in it.

The United States has a dominant political culture, sometimes referred to as the American creed. The main ideas and values that make up the creed are individualism, democracy, equality, and liberty, as well as respect for private property and religion. Most Americans strongly embrace these concepts in the abstract, and often in specific cases as well. Often these values, however, can clash with one another. For example, does equality dictate that everyone in America should have equal incomes? Not necessarily. When Americans express their belief in the value of equality, they generally mean equality of opportunity—everyone having an equal chance to rise as high as their talents will carry them. This is not the same, however, as everyone enjoying equal outcomes.

American political culture gives a sense of what is politically possible in the United States: what the American people demand, expect, and will tolerate from government; which public policy undertakings are likely to be viewed favorably and which negatively; which political messages are consistent winners and losers with American voters; and which social, political, and demographic trends are likely to put pressure on government.

The American political culture is not a perfectly harmonious set of beliefs. When it comes to specific cases, some values and ideas in the culture clash, and others give way to more practical considerations. Although it establishes some clear boundaries for American political discourse and governmental action, those boundaries are fairly expansive. Chapter 2 will explain the American political culture in comparative and historical contexts, and this text throughout will periodically invoke American political culture as a useful lens through which you can view U.S. politics and government.

Chapter Summary

In this chapter you have learned to:

1-1 Assess the challenges that researchers face when studying causal relationships within politics.

Political science focuses on politics and government and how government leaders and citizens behave. Political scientists typically try to determine what factor, or combination of factors, produced a particular outcome. Political scientists strive to be rigorous, thorough, and scientific researchers. To be good citizens and understand how your government and society work, students of American politics should also understand some basic rules of rigorous thinking. One important rule, often violated by politicians and pundits alike, is the fact that correlation does not equal causation. Just because two factors may move together—ice cream sales and burglaries, number of firefighters and fire damage—does not mean that one is causing the other.

1-2   Analyze the purposes of government and explain why government is necessary.

Government is necessary because only government has the broad right to force citizens to do things they otherwise might not do. Citizens grant government this monopoly on force and coercion in order to gain public goods such as roads, military defense, clean water, and education, and to protect themselves against fellow citizens trying to enforce their wills through coercion or violence. Individuals give up any claim to use force to get what they want and, in return, get security for themselves, their families, and their property. Still, in a democracy, government receives its power from the people—citizens decide, through a social contract with their leaders, which rights and authorities they will relinquish to government and which they will retain for themselves. Politics in America is a competition about which rights and authorities are best handled by government and what government will do with its authority. America is a constitutional democracy in which the U.S. Constitution identifies the responsibilities of each branch of government: executive, legislative, and judicial. The Constitution also makes clear, through the Bill of Rights, that the government may not do certain things—abridge freedom of speech, religion, or assembly, for example—and that it must do certain things, such as ensure that criminal defendants receive speedy and fair trials.

1-3   Compare and contrast the U.S. government to other democratic systems, and identify core values and beliefs within American political culture.

The American model of government is one sort among many. By studying models and practices in other countries, we can learn a great deal about our own. America is a democracy and like all democracies is committed to majority rule through elections. Differences in governmental structure and the core values of citizens influence the path of politics in different democracies. Understanding the major features of American politics and the major factors that drive political decisions and outcomes can be made easier by comparing our system to government systems in other countries. American politics and government are influenced by the uniquely American, dominant political culture, sometimes referred to as the American creed. The main ideas and values that make up the creed are individualism, democracy, equality, and liberty, as well as respect for private property and religion.

MyPoliSciLab® THINKING ABOUT AMERICAN POLITICS
Apply what you learned in this chapter on MyPoliSciLab.

Read on **mypoliscilab.com**

> **eText:** Chapter 1

Study and **Review** on **mypoliscilab.com**

> **Pre-Test**
> **Post-Test**
> **Chapter Exam**
> **Flashcards**

Watch on **mypoliscilab.com**

> **Video:** The Bailout Hearings
> **Video:** Vaccines: Mandatory Protection

Explore on **mypoliscilab.com**

> **Comparative:** Comparing Political Landscapes

KEY TERMS

authoritarian (or totalitarian) system, p. 11
autocracy, p. 13
causal question, p. 3

causation, p. 5
constitutional democracy, p. 14
correlation, p. 5
democracy, p. 13

direct democracy, p. 13
government, p. 8
parliamentary system, p. 15
political culture, p. 16

politics, p. 12
presidential system, p. 15

public goods, p. 11
representative democracy, p. 14

social contract, p. 10
spurious relationship, p. 5

SUGGESTED READINGS

David Friedman. 1996. *Hidden Order: The Economics of Everyday Life.* New York: Harper Business. Argues that economics can explain everything from general wants, choices, and values to consumer preferences, street crimes, financial speculations, and political campaign spending.

John Gerring. 2001. *Social Science Methodology: A Critical Framework.* New York: Cambridge University Press. An introduction to social science methodology suggesting that task and criteria, not fixed rules of procedure, lead to methodological adequacy.

Gary King, Robert O. Keohane, and Sidney Verba. 1994. *Designing Social Inquiry: Scientific Inference in Qualitative Research.* Princeton: Princeton University Press. A unified approach to developing valid descriptive and causal inference, arguing that qualitative and quantitative researchers face similar difficulties that can be overcome in similar ways.

Steven Levitt and Stephen Dubner. 2006. *Freakonomics: A Rogue Economist Explores the Hidden Side of Everything.* New York: William Morrow. Looks at different puzzles in American society, providing a good illustration of how one social science method can help us understand vexing social issues.

Michael M. Lewis. 2003. *Moneyball: The Art of Winning an Unfair Game.* New York: Norton. How Billy Bean, manager of the Oakland Athletics baseball team, took a modernized, statistics-heavy approach to running an organization and recruiting valuable players overlooked by better-resourced teams.

SUGGESTED WEBSITES

FREAKONOMICS BLOG:
www.freakonomics.blogs.nytimes.com

The authors of Freakonomics continue their search for new and interesting social science puzzles.

UNITED KINGDOM PARLIAMENT:
www.parliament.uk

Information on the workings of the British government as well as links to the House of Lords and House of Commons.

CONSTITUTION FOR ISRAEL:
www.cfisrael.org//home.html

Explains the continuous work of the Constitution, Law, and Justice Committee of the Knesset toward drafting a constitution for the State of Israel.

ROBERT WOOD JOHNSON FOUNDATION: COVERAGE FOR THE UNINSURED:
www.rwjf.org/coverage/index.jsp

Information about various health care issues and health reform plans by a major foundation in the medical policy field.

INITIATIVE AND REFERENDUM INSTITUTE AT THE UNIVERSITY OF SOUTHERN CALIFORNIA:
www.iandrinstitute.org/statewide_i&r.htm

Describes the government processes for placing issues on the ballot in each of the 50 states.

Political Culture

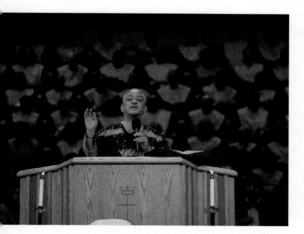

FAITH BECOMES A POLITICAL ISSUE Provocative statements by Reverend Jeremiah Wright created shockwaves in the 2008 presidential nomination contest. Wright was the pastor at the church long attended by Barack Obama, and the Democratic candidate considered him a spiritual mentor. In his response, Obama explained the historical context for his pastor's remarks while at the same time rejecting them.

CHAPTER LEARNING OBJECTIVES

After reading this chapter you will be able to:

2-1 Define political culture and explain how certain values and beliefs achieve dominance within a society.

2-2 Illustrate how the key values and beliefs of the American creed shape politics and government today.

2-3 Evaluate the consequences of American political culture such as limited government and a weak sense of sovereign power.

2-4 Identify the major challenges and alternatives to the dominant political culture.

The words were stunning and, to many Americans, shocking.

"The government . . . wants us to sing 'God Bless America.' No, no, no, not God Bless America. God damn America—that's in the Bible—for killing innocent people. God damn America, for treating our citizens as less than human."

These comments by Reverend Jeremiah Wright, senior pastor of Chicago's Trinity United Church of Christ through early 2008, exploded into the 2008 presidential nomination battle. Wright's remarks posed a difficult challenge for Barack Obama. The Democratic contender had a close relationship with Wright. Wright had officiated at Obama's wedding, baptized his two children, and one of his sermons served as the inspiration for the title of Obama's memoir, *The Audacity of Hope*. Obama had been a member of Wright's church for over 20 years.

At first, Obama tried a middle-ground approach. He repudiated Wright's most inflammatory comments, endorsed the positive role and message of the pastor in other respects, and said the excerpts were not reflective of Wright's typical message. When the controversy did not die down, the candidate gave a major speech on race in which he placed Wright's comments, particularly those touching on race, in historical context. Soon after the speech, Wright made several media appearances in which he amplified the most controversial of his rhetoric, leading Obama to denounce Wright more strongly and ultimately resign his membership in Trinity United.

American political culture and the national identity entwined within it can have significant effects in politics. Candidates work hard to demonstrate that they are in the mainstream and embrace a shared set of values with voters. More so than in most other economically advanced countries, religious belief is an important part of America's self-perception.[1] Reverend Wright's comments had a particularly strong impact on the presidential campaign precisely because he was a man of religion. Had the comments been made by Obama's longtime electrician or accountant, they would not likely have had the same effect.

Religion is only one aspect of American political culture. Beliefs in individualism, democracy, liberty, and property rights also guide people in how they vote, how they want the government to spend their tax dollars, and who should benefit from such spending.

Strongly held beliefs seem natural to those who hold them. Most Americans do not, for example, spend much time thinking through the costs and benefits of freedom of speech to decide whether it is a good thing. "Of course" freedom of speech is good, they would think. Sometimes, however, the assumptions and habits of "of course" are challenged. Of course free speech is deeply cherished, but what about speech that is vile and hateful toward particular groups? Of course religion has an appropriate place, but to what degree should a public official bring his or her religious values into decisions about public policy or be held accountable for the beliefs of a particular religion? As happened in 2008, religious and other beliefs often present the public and candidates for public office with difficult choices and questions that affect Americans' self-identity. ■

What Does It Mean to Be an American?

2-1 Define political culture and explain how certain values and beliefs achieve dominance within a society.

What makes Americans *American?* For most Americans, what defines being an American is a set of beliefs or ideals. The idea that individuals pursuing opportunity can make a better life for themselves, often referred to as the American Dream, is widely shared. This is part of American political culture.

Culture refers to a way of thinking or mode of behavior. **Political culture** refers to the basic values, beliefs, attitudes, predispositions, and expectations of citizens toward the political system and toward themselves as participants in it. For example, survey results over a long period of time suggest that freedom of speech is a bedrock value in the United States, with 90 percent or more of the public agreeing with statements such as "I believe in free speech for all no matter what their views might be." When evaluating an issue concerning speech, most Americans start from the premise that free speech is important and should be encouraged and that they have a right to speak their minds. Freedom of speech is part of American political culture. Unlike public opinion, which focuses more on the issues of the day and is more susceptible to quick change, political culture is a broader, more permanent set of beliefs.

political culture the values and beliefs of citizens toward the political system and toward themselves as actors in it.

Political culture provides a framework for political evaluation.

Political culture does not necessarily explain how Americans will respond to every situation. For instance, we noted that over 90 percent of Americans say they believe in free speech for all, but in specific situations the support for free speech may be lower.

Often there are significant inconsistencies when moving from abstract beliefs to concrete decisions and issues. But abstract principles still matter. Most likely, you believe that people should obey the law, that laws should be enforced, and that enforcement of the law should be done fairly. Yet, most of us who drive have probably found ourselves, on occasion, driving over the posted speed limit when there were no police watching (we plead guilty).

Does that inconsistency mean your general belief that people should obey the law is a farce? No. You start with that policy when you evaluate what to do. The belief provides a framework for decision making. Political culture works the same way—it provides a general framework and a starting point to evaluate issues, candidates, and the actions of public officials.

The American creed is the dominant political culture in the United States.

The dominant political culture in the United States consists of beliefs in individualism, democracy, liberty, property rights, and religion, all tied together by the value of equality. This set of beliefs has been labeled with many terms; we will call it the **American creed**.[2] It provides the frame of reference most Americans use to evaluate candidates and specific issues. For that reason, politicians make heavy use of this frame of reference to reach Americans, which then reinforces its importance.

American creed the dominant political culture in the United States, marked by a set of beliefs in individualism, democracy, liberty, property, and religion, tied together by the value of equality.

To say there is a widely shared political culture is *not* to say that Americans agree on all the specifics about politics or that these beliefs always describe the political reality for all groups. Even a passing glance at American political history reveals that not all groups have had full property rights or access to democratic politics. Instead, to say that there is a strong, widely held political culture is to say that most Americans share a set of general presumptions about politics and that most political debate operates within those general boundaries.

In many countries, including those with far less diverse populations than the United States, competing political cultures are at the core of politics. There might be competition between a capitalist orientation and a socialist orientation, between a secular and a religious outlook, or even between one region of the country and others. European countries such as Spain and France regularly pit evenly matched socialist parties against capitalist parties. Canada has weathered deep regional splits based in language and cultural differences between French-speaking Quebec and the remaining provinces. These different perspectives offer fundamentally different beliefs to guide citizens and politicians.

The population of the United States is among the most diverse of any country in history. Americans named over one hundred ethnicities when identifying their ancestry in the 2009 American Community Survey conducted by the U.S. Census. In some parts of the country, notably California and Texas, the terms "minority" and "majority" are becoming outmoded as the non-Hispanic white majority becomes a minority of the population and current minority groups such as blacks, Hispanic whites, and Asians together become the majority, a development that is likely to be mirrored elsewhere.[3] This extraordinary diversity makes American political culture all the more interesting.

Considering the varied backgrounds of the American population, the agreement in the United States around a set of general political beliefs is remarkable. However, that agreement has not been without significant racial, ethnic, and religious strife. Through all the waves of immigration, there have been charges that new immigrants were too "different" to fit into American life. As the children and grandchildren of immigrants grow up within American culture, they often find themselves culturally at odds with their ancestors. Efforts to "Americanize" immigrants through instruction in values,

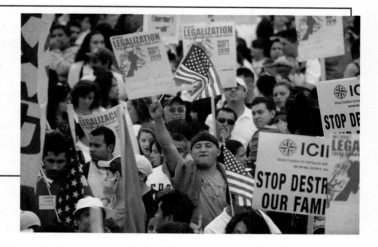

DOES IMMIGRATION THREATEN NATIONAL COHESION?

While acknowledging the contributions of immigrants to society, and often being children or grandchildren of immigrants themselves, many Americans worry that immigration threatens the sense of national identity conveyed by shared values. Advocates for expanded immigration stress that the historical record shows that immigrants are united around core American creed beliefs.

culture, language, childrearing, household management, and dress were explicit in past immigration waves and implicit in more recent attempts to make English the official language of the United States.

American creed beliefs became dominant for several reasons.

Why would one particular set of values and beliefs become dominant in the face of such diversity? One explanation is that Americans hear numerous messages from politicians, economic leaders, and educators that reinforce and tout the superiority of those beliefs. Other messages that reinforce political culture come from outside politics, for example, the entertainment media. Popular culture, whether fictional or based on actual events, tends to embrace the individualistic ideals and wants of Americans, celebrating the self-reliant individual who overcomes the odds.

This explanation is helpful, but it does not tell us why Americans believe and "buy into" these repeated messages. Why has socialism had less support in the United States than in other countries? One scholar offered three reasons.[4] First, because voting rights spread early to white men, the political system in the United States was relatively more open to working-class influence than in other countries. Second, prosperity in the United States made it difficult for competing political cultures to take firm root; the creed seemed to work. And last, the United States did not experience the same history of class relations as did European countries, which may have been necessary for an alternative to the creed to take root.[5]

Other scholars have been less optimistic, arguing that government use of repressive tactics and judicial rulings played a stronger role in thwarting opposition to the creed than these interpretations suggest. They point to examples

Thinking Causally Given the tremendous diversity of groups in the American population, how would one particular set of values and beliefs become dominant?

ranging from nineteenth-century labor activists being beaten and jailed, to investigations like those launched by Senator Joseph McCarthy in the 1950s to root out suspected communists in government, entertainment, and other industries, as evidence that the government has often taken action to squelch dissent against the American creed.[6] These competing explanations are insufficient on their own, but together they show there are many factors at play that sustain the preeminence of the American creed. A widespread popular mindset, based on life experience, that the creed works and produces individual opportunity is the broad foundation for the creed's success.

In sum, it is reasonable to describe American political culture as one based in the American creed, but—as this chapter will show—consensus does not eliminate conflict. There is substantial conflict in American politics within the confines of the creed. How much weight to place on each belief and what the beliefs themselves mean are often up for debate. In addition, other competing beliefs have had important impacts on American political life. These alternative approaches have mixed and mingled with the beliefs of the creed, proving that American political culture is dynamic and changing.

The Beliefs of the American Creed

2-2 Illustrate how the key values and beliefs of the American creed shape politics and government today.

equality the value that all Americans should be treated the same under the law, be able to influence government, and have equal opportunity to succeed in life.

The central value of the American creed is **equality**. A sense of equality underlies each of the specific beliefs of the creed—individualism, democracy, liberty, property, and religion.[7] Americans value the idea of every person being treated the same under law, being able to influence government, and having an equal opportunity to succeed in life. These expectations do not mean that everyone will or should have equal results, but that all people should play by the same rules. The American experience has fallen short of these ideals many times in many places, however. As you read the descriptions below, remember that the emphasis in this part of the chapter is on the general ideals to which Americans say they aspire and how they affect the ways Americans think about politics and government.

Individualism: People should choose their own path through life.

individualism a belief that all individuals should be able to succeed to the maximum extent possible given their talents and abilities, regardless of race, religion, or other group characteristics.

For Americans, individuals—not groups or classes—are the fundamental political unit. Americans believe in **individualism**, meaning that all individuals should be able to succeed to the maximum extent possible given their talents and abilities. The leading example of what Americans mean by freedom is the ability of individuals to choose their own path in life (see Table 2-1).

TABLE 2-1 What Freedom Means to Americans (in percentages)

Characteristics of Freedom	One of the Most Important Things about Freedom	Extremely Important	Very Important	Moderately, Somewhat, or Not Too Important
Having the power to choose and do what I want in life	45%	27%	22%	6%
Being able to express unpopular ideas without fearing for my safety	40	29	24	7
The right to participate in politics and elections	36	27	26	11
Having a government that doesn't spy on me or interfere in my life	30	26	32	12
Being left alone to do what I want	27	23	28	22

Note: Percentages add across each row. Survey respondents were asked for each characteristic of freedom whether it was one of the most important things about freedom, extremely important, very important, or moderately, somewhat, or not too important an aspect of freedom.
Source: General Social Survey 2000.

Organizations, even those that epitomize teamwork, recognize the power of this cultural belief. From 1980 through 2000, the U.S. Army used "Be All You Can Be" as its main recruiting slogan. This is precisely what Americans think of when they think about individualism—which is, of course, why savvy marketers tapped into this message. From 2001 to 2006 the Army replaced this slogan with another that tapped into individualism: "An Army of One." (The current slogan is "Army Strong.")

Presidential candidates are similarly not shy about casting their biographies as triumphs of American individualism. From Ronald Reagan's rising from his modest, Midwestern roots, through Barack Obama as a mixed-race child raised primarily by a single parent and grandparents, candidates hope their stories are relatable to voters as examples of American opportunity and success.

Democracy: Government actions should reflect the will of the people.

The second belief of the American creed is that government should adhere to democratic principles. Democracy, as described in Chapter 1, is a form of government in which the people rule. This rule can take place directly, through participation by the people in actual lawmaking, or indirectly, through free elections in which the people choose representatives to make laws. Between elections, people have indirect input in democracy through a variety of means—hearings, writing to public officials, signing petitions, and lobbying, for example. To Americans, the ideal suggests four criteria in particular.

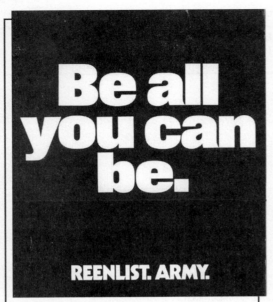

Be all you can be.

REENLIST. ARMY.

THE MARKETING APPEAL OF INDIVIDUALISM

The Army's "Be All You Can Be" recruitment campaign effectively tapped into American political culture's emphasis on individuals reaching their maximum potential and seeking to achieve their personal dreams.

The will of the people   First, government actions should reflect the will of the people. The people's wishes are not always easy to identify, but the general principle is that government should be guided by them as much as possible.[8] Frequent elections allow the people to remove officials who have not lived up to this standard.

The consent of the governed   Second, and closely related, power is granted to public officials by the consent of the governed. In this view, power that is exercised by a public official is always an extension of the public will and can potentially be reclaimed by the people. At its most extreme, the notion of consent means that citizens have a right to abolish the government altogether if they conclude that it is using power inappropriately.[9]

Equal opportunity to influence government   Third, to Americans, democracy also means an equal opportunity to influence government. This includes not only the opportunity to vote, but also access to government by citizens from all walks of life. Americans are uneasy with the idea that some individuals or groups may appear to have "inside connections" with public officials that may make their views more influential than those of the "average" person.[10] Candidates and public officials go to great lengths to clobber their opponents for being cronies of "special interests."

Equal treatment by the law   Fourth, to Americans, democracy means equal treatment by the law. Laws, regulations, and penalties should be enforced regardless of the social stature of the individual. This means that the same actions taken under the same set of circumstances should result in equal penalties or benefits, regardless of the social status, religion, ethnicity, race, income, or other characteristics of the individuals involved. Americans recognize and criticize when these ideals are violated.

Liberty: Government restraint on individual behavior should be minimal.

liberty the belief that government should leave people free to do as they please and exercise their natural rights to the maximum extent possible.

The third belief in the American creed is liberty. Americans often define **liberty** as freedom from government restriction on the exercise of one's rights; that is, whenever possible, government should let people do as they please. Government's obligation, in this view, is not to make decisions for you about

HOW CLOSE IS TOO CLOSE?
The linkage of business and government troubles many Americans. Here, Barack Obama shakes hands with Verizon CEO Ivan Seidenberg at a 2010 meeting of the Business Roundtable, a group of the country's largest corporations. Is this unfair access, or is a president right to lend an ear and share his thoughts with the heads of companies employing thousands of Americans and generating billions of dollars in revenue?

what would make your life better, but to protect your right to decide what a "better life" is and to protect your freedom to go for it.

Natural rights Associated with this belief is the conviction that government does not grant rights. Rather, rights are inherent and part of what makes people human: these are **natural rights**. The Declaration of Independence provides a clear statement of this idea: "we hold these truths to be self-evident, that all men are created equal, that they are endowed by their Creator with certain unalienable rights, that among these are life, liberty, and the pursuit of happiness." Government's job is to protect these rights from other citizens and from government at other levels.

> **natural rights** rights inherent in the essence of people as human beings; government does not provide these rights but can restrict the exercise of them.

Government's role in securing liberty To Americans, government secures liberty either by not restricting rights or by restricting them only when their expression imposes excessively on the rights of other individuals. Slanderous and libelous speech can lead to punishment. Marching and demonstrating without a permit can result in fines or other sanctions. And, when they believe national security is threatened, Americans often tolerate what would be considered unacceptable infringements on liberty at other times. All these limitations can be a matter of great political controversy.

Individuals in other countries view liberty in somewhat different ways from those in America. In Scandinavian countries, for example, liberty requires being given something by government in order to thrive fully as a human being. This may mean health care, education, housing, or any number of other services. In this view, the freedom to speak or to earn a living is weak unless citizens are given the tools to use these freedoms effectively.

In the United States, the perspective is a different one. Many Americans may agree that universal health care and quality education are important goals for government. However, relatively few Americans would say that liberty is absent if these government services are not provided.

Property: Individuals should be free to acquire, own, and use goods and assets.

property rights the belief that people should be able to acquire, own, and use goods and assets free from government constraints, as long as their acquisition and use does not interfere with the rights of other individuals.

Americans believe in extensive **property rights**—that people should be able to acquire, own, and use goods and assets free from government constraints, so long as their acquisition and use does not interfere with the rights of other individuals. Property rights are therefore twofold: freedom to acquire property and freedom to use property.

Freedom to acquire property First, people should have the right to acquire private property without limitations. This means that individuals should be paid whatever they can command in the economic marketplace for their goods or their work. You may think it excessive that a professional athlete or movie star makes $20 million per year, or that a corporate executive receives $20 million in total compensation, but Americans generally do not believe that these levels of pay should be prohibited.

Freedom to use property Second, individuals should be free to use property with few restrictions. Some restrictions are tolerated to protect the property of others or protect some societal interest. Most communities have noise ordinances of some type, for example, and you cannot build your house on sensitive wetlands.

Exactly how property rights coexist with democracy in the confines of a single political culture is an enduring puzzle. Historically, one prominent school of thought feared that the growth of democracy would lead to property rights being tossed aside. The Framers of the U.S. Constitution shared this fear. Because democracy might pose a risk to property rights, they believed a careful structure of institutions, rules, and procedures was needed to protect property from the people's "passions." Another approach saw property rights and political freedoms as mutually reinforcing.[11] The individual freedoms prized in a market economy are attractive as political liberties as well.

Thinking Causally How do democratic rights and property rights, which are potentially at odds, coexist?

Political scientists have noted a third way in which the two can fit together: Property rights as expressed in activities such as shopping could lead to skepticism about government, as individuals might see the free market as ultimately more democratic and equal than the political system. In the market, you can buy the product—like anyone else—if you can afford it. With government, on the other hand, the process for you to get an economic benefit can appear to be much more time consuming, complicated, and conflictual. This perceived difficulty of getting economic gains through government may reduce the number of demands placed on government to take property from one group and give it to another.[12]

Religion: Individuals should be free to practice their religious faith.

Americans believe in **religious freedom**, the idea that individuals should be free to choose and practice their religious faith and that government should not establish any particular religion as the official or preferred religion.[13]

Freedom of religious expression Americans view the freedom to practice one's religion as akin to the right to free speech. Early in the nation's history, so-called dissenting Protestants emigrated to the colonies in part as a way to practice their faith. They fled societies, England in particular, where official government religions made it difficult for individuals with other religious beliefs to practice their faith. The idea that government should remain neutral among religions was therefore closely linked to the idea of freedom of religious practice. In this perspective, freedom of religious expression was likely only if government did not take sides. The twin beliefs in freedom of expression and noninterference by government were enshrined in the Constitution and have grown gradually over time.

Importance of religion in American political life Religious belief has been central to American political discourse. Major efforts such as the anti-slavery, civil rights, and anti-abortion movements relied on religious language and principles. Presidents of both parties have sprinkled religious language in their speeches and ended major addresses with the exhortation "God Bless America." American beliefs lean against the idea of an official religion or church, but *religiosity*, the tendency of people to have some sort of religion, pervades political culture.

Survey results provide a sense of just how important religion is to Americans today. Over 80 percent of Americans in 2009 said they completely or mostly agree that they never doubt the existence of God, while nearly that many said that prayer is an important part of their daily life, and that everyone will have to answer to God for their sins.[14] Nearly three-quarters of Americans in 2008 said it was important for a president to have strong religious beliefs, and only about 30 percent thought politicians expressed their religious faith too much.[15]

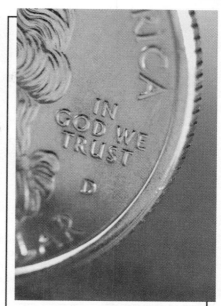

FAITH AS AN AMERICAN TOUCHSTONE
References to faith appear frequently in American political culture. Presidents routinely end their speeches by saying "God bless the United States of America," and other references abound in places such as the Pledge of Allegiance, the Declaration of Independence, and U.S. currency.

religious freedom a belief that individuals should be free to choose and practice their religious faith and that government should not establish any particular religion as the official or preferred religion.

The American creed provides a starting point for most Americans to evaluate issues, candidates, and government actions.

The five beliefs of the American creed have endured even though these ideals have not always been honored in practice. For much of the nation's history, not all groups have shared equally in the promises and benefits of creedal beliefs or

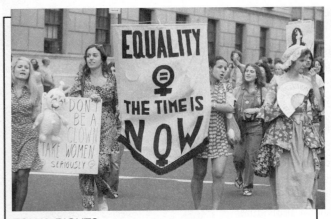

EQUAL RIGHTS

Marchers in New York supporting the addition of the Equal Rights Amendment to the U.S. Constitution. Although the attempt to ratify the amendment fell short by three states, the women's rights movement had a profound effect on American laws, business practices, and society.

the overarching value of equality. During the Revolutionary era, only about 15 to 30 percent of the adult population could take full advantage of the promises of life, liberty, and the pursuit of happiness. Laws and customs made sure that women, blacks, white indentured servants, and nonpropertied adult white males could not.[16]

Despite this widespread exclusion, the remarkable fact is that these groups still believed in the promise of the American creed. They did not argue that this set of beliefs should be discarded. Instead, women, white men without property, blacks, and other racial and ethnic minorities demanded to be included in the promises of the creed. These groups engaged in massive social movements for individual rights, liberty, property, and participation in the democratic process, a testament to just how powerful these beliefs were to those on the outside looking in. By championing the equality promised by the American creed, these movements had a strong impact on public opinion concerning equal treatment across race, gender, and group. Figure 2-1 shows that, in the case of equal roles for women, equality

FIGURE 2-1 Support for Women's Equal Role.

In 1972, nearly half the U.S. population held neutral views or believed a woman's place was in the home, but by 2008 less than one-sixth of the population held those views.

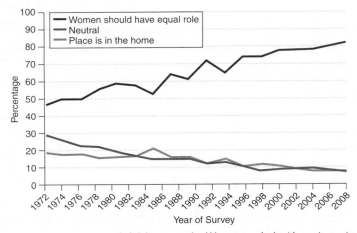

Year of Survey

Note: Answers to the question: "Some people feel that women should have an equal role with men in running business, industry and government. Others feel that women's place is in the home. Where would you place yourself on this 7-point scale or haven't you thought much about this?" "Equal role" indicates respondent chose point 1, 2, or 3 on the 7-point scale; "Neutral" is point 4; "In the home" is point 5, 6, or 7. Remaining percentage had no opinion. Questions not asked in 1986, 2002, 2006. Any opinions, findings, and conclusions or recommendations expressed in these materials are those of the author(s) and do not necessarily reflect the views of the funding organizations. *Source:* The American National Election Studies (www.electionstudies.org). THE 1948–2004 ANES CUMULATIVE FILE [dataset]. Stanford University and the University of Michigan [producers and distributors], 2008.

as defined by the women's rights movement has gained support from the American public.

Consequences and Implications of the American Creed

2-3 Evaluate the consequences of American political culture such as limited government and a weak sense of sovereign power.

Political scientists ask the "so what?" question: why should we care about political culture? The American creed matters because its consequences and implications are far-reaching. A brief survey of some of these consequences and implications will demonstrate the important influence of political culture on American life.

Americans prefer government to be limited in the scope of its activities.

One consequence of the American creed is a preference for the idea of **limited government** rather than a large, active government. This means government is seen as a last resort to solving problems. Americans tend to rely first on other arenas—family, church, the marketplace, nonprofit institutions, self-improvement—and they turn to government when these alternatives fail or are overwhelmed by the scope of a problem.

limited government the idea that the scope of government activities should be narrow and that government should act only when the need is great and other sectors of society are unable to meet the need.

Some political scientists describe American opinion as philosophically conservative but operationally liberal, meaning that Americans may genuinely believe in limited government while simultaneously supporting specific government programs.[17] Surveys show that across nearly all issues, the public is reluctant to cut federal spending significantly, even when the budget deficit is high and the public believes government is inefficient and wasteful.[18]

The dedication to the idea of limited government is stronger in the United States than in other industrialized democracies. In general, governments in these countries are larger and have more control over society and the economy than is true in the United States. We need to interpret these comparisons with caution, as there are many different ways to measure government's role. Nonetheless, when we compare the size of government to the size of the economy, especially when focusing on domestic rather than military spending, the United States regularly falls at the low end of the list. Government in the United States often hires private sector firms to do a wide range of work, including counseling, job skills training, rubbish collection, and more, that in other countries might be done by government employees. Faith-based organizations, for example, have been involved in providing services and training to welfare recipients to ready them for the labor force. In the United States, expanding government's reach through the use of private sector firms and organizations can be less politically controversial than hiring scores of new public employees.[19]

FIGURE 2-2 Percentage of Americans Saying They Trust the Federal Government to Do the Right Thing Just About Always or Most of the Time.

Americans' trust that the federal government will do the right thing has dropped from the high levels recorded 50 years ago by the American National Election Studies. Despite fluctuations and differences between partisan groups, the general trend is a decline in trust since the mid-1960s.

Source: Data from Pew Center on the People and the Press.

Americans often do not trust that government will do the right thing.

A second consequence of the American creed has been a pervasive skepticism about the effectiveness of American government. At some times in U.S. history this skepticism has been deeper than at others. In 1958, according to the American National Elaection Studies, a major academic public opinion survey, about three-fourths of Americans believed they could trust the federal government to do what is right most or all of the time. In 2010, fewer than one-fourth believed so (see Figure 2-2).[20]

What might explain this decline in trust? A succession of difficult events in American politics plays some role. But, as we cautioned in Chapter 1, political life tends to be complicated. Thus, political scientists have proposed and established some validity for a variety of factors:

Thinking Causally Why has trust in government declined?

- Trust was artificially inflated in the years after the Great Depression and World War II. After those calamities were overcome and the United States stood atop the world in economics, science, and many other categories, trust was high. This high trust may have been the anomaly, and trust has simply declined to more "normal" levels.

- American politics at the elite level has become more divisive, and news coverage in turn has focused disproportionately on conflict and stalemate rather than cooperation and accomplishment.

- American economic life has become less secure, traditional moral values have been challenged, and government has been unwilling or unable to do much to reverse these trends.

- Respect for all large institutions, not simply government, has declined.

- Trust across advanced industrial democracies has declined, suggesting some causes not specific to America may play a role also.[21]

Governing within the American constitutional system of separation of powers and checks and balances has never been easy. Low levels of trust may complicate the jobs of political leaders.[22] High levels of distrust can increase the difficulty of making necessary and tough policy decisions, thus reinforcing the skepticism about government's ability to perform effectively.

There is a weak sense of sovereign power in the United States.

A third consequence of the American creed is that there is a weak sense of sovereign power in the United States. **Sovereign power** suggests a final authority, a final decision maker. In the United States, it is difficult to think of any truly "final" authority. American government is structured so that one part of government can challenge and check other parts of government. For example, Congress can pass legislation, but the president can veto it. The Supreme Court can declare unconstitutional the actions of both Congress and the president. There is no ultimate seat of power in the system at the national level.

sovereign power the individual or institution in a political system whose decisions are binding and unable to be overturned by other individuals or institutions.

But what about the claim that the American people are sovereign? In the abstract, this is true. However, on a practical, day-to-day level, it is a limited sovereignty. American government is designed to hear the voice of the people, but not to translate that voice into immediate action. Similarly, there is never a time when Americans can vote out all members of government in a single election. And members of the federal judiciary and bureaucracy, who are unelected, are never up for direct public removal.

Competing ideas are viewed with suspicion.

A fourth consequence of the American creed is that competing ideas are often viewed with suspicion. In general, the American people and their leaders tend to assume the superiority of the creed's values. Only rarely do U.S. policy makers, at least publicly, seriously talk about the policies and programs of other countries as examples to be followed, the assumption being that the underlying values and beliefs guiding these programs would not be relevant in the American context.

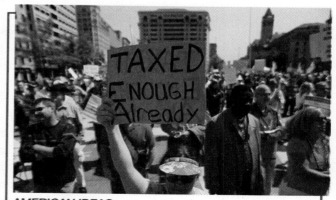

AMERICAN IDEAS

American national identity is closely linked to the widely shared beliefs of the American creed. Political activists use this linkage to suggest that some ideas are not simply wrong, but directly violate the country's founding principles and basic beliefs. Supporters of the Tea Party movement, as seen here in April 2010, argue that the actions and policies of the federal government have become inconsistent with the Constitution, the intentions of the Framers, and the American creed.

"Un-American" beliefs Competing ideas not only challenge the American creed but also are sometimes deemed "un-American." In few countries is a set of political beliefs so intertwined with national identity that to oppose or challenge these beliefs can sometimes be perceived as a challenge to the nation itself.

In the 1950s, the House Un-American Activities Committee investigated a large number of individuals suspected of holding or being sympathetic to un-American ideas, chiefly socialism and communism. At other points in American history, efforts to remove immigrants and to restrict the future flow of immigration were based on the idea that these individuals brought disruptive beliefs and values to the United States. Liberals and conservatives alike criticize the ideas of their opponents as un-American.

Appeals to social class Attempts to appeal to Americans as members of social classes are often considered a danger to national harmony. With the exception of references to the middle class—a widely used term that tends to be defined broadly—directly appealing to class interest is often denounced. The concerns that policy is being devised to promote one class at the expense of another are often sincerely held, as are the fears that class-based politics invite disharmony and division. But the provocative charge that the rich are warring on the poor or the poor are warring on the rich can also be a strategy for halting serious discussion about a particular policy.

Appeals to the public interest are difficult in an individualistic political culture.

A fifth consequence of the American creed is that it can be difficult for politicians and the public to act in the public interest or even to define it. In a nation in which individualism and skepticism toward government are strong, references to "the public" might be interpreted by many people as a rhetorical gloss employed to make someone's individual interest sound more noble. When advocating policies, politicians and political activists continually wrestle with the tension between appealing to the interests of the community and the interests of the individual.

Alexis de Tocqueville, a French historian and political theorist, visited the United States in the 1830s and wrote a sweeping analysis of the nature of American politics and society that is still considered one of the most perceptive studies ever written about the United States. He was particularly interested in the interplay of liberty, individualism, democracy, and equality in the young American republic. In his famous *Democracy in America*, published in 1835 when he was 30 years old, Tocqueville suggested that Americans engage in "self interest rightly understood." In Tocqueville's view, one way Americans reconciled the conflict between pursuing their self-interest and sacrificing for the public interest was by seeing how engaging in kind acts toward others and being concerned about the public interest could also serve their self-interest. Help others, and you will feel good about yourself. Volunteer for community service and do good things, and you will have another impressive line on your résumé.

Political conflict emerges from tension among the creed's beliefs and from debate over the meaning of the beliefs.

An important and ironic final consequence of the widely shared American creed is that it produces intense political conflict. The creed creates political conflict because, first, its beliefs are often in tension with one another, and second, the meaning of the individual beliefs is open to debate.[23] Americans vigorously debate the proper meaning and weight of the beliefs and what the appropriate role for government should be.

Tension among the creed's beliefs Consider a low-income high school student. She is an excellent student, qualified for admission at a prestigious university. Her ability to maximize her potential depends on her going to the most prestigious institution for which she is qualified. Being poor, however, she cannot afford such a university. Her situation poses a conflict between two beliefs. According to the belief in individualism, this young woman should be able to achieve all she can achieve without any artificial barriers. On the other hand, according to the belief in property, when you work hard to earn income, that money is yours. If you want to donate voluntarily to a scholarship fund, you can do that, but you should not be forced by government to give your money to someone else.

As a society, Americans have resolved this particular conflict between American creed beliefs by deemphasizing property rights to elevate individual opportunity. That is, we have created federal financial aid programs that take tax dollars and redistribute them to individuals like this student. This example reinforces the point made earlier that beliefs can prevail at the abstract level but weaken in specific circumstances.

Cultural differences across regions When the beliefs of the American creed are in conflict, there is no balance that is inherently right or wrong. Instead, there is a balance that can gain the strongest political support nationally at a particular moment in time. But what does this national balance mean at the state or regional level? Even a quick glance at the United States shows significant variation across the states in partisan strength, public opinion, and the content of laws and policies. If national political culture is important, why do states vary? Is the variation simply random, or do particular factors contribute to it? More specifically, does political culture play a systematic role in this cross-state variation?

The regional variety in laws and political behavior has led some political scientists to suggest that the balance among creedal beliefs varies systematically from region to region, state to state, and even within states. Migration and immigration have contributed to this variation. Ethnic groups and nationalities are distributed unevenly across the country, and their heavy presence in a

Thinking Causally If national political culture is so important, why do we see variations across the states in party strength, public opinion, and laws?

Case Study

Defining Democracy When Drawing District Lines

Political tension results not only from the conflict between beliefs, but also from different interpretations of beliefs in the American creed.[24] Consider the process of redistricting, which refers to the drawing of boundaries around legislative districts. Each district elects one legislator.[25] Prior to 1964, congressional and state legislative district boundaries often followed county lines. They were redrawn for U.S. House districts only when the U.S. Census, taken every 10 years, indicated that a change in a state's share of the national population meant it should have more or fewer representatives than it currently had. Under this system, districts could vary enormously in population from one House district to another or one state legislative district to another, yet each would have the same number of legislators: one.

What does a seemingly technical matter like redistricting have to do with the American creed or beliefs in democracy? A lot, as it turns out. In 1964, the Supreme Court, in two famous decisions, concluded that democracy hinges on the principle of "one person, one vote"—the idea that every citizen has one vote, each voter is equally powerful in selecting legislators, and each voter is equally represented in the legislature.[26] If one district had 1,000 potential voters and another had 100,000, the power of each voter in selecting a representative in the first district would be 100 times greater than in the second. To the Court, such unequally sized districts, although common in 1964, violated constitutional norms of equality that were fundamental to the American democratic process. Moreover, given residential patterns in which populations of minority racial and ethnic groups tend to be clustered together, district lines can either deliberately attempt to keep these groups in a single district, disperse them across districts, or not take account of race or ethnicity at all when drawing the lines.

The Court's one person, one vote principle provides no explicit guidance about how to draw the lines that separate districts. Is democracy better served if lines are drawn in a way that some districts are likely to be heavily Republican and others

heavily Democratic? The individuals elected to the legislature in these districts are apt to represent their citizens very well because they tend to share common viewpoints. However, competitive elections will be rare in these districts—the weaker party is unlikely to have any chance to win, so voters might not have much real choice. If the lines are drawn with an intent to spread Democratic and Republican voters about equally across the two districts, elections may be more competitive—considered by many people to be a fundamental sign of a healthy democracy—but large numbers of people in the districts may feel they share few beliefs and values with the elected officials who represent them in the legislature. They might feel unrepresented, and that hardly seems democratic.[27]

Every decade, after the census is finished, there are bitter battles to draw up district lines. In most states, the job falls to the legislature. And most often, the pattern is predictable. First, lines are drawn in a way to protect incumbents (those already in elected office) of both major parties. Then, the majority party seeks to draw lines around remaining districts in such a way as to maximize the number of seats the party will win. This process, known as gerrymandering, often produces districts with contorted, convoluted boundaries.

The most widely publicized dispute in recent years over district lines occurred in Texas. Following the 2000 census, the Texas legislature, with one house controlled by each party, was unable to agree on a new districting plan and, under state law, the districting process went before a panel of federal judges. The judges drew new lines that kept in place a Democratic majority in the Texas delegation to the U.S. House. In the 2002 Texas state legislative elections, however, Republicans gained control of the legislature and in 2003 passed a new district map much more favorable to Republican candidates. Predictably, in the 2004 U.S. House election, the Republicans won 21 seats, compared to 15 in 2002.

Challenges to the new Texas district lines landed in the U.S. Supreme Court in 2006, arguing two points.[28] First, Democrats charged there was no lawful reason

Case Study Defining Democracy When Drawing District Lines

to change the lines that had just been established in 2001. Second, minority groups claimed that the Texas legislature illegally sought to distribute Hispanic and black voters across districts in order to decrease the likelihood of electing Democrats to the House. Since the late 1980s, the Supreme Court has frowned on using race as a primary factor in drawing district lines, including deliberate attempts to weaken the voting clout of minority groups. In 2006, the Court concluded that the critics of the plan had not established that the partisan rearrangement was inherently unequal or undemocratic, but it did strike down one district for unconstitutionally weakening minority voting power.

These conflicts show again that Americans believe in democracy in general but can disagree on precisely what that belief requires them to do in the specific case of drawing district lines. In the real world of

politics, ideals about democratic principles and values often jostle with hardheaded aspirations for political power. Most Americans share the general ideals of the American creed, but the tension inherent in the creed leaves plenty of room for political debate, conflict, and struggle.

Thinking Critically

1. In your view, what considerations should line drawers have in mind if they want to draw the most democratic, equal district lines?

2. In a democracy, should district lines be drawn to maximize the competitiveness of elections, even if that means about one-half of the residents will not believe their elected officials represent their policy viewpoints?

particular state or city encourages further immigration to that area. This was as true of European immigrants in the 1890s as it is of Asian and Latino immigrants today. In one part of the country, property rights might get more emphasis; in another, it might be religious freedom. These areas are then appealing relocation destinations for other Americans who share those preferences. This geographical variation in political culture is one factor that helps explain differences in state laws and politics.

One famous classification speaks of moralistic, traditionalistic, and individualistic subcultures that dominate or mix in different parts of the United States.[29] The moralistic subculture, present in northern states and the Pacific Northwest, views government as a positive force and tends to place heavy emphasis on the needs of the community and government's ability to satisfy those needs. A traditionalist subculture, found in southern states, favors limited government that works to sustain the current social relations and values in society and the economy. The individualistic subculture, encountered in the middle tier of states and in California, sees politics neither as a means to transform society (like moralism) nor to preserve society (like traditionalism), but a mechanism through which private interests are advanced and in which government is expected to encourage, enable, and support private initiative. Political scientists have used these regional cultural differences as one factor among many to try to explain differences in voting turnout, election outcomes, and social policy across states.

Challenges to the American Creed

2-4   Identify the major challenges and alternatives to the dominant political culture.

Although the American creed has had strong allegiance, alternative beliefs have also challenged the creed. At different points in U.S. history, beliefs in communitarianism, discrimination, multiculturalism, and libertarianism have influenced American politics and American political culture.

Communitarianism emphasizes the contributions and interests of the community.

communitarianism the view that the needs of the community are of higher priority in government than the needs of the individual, even if the result is a restriction of individual liberties.

Whereas the American creed gives primacy to the individual in society, **communitarianism** focuses on society and the community.[30] In the communitarian view, individuals are not self-made; society makes us and we owe something to society in return. The communitarian approach does not dispute that individuals are personally responsible and need to work hard. But it would point out that we all depend on the resources provided by others and by the community, whether education, transportation, or the bounty of the earth and water. These resources do not determine whether we will reach our goals, but they influence our ability to reach them, and we rely on others to provide them.

Communitarian beliefs in American history Communitarianism has been influential throughout American history. In the colonial and Revolutionary eras, this was the dominant mode of thought, often referred to by historians and political scientists as classical republicanism.[31] Political rhetoric of those eras placed great emphasis on having self-sacrificing virtuous people—those who would pursue the common good—as political leaders. It was common practice for government to regulate wages, prices, and the entry of new businesses into the marketplace, all to maintain social stability and, it was believed, to produce a just society. Gradually, individualistic beliefs gained ascendancy. Communitarian ideals survived, but in a less prominent position than previously.

Periodically, these ideals flourished in the advocacy of social, political, or economic reform. Populists from 1875 through 1900 expressed deep concern about the disruption of communities by industrial capitalism and proposed many reforms to rectify the perceived exploitation of government by private interests. Major reform movements like Progressivism (1904–1918), the New Deal (1930s), and the Great Society (1960s) were similarly infused with the idea that politics or economics needed to be reformed for the greater interest of the community.

Private interest and the public good To communitarians, the rights of individuals and the interests of the community are not necessarily in conflict. But when they are, the public good should trump private interest.[32] For example, in some states and municipalities, police set up sobriety checkpoints and stop drivers at random to screen them for drunk driving. Sobriety checkpoints are clearly an infringement on the privacy rights of individuals, but they have been defended as serving the community's interests. If drivers realize they might get pulled over even when they are not driving erratically, they will be more cautious about drinking and driving, thereby enhancing everyone's safety and reducing the social costs involved with car crashes, injuries, and loss of life.[33]

Refining the American creed One way to look at communitarianism is that it refines the American creed without necessarily rejecting it.[34] On their own, creedal beliefs about individualism can appear harsh, advocating a "sink or swim" society in which individuals either succeed or fail, with little compassion for those who fall behind. Communitarian ideas remove this harsh edge by supporting government programs to provide social resources and services for individuals who are struggling, if that is in the community's interest.

HOW DO WE KNOW?

Why Was the Path to Universal Health Insurance Coverage So Difficult?

The Question

In nearly all industrialized countries, health care coverage for every individual is guaranteed by the national government, either by the government paying for private health care services, the government directly providing services, or some combination of these two. In the United States, private expenditures are a far larger share of the total spent on health care than is true elsewhere (see Figure 2-3). In 2010, after nearly a century of attempts and after a bruising legislative battle, the United States adopted a set of reforms designed to provide nearly universal health care coverage. Why was the path to universal health insurance coverage so difficult? How do we know?

Why It Matters

In recent years, nearly 47 million Americans, or about 16 percent of the population, had no health insurance. These figures are a matter of dispute, as they include not only those who are unable to find insurance they can afford, but individuals who have chosen not to purchase insurance (for example, the young and healthy), those who qualify for health insurance from their employer or government but do not sign up, and individuals in the United States illegally. Nonetheless, they are the most widely cited figures. In public opinion surveys, Americans frequently express fears that they will lose their insurance and will not be able to afford their medical expenses.[35] Whether you believe that universal health insurance is crucially important to individuals' health and life opportunities, or you believe that it will harm medical care overall more than help it, the answer to the question matters.

Investigating the Answer

For political scientists, explaining why something did not happen is similar to explaining why something did happen: a researcher needs to come up with an idea

(continues)

HOW DO WE KNOW? Why Was the Path to Universal Health Insurance Coverage So Difficult? *(continued)*

FIGURE 2-3 Public and Private Health Care Expenditures as a Percentage of Gross Domestic Product, 2010

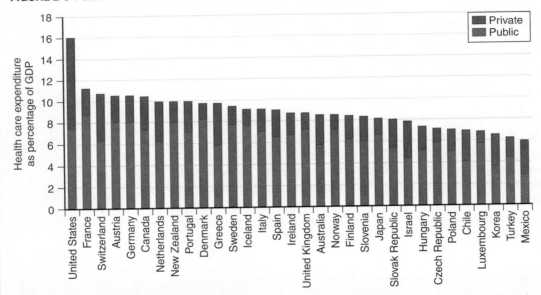

The United States devotes a much larger share of its economy to health care expenditures than other countries and has a much larger role for the private sector. American national and state governments also spend substantial sums on health care.

Source: Organisation for Economic Co-operation and Development, OECD Health Data 2010. Updated October, 2010.

that connects the outcome to factors that might explain it. The outcome we are interested in is the absence or presence of national health insurance that covers all individuals. The possible cause we are especially interested in is political culture. The hunch is that the American creed's emphasis on individualism, liberty, and property is incompatible with the idea that health care should be considered a federal government responsibility. Individualism demands personal responsibility. Liberty means allowing choices, and if some people choose not to have insurance, why force it on them? Moreover, in the American free enterprise economy, health insurance has been a benefit offered by employers to entice prospective employees and to retain their current workers. This competition might give employers the incentive to offer more generous insurance packages as they compete for employees. If different jobs provide different levels of benefits, workers have choices. They might trade health insurance for higher income, more flexible work schedules, or overtime opportunities.

One way to test this idea is through examining public opinion. Depending on the survey, half to three-quarters of Americans say they favor "providing health care coverage for all," even if it means raising taxes. However, in one survey, support for national health insurance dropped off if the program would limit one's choice of doctors or if there were waiting lists for nonemergency treatments or if the respondent personally had to pay higher taxes. During the 2009–2010 debate, the measurement of public opinion on health reform was highly susceptible to question wording and the information provided to respondents. About 90 percent of Americans in mid-2009 expressed support for "fundamental changes" in or "completely rebuilding" American health care, but when asked about their personal situation, nearly as high a percentage reported being satisfied with their health care.[36]

The idea that there was no support for universal health insurance certainly is not correct, but support for a national plan was vulnerable to political arguments—and survey question wording—about service quality,

HOW DO WE KNOW? Why Was the Path to Universal Health Insurance Coverage So Difficult?

availability, and choice. So it is fair to say that American political culture did not rule out national health insurance, but it also did not lend clear support for it if advantages of the current system might be lost.

Although the United States has not had universal national health insurance, and the new plan will not be fully in place until 2014, America does have the Medicare and Medicaid programs, which provide insurance for the elderly and the poor, respectively. U.S. national and state governments spend huge sums on health care (see Figure 2-3). If American political culture prior to 2010 simply would not allow any form of national health insurance, the existence of these two programs and all that spending would be a real puzzle. What if the explanation was modified to say that Americans opposed government-funded health insurance except for those individuals who are unable to provide for themselves? That seems to fit Medicare. But what about Medicaid? American creedal beliefs in individualism might argue that low-income persons, unlike the elderly, are in a position to better their financial standing and acquire health care, so government should not provide it. But government has, for decades.[37]

Given the mixed public opinion results and the presence of these two partial forms of national health insurance in the United States, how might we further try to explain the long, difficult path toward universal health insurance? One possibility is to add another factor: American political institutions.[38] For something as massive as national health insurance—which entails changes throughout the health care industry—the president, Congress, different parts of the federal bureaucracy, state governments, and possibly even the Supreme Court would be involved in the policymaking process. The health care industry is huge and well established, so efforts to change it are necessarily long and complicated, requiring a great deal of political dedication throughout multiple levels of political power. With influence dispersed across institutions and across majority and minority parties, there are many locations in the American political process where legislation can be defeated.

The political activity of "special interests" is another factor to consider.[39] Traditionally, one part of the health care industry or another was likely to oppose movements toward national health insurance because they feared bureaucratic oversight of their business practices,

interference with patient care, and depression of prices and salaries that would make the industry less efficient economically and less desirable as a career.[40] The interests opposed to national health insurance were likely to be already very well organized and very persistent on the issue because they had a lot at stake financially. Those individuals or groups in favor of national health insurance, on the other hand, needed to get organized to fight this battle, frequently had many different points of view, and often did not have as intense an interest in creating national health insurance as opponents had in stopping it.[41] A battle between a movement divided across several different reform plans and groups relatively unified to protect their turf will usually be won by the latter, even if there are more people in the former.

Thinking Critically

1. If you were a political strategist, how would you convince Americans that universal health care coverage guaranteed by the federal government is consistent with American political culture?

2. Do any of these causal factors—culture, institutions, or interests—seem more important than the others, or does each seem about equally important in explaining the long path toward universal coverage?

3. The two major parties were unable to agree on the principles and details that should guide reform of the American health care system. How important, if at all, is it that both major parties be in agreement when government is considering large-scale policy reforms?

The Bottom Line

Political culture, institutional features of American government, and the politics of special interests historically formed a thicket of obstacles to the adoption of national health insurance. So what made 2010 different from past years? The role of culture in 2010 ultimately is best thought of as neither as advancing nor defeating universal health insurance, but as shaping the construction of the program. Coverage for illegal immigrants, for example, was not included, and efforts to create a new government-run insurance company were defeated. Where the health care reform effort in 2009–2010 differed most from previous experiences

(continues)

HOW DO WE KNOW? Why Was the Path to Universal Health Insurance
Coverage So Difficult? *(continued)*

is in the institutions involved with it. Lowering some of the institutional barriers to reform were a president who made health insurance a major priority, the substantial majority of seats held by his party in the House and Senate, adroit use of legislative procedures by Democratic leaders, and a fear that failure would lead to deep discontent among their staunchest party activists and supporters. As for interests, the growing worry, even among former opponents of reform, that health care costs had become economically unsustainable for businesses, governments, and individuals, prodded a recalculation about the desirability of some kind of universal coverage. Organizations representing senior citizens, physicians, pharmaceutical companies,

hospitals, businesses, labor, and many others, including even the insurance companies themselves, committed early in the process to work with, or at least not actively oppose, the reform efforts. The change of heart among former opponents was due in part to the odds looking better than on previous occasions that reform might pass—better to be on the reform bus and try to steer its path rather than be run over by it. Despite this historically friendly institutional and interest environment in 2009–2010, the path to reform was still extraordinarily difficult, in part because of the mobilization of those Americans who saw government-guaranteed health insurance coverage as likely to infringe on their personal freedom and choices.

Public support for communitarianism Public opinion reveals the persistence of communitarian ideals today. Americans are not anti-business. In 2009, over 75 percent believed that "the strength of this country today is mostly based on the success of American business." Over half believed government regulation of business usually does more harm than good. However, about three-fifths of Americans charged that business fails to strike "a fair balance between making profits and serving the public interest." And the same proportion concluded that "business corporations make too much profit."[42] The very notion of "too much profit" is telling. In the creedal beliefs of property, liberty, and individualism, the idea of "too much" profit makes no sense. If an individual or business is clever enough to make a product for which there is high demand, how can we say "too much" profit is being made? Assuming you have choices, you are not forced to buy the product. If you believe the price is too high, you should not purchase it. Whereas the creedal view holds that substantial profit indicates a good business plan, communitarianism worries that businesses may be taking advantage of customers individually and society more generally. When investment bankers in 2008 and 2009 received large bonuses even while their banks received taxpayer assistance to stay afloat as the economy soured and foreclosures soared, many Americans saw this as disregarding the interest of the community.

Discrimination stresses that not all groups deserve equal treatment.

discrimination the view that not all groups in society are deserving of equal rights and opportunities.

Another challenge to the American creed, particularly the value of equality, is **discrimination**. According to this view, society is a hierarchy where not all groups deserve all the rights and benefits the American creed can offer—some groups are favored and others are disfavored. The most glaring example of discrimination in American history was the treatment of racial minorities, especially blacks. Those holding hierarchical ideas considered blacks inherently inferior to whites. Some of the language used to describe blacks in comparison to whites was degrading and offensive, depicting blacks as anything from children to savages. Racism was so pervasive in American history that even many of those who opposed slavery did not consider blacks fully equal and fully deserving of the same rights as whites.

Discrimination cannot be dismissed as an inconvenient blip on history, or an unpleasant set of ideas held by relatively few people on the bottom rungs of society, or the distorted worldview of a few white supremacist organizations such as the Ku Klux Klan. Political, educational, and business leaders believed in these ideas. Well into the twentieth century, American public policy at the national and state levels was greatly influenced by the racist, anti-equality premises of discrimination, denying minorities equal access to the opportunities in America's society, economy, and polity.

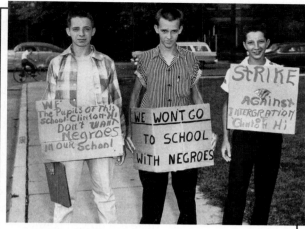

NO WELCOME MAT
Efforts to integrate the nation's schools during the civil rights movement faced strong opposition in some areas of the country.

The same group inferiority and social hierarchy arguments that limited the individual rights of blacks were also historically used against other ethnic groups, Native Americans, and women. Some people today argue that homosexuals face some of the same kinds of unequal treatment. Visions of the United States as a social hierarchy are still part of the mixture of American political culture, but not in the same bold, public, and widespread manner as in previous eras.[43]

Multiculturalism questions the desirability of a common American political culture.

Multicultural thought began sweeping through the United States in the 1980s, particularly on college campuses and in popular culture. The defining characteristics of **multiculturalism** are a belief that American society consists of multiple cultures and that group identity should be as prominent in Americans' thinking as the individualism strongly emphasized in the American creed. Advocates of multiculturalism are skeptical about the notion of any common American political culture. Some multiculturalists contend not only that national political culture is highly diverse rather than unified, but that individuals themselves hold multiple competing cultural beliefs.

multiculturalism the view that group identity influences political beliefs and that, because groups are naturally diverse in their beliefs, the idea of a shared or dominant political culture merely reflects the imposition of a dominant group's beliefs on subordinate groups.

Recognition and tolerance of diversity   In its least controversial version, multiculturalism simply calls for a recognition that the United States is composed of many different ethnic, racial, religious, gender, sexual preference, class, and nationality groups with distinctive contributions to bring to American society. If we view it in this way, it is possible to conceive of the American creed as a national political culture, even while acknowledging that many other aspects of culture and behavior might differ from one group to another. It is from this version of multiculturalism that frequent calls for toleration, diversity, and "embracing our differences" are heard in public discourse.

Rejection of a common culture   In a more controversial version, multiculturalism means that any concept of a unified national political culture is false and is inherently an attempt by dominant groups to exert their power. If there is a unified culture, it is seen as reflecting the domination of one group in society—white men of European descent in particular—over other groups. In this view, as groups become more aware of how the dominant culture has cemented their subordinate position in society, they become more determined to protect and advocate their separate group identity and culture. They may interact with "mainstream" American society, but they also wish to preserve their distinctive language, customs, and beliefs.[44] "Identity politics" is a recent term used to describe such political activity.

Conflict with the American creed   Multiculturalism can lead to direct conflicts with beliefs in the American creed. One area that has been especially controversial and delicate is how multiculturalism intersects with the focus on equality and individualism in the American creed. For example, the nature of gender relations in some cultures has led to the rise of "cultural defenses" in court cases.[45] Some cases have involved men charged with kidnap and rape who defended their actions as part of a particular marriage custom in their culture, and men who explained their murder of their wives as a culturally sanctioned response to their wives' adultery or abuse. In other cases, mothers who killed their children have explained their actions as instigated by the shame of a husband's infidelity and as part of a cultural practice of mother-child suicide. Expert testimony about a defendant's cultural background has sometimes led to dropped or reduced charges or reduced sentences.[46]

Cases like these raise challenging questions. Advocates of the American creed would ask whether equality is better served by emphasizing the equal and free status of each individual or by emphasizing the equal status of different cultural beliefs, which might differentiate between the rights accorded to men and women. Advocates of multiculturalism would ask whether these defenses are any different from those offered earlier in American history by individuals whose cultural heritage was European. For a long time in the United States, they note, legal rights were sharply different for men and women, largely because of Western cultural understandings about gender relations.

Libertarianism argues for a very limited government role.

Libertarianism argues that individuals are responsible for their own lives, and society is best off with individuals maximally free from government restraints. Government's responsibilities, libertarians argue, are to defend the country militarily, to protect individuals from crime, and to ensure that people fulfill contracts entered into freely. Outside these core responsibilities, each and every act of government compromises individual freedom. For example, if Americans believe that providing financial assistance to potential college students is valuable, they should be free to provide funds voluntarily to organizations interested in this cause, rather than be forced by government to support this cause through mandatory taxation.

In the United States, many citizens and

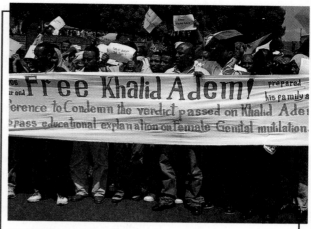

CULTURAL DEFENSES

In a society that wishes to embrace diverse groups and backgrounds, what happens when that diversity clashes with established legal standards? Khalid Adem, an Ethiopian immigrant to the United States, was convicted for cruelty to children for the circumcision of his two-year-old daughter, though he denied being responsible for the act. Defenders of Adem argued that his behavior needed to be understood within the context of his cultural heritage, which was more accepting of female circumcision than was the case in the United States.

politicians of both major political parties profess to hold some libertarian beliefs. This pick-and-choose method is usually unsatisfactory to libertarians: the American creed prizes individualism and limited government, but to libertarians the creed tolerates too big a role for government and too many ways for groups with political clout to use the power of government to advance their interests.

libertarianism a view that emphasizes the importance of individual choice and responsibility, the private sector, and the free market, in which government's primary obligations are to defend the country militarily, protect individuals from crime, and ensure that people fulfill contracts entered into freely.

American political culture is a mosaic of beliefs.

The beliefs of the American creed have been powerful guides for public thinking about politics. Americans may be convinced to change their understanding of the meaning of these beliefs, or they may find the beliefs in severe tension and have to determine the acceptable balance between them. They may in some cases simply choose to ignore, or be persuaded to ignore, one of the beliefs that they profess to support.

For some Americans, American creed beliefs may be displaced by alternative sets of beliefs. More common, however, is that Americans hold many of these beliefs simultaneously and in some tension—supporting the American creed's beliefs, for example, but also holding strong communitarian beliefs or even views supportive of discrimination. Perhaps some hold beliefs from all three of these streams—American creed, communitarianism, discrimination—simultaneously. Or they could embrace the joining of other beliefs like multiculturalism or libertarianism with the American creed beliefs.

The beliefs of the American creed—democracy, individualism, liberty, property rights, religion—and the fundamental value of equality are powerful touchstones in American politics that guide the way most individuals think about politics and government, but they do not preclude other beliefs and ideals holding important places in the mosaic of American political culture. Each generation works with the political culture template left by previous generations and makes its own adjustments, either minor or major, to what is permissible and impermissible, proper and improper, in American politics and government. The remarkable and dynamic mosaic of American political culture endures but also is periodically redefined and reshaped.

Chapter Summary

In this chapter you have learned to:

2-1 Define political culture and explain how certain values and beliefs achieve dominance within a society.

Political culture consists of the basic values, beliefs, attitudes, predispositions, and expectations within which politics operates. It is where citizens start as they process and assess issues, causes, groups, parties, candidates, and public officials. Political culture provides a language used by politicians in speaking to the public.

2-2 Illustrate how the key values and beliefs of the American creed shape politics and government today.

The American creed is built around beliefs in individualism, democracy, liberty, property rights, and religion, all tied together by the value of equality. These beliefs are frequently discussed during the formation of public policy. One of the key storylines of American history is that over time additional groups, such as racial minorities and women, demanded that they, too, be able to receive the benefits of the creed.

2-3 Evaluate the consequences of American political culture such as limited government and a weak sense of sovereign power.

Several consequences emerge from the creed's dominance in American political culture, including a preference for limited government, a weak sense of sovereign power, tension between private and public interests, and concern about the impact of competing beliefs. The beliefs of the creed can sometimes conflict. The belief in liberty might lead toward one policy solution, but the belief in democracy might lead toward another. Tension also arises because the beliefs themselves may be defined differently or might change over time. A term like "democracy" or "liberty" might mean different things to different people. Tension between beliefs and over the definition of each belief creates much of the debate in American politics.

2-4   Identify the major challenges and alternatives to the dominant political culture.

Throughout American history other views have challenged the creed. Alternative modes of thinking about political life have had important effects in the United States. Communitarianism emphasized the role of society or community rather than the centrality of the individual. Communitarianism was prominent during the colonial and Revolutionary periods and continues to influence politics. Discrimination also has had a profound influence on American politics. Justification and defense of social hierarchy and inequality, particularly inequality based on race and gender, have had a long place in American history. Multiculturalism questions the desirability of a consensus in political culture, arguing that any such consensus is more likely the imposition of the values and beliefs of dominant groups upon groups that are weaker. Libertarianism tolerates only the most minimal role for government.

CHAPTER TEST

1. What is the difference between political culture and public opinion?

2. Why has the United States had a shared political culture despite the country's extensive diversity?

3. How does the value of equality tie together the five beliefs of the American creed?

4. What expectations about politics and government are contained in the American creed's belief in democracy?

5. How can the preference for limited government in the American creed coincide with the existence of an array of government programs?

6. In what ways is the sense of sovereign power in the United States weak?

7. How do tension among American creed beliefs and different interpretations of the meaning of the beliefs create conflict in the United States, despite a shared political culture?

8. How do the major communitarian beliefs compare to the American creed, and how prominent has this alternative outlook on politics been in the United States?

9. What are the chief conflicts between multiculturalism and the American creed?

10. In what ways might American political culture be thought of as a mosaic of beliefs?

MyPoliSciLab® POLITICAL CULTURE
Apply what you learned in this chapter on MyPoliSciLab.

Read on mypoliscilab.com

    eText: Chapter 2

Study and Review on mypoliscilab.com

    Pre-Test
    Post-Test
    Chapter Exam
    Flashcards

Watch on mypoliscilab.com

    Video: Facebook Privacy Concerns
    Video: The President Addresses School Children

Explore on mypoliscilab.com

    Simulation: What Are American Civic Values?
    Timeline: Major Technological Innovations that Have Changed the Political Landscape
    Visual Literacy: Using the Census to Understand Who Americans Are
    Visual Literacy: Who Are Liberals and Conservatives? What's the Difference?

KEY TERMS

American creed, p. 22
communitarianism, p. 38
discrimination, p. 42
equality, p. 24
individualism, p. 24

libertarianism, p. 45
liberty, p. 26
limited government, p. 31
multiculturalism, p. 43
natural rights, p. 27

political culture, p. 21
property rights, p. 28
religious freedom, p. 29
sovereign power, p. 33

SUGGESTED READINGS

Alexis de Tocqueville. 1835. *Democracy in America*. Still a remarkably perceptive and insightful analysis of the nature of American society, politics, and identity and how they differ from other countries.

Jennifer L. Hochschild. 1981. *What's Fair: American Beliefs About Distributive Justice*. Cambridge, MA: Harvard University Press. Argues that support for equality thrives in political and private life, but that there is less support for equality in economic matters.

Samuel P. Huntington. 1981. *American Politics: The Promise of Disharmony*. Cambridge, MA: Harvard University Press. Suggests that American politics has been cyclically driven by gaps that emerge between the ideals of the American creed and the reality of American institutions, and that the timing of the cycle is related to the rise and fall of religious "great awakenings."

Seymour Martin Lipset. 1996. *American Exceptionalism: A Double-Edged Sword*. New York: W. W. Norton. Examines whether America is distinctive from other societies in culture, economics, and politics, and concludes that overall it is.

Benjamin I. Page and Lawrence R. Jacobs. 2009. *Class War? What Americans Really Think About Economic Inequality*. Chicago: University of Chicago Press. Argues that Americans are more supportive of measures to address income inequality than is typically assumed.

SUGGESTED WEBSITES

E PLURIBUS UNUM: THE BRADLEY PROJECT ON AMERICA'S NATIONAL IDENTITY
www.bradleyproject.org/bradleyprojectreport.html

Data and analysis exploring the idea of a shared national identity, perceived threats to that identity, and differences between demographic groups.

U.S. RELIGIOUS LANDSCAPE SURVEY
religions.pewforum.org

A survey of over 35,000 adult Americans on their religious practices, beliefs, and opinions on issues.

TRENDS IN POLITICAL VALUES AND CORE ATTITUDES: 1987–2009
people-press.org/report/517/political-values-and-core-attitudes

A survey of American attitudes across an array of fundamental beliefs as well as some specific policy areas.

PUBLIC AGENDA
www.publicagenda.org/citizen

Of particular interest are the issue guides, which examine major issues and present the basic policy choices. The choices provide a good sense of different tradeoffs in American creed beliefs, as well as competing beliefs such as communitarianism and libertarianism. See also the surveys of immigrants in 2002 and 2009 ("A Place to Call Home").

WORLD'S SMALLEST POLITICAL QUIZ
www.theadvocates.org/quizp/index.html

A quiz published by the Advocates for Self-Government, a libertarian group. The quiz analyzes your answers and labels your political ideology.

The Constitution

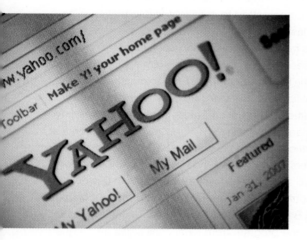

TRACKING COMMUNICATIONS Federal government arguments that it has the right to access e-mail messages and records of the location of cell phone calls as part of the executive branch's national security duties have been highly controversial. In 2010, the Justice Department dropped its demand that Yahoo! provide e-mail messages to investigators, but maintained that it had a right to the messages.

CHAPTER LEARNING OBJECTIVES

After reading this chapter you will be able to:

3-1 Trace developments from events leading to the American Revolution through problems with the country's first constitution.

3-2 Outline the problems the Framers of the Constitution attempted to resolve and the solutions they devised.

3-3 Compare and contrast the arguments of Anti-Federalists and Federalists.

3-4 Explain the processes of constitutional change.

By shaping and constraining the actions of the three branches of government, the U.S. Constitution has direct causal effects on American politics. Ironically, because the Constitution constrains, it also leads these branches to take actions to expand their authority and influence.

In December 2005, the *New York Times* revealed the existence of a program in which the National Security Agency, without authorization from the courts, monitored communications that the Bush administration said involved individuals and members of terrorist organizations in the United States. Under the 1978 Foreign Intelligence Surveillance Act (FISA), the government is normally expected to obtain a warrant from the Foreign Intelligence Surveillance Court to eavesdrop on the international communication of individuals in the United States when at least one party to the communication is suspected of having ties to terrorism.

The revelation that the government had been conducting surveillance without requesting warrants prior to intercepting messages provoked a firestorm of protest. Moreover, although a few members of Congress had been informed about the program, they were not permitted to divulge any information to their colleagues, so Congress as an institution had no knowledge of the surveillance.

The president's position was that Congress's authorization of military action to root out terrorism after September 11, 2001 implicitly gave him wartime authority as commander in chief to order the National Security Agency to monitor suspicious e-mail and telephone calls. Specifically, these would be communications in which one of the persons involved—either in the United States or abroad—might have terrorist links. To critics, the president was taking unilateral, unchecked action that threatened the constitutional balance between the branches. The president's theory of his commander in chief powers, they charged, had no logical stopping point, and yet the U.S. Constitution is all about providing stopping points to power.[1]

Many of these critics thought that a new president would mean a change in these policies. But President Barack Obama's Department of Justice has repeatedly defended the surveillance program from legal challenges and argued that being required to reveal any information gathered by the program would cause substantial harm to national security.

The administration has defended warrantless searches in other cases, as well. In spring 2010, the Department of Justice filed suit against Yahoo! to obtain messages in its Yahoo! Mail service, stating it did not need a warrant to obtain the mail. The dispute turned in part on whether e-mails that had been opened and read were in "electronic storage" and therefore required a warrant to search. The Justice Department argued they were not, and thus no warrant was needed. A large coalition of groups opposed the demand, including Yahoo!, Google, and the Computer and Communications Industry Association. The department ultimately dropped its demand, but not its position that it had a right to the mail.

Other cases have involved the authority of government investigators to demand, without a search warrant, records from cell phone companies recording the location of cell phone calls as determined by cell tower tracking information. The administration has argued that individuals' constitutional rights are not violated when a phone company, responding to a government demand, provides records showing where a cell phone made or received a call. However, the administration's position on cell phone tracking has alarmed civil liberties groups, who argued the administration was unconstitutionally prioritizing executive branch authority over individual citizen privacy.[2]

Although the Framers of the U.S. Constitution could not have foreseen the precise issues leading to the recent battles over warrantless searches, or imagined the new technologies available to store and transmit information, the questions raised by the controversies are the same kinds the Framers wrestled with nearly 225 years earlier. What are the responsibilities of the different branches of government? How can the Constitution ensure that no one part of American government becomes too powerful or too unchecked in its exercise of power? In this chapter, we explore how the Framers answered these questions as they wrote the Constitution. Based on their experience with Great Britain, as well as their experience in governing the new country after the Revolution in 1776, the Framers were deeply concerned with power—its use, abuse, extent, and proper exercise—as they designed a new system of government. Over the centuries since, public officials have sought to work within the Constitution's constraints but also, in turn, to reshape and redefine those constraints. ■

From Revolution to Constitution

3-1   Trace developments from events leading to the American Revolution through problems with the country's first constitution.

Momentous in its impact, the American Revolution has been difficult for historians to classify. Unlike other revolutions, it was not a revolt of one social class against another or a replacement of one economic system by another. If it was not a revolution in these ways, then what was it?

The American Revolution changed ideas about governance.

One answer provided by political scientists and historians is that the American Revolution was an "ideological" revolution, which is to say a revolution most notably in ideas and philosophy of government. To colonial leaders, power tended to be too aggressive and to extend beyond its legitimate boundaries due to human corruption. To defend liberty and thwart excessive power required vigilance and virtue from ordinary people.

The colonists drew insights from their own experience and borrowed liberally from various political theorists and writers. British political theorist John Locke's ideas on limited government and social contracts were especially influential. The idea of the social contract was that the relationship between the governed and those in power was equivalent to a business contract in which each side had obligations to fulfill or the contract would become void.[3]

From this basis, the colonists built a new understanding of politics based on the concepts of representation, guaranteed rights, and sovereignty. The expression "no taxation without representation" highlights one of the most famous demands from the American Revolution. British government officials attempted to convince the colonists they were "virtually represented": the colonists did not elect members of Parliament, but members of Parliament in effect represented the colonists' specific interests by tending to the interests of the British Empire in general, and these two sets of interests were said by the British to be the same. The colonists, instead, touted the concept of direct representation: the job of the representative was to reflect faithfully the opinions of the constituents who elected him or her.

In addition, the colonists believed that constitutions should mark the boundaries of legitimate government power. People had natural, inherent rights that preceded any government action, and written constitutions were needed to protect and guarantee these rights.

Lastly, the colonists challenged the dominant view of sovereignty. In Britain, the idea that there could only be one final, ultimate authority— sovereignty—was undisputed. The colonists, however, argued that sovereignty could be divided. Authority could be divided by different geographical locations, for example at the local and national levels, as well as in different institutions, such as the executive and legislative branches.

The combination of these beliefs generated a new view of the people as self-governing. The people's role had been transformed from occasional watchdog to participant: the people were not only a check on government, they in effect were the government.[4]

The colonists rebelled against taxes imposed unilaterally by the British government.

The immediate impetus for the revolution was a series of economic and political events, many of which received prominent billing in the Declaration of Independence. But, the causal forces are difficult to disentangle. Would the events have had such resonance in the absence of new ideas about the right of the people to self-govern? For decades, the colonists had been out of practical reach of British rulers and had been allowed to operate with extensive freedom. This experience built their confidence in their ability to self-govern. So we can flip the question and ask: would those ideas about self-government have flourished as thoroughly in the absence of a set of provocative events?

Thinking Causally Did powerful ideas or dramatic events push the colonies toward revolution?

The best resolution to these questions is to see the events and ideas as mutually reinforcing. When Britain began to clamp down on the colonies, the colonists believed the freedom they had already achieved was being threatened, and this threat reinforced the appeal of self-governance. To colonists, the revolution was needed to maintain their freedom, not to create it. These causal factors—ideas and events—cannot be completely separated, as each furthered the other and both in turn fostered sentiment for revolution.

The two most influential economic groups of the day were New England merchants and southern planters. These two groups had long been fiercely loyal to the British government, and by controlling key positions of power in the colonies they prevented more radical elements in the colonies from pushing toward conflict with the mother country. Now, however, they were agitated by recent changes in British policies, particularly tax policies. For seven years, Britain had been engaged in the French and Indian War, an engagement that depleted the British treasury. Believing that many of its costs were related to maintaining the safety of the American colonists, the British government instituted new policies designed to extract some revenue from this growing part of its empire.

Stamp Act   The Stamp Act, passed by Parliament in 1765, required all legal documents, licenses, commercial contracts, newspapers, and pamphlets to obtain a tax stamp. The colonists rebelled. Stamp agents were attacked by mobs, and many had their property destroyed. Several colonial assemblies passed resolutions of protest against the act. A boycott of British goods finally led Parliament to repeal the tax.

Revenue Act   Passed in 1767 as one of the set of measures known as the Townshend Acts, the Revenue Act imposed customs duties on colonial imports of glass, lead, paint, paper, and tea. Generally, the cost of these fees was passed along to the colonists by raising the price tag on these products. Resistance to the Revenue Act was considerable. The Massachusetts Assembly, indicating its unwillingness to enforce the law, was disbanded by the British in 1768. Tensions rose over the next 18 months, culminating with the Boston Massacre in March 1770. British soldiers, enduring another day of taunting from a crowd gathered at the Customs House, killed five colonists. The event and the subsequent acquittals further agitated the colonists. Ultimately, boycotts and merchants' refusal to import goods led to the repeal of all the duties except that on tea.

Tea Act   Following a three-year lull, the British government enacted a particularly controversial new economic policy in 1773, the Tea Act. Tea was an extremely important industry in that era. Leaders of the economically advanced countries of the day believed that tea stimulated the national economy. Nearly every country wanted a piece of this industry. The Tea Act allowed the British-controlled East India Company to export its tea to America without paying the tea duty that had been imposed by the Revenue Act. The colonial merchants were squeezed out by the new law, because the East India Company would use its own British agents, not colonial merchants, to sell the tea.

The colonists' response was the incident known as the Boston Tea Party. In December 1773, protesters prevented the unloading of the East India

Company tea and threw the tea in the harbor. The British government viewed the Tea Party as an act of terrorism. To Americans, however, the Tea Party became a symbol of reaction against powerful government. The Tea Party movement that emerged in 2009 is the latest in a long line of protests that use Boston Tea Party imagery to link back to this iconic event.

The British government retaliated with what colonists referred to as the Intolerable Acts. These acts closed the port of Boston, restricted the power of the Massachusetts Assembly, quartered troops in private houses, and exempted British officials from trial in Massachusetts. In response, 12 of the 13 colonies banded together to establish the First Continental Congress in September and October 1774.[5] The Congress issued demands to the king in the form of a Declaration of Rights and Grievances and developed plans for colonial resistance to what they deemed an overbearing imperial government.

The Declaration of Independence aimed to build a nation.

The Continental Congress met again from May 1775 through December 1776 in a charged atmosphere. In April 1775, skirmishes had broken out in Lexington and Concord, Massachusetts. Parliament had rejected the First Continental Congress's Declaration of Rights and Grievances, which set out the colonists' complaints about economic policies, lack of representation, British domination of the colonial judicial system, and disbanding of colonial legislatures. Communications within and between the colonies about the trouble with the British government were frequent and impassioned, with writers like Thomas Paine using pamphlets and his book *Common Sense* to arouse opposition to the royal government.

Recognizing the drift of events and opinion, the Second Continental Congress began the process of building a new government by creating an army, approving the issuance of currency, and establishing diplomatic and trade relations with other countries. On July 4, 1776, their efforts bore fruit, as the Second Congress approved the **Declaration of Independence** drafted by Thomas Jefferson. (An annotated Declaration of Independence can be found at the end of this book, in the Appendix.)

Declaration of Independence document announcing the intention of the colonies to separate from Great Britain based on shared grievances about the treatment of the colonists by the British government.

nation a shared sense of understanding and belonging among a people,that they are different and separate from other peoples with particular characteristics and that they have a right to self-government over a defined territory.

The Declaration asserted that rights of life, liberty, property, and the pursuit of happiness were "unalienable," meaning they cannot be given away. Similarly, as expressed earlier by John Locke, these rights were natural—born in people as an essential part of their being. Government did not provide these rights—the most it could do was restrict them. When it restricted them arbitrarily and unjustly, then revolution was an appropriate response. The Declaration was also an attempt to find common ground that would join the colonists as "Americans." Although "nation" is often used as synonymous with "country," from a political science perspective a **nation** refers to a shared sense of understanding among a people that they are different and

THE DECLARATION OF INDEPENDENCE

The Declaration was adopted by the Second Continental Congress on July 4, 1776. It sought to build a sense of national unity. Creating a nation, and the shared goals and sacrifices that go with it, was one contributing factor in the success of the revolutionary effort.

separate from other peoples; that basic principles, values, and outlooks unite them; and that they have a right to self-government over a territory. The Declaration attempted to inspire that sense of nationhood.

The Articles of Confederation aimed to build a government.

The next step was to build a set of government institutions infused by fundamental principles, rules of operation, values, and beliefs.[6] Constructing a government that can rule effectively and is consistent with a population's sense of nationhood was a significant challenge in 1776, just as it is in emerging democracies today. Rules and procedures guide how governments operate. And rules laid down early can be difficult to change later.

The first attempt to devise governing principles and draft a national constitution was the **Articles of Confederation.** This document reflected a deep fear of centralized political power, a fear born from the Americans' experience with Parliament and British monarchs, and so provided a leading role for the states. The Articles were approved in November 1777 by the Third Continental Congress, which had begun meeting in December 1776. Each of the former colonies, now called states, had to ratify the document. The ratification process was completed in March 1781, and the Articles remained in effect until 1789. The Revolutionary War, which had begun in April 1775, ended in April 1783.[7]

Under the Articles, the national government was based in Congress. Members of Congress were selected by state legislatures, paid by the states, and able to be recalled and removed from office by the states. There was neither an executive branch nor a judiciary. It was difficult for Congress to pass legislation. For a bill to pass, a simple majority of 7 of the 13 states was not enough. Instead, a supermajority—a set amount that is more than a simple majority—of 9 states had to agree. Changing the Articles required the approval of all 13 states.

Articles of Confederation the first constitution of the United States, which based most power in the states.

There were problems with the Articles as a governing framework.

Difficulties set in almost immediately. Congress's powers were limited. Although this was consistent with American ideas about limited government, the government also needed to perform basic functions. Congress could declare war, but there was no standing national army. It could not regulate trade between the states. It could borrow money or coin money, but it could not institute taxes. The national government was almost entirely dependent on the voluntary cooperation of the states.

In addition, the government had no coherent way to deal with other countries. Economic treaties were a free-for-all, with states making their own arrangements. And internally, politicians, merchants, and creditors were shaken by domestic upheaval during the 1780s. Many events worried them. For example, Rhode Island printed paper money for use in repaying debts, which was popular among the citizens who owed money, but creditors considered the money worthless.

Shays's Rebellion a protest by farmers in western Massachusetts in 1786–1787 to stop foreclosures on property by state courts; it convinced many political leaders that the Articles of Confederation were insufficient to govern the United States.

In the view of government and business leaders, all that was wrong under the Articles was evident in the incident known as **Shays's Rebellion** from 1786–1787. Daniel Shays was a former army officer angered by the growing number of people being thrown off their land in western Massachusetts, mostly for inability to pay land taxes. To prevent further foreclosures, Shays joined and led like-minded men in assembling outside courthouses to prevent the courts from opening. His supporters then attempted to raid the federal arsenal in Springfield, where weapons were stockpiled. Massachusetts officials asked the Continental Congress for assistance, but the national government was ill equipped to pull together either financial resources or military personnel. The state itself had no permanent militia. To displace Shays and his supporters, Boston businessmen raised private money to fund the state militia. Although Massachusetts successfully put down the rebellion within a few days after the militia was formed, the incident sent shockwaves around the country.

The political system created by the Articles of Confederation seemed unable to manage either international or domestic affairs. As a result, political and economic leaders concluded that the new nation's first constitution had already failed.

Frustration with the Articles led to the writing of the Constitution.

Shocked by Shays's Rebellion, Congress called on each state to send delegates to Philadelphia in May 1787 to discuss revision of the Articles. Every state except Rhode Island participated. They met with a sense of crisis in the air: the national government appeared to be unable to handle international disputes, establish civility and cooperation between the states, or react to domestic insurrection. The delegates quickly concluded that revision of the Articles was pointless. They decided to start over and establish a new set of ground rules for an effective American government.[8]

Those efforts would culminate in the Constitution, the young country's second attempt to build a government that would rule effectively and unify the new American nation. (An annotated Constitution is found in the Appendix.) Although still concerned about threats to personal liberty posed by the concentration of too much power in a national government, the delegates now believed that too weak a national government was just as severe a threat. As they struggled to devise a new set of rules for the national government, the Framers would need to find a way to blend power with liberty, freedom with order, and national authority with state sovereignty.

Crafting the Constitution

3-2   Outline the problems the Framers of the Constitution attempted to resolve and the solutions they devised.

Although Americans may often be skeptical about the individuals in power, they tend to be proud of their Constitution and the system of government, liberties, and responsibilities it created. People may be critical of politicians, but they believe that the constitutional system works fairly and effectively.

For the most part, this satisfaction is reasonable. The U.S. Constitution is now the oldest national written constitution in the world, and the vast majority of countries have followed the American model of a written constitution. In the United States and other countries with written constitutions, such as Canada, Mexico, France, and Germany, the interpretation of the text might change, but "the constitution" is a well-defined, explicit document. Similarly, the means to amend it are precisely stated, normally requiring a procedure that differs from the one used to pass legislation. In contrast, Great Britain provides the primary example of an unwritten constitution. The British constitution might be thought of as "an understanding" that has emerged from statutes and traditions.

Fashioning a constitution is a complex exercise in problem solving that reflects the particular circumstances present at the document's creation. The more detailed and complicated the document, the higher the risk that it may institutionalize ideas that have only passing or temporary allegiance. This criticism has been lodged against state constitutions in the United States. Too thin a framework, however, runs the risk that the document will not be taken seriously as a guide to behavior or a limit on the abuse of power.[9]

There are many ways to think about and categorize the results of the deliberations of the Framers at the convention. Table 3-1 lists the seven articles

TABLE 3-1 The Constitution

Article I: The Legislative Branch

Bicameral legislature

Nature of election

Powers and duties

Article II: The Executive Branch

Nature of election

Qualifications

Powers and duties

Article III: The Judicial Branch

Nature of appointment and tenure

Creation of Supreme Court

Types of cases

Article IV: National Unity

"Full faith and credit" to acts of other states

All "privileges and immunities" to be same whether or not a state's citizen

Guarantee of republican government

Admitting new states

Article V: The Amending Process

Procedures to amend Constitution

Article VI: National Supremacy

Constitution to be "supreme law" of the land

No religious test for public office

Article VII: Ratification Process

Procedure to ratify Constitution

of the Constitution. Rather than review the Constitution article by article, however, we will discuss the crafting of the new constitution as an exercise in problem solving. In particular, the Framers had five major objectives:

- Overcoming fundamental disputes over representation in the new government.
- Encouraging public input while limiting both "excessive" democracy and concentrated power.
- Protecting commerce and property.
- Creating legitimacy for the new system.
- Providing a coordinated approach to international relations and national defense.

The Great Compromise and Three-fifths Compromise resolved fundamental splits over representation.

Two issues facing the delegates absolutely had to be resolved for the convention to succeed. Both involved the distribution of political power. The delegates' compromise solutions did not guarantee success, but without them failure was assured.

More so than many of us can understand or appreciate today, the delegates were oriented toward their individual states. Political history, tradition, and loyalty, as they knew it, had much more to do with their colonies (now states) than with the American nation at large.

The large state–small state split Given this strong allegiance to the states, the relative influence of the various states in the new system rose immediately as a contentious issue. The first split was the division between large and small states. If the new system were to be based at least in part on a representative legislature, how would states be represented in that body?

The battle lines were predictable. Large states gravitated around the **Virginia Plan** offered by Virginia governor Edmund Randolph.[10] This plan called for state representation in the national legislature to be based on state population: the larger a state's population, the more representatives it would have in the legislature. The so-called lower house would be elected by the people; in turn it would select the members of the upper house, based on lists of candidates provided by state legislatures.

Delegates from small states saw this plan as an unacceptable push toward large-state domination of the new political system. Their response was the **New Jersey Plan,** introduced by William Paterson (who would go on to become a justice on the U.S. Supreme Court). The New Jersey Plan called for equal state representation in a single-house legislature. Each state would send the same number of representatives to the legislature, regardless of population.

With the two plans on the table, each side took a strong stance. The large-state delegates held that if the small states wanted to destroy the Union, then so be it. The small states declared that if the large states wanted to throw their power around, any number of foreign countries would be more than happy to create a new government with the small states. The convention and the task of writing a new constitution faced a deep fracture, but returning to what nearly all the delegates concluded was a defunct and ineffective status quo was not a reassuring prospect for either side, so they were open to compromise.

The solution to the big state–small state split came in the form of the Connecticut Plan, also known as the **Great Compromise.** Under this plan, representation in the House of Representatives would be based on population, as the large states preferred, and legislators would be elected by the people. A second legislative body, the Senate, would have equal representation of all the states, as the small states preferred, and be elected by the state legislatures. The

Virginia Plan one of the rival plans at the Constitutional Convention, it argued for a two-house legislature with representation based on a state's population; the lower house would be elected directly by the people, and that house would then select the members of the upper house.

New Jersey Plan one of the rival plans at the Constitutional Convention, it called for, among other things, equal representation of the states in a single-house legislature.

Great Compromise the agreement between small states and large states that representation in the Senate would be equal for each state, as small states preferred, and representation in the House would be based on population, as large states preferred.

idea of a bicameral, or two-house, legislature itself was not new: Great Britain had a House of Commons and House of Lords, and the existence of two legislative houses was the norm in the colonies and in the states.

The slave state–free state split Similar calculations drove the other critical division between political leaders: the split between states where slavery was forbidden and states where slavery was allowed (a split between northern and southern states, respectively). If representation in the House of Representatives were to be determined by a state's population, how would population itself be determined? Southern states argued that slaves should count as part of the population. Delegates from northern states saw this as hypocrisy, since slave states considered slaves to be property, not people, for all other political purposes.

Once again, both sides were concerned with the balance of power in the new legislature. There were more free states than slave states, so the South was disadvantaged in the Senate. And the population of the North exceeded that of the South, so the South faced the prospect of being outvoted in the House as well. Southern delegates made it clear that this was a make-or-break issue: either include slaves in the population count or the convention ends.

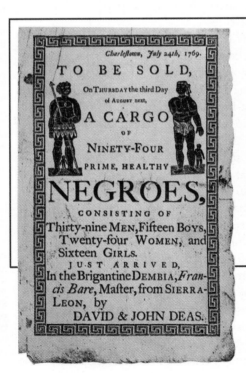

PEOPLE AS PROPERTY

Delegates from slaveholding states wanted to count slaves toward their state population to boost their representation in the House of Representatives. Delegates from other states saw this as inconsistent with the slave states' usual treatment of slaves as property, not people. Why, they asked, should these states now benefit from treating slaves as people for the purpose of gaining more representation in the House? The dispute was resolved by the Three-fifths Compromise.

A resolution was reached through the **Three-fifths Compromise.** Under this plan, sixty percent of a state's slave population would be counted toward the state's overall population. Sixty percent was chosen because this number would balance representation between the North and South in the House. Neither side could dominate the other.[11]

It is a popular misconception that the lack of direct discussion of slavery in the Constitution means that the delegates ignored the issue and were uniformly uninterested in the plight of slaves. This contention makes the analytical mistake of assuming that what we can see is a reliable indicator of what matters most to politicians. Rather than ignore slavery, the delegates were actually consumed by the issue. Some were ardent defenders of slavery. Others opposed the practice on economic or moral grounds. Individual states had wrestled with the issue in years prior to the convention. It was ironically the importance of the issue, not the lack of interest in it, which led to its being given less visibility in the Constitution than critics today might wish.

Believing that politicians usually act strategically in important situations, political scientists would reframe the question: if it was not due to lack of interest or concern, what would cause the Framers to avoid placing heavy emphasis on slavery in the Constitution? The answer is the immediate strategic imperative of crafting a constitution—this is the causal force contributing most heavily to slavery's lack of prominence in the Constitution. The Framers had to find a way to address the issue of slavery in a way that did not undermine their interest in producing a new document. Would a constitution have been possible if opponents of slavery were determined to use the document to eliminate it? Most of the Framers thought not. In the twenty-first century, our moral revulsion against slavery makes it deeply disturbing to even think about this kind of tradeoff, but that was the real-world situation as the Framers perceived it.[12]

Although the terms *slave* and *slavery* do not appear in the Constitution, three provisions directly concerned slavery. The first is the Three-fifths Compromise, which boosted southern representation in the House of Representatives. Second, the Constitution forbade Congress from prohibiting the importation of slaves prior to 1808. And third, any slave escaping to a free state would have to be returned to his or her master. Those who opposed slavery were frustrated by these provisions, but they also realized that no new government would be formed if they pressed the issue. Their hope was that the new government would, over time, devise a way to deal with this problem.

Three-fifths Compromise an agreement between slave states and free states that a state's slave population would be counted at 60 percent for purposes of determining a state's representation in the House of Representatives.

Thinking Causally Does the lack of emphasis on slavery in the Constitution demonstrate the Framers' lack of interest in the plight of slaves?

The Framers wanted public officials to hear the voice of the people but also wanted to prevent "excessive" democracy.

The Framers believed that the people should have a voice in government, but they did not believe that the people's voice should dictate the behavior of public officials. The people's input should influence the decisions of government, they concluded, but there must be a buffer between the people's demands and the government's actions. They feared that a government that was too close to the people would weaken the rights of the minority in general, and the minority that owned significant amounts of property in particular.[13]

For these reasons, the Framers did not create a democracy in the technical sense, in which the people themselves directly rule. Rather, they created a representative democracy or **republic,** in which the people select representatives who are entrusted to make the laws.[14] Preventing excessive democracy meant not only protecting government from the people's passions, but also protecting citizens from each other. The Framers accomplished these goals in several ways.

republic a system in which people elect representatives to make policy and write laws; also known as a representative democracy.

Selection of public officials The Constitution provides for staggered terms of office for elected officials (Articles I, II). House members serve two-year terms; senators serve six-year terms, with one-third of the senators up for election in any given election year; and the president serves a four-year term. This arrangement means that Americans can never dismiss all government officials at once because all officials are never up for election in the same year. Regardless of the passions that may be stirring the public, it would take six years before they could completely replace all the elected officials in the national government. And the public has no direct way to choose federal judges. Once nominated by the president and confirmed by the Senate, federal judges—unlike judges in many states—have lifetime tenure and do not face elections.

indirect election an election in which voters select other individuals who directly vote for candidates for a particular office; U.S. Senate and presidential elections were of this type in the Constitution, but Senate elections are now direct elections.

In the Constitution as ratified, the people directly elected only the members of the House of Representatives. Senators were selected by state legislatures. The people voted for state legislators, who then selected the state's U.S. senators, a process known as **indirect election.** Not until the passage of the Seventeenth Amendment in 1913 did the people directly elect their U.S. senators. Presidents were also elected indirectly. The public in a state voted for electors, and these electors then met in their states in the Electoral College to cast ballots for president and vice president. The candidate who received a majority of the electoral vote would be the president. Even today, although ballots list the presidential candidates, voters are technically voting for a group of electors who have pledged to cast their electoral vote for the particular candidate. The logic was that the people could select the electors, but the electors, presumably individuals who were wise, knowledgeable, and distinguished, would evaluate the presidential candidates more carefully.

Separation of powers The Framers also attempted to protect against the effects of excessive democracy with separation of powers and checks and balances. The idea of balancing power was not new. The colonies had relied on the idea of balancing power against power, with legislators checking the power of the governor, who served on behalf of Britain. The Framers drew heavily upon the ideas of political thinkers such as Montesquieu (1689-1755), a French political thinker who wrote at length about separation of powers.

In the Constitution the Framers provided for three independent centers of authority in a legislature, executive, and judiciary (in Articles I, II, and III, respectively). **Separation of powers** means that the major branches of government would have different primary functions and responsibilities—the legislature would make law; the executive would implement law; and the judiciary would interpret law (see Figure 3-1). The separation would be reinforced by alternative methods of selecting the leadership of each branch. In practice, the division in functions has not been quite this neat and tidy, so some observers suggest that a better description of separation of powers is "separated institutions sharing powers."

separation of powers the principle that the executive, legislative, and judicial functions of government should be primarily performed by different institutions in government.

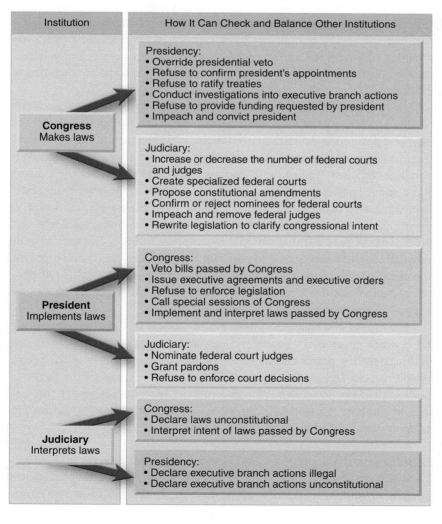

Institution	How It Can Check and Balance Other Institutions
Congress Makes laws	Presidency: • Override presidential veto • Refuse to confirm president's appointments • Refuse to ratify treaties • Conduct investigations into executive branch actions • Refuse to provide funding requested by president • Impeach and convict president Judiciary: • Increase or decrease the number of federal courts and judges • Create specialized federal courts • Propose constitutional amendments • Confirm or reject nominees for federal courts • Impeach and remove federal judges • Rewrite legislation to clarify congressional intent
President Implements laws	Congress: • Veto bills passed by Congress • Issue executive agreements and executive orders • Refuse to enforce legislation • Call special sessions of Congress • Implement and interpret laws passed by Congress Judiciary: • Nominate federal court judges • Grant pardons • Refuse to enforce court decisions
Judiciary Interprets laws	Congress: • Declare laws unconstitutional • Interpret intent of laws passed by Congress Presidency: • Declare executive branch actions illegal • Declare executive branch actions unconstitutional

FIGURE 3-1 Separation of Powers and Checks and Balances.

With separation of powers and checks and balances, each branch of government has distinct but overlapping responsibilities.

checks and balances the principle that each branch of the federal government has the means to thwart or influence actions by other branches of government.

judicial review the power of the judiciary to interpret and overturn actions taken by the legislative and executive branches of government.

federalism a form of government that distributes power across a national government and subnational governments and ensures the existence of the subnational governments.

Checks and balances The system of **checks and balances** provides the main set of mechanisms through which the branches monitor each other. Checks and balances means that each branch of government has a way to affect and, in some instances, to stop, the actions of the others. Many of the checks and balances techniques are likely familiar; they are listed in Figure 3-1. They reinforce the idea of separated institutions sharing power. Lawmaking, for example, is not the province of Congress alone. The president has to approve any bills before they can become law.[15] And, because of legislative bicameralism—Congress is divided into two houses, each of which must approve the same version of a bill before it can be sent to the president for approval—Congress has internal checks and balances. Lastly, although the judiciary's power was only thinly described in the Constitution, this branch soon asserted the power of **judicial review,** meaning it would decide whether the laws and other actions of government officials were constitutional. The judiciary could strike down a federal or state law and overturn nonlegislative actions such as a policy or procedure implemented by an executive branch agency. As for checks on this branch, Congress and the president can counteract the judiciary's power through constitutional amendments, new appointments to the courts, and restructuring of the courts.[16]

There were competing views early in the convention on how to check and balance power. Both the Virginia and New Jersey plans gave the legislature the strongest position in American government, and the Framers ultimately concurred. Congress is the focus of Article I in the Constitution and is the institution with the most detailed list of responsibilities and duties. But the Framers also dispersed power and increased the independence of the other branches.[17] They wanted to make sure that any pressure from the people was heard by government, but that it was diffused across the three branches. Moreover, the Framers wanted a strong national government, but they also wanted to be sure that it would not become so powerful as to threaten liberty and property. The proposed government was designed to thwart the power-grabbing tendencies of human nature, according to James Madison. "If men were angels," he wrote, "no government would be necessary."[18]

The checks and balances system was one aspect of the careful balancing act between government power and personal freedom. As the Framers saw it, disaggregating power this way both protected against abuse of the people by government and made it more difficult for any one part of the public to capture all of the power centers in government. Madison referred to this system, in combination with federalism (described in the following section), as a "double security" against tyrannical government.[19]

Federalism Despite differences concerning the relative power and authority of the national and state governments, delegates agreed that federalism would be an underlying principle of the new system. **Federalism** is a governing arrangement that provides multiple levels of government with independent ruling authority over certain policy areas, and guarantees the survival of these different levels of government. Federalism was a bulwark against the risk of concentrated power and excessive democracy. The states check the power of the national government, but the national government checks the power of the states. We will have much more to say about federalism in Chapter 4.

The parliamentary system as an alternative distribution of power

The choices made by the Constitutional Convention delegates differ significantly from the choices made in later years in other parts of the world. In Europe, especially, the parliamentary system was the structure of choice for those constructing governments. In a **parliamentary system**, the prime minister, who serves as the chief executive, is selected from the parliament (the legislature) by other members. The prime minister then selects department heads from among fellow partisans in the legislature. Typically in a parliamentary system, the legislature is supreme, and the notions of checks and balances and separation of powers are not particularly relevant.

parliamentary system
a political system in which the head of the executive branch is selected by members of the legislature rather than by popular vote.

Opponents of the parliamentary system charge that it puts too much power in the hands of the majority party. Control of the executive branch and the legislature cannot be split between two parties, even if that would be the voters' preference. Advocates of the parliamentary system respond that it is a government that is not at cross-purposes with itself. Rather than checking and balancing power, and having branches of government intentionally frustrate each other and the majority's will, the parliamentary system enables the leading party in the legislature to take swift action. The Framers of the American Constitution were wary of giving any entity, including the majority of the population, so much power.

Numerous constitutional provisions were designed to protect commerce and property.

Events in the states in the 1780s, such as Shays's Rebellion and the printing of currency of questionable worth, panicked New England merchants, southern planters, and the entire spectrum of businesspeople in between. Therefore, one chief concern of the Framers was to protect commerce and property from the designs of the national government, the state governments, and states pitted against states.

First, the Framers established that the national government would have primary regulatory control over commerce and finance. The national government would regulate commerce between the states and with other countries and be responsible for producing coinage and currency, establishing bankruptcy laws, and creating protections for copyrights and patents (Article I in the Constitution). This arrangement still allowed differences between the states, but it prevented states from creating alliances with each other or with another country that harmed the commercial or property interests of citizens in other states. It also prevented states from inflating currency or devising other schemes to make it easy for their citizens to escape from debt obligations.

supremacy clause a clause in the Constitution that declares that national laws and treaties have supremacy over state laws and treaties.

Second, the Constitution's **supremacy clause** declared that national laws and treaties would have supremacy over state laws and treaties (Article VI). State laws could differ from the national law, but they had to be consistent with it. For example, states can enact anti-pollution laws more stringent than those the federal government requires, but not more relaxed. Federal law can, however, preempt the states from deviating from federal standards. For example, the Federal Cigarette Labeling and Advertising Act imposes national rules on cigarette advertising and prohibits state governments from imposing additional advertising regulations.[20]

full faith and credit clause a clause in the Constitution stating that states are to honor the official acts of other states.

equal privileges and immunities clause a clause in the Constitution stating that states are to treat equally their citizens and the citizens of other states.

States were also to be nondiscriminatory toward each other (Article IV). Through the **full faith and credit clause,** states are to honor the official acts of other states, such as public records and the results of judicial proceedings. Under the **equal privileges and immunities clause,** states are to treat their citizens and citizens of other states similarly. Congress and the president can override these provisions if they choose to do so. Such an override happened in 1996 with the passage of the Defense of Marriage Act, which stipulated that states need not honor same-sex marriages performed in other states. Normally, the free faith and credit clause would dictate that a marriage that is legal in one state will be recognized as legal in the others, but states were given an exemption in this instance.

The Constitution included additional protections for commerce and property. Article VI stipulated that any contracts entered into before the Constitution must still be honored after the Constitution was ratified. This provision was motivated chiefly by concern that debts incurred during the Revolutionary War be paid, but it applied to debts incurred after the war also. The national government also guaranteed each state a republican—that is, representative—form of government and pledged to protect the states against domestic violence, a reaction to Shays's Rebellion.

Lastly, the Framers provided for a president who would be a counterweight to Congress. As the Framers saw it, representatives would often allow the narrow interests of their districts to guide their decisions, whereas senators would have the somewhat broader but still biased self-interests of their states in mind. Only the president would represent the country as a whole and have an ongoing commitment to the national interest rather than to any special interest of a state or district.

Certain measures and principles were emphasized to enhance the proposed system's legitimacy.

Legitimacy is about trust. When you believe that an arrangement is legitimate, you may not trust individual officials, but you trust the system. To the Framers, establishing legitimacy for the new government was critical, and they addressed the challenge in three ways.

First, they emphasized the representativeness of the new government. The House, the Senate, and the presidency, they noted, represented distinct parts of society—parts of states, entire states, and the country, respectively. Direct popular election of the House of Representatives was another legitimacy-building feature. The House would be the "people's house." And, because of the system of checks and balances, much of the work of government would have to pass through the people's house and some, particularly matters concerning taxation, would have to begin there.

Second, the Framers built the case for legitimacy around the notion that the new government would have constrained power. The checks-and-balances system would prevent government from acting recklessly. The Constitution, the Framers noted, was a social contract between rulers and ruled. If the rulers violated this contract, the people had a right to remove them. Further, the Framers promised that a bill of rights guaranteeing personal liberties would be added to the Constitution as the first order of business after ratification.

Third, they created an enduring but flexible framework for government. They wanted the people to be confident that the Constitution had roots—that its meaning and content would have some stability—but they also wanted the people to believe that the system could be changed if necessary. By providing for amendments, the Framers created a document that would be flexible. By making the amending process difficult, they created a document that would be enduring.

Balancing stability and flexibility was also achieved by writing a constitution that provided a basic framework for government and politics. The Constitution lays down the essential rules of how government will work and how officials will be selected. It also indicates the responsibilities of government officials. It presents a general outline for how public policy will be made, but it contains very little actual policy. The Framers left the details of policy to the branches of government to work out in the form of laws. They realized that preferences about particular issues would change over time, so enshrining them in the Constitution would be problematic.

The Civil War provides the most glaring exception to Americans' beliefs that their political differences can be worked out through constitutional provisions. The Constitution could not contain the depth of division between North and South. In addition, for much of American history the Constitution was seen as compatible with discrimination of the rankest sort against racial, ethnic, and religious minorities and women. Americans today, however, are more likely to fault the people and the politicians in power during those times rather than the Constitution itself, because the Constitution also provided the means to change these patterns.[21]

The new system provided the means for a coordinated approach to international relations and national defense.

The foreign threats facing Americans in the 1780s were significant. Britain controlled the territory around the Great Lakes. Aside from Britain's own disagreements with the United States, the tension between Britain and France meant that being caught in their crossfire was a distinct possibility. Spain controlled Florida and areas to the west. Skirmishes with Native American tribes were frequent. The Constitution provided the promise of executive and legislative leadership and coordination to respond to these challenges. The president would be the operational head of military actions and the representative of the United States to other countries. He would appoint ambassadors and negotiate treaties, but both of these would require the Senate's approval. Congress's control over military budgets and taxes and the declaration of war was intended to make foreign policy a cooperative venture. States would have to follow the national lead on military matters, including those with Native American tribes. They could not enter into treaties or alliances with other countries or tribes, arrange discriminatory tariffs, or enter into military conflict unless invaded or facing a similar immediate emergency.[22]

The Battle for Ratification

3-3 Compare and contrast the arguments of Anti-Federalists and Federalists.

Sending the Constitution to the states for ratification was a risky gambit. The Framers could not look to other countries to see how a national ratification effort would fare, or what the risks and rewards were for giving the people this much influence. However, supporters of the Constitution believed that ratification in the states was a political necessity. It was also, they realized, an opportunity for opponents to derail the document.

Battle lines over ratification of the Constitution were drawn between the **Federalists,** who supported ratification, and the **Anti-Federalists,** who opposed it.[23] The central debate concerned what kind of governmental arrangement would best preserve liberty.

Federalists individuals who supported the proposed Constitution and favored its ratification.

Anti-Federalists individuals opposed to the proposed Constitution, fearing it concentrated too much power in the national government.

Anti-Federalists argued that the Constitution threatened liberty.

Anti-Federalists argued that the proposed Constitution threatened the people's liberty. Distant from the people, this kind of government might begin to tax heavily, override state court decisions, have a permanent army at its disposal, or absorb functions performed by the states—fears that history shows were not

HOW DO WE KNOW?

What Motivated the Framers of the Constitution?

The Question

The men sent to the Constitutional Convention in Philadelphia in 1787 had risen to prominence in their respective states. Overall, however, the U.S. Constitution reduced the autonomy of the states. For political scientists, this outcome raises a research puzzle: why would ambitious, intelligent political leaders agree to a system that might reduce the power of the states in which they had been politically influential? What motivated the Framers of the Constitution? How do we know?

Why It Matters

Why should any of us care what motivated the Framers of the Constitution so long ago? The reason is simple: if Americans wish to know whether contemporary American politics and government live up to founding values, they must know why the system was designed the way it is.

Investigating the Answer

One answer, offered by economist Charles Beard early in the twentieth century, is that the Constitution reflected the economic self-interest of those drafting and voting for it.[24] Beard complained that previous accounts of the Constitution had been based on ideals and wishful thinking. He called for social scientists to conduct hardheaded, systematic analyses of the world as it was.

Beard wanted to explain the votes of delegates at the Constitutional Convention. Assuming that political action is guided by self-interest, Beard hypothesized that delegates' financial self-interest determined how they voted on the Constitution. By analyzing the financial holdings and economic interests of the delegates, he concluded that the Framers protected their commercial interests. Opponents in the convention, he argued, were also influenced by their self-interest and were mostly farmers who had land holdings, those without property, and those in debt. Knowing the economic interests of those who supported or opposed the document, he argued, reveals the motivations of the document's writers.[25]

Beard's critics offer a different answer. They saw the Framers' actions as grounded more in their practical political assessment of what was necessary to keep the country united and afloat, or in their sincere interest in the political ideals they were espousing.[26] To the critics, Beard mistakenly assumed that correlation equals causation: the fact that delegates' financial self-interest and their votes in the convention were correlated did not prove that the interests caused the votes.

Reanalysis of Beard's data showed that the delegates in favor of the Constitution also had substantial land ownership, which was a prime characteristic Beard identified among the opponents. In fact, those favoring the Constitution had more land ownership than ownership of commercial interests.[27] If landholders had a self-interest in opposing the Constitution, even the supporters of the Constitution should have opposed it because they had a larger financial stake in land than in commerce.

But by assuming that the ideals of those who supported the Constitution were unified and that therefore their motives were the same, Beard's critics may also have erred. For example, James Madison and Alexander Hamilton wrote the bulk of the *Federalist Papers*, but within a few years it was clear that their political ideologies were radically different from one another.[28] They may have both supported the Constitution, but their motivations were likely not identical.

Rather than looking at a political outcome and then assuming that the result reflects some group's motives, political scientists can look to the historical record—memoirs, journals, interviews, and other sources—to determine what drove individuals to take particular actions. Individuals may not be completely aware of or candid about their motivations, but this approach can reveal important insights. In a study of the crafting of the Constitution, for example, one political scientist concluded that the final document was a defeat for some of its most ardent proponents, such as Madison.[29] Throughout the convention, Madison unsuccessfully pushed for a more powerful national government than created in the final document. Careful analysis of the day-by-day proceedings shows Madison to be frequently on the defensive. Rather

(continues)

HOW DO WE KNOW? What Motivated the Framers of the Constitution? *(continued)*

than Madison's rhetoric in the *Federalist Papers* being a completely clear signal of his true preferences, he shaped his argument around the Constitution that was approved by the convention.

Such analysis highlights the importance of sequence and timing in explaining political outcomes. Early decisions, even small ones, can have tremendous impact because they begin a process that influences future decisions. Once the delegates decided on an elected presidency, for example, that decision affected their votes on other aspects of the Constitution, and rethinking that decision would have been very difficult, because everything else afterward depended on it. The Constitution was created by a series of decisions that produced a document much more deferential toward the states than Madison and many others wanted. And yet, after the Constitutional Convention sent the document to the states for ratification, Madison strongly supported the document, and scholars ever since, influenced by that strong support, have seen the Constitution as a victory for him.

Thinking Critically

1. In what ways might you imagine the American political system would be different if the delegates had decided early in their deliberations to have a president elected for a single six-year term?

2. Offer your strongest argument for having delegates at the convention vote by state rather than each delegate casting an individual vote. How about the other way around?

3. When is it acceptable or unacceptable for a representative—for example, a delegate to a convention or a legislative body—to vote in a manner consistent with his or her economic interests?

The Bottom Line

The Framers of the Constitution were motivated by a number of factors, including political ideals and principles, a belief that the status quo was unacceptable, concerns about what would be politically palatable to the states, and likely some political and economic self-interest as well. But to correlate the convention votes with economic self-interest and then assume that self-interest was the primary causal motivation behind the Constitution is faulty social science. In political analysis, it is important to consider multiple causal factors and to realize that the sequence and timing of decisions, as well as the rules for making decisions, affect the outcome. These factors can even lead an individual to support something he or she believes falls short. Just as Madison vigorously supported a document that did not entirely reflect his preferences, a president must sometimes sign legislation that does not precisely reflect his or her leanings.

THE CONSTITUTIONAL CONVENTION, 1787 Delegates gathered in Philadelphia to revise the Articles of Confederation, but quickly concluded that a new constitution was necessary. The crafting of the Constitution involved a sequence of decisions, and scholars have examined the evidence to disentangle causality from correlation in explaining the outcome of the convention.

far-fetched. Legendary patriots such as Patrick Henry, a stalwart supporter of the Revolution, saw the proposed Constitution as a counterrevolution, pushing back toward more central authority, reducing democratic influence on government, and protecting the interests of political and economic leaders.

The Anti-Federalists argued that the government should have many restrictions on its power. For example, they suggested reducing the range of cases the Supreme Court could hear; creating a council to review all presidential decisions; leaving military affairs to state militias; enlarging the House of Representatives; and adding a "bill of rights" to protect individual freedoms.

The Anti-Federalists were only successful on this last item. Supporters of the Constitution initially argued that a bill of rights was unnecessary and that a listing of rights or liberties could effectively become a limitation on rights and liberties if misinterpreted as a comprehensive list. In the climate of the ratification debate, however, a strong symbolic statement was needed, so the proponents of ratification agreed to a bill of rights. They knew their best chance of success would be if states were forced to make an up-or-down vote—this document or nothing. As ultimately ratified by the states, the **Bill of Rights** refers to the first 10 amendments to the Constitution, which focus on preserving individual freedoms.

Bill of Rights the first 10 amendments to the U.S. Constitution, intended to protect individual liberties from federal government intrusion.

Madison responded in the *Federalist Papers* that a large republic is the best defense for liberty

The argument between Federalists and Anti-Federalists was fought out in speeches, handbills, and newspaper columns. The most famous of all these was a set of newspaper opinion columns penned under a pseudonym by James Madison, Alexander Hamilton, and John Jay. Collectively, these columns would come to be called the *Federalist Papers*. These columns presented the theoretical basis of American government, discussing such concepts as federalism, the separation of powers, and checks and balances.

The Anti-Federalist argument about the desirability of democracies and small republics was rejected in the most famous of the *Federalist Papers*—number 10. (An annotated *Federalist 10* appears in the Appendix.) In *Federalist 10*, James Madison argued that liberty is actually most at risk in direct democracies and small republics. It is safest in precisely the kind of large republic being proposed in the Constitution.

Like politicians today, Madison was making causal claims. The outcome to be explained is the preservation of liberty. Madison begins by stating that the most severe threat to liberty is the presence of factions, which threaten the rights of other citizens. Factions are natural, Madison argues, as people naturally cluster with like-minded individuals. The real question, therefore, was how to control factions and their effects, especially their effects on property rights.

Thinking Causally What best preserves liberty?

Madison believed that the proposed republic, and not a democracy, would be the best way to control excessive factional influence. This is Madison's key causal link between the proposed Constitution and the protection of liberty. First, in Madison's view, having a relatively small number of representatives increases the likelihood that voters are selecting individuals of honor, merit, and virtue for public office. Second, larger, more diverse districts will send mixed policy messages to representatives, encouraging them to sift out the bad ideas and keep the good. Third, in a geographically large political system, more opposing interests will be vying for attention; as interest battles interest, a majority faction is less likely to form.

The bottom line of Madison's argument was a remarkable rejection of the conventional causal wisdom of his day. Rather than holding onto communitarian hopes about civic virtue—selfless political participants concerned only for the common welfare—Madison suggested the country allow self-interest to serve public ends. Each individual's self-interest, he reasoned, gives that person an incentive to ensure that other individuals do not abuse power, thus producing precisely the best outcome for society. Madison took this argument one step further in *Federalist 51* (an annotated version appears in the Appendix), in which he noted that governmental power would be distributed across the national and state governments and across the three major branches of government, whose officials would challenge each other and thus prevent the monopolization of power. Their self-interest would protect liberty.[30]

Belief that change was necessary assisted the Federalists' ratification campaign.

Citizens in the states voted for delegates to attend state ratifying conventions. Nine states needed to approve the Constitution for it to be in effect. The first state to ratify was Delaware, in December 1787. Seven months later, when New Hampshire became the ninth state to approve, the Constitution was ratified.

In the end, the Federalists won the debate. The main causes are straightforward. In part, this victory appears to be due to the more convincing arguments of the Federalists. In part, it owes to the absence of a comprehensive Anti-Federalist alternative. Many who voted for the Constitution might well have shared some of the Anti-Federalists' fears about a strong central government, but they also feared domestic disturbances and foreign threats. At bottom, the decision became whether to adopt the Constitution, stick with the Articles, or start over again. Given the sense that the young country faced both foreign and domestic challenges, the appeal of continuing with the Articles or renewing the debate was limited. Change was needed, most people believed, and the Constitution provided that change.

Amending the Constitution

3-4 Explain the processes of constitutional change.

The structure of the constitutional system sometimes frustrates Americans. Features usually thought of as strengths can sometimes be seen as negatives, especially when they slow government responses to important national problems. However, on the whole, any frustration is outweighed by a belief among Americans that the system works.

Part of the process of establishing legitimacy for the Constitution was providing a procedure by which it could be revised. The underlying premise of the Constitution's amendment process is that any change in the Constitution has to have broad consensus throughout society.

Amendments should have broad societal acceptance.

The introduction of amendments is essentially a national-level process, while the ratification of amendments is a state-level process (see Figure 3-2). Moreover, supermajorities are a requirement of all four paths to amendment. Amendments will not be added to the Constitution unless they receive supermajority support at two stages. The premise that amendments should have broad social acceptance is therefore built into the process, and the presence or absence of such acceptance is often a chief point of debate.[31]

In the two paths used for the introduction of all amendments to date (paths A and C in Figure 3-2), two-thirds of the members of the House (representatives of the entire population) and two-thirds of the members of the

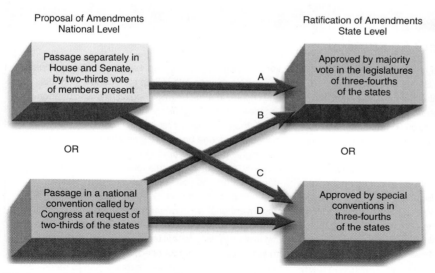

Proposal of Amendments
National Level

Ratification of Amendments
State Level

Passage separately in House and Senate, by two-thirds vote of members present

Approved by majority vote in the legislatures of three-fourths of the states

OR

OR

Passage in a national convention called by Congress at request of two-thirds of the states

Approved by special conventions in three-fourths of the states

A
B
C
D

FIGURE 3-2 Paths to Amending the Constitution.

The amending process is based on supermajorities at both the proposal and ratification stages.

Note: Congress chooses which path is used. Path A: Used for 26 Amendments. Path B: Never used. Path C: Used for one amendment (21st). Path D: Never used.

Senate (representatives of the states) who are present and voting are needed to approve a proposed constitutional amendment.

The constitutional rules for introduction of an amendment using paths B and D are less clear, as these methods have never been used. The Constitution does not indicate whether votes at a national convention would need to be supermajorities. Most likely, given that the Constitution gives Congress the power to call the convention if two-thirds of the states request it, Congress would set the rules for how the convention would be run.

At the ratification level, we again see the Framers' desire that constitutional changes have broad societal acceptance. Three-quarters of the states, or 38 today, either in the state legislature or specially convened state conventions, are needed to ratify an approved amendment. Members of Congress have little incentive to approve a proposed amendment that seems to lack sufficient support in the states to be ratified. On some occasions, however, initial supportive conditions can deteriorate as opponents mobilize against the proposal. When members of Congress sent the Equal Rights Amendment (ERA) to the states in the 1970s, they had good reason to believe it would be ratified. After a rapid string of state ratifications, however, the ERA proved susceptible to the arguments of opponents in some states that its implications were vague and its interpretation so uncertain that extensive litigation would be a likely result.[32] Supporters were unable to build sufficient societal consensus in the wake of these critiques.

Congress has the responsibility to decide which ratification path a proposed amendment will take. Congress also determines whether proposed amendments have any time limits attached to their ratification. The most

Case Study

Lowering the Voting Age to 18

The uniform adoption of an 18-year-old voting age across the United States was accomplished through the ratification of the Twenty-sixth Amendment in 1971. A handful of states had lowered their voting ages before this, at least for some elections. Most states, however, still had 21 as the legal age for voting entering the 1970s. This was consistent with the societal consensus that 21 was the age of maturity.[33]

War provided one key catalyst to changing thoughts about the age of maturity. Eighteen- to twenty-year-olds were dying in the Vietnam War in large numbers, but they did not have the right to vote. Similar pressure had arisen following previous wars, but support for a voting age amendment went nowhere. In part, this failure was because the support was not overwhelming, and many Americans saw the ages of 18 to 20 as those of rebel-

lion, uncertainty, and susceptibility to emotional appeals and rabble rousing rather than sober and thoughtful citizenship. In addition, most legislators who supported the idea also had higher-priority concerns.

Vietnam changed everything. Unlike the previous conflicts, this one became tremendously controversial and highly unpopular among large, though not always majority, parts of the population. It was especially unpopular among younger Americans, at least in part because of the military draft. Youth protested in unconventional ways rather than through the ballot box, because they could not vote. The contradiction between eligibility for military service and ineligibility to vote was more pronounced, at least symbolically, under these circumstances. States began to reconsider their laws, and support grew again at the national level

Case Study Lowering the Voting Age to 18

for an amendment. In addition to the organizations that had supported the idea for decades, a number of the youth organizations that emerged during the war pressed for the 18-year-old vote, as did labor unions, some church groups, and organizations linked to the civil rights movement. The societal consensus for an 18-year-old voting age had grown.

The path to an amendment was accelerated in 1970, with the addition of a provision in the Senate's renewal of the Voting Rights Act (originally passed in 1965) that lowered the age for all elections to 18. Although many members of the House suspected the provision was unconstitutional, they agreed to it so that the renewal of the Voting Rights Act would not be derailed. President Nixon, similarly skeptical about the provision's constitutionality, nonetheless signed the bill.

A challenge to the provision quickly reached the Supreme Court. In *Oregon v. Mitchell* (1970), in a closely divided 5-4 decision, the Court concluded that Congress could set the age for federal elections but not state elections. Therefore, the country was now faced with an 18-year-old voting age for federal elections (president, U.S. House, U.S. Senate) and whatever age each state set for its own elections.

This scenario promised a very difficult election in 1972. Many states would have to monitor different voting ages for different parts of the ballot. Even if they wanted to change their voting age to 18, in many states that change required voter approval of a proposed state constitutional amendment at two subsequent elections. The nation was now near consensus that lowering the voting age uniformly was right, whether on policy grounds or because of the horrors facing election administration without a uniform age.

FIT TO SERVE BUT NOT TO VOTE Young American soldiers of the 9th Infantry fire at enemy troops along the South Vietnamese–Cambodian border in May 1970. The contrast between young adults aged 18 to 20 serving in combat but being unable to vote led to demands, as during previous wars, that the voting age be lowered. One reason the demand succeeded at this time and not the others was the controversy over the war itself. Not only were the troops unable to vote, but the young adults who marched in large numbers against and for the war were also shut out of the ballot box.

Spurred by the Court's action, Congress moved quickly. Within a month of the *Oregon v. Mitchell* decision, Randolph Jennings, who had proposed the first constitutional amendment on the issue in 1942, introduced another constitutional amendment to lower the voting age. The amendment was approved unanimously in the Senate, with fewer than 20 dissenting votes in the House, and sent to the states for ratification. The amendment needed quick passage to be in effect for 1972. In the states, ratification was accomplished in record time. A little over three months after being sent to the states, the Twenty-sixth Amendment had been ratified and added to the Constitution.

The quick response across the states marks this amendment as unusual—ratification looked much the same in every state. In the importance of causal factors such as societal consensus, interest-group pressure, and politicians who believed in the proposal for reasons of good policy or electoral advantage, or both, however, the story of the Twenty-sixth Amendment looks like those of other successful amendments.[34]

Thinking Critically

1. Some reformers have proposed that the voting age today be lowered to 16. What criteria would you use to decide whether this is a good idea?

2. In your view, what are the valid reasons, if any, to deny someone the ability to vote? Should that denial be permanent or temporary?

3. War was a key causal factor in lowering the voting age to 18. Should we generally expect war to lead to social change or instead to preserve the status quo?

recent amendment, the Twenty-seventh, which states that a congressional pay raise cannot take effect until after the next election, was actually introduced at the same time as the Bill of Rights but did not gather enough state support to be ratified—mostly because it had been forgotten—until 1992.

Twenty-seven amendments have been added to the Constitution.

The proof that the federal amending process is difficult is in the numbers. Since 1789, over 10,000 proposals for constitutional amendments have been introduced in Congress. Of these, only 27 have been ratified. Ten were ratified almost immediately, as part of the Bill of Rights. Since 1791, only 17 amendments have been added to the Constitution, less than one per decade on average. The country can go long periods without any amendments, and then have a number of amendments over a short period. Over 60 years elapsed between the Twelfth and Thirteenth Amendments, and over 40 between the Fifteenth and Sixteenth Amendments, but between 1961 and 1971 four amendments were added to the Constitution.[35]

As Table 3-2 shows, amendments have followed the logic of the articles of the Constitution, emphasizing the basic framework of government, the powers of government, the size of the electorate, and the relationship between people and government. The amendments have generally not dealt with matters of social or economic policy, with three exceptions: the elimination of slavery, the approval of a federal income tax, and the prohibition—and then repeal of the prohibition—of alcohol production and sales. Slavery and taxation were issues addressed in the Constitution, implicitly and explicitly, respectively, so these amendments did not address new areas. The failure of Prohibition is often considered a prime example of why specific social policy should not be included in the Constitution.[36]

Although the amending process provides flexibility to the Constitution that enhances system legitimacy, it is, as we have seen, infrequently successful, and the country can go long periods without any formal change to the Constitution. Whether the Framers expected this degree of structural stability in the Constitution is difficult to say. After all, they saw the Constitution amended 10 times—the Bill of Rights—within two years. By 1804, another two amendments had been ratified, so 12 of the 27 amendments, or nearly 45 percent, had been added to the Constitution within 15 years of its adoption.

Thinking Causally Why has the Constitution been amended so infrequently?

The infrequent amendment of the Constitution since those first 15 years presents a puzzle. The easy answer, often given, is that the Framers disdained the idea of frequent revision of the document and provided a role model of appropriate behavior for later generations. From the view of political science, however, the empirical record is difficult to match up with this answer. Americans are sometimes so swept up with notions of wise, philosophical Framers that they neglect how astute and capable the Framers were as politicians. In

TABLE 3-2 Amendments to the Constitution

Amendment	Purpose	Year Adopted
Relationship of People and Government		
1st	Freedom of religion, speech, press, assembly, petition	1791
2nd	Right of people to keep arms	1791
3rd	No housing of militia without due process	1791
4th	Restrictions on search and seizure	1791
5th–8th	Rights in judicial proceedings	1791
9th–10th	Non-enumerated rights reserved to the states or people	1791
13th	Slavery prohibited	1865
14th	Civil liberties and civil rights protections extended to states	1865
Government Structure		
12th	Changes in Electoral College process	1804
17th	Direct election of U.S. senators	1913
20th	Starting dates for terms; procedure when president-elect dies	1933
22nd	Presidents limited to two terms	1951
25th	Succession in cases of president's death or disability	1967
27th	Congressional pay raises require intervening election	1992
Size of the Electorate		
15th	Extend voting rights to all races	1870
19th	Extend voting rights to women	1920
23rd	Extend voting rights to residents of District of Columbia	1961
24th	Eliminate payment of "poll tax" as requirement to vote	1964
26th	Extend voting rights to citizens 18 years of age and over	1971
Powers of Government		
11th	Restricts federal courts' role in cases involving states	1795
16th	National income tax	1913
18th	Prohibition of sale, manufacture, and transportation of alcohol	1919
21st	Repeal of 18th Amendment	1933

the world of practical politics, they were not adamantly opposed to the idea of amending the document to achieve their goals. The bottom line is that if the Framers were setting an example by their actions for future generations to follow, it was not one of restraint in the amendment process.

If infrequent amendments cannot be attributed to the Framers as role models, what other factors might be important? One key factor noted by political scientists is that the supermajority processes involved in the proposal and ratification stages create a high barrier to adding new amendments.

The Constitution can be "amended" through judicial interpretation.

Another reason identified by political scientists for the infrequency of amendments is that the formal amending process is not the only means of constitutional change. When the Supreme Court interprets the Constitution, it can change the meaning of the Constitution. Most likely, the causality runs both ways: the difficulty of the formal amending process leads individuals to look to the Supreme Court for new interpretations of the Constitution, and because the Court engages in constitutional interpretation, individuals may see less need to engage in the lengthy formal amendment process.

Consider the Court's *Plessy v. Ferguson* decision of 1896. The Supreme Court declared that racial segregation was legally permissible under the Constitution. Nearly 60 years later, however, in the *Brown v. Board of Education* decision, the Court concluded precisely the opposite. The language of the Constitution had not changed with regard to this issue, yet the Court, with different members, in a different time, read the meaning of the Constitution differently.

Think of the amending process detailed in the Constitution as producing formal amendments: they actually change the text of the document. Constitutional interpretation as performed by the courts produces what might be considered informal amendments: the constitutional text remains the same, but the meaning of that text is read differently. To some observers of American politics, this practice creates the risk of allowing judges to insert their policy preferences into the Constitution, by decreeing the Constitution requires or prohibits something that had previously been left to elected officials to decide. In this view, too much power is placed in the hands of unelected federal judges, rather than the elected officials who would have to pass constitutional amendments. On the other hand, informal amendments undeniably provide additional adaptability to the system, which was a goal of the Framers. Most likely, it would have proved impossible to pass a formal constitutional amendment between 1896 and 1954 stating that segregation was unconstitutional, but through a change in interpretation, the Constitution was, in effect, amended.

Chapter Summary

In this chapter you have learned to:

3-1 Trace developments from events leading to the American Revolution through problems with the country's first constitution.

Although scholars still debate the causes and effects of the American Revolution, we can safely say that ideas about liberty and democracy were prominent rallying cries of the colonists. After a series of acts by the British government led to support for independence, the Americans turned their attention to building a structure of governance. The first attempt at a constitution, the Articles of Confederation, proved to be insufficient in building a national government with adequate power and authority over the states.

3-2 Outline the problems the Framers of the Constitution attempted to resolve and the solutions they devised.

The Framers focused on resolving five problems: overcoming fundamental disputes on representation in the new government; allowing for public input while limiting "excessive" democracy and concentrated power through election procedures, separation of powers, checks and balances, and federalism; protecting commerce and property; creating legitimacy by constructing an adaptable but stable governing framework; and providing for national defense. As they wrote a new constitution, the Framers sought to meld power and liberty, freedom and order, and national authority and state sovereignty.

3-3 Compare and contrast the arguments of Anti-Federalists and Federalists.

Federalists and Anti-Federalists debated the system of government set out in the Constitution. The Federalists argued that the best protection for liberty would be a stronger national government, a large republic rather than a small democracy, and a system with some distance between the people and government power, so that any "passions" that swept through the population would not immediately find their way into law. The Anti-Federalists favored a system closer to that provided by the Articles of Confederation—a loose union of the states in which the national government was clearly subordinate. At the very least, they wanted a national government that was very close to the people and had many checks on its power.

3-4 Explain the processes of constitutional change.

The amending process includes introduction or proposal of an amendment, which happens at the national level, and the ratification of a proposed amendment, which happens at the state level. Through this two-level process, and through the use of supermajorities in Congress and the states, the Framers hoped to ensure that only those amendments with broad societal approval would be added to the Constitution. To date, only 27 out of more than 10,000 amendments proposed have made it through both levels of the amending process. The Constitution does not change only when the text is changed, however. When judges interpret the Constitution, they give it specific meaning. When those interpretations change, the meaning of the Constitution changes also, even though the text remains unchanged.

CHAPTER TEST

1. In what ways did the Articles of Confederation make it difficult for national government to act?

2. How did the Declaration of Independence, the Articles of Confederation, and the Constitution differ in purpose?

3. What were three key problems the Framers sought to address in the Constitution, and what were some of the ways they did so?

4. How would the Framers respond to someone who argued "American government is supposed to be about 'the will of the people'"?

5. With what provisions does the Constitution attempt to improve relations among the states?

6. What were the major steps the Framers took to protect commerce and property?

7. Would Federalists or Anti-Federalists be more likely to support the idea of having all senators, representatives, and the president serve the same length term and be up for election at the same time, and why?

8. How, in the Federalists' view, would the Constitution defend liberty?

9. How do the paths to amend the Constitution provide for a high degree of consensus before the document is changed?

10. What are the differences between formal and informal amendments?

MyPoliSciLab® THE CONSTITUTION
Apply what you learned in this chapter on MyPoliSciLab.

Read on mypoliscilab.com

eText: Chapter 3

Study and Review on mypoliscilab.com

Pre-Test
Post-Test
Chapter Exam
Flashcards

Watch on mypoliscilab.com

Video: Animal Sacrifice and Free Exercise

Video: Polygamy and the U.S. Constitution

Explore on mypoliscilab.com

Simulation: You Are James Madison
Comparative: Comparing Constitutions
Timeline: The History of Constitutional Amendments
Visual Literacy: The American System of Checks and Balances

KEY TERMS

Anti-Federalists, p. 68
Articles of Confederation, p. 55
Bill of Rights, p. 71
checks and balances, p. 64
Declaration of Independence, p. 54
equal privileges and immunities
   clause, p. 66
federalism, p. 64

Federalists, p. 68
full faith and credit clause, p. 66
Great Compromise, p. 59
indirect election, p. 62
judicial review, p. 64
nation, p. 54
New Jersey Plan, p. 59
parliamentary system, p. 65

republic, p. 62
separation of powers, p. 63
Shays's Rebellion, p. 56
supremacy clause, p. 66
Three-fifths Compromise, p. 61
Virginia Plan, p. 59

SUGGESTED READINGS

Robert A. Dahl. 2002. *How Democratic Is the American Constitution?* New Haven: Yale University Press. A comparison of the U.S. Constitution to others around the world.

Alexander Hamilton, John Jay, and James Madison. 1787–1788. The *Federalist Papers*, any edition. Considered by many political scientists to be the single best distillation of American political philosophy, *The Federalist Papers* presented arguments in favor of the proposed Constitution.

David Brian Robertson. 2005. *The Constitution and America's Destiny*. New York: Cambridge University Press. An account of the Constitutional Convention that emphasizes the practical politics as well as principles involved in shaping the Constitution, profiling the defeats suffered by James Madison to delegates wary of national government power.

Herbert J. Storing. 1981. *What the Anti-Federalists Were For: The Political Thought of the Opponents of the Constitution*. Chicago: University of Chicago Press. A brief overview of the philosophy and principles that drove the Anti-Federalists and gave them lasting relevance in American politics.

Gordon S. Wood. 1969. *The Creation of the American Republic, 1776–1787*. New York: W.W. Norton. A beautifully written account of the events between independence and the Constitution, focusing especially on the significance of the classical republican, communitarian vision in America.

SUGGESTED WEBSITES

CONGRESSIONAL RESEARCH SERVICE ANNOTATED CONSTITUTION
www.law.cornell.edu/constitution

A helpful guide that includes commentary, background, historical developments, and relevant court cases for each article, section, and amendment of the Constitution.

AVALON PROJECT: THE U.S. CONSTITUTION
www.yale.edu/lawweb/avalon/constpap.htm

An outstanding collection of documents related to the development of the Constitution. From the Avalon Project home page you can access document collections on many other topics in American politics and law.

CONSTITUTION FINDER
confinder.richmond.edu

Constitutions from around the world.

CONSTITUTION OF THE CONFEDERATE STATES OF AMERICA
www.civilwarhome.com/csconstitution.htm

The Confederate Constitution used the U.S. Constitution as a framework. This site shows where the two constitutions matched and where they diverged.

AMERICAN LAW SOURCES ONLINE
www.lawsource.com/also

Provides a gateway to state constitutions and other state legal documents and information.

4

Federalism

MARRIAGE AND FEDERALISM The debate over
same-sex marriage has occurred at the national and
state levels. Protesters outside a federal courthouse in
California in 2010 support overturning California's ban on
same-sex marriage. The first successful federal challenge
to state laws prohibiting gay marriage, the case could
ultimately end up before the U.S. Supreme Court.

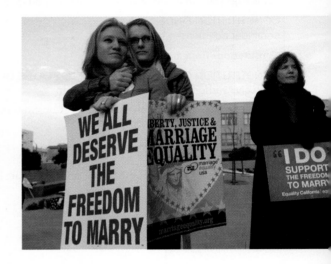

Among the issues that gay and lesbian advocacy groups currently see as fundamental to equality, the most publicly prominent has been same-sex marriage. Same-sex marriage illustrates several causal questions at the heart of federalism. How is federal policy influenced by state policy, and how is state policy influenced by federal policy? Under what conditions are federal policy makers likely to intervene to impose uniform rules and regulations across the states? How do outcomes at the federal level or in one state affect groups' political strategies and calculations?

Marriage confers favorable treatment in a range of areas—inheritance, taxation, health care, child custody, immigration, property rights, hospital visitation, and Social Security survivor benefits. Over 1,000 federal laws include reference to marital status.

The issue of same-sex marriage first entered national political conversation in the mid-1990s when it appeared the state of Hawaii might legalize this type of marriage. The 1996 Defense of Marriage Act (DOMA) signed by President Clinton was the federal response. This act stipulates that, for the purpose of federal programs and benefits, marriage consists of "the legal union between one man and one woman as husband and wife." As the Constitution allows, the law also creates an exemption to the usual requirement that states honor the official acts of other states, by specifying that they need not honor same-sex marriages that are legal in another state. Because of the heterosexual definition of marriage in DOMA, same-sex marriage is not recognized by federal programs like Social Security.

Because marriage has traditionally been a state-level issue, gay and lesbian civil rights organizations have focused most of their attention on this issue in the states. In 2004, the Massachusetts Supreme Judicial Court was the first to decide that banning same-sex marriage violated the state constitution's guarantee of equal protection under the law. As of 2011, six other states and the District of Columbia permit same-sex marriage, and eight others allow some form of "civil union" or "domestic partnership."

Unions or partnerships are a legal status that can provide nearly all of the benefits of marriage. Unlike marriage, however, civil unions and domestic partnerships have no meaning outside the state in which they were created; other states do not acknowledge them.

Although marriage is usually a state issue, the U.S. Supreme Court has upheld the federal government's authority to pass laws banning certain state-approved marriage arrangements, such as polygamy. It has also struck down some state marriage restrictions. In *Loving v. Virginia* (1967), the Court declared Virginia's ban on interracial marriage to be a violation of the U.S. Constitution's promise of equal protection of the laws. Gay and lesbian civil rights activists point to the ban on same-sex marriage as presenting precisely the same discriminatory issues as *Loving*. Opponents of same-sex marriage reject this parallel, claiming that the banning of same-sex marriage is about the basic definition of a social institution.[1]

Accordingly, these critics have led a countermovement designed to stop the legal recognition of same-sex marriages. Part of the strategy has been passage of laws and constitutional amendments in the states to prohibit same-sex marriage. These efforts have been highly successful, while an amendment to the U.S. Constitution to prohibit same-sex marriage has not.

Gay and lesbian rights advocates see same-sex marriage as a matter of civil rights and equality. They have focused their strategy largely at the state level, but in 2010 they won a major victory when a federal district court in California ruled that the state's prohibition on same-sex marriage—enacted by voters in a referendum—violated the U.S. Constitution. The decision was appealed and both the proponents and opponents of same-sex marriage expect the case will ultimately arrive at the U.S. Supreme Court.

Same-sex marriage illuminates the principles and practices of federalism and the fault lines in American politics between different levels of government and among different institutions. It raises questions about where the responsibilities of the state governments end and the federal government begins. And it shows us how federalism has strong causal effects in American politics.[2] This chapter explores these principles and practices of federalism and the politics surrounding them. ■

The Nature of the Union

4-1   Show how the Constitution serves as a framework for federalism and why debates remain.

When the Constitution was written and sent to the states for ratification, the debate between Federalists and Anti-Federalists was about the interaction of liberty and federalism. This clash was about ideas, but it was also an intensely political battle. Both groups had views about public policy, and they realized some arrangements of national and state power would be more likely to advance these policies than would others. This clash started a long trend of federalism being a political battleground on which politicians, judges, and activist groups jostle to advance their positions. Politicians frequently evoke federalism to justify particular policies or to argue against their opponents. Those arguments can be inconsistent, arguing for more national control in one area and more state control in another. Politicians can also be federalism opportunists, willing to support strengthening Washington or strengthening the states depending on how the issue suits their own policy preferences, ideology, or reelection prospects. Federal judges also can be influenced by

PRESIDENT OBAMA ADDRESSING THE NATIONAL GOVERNORS ASSOCIATION, FEBRUARY 2011

The nation's governors meet annually to share ideas on education, transportation, budgets, and other issues they have in common. They also discuss the appropriate relationship between the national and state levels of government. Governors welcome federal assistance but worry about too much federal control of their activities.

ideology or by particular outcomes they wish to see. Federalism is not a settled topic of constitutional doctrine—it is a matter of intense debate that brings together philosophy, power, politics, and policy.

Confederal and unitary arrangements are two ways to organize power between national and subnational governments.

What was the appropriate relationship between the state governments and the national government? The question was important mainly because it had significant implications for liberty. To the Anti-Federalists, a system with a powerful, remote national government was likely to lead to the erosion of individual liberty. State governments could be better monitored and controlled by the people and, thus, were less a danger to liberty. Anti-Federalists therefore preferred a **confederation**. In this type of government, independent entities join together to pursue some common purposes. The joint government in a confederation tends to have very limited authority over the individual member governments. Under the Articles of Confederation, for example, state governments selected their representatives in the national Congress. However, governing a confederation can be a challenge. Member governments are frequently in competition, trying to best or disadvantage each other, especially economically.

The Framers did not share the Anti-Federalists' enthusiasm for a confederal arrangement that made the national government dependent on the states, but neither did they construct a **unitary system** that would make the states subordinate to the national government with little, if any, independent governing authority. In a unitary system, the upper-level government is free to create, combine, or disband lower-level governments.

State governments are essentially unitary systems with respect to local municipalities. Typically they allow substantial independence to the localities within their borders, but this arrangement is at the convenience of the state government. The Constitution makes no mention of cities and counties or other substate governments, nor does it guarantee their existence.

Around the world, the unitary system of government is the norm. France, Great Britain, The Netherlands, Japan, and Italy are unitary systems, and South America and Africa are dominated by unitary systems as well. The amount of independence granted to lower-level governments is determined by the national government. In the United States, by contrast, a functioning set of state governments already existed when the Constitution was being debated, making a move to a unitary form of government difficult.

confederation a loose grouping of independent political units, such as states or countries, whose main purpose is to govern the relationship between those units.

unitary system a form of government in which government at the highest level has the power to create, combine, or disband lower-level governments and determine what powers will be allowed at the lower levels.

The Constitution provides the framework for intergovernmental relations through federalism.

The Framers steered a middle course between a confederation and a unitary government. They were not unanimous in their vision. Federalism was a middle-ground position between the unitary and confederal extremes (see Figure 4-1).

FIGURE 4-1 Flow of Power in Three Systems of Government.

The confederal, federal, and unitary systems of government provide alternative distributions of political power. The confederal system places sovereignty in the subnational governments, while the unitary system places it in the national government. The federal system is blended, with sovereignty at both the national and subnational levels.

Confederal

Subnational governments create the national government and grant it some limited areas of responsibility. The national government relies on the subnational governments for funding and to implement decisions made by the national government. The national government typically lacks enforcement mechanisms and relies on the voluntary compliance of the subnational governments. Sovereign power (the ultimate decision maker) is at the subnational level.

Federal

Both the national government and the subnational governments have areas in which they hold primary sovereign power and have their own sources of funds and ability to implement policies. They have some areas of shared authority and may compete for control. The existence of the subnational governments is guaranteed. Sovereign power exists at both levels.

Unitary

The national government creates the subnational governments. It may grant governing authority to the subnational governments in certain policy areas, but this authority is not independent or guaranteed—it can be eliminated by the national government, as can the subnational governments themselves. Sovereign power is at the national level.

federalism a form of government that distributes power across a national government and subnational governments and ensures the existence of the subnational governments.

reserved powers Tenth Amendment guarantee to state governments of any powers other than those granted to the national government or those specifically prohibited for the states.

Federalism is a system that distributes political power across a national government and subnational governments. In the United States, these subnational governments are the states. Federalism ensures that the subnational units have their existence protected. In addition to the United States, other federal systems include Austria, Australia, Brazil, Canada, Germany, India, Mexico, and Tanzania.

According to the *supremacy clause* of the Constitution, when the national and state governments are in conflict, national laws overrule state laws. In addition, powers delegated to the national government are not available to the states. However, the Tenth Amendment provides that powers not delegated to the national government by the Constitution, and not prohibited for state governments, are reserved for the states or for the people—the **reserved powers**. States also are guaranteed equal voting rights in the U.S. Senate, protection against domestic insurrection and foreign invasion, and the preservation of a representative form of government.

The Constitution also mandates fair play between the states with three crucial provisions that are intended to prevent states from discriminating against one another or cutting special deals that would aggravate relations with other states or potentially other countries. The *full faith and credit clause* requires states to honor the official acts of other states, such as public records and the results of judicial proceedings. The *equal privileges and immunities clause* requires states to treat similarly their citizens and citizens of other states. And the *commerce clause* places the regulation of interstate commerce and foreign economic trade within the national government, not the individual states.

Federalism and the "federal system" refer to the arrangement of power distributed across the national and state levels. In common everyday usage, however, references to the "federal government" or to the "national government" both mean the government created by the Constitution and based in Washington, D.C.

The appropriate balance of national and state power creates significant debate.

Ratification of the Constitution did not end disputes over the nature of the new system. From the start, the question of precisely how much control the national government had over the states was a matter of contention. Sovereignty was a key point of difference. **Sovereignty** refers to a government having the ultimate authority to make decisions about what happens within its borders, free from interference by other governments. Advocates of a limited national role preferred a **compact theory** of federalism, which suggested the states were sovereign entities that joined together. The states gave up some limited and specific powers, but they retained their sovereignty. Except in ways that they explicitly consented to, the states were to be left alone.

This approach to understanding federalism was particularly prominent in the South, where it led to the doctrine of **nullification**—the idea that states could nullify national government laws with which they disagreed and which they believed violated the letter or spirit of the U.S. Constitution. Identified most strongly with Vice President John Calhoun of South Carolina (1825–1832), nullification was frequently and controversially employed in the decades prior to the Civil War, especially with regard to the slavery issue, but it had been present in political circles long before that.[3]

In later years, the compact theory would sometimes be referred to as the "states' rights" position. This became a controversial term in the 1950s and 1960s when it was most commonly invoked to thwart the push of the national government to end racial segregation, particularly in southern states. The compact view of federalism, however, should not be seen as limited to issues concerning civil rights, nor does it inherently advocate a limited, minimalist government. State governments could be quite active within the compact framework.

The **nationalist theory**, more prominent in northern states, provided an alternative to the compact theory. This approach stressed that the Constitution represented the people, not the states, coming together. The very language of the preamble "We the people," according to the nationalist view, indicates that the Constitution's purpose is to provide the institutions and rules by

sovereignty having the ultimate authority to make decisions within one's borders, without interference by other governments.

compact theory a theory of the founding of the American government that argues states were sovereign units that joined together in the new national government but did not give up their status as sovereign, independent governments.

nullification the theory that states have the right to nullify national laws to which they object and believe violate the U.S. Constitution.

nationalist theory a theory of the founding of the American government that sees the Constitution more as the joining together of the people than the joining together of the states.

which a nation of people, rather than a collection of states, can be governed. At times, states will have to accept national direction and demands, regardless of their approval or disapproval of those demands, especially if the national action can be portrayed as promoting the general well-being of the country.

Strongly identified with this view is Alexander Hamilton, secretary of the Treasury under President Washington. Among executive branch officials in the early years of the republic, Hamilton had the most expansive vision for national government power. He proposed that the national government establish a bank and that it invest heavily in building the roads, canals, and other infrastructure that would help unite the new country and advance economic development.

Given the unhappy experience of centralized British power during the colonial era, how could Hamilton go about creating the political coalition to support such a plan? His answer was to mastermind a deal in which the federal government assumed all the debt that state governments had incurred in fighting the Revolutionary War. This plan would link wealthy individuals and institutions in financial arrangements with the national government rather than with the states.

Across the course of American politics, debate has flourished concerning the appropriate balance of power between the national and state governments. This debate matters in very concrete ways. Issues as diverse as slavery, punishment for violence against women, regulation of business, environmental protection, minimum wages, end-of-life decisions, enforcement of anti-discrimination statutes, and health care reform, among many others, are influenced heavily by interpretations of federalism. People who care about these issues need to care about federalism, because in the American political system prevailing interpretations of federalism will strongly shape what, if anything, government can or should do about these matters, and which level of government should do it.

Dual Federalism

4-2 Outline the principles of dual federalism and their basis in the Supreme Court's traditional understanding of interstate commerce.

dual federalism a form of federalism in which the national and state governments have distinct areas of authority and power, and individuals have rights as both citizens of states and citizens of the United States.

Distinct lines separating the national and state governments are the hallmark of the system of **dual federalism**, which dominated American politics through the mid-1930s. This model of federalism embraces the ideas of dual sovereignty and dual citizenship. Sovereignty refers to a final say—the sovereign power is the one who speaks last and most authoritatively. In dual federalism, the national government is sovereign in some areas and the state governments are sovereign in others. The essence of dual federalism is the idea of a constitutional division of labor between the national government and state governments.

Dual sovereignty provides separate areas of authority for the national and state governments.

Dual sovereignty is the idea that both the national and state governments have the final say over different policy areas and functions. In the nineteenth century, the federal government had control over setting tariffs on foreign goods, granting patents and copyright protection, managing the country's currency, establishing agreements with other countries, and providing defense and postal services. Some concurrent powers were shared by the two levels of government: both could collect taxes, establish courts, create roads and other internal improvements, and borrow and spend money. States were concerned with pretty much everything else: banking and insurance law, family and morals regulation, public health, education, criminal law, construction codes, water use, health, safety, and environmental regulations, and so on. Collectively, this list of duties is often referred to as the **police power** reserved to state governments by the Tenth Amendment—protection of public safety, health, welfare, and morality.

> **dual sovereignty** the idea that both the national and state governments have sovereignty, but over different policy areas and functions.

> **police power** the protection of public safety, health, welfare, and morality by a government.

The U.S. Constitution falls short of 9,000 words, while several state constitutions exceed 90,000. Why are state constitutions longer? Two factors help explain why state constitutions are longer: the reserved powers, plus the idea that the states are closer to the people than is the national government. First, the list of state areas of responsibility, as the scope of the police power implies, is extensive. In addition, there are about four dozen references to the states in the U.S. Constitution, and many of these references are shorthand for areas that state constitutions would need to fill out in detail. Second, because state governments were seen as closer to the people, their constitutions were made easier to amend than is the federal constitution. If the amending process is not inordinately difficult, then legislators have an incentive to put policy provisions into constitutions, as they will still be harder for future legislators to change than a law would be.[4]

> **Thinking Causally** Why are state constitutions typically much longer than the U.S. Constitution?

MIXING OIL AND WATER

Due to the 2010 oil spill in the Gulf of Mexico, authorities in Escambia County, Florida, issued a health advisory for beach visitors. This action is an example of the "police power" reserved for states under the Constitution. Construction standards and zoning laws are other examples of areas left to the states under their police power.

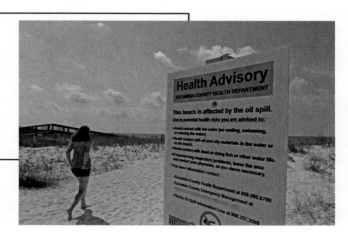

Health Advisory
ESCAMBIA COUNTY HEALTH DEPARTMENT

This beach is affected by the oil spill.

Dual citizenship ensures that citizens of the United States are also citizens of a state.

dual citizenship the idea that an individual is a citizen of both his or her state and the United States. Rights and responsibilities can vary from state to state and can be different on the state and national levels.

Dual citizenship is the idea that if you are a U.S. citizen, you are also a citizen of a state.[5] As a citizen of the United States, you have the same rights as other citizens of the United States. As a citizen of your state, you have rights and responsibilities that may be different from citizens of another state. The ability to purchase alcohol legally, to be married, to drive a car, and so on, varies from state to state.

The case of *Barron v. Baltimore* (1833) illustrates the principle of dual citizenship under dual federalism. John Barron operated a commercial wharf in Baltimore. During construction projects, the city began dumping dirt and fill in the harbor. With ships facing great difficulty navigating in or out of the area near Barron's wharf, his business collapsed. Barron sued the city, arguing that the Fifth Amendment to the U.S. Constitution guarantees that citizens will be compensated when government takes their property for public purposes (known as the *takings clause*). The U.S. Supreme Court determined that Barron was not entitled to any compensation. In the Court's view, the Fifth Amendment—indeed, the Bill of Rights as a whole—applied only to Barron as a citizen of the United States, not as a citizen of Maryland. In this case, Barron was not injured by the U.S. government, he was injured by a state government. If Maryland's constitution had a "takings" clause, then Barron would have recourse through the state's courts.

Interpretation of the commerce clause affects national government power.

commerce clause a provision in the U.S. Constitution that gives Congress the power to regulate commerce with other countries, among the states, and with Indian tribes.

Interstate commerce has been a central political and legal battleground on which the meaning of federalism has been fought. The Constitution's **commerce clause**, in Article 1, section 8, gave Congress the power to "regulate commerce with foreign nations, and among the several states, and with the Indian tribes." Intrastate commerce, on the other hand, was implicitly under the jurisdiction of the states.

Regarding interstate commerce, the Supreme Court confirmed the national government's primacy in this policy area in its decision in *Gibbons v. Ogden* (1824). The state of New York required boats entering from another state to obtain a permit to navigate on New York waters. A steamboat owner whose business required him to travel between New Jersey and New York challenged this law. In its decision, the Supreme Court under Chief Justice John Marshall concluded that, because of the Constitution's supremacy clause, New York's licensing requirement was overridden by a federal law that regulated coastal trade.

Gibbons v. Ogden was a judicial victory for national commercial authority over the states. The Sherman Anti-Trust Act of 1890 was a legislative victory. The law was a response to the growth of huge corporations that monopolized sales in their particular industries. As monopolies, or nearly so, they could price their products excessively high to gain extra profit, or they could price excessively low to drive out any remaining competitors. In response, the Sherman Anti-Trust Act prohibited contracts, mergers, or conspiracy that restrained trade or commerce between states or with other countries.

In a blow to the federal government's regulation over interstate commerce, however, the Supreme Court ruled in 1895 that "commerce" did not include manufacturing and that the Sherman Act only applied to the actual sale and moving of goods across state lines, not to monopolies in manufacturing.[6] Although the Court recognized that monopoly over manufacturing might be linked to restraint of commerce, it sought to keep the two separate in the interests of dual federalist principles. States, but not the federal government, could regulate manufacturing; the federal government, but not the states, could regulate interstate commerce.[7]

Although this judicial definition of interstate commerce placed limits on what the federal government could do, it did not leave the government powerless. In the early twentieth century, the federal government expanded its reach into economic matters. The Pure Food and Drug Act of 1906 gave the federal government the regulatory authority to monitor food and drug safety and, in particular, to ensure that labeling of these products was accurate. The Federal Trade Commission (FTC) is another example of increased federal power under the traditional definition of commerce. Created in 1914 in the Federal Trade Commission Act, the FTC monitors false and deceptive advertising as well as corporate mergers with implications for commerce.

Cooperative Federalism

4-3   Trace the evolution from dual to cooperative federalism, and identify methods of cooperative federalism.

Dual federalism's sharp line of separation between national and state responsibilities was blurred by **cooperative federalism**, which rose to prominence beginning in the 1930s. In this form of federalism, still prominent today, the national and state governments share many functions and areas of authority. For the liberal reformers of the 1910s and especially the 1930s, this new way of thinking about federalism opened the doors to policy successes that were impossible as long as dual federalism held sway.

cooperative federalism a form of federalism in which the national and state governments share many functions and areas of authority.

Many of the new social programs adopted by the national government during the 1930s, including welfare, unemployment insurance, and jobs programs, were jointly financed and administered by the national and state governments. This is a puzzle. Why would power-seeking national politicians place partial control of these programs at the state level? Political scientists have suggested that the national–state blend was often done for practical political reasons rather than for reasons of grand philosophy. The national government in the early

Thinking Causally Why would power-seeking national politicians share control of important government programs with politicians at the state level, rather than centralizing all control in Washington?

1930s was small. The New Deal, as the collection of new programs in the 1930s was known, called for a significant expansion of the role of the national government in American life. Instantly expanding federal agencies would be difficult, so state agencies could be helpful in launching programs. And state officials were sure to be reluctant to give up power. So a joint program might have been necessary in some instances to ensure passage through Congress.

Often, the support of state officials hinged on whether they would have a piece of the action in administering the new program. If benefits were to be distributed to their constituents, they wanted some say in the matter and some of the political credit. In other cases, if a program seemed likely to have significant and possibly disruptive social and economic effects, state officials would want to have some flexibility in managing the program.

Since the 1930s, minimum wage policy has been consistently cooperative. The national government sets minimum wage standards that states have to meet. States, however, are free to exceed those wages if they so choose and may establish minimum wages for workers not covered under federal law. Figure 4-2 shows how states vary on the minimum wage. Where the map indicates the state level is lower, the federal rate prevails except for workers who are not covered by the federal minimum wage law (generally workers at non-interstate businesses that gross less than $500,000).[8]

The practice in minimum wage is similar to that in other contentious policy areas, such as welfare. Prior to 1996, the national government had specific

FIGURE 4-2 Differences in State Minimum Wages, 2011.

State minimum wages can match or exceed the federal wage. For work categories not covered by the federal law, states may set a minimum wage below the wage assigned for categories that are federally covered, or can go without a minimum wage. Until the federal minimum wage was increased to $7.25 in 2009, many more states exceeded the federal wage than is true today.

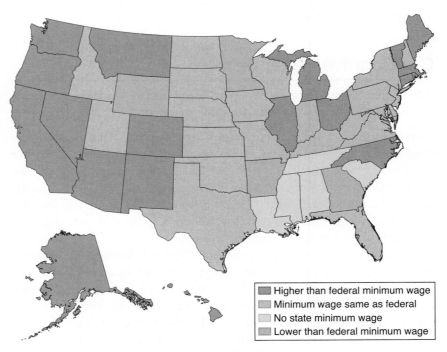

Higher than federal minimum wage
Minimum wage same as federal
No state minimum wage
Lower than federal minimum wage

Source: US Department of Labor, www.dol.gov/esa/minwage/america.htm.

programs designed to address the needs of poor families with children. The states, however, had substantial leeway in administering these programs, including the benefit levels. After the passage of welfare reform legislation in 1996, state-by-state variation became even more pronounced. National law set a few guidelines for states to work within. Most importantly, there were national limits on the number of years an individual could receive welfare benefits, and state programs needed to focus on moving recipients from welfare to work. The programs themselves, however, were entirely the creation of the states. Before 1996, states administered one national program but in 50 different ways; now states are administering 50 different state programs within broad national guidelines. Each of these two approaches is an example of cooperative federalism.

Implied powers increased the scope of permissible federal government activity.

Changes in constitutional interpretation were necessary to facilitate the evolution from dual federalism to cooperative federalism. One important step happened early in American history, in the case of *McCulloch v. Maryland* (1819). The case involved the Second Bank of the United States. The bank, chartered by Congress, had a branch in Baltimore, Maryland. Traditionally, states had chartered banks, so this new national role was eyed warily by the states. In response, Maryland taxed the bank. The U.S. government challenged this tax and filed suit against Maryland in the Supreme Court.

The Court had to resolve two questions. Could Congress charter a national bank? And, if so, could Maryland tax the bank? The Court's answer to the first question was yes. Its justification was twofold. First, Chief Justice John Marshall argued against the compact theory of the Constitution in favor of the nationalist theory. Marshall claimed that it was not the states, but the people, who had formed the national government, and the national government therefore did not require the consent of the states to carry out its powers, nor was it subordinate to the states.

Second, the Court pointed to the **necessary and proper clause**, sometimes referred to as the *elastic clause*. Article 1, section 8, of the Constitution gives Congress the authority "to make all laws which shall be necessary and proper for carrying into execution the foregoing powers, and all other powers vested by this Constitution in the Government of the United States, or in any Department or Officer thereof." The "foregoing powers" refers to a list of duties prescribed in Article 1 as the responsibilities of Congress. These listed duties, specifically mentioned in the Constitution, are known as Congress's **enumerated powers**.

What the Court said in *McCulloch* is that the necessary and proper clause gave Congress **implied powers**, meaning it could make laws needed to carry out its enumerated powers. It was reasonable, in the Court's view, for a Congress

necessary and proper clause a provision in the U.S. Constitution that gives Congress the authority to make the laws needed to carry out the specific duties assigned to Congress by the Constitution.

enumerated powers the specifically listed duties that the U.S. Constitution assigns to Congress.

implied powers functions and actions that Congress or the president could perform in order to implement and exercise its enumerated powers.

given the power to pay debts, borrow money, regulate commerce, and coin money, to create a bank to facilitate the performance of these duties.

Having answered the first question by ruling that the bank was constitutional, the Court now had to answer the second question—whether Maryland could tax the bank. The Court's answer was no. The power to tax, the Court famously stated, is the power to destroy. Under a federal system, a single state government has no right to destroy an entity of the national government. Maryland could not force the national government out of banking by onerous taxation. The *McCulloch* decision opened the door for Congress to expand the reach of the national government and chip away some of the wall separating state and national government functions and responsibilities.[9]

Redefining interstate commerce expands federal government power.

If the door to cooperative federalism cracked open in 1819, it swung fully open in 1937. In *National Labor Relations Board v. Jones & Laughlin Steel Corporation* (1937), the Supreme Court expanded the scope of what was meant by interstate commerce.

Jones & Laughlin had fired workers for labor union activity. The recently enacted National Labor Relations Act (1935) prohibited employers engaged in interstate commerce from taking such actions. The act declared that labor-management relations were an aspect of commerce and thus subject to federal government regulation. When challenged by the National Labor Relations Board, which was created by the 1935 law, the steel company argued that labor-management relations were not part of commerce and therefore were not subject to federal regulation. Traditionally, the Supreme Court interpreted interstate commerce to mean not what happened inside a factory—that was manufacturing, not commerce—but what was involved in the transfer of products from one state to another.

In its decision in *Jones & Laughlin*, the Supreme Court concluded that this conception was too narrow. Instead, a company that uses any interstate products in its business or sells any product interstate is part of the stream of interstate commerce. Poor labor-management relations can lead to industrial strife, and this strife can affect the stream of commerce. In addition, if a company's intrastate activities taken all together had a "substantial relation" to interstate commerce, they could be regulated.

The *Jones & Laughlin* decision meant, in effect, that national government action on issues such as worker safety, environmental controls, health codes, work hours and conditions, and overtime pay were justified by the government's responsibility to regulate interstate commerce.[10]

Although the Court cautioned that its new definition of interstate commerce must be "a matter of degree," the principle of the stream of interstate commerce provided a nearly limitless range to congressional action. The Court declared that it was up to Congress to decide the appropriate use of its newly expanded interstate commerce powers.[11] The constitutional basis of cooperative federalism was now firmly established, the role of Congress and the president in deciding what activities came under the interstate umbrella was in place, and the scope of federal government activity in society and in the economy was poised to grow accordingly.

The scope of activity and the debate over it continue to this day. The interpretation of the federal government's role in regulating interstate commerce has, for example, been a central point of debate since the passage of health care reform legislation in early 2010. The federal requirement that individuals purchase insurance is a particular flashpoint. If insurers must provide coverage to individuals with preexisting health conditions, everyone, healthy or not, needs to be in the insurance market to pay for it. Until health care reform, the federal government had not used an interstate commerce justification to compel someone to purchase a product or service under threat of penalty. To opponents of the health care reform law, forcing an individual to enter interstate commerce by buying insurance when he or she does not choose to do so is not consistent with the Framers' vision of regulating commerce between the states. Governors or attorneys general in over 25 states cited this mandate as one way the law violates the commerce clause, and filed lawsuits to block it. To supporters, this mandate is a "necessary and proper" action for Congress to take as part of its enumerated power of regulating interstate commerce. In their view, individuals' failure to buy insurance ultimately has a substantial effect on the health care market and is thus a form of economic activity. Ultimately, the Supreme Court will decide the matter.

The federal and state governments collaborate to implement policy in some issue areas.

The regulation of Indian gaming (see Case Study) indicates the complexity that arises when multiple levels of government are involved in the same policy area. The national–state relationship in cooperative federalism can likewise take on different forms: *collaboration*, *mandates*, and *persuasion*.

To understand collaboration, consider environmental policy. State governments and the national government collect and share significant amounts of data and information on the environment. They work together to identify and create rules to protect endangered species. They respond jointly to disasters such as the massive oil spill in the Gulf of Mexico in 2010. State offices often provide personnel who implement, at the state level, programs that are created at the national level, such as water and air pollution control.

As a form of collaboration, the national government may set standards and then allow states to exceed those standards, as is the case in air pollution control. A provision added to the Clean Air Act in 1967 allowed California

Case Study

Federalism and the Regulation of Native American Casinos

Long before the Founding Fathers led a revolution and crafted a constitution, Native Americans governed territory in what would become the United States. This history created a particularly difficult problem for governance in the United States: how would these Native American, or Indian, nations be incorporated into the American political system? The answer was to grant tribes some degree of sovereignty within the United States and within the states. The tribes, in other words, are part of the American system of federalism.

American Indians are citizens of their tribes, the state they live in, and the United States. They pay individual federal income tax and pay state income tax unless they work for the tribe and live on tribal lands. As governmental entities, the 564 federally recognized tribes do not pay taxes to other governments, just as the federal and state governments do not pay taxes to each other.[12]

The questions raised by tribal sovereignty are similar to those raised by the relationship between states and the national government in American federalism. In what areas does the national government prevail? How do the states fit in?

In recent years, the status of American Indians in the federal system has been particularly salient because of gambling and the revenues it generates. From 1987 to 2009, revenues from tribal-owned casinos increased from barely $100 million to more than $26 billion.[13] The world's largest casino is the tribal-owned Foxwoods Resort in Connecticut.

INDIAN GAMING AND FEDERALISM
Indian tribes, as a part of American federalism, often need to negotiate with the federal and state governments. Gaming is no exception. Under a federal law, the tribes enter into agreements with state governments concerning the nature of the gaming and the share of the proceeds that will go to the state. This profit sharing encourages states to sign the agreements.

One of the controversies in federalism raised by Indian gaming is the ability of state governments to regulate tribal-run casinos. In 1987, the Supreme Court ruled that a state could not enforce its gaming laws within tribal reservations, unless Congress had specifically given the states that authority.[14] In this case, the Court said that state restrictions on Indian casinos conflicted with the federal government's attempt to further tribal self-sufficiency and economic development through tribal gaming.[15]

Recognizing the difficult political issues that might arise with the expansion of tribal gaming in the states, the federal government provided a role for the states in regulating this gambling. The Indian Gaming Regulatory Act (IGRA), signed into law in 1988, established three classes of Indian gambling activity: (1) social and traditional games with stakes or prizes of minimal value, commonly associated with tribal customs or celebrations; (2) bingo and other games played against other players, not against "the house"; and (3) any games not in the first two groups, such as slot machines, blackjack, and roulette. Tribes are essentially free to offer the first two classes of games; the third requires the tribes to negotiate a "compact" with a state that would determine casino size, games, hours, and the share of the profits that would go to the state. Intended to regulate gambling on Indian reservations, the IGRA also gave the states some incentive to encourage, or at least not

Case Study Federalism and the Regulation of Native American Casinos

discourage, Indian gaming, because now states would receive a portion of the profits.

To its critics, IGRA was a disaster. They described it as reckless—in effect establishing a national policy that encourages loose affiliations of Native Americans to petition the Bureau of Indian Affairs to be declared tribes in order to enter into casino gambling operations. Once acknowledged as tribes, sovereignty leaves them free to develop their lands without being subject to state environmental, safety, zoning, or other ordinances.

States seemed to regain some leverage in 1996. The Seminole tribe in Florida filed suit in federal court, complaining that the state had violated IGRA by not bargaining in good faith to establish a gaming compact. In *Seminole Tribe v. Florida*, the Supreme Court rejected the tribe's case. The Court concluded in a 5–4 decision that the Eleventh Amendment gave states, as sovereign bodies, immunity from lawsuits in federal courts without their consent.[16]

As it turns out, with significant financial resources likely to flow from gambling, states did not use the *Seminole* decision to prevent Indian casinos. Instead, they used the decision as leverage to negotiate more lucrative agreements with the tribes. Suffering from revenue shortfalls, states saw casino gambling on reservations as a potential windfall, now that they could force better deals.

The sovereign status of Indian tribes intersects American federalism at both the national and state levels. Although states sometimes complain that Indian sovereignty compromises their own sovereignty, they have been able to use the *Seminole* decision—itself based on state sovereignty—to wrest more profitable deals with the casinos in difficult budgetary times. At the same time, states without casinos or with less attractive gaming options see their citizens and other tourists pouring into neighboring states to gamble at Indian casinos. This gives some negotiating power back to the tribes. Within states, Indian casino gambling has emerged as a political football as governors and legislatures battle to determine who has the authority to negotiate and sign the gaming compacts.

Thinking Critically

1. Should states or the federal government have the primary regulatory role regarding Native American tribes? Why?

2. Should tribes have to negotiate with states or should they, as sovereign entities, be free to determine how they will run their gaming enterprises?

3. Consider the case of tribes that have members scattered geographically and do not control any land as a group. Are these the equivalent of tribes on reservations? Should these individuals, because of tribal sovereignty, have a right to receive land from the federal and state governments for the purpose of establishing casino operations? Why or why not?

---

to seek exemptions from federal air pollution rules. If these exemptions were granted, other states then had the option of following the federal or California standards, whichever were more stringent. In 2010, the EPA folded the stronger California standards into new national emissions and fuel mileage standards that apply across the country.[17]

Even while collaborating, the state and national governments will often have separate areas of responsibility, the hallmark of dual federalism. For example, the federal government sets policy on which pesticides can be made, but a state, or a city if allowed by the state, can decide which of these allowable pesticides can be used within its borders and in what ways.

Immigration has been another area of federal and state collaboration. In the first three months of 2011, states passed over 60 laws concerning immigration.

Federal law is supreme, but states have enforcement roles and can make decisions about which benefits and services immigrants may receive. Although laws requiring strict enforcement and verification of legal immigrant status receive the most publicity, many of the laws enacted offer benefits to immigrants. Similarly, laws are not always about illegal immigration, but about the obligations and privileges of legal immigrants or issues that arise because of immigration.[18]

The federal government may enact policy mandates to direct the states to take certain actions.

mandate an order from the federal government that requires state governments to take a certain action.

Another possibility is for the national government to issue a **mandate** that orders state governments to take certain actions. Beginning in the 1960s, the volume of federal government mandates upon the states increased sharply. For example, in the area of education, states must follow the rules established by the national government in the Individuals with Disabilities Education Act. This law sets out the kinds of services that states and localities must provide to students with learning or other disabilities and provides some federal funding. Here "cooperative" federalism need not mean that there is harmony and agreement between the two levels of government. Instead, the national government may set the rules that states are required to follow, regardless of the view of the states toward these rules. Some analysts refer to this practice as "coercive federalism."

Federal mandates have rankled state officials for two reasons. First, the mandates may force states to do things they would prefer not to do or for which there is only modest support from state residents. Second, mandates impose demands on the states but often do not provide federal financial assistance to carry out the demands. **Unfunded mandates** are federal requirements that states take some action, but without provision of sufficient resources to do so.

unfunded mandate a law requiring certain actions without appropriating the necessary funds to carry them out.

Lengthy controversy and extensive lobbying by groups such as the National Conference of State Legislatures and the U.S. Conference of Mayors led to the 1995 Unfunded Mandates Reform Act. The bill required congressional committees to get estimates of the cost of proposed legislation that would mandate new expenses on states, localities, or businesses. If the cost exceeded $50 million on states and localities or $100 million on the private sector, adjusted over time for inflation, legislators could then be required to vote that the benefits of the bill exceeded the costs. The act did not apply to mandates that protected the constitutional rights of individuals, prohibited discrimination, or were labeled emergency legislation.

Unfunded mandates seemingly declined after the act was passed. However, this correlation between the law and the drop in unfunded mandates may be misleading. Evidence on the effectiveness of the act has been mixed. One account argues the law looked effective only because its exemptions allowed major new unfunded mandates that simply were not labeled as such, including education reforms in the No Child Left Behind Act, education services for disabled children, Medicaid, and a requirement after 2000 that states meet standards for voting technology.[19] The U.S. Government Accountability Office noted in its examination of unfunded mandates that the most common complaint was that the law defined unfunded mandates too narrowly, rather than actually reducing the fiscal burden imposed on states.[20]

Similar to mandating that states take some action, the federal government can pass **preemption legislation** that declares, or mandates, certain actions off-limits for state governments. For example, federal law passed in 2005 prohibits certain kinds of liability suits from being filed against firearms manufacturers in state courts.[21] In addition, the Family Smoking Prevention and Tobacco Control Act of 2009 preempts state laws in areas such as tobacco product standards—flavored cigarettes except for menthol, for example, are prohibited—and warning labels. And the health care reform legislation enacted in 2010 (the Affordable Care Act) contained an extensive array of new requirements on health insurance companies that preempt state law, such as who is eligible for benefits, the particular benefits that insurance policies must offer, and the allowable rate differentials in individual insurance policies for different groups of individuals (such as younger and older policy holders).

preemption legislation legislation that declares, or mandates, certain actions off-limits for state governments.

The federal government may use fiscal persuasion to influence states' behavior.

In addition to collaboration and mandates, cooperative federalism can work through persuasion. The national government might try to influence or persuade a state government to take some action in the area of education, the environment, or some other policy area, but not require it. Typically, this will involve providing some incentive for states to agree to take the desired action.

One of the best incentives is money. **Fiscal federalism** refers to the national government's use of its financial resources to persuade the states to take particular actions. The restrictions on the use of the money might be specific or general. With a **categorical grant**, the federal government provides money that is to be used for very specific purposes. As Table 4-1 shows, the tools the federal government can employ can make it difficult for a state not to comply with federal demands. Various rules about discrimination, environmental protection, and employment and contract requirements, for example, are built into a large group of federal grants. A state not willing to accept any one of these rules is shutting itself out of dozens or hundreds of programs.

fiscal federalism a technique of persuasion in which the federal government offers resources to states that agree to take certain actions.

categorical grant funds provided by the federal government to a state or local government for a specific, defined purpose.

Categorical grants can be either formula based or competitive. Formula-based grants are, as the name suggests, based on a formula that determines the amount of funds a state will receive. Precisely what should be in the formula

TABLE 4-1 Tools of Federal Influence Over State Governments

Tools	Description
Mandates	**States are required to follow federal policy orders**
Direct orders	An order is imposed by the federal government on a state government requiring that it carry out a federal policy or program
Total preemption	A state is prohibited from implementing its own program or law in a policy area
Partial preemption	A state is partially prohibited from implementing its own standards and regulations in a policy area—typically it may implement a standard higher than the federal standard but not below the federal standard
Persuasion	**States are prodded to follow federal policy preferences through financial inducements**
Conditions on grants	A state must meet conditions and requirements established by the federal government in order to receive a federal grant
Crosscutting requirements	The federal government places the same set of requirements across a large number of grant and funding programs, making it more difficult for a state to choose not to meet the requirement
Crossover sanctions	The federal government requires compliance with requirements on small grant programs in order for a state to continue to receive federal funds in larger, often unrelated, federal funding programs

Note: The federal government imposes these tools directly on local governments as well. Within states, state governments use similar tools in relation to local governments.
Source: Paul L. Posner, *The Politics of Unfunded Mandates: Whither Federalism?* Washington, DC: Georgetown University Press, 1998.

is the focus of intense political maneuvering. Usually, several factors are included, and each will reward some states more than others.[22]

block grant funds provided by the federal government to a state or local government in general support of a broad government function such as education or transportation.

Block grants, which began during the presidency of Richard Nixon (1969–1974), are more general and provide greater flexibility to the states. These grants are for broad categories of spending: transportation funds, welfare program funds, homeland security, and so on. States are free to spend those funds more or less as they please, within those particular policy areas, and the amounts states receive are based on formulas determined by the federal government. Block grants can come with conditions, however. For example, states that do not comply with portions of the federal Clean Air Act will lose some of their highway funding.

Since 1987, the federal government has provided funds to state and local governments through block grants and categorical grants that comprise over 20 percent of all state and local expenditures.[23] This proportion recently spiked up because of the large infusion of federal stimulus and economic recovery funds sent to state government beginning in 2009. The most rapidly growing area of federal aid to states and localities has been assistance for medical expenses, increasing from about $44 billion in 1990 to a projected $350 billion in 2015.[24] Although the percentage of state and local budgets financed by federal aid stayed about the same over the past two decades, much more of that aid is now dedicated to medical expenses (see Figure 4-3).

To state governments, fiscal federalism is attractive. It provides states with funding to do things they otherwise would be unable to do. But fiscal federalism creates problems as well. One problem is that these cash infusions may come with strings attached, so the state may be creating some programs or services primarily because there is money available to do so, rather than because it is a priority of the state government or the people of the state.

Another problem with fiscal federalism is that states may battle each other to get a larger share of federal funds. The criteria used by federal officials to distribute aid will benefit some states more than others, so they are hotly debated. In the competition for the Race to the Top education grants, states had to agree to certain requirements—allowing teachers to be evaluated in part by student achievement, for example. States that already had those provisions in place were better positioned to focus on burnishing other aspects of their proposals for funding, possibly giving them a competitive edge. In effect, states that win grant competitions like these are being subsidized by the federal tax payments made by citizens of the losing states.[25]

A final problem with fiscal federalism is the dif-

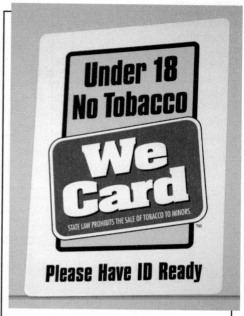

PERSUASION THROUGH FISCAL FEDERALISM

In order to receive their full share of federal substance abuse prevention and treatment block grant funds, states have to prohibit tobacco sales to minors. States that do not, or that inadequately enforce the law, can lose up to 40 percent of their block grant funds. Should the federal government put conditions on the receipt of its funds?

ficulty of a state or city in speaking with one voice. Officials at the highest levels of state and local government, such as governors or mayors, typically prefer the flexibility of block grants and lobby the federal government for more. Officials in state and city agencies, however, as well as organized interest groups, are often equally determined to obtain categorical grants that they know will be used for a defined purpose. The availability of specialized funds can lead employees in different parts of the same agency to remain isolated as they seek to win these narrowly targeted funds—known as the policy silo problem.

In addition, states and city officials can have different political incentives. In particular, to the extent that federal grants go directly to cities, state political leaders will not receive political credit for new programs and spending. Moreover, the funds being received by the city might, in the view of state officials, be put to better use elsewhere. One of the reasons federal officials

FIGURE 4-3 Federal Aid to States and Cities by Function.

Federal grants to the states for medical expenses have been an increasing share of all federal aid provided to states and cities.

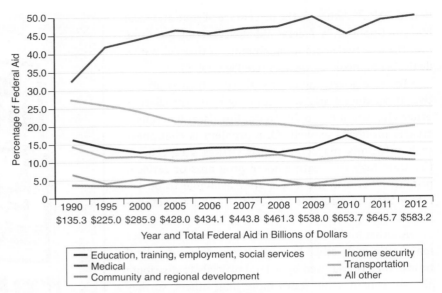

Note: Data for 2010–2012 are estimates provided in the 2011 U.S. Budget.
Source: Budget of the United States Government: Historical Tables Fiscal Year 2011

sometimes wish to funnel funds directly to cities is precisely because they are concerned that states will shortchange them.

So which are better—categorical grants or block grants? The answer will vary depending on whom you ask. Categorical grants reveal the national government's priorities, or at least the priorities of those members of Congress who voted in favor of a federal agency's budget. With block grants, the national government has money spent generally where it wants, but the states decide how they want to spend it. Thus, national lawmakers can be less sure that funds are being spent in specific ways they would desire. For federal lawmakers, the tradeoff is between the close national-level control of categorical grants and the potential state-level innovation and effectiveness of block grants. Elected officials in the states will rarely turn down what appears to be "free" federal money, however, whether block or categorical.[26]

Federalism can create both problems and solutions.

The more general question raised by the choice between categorical grants and block grants is what type of relationship one desires between the national and state governments. For those who favor more national standards and control, there are multiple concerns with allowing the states a great degree of independence in setting policy. States may simply not have access to the same expertise available to the federal government. One state's solutions may create problems for bordering states. If states are not required to meet high national standards,

HOW DO WE KNOW?

Are States Engaged in a Race to the Bottom?

The Question

Critics of welfare policy argue that states with generous welfare benefits risk becoming "magnets" that attract the poor. Furthermore, the higher taxes resulting from these policies may be a disincentive to businesses looking to locate in the state. Defenders of these policies worry that this logic leads states to compete economically by decreasing welfare benefits to the level of neighboring states, which they refer to as a "race to the bottom." Are states engaged in a race to the bottom? How do we know?

Why It Matters

The race-to-the-bottom question is one of the most contentious in the study of federalism. The policy consequences are significant for welfare recipients, taxpayers, and economic development. Philosophically, the question engages the very strong and competing points of view researchers may have about the desirability of welfare programs for individuals. And the concern about magnets and policy races in American federalism appears in other policy areas.[27]

Investigating the Answer

The premise of the race-to-the-bottom debate is that states offering generous welfare policies put themselves at risk by becoming welfare magnets. With more generous policies, there will be an influx of welfare recipients because of higher benefits and an outflow of business because of higher taxes. States respond to this dilemma by reducing welfare benefits, which prompts surrounding states to do the same. The result is a downward spiral in which states follow each other toward low benefits.

The basic approach in studies of the race to the bottom is twofold. One group of studies focuses on state government behavior. The outcome to be explained is whether surrounding states adjust their level of welfare benefits in reaction to changing levels of benefits by their neighbors. The causal relationship being tested by the researchers is whether lower benefits in one state lead to lower benefits in surrounding states. This requires tracking benefit levels over time.

These researchers may also seek to determine whether a state is a "welfare magnet" by looking at states that make benefits more generous and then seeing whether the poverty level in those states changes. The logic is that if increased benefits lure the poor, then at least initially a state's poverty rate would increase after benefits were raised because poor residents from other states will have migrated to the generous state.

Any investigation of state government welfare benefits needs to take into account a number of factors other than the actions of other states that might affect a state's benefit levels. Wealthier states can more easily afford higher benefits per person, because they have a smaller percentage of their population receiving benefits than do poorer states. States with more liberal public opinion might also be expected to have higher spending. On the other hand, states with declining wages might reduce welfare benefits to discourage workers from leaving jobs to enter the welfare system.

A second set of studies focuses on the behavior of individuals rather than state governments. These studies seek to determine why low-income individuals move from one state to another and, in particular, whether welfare benefits are part of that decision. Researchers tracking the movement of individuals from one state to another need to consider other factors that may lead individuals to move, particularly family concerns and greater work opportunities in another state. The latter is particularly important. A low-income individual might move to a higher-benefit state not because of the higher benefits, but because that state is more likely to be prosperous and have more available jobs. Thus, the increased economic opportunity, not the generous welfare policy, would be the magnet. Although there would be a correlation between welfare benefits and migration, the benefits would not actually be causing the migration.

Research on the race-to-the-bottom thesis faces other complications. Most studies, for example, assume that neighboring states are the relevant set of states—these are the states that a government is "competing with" in terms of welfare benefits and also the states from which migration is most likely. However,

(continues)

HOW DO WE KNOW?   Are States Engaged in a Race to the Bottom? *(continued)*

this assumption is not always accurate. California, for example, has more migrants from Texas, New York, Illinois, and Florida than from neighboring Oregon. Also, what if state officials set their benefits not in reaction to actual reductions in other states but in anticipation that other states will reduce their benefits? As a result, the cause of their behavior may well be behavior in other states that has not even happened yet and thus would be hard to demonstrate by a researcher. A similar problem is that states may reduce their welfare benefits to be more in line with nearby states even if individuals do not behave in the manner presumed by the welfare magnet thesis. State government officials might assume that individuals will migrate for benefits and therefore reduce their state welfare expenditures to preempt migration. In this scenario, state policy makers are influenced by the threat of movement, rather than by any demonstrated fact that individuals do move for welfare reasons. And while most studies focus on benefit levels, states could compete in other arenas as well. They could keep benefits per recipient largely unchanged, for example, but make access to a program more difficult.

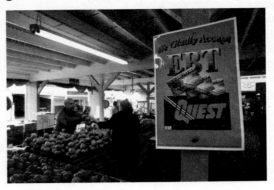

MAGNETIC BENEFITS? Although food purchase assistance is a federal program, states are allowed some leeway on benefits and eligibility. Supporters of generous program benefits worry that states have incentives to match their neighbors by decreasing benefits, while opponents are concerned that generous states become magnets attracting more beneficiaries. This farmers market in California accepts the electronic benefit transfer cards used by Supplemental Nutrition Assistance Program recipients.

Thinking Critically

1. You are a state legislator and an advocacy group wants you to support a proposal to substantially increase benefits and services for students with severe developmental disabilities—services that tend to be very expensive. Would your decision about supporting the proposal depend at all on concerns that families will move to your state to receive these benefits? Why or why not?

2. Can you think of any policy areas in which a state might provide higher benefits to encourage migration to the state?

3. If a state was determined to spend a fixed amount on income assistance programs, would you recommend higher benefits but less access, or lower benefits but more access?

The Bottom Line

Despite these research challenges, political scientists have reached some conclusions on the race-to-the-bottom theory. Overall, research has found support for the notion that states compete on benefit levels.

States tend to follow each other as benefits are lowered, but they do not seem to follow each other if benefits are increased. Studies vary regarding whether states match benefits changes in other states in full or just a few cents to the dollar.[28]

There have been fewer studies on whether individuals move to welfare magnets, but these generally conclude that factors other than welfare benefits are more important in determining the location decisions of low-income individuals. For policy makers, it may not matter whether welfare benefits are the only reason an individual moves or a major reason: what might matter is simply whether welfare benefits influence location decisions to any degree.[29]

The Obama administration has urged states to think more regionally about economic development, and to see these regions as being in competition with other countries rather than with each other or with other states. Achieving such a change on any large scale would require a significant shift in the thinking of both politicians and citizens. It would also require the federal government to change its practices significantly, as much of its funding flows to states and inherently pits states in competition with each other.[30]

there may be a "race to the bottom" in which states try to provide minimal services and cut taxes and regulation in an attempt to attract business.

Political power is a factor as well. If particular ideas and politicians dominate national politics—whether conservative or liberal—these politicians may be tempted to use that opportunity to implement uniform conservative or liberal policies, respectively, across the country. Even ardent advocates of a strong role for the states can be attracted to the idea of writing national policies and rules that the states must follow, especially if they believe their political opponents have a foothold in state governments.

For those who favor allowing states more flexibility and leeway, the advantages are also multiple. Allowed flexibility in solving problems, the states become "laboratories of democracy," a phrase coined by Supreme Court Justice Louis Brandeis early in the twentieth century to describe an environment in which numerous policy proposals can be implemented and tested. States vary tremendously in the substance of their policies in areas such as education, welfare, consumer protection, health care, and many more. States also vary in their political processes. Ultimately, the nation gains because other states can borrow those policy reforms that prove to be effective, efficient, or popular.

Some examples of state innovations that were adopted by many states—known as policy diffusion—include raising standards and creating charter schools in education and "three strikes" laws and minimum sentencing standards in criminal justice. Citizens also have the advantage of choice—they can choose where to live based on a number of factors, including the different styles and roles of government across the states.[31]

Federalism in Flux

4-4   Assess the extent and nature of changes in federalism over the past two decades.

Since the early 1990s, American federalism has changed. "Revolutionary" is probably too strong a term to describe the change, but certainly there has been a significant departure from previous decades in the way elected officials and the judiciary have interpreted and implemented American federalism.

Elected officials have initiated changes in federalism.

Congress and Presidents Bill Clinton and George W. Bush instigated part of the shift. After Republicans won control of the House and Senate in the 1994 congressional elections, they pushed an agenda of devolution and block grants. **Devolution** refers to the transfer of authority over program details and implementation from a higher level of government to a lower level of government. This transfer could be from federal to state, from state to local, or from federal to local, depending on the issue. In the devolution starting in the 1990s, transfer from

devolution a process in which the authority over a government program's rules and implementation is largely transferred from a higher-level government to a lower-level government.

the federal to state level was especially prominent. For example, by the end of the 1990s, the federal Environmental Protection Agency had shifted the authority for nearly 760 federal environmental programs to the states. Over 80 percent of the programs related to the Clean Air Act are now run by state governments.

Another way in which Congress has shifted authority to the states is through a process known as negotiated rulemaking. Here, Congress inserts into legislation a requirement that federal agencies negotiate with states over the content of the federal regulations that will implement the law. This requirement does not give states veto power over agency regulations, but it ensures them a formal, ongoing role in the process when regulations are developed.[32]

The Supreme Court has redefined contemporary federalism.

Even more dramatic than the changes initiated by elected officials were the changes produced by the Supreme Court. In a series of controversial decisions starting in the mid-1990s, the Court began to redraw the boundaries between federal and state responsibilities and authority. It did this by scaling back Congress's use of the interstate commerce clause to justify legislation and by reasserting dual sovereignty ideals.

Reining in Congress's use of the commerce clause Following the Supreme Court's 1937 decision in *National Labor Relations Board v. Jones & Laughlin Steel Corporation*, Congress used the Court's new interpretation of the interstate commerce clause to move the federal government into areas previously relegated to the states. Until 1995, the Supreme Court acceded to this expansion of federal power. That year, however, in *United States v. Lopez*, the Supreme Court signaled a change in direction.

The Gun-Free School Zones Act of 1990 prohibited the possession of firearms within 1,000 feet of a school. Congress justified its intervention in this area by arguing that guns were an item of interstate commerce, but the Court struck down the law.[33] In the Court's view, Congress was improperly involving itself in matters of local policing and using the interstate commerce clause as a thin and unconvincing rationale for its action. If states and localities wished to pass such restrictions on firearm possession, they were free to do so, but this was not a matter for federal government involvement. For the first time in nearly six decades, the Court refused to agree to Congress's use of the interstate commerce clause to expand federal power. The Court reached a similar decision in *United States v. Morrison* (2000) declaring that portions of the Violence Against Women Act were not substantially connected to Congress's commerce clause powers.

Reasserting dual sovereignty Another issue in the Court's new federalism offensive was whether states could be sued by private parties, such as individuals or organizations, in federal court. In a set of controversial decisions, the Court concluded that under the Eleventh Amendment, states had **sovereign immunity** against these suits—in essence, the states could not be sued in federal court unless they chose to allow themselves to be sued or Congress made a compelling case that it should be able to override this immunity.[34] The Court majority in these decisions reaffirmed the compact theory, adding that even without the Eleventh Amendment, the states were sovereign entities prior to the creation of the Constitution and had not given up that status.

Some decisions were designed to limit the federal government's ability to impose its will on the states. In *Printz v. United States* (1997), the Court concluded that the Constitution's necessary and proper clause did not entitle Congress to compel state or local law enforcement officials to perform federal tasks without their consent, in this case background checks for handgun purchasers. And in *Gonzales v. Oregon* (2006), the Court concluded that the federal government did not have the authority, under the Controlled Substances Act, to prohibit the use of regulated but legal drugs for physician-assisted suicide in Oregon.

The cumulative effect of the Court's jurisprudence in this era was to send Congress and the president stark messages that they had to tread carefully in their attempts to intervene in states' relationships with their citizens and other areas traditionally established as matters of state concern. It was a clear attempt to restore the influence of dual federalist principles and the ideas of the compact theory, described earlier in this chapter. The narrow 5–4 majorities on many of the decisions heightened the political tension surrounding future Supreme Court nominations.

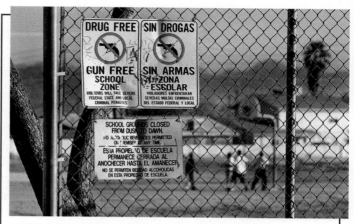

GUNS PROHIBITED NEAR SCHOOL PROPERTY
The Supreme Court went nearly 60 years after the *Jones & Laughlin* decision before objecting to Congress's use of the commerce clause to justify a law. In 1995, the Court did so, striking down the Gun-Free School Zone Act of 1990. The following year, a new version of the law was passed that, in the view of Congress and the president, provided a stronger justification for the law's connection to interstate commerce. The new law still stands and has not been challenged in court.

sovereign immunity the principle that state governments cannot be sued by private parties in federal court unless they consent to the suits or Congress has constitutionally provided an exemption that allows suits to be filed.

State officials have implemented significant new policy.

As law and constitutional interpretation shifted at the federal level, policy innovation in the states expanded in the 1990s and the first decade of the twenty-first century. In areas as diverse as the minimum wage, greenhouse gas emissions, health care coverage, prescription drug imports, and embryonic stem-cell research, state governments enacted significant legislation. In some of these areas, states acted because of their dissatisfaction with national government policies. In other areas, the federal government's involvement had waned as government officials' concerns were focused elsewhere.

Has there been a revolution in federalism?

Given these strong moves by Congress, the president, the Supreme Court, and the states, why consider the change in federalism to be anything short of a revolution? Many media and advocacy group critics of the moves describe the changes precisely that way, especially the Court's decisions. These conclusions, however, tend to generalize from only part of the evidence—particular laws or decisions that rankled the critic. Bringing a wider body of evidence into the analysis suggests that "revolution" is too strong a word to describe the changing balance of national and state power.

> **Thinking Causally** Have elected officials and the Supreme Court produced a revolution in the balance of national and state power?

One reason is that the federal government still remains involved in those policy areas known for devolution, such as welfare. States are free to design their programs as they wish, but they are not free to eliminate those programs. Also, federal involvement in new policy areas is possible.

One example of the pull and tug of federalism links terrorism and driver's licenses—two seemingly distinct areas of federal and state responsibility, respectively. Congress, in the REAL ID Act of 2005, sought as an antiterrorism measure to require all states to demand proof of permanent residency before issuing driver's licenses. Ten states had no such requirements. In addition, licenses were to be standardized in certain ways across the states, such as the information stored on the machine-readable cards. State license databases would need to be linked to a national database. If a state's licenses were not consistent with the federal standard, individuals holding those licenses would not be able to use them for identification purposes with federal agencies, such as the Transportation Security Administration, which handles security at the nation's airports. Proponents of the law argued that these provisions would make it more difficult for terrorists to operate in the United States and more difficult for illegal immigrants to get legal employment. Some of the hijackers involved in the September 11, 2001, attacks had acquired driver's licenses and been able to board planes despite being in the United States illegally.

Opposition to the REAL ID Act spread through states in early 2007. Legislators in many states objected to this federal intervention in traditional state responsibility, its perceived threats to privacy, and the cost imposed on state governments. State governments estimated the cost to them to be $11 billion nationwide, while the federal government put the cost at $3.9 billion. Congress had allocated only about $200 million to implement the law.[35] Quickly, a majority of states passed resolutions objecting to the law and pledging not to implement it.[36]

By the end of 2007, the federal government had softened its demands in an attempt to increase support from state officials, and the original May 2008 deadline to meet the act's requirements was extended. The deadline was extended again in 2009, and measures to repeal REAL ID were introduced in the House and Senate. President Obama's Secretary of Homeland Security, Janet Napolitano, an opponent of REAL ID, supported the Senate legislation known as PASS ID (Providing for Additional Security in States' Identification Act). The proposed PASS ID would still require state licenses to conform to a national standard, but numerous mandates in REAL ID would be dropped, and state privacy laws would not be preempted.

The federal government's role has also become more pronounced in other areas.[37] The most notable example in the past decade of an expanded federal role has been in education, long a bastion of state and local governments. The No Child Left Behind Act championed by President Bush and passed by Congress in 2002 required school districts to test each child in grades 3 through 8 and specified penalties for schools whose students do poorly and are not improving. President Obama's Race to the Top program aims to reward states with competitive grants for innovations in curriculum standards, student assessment, teacher training, rewarding effective teachers, and improving the performance of unsuccessful schools.[38]

The increased federal role across policy areas has had multiple causes—partisan goals, interest group activism, reactions to crises, similarity of goals among federal and state officials, and disorganized state officials being outmaneuvered by unified legislators at the national level.[39] Federalism remains a political battleground where politicians take advantage of the opportunities they have in front of them. That may mean preferring national solutions in some instances and state solutions in others.

Another reason not to overstate the extent of the new federalism "revolution" is that the Court did not completely defer to the states in its decisions about sovereign immunity from lawsuits. For example, when cases have involved Fourteenth Amendment issues of equal protection, particularly in the areas of race and gender, the Court has allowed states to be subject to federal authority. In one decision, the Court concluded that an individual could sue a state in federal court for that state's alleged gender-based discrimination in implementing the Family Medical Leave Act, and that these suits were consistent with Congress's intent when it passed the act.[40]

This idea, that Congress could respond to widespread and persistent discrimination, was also at the core of *Tennessee v. Lane* (2004). The case concerned a paraplegic who could not attend a court case because of a lack of elevators in the court building. To the Supreme Court, the fundamental importance of citizen access to the courts overrode the state's claim to immunity from a discrimination lawsuit. If the Court believes a right is of special gravity, it will give Congress more leeway to force states to comply with federal rules that might otherwise be seen as exceeding federal constitutional authority.[41]

The Supreme Court also has been willing to trim state power. In *Gonzales v. Raich* (2005), Congress's power to prohibit the personal growing and possession of marijuana for medical use was upheld, superseding a 1996

WOULD YOU LIKE SOME HIGHS WITH THAT?

In 2000, Colorado voters supported the use of marijuana for medicinal purposes. Medical marijuana shops soon emerged. A U.S. Supreme Court decision in 2005, however, upheld Congress's power to prohibit the growing and possession of medical marijuana, even for one's personal use, superseding the Colorado law. The U.S. Justice Department announced in 2009 that it would no longer prosecute the use of medical marijuana in states that allowed it. How aggressive should federal government enforcement be when state laws contradict federal laws?

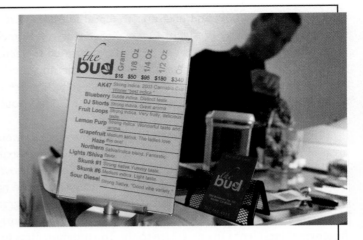

California law that allowed such use. The federal Controlled Substances Act did not allow exemptions for medical use of marijuana, the Court held, and the federal government could regulate those products involved in interstate commerce. Although growth for personal medicinal use might appear to be entirely local and thus not an area for federal regulation, the Court concluded that personal medicinal use nonetheless affected supply and demand and was in effect a part of the national marijuana market. Therefore, it was subject to the national government's interstate commerce power.

So where does federalism stand today? Early in the second decade of the twenty-first century, federalism continues to evolve. It has not returned to the dual federalism of the nineteenth century, as the federal government's intervention into areas like education, traditionally thought of as a local and state responsibility, makes clear. But it is also not simply the cooperative federalism of much of the twentieth century. Today's federalism remains cooperative in many respects but does so within dual federalism boundaries that have been reasserted by elected officials and by the Supreme Court.

Today's federalism is a constrained cooperative federalism, restricted and limited by the Court's enforcement of dual federalist principles via the Tenth and Eleventh Amendments. However, it does not sit still. Politicians and judges push and pull it in multiple directions. Today's federalism is united with past federalism in that politicians and judges mix philosophy with desired policy outcomes as they wrestle with the balance of national and state power.

Although it is uncertain how President Obama's appointments to the Supreme Court will affect this blend of dual and cooperative federalism, they will most likely not lead to a major new direction. The president's first two appointments to the Court replaced liberal justices with new justices who are also liberal, thus suggesting the Court's overall view on issues concerning the balance of national and state power would remain about the same as previously. Among the president's legislative achievements, universal health insurance, which requires states to comply with new national standards and uses interstate commerce regulation to mandate that individuals purchase insurance, may produce the most highly charged federalism case that will reach this new Court.

Chapter Summary

In this chapter you have learned to:

4-1   Show how the Constitution serves as a framework for federalism and why debates remain.

The Constitution defines the framework within which American federalism operates, identifying areas where the national government is supreme to the states. But disputes about the role of the states in the federal system have never gone away. Differing interpretations of the formation of the United States contribute to the dispute. To some, the Union was a joining together of "the people," which weakens the primacy that states should have in federalism. To others, the Union was a joining together of the states in which states reserved a substantial amount of the sovereignty they held prior to creating the United States.

4-2   Outline the principles of dual federalism and their basis in the Supreme Court's traditional understanding of interstate commerce.

Dual federalism delineates separate and independent spheres of function and responsibility for the federal and state governments. All citizens have dual citizenship, being a citizen of both their state and the country. Prevailing Supreme Court interpretation of Congress's power to regulate interstate commerce reinforced dual federalism.

4-3   Trace the evolution from dual to cooperative federalism, and identify methods of cooperative federalism.

Redefining interstate commerce played a significant role in expanding the scope of federal government responsibility and moving the country from dual to cooperative federalism. Rather than relying on strict spheres of federal and state duties, cooperative federalism allows for many areas of overlapping responsibilities for these two layers of government. Collaboration, mandates, and persuasion in the form of fiscal federalism are types of federal–state interaction in cooperative federalism. Generally, the federal government was the more powerful in this "cooperative" arrangement; thus, cooperative did not always mean harmonious. Mandates are sometimes described as coercive federalism, and fiscal federalism can apply pressure on state officials to follow federal government wishes.

4-4   Assess the extent and nature of changes in federalism over the past two decades.

Over the past two decades, the relationship between the federal and state governments has shifted. State officials became more active in policy areas where they had previously deferred to national leadership. At the national level, elected officials sought to provide states with more flexibility and responsibility over some policies. In a number of important decisions, the Supreme Court clamped down on Congress's use of the interstate commerce justification, concluded that the federal government had become improperly involved in areas of state government responsibility, and asserted the argument that the sovereignty of state governments shielded them from some federal government regulation. Not everything has moved in the direction of more state authority, however. In few policy areas has the federal government fully withdrawn, and it has inserted itself into new areas that had traditionally been the purview of the states.

CHAPTER TEST

1. What are the main differences between the confederal, unitary, and federal systems of organizing government?

2. How would advocates of the nationalist and compact theory views of American government evaluate the confederal, unitary, and federal systems?

3. What is the difference between dual sovereignty and dual citizenship?

4. What were the main areas of responsibility thought to be distinctively the authority of the federal government and distinctively the authority of the state governments under dual federalism?

5. How did the interpretation of interstate commerce change, and how did this matter for the evolution of federalism?

6. As a federal official, what would influence your decision on whether to use a form of collaboration, mandate, or persuasion in dealing with the states?

7. As a governor of a state, how would you rank the forms of federal financial assistance from most to least attractive?

8. In what areas would you argue that states should and should not have a great degree of flexibility rather than following national standards in establishing public policy? What are your criteria for making those distinctions?

9. What were the main themes of Supreme Court pro-state federalism decisions over the past two decades?

10. What are the strongest arguments that there has not been a revolution in federalism?

MyPoliSciLab® FEDERALISM
Apply what you learned in this chapter on MyPoliSciLab.

Read on mypoliscilab.com
   eText: Chapter 4

Study and Review on mypoliscilab.com
   Pre-Test
   Post-Test
   Chapter Exam
   Flashcards

Watch on mypoliscilab.com
   Video: The Real ID
   Video: Water Wars
   How Do We Know Video: Are states engaged in a race to the bottom?

Explore on mypoliscilab.com
   Comparative: Comparing Federal and Unitary Systems
   Simulation: You Are a Federal Judge
   Simulation: You Are a Restaurant Owner
   Timeline: Federalism and the Supreme Court
   Visual Literacy: Federalism and Regulations

KEY TERMS

block grant, p. 100
categorical grant, p. 99
commerce clause, p. 90
compact theory, p. 87
confederation, p. 85
cooperative federalism, p. 91
devolution, p. 105
dual citizenship, p. 90
dual federalism, p. 88

dual sovereignty, p. 89
enumerated powers, p. 93
federalism, p. 86
fiscal federalism, p. 99
implied powers, p. 93
mandate, p. 98
nationalist theory, p. 87
necessary and proper clause, p. 93
nullification, p. 87

police power, p. 89
preemption legislation, p. 99
reserved powers, p. 86
sovereign immunity, p. 107
sovereignty, p. 87
unfunded mandate, p. 98
unitary system, p. 85

SUGGESTED READINGS

Martha N. Derthick. 2001. *Keeping the Compound Republic: Essays on American Federalism*. Washington, DC: Brookings Institution Press. The evolution of federalism in the United States and an analysis of a range of issues concerning federalism and intergovernmental relations.

Alison LaCroix. 2010. *The Ideological Origins of American Federalism*. Cambridge, MA: Harvard University Press. Views American federalism as not so much an adaptation to circumstances that Americans backed into, but as a major theory and ideology that held a prominent position in American political thought in the eighteenth century prior to the Constitution.

Paul Manna. 2006. *School's In: Federalism and the National Education Agenda*. Washington, DC: Georgetown University Press. How the increased role of the federal government in education was a result of building on state-level fiscal and administrative capacities created by education reformers in previous decades.

Paul E. Peterson. 1995. *The Price of Federalism*. Washington, DC: Brookings Institution Press. An exploration of the ways in which federalism works well and the political pressures that can push legislators away from it.

Deloria Vine, Jr., and Clifford M. Lytle. 1998. *The Nations Within: The Past and Future of American Indian Sovereignty*. Austin: University of Texas Press. Through a close accounting of the politics surrounding an important bill, the book explores the complexity of tribal sovereignty in the American federal system.

SUGGESTED WEBSITES

NATIONAL CONFERENCE OF STATE LEGISLATURES
www.ncsl.org

Excellent resource with policy analysis, election results, and a range of other helpful data comparing states and examining federal–state issues.

LIBRARY OF CONGRESS, AMERICAN MEMORY PROJECT: TO FORM A MORE PERFECT UNION
memory.loc.gov/ammem/collections/continental/intro01.html

Original documents related to federalism and the relationship of the states to each other and the national government. Focus on Revolutionary War era and the making of the Constitution.

GRANTS.GOV
www.grants.gov

Easy-to-use searchable database of federal grants.

STATISTICAL ABSTRACT OF THE UNITED STATES
www.census.gov/compendia/statab

Terrific collection of data published by the U.S. Census Bureau that includes hundreds of tables and downloadable spreadsheets, many at the state level, and data on intergovernmental finances.

URBAN INSTITUTE
www.urban.org/government/federalism.cfm

Good collection of studies on a wide range of issues facing federalist systems in the United States and around the world.

5

Civil Liberties and Civil Rights

CENTER OF ATTENTION Justice Samuel Alito (center) sits with five other justices during President Obama's State of the Union Address, 2010. The president had just rebuked the Supreme Court for its decision in *Citizens United v. FEC*, bringing senators and administration officials to their feet in applause. Alito silently mouthed "not true" in response to the president's critique.

The scene was extraordinary. Before a national television audience and in front of the assembled members of Congress, President Barack Obama directly criticized the U.S. Supreme Court in his State of the Union Address, with six of the justices seated before him. One of those justices, Samuel Alito silently mouthed the response "not true" to the president's criticism.

In January 2010, a bitterly divided Supreme Court ruled 5–4 that corporations have a right to spend their funds independently to support or oppose candidates by running television ads or other forms of communication. At issue was *Hillary Clinton: The Movie*, a critical documentary produced by Citizens United, a small nonprofit corporation funded mostly by individual contributions. Hillary Clinton was running for the Democratic Party's 2008 nomination for the presidency. Fearing the Federal Election Commission (FEC) would consider the documentary and ads to promote it to violate the Bipartisan Campaign Reform Act of 2002 (BCRA), Citizens United sought an injunction against any FEC action. BCRA prohibits corporations from using their general treasury funds for independent electioneering activities—that is, any broadcast, cable, or satellite communications within 30 days of a primary election or 60 days of a general election that specifically mentions a candidate for federal office. Citizens United lost and the case moved to the Supreme Court.

The response to the Supreme Court's decision was thunderous. Critics denounced the ruling in *Citizens United v. Federal Election Commission* as a devastating blow to democracy and fair elections: "This appalling decision . . . will further weaken the quality and fairness of our politics. The Court has given lobbyists, already much too powerful, a nuclear weapon. . . . The conservative justices savaged canons of judicial restraint they themselves have long praised." Supporters cheered the decision as a stirring victory for free speech: "Hopefully, this ruling marks an end to 20 years of jurisprudence in which the Court has provided less protection to core political speech than it has to Internet pornography . . . flag burning, commercial advertising, topless dancing, and burning a cross outside an African American church."

Praise for and condemnation of the Supreme Court's reasoning, and impassioned debate over what the First Amendment demands regarding free speech, were the basis of one major post-decision debate. The other major debate concerned causality. What would be the result of the Court's decision?

Critics charged that corporate speech would "drown out" speech from candidates and other sources. Some argued that legislators would live in fear that casting a difficult vote might unleash a large war chest of independent corporate or union spending against them.

Supporters claimed that the ruling would lead to more vibrant campaigns—speech begets more speech in response, and the public is ultimately the beneficiary. Many also argued that it is corporations that have more to fear from government power, so corporate campaigning would more likely be defensive moves responding to government actions rather than prompting such actions.

Prior to *Citizens United*, about half the states already allowed unlimited campaign spending by corporations and unions. These are funds spent independently by these organizations on campaign ads, for example. One analysis soon after the Court decision found little significant difference between this set of states and the other states on party control, business climate, or policy of interest to business. Why? Perhaps business spending motivates labor and consumer groups to be more involved. Maybe different businesses are on opposite sides in a particular race. Or many businesses may fear the reputational backlash of heavy involvement in campaigns.[1]

The debates over the propriety of the Supreme Court's decision, as well as its causal impact on politics, will continue. Constitutional guarantees such as freedom of speech, freedom of religion, and the right to assemble are general principles, but politics is also about specifics, and these specifics lead to conflict. In these conflicts, choices must be made, either through law, executive action, or court decision, each of which are examined in this chapter. You will see how Court decisions prompt legislative action, to which the Court may have to respond in the future.

In addition to conflict, another constant of civil liberties is change. What is considered appropriate at one time might not be considered so at another. This feature is also true for civil rights. This chapter will emphasize how the scope of civil liberties and civil rights protections have changed across time, and the role of the courts, Congress, presidents, and political pressure in bringing about these changes. ■

Civil Liberties in American Politics and the Constitution

5-1   Define the civil liberties guaranteed by the Constitution and trace the process by which they became binding on state governments.

We can safely say that few words are more important to Americans' understanding of their political system than *rights*. Political rhetoric in America is full of references to rights, whether individual rights, like the right to speak freely, or collective rights, such as the right of the people to assemble. American political culture, with its emphasis on individual independence, liberty, property ownership, religious freedom, and democratic government, is infused throughout with individual rights.

Civil liberties identify areas in which government should not interfere.

civil liberties individual rights and freedoms that government is obliged to protect, normally by not interfering in the exercise of these rights and freedoms.

In the United States, **civil liberties** focus on individual rights that government is obliged to protect, normally by standing back and not interfering. When Americans talk about civil liberties, they are typically talking about places government should not go: speech, the press, religious expression, organizing for political purposes, and so on.[2] American political culture, and its understanding of liberty, suggests that these rights are not *granted* to us or *given* to us by government—they are inherent in us as people. What government can do is protect or restrict the exercise of these individual rights.[3]

In some instances, Americans will tolerate limits on civil liberties to preserve public safety, order, or other important societal goals. For example, Americans have the right to assemble, but that does not extend into a right to assemble in the middle of a city street and stop traffic. Part of civil liberties protection, therefore, is that when government restricts the exercise of rights, it does so with **due process**. The Fifth Amendment to the Constitution states that no person shall "be deprived of life, liberty, or property, without due process of law." This clause means that there must be procedural safeguards in place prior to the restriction of rights. In the case of gathering in the street, for example, there are procedures by which a group can get a permit to assemble and march.

due process procedural safeguards that government officials are obligated to follow prior to restricting rights of life, liberty, and property.

In general, civil liberties protections are strongest in Europe and the Americas and weakest in Asia and Africa. These patterns correlate roughly with the distribution of prosperity around the globe, prompting social scientists to examine whether civil liberties result from prosperity or create prosperity. Their research suggests that both processes are present: civil liberties encourage economic growth, and economic growth encourages civil liberties.[4] The relationships are not automatic, however. Economic prosperity varies among countries with strong civil liberties protection, and countries with increasing prosperity, such as China, do not necessarily support civil liberties strongly.

Thinking Causally Do protections for civil liberties lead to prosperity or do they result from prosperity?

The Constitution protects civil liberties.

When Americans think about the constitutional protection of civil liberties, they think first of the Bill of Rights. But this is only one of the Constitution's protections of liberty. To the Framers, the structural principles in the articles of the Constitution—separation of powers, checks and balances, federalism, and limited government—all worked to enhance the general protection of the people's liberty. The Framers also included specific civil liberties protections in the articles of the Constitution. For example, the Constitution declares that only courts and juries—not the legislature—can determine whether an individual is guilty of a crime. The intent is to ensure that, before any rights are restricted, the proceedings that might lead to that outcome are fair, impartial, proper, and not subject to the political pressures that exist in a legislature. Similarly, an individual cannot be tried based on *ex post facto* ("after the fact") laws passed by state governments or the federal government, meaning that you cannot be tried for an act that was not illegal at the time you committed it.

Freedom of expression and the rights of the accused are the two main areas of civil liberties protection in the Bill of Rights.

The Bill of Rights is at the heart of constitutional civil liberties protections. The provisions in the first eight amendments of the Bill of Rights provide protection against the actions of the legislative, executive, and judicial branches of government. The protections overwhelmingly regard two categories: freedom of expression and the rights of those accused of crime. A final category consists of three provisions that do not fit into the previous two categories. Two of these—the right to keep and bear arms and the compensation for public appropriation of one's property—have been the subject of extensive political and legal debate. The Ninth Amendment states that the failure to list rights in the preceding amendments should not be presumed to mean that the people do not have additional rights. The Tenth Amendment declares that powers not given to the federal government are reserved for the states or the people.[5]

Nationalization of the Bill of Rights protected individuals against the actions of state governments.

The Bill of Rights had a more limited effect on American politics during the nineteenth century than it does today. During that time, government was much more active on the state level. Many states had their own bills of rights to protect their citizens from state government actions, but the U.S. Constitution's Bill of Rights was considered to apply only to the actions of the national government. Beginning in 1897, the Supreme Court began to see the Bill of Rights as limiting the actions of state governments as well as the national government. This revolutionary shift opened the door for increased federal government authority and changed the scope of civil liberties protection.[6]

incorporation process the application, through the Fourteenth Amendment, of the civil liberties protections in the Bill of Rights to state governments.

Incorporation and the Fourteenth Amendment   The Supreme Court used the **incorporation process** to apply the Bill of Rights to the states. The Fourteenth Amendment was key to this process. Stated technically, the Bill of Rights was incorporated into the Fourteenth Amendment and through this inclusion became binding on the states.

The amendment was ratified in July 1868 as part of the post–Civil War reconstruction of American government and society. It was the first amendment to limit state action directly, declaring that "no State shall make or enforce any law which shall abridge the privileges or immunities of citizens of the United States; nor shall any State deprive any person of life, liberty, or property, without due process of law; nor deny to any person within its jurisdiction the equal protection of the laws."

If we consider the battle over state versus national power during the framing of the Constitution, and the many protections for state sovereignty in the

Constitution and in law, this declaration was a remarkable turnabout. Why would three-quarters of the states vote to limit their independence? Political scientists often point to the importance of ideas, interests, and institutions in explaining political change, and all three can be brought to bear on this puzzle. Some of those legislators voting to ratify the amendment may have done so based on a sincere belief in the idea that the Union needed to have some consistent civil liberties standards to protect all citizens, but especially the recently emancipated slaves.

Given that the collapse of a unified nation contributed to the descent into a horrific war, it is understandable that a majority of politicians and the public supported constitutional provisions that could prevent states from straying too far from fundamental protections of life, liberty, and property—it was in their self-interest. An important institutional rule further helps explain the amendment's success: southern states were required to accept the amendment prior to being readmitted to the Union, and they were not allowed representation in Congress until they were readmitted. Even if they opposed the content of the amendment, self-interest ultimately led them to ratify it.

Selective incorporation The Supreme Court began the process of incorporation with a decision concerning property. In 1897, the Court decided that, in order for the Fourteenth Amendment's general protection of property to be a meaningful concept, it required compensation when property was taken for public use. The Fifth Amendment's "takings clause," which states that private property cannot be taken for public use unless the property owner is compensated, was thus incorporated into the Fourteenth Amendment and, therefore, now applied to the states.

Over a quarter-century would pass before the Court took another incorporation step. In 1925, the Court decided that the Fourteenth Amendment's protection of "liberty" must include a free speech guarantee—free speech was fundamental to the concept of liberty. The First Amendment's free speech guarantee was thus incorporated into the Fourteenth Amendment's protection for "liberty" and now it, too, applied to the action of state governments.[7]

Notice that these two cases incorporated only part of the Bill of Rights guarantees into the Fourteenth Amendment. In practice, the Supreme Court has proceeded through **selective incorporation**, meaning that it incorporated civil liberties guarantees in bits and pieces. As cases raised issues concerning particular parts of the amendments that comprise the Bill of Rights, the Court would decide whether that particular right was fundamental enough to the Fourteenth Amendment's protection of life, liberty, and property that it should now apply to the states. Table 5-1 shows that selective incorporation has been a lengthy process.

The Second Amendment right to keep and bear arms Incorporation is an ongoing process. Only recently has the Second Amendment right to keep

Thinking Causally Why would state legislators ratify the Fourteenth Amendment, an amendment that was likely to limit their independent authority?

selective incorporation the process by which protections in the Bill of Rights were gradually applied to the states, as the Supreme Court issued decisions on specific aspects of the Bill of Rights.

TABLE 5-1 Selective Incorporation of the Bill of Rights into the Fourteenth Amendment

Amendment	Issue	Year	Key Case
Amendments Fully Incorporated			
1st	Freedom of speech	1925	*Gitlow v. New York*
1st	Freedom of the press	1931	*Near v. Minnesota*
1st	Freedom of assembly	1937	*De Jonge v. Oregon*
1st	Freedom of religious exercise	1940	*Cantwell v. Connecticut*
1st	No establishment of religion	1947	*Everson v. Board of Education*
1st	Freedom of association	1958	*NAACP v. Alabama*
1st	Right to petition	1963	*NAACP v. Button*
2nd	Right to keep and bear arms	2010	*McDonald v. Chicago*
4th	No unreasonable search and seizure	1949	*Wolf v. Colorado*
4th	No search and seizure without warrant	1961	*Mapp v. Ohio*
6th	Right to counsel in capital punishment cases	1932	*Powell v. Alabama*
6th	Right to public trial	1948	*In re Oliver*
6th	Right to counsel in felony cases	1963	*Gideon v. Wainwright*
6th	Right to confront witnesses	1965	*Pointer v. Texas*
6th	Right to impartial jury	1966	*Parker v. Gladden*
6th	Right to speedy trial	1967	*Klopfer v. North Carolina*
6th	Right to compel supportive witnesses to appear in court	1967	*Washington v. Texas*
6th	Right to jury trial for serious crimes	1968	*Duncan v. Louisiana*
6th	Right to counsel for all crimes involving jail terms	1972	*Argersinger v. Hamlin*
Amendments Partially Incorporated			
5th	Compensation for public taking of private property	1897	*Chicago, Burlington, and Quincy Railroad v. Chicago*
5th	No compulsory self-incrimination	1964	*Malloy v. Hogan*
5th	No forced confession	1964	*Escobedo v. Illinois*
5th	Right to remain silent	1966	*Miranda v. Arizona*
5th	No double jeopardy	1969	*Benton v. Maryland*
5th	Right to grand jury hearing in criminal cases	Not incorp.	
8th	No cruel and unusual punishment	1962	*Robinson v. California*
8th	No excessive bail or fines	Not incorp.	
Amendments Not Incorporated			
3rd	Limits on quartering of soldiers	Not incorp.	

and bear arms been seen as an individual right, and not until 2010 did the Supreme Court incorporate this right and apply it to the states.[8]

The Second Amendment states, "a well regulated Militia, being necessary to the security of a free State, the right of the people to keep and bear Arms, shall not be infringed." The Supreme Court traditionally considered this language a collective guarantee of the self-defense of the states, rather than a guarantee of individual ownership. In 2008, however, in a case involving the prohibition of handgun ownership in the District of Columbia, the Supreme

Court declared for the first time that the Second Amendment protected an individual's right to have a gun in his or her home.

The decision struck down the handgun ban in Washington, D.C., and the National Rifle Association, the country's leading advocacy group for gun owners, quickly filed challenges to gun control laws in Chicago and other cities. Because the District of Columbia is a federal entity and not a state, the Court needed to decide in a subsequent case whether its decision in *District of Columbia v. Heller* should be incorporated and thus apply to the states and their cities. It did so in *McDonald v. Chicago* (2010). That decision does not end the story, however. We can expect causal reactions between judicial and legislative action. Future cases will continue to determine the scope and limits of an individual's right to possess firearms and government's ability to regulate them.

The right to privacy has revolutionized the law concerning birth control, abortion, and same-sex relationships.

Some of the most momentous civil liberties decisions of the past four decades have been based on a right that is not even explicitly guaranteed in the Constitution, the right to privacy. Court decisions concerning birth control, abortion, and homosexual behavior have all focused on individuals' rights to privacy. This right connects deeply to beliefs in individualism and liberty in American political culture. The Court used the Ninth Amendment to discover this right.[9]

Birth control   In 1961, the Planned Parenthood League of Connecticut opened a birth control clinic in defiance of state law. The clinic provided information and instruction on contraceptive use to married couples. Ten days after opening the clinic, Estelle Griswold, the league's executive director, and Charles Lee Buxton, the medical director, were arrested and convicted for violating Connecticut's law barring the dissemination of information about birth control devices and techniques.

Four years later, in *Griswold v. Connecticut* (1965), the U.S. Supreme Court overturned the convictions and declared by a 7–2 majority that there was a constitutional right to privacy for married couples, later extended to unmarried heterosexual couples.[10] The Court's majority concluded that even though the word *privacy* does not appear in the Constitution, the Ninth Amendment, combined with provisions of the First, Third, Fourth, and Fifth Amendments, implicitly suggested that the Constitution contained a right to privacy.[11] Protections in these amendments create "zones of privacy" in the Constitution. The dissenting justices in *Griswold* argued unsuccessfully that, by declaring a general right to privacy beyond the specific privacy protections mentioned in the Constitution, the unelected justices of the Supreme Court were displacing the appropriate role of elected officials in the states and of the voters who elected them.

Abortion *Roe v. Wade* (1973) demonstrated the extensive impact of the *Griswold* decision. Abortion had been illegal by law in Texas since 1854, unless medical personnel determined it was necessary to save the life of the mother. Similar laws existed in almost every state by the 1950s. Norma McCorvey— known in the legal case as "Jane Roe"—wishing to terminate her pregnancy legally, filed a challenge to Texas's law in 1970. Building from the *Griswold* decision, the suit contended that the statute violated McCorvey's right to privacy.

The Supreme Court, by a 7–2 majority, agreed. A woman's privacy right was not absolute, however. The Court determined that the right to privacy in the abortion decision could be conditional upon important government interests in health, medical standards, and protecting potential life. The privacy interest dominates at first, but as pregnancy advances, these government interests begin to balance the woman's privacy interest. Based on this framework, the Court established a trimester arrangement. During the first three months of pregnancy, women were free to obtain abortions. During the second trimester—after the first three months but before the fetus could potentially live outside the mother's womb—*Roe* allowed the state to regulate abortion in a manner consistent with its interest in protecting maternal health. During the final trimester, a state could regulate or prohibit abortion, consistent with its interest in protecting potential human life.[12]

In later years, the Court would allow states to adopt some first-trimester restrictions consistent with their interest in protecting potential life, but none that could put an undue burden on a woman's right to obtain an abortion.[13] The Court defined an undue burden as a "substantial obstacle in the path of a woman seeking an abortion before the fetus attains viability." By this standard, in *Planned Parenthood v. Casey* (1992) the Court accepted a mandatory 24-hour waiting period before an abortion procedure could be performed, requiring doctors to counsel women on alternatives to abortion, and requiring minors to get parental consent or a judge's approval as reasonable and constitutional restrictions on abortion access. No state can deny access to abortion completely, but some have made it more difficult to exercise this right than others. In 2010, Nebraska became the first state to restrict abortions on the basis of fetal pain, and in Oklahoma, the legislature passed, over the governor's veto, a law that requires providers of abortion services to set up an ultrasound monitor so that the woman can see and hear the description of the fetus's heart, limbs, and organs.

Sexual activity The Supreme Court's 2004 decision in *Lawrence v. Texas* was not based on privacy considerations relating to homosexual activity, but rather on the broader grounds of what the guarantee of "liberty" in the Fourteenth Amendment protects. It nonetheless had the effect of overturning *Bowers v. Hardwick* (1986), in which the Court upheld an anti-sodomy law in Georgia. But in *Lawrence*, the Court sharply repudiated its previous decision, declaring that the previous court, by defining the issue narrowly as the "right to engage in sodomy," minimized the liberty at stake. Liberty, the Court concluded, demanded that homosexuals not lose "their dignity as free persons" because of their sexual behavior in the confines of their own homes.

Legislative protection of the right to privacy Privacy need not be a constitutional right for government to protect it. Government can choose legislatively or administratively to protect aspects of privacy if it wishes. For example, the Privacy Act places restrictions on how government agencies use personal information about individuals. The Family Educational Rights and Privacy Act protects the privacy of students' educational records. The Right to Financial Privacy Act governs how financial institutions collect and disclose personal financial information and how individuals can limit that disclosure.

The privacy of consumer information online is one area in which legislation will likely be considered over the coming years.[14] What kind of privacy employees can expect may be another. In 2010, the Supreme Court ruled unanimously that police employees in Ontario, California, who were given pagers for their jobs, could not assume they have an expectation of privacy when sending text messages on the pagers.[15] The constitutional right to privacy will remain contentious because it implies a much broader scope of privacy than these legislative enactments provide, and a scope that will be determined not by elected officials but by judges.

Speech, Religion, and the Rights of the Accused

5-2   Analyze the different standards by which the Supreme Court has evaluated freedom of speech and religion and the rights of the accused.

To Americans, freedom of speech is the most prized of all the rights guaranteed by the Constitution and perhaps the most definably *American* right. The freedom to speak one's mind is a hallmark of America's political and popular culture.

Government can attempt to limit speech before and after its utterance.

Government action limiting speech is of two types. Action that prevents the publication or utterance of material the government finds objectionable is referred to as **prior restraint**. This is censorship in its truest form. Most often this kind of restraint has concerned the news media. The Supreme Court today is reluctant to tolerate restraint of this type.

The Court first established its position in *Near v. Minnesota* (1931), in which a Minnesota law that allowed government to prevent the publication

prior restraint government intervention to prevent the publication or utterance of material it finds objectionable.

of malicious material was struck down as a violation of the First Amendment. The most famous prior restraint case is *New York Times v. United States* (1971). The U.S. government attempted to prevent the newspaper from printing the "Pentagon Papers," a history of the Vietnam War based on State Department documents that had been leaked to the *Times* and the *Washington Post* by a former State Department official. Despite the government's argument that publishing the documents threatened national security, the Court agreed with the newspaper's contention that the public had a right to the information.[16]

The "preferred position" standard presumes the unreasonableness of restrictions on speech.

preferred position the idea, endorsed by the Supreme Court, that protection of First Amendment rights predominates over other rights.

Change in membership on the Court in the 1960s led to the strongest support yet for the protection of free speech rights. The Court had maintained for decades that the First Amendment and its protection for freedom of speech, the press, and religion held a "preferred position" among the amendments.[17] A **preferred position** means that First Amendment freedoms should be abridged only with great reluctance, and that if these freedoms are in conflict with other rights, the First Amendment protections, such as free speech, should prevail. But only in the late 1960s, in *Brandenburg v. Ohio* (1969), did the Court explicitly adopt preferred position as its primary free speech standard.

Clarence Brandenburg, a speaker at a Ku Klux Klan rally in 1964, was convicted under an Ohio law that made it illegal to advocate or assemble with those who promote criminal behavior in the pursuit of political or economic reform. The Court concluded that Ohio's law was unconstitutional. The decision established a two-part rule to determine whether speech acts could be considered criminal: First, was the speech "directed at inciting or producing imminent lawless action"? Second, was the speech "likely to incite or produce such action"? If the answer was yes to both, then government could restrict the speech. The Court concluded that the Ohio law ignored the second part of this test. Advocating that people commit illegal acts was not in and of itself an illegal act, unless it was highly likely to result imminently in that lawbreaking.

With its strong statement in *Brandenburg*, the Court had effectively moved the burden of proof in free speech cases from the individual to the government. With the

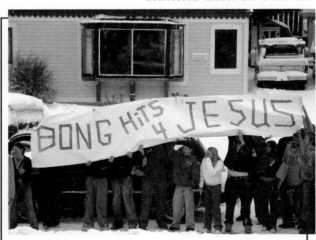

HIGH SCHOOL

In *Morse v. Frederick* (2007), the Supreme Court upheld a Seattle school principal's right to suspend an 18-year-old student for holding up this banner during a school-sponsored event, because the message contradicted the school's anti-drug policy. The students were watching an Olympic torch relay parade. Should a school principal be able to discipline students for their speech?

preferred position standard, government now had the burden to show, through a stringent two-part test, that limiting speech was necessary and desirable.

The Supreme Court determines which categories of speech merit constitutional protection and which do not.

The Supreme Court has determined that some categories of speech do not merit constitutional protection. Fighting words or inflammatory words that create an immediate threat to public safety are not constitutionally protected.[18] Defamation means speaking (slander) or writing (libel) a false statement that is heard or read by a third party and harms the target's reputation.[19] For public figures, defamation also requires that the person who spoke or wrote the offensive words did so knowing they were false.[20] Commercial speech has gained growing protection from the courts, as it, like political speech, transmits information. Unlike political speech, however, the government can regulate commercial speech to be sure it is accurate and not misleading.[21]

Governments have also passed numerous laws attempting to thwart the distribution of obscene materials, and challenges to these laws have generated a lengthy trail of court decisions. In 1973, a 5–4 Court ruling revised the definition of obscenity (material mainly appealing to prurient interest) and, in the process, increased the range of speech protected by the Constitution.[22] The Court now added that to be obscene and thus subject to government restrictions, a work also must depict or describe sexual conduct "in a patently offensive way" and have no serious literary, artistic, political, or scientific value. Federal law and court rulings have established that any sexually explicit depictions of children or depictions of children in sexual acts inherently violate these guidelines and are not constitutionally protected.[23] The difficulty of defining obscenity in other instances was most famously reflected in the comment of Justice Potter Stewart when he wrote that although he could not easily define hard-core pornography, "I know it when I see it."[24]

Controlling the spread of obscene materials in the Internet era provides a test of the Supreme Court's impact on political outcomes and on society—known to political scientists as judicial impact studies. The question is twofold. Did a Court ruling prompt elected officials to take new actions? And did the ruling prompt major societal changes?

Thinking Causally Do Supreme Court actions change political outcomes?

The Communications Decency Act (CDA) of 1996 prohibited making available to minors online any obscene or indecent material that shows or describes "sexual or excretory activities or organs" in a way that would be considered offensive by community standards. The act launched the kind of causal chain reaction common in civil liberties: Congress passes a law, the Court responds, Congress often replies by revising its law, and the Supreme Court weighs in again.

Responding to CDA, the Supreme Court in 1997 strongly declared the law to be an unconstitutional limit on free speech.[25] Including "indecent" materials, the Court ruled, made the law overly broad and intruded too far on the speech rights of adults. Congress responded with the Children's Online Protection Act of 1998, which required websites to provide age-verification systems (for example, providing credit card information) to keep harmful content from minors.[26] Dissatisfied, the Court suspended enforcement of the act unless Congress could demonstrate that there were no other methods available to achieve its goals that would be less intrusive on personal privacy. This time, Congress responded with a law more modest in scope than either of the previous laws. The Children's Internet Protection Act of 2000 required public libraries that received federal funds to install filtering software on their publicly accessible computers. The Supreme Court upheld the law, concluding that it did not violate patrons' First Amendment rights.[27]

So what was the judicial impact? Overall, we do see the Court prompting action by elected officials, but it does not appear that the Court has prompted societal change. Few would declare that the spread of obscene materials on the Web has declined or that it is significantly difficult for minors to access it. But societal change may not have been the Court's direct intent—the justices in the majority in these decisions might argue that their job is not to stop the spread of obscenity per se, but to make sure that government attempts to do so do not violate other rights.

Establishment clause cases have been decided using the *Lemon* test.

establishment clause a clause in the First Amendment that prevents government from establishing an official religion, treating one religion preferably to another, proselytizing, or promoting religion over nonreligion.

free exercise clause a clause in the First Amendment that prohibits government from interfering with individuals' practice of their religion.

***Lemon* test** a three-part establishment clause test used by the Supreme Court that states that, to be constitutional, a government action must have a plausible nonreligious purpose; its primary or principal effect must be to neither advance nor inhibit religion; and it must not foster excessive government entanglement with religion.

As with speech, the First Amendment sets out the Constitution's basic principles regarding freedom of religion. The amendment states, "Congress shall make no law respecting an establishment of religion, or prohibiting the free exercise thereof." "Respecting an establishment of religion" is referred to as the **establishment clause**. Government is not to designate any official religion, appear to embrace some religions at the expense of others, become involved in religious teaching, or, as interpreted by some scholars and justices, favor religion over nonreligion. "Prohibiting the free exercise thereof" is referred to as the **free exercise clause**. This clause declares that government should not interfere with the individual practice of religious beliefs. Because of incorporation, the establishment and free exercise clauses also apply to the states.

The Court's current standard on establishment clause issues is provided by the ***Lemon* test**, drawn from its decision in *Lemon v. Kurtzman* (1971). In this ruling, the Court used standards from previous cases and applied a three-part test to determine whether a government action was permissible. First, the law or action must have a plausible secular—that is, nonreligious—purpose. Second, its primary effect must not be to either advance or inhibit religion.

Third, it must not foster "excessive government entanglement with religion." A law or action violating any of these three precepts would be considered unconstitutional under this test.

Establishment clause cases   Many issues test the establishment clause. Two important ones are school prayer and public religious displays. In a long line of cases, the Court has ruled that public school prayer or similar activities constitute establishment of religion if they rely on public resources or imply the sponsorship or endorsement of the school. The Court has disallowed prayer time in classrooms, classroom Bible reading exercises, prayers delivered at graduation events, and student-initiated and student-led prayers at sporting events.[28] Individual student decisions such as wearing religious symbols to public school or praying privately while in school are not considered establishment.

Evaluating two religious displays in 2005, the Court concluded by a 5–4 vote that a Ten Commandments display in Austin, Texas, was constitutional because it had a valid secular purpose, was part of a large number of statues, and had been on display for over 40 years without complaint that it was advocating a particular religion. In contrast, the Court determined that a courthouse display in Kentucky was unconstitutional because it had clearer religious intent, having been posted initially in courtrooms without any other historical documents and being modified later only after complaints were lodged by the American Civil Liberties Union.[29] A 2009 Court decision clarified unanimously that governments are not required to accommodate every religious group wishing to add a religious symbol to a public display. In *Pleasant Grove City v. Summum*, the Court also rejected the argument that a group's free speech rights are violated if its symbol is not added to a display.

A CROSS IN THE DESERT

This cross was placed in the Mojave National Preserve in California in 1934 as a memorial to fallen soldiers. A legal challenge to its placement on public land led Congress to arrange a land swap—placing the land around the cross in private ownership while receiving an offsetting amount of property to add to the preserve. In *Salazar v. Buono* (2010), the Supreme Court did not rule directly on the constitutionality of the placement of the cross but said the lower courts had not conducted the appropriate legal analysis when they concluded that the land swap was improper. The case was sent back to federal district court.

The balancing standard carved out a zone of protection for religious free expression.

In addition to prohibiting any establishment of religion, the First Amendment also guarantees the free exercise of religion. Are restrictions on free exercise ever permissible? If so, when and why?

As with establishment cases, the Court has answered these questions with standards that it then applied to subsequent cases. From

balancing test used by the Supreme Court in free exercise of religion cases, this two-part test first determined whether a government action or law was a burden on religious practice and, if it was, whether a compelling government interest was at stake that would make the burden constitutionally acceptable.

1963 through 1990, the Court relied on the **balancing test**, introduced in *Sherbert v. Verner* (1963). Adeil Sherbert, a Seventh-day Adventist, lost her job when she refused to work on Saturday, her Sabbath Day. After she was unable to find other work for the same reason, she applied to the state of South Carolina for temporary unemployment benefits. The state denied her any benefits, because the state believed she could have taken a job requiring Saturday work.

The Supreme Court applied a two-part test to resolve the dispute. First, did the government law or policy impose a significant burden on religious exercise? The Court concluded in this instance that South Carolina's eligibility requirements for unemployment compensation did significantly burden Sherbert's ability to practice her faith. With that established, the Court turned to the second part of the test: was a compelling government interest served by this burdensome law or policy? If it was, then the policy or law would be constitutional despite its interference with religious expression. Here, the Court determined that there was no compelling state interest that justified the burden on Sherbert's religious practice. On the basis of the two-part test, the Court ruled in favor of Sherbert.

The neutrality standard narrows the scope of religious free expression.

The two-part balancing test survived for nearly three decades before being demoted in favor of a new test.[30] The new standard made it surprisingly more difficult to carve out space for religious expression. The case establishing the new standard involved Alfred Smith and Galen Black, who participated in Native American church ceremonies that involved the ingestion of peyote, an illegal hallucinogen. Unlike many other states, Oregon law provided no exception for use of the drug for sacramental purposes. Smith and Black were fired from their jobs at a private drug rehabilitation center because their drug use was considered work-related misconduct. They were denied state unemployment benefits on those grounds.

In *Employment Division v. Smith* (1990), the Supreme Court upheld Oregon's refusal to provide unemployment benefits. In a striking shift away from the balancing test established in *Sherbert*, the decision introduced the

neutrality test the Supreme Court's most recent approach to deciding free exercise of religion cases, this test declares that a government law or action with a neutral intent and application is constitutional, even if it burdens religion and there is no compelling government interest at stake.

Court's **neutrality test** for free exercise cases: a neutral law applied in a neutral way can validly impose a burden on religious practice, even if there is no compelling government interest at stake.

In the Court's view, the law prohibiting peyote and other drugs validly regulated something that government is allowed to regulate, and it did so in a neutral way. Its enactment was not targeted at any one group, and it was applied equally across groups. Restriction of religious expression was an "incidental effect" of the law, not an intentional goal.

Responding to a massive outcry among religious groups, Congress responded to the Court's new neutrality test by passing the Religious Freedom

Restoration Act (RFRA) of 1993. Referring directly to the Court's *Smith* decision, RFRA attempted to erase the Court's use of the neutrality test by prohibiting the federal and state governments from restricting an individual's free exercise of religion unless such restriction served a compelling government interest and was narrowly tailored to meet that interest. In short, with RFRA Congress was telling the Court that balancing, not neutrality, was the standard by which to judge religious practice cases. But, in 1997, the Supreme Court invalidated the underlying premise of RFRA, saying the law intruded too far into the judiciary's responsibilities in the American separation of powers system. The Court also declared the application of RFRA to the states to be unconstitutional.[31] But the Court said Congress could use its budgetary control over federal agencies to direct them that any burden imposed on religious practice by an agency regulation or action must be justified by the need to advance a compelling government purpose.

The Court's most significant recent ruling on free exercise came in 2010. A Christian group at the University of California's Hastings Law School was denied recognition as a registered student organization because it required adherence to a particular set of beliefs and behaviors for voting members and officers. This policy ran afoul of the university's nondiscrimination rule, which was based on state law. The student group challenged the university in federal court, arguing its constitutional free speech, freedom to associate with others of like-minded interests, and free exercise rights were violated. In a 5–4 decision, the Court disagreed and upheld the constitutionality of the university's rule, determining that the rule was created and applied neutrally and was not targeted toward religious beliefs in general or Christian beliefs in particular.[32]

The Constitution protects the rights of accused during investigations, trials, and sentencing.

As with freedom of speech and freedom of religion, the scope of rights accorded to individuals accused of a crime has changed significantly over the past 50 years. Table 5-2 lists these rights, ordered from initial investigation to subsequent trial and sentencing.

Illegally obtained evidence In 1914, the Supreme Court prohibited federal courts from basing decisions on evidence obtained improperly—a principle known as the **exclusionary rule**. According to this rule, evidence that is gathered during an illegal search cannot be introduced in a trial, even if that evidence is absolutely necessary to obtain a conviction. In 1961, the Supreme Court applied the rule to the states also.[33] Even after a trial, a conviction can be overturned if a defendant can convince an appeals court that the evidence used for conviction was obtained improperly and should not have been introduced at trial.[34]

exclusionary rule principle established by the Supreme Court, according to which evidence gathered illegally cannot be introduced into trial, and convictions cannot be based on this evidence.

TABLE 5-2 Constitutional Rights of the Accused from Investigation to Sentencing

Investigation and Arrest
- No unreasonable or unwarranted searches and seizures (4th Amendment)
- No arrest without probable cause (4th)
- No entrapment (4th)
- Be informed of rights (to remain silent, to counsel) (5th)
- No coerced confession and no illegal interrogation (5th)
- No self-incrimination during arrest or trial (5th)
- Be informed of charges (6th)
- Prompt arraignment (6th)
- Legal counsel (6th)
- No excessive bail (8th)
- Grand jury hearing to determine if case is viable (5th)

Trial
- Trial before a judge (Article I, Section 9)
- Speedy and public trial before an impartial jury (6th)
- Trial atmosphere free from prejudice and external interference (6th)
- Evidence obtained by illegal search not admissible during trial (4th)
- Right to confront witnesses (6th)
- No double jeopardy (5th)

Sentencing
- No cruel and unusual punishment (8th)
- Opportunity to appeal verdicts (8th)

Over time, the Court has become flexible in its enforcement of the exclusionary rule. The Court has allowed evidence that was technically collected improperly, but that police exercised "good faith" to collect properly or, in a 2009 decision, was collected as a result of a simple police error. In addition, if a person agrees to a search even without a warrant, these searches are legal so long as the individual did not feel intimidated into complying with the police request. Police do not need to obtain warrants to seize illegal goods that are in open view—firearms, for example. And in 2011 the Court ruled 8-1 that police can enter premises without a warrant if they suspect that evidence is being destroyed.[35]

The Fifth Amendment and self-incrimination As any viewer of television dramas knows, police are required to read suspects their rights when placing them under arrest. One of these rights is the right to remain silent. The basic idea is that individuals should not be coerced or intimidated into offering a confession; that individuals must be informed that they are not required to speak to the police except to respond to basic questions of identification; that anything they say can be used against them in court; that they have a right to have an attorney present during questioning; and that an attorney will be provided if they cannot afford one. Confessions made in the absence of these conditions would be inadmissible in court. This procedure is known as the **Miranda warning**, based on the Court's 1966 decision in the case of *Miranda v. Arizona*. It emerged from the Fifth Amendment's guarantee that no citizen "shall be compelled in any criminal case to be a witness against himself" and the Sixth Amendment's guarantee of the right to legal counsel.

Despite occasional congressional attempts to overturn it, the *Miranda* warning remains binding on police during investigations. Over time, however, the Court has made the burden on the police less restrictive—for example, unless individuals explicitly request to speak to an attorney, police need not assume that they would like to do so.[36] Two recent 5–4 rulings continued this trend. In *Montejo v. Louisiana* (2009), the Court ruled that police may continue questioning a suspect after the suspect has requested to consult with legal counsel. And in *Berghuis v. Thompkins* (2010), the Court ruled that a suspect must state to police that he or she is invoking the right to remain silent—not talking for an extended period does not itself invoke the right.

> *Miranda* **warning** ruling that requires police, when arresting suspects, to inform them of their rights, including the right to remain silent and have an attorney present during questioning.

The Sixth Amendment and the right to counsel

One of the rights guaranteed by the Constitution and mentioned in the *Miranda* warning is the right to have the advice of legal counsel during questioning and trial. As it selectively incorporated the Sixth Amendment, the Court broadened the range of cases that fit within the right to counsel. Moreover, the Court made the individual's right to counsel an obligation upon governments to *provide* counsel for defendants who could not afford an attorney. The defining case was *Gideon v. Wainwright* (1963). Clarence Earl Gideon defended himself at trial and was convicted and sentenced. Gideon appealed to the Supreme Court, and the Court unanimously concluded that lawyers in criminal cases are not a luxury but, rather, a necessity for a fair trial. The broad right to counsel established in this case was extended even further in subsequent years, with defendants able to challenge convictions based on the poor quality of publicly provided legal representation they received.

The Eighth Amendment and cruel and unusual punishment

Once a defendant is found guilty, a judge or jury must declare an appropriate sentence. The Constitution forbids "cruel and unusual" punishment. A punishment can be cruel but not unusual, or unusual but not cruel. The Supreme Court is most concerned when it is both.

Capital punishment—the death penalty—is the area that most often reaches the Supreme Court for review under the Eighth Amendment's prohibition against cruel and unusual punishment. Though opponents of the practice decry it as inhumane, the Court has never declared the death penalty in general to constitute cruel and unusual punishment. It has prohibited capital punishment in cases of rape, including rape of a child,[37] for individuals with severe mental developmental disabilities and for minors.[38] In 2010, the Court added in a 5–4 vote that life terms without parole also constitute cruel and unusual punishment for minors.[39]

For individuals outside the categories of minors and the mentally challenged, the Court has sought to ensure that defendants' due process rights were adhered to rigorously in capital punishment cases. Although it is uncommon, the Court will, for example, overturn death sentences if it believes a defendant received a defense so inadequate that it violates the constitutional right to counsel.[40] The Court also considers whether the method of execution is cruel and unusual. In April 2008, the Supreme Court ended its eight-month moratorium on the death penalty when it decided that death by lethal injection—the primary method used in the 35 capital punishment states—did not constitute cruel and unusual punishment.

The public balances its concerns for liberty and security in times of stress.

The historical record indicates that the public may well be willing to sacrifice some liberty if it is given a convincing security rationale. This is not isolated to September 11 and subsequent terror threats. In fact, study of similar historical cases suggests it would have been puzzling if Americans had not been supportive of civil liberties restrictions following the 2001 terrorist attacks.[41] Throughout American history, particularly when war or foreign disruption of American life was feared, the national government has imposed restrictions on civil liberties that usually received at least passive support from large segments of the public.

As part of the "war on terror" after September 11, 2001, "enemy combatants" were indefinitely detained at Guantanamo Bay, Cuba; the National Security Agency engaged in surveillance without judicial approval; "extraordinary rendition" led to suspects being sent to other countries for potentially harsh interrogation techniques; and the Patriot Act allowed the government to engage in searches and investigations without the judicial approval typically required for other investigations. The act was revised modestly and reauthorized in 2006 and again in 2011 for four years.

Equality and Civil Rights

5-3   Explain the demise of the separate but equal doctrine and the creation of civil rights laws and regulations.

Barack Obama, an African American of mixed racial heritage, is president of the United States. His victory does not end the American civil rights story. It does, however, shine a bright light on dramatic changes in American politics and society. A momentous election year saw African American, Hispanic, Mormon, and women candidates vie seriously for major party presidential nominations.

To understand the significance of President Obama's accomplishment requires a close look at the politics and evolution of civil rights in the United States. **Civil rights** are the guarantees of government to provide equal opportunities, privileges, and treatment under the law for all individuals. They entail sharing in the equal rights and responsibilities of citizenship and being fully part of the American nation. When Americans claim that civil rights have been violated, they usually mean that the government needs to defend the rights of an individual or group that has been denied some form of access or opportunity based on their race, ethnicity, sex, religion, sexual orientation, or other group characteristic.

civil rights guarantees of equal opportunities, privileges, and treatment under the law that allow individuals to participate fully and equally in American society.

In American politics, discriminatory treatment toward different groups has led to angry and sometimes bloody conflict over civil rights. This experience has torn through the history of many groups. But, most civil rights laws and court decisions arose originally in the area of black–white relations and set the framework for the legal status of other groups. Because the black civil rights movement was also the earliest to be extensively organized, it provides a historical example that has played a key role in the evolution of American civil rights for other groups.

The Civil War amendments bring civil rights into the Constitution.

Slavery was not prohibited by the Constitution. Thus, for the 70 years following ratification of the Constitution, slavery repeatedly flared up as an issue. One particularly dramatic development brought the issue to the Supreme Court. Dred Scott, a slave from Missouri, traveled with his owner to Illinois, a free state, and to other free territories north of the line established by the Missouri Compromise of 1820. Scott and his owner lived in these free areas for seven years, ultimately returning to Missouri, a slave state. When his owner died, Scott filed a lawsuit in Missouri, arguing that he should be considered a free man because he had been living on free soil.[42]

In one of the most notorious opinions in its history, the Supreme Court ruled in ***Dred Scott v. Sandford*** (1857) that Scott could not bring his case to federal court. To Chief Justice Roger Taney, the question was straightforward: "Can a negro, whose ancestors were imported into this country, and sold as slaves, become a member of the political community formed and brought into existence by the Constitution of the United States, and as such become entitled to all the rights, and privileges, and immunities, guaranteed by that instrument to the citizen?" Taney's answer was no: slaves could not be citizens, and neither could the descendants of slaves, whether free or not. When the Constitution was written, the Court concluded, blacks were considered "subordinate and inferior" to the "dominant race." Therefore, they could not possibly be considered citizens or part of "the people" as understood by the authors of the Constitution. The

Dred Scott v. Sandford Supreme Court decision in 1857 declaring that neither slaves nor the descendants of slaves could be U.S. citizens.

Dred Scott decision also declared the Missouri Compromise an unconstitutional use of congressional power because it deprived slaveholders of their property without due process of law. The political firestorm it triggered was one of the contributing factors to the country's move toward civil war.

By mid-1865, when the Civil War drew to a close, a nation disassembled by war needed to be put back together—not on its old terms, but recast, with African Americans as citizens. From 1865 through 1877, this process, known as Reconstruction, repeated the efforts of the revolutionary and constitutional eras to build both a sense of shared nationhood and a government capable of delivering the war's hard-won gains to blacks.

Following the Civil War, the Thirteenth, Fourteenth, and Fifteenth Amendments—commonly referred to as the Civil War amendments—were added to the Constitution. All concerned civil rights for blacks. The Thirteenth Amendment, ratified in December 1865, made slavery unconstitutional anywhere within the United States. The Fifteenth Amendment, ratified in March 1870, made it unconstitutional for the national government or state governments to deny someone the right to vote based on race, color, or whether the individual had previously been a slave or was descended from a slave.

The Fourteenth Amendment, ratified in July 1868, has had an extraordinary impact on American politics and life. It establishes that anyone born or naturalized in the United States is a citizen of the United States and also the state in which he or she lives. This edict made it clear that former slaves were fully citizens. It then declares that no state shall "deny to any person within its jurisdiction the equal protection of the laws." This **equal protection clause** would be the basis of much of the subsequent legislation and many of the court decisions concerning civil rights.

equal protection clause clause in the Fourteenth Amendment stating that states are not to deny any person equal treatment under the law.

In addition to the Civil War amendments, Reconstruction included other legislation that assisted the promotion of black civil rights. The Freedmen's Bureau, created in 1865, provided food, clothing, and fuel; established schools; supervised labor–management relations; and created a system by which blacks could become landowners. The Civil Rights Act of 1866 guaranteed blacks the same property and legal rights as whites.[43] It also provided for the punishment of those who violated an individual's rights because of race or color.[44] The final legislative action was the Civil Rights Act of 1875, which concerned the private sector. It promised blacks the "full and equal enjoyment" of hotels, transportation, and places of entertainment such as theaters.

In the *Civil Rights Cases* (1883), the Court consolidated five cases from California, Kansas, Missouri, New Jersey, and Tennessee in which blacks had been denied service in private establishments. The Court declared the 1875 Civil Rights Act to be unconstitutional because it concerned discriminatory private action, as opposed to government action.[45] The Fourteenth Amendment, in the Court's view, applied to the actions of governments: it did not apply to discriminatory private behavior between individuals.[46] This **state action** view of the Fourteenth Amendment has remained a binding standard for Court decisions.

state action Supreme Court interpretation of the equal protection clause that holds the clause prohibited unfair discriminatory actions by government, not by private individuals.

JIM CROW IN DURHAM, NORTH CAROLINA, 1940

The separate but equal doctrine was the cornerstone of racial segregation. The Supreme Court validated the doctrine in 1896, but in *Brown v. Board of Education* in 1954, it declared that mandatory racial separation is inherently unequal and unconstitutional.

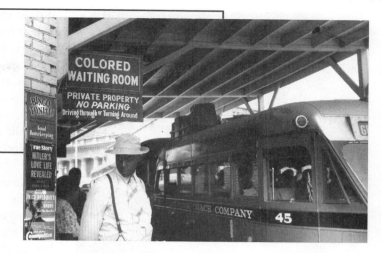

Beginning in the late 1880s, southern states enacted laws that required blacks and whites to be separated when they used public accommodations. Referred to as **Jim Crow laws**, the statutes covered a wide range of circumstances. From parks to schools, hotels, restaurants, hospitals, prisons, funeral homes, cemeteries, sporting events, restrooms, entrances, exits, transportation, and more, the laws required separate facilities for blacks and whites. In **Plessy v. Ferguson** (1896), the Supreme Court upheld these laws and ruled there was nothing inherently discriminatory in separating the races, as long as each race was accommodated. The decision established the **separate but equal doctrine**, which argued that it was constitutional to require separate facilities for the races, as long as the facilities were substantially equal, even though not identical.

Jim Crow laws system of laws that separated the races in schools, public accommodations, and other aspects of daily life.

Plessy v. Ferguson Supreme Court decision in 1896 upholding the constitutionality of laws and government policies that required segregated facilities for blacks and whites.

separate but equal doctrine Supreme Court doctrine that laws or policies requiring segregated facilities for the races are constitutionally acceptable as long as the facilities are of equal quality.

Segregation is declared unconstitutional in *Brown v. Board of Education.*

An emerging civil rights movement achieved some victories in the 1940s. Presidents Franklin Roosevelt and Harry Truman each used their unilateral authority to issue executive orders advancing civil rights. With these victories, and victories in courts, the stage had been set for an assault on the separate but equal doctrine. Four cases in 1951 and 1952, from Kansas, South Carolina, Virginia, and Delaware, challenged the doctrine in education. The Supreme Court consolidated these cases and considered them together as **Brown v. Board of Education** of *Topeka, Kansas* (1954). The lead case was prompted when Oliver Brown attempted to enroll his daughter for third grade in an all-white school and was turned away. Arguing the case on behalf of Brown was Thurgood Marshall of the NAACP, who later became the first black Supreme Court justice.

Under the leadership of Chief Justice Earl Warren, the Court unanimously struck down the separate but equal doctrine. Avoiding any definitive stand on what the Fourteenth Amendment required in public education, the Court

Brown v. Board of Education Supreme Court ruling in 1954 that in public education, mandatory separation of children by race leads to inherently unequal education. The decision overturned the separate but equal doctrine.

AN INTEGRATION PIONEER IN LITTLE ROCK, ARKANSAS, 1957

Elizabeth Eckford arrives for her first day of class at Little Rock Central High School. A federal court ordered the school to enroll her and eight other black students. The court's order was prompted by a lawsuit filed by the NAACP.

instead emphasized the importance of education in modern society and asked whether segregating the races provided equal opportunity for black children. Referring to psychological studies, the Court concluded that segregation could generate a permanent "feeling of inferiority as to their status in the community." In public education, the Court famously ruled, "the doctrine of 'separate but equal' has no place. Separate educational facilities are inherently unequal."

The *Brown* decision was an earthquake, bringing down the legal and constitutional edifice of enforced segregation. It struck down the laws of 21 states.[47] In practical terms, however, change was not as swift. Aware of the potential explosiveness of its decision, the Court did not set any timetable in *Brown*. In a follow-up opinion in 1955, referred to as *Brown II*, the Court stated that school districts should move with "all deliberate speed" to desegregate their schools.[48]

Massive resistance, especially in the South, blunted the speed of change. A decade after *Brown*, barely 3 percent of southern black children were in schools where a majority of students were white. In response to this foot dragging, the federal government began threatening to initiate lawsuits and withhold federal funds from states and districts that were not making progress in implementing desegregation. These tactics were effective. By 1970, about one-third of southern black children were in white-majority schools and 90 percent were in schools with at least some white students.[49]

de jure segregation racial segregation that occurs because it is written into law, policy, or government procedures.

de facto segregation racial segregation that results not from explicit laws, policies, or procedures, but from patterns of behavior that have the effect of segregating the races.

Activists in the black civil rights movement pushed courts to address instances both of **de jure segregation** and **de facto segregation**. *De jure* segregation refers to segregation explicitly written into laws and regulations. *De facto* segregation occurs, in practice, because of patterns of behavior. If residential patterns are highly skewed racially, for example, and all children attend the school nearest to them, then schools would automatically remain highly segregated. In 1974, by a 5–4 vote, the Supreme Court concluded that the Fourteenth Amendment's equal protection guarantee did not extend to *de facto* segregation if there was no evidence that a school district intended to discriminate.[50]

In *PICS v. Seattle* (2007) the Supreme Court went further and struck down racial balance plans initiated voluntarily in Seattle, Washington, and

Louisville, Kentucky, as an unconstitutional violation of equal protection. School districts could not make an individual student's enrollment in a school dependent on his or her race.

The debate over how best—or whether—to achieve racial integration in education will continue as districts devise plans they hope will meet the Supreme Court's approval. One challenge for architects of even the most creative integration and diversity plans will remain finding public support for their efforts. Public opinion data consistently show that people of all races are more concerned about the quality of education than about the racial diversity of students in schools.

New laws and executive orders expand civil rights protection.

During the 1960s, civil rights also advanced in other spheres of public and private life. As with the education system, public officials employed both legislation and executive orders in this process.

Legislation The Civil Rights Act of 1964 is the centerpiece of American antidiscrimination law. The law prohibited discrimination in public accommodations and in private employment on the basis of race, color, religion, sex, and national origin.

Congress justified the Civil Rights Act of 1964 not in terms of the equal protection guarantee of the Fourteenth Amendment, but by linking it to Congress's power to regulate commerce. As noted in Chapter 4, the Supreme Court in 1937 established a generous definition of interstate commerce that vastly expanded the power of the federal government. As a result, if Congress could link discrimination to the flow of commerce, it could regulate discriminatory actions in the private sector.

Grounding Congress's action in an established constitutional power like regulation of interstate commerce opened new horizons for civil rights legislation. The Civil Rights Act of 1964 also set the mold in another way: it denied federal funds to any program or activity that discriminated. After 1964, Congress justified all civil rights legislation that affected the private sector either on interstate commerce grounds or as an extension of Congress's control over federal spending.[51] By doing so, Congress bypassed the restrictions of the state action doctrine.

Another signal legislative achievement was the Voting Rights Act of 1965, which prohibited the use of discriminatory methods, such as literacy tests, intended to weaken the voting power of blacks. States or parts of states with a history of such methods were required to clear any changes in their voting laws with the Department of Justice. The preclearance requirement is subject to periodic reauthorization by Congress and the president and remains in place today.[52] Black access to voting was enhanced with the abolition of **poll taxes**

poll tax fee assessed on each person who wishes to vote; prohibited by the Twenty-fourth Amendment in 1964.

(or fees to vote) in federal elections by the Twenty-fourth Amendment in 1964 and subsequently in state elections by the Supreme Court in 1966.[53]

These changes had a significant effect. The number of black voters increased substantially. Black candidates began winning elected office. The Supreme Court's "one person, one vote" mandates of the 1960s, which improved the representation of urban areas within states, further boosted black political participation and candidate success. Without these changes, Barack Obama's achievement would have been impossible.

Executive orders   As noted earlier, Presidents Roosevelt and Truman began using executive orders to advance civil rights—a practice continued by later presidents. Presidents Eisenhower and Kennedy, for example, used executive orders to activate National Guard units in Arkansas, Mississippi, and Alabama to enforce school desegregation. President Kennedy ordered the creation of compliance mechanisms for nondiscriminatory employment policies by federal contractors. Orders by later presidents enhanced these mechanisms. Additional categories of protection were added as well, including discrimination based on sex (President Johnson), disability and age (President Carter), and sexual orientation and status as a parent (President Clinton).[54]

Affirmative action   Despite becoming one of the most controversial civil rights policies, affirmative action started out quietly in executive orders issued by Presidents Kennedy, Johnson, and Nixon in the 1960s to combat discrimination in federal hiring and contracts.[55] On its face, **affirmative action** calls for aggressive outreach efforts targeted to groups traditionally underrepresented in particular jobs and college admissions. Since 1989, however, the Supreme Court has been reining in the scope of these efforts.

affirmative action efforts to reach and attract applicants for jobs, college admissions, and business contracts from traditionally underrepresented groups, ranging from extensive publicity and outreach to quota plans.

In *Richmond v. Croson* (1989), the Court struck down "set-aside" programs that required contractors on city projects to subcontract 30 percent of the business to minority businesses. In *Adarand v. Pena* (1995), a case concerning extra payments supplied by the federal government to contractors who hired minority firms, the Court decreed that all racial classifications at all levels of government would be subject to strict scrutiny, meaning the Court would have to be convinced that the classification was absolutely necessary to meet a compelling government interest, and that this interest was being achieved in the least intrusive, narrowest manner possible. And a 5–4 decision in 2009 concluded that in New Haven, Connecticut, officials could not throw out the results of a firefighter promotion exam simply because they feared being sued when few minorities did well.

Regents of the University of California v. Bakke Supreme Court decision in 1978 that a rigid quota plan for admissions violates the Constitution's equal protection guarantee, but race could be considered a "plus factor" in college admissions to increase student body diversity.

Affirmative action affected college admissions as well. In ***Regents of the University of California v. Bakke*** (1978), while prohibiting racial quotas for college admissions, the Court ruled that race could be a "plus" factor considered along with other admissions criteria. More recently, the Supreme Court in *Grutter v. Bollinger* (2003) upheld in a 5–4 vote the University of Michigan Law School's "holistic" use of race to foster viewpoint diversity at the school. That same year, in *Gratz v. Bollinger* (2003), however, the Court rejected an undergraduate admissions policy at the University of Michigan that automatically granted 20 points of the 100 needed for admission to every African American, Hispanic, and Native American applicant. The Court concluded that this approach was not a narrowly-tailored solution to the problem of diversity in college admissions.

The Politics and Extension of Civil Rights

5-4   Describe legal and legislative actions to extend equal protection guarantees to other groups.

By the end of the 1960s, the United States had been through a civil rights revolution. The equal protection clause had been used to challenge discrimination by government. Congress advanced civil rights in the private sector through its commerce clause and spending powers. Presidents used unilateral executive power to prod civil rights in the federal government and among those doing business with it. The Supreme Court added its first black justice, Thurgood Marshall, in 1967. In later years, blacks, women, Hispanics, and other minorities would reach the highest levels of American government. Barack Obama's election in 2008 provided an exclamation point to this journey. Inequities in quality of life remained then and remain today, but the country had changed radically.

How did these seismic changes happen? Some political scientists argue that the success of civil rights resulted from political opportunities that created the possibility for change. Others focus on effective appeals to American creedal beliefs. Still others emphasize overcoming the difficulties in organizing people for political action. All of these factors are important, and their reversals featured prominently in the struggles civil rights advocates faced after these major successes.[56] As is common in politics, no single explanation is sufficient.

Thinking Causally What were the key political factors that led to the dramatic changes in civil rights?

The civil rights movement led to civil rights successes for blacks.

The pressure created by the civil rights movement contributed to the legal, legislative, and administrative successes gained by blacks. Organizations advocating for black civil rights led to significant legal victories in the first half of the twentieth century. In December 1955, the NAACP encouraged a year-long boycott of the bus system in Montgomery, Alabama, to protest segregation of public buses. The boycott drew national attention. Rosa Parks, an NAACP member who refused to change her seat, became a household name. Martin

A LONG ROAD

It took a century after the Civil War for black Americans to gain fully equal voting rights. These marchers walked from Selma to Montgomery in 1965 to demand equal suffrage rights for blacks. Rev. Martin Luther King, Jr. led the march.

civil disobedience strategy of breaking a law nonviolently, risking arrest, in order to draw attention to the injustice of the law.

Luther King Jr., a Baptist minister, similarly became nationally known. King advocated a strategy of **civil disobedience**, in which unjust laws would be violated to draw attention to them. Being arrested for sitting at segregated lunch counters is one example. King also argued for the use of nonviolent tactics such as marches and demonstrations to sway public opinion and pressure public officials. Prior to the late 1950s, mass protests had been infrequent. Inequalities and injustice were severe, but organizing and encouraging mass participation in the face of entrenched and powerful opponents was not easy. Participants risked their jobs and even their lives. Each victory was important, and each victory gave future participants the sense that direct political action could succeed.

The civil rights movement was aided by the transformation of the Democratic Party. In the period following the Civil War, just as the Democratic Party dominated southern politics, the South dominated Democratic Party politics. The grip of the South over the Democratic Party began to weaken in the 1930s. The Great Migration of blacks from the South, where they typically could not vote, to the North, where they could, gave northern Democratic politicians increased interest in cultivating the black vote. Recognizing that the party's geographical center was increasingly moving north, every Democratic presidential nominee after 1936 expressed support for civil rights, and the party added civil rights to its 1948 platform.

Southern Democrats' grip on Congress slowly weakened as well. With the northern share of congressional Democrats growing, and with this share dominated by urban, liberal representatives, support for civil rights legislation increased and made it possible for the civil rights and voting rights acts to pass in the 1960s.[57]

The civil rights achievements of the 1960s were monumental. But as the decade wore on, the politics of gaining additional civil rights advances grew daunting. Why did the political environment become so unfavorable so quickly? Political scientists focus, with varying emphasis, on three igniters of this trend. First, unity in the civil rights movement disintegrated. Second, new issues raised by the movement troubled many whites who had supported, or at least not opposed, the breakthroughs of the early 1960s. Third, blacks had the support of the Democratic Party, and the party had the support of black voters, and this mutual support created challenges as well as opportunities. The combination of these three factors created particular problems for the civil rights agenda.[58]

Thinking Causally What led to the political environment for civil rights becoming unfavorable so quickly?

Debate continues over how to enhance minority electoral power.

One question facing minority groups is how best to enhance their political power. Would an effective strategy be to spread minority voters out across districts so that they are a sizable and potentially influential bloc but not necessarily a majority of the district population? Or would minority interests be better served by concentrating minority voters in a small number of districts and virtually ensuring that a minority candidate will be elected? Districts where boundaries are drawn to ensure that a majority of potential voters are minority—that is, a historically disadvantaged racial or ethnic group—are known as **majority-minority districts**.

Starting in the late 1980s, the U.S. Supreme Court issued decisions in a series of cases that challenged the constitutionality of creating district lines for the express purpose of creating a majority-minority district. The conclusion of these decisions was that race or ethnicity could not constitutionally be the predominant factor in drawing district lines, but they could be taken into account as one of several factors.[59]

majority-minority districts legislative districts in which boundaries are drawn in a manner to ensure that a majority of the district residents are members of minority groups, intended to increase the probability of minorities being elected.

Whether the creation of majority-minority districts assists minority political influence has become hotly debated. One study suggests that spreading minority voters across districts had not been an optimal strategy for minority political influence in the 1970s or 1980s, but it had become so by the 1990s. In part, reduced bloc voting by whites meant that even in districts where the minority population is 40 to 50 percent rather than a majority, a minority candidate can win about two out of three times.[60] Even if a minority does not win, this argument suggests, his or her strong share in the electorate may influence the winning candidate's voting behavior as a legislator.[61] The debate over the "best" strategy for minority influence will continue, but this research suggests the answer may change over time.

The way forward will also depend on the Supreme Court. The Voting Rights Act required redistricting when a majority-minority district could be formed to address minority vote dilution, which refers to minority voting power and influence being reduced by spreading minority voters in small percentages across districts. But what about a situation in which a district could be created with a larger, but not majority, share of minority voters? In 2009, the Court decided 5–4 that the Voting Rights Act did not require redistricting to create a minority-influence district (sometimes called a coalition district) in which minority voting power would be enhanced but the minority presence would fall below 50 percent.[62]

Thinking Causally Is minority group political power best advanced by distributing minority voters across legislative districts, or by concentrating minority voters in a smaller number of districts so that they are a majority of voters in those districts?

The Supreme Court classifies discrimination cases into three types.

Many of the political and social accomplishments of the black civil rights movement had benefits for other groups. In addition to race and color, the legislative and administrative actions of the 1960s have been applied to religion, national origin, sex, disability, age, and sexual orientation.

Most Americans consider different treatment of individuals based on race, gender, or other factors offensive. How do the federal courts determine which kinds of group classifications resulting in differential treatment are acceptable and which are not? The courts divide these cases into three types.

The first type concerns "suspect categories," namely race and ethnicity. Here, the courts employ "strict scrutiny," meaning government officials would need to prove that there was a *compelling* governmental interest at stake that *required* the distinction between racial or ethnic groups. This is normally very difficult to prove.[63]

A second type of case involves "quasi-suspect categories." Cases involving classification on the basis of sex are the prime example. Government would have to show that classifying by sex had a *substantial* relationship to an *important* government interest.[64]

The third type of case involves most other classifications, such as age, income, and disability. They are evaluated on what the courts call a rational basis standard; that is, does the classification have some *rational* connection that *contributes* to the goal of the law or policy?[65] This is an easier test for government officials to meet, and the courts will be more easily convinced that these classifications were necessary than they will for race and ethnicity. For example, the courts allow the federal government to impose higher tax rates on wealthier individuals in order to fund programs and redistribute income across income levels, but it would not allow higher tax rates to be imposed on the basis of race.

Latinos, Asians, and Native Americans have experienced unique histories of discrimination.

Other racial and ethnic groups have experienced severe discrimination throughout U.S. history. Many states and municipalities enacted laws specifically targeting groups for differential treatment. When these laws have been challenged on constitutional grounds, the Supreme Court has generally applied reasoning similar to that in cases involving black civil rights. Segregation, until 1954, was acceptable. Laws that treated groups differently, however, were suspect. For example, in 1886 the Court struck down a San Francisco law that, despite appearing neutral on its face, the justices interpreted as intended to drive Chinese laundries out of business. The Fourteenth Amendment's guarantees of equal protection, the Court declared, "are universal in their application."[66] Similarly, legislation and presidential orders enacted as a result of the black civil rights movement in the 1960s also benefited other groups.

Each group has had its own particular history and specific issues, as well as its own interest groups to represent its concerns. Ethnic groups such as Asians and Latinos—the largest minority group in the country—are not randomly distributed throughout the country. As a consequence, laws targeting

HOW DO WE KNOW?

Is White Opposition to Affirmative Action Racist?

The Question

The opinions of whites and blacks are often far apart on policies like affirmative action, school desegregation, and spending on social programs. Such a gap could be explained by genuine principled opposition among whites to certain roles for government. It could also be explained by white racism. If whites hold inherently negative and generalized views toward racial minorities, they might be more likely to oppose policies that seem to disproportionately benefit minority groups. Is white opposition to affirmative action and similar programs racist? How do we know?

Why It Matters

Whether white opposition to policies benefiting minorities is based on bigotry or other factors matters for at least two reasons. First, as discussed in Chapter 2, political culture is negotiable. If policy opposition is based on political culture, there is some prospect that opponents and proponents can engage in dialogue. However, if policy opposition is based on racism, this more deep-seated resistance will be hard to change. Second, if bigotry, rather than different weighting of beliefs in the American creed, is the primary reason for opposition to certain policies, then the prospects for civil rights and racial and ethnic harmony would seem dim.

Investigating the Answer

Political scientists have explored this question largely through research on black and white public opinion, so that is the focus here.[67] The outcome analyzed is white opposition to affirmative action. The two competing factors that may explain the outcome are racist beliefs and general philosophical beliefs about government's appropriate role.

Public opinion data show substantial differences between whites and blacks. The differences between the races' attitudes toward race-related policies, income redistribution programs, and the fairness of American life are often larger than those of class, gender, and religion.[68]

Exploring the extent to which racial considerations drive white opinion has been a large, complex, and heated area of debate in political science research.[69] One group of scholars points to the significance of what they call *racial resentment*.[70] Traditional racism was cruel and blunt and built around an explicitly stated belief in white racial superiority. The success of the civil rights movement, however, blocked that kind of racism from entering public discourse.

In its place, however, arose a more subtle racism in which blacks were not seen as inherently inferior but were critiqued for not making the best of the opportunities given to them. This racism blends traditional beliefs of American political culture, especially individualism, with disaffection for blacks or what is considered "black behavior." Discrimination, in this view, is not a significant problem and is used as an excuse by blacks. Black progress is stunted by blacks themselves—their failure to work and study hard and their expectation that government should take care of people even if they make poor choices in life. This racism is hard to detect in surface behavior, but underneath lies suppressed racist views. Extensive analysis of survey research has led scholars in this school to conclude that white attitudes toward affirmative action and similar programs are strongly determined by this racial resentment.

Another group of scholars believes the racial resentment argument goes too far in blaming racism for white opposition to programs like affirmative action. This view claims that the impact of any white racism on policy attitudes has been overstated and is less important than general ideological predispositions about government. In this view, opposition to certain programs would exist because of ideological positions favoring limited government, regardless of whether the beneficiaries were white or black. To the extent that the racial resentment argument presumes that liberal positions favor racial equality and conservative positions do not, white public opinion will be wrongly interpreted as racist when in fact whites are simply more ideologically conservative than blacks, on average, but are no less committed to equality.

One technique employed to test this possibility—the survey experiment—changes the wording of a public

(continues)

HOW DO WE KNOW?   Is White Opposition to Affirmative Action Racist? *(continued)*

opinion survey question and compares responses. For example, in one study whites were split into two groups. The first group was asked if, because of past discrimination, blacks should be given preference in college admissions. Only 26 percent of whites supported this idea. The second group was asked instead whether an extra effort should be made to ensure that qualified blacks applied for college admission. About 65 percent of whites supported this form of affirmative action specifically aimed toward blacks.

Another experiment divided respondents into three groups. All three were asked about government assistance for those born into poverty. For the first group, the program was said to help blacks as a matter of racial justice for past wrongs: 31 percent of whites approved of such a program. For the second group, the program was said to help blacks, but the justification was equal opportunity rather than racial justice: 42 percent of whites supported this program. And for the third group, the program was said to help poor people, with no race indicated: 49 percent of whites supported this program. This suggests that programs that are justified by reference to American creed beliefs and that do not single out particular racial or ethnic groups as beneficiaries receive greater support from whites.

Finally, an experiment dividing respondents into two groups asked one group about blacks and the other about new immigrants from Europe. Whites were equally likely to say these two groups should "work their way up without special favors." White views appeared more driven by ideology than by who benefited from government help.

RACIAL PROFILING OR APPROPRIATE POLICE RESPONSE? To some Americans, the 2009 arrest of Harvard Professor Henry Louis Gates at his home was an illustration of subtle racial bias—a neighbor and police saw a black man attempting to enter a house and assumed the worst. To others, this interpretation racialized what was a simple matter of police responding to what looked like an attempted break-in.

because they provide public officials with tools to manipulate public opinion?

Thinking Critically

1. In a survey experiment, participants are not saturated with the media messages they might receive in a real-world setting. Does this difference make these experiments more or less useful guides of individuals' true beliefs?

2. When, if ever, are generalizations about a group's behavior acceptable in either designing or evaluating public policy?

3. Would you consider the results of survey experiments helpful, because they show public officials what resonates with the public, or dangerous,

The Bottom Line

The debate over the concept of racial resentment has been extensive and deeply felt among political scientists. The perceived stakes are high. Studies continue to support each side in the argument—some finding that racial resentment is a key driver of white public opinion, and others finding that belief and ideology are more important than attitudes toward blacks.[71] Many Americans are conflicted in their views, believing that individuals are responsible for improving their condition, but also believing that society may need to provide assistance under certain circumstances.[72]

Virtually all scholars agree that racism at some level remains a force in American society and that bigotry continues as an everyday problem facing blacks and other minorities. Although it is complicated to measure

---

HOW DO WE KNOW? Is White Opposition to Affirmative Action Racist?

and analyze, clear and incontrovertible evidence that racism is the predominant driver of white public opinion is lacking. Evidence in some studies shows that white public opinion is open to persuasion and appeals to principle, which seems unlikely if racism thoroughly dominated white opinion on racially oriented policies.[73] Scholars are careful to note, however, that such evidence does not mean that negative racial attitudes cannot be activated among some individuals by the way that issues are portrayed or symbolized, including in news coverage.[74] Nor does it mean that we can always be certain that the results obtained in experimental settings will apply directly to real-world situations.[75]

Latinos were more common in the Southwest, while laws targeting Asians were more common on the West Coast.

Because of the ways their histories in the United States differ from the history of blacks—most notably the absence of slavery—the umbrella terms *Hispanic* and *Asian* may mean less for individuals in these categories than do national identities such as Mexican, Argentinean, Cuban, Japanese, Korean, or Chinese. "Hispanic" or "Latino" and "Asian" have not provided the same kind of common identity and widely shared political outlook that has been prevalent among African Americans. That heterogeneity has made political organization of these groups more difficult, and cross-ethnic group coordination—black, Hispanic, Asian—has been minimal. On some issues, such as immigration and language accommodation, individuals in these three groups often see more conflict than commonality among their interests.[76]

The experience of Native Americans has its own distinctive features. Prior to the passage of the Indian Citizenship Act in 1924, Native Americans were not considered U.S. citizens. As members of sovereign nations, they had to go through the same citizenship application procedures as individuals from other countries. Attempts to use the Fifteenth Amendment as a basis for the right to vote failed because of this lack of citizenship.[77] With the passage of the act, Native Americans were considered U.S. citizens without any special procedure required. This status entitled Native Americans to the rights and responsibilities of U.S. citizenship, but as with other groups, rights did not instantly materialize. They required political action.

The case of Native Americans differs from other groups in that they are considered U.S. citizens and also members of sovereign nations

ORGANIZING FOR HISPANIC CIVIL RIGHTS
Like blacks, other groups have had advocacy organizations play a large leadership role in advancing their civil rights. Increasing Hispanic political participation has been a recent focus, as in this voter registration drive at an immigration reform rally in Florida in 2010.

that exist within the United States. Native Americans are protected by the anti-discrimination statutes and regulations that cover other groups. They also have tribal rights and responsibilities that differ among the various tribes and are determined by tribal authorities. Tribes have been actively involved in court cases and legislation seeking to preserve and restore their interests in land, mineral, and water resources, and defending traditional customs even if they conflict with state or national law.

Pervasive sex discrimination in law has eroded.

The movement for women's equality had two distinct phases. The early phase culminated in 1920 with the Nineteenth Amendment, which gave women the right to vote. An extensive array of legal restrictions on women remained, however, and these became the focus of women's rights organizations in the second phase, beginning in the 1960s.

Like the civil rights movement, the women's movement used legal and legislative strategies to challenge laws and policies that differentiated between men and women. The women's movement also engaged in "consciousness raising" designed to help women understand their identity and their status in law and society. Sometimes criticized as being geared toward the needs of white upper-middle-class women, this self-awareness and its call for "women's liberation" likely generated important organizational benefits by contributing to fund-raising and support for the efforts of women's rights organizations. These funds would be instrumental in filing court cases and lobbying for legislative changes. One of the key organizations involved in these efforts, the National Organization for Women (NOW), was founded in 1966.

Supreme Court rulings Prior to the 1970s, the Supreme Court had tended to uphold gender-based distinctions in law. It had sustained laws that denied women the right to vote prior to 1920, restricted their working hours to "protect the weaker sex," and prohibited admission to trades and professions. Fundamental rights and responsibilities of citizenship, such as participating on juries, were often denied to women.[78] After 1970, the Court overturned many gender-based state laws. Examples of the kinds of gender distinctions in law that the Court rejected included different treatment of men and women when calculating Social Security benefits, different ages for consuming alcohol, and permitting unwed mothers but not unwed fathers to withhold consent on the adoption of their children.

While striking down most sex distinctions, the Court has upheld those that furthered important government interests. It has upheld limiting the military draft to men, for example. It has also supported regulations and policies that do not formally distinguish between men and women but in practice will have the effect of doing so. Giving preferences to veterans in state and federal government employment will tend to advantage men disproportionately, but the Court has upheld these as furthering an important government interest.

Actions by Congress and presidents Congress and presidents have also addressed sex discrimination issues. The 1963 Equal Pay Act required equal pay for equal work, and the 2009 Lilly Ledbetter Fair Pay Act stated that the 180-day clock for filing a pay bias case starts again with each new paycheck, not just the first one. The Civil Rights Act of 1964 prohibited employers, employment agencies, and labor unions from discriminating on the basis of sex. Amendments to the Higher Education Act in 1972, specifically that portion of the act known as Title IX, denied federal funds to universities that discriminated against women in any respect, including admissions, course availability, athletics, and advising.

Women's rights activists have argued that full equality sometimes needs to take account of differences. Expanded government support for child care, for example, has been advocated on gender equality grounds, so that women can more fully enter the workforce. In the United States, the need to accommodate the special demands placed on women inspired the Family and Medical Leave Act of 1993, which provides women with 12 weeks of unpaid leave following childbirth. New fathers can take this time off also, as can same-sex partners (as of 2010) and individuals needing to care for a sick family member.

Proposed annually since 1923, the Equal Rights Amendment (ERA) finally passed both houses of Congress in 1972 after heavy lobbying by NOW and the National Women's Political Caucus. The proposed amendment stated, "Equality of rights under the law shall not be denied or abridged by the United States or by any State on account of sex." It was sent to the states for ratification, with 1979 set as the deadline. Twenty-two states ratified the amendment in the first year. By 1978, the amendment was three states short of the 38 needed for ratification. Congress controversially extended the ratification period through 1982. But by 1982 the amendment was still three states short, and five states that had approved the amendment rescinded their approval. The constitutionality of the rescissions was unclear; nevertheless, the proposed amendment was never able to obtain enough state approval to add it to the Constitution. Why not?

Thinking Causally What factors contributed to the stalling of the Equal Rights Amendment?

The rise of a conservative opposition, division among women, and a legacy of prior success help explain what happened. First, the ERA faced concerted opposition by religious and conservative groups, which had used this issue to build very effective political organizations. Ironically, these groups may have actually benefited from the quick approval of the ERA in 35 states. They were able to concentrate their resources and lobbying on the remaining states, rather than fighting a national battle.[79] Second, division among women meant the pro-amendment forces were unable to marshal the same focused intensity as the opponents. Some women thought the amendment did not go far enough. Others thought women would lose some rights in the workplace—for example, accommodations for pregnancy—or would not be able to obtain support from ex-husbands. Third, the amendment may have been weakened by a perception that much of what the amendment was intended to achieve had already been accomplished by law, unilateral presidential action, and Supreme Court application of the Fourteenth Amendment's equal protection guarantee and its interpretation of civil rights laws. Together, these factors stalled the drive for the ERA.

Age and disability discrimination are subject to standards of review different from race and sex.

Not considered suspect or quasi-suspect classifications requiring the Court's strict scrutiny, the use of an age or disability classification in law must have some rational connection to the goal of the law. For example, the Court upheld Missouri's mandatory requirement that public officials retire at age 70.[80] Similarly, certain rights, such as voting, are limited to adults.

Laws passed by Congress and executive orders issued by presidents have also addressed discrimination based on age and disability. The Age Discrimination in Employment Act of 1967 prohibits employment discrimination against individuals between the ages of 40 and 70, but a court decision in 2009 said that an age bias case against an employer had to show that age was the decisive factor in an adverse employment decision, not just a factor.[81] Two major laws have advanced civil rights for the disabled. The Rehabilitation Act of 1973 prohibited discrimination in federal employment on the basis of physical or mental disability, required the federal government to make reasonable accommodations for disabilities, and mandated affirmative action in hiring.

Years of lobbying, litigation, and protest led to the Americans with Disabilities Act (ADA) of 1990. This act placed the same requirements on the private sector as the Rehabilitation Act had placed on the government. The law prohibits discrimination in employment, in all programs and services of state and local governments, and in public accommodations. Many cases have reached the courts in an attempt to sort out what is and is not reasonable with regard to accommodations and what type and severity of disability leave a person qualified or unqualified for a particular job. In response to court decisions, the ADA was amended in 2008 to clarify that Congress intended the courts to take a broad rather than narrow view of what constituted a disability under the law.

Gay and lesbian equality has involved both civil liberties and civil rights.

Rights campaigns for gays and lesbians have concerned both civil liberties and civil rights. Regarding civil liberties, many states had prohibitions against homosexual sexual activity. The Supreme Court upheld these restrictions in 1986 but overturned them as violating basic concepts of liberty in the *Lawrence v. Texas* decision of 2003.

Regarding civil rights, most states, many cities, and the federal government have adopted anti-discrimination hiring policies that include sexual orientation. These cover government employees and companies doing business with the government. Which aspects of federal civil rights law apply to gays and lesbians has been handled by the Supreme Court on an issue-by-issue basis. For example, the Supreme Court ruled in 1998 that same-sex sexual harassment is forbidden by the 1964 Civil Rights Act.[82] On the other hand, the Court in 2000 upheld the Boy Scouts of America's right to prohibit gays from serving as troop leaders because it conveyed a message contrary to the organization's beliefs.[83]

During his first two years in office, President Obama took unilateral steps through executive orders, proclamations, and administrative rulings to promote lesbian, gay, bisexual, and transgender rights. Sexual orientation was added as a protected class under hate crimes law. The Violence Against Women Act, which in practice also covers domestic violence against men, was expanded to include victims in same-sex relationships of either gender. Some advocates for LGBT rights, however, were critical of what they saw as the administration's slow movement on a range of issues. As a presidential candidate, Obama had not supported same-sex marriage, and gay and lesbian groups were disappointed that his administration defended the Defense of Marriage Act in federal court. Activists also criticized what they considered slow movement on the issue of homosexuals serving in the military. Movement on these issues, however, was swift in late 2010 and early 2011. President Obama signed into law a repeal of the ban on openly homosexual individuals serving in the armed forces, and the administration announced that it would no longer defend the Defense of Marriage Act in federal court.

REACHING NEW HEIGHTS
Previously a test pilot for Raytheon, Amanda Simpson was named by President Obama as senior technical adviser in the Commerce Department's Bureau of Industry and Security, monitoring U.S. weapons technology exports. She is the first openly transgender presidential appointee.

Noncitizens share some of the rights of citizens, but not all.

Whether or not individuals are citizens or they are in the United States legally, they are covered by the Constitution's freedom to practice one's religion, equal protection of the laws, due process provisions when charged with a crime, and prohibition against cruel and unusual punishment, among other protections.[84] The major provisions of the Bill of Rights apply to citizens and noncitizens alike.

Although individuals who are in the United States illegally may have constitutional rights, they remain subject to deportation for having violated

Case Study

Gays in the Military

At the national level, one of the most prominent civil rights issues concerns homosexuals serving in the military. Early in American history, homosexuals or bisexuals were not explicitly prohibited from military service, but engaging in same-sex sexual activity was considered grounds for dismissal. In one form or another, this policy was effectively in place for most of American history. During World War I and World War II, revisions to discharge policy added provisions for removal for homosexual status as well as conduct, and psychological prescreening aimed to bar homosexuals from military service. A Department of Defense directive issued in 1982 reaffirmed the policy that homosexuality was incompatible with military service.

The ban on gays in the military became a major issue advanced by gay advocacy groups in the 1980s. The groups argued that the policy violated the civil rights of homosexuals, by preventing them as a class from this aspect of citizenship. They also argued the policy was inconsistent, because thousands of gays had in fact served in the military without being discharged, while others were discharged or not allowed to enlist.

During the 1980s, gay and lesbian groups were becoming important parts of the Democratic Party voter and financial base. This more prominent role led many Democratic candidates to call for a change in the military's policy. In his 1992 presidential campaign, Democratic nominee Bill Clinton advocated an end to the ban on gays serving in the military.

The issue became one of the earliest and most controversial tackled by the Clinton administration upon taking office in 1993. When it became apparent that a complete removal of the ban was politically unlikely, the administration later in the year adopted a compromise policy known as "don't ask, don't tell." Under this policy, military personnel were not to be asked about their sexual orientation nor are they to disclose it, the logic being that unit cohesion and discipline would thus be protected. Revealing that one is homosexual could lead to dismissal. According to military guidelines as of March 2010, the dismissal would be not for homosexual sexual orientation itself, but because of the risk of homosexual conduct.[85] Although this policy allowed gays and lesbians to serve in the military, it did not allow them to do so openly.

ENDING "DON'T ASK, DON'T TELL." With a former naval officer, a Marine staff sergeant, and House Speaker Nancy Pelosi looking on, President Obama signs the repeal of the Don't Ask, Don't Tell policy in December, 2010. The policy had been in place since 1993. Its repeal was a longtim`e objective of gay and lesbian civil rights advocates.

Public opinion on the issue has shifted over time, with most surveys now showing majority support for gays and lesbians serving openly. President Obama said during his campaign in 2008 and his State of the Union Address in 2009 that he wanted to end the policy. In 2010, a federal judge struck down the policy, but the Obama administration, preferring a legislative solution, successfully requested the implementation of the ruling be put on hold pending an appeal. After two unsuccessful efforts in Congress, President Obama signed the repeal of "don't ask, don't tell" in December 2010. Following Defense Department certification that repeal would not harm military readiness or unit cohesion, the ban on gays in the military expired in September 2011.

> ## Case Study Gays in the Military
>
> ### Thinking Critically
>
> 1. Imagine you are a legislator, and rank the influence of the following in determining how you would vote on repealing "don't ask, don't tell": arguments made by advocacy groups supportive of or opposed to allowing gays and lesbians in the military, the opinions of military leaders, the opinions of military rank-and-file, and public opinion.
>
> 2. What would you identify as the major factors explaining why the political environment today is more favorable than it was previously toward overturning the prohibition on homosexuals serving in the military?

immigration law. For this reason, there has been great controversy around the country as to what extent government officials should, when they are not directly involved in immigration enforcement, inquire whether someone is in the United States legally. This simmering debate boiled over in 2010 due to a new Arizona law intended to increase these inquiries. The U.S. Justice Department responded by filing a successful lawsuit in federal district court to block implementation of the law, arguing that portions of the legislation violated the national government's supremacy in immigration policy. Arizona appealed the ruling, and a decision was expected in 2011. In the meantime, Arizona filed a countersuit in February 2011 against the U.S. government for failure to secure the border with Mexico.

Noncitizens do not have all the same rights and privileges as citizens. They cannot, for example, run for certain public offices and cannot vote in federal elections. Access to federal programs and funds may in some instances be limited. And because of national security concerns, there are limits placed on the length of time noncitizens can be in the United States and the types of jobs they may hold. In addition, immigrants in the country illegally are subject to long detentions prior to hearings or possible deportation. Generally, the Supreme Court has applied an intermediate to high level of scrutiny in examining cases concerning classification by citizenship status, which means that the Court is usually inclined to reject classifying by citizenship unless a compelling government interest is at stake and the classification is necessary to achieve it. The Court has ruled, for example, that public schooling cannot be denied based on whether one is a citizen.[86]

Chapter Summary

In this chapter you have learned to:

5-1 Define the civil liberties guaranteed by the Constitution and trace the process by which they became binding on state governments.

Civil liberties are guaranteed in the U.S. Constitution— in the articles and in the Bill of Rights. Civil liberties address concerns such as speech, the practice of one's religion, and the use and ownership of property, with Americans usually believing that these are areas in which government should not interfere unless there are fundamental and compelling reasons to do so. Through selective incorporation, the Bill of Rights gradually became binding upon the states.

5-2 Analyze the different standards by which the Supreme Court has evaluated freedom of speech and religion and the rights of the accused.

Free speech protection has generally expanded over time. The Constitution's religious freedom guarantee is two-fold: Individuals are to be free to exercise their religion, and government is not to establish religion. Individuals accused of crimes have rights in place from the time of police investigation through sentencing by a judge.

5-3 Explain the demise of the separate but equal doctrine and the creation of civil rights laws and regulations.

In the twentieth century, black civil rights organizations began to challenge discriminatory laws in court and at all levels of government. The rejection of the separate but equal doctrine by the Supreme Court in *Brown v. Board of Education* prompted a broader movement to press for civil rights. Major legislation challenging discrimination in the private sector and government, significant executive orders introducing affirmative action policies, and a constitutional amendment prohibiting use of the poll tax produced a civil rights revolution in the United States. Congress used its interstate commerce powers and spending powers to avoid Supreme Court concerns that the Fourteenth Amendment did not apply to the private sector.

5-4 Describe legal and legislative actions to extend equal protection guarantees to other groups.

Although covered by the same laws, court decisions, and presidential actions that aided black civil rights, groups based on ethnicity, sex, religion, age, and sexual orientation, among other categories, have each faced distinctive issues of discrimination and formed their own organizations to challenge discriminatory laws and practices. The doctrine of equal protection extends to these groups, although the Supreme Court does not treat every classification the same. Race and ethnic classifications in laws and regulations are reviewed the most strictly, followed by classification by sex.

CHAPTER TEST

1. How did selective incorporation change the impact of the Bill of Rights on American government and society?

2. Why was the Fourteenth Amendment so significant?

3. How do the balancing and neutrality standards in religious practice cases differ?

4. How has the Supreme Court's view changed on whether and when capital punishment is potentially cruel and unusual?

5. Why did the Supreme Court determine that Americans had a constitutional right to privacy despite that term not appearing explicitly in the Constitution, and what are some of the major issue areas affected by this right?

6. What was the separate but equal doctrine, and how did the Supreme Court overturn it in *Brown v. Board of Education*?

7. What is the significance of the Civil Rights Act of 1964?

8. How did Congress apply civil rights statutes to the actions of private individuals and organizations rather than only to governments?

9. In what ways have strategic challenges facing civil rights movements for other groups differed from the movement for African Americans?

10. What categories has the Supreme Court constructed to guide its decisions about discrimination in cases based on race, sex, age, and other categories?

MyPoliSciLab® CIVIL LIBERTIES AND CIVIL RIGHTS
Apply what you learned in this chapter on MyPoliSciLab.

Read on mypoliscilab.com

eText: Chapter 5

Study and Review on mypoliscilab.com

Pre-Test
Post-Test
Chapter Exam
Flashcards

Watch on mypoliscilab.com

Video: D.C.'s Right to Bear Arms
Video: Funeral Protestors Push the Limits of Free Speech
Video: Supreme Court: No Race-Based Admissions

Explore on mypoliscilab.com

Comparative: Comparing Civil Liberties
Comparative: Comparing Civil Rights
Simulation: You Are a Police Officer
Simulation: You Are the Mayor and Need to Make Civil Rights Decisions
Timeline: Civil Liberties and National Security
Timeline: The Civil Rights Movement
Visual Literacy: Race and the Death Penalty

KEY TERMS

affirmative action, p. 138
balancing test, p. 128
Brown v. Board of Education, p. 135
civil disobedience, p. 140
civil liberties, p. 116
civil rights, p. 133
de facto segregation, p. 136
de jure segregation, p. 136
Dred Scott v. Sandford, p. 133
due process, p. 117

equal protection clause, p. 134
establishment clause, p. 126
exclusionary rule, p. 129
free exercise clause, p. 126
incorporation process, p. 118
Jim Crow laws, p. 135
Lemon test, p. 126
majority-minority districts, p. 141
Miranda warning, p. 131
neutrality test, p. 128

Plessy v. Ferguson, p. 135
poll tax, p. 137
preferred position, p. 124
prior restraint, p. 123
Regents of the University of California v. Bakke, p. 138
selective incorporation, p. 119
separate but equal doctrine, p. 135
state action, p. 134

SUGGESTED READINGS

Amitai Etzioni. 1999. *The Limits of Privacy*. New York: Basic Books. Argues, from a communitarian perspective, that sometimes community interests need to trump the privacy concerns of individuals.

F. Chris Garcia and Gabriel R. Sanchez. 2008. *Hispanics and the U.S. Political System: Moving into the Mainstream*. New York: Pearson/Prentice Hall. A helpful examination of Hispanic politics and civil rights issues today.

Jane J. Mansbridge. 1986. *Why We Lost the ERA*. Chicago: University of Chicago Press. Highlights the organizational, ideological, and strategic reasons the Equal Rights Amendment was not ratified.

Martha Nussbaum. 2008. *Liberty of Conscience: In Defense of America's Tradition of Religious Equality*. New York: Basic Books. An accessible and wide-ranging analysis of conflicts over religious liberty and freedom across American history.

C. Vann Woodward. 1957. *The Strange Career of Jim Crow*. New York: Oxford University Press. A classic account of the system of Jim Crow laws that prevailed throughout the southern states until the 1960s.

SUGGESTED WEBSITES

AMERICAN CIVIL LIBERTIES UNION
www.aclu.org

The largest civil liberties advocacy group in the United States, active both in legislation and lawsuits. Site provides overviews of key civil liberties issues. The ACLU is generally more aligned with liberal perspectives.

INSTITUTE FOR JUSTICE
www.ij.org

A major civil liberties advocacy group. The IJ is generally more aligned with conservative perspectives.

FIRST AMENDMENT CENTER
www.firstamendmentcenter.org

Excellent starting point for research. "First Amendment Topics" provides gateway to description, overview, and analysis of a wide range of civil liberties issues.

AMERICAN CIVIL RIGHTS INSTITUTE
www.acri.org

Website of an organization dedicated to ending racial and gender preference policies around the country and challenging the philosophy of other civil rights organizations.

HUMAN RIGHTS CAMPAIGN
www.hrc.org

One of the leading advocacy organizations for lesbian, gay, bisexual, and transgender rights.

Public Opinion and the Media

GUESSING WEIGHTS This team of oxen is not unlike those to be found at a country fair weight-guessing competition. On average, a crowd not only may be very close to guessing an ox's correct weight but also may collectively exercise good judgment in a political context.

CHAPTER LEARNING OBJECTIVES

After reading this chapter you will be able to:

6-1 Define public opinion, and outline the process and agents of political socialization.

6-2 Establish how American democracy functions despite the public's low levels of political knowledge.

6-3 Evaluate the unique role that the media play in American politics and society.

6-4 Identify the legal constraints on American media.

6-5 Analyze the nature of media coverage of politics and government.

6-6 Assess the effect of the media on political attitudes and behaviors.

One day in the fall of 1906, British scientist Francis Galton left his home in the town of Plymouth and headed for a country fair. As he walked through the exhibition that day, Galton came across a weight-judging competition. A fat ox was on display and members of a gathering crowd were lining up to place wagers on the weight of the ox.

Eight hundred people tried their luck. They were a diverse lot. Many of them were butchers and farmers, who were presumably expert at judging the weight of livestock, but there were also quite a few people who had no special knowledge of cattle. "Many nonexperts competed," Galton later wrote in the scientific journal *Nature*, "like those clerks and others who have no expert knowledge of horses, but who bet on races, guided by newspapers, friends, and their own fancies."

When the contest was over and the prizes had been awarded, Galton borrowed the tickets from the organizers and ran a series of statistical tests. He undoubtedly thought that the average guess would be way off the mark. After all, mix a few very informed people who may be expert at guessing weights of livestock with a slew of less well informed folks, and it seems likely the result would be a wrong answer. But Galton was wrong about getting a wrong answer. The crowd as an average had guessed that the ox, after it had been slaughtered and dressed, would weigh 1,197 pounds. After it had been slaughtered and dressed, the ox weighed 1,198 pounds. In other words, the crowd's judgment was essentially perfect.[1]

What Galton discovered that day was something of a paradox: a group of people, many of whom have little interest or expertise in a particular subject matter, can still, collectively, make appropriate judgments about it. This chapter will consider this paradox as applied to American politics. Although most Americans have no great interest or expertise in politics or policy, somehow they tend to make appropriate, reasonable, and logical judgments about political life. These judgments fall under the heading of "public opinion," one of the most commonly used phrases in any discussion of politics and policy.

Political leaders focus on public opinion and strategists focus on influencing the content and direction of what people think and know. The fact that public opinion has an important role in American politics comes from our political culture and the value it places on democracy, representation, and civil liberties. Compared to other political systems (even other democratic ones), Americans seem to have a greater opportunity for their opinions to matter. ■

The Nature of Public Opinion and Political Socialization

6-1 Define public opinion, and outline the process and agents of political socialization.

Public opinion is one of the most commonly used phrases in the discussion of politics and policy. But, what, in fact, is public opinion? First we'll examine what public opinion is and how it can be measured, and then we'll examine the sources of public opinion and how individuals acquire their political values and attitudes through the process of political socialization.

Public opinion has four basic traits.

Public opinion can be measured, obeyed, manipulated, ignored, and even misunderstood. Public opinion is the collective political beliefs and attitudes of the public, or groups within the public, on matters of relevance to government. Public opinion has four basic traits: salience, stability, direction, and intensity.

public opinion the collective political beliefs and attitudes of the public, or groups within the public, on matters of relevance to government.

Salience indicates an issue's importance to a person, or to the public in general. The public can feel strongly about an issue yet not rate that issue as particularly salient in their lives or political calculations.

salience an issue's importance to a person or to the public in general.

When politicians decide whether to attempt to change public opinion or whether to follow the message the public appears to be sending, they need to consider the **stability** of public opinion. Is public opinion on an issue likely to change and, if so, is change likely to be gradual or rapid? Once changed, is opinion likely to solidify around that new position, or is this an issue on which one might expect changes to be frequent? These are crucial questions for politicians.

stability the speed with which the change will occur, and the likelihood that the new opinion will endure.

The **direction** of the public's opinion about something refers to whether the public favors or opposes it. Any indication of agreement or disagreement, approval or disapproval, favor or opposition, is an example of direction.

direction in public opinion, the tendency for or against some phenomenon.

The **intensity** of the public's opinion measures the strength of the direction. For example, some people strongly favor or oppose abortion, whereas others may not harbor such strong feelings on the issue.

intensity the strength of the direction of public opinion.

It is important for politicians to recognize how public opinion breaks down among various groups within the population, so they can better understand the impact of different policies on different demographics. The same-sex marriage debate illustrates this perfectly. When Proposition 8 was put on the ballot in California in 2008 to make same-sex marriage unconstitutional, liberals assumed that the strong turnout to elect Barack Obama would also help defeat the proposition. What they did not foresee was that African Americans would turn out in such force for the proposition. The measure passed, thus defining marriage in California as between a man and a woman only, in large part because of the black vote. It was bitter irony for the Democrats that the same people who voted so heavily to elect the more liberal presidential candidate also voted so heavily with conservatives against same-sex marriage.

Thinking Causally Why did the same people who voted to elect the more liberal presidential candidate in 2008 also vote with conservatives against same-sex marriage in California?

Public opinion on specific policy issues varies greatly among different demographic groups. Race, gender, income, and political affiliation are all factors in how an individual forms an opinion on a certain issue.[2] It is important for politicians to understand how these opinions differ among these groups so they can strategically appeal to each group.

Politicians do not always base their actions on public opinion, and representative democracy does not demand that office holders always follow public opinion. Still, in a well-functioning representative democracy, policy-making should generally follow the contours of public opinion on most issues.

Furthermore, most politicians like to be on the "80 side of 80–20 issues." In other words, office holders who are too often on the wrong side of public opinion risk great political cost and face electoral danger.

Political socialization is a learning process that is governed by primacy and persistence.

political socialization the learning process in which individuals absorb information and selectively add it to their knowledge and understanding of politics and government.

primacy the principle that what is learned first is learned best and lodged most firmly in one's mind.

persistence the principle that political lessons, values, and attitudes learned early in life tend to structure political learning later on in life.

ideology a consistent set of ideas about a given set of issues.

Political socialization is a learning process, one in which individuals absorb information about the political world and add it, selectively, to their stock of knowledge and understanding of politics and government. This learning tends to be governed by two important principles: primacy and persistence. **Primacy** means that what is learned first is learned best. **Persistence** means that political lessons, values, and attitudes learned early in life tend to structure political learning later on in life. In keeping with these two principles, what children learn about politics at a young age becomes an important determinant of the values, attitudes, and beliefs they will hold in later life.

The most common expression of values, attitudes, and beliefs is the identification of an individual's ideology. **Ideology** can be described as a consistent set of ideas about a given set of issues. The two most commonly used ideological categories are "liberal" and "conservative." Although there are no hard and fast definitions for what makes an individual "liberal" or "conservative," a liberal would generally favor a government that is active in promoting social equality and economic welfare. A conservative would generally favor a smaller government that interferes minimally in the economic sphere but actively promotes social morality. Of course, many people do not fall squarely in either of the two camps. People who favor a smaller government that interferes minimally in the economy and does not interfere in social morality are often call "libertarians." Those who support an active government role in both the economy and social morality are sometimes dubbed "populists."

Political sophistication grows as children grow up.

Political socialization plays a crucial role in determining which ideology an individual will support. Children begin learning about politics and government surprisingly early. In their preschool years, the first representative of government that they become familiar with is often the police officer. Preschoolers generally consider the police officer to be a helpful, benevolent authority figure.[3] In early grade school, children generally become familiar with the president, believing him to be an honest, trustworthy, and virtuous figure.[4]

These generally positive sentiments are by no means universal, however. There are certain subgroups of children who do not view political authority as favorably—for example, African Americans, Hispanics, and the low-income, white children of Appalachia.[5]

In the later grade school years, a child's awareness of political figures begins to expand. To the short list of police officer and president, many children add figures such as firefighters, soldiers, mayors, and governors.[6] At the same time, the child begins to think of government in terms of institutions and activities.[7]

During the later grade school years, children come to understand the differences in the roles played by, for example, the president, the Supreme Court, and members of Congress.[8] They also begin to view some political figures more favorably than others[9] and to transition toward a more realistic, less heroic view of specific political figures.[10] During these years, children also begin to gain a basic understanding of the concept of "policy," of conflict over specific issues, and of the idea of competition between the political parties.[11]

Beyond basic political knowledge, grade schoolers also develop a concept of the elements of good citizenship. Their earliest thoughts on the subject consist primarily of being a "good person." In later years, children expand the concept of good citizenship to include showing an interest in governmental affairs and participating in politics by voting,[12] although most children often have a hard time understanding the differences between the two parties.[13]

Further political maturity comes with adolescence. High school students begin to understand major policy issues and take sides on them. They also gain an understanding of the place of interest groups in the political process, and of which groups are involved with which issues.[14] In the high school years students also make significant progress in understanding differences between Democrats and Republicans.[15]

The adolescent's concept of good citizenship remains centered on the ideas of attention to public affairs, participation in the political process, and obedience to the laws.[16] One thing that does change, however, is the adolescent's sense of trust in the political system. In the high school years, idealistic views begin to give way to some distrust and cynicism.[17]

What are the sources of these attitudes that children have toward the political world? Political scientists tend to think in terms of agents of socialization, that is, individuals or institutions that help confer political knowledge, and events that help socialize people to politics.

Family The single most important socialization agent is the family, particularly parents. Even with the myriad distractions of work and modern life, children still spend a tremendous amount of time with their parents, and the bonds between parent and child are usually very close. Furthermore, parents are likely to reveal their own political beliefs in front of their children more frequently and openly than other socializing agents—teachers and peers, for example.[18]

The most reliable area of transmission from parent to child is identification with a political party—that is, whether one considers oneself a Democrat,

Republican, independent, or something else.[19] One reason that partisanship tends to be "inherited" more easily than specific issue positions is that a parent's partisanship is much easier for a child to grasp than a parent's position on, say, Social Security reform. Finally, partisanship is often deeply held and highly salient to adults. Such core beliefs tend to be transmitted most reliably.[20]

Religious institutions and traditions   Family religious traditions may also influence a child's political learning. Different religions and denominations teach different values with respect to punishment and mercy, social justice, the importance of law and authority, equality, and so on. These values, adopted by the child in a religious context, can also play an important role in thinking about politics.

Furthermore, adherents of different religious traditions have historic affiliations with different parties and socioeconomic groups.[21] Jews, for example, tend to be Democrats, while evangelical Christians are more likely to be Republicans. In cases such as these, parents who pass their religion on to their children also may pass along part of their politics.

Peer groups   The child's peer group (the friends that a child most closely associates with) will likely impact the development of political views. This influence is particularly strong during adolescence, when children begin the transition to adulthood and spend more time with their friends, away from their parents. However, the salience of politics to adolescents is generally low and is largely unrelated to a child's status within peer groups.[22]

Educational system   Another potentially important socialization agent is the educational system. Public schools actively seek to inculcate students with a respect for the law, authority, and democratic values; an appreciation of the American political system; a sense of the meaning and importance of active democratic citizenship; and the political knowledge necessary for active, effective political participation. They also teach some of the rituals and symbolism of politics—flying the flag, reciting the Pledge of Allegiance, voting in student elections, writing to elected officials, and so on.

The media   Political socialization depends on politically relevant information, often provided by the media. What the media choose to cover, how they choose to cover it, and the accessibility of their coverage are all important political socialization questions.

Events that socialize can have generational, period, or life cycle effects.

Thinking Causally What types of events might influence political learning?

Events as well as agents contribute to political socialization. Whereas socialization by agents typically revolves around the socialization of children and young adults, events can influence the political learning of older individuals as well.

Generational effects One kind of effect that political events can exert on public opinion is a generational effect. When a **generational effect** occurs, younger members of the body politic are influenced by events in a way that makes their attitudes and beliefs different from those of older generations. Consider the tumultuous political period of the 1960s and early 1970s, for example. For many young people coming of age in these years, the defining political events were the Vietnam War and the protest movement surrounding it. Not surprisingly, in general, those who lived through this era as young men and women, and particularly those who participated in protest politics, ended up with a distinctive—and more liberal—set of political beliefs.

Period effects Sometimes events exert a noticeable impact across political generations and affect the political socialization of citizens young and old. This is known as a **period effect**. Consider, for example, responses to the following survey question:

> There is much discussion as to the amount of money the government in Washington should spend for national defense and military purposes. How do you feel about this? Do you think we are spending too little, too much, or about the right amount?

In the early 1970s, only a small percentage of Americans thought that the country was spending too little on national defense. But by the mid-1970s, the number of Americans who held that belief doubled once, and then, surprisingly, doubled again. What caused this dramatic shift? One political scientist suggests it was a combination of two factors. First, this period saw a substantial decline in defense spending as a percentage of the federal budget and as a percentage of gross domestic product. Second, a series of disturbing foreign policy events rocked the world: the fall of South Vietnam, Cambodia, and Nicaragua to communist forces; the Soviet military build-up and takeover of Afghanistan; and the hostage crisis at the American embassy in Iran.[23] This shift in public opinion is a clear illustration of the period effect.

Life cycle effects Finally, individuals tend to get more conservative as they grow older and more secure in their political beliefs. This is known as the **life cycle effect**. Consider Americans' description of themselves as "liberal" or "conservative." As they

generational effect the situation in which younger citizens are influenced by events in such a fashion that their attitudes and beliefs are forever rendered distinct from those of older generations.

period effect an event that influences the attitudes and beliefs of people of all ages.

life cycle effect attitudes or physical characteristics that change as one ages, no matter the time period or generation. The graying of one's hair is a life cycle effect.

POLITICAL EXPERIENCE OFTEN SHAPES POLITICAL BELIEFS

Those involved in the Vietnam War protest movement adopted a distinctive and more liberal set of political beliefs than others in their generation.

HOW DO WE KNOW?

Can Surveys Accurately Gauge the Opinions of Almost 300 Million Americans?

The Question

Discussions of public opinion are a routine part of American political life. During election season, scores of polls report who is ahead and behind virtually every day. At other times, news reports frequently mention the public's perception of the president's job performance and whether the country is heading in the right direction. If the president or a member of Congress makes a significant policy proposal, major media outlets survey Americans for their reactions. Politicians seldom rely on media polls; they conduct their own surveys. Presidents have extensive polling operations. Typically they take the pulse of the nation before, during, and after a campaign, an important speech, or the introduction of a major policy initiative. Political scientists, too, use surveys to gauge the collective consciousness of the American people.

Not all surveys are created equal, however. A well-designed survey can provide accurate information on public opinion, but a poorly done one can lead to false conclusions and be essentially useless. The question is: can surveys accurately gauge the opinions of almost 300 million Americans? How do we know?

Why It Matters

Agreement between public opinion and government action is one measure of a democratic government. However, it is not always a good one. Sometimes the opinion "snapshot" in a survey obscures important momentum—at the time of the survey, government may be in the process of moving toward the public's position, or vice versa. And sometimes what the public wants may be ill-advised or even unconstitutional. However, a critical starting point in our assessment is understanding how surveys work.

Investigating the Answer

Imagine you are making a pot of soup for some friends. You add water, chicken, vegetables, and

THE PIECES OF PUBLIC OPINION Hoping to influence election and legislative outcomes, politicians and political strategists must consider the stability, direction, and intensity of public opinion. Here, Senior Advisors Valerie Jarrett, David Axelrod, and Director of Communications Dan Pfeiffer meet with President Barack Obama in 2010.

HOW DO WE KNOW?   Can Surveys Accurately Gauge the Opinions of Almost 300 Million Americans?

spices, and let the soup simmer for a couple of hours. Before serving it, you want to make sure it tastes good, so you take a small spoonful. If you took the spoonful from the top, you might think the soup needed more seasoning. If you took a spoonful from the bottom, you might think the soup needed more water. A good cook mixes the soup before taking a sample spoonful to make sure all parts are represented.

The same logic applies to survey **sampling**, the process of choosing a small group of people to interview for a survey. A survey sample should represent all elements of the population—men, women, young, old, Democrats, Republicans, and other groups—in rough proportion to their population percentages. Such representation is accomplished by using a **random sample**—a sample of the population in which every member of the population has an equal chance of ending up in the sample.

Particularly with large populations, the sampling procedures for a random sample can become very complex. But consider this simple example. We begin with a population of 100 people, half men, half women. We want to take a random sample of 20. To do this, we give each man and woman a slip of paper with a number, 1 through 100. Each number is used only once. Then we have a computer generate 20 random numbers between 1 and 100. As the computer generates each number, the person holding the number is asked to step forward. Once the computer has provided 20 numbers, we have our random sample.

This sample should end up with roughly half men and half women, and in that respect be representative of the total population of 100, because every man and woman in our population had an equal probability, or chance, of being sampled. We can then have some confidence that if we pose questions to members of the sample, their answers will be very similar to the ones we would get if we posed them to the entire population.

Even in perfectly drawn samples, unavoidable **sampling error** occurs because no sample is an exact match for the population. Sampling error is reported in most surveys as the **margin of error**. To understand what this means, suppose that 55 percent of

respondents in a survey approved of the president's job performance and the survey claims a margin of error of plus or minus 5 percentage points. Thus, if we had talked to the entire population, we would have found that somewhere between 50 percent and 60 percent approved of the president's performance—55 percent plus or minus 5 percentage points. So the result from interviewing a random sample is close to what we would get if we spoke with the entire population.

One influence on sampling error is the size of the sample. The larger the sample, the smaller the sampling error. If you flipped a coin several times, you should get a roughly equal proportion of heads and tails, but you could get all heads or all tails. The more times you flip the coin, the more likely the proportion of heads to tails will be nearly equal. Try it! The same applies to survey samples. If researchers picked just 1 person at random, or 10, or even 100, to represent the entire U.S. population, the sampling error would be enormous. But if they picked 1,000 people at random, the sampling error would be 3 or 4 percentage points, a margin most researchers are comfortable with. With 1,000 people in the sample, there would likely be a fair mix of men, women, young, old, Democrats, Republicans, whites, nonwhites, and so on. In other words, 1,000 people are a large enough group to be broadly representative of the entire U.S. population.

Sampling error also can result from the diversity of the population studied. To take an extreme example, suppose you knew everyone in a state had the same opinion on every issue. If you wanted to measure public opinion on an issue in that state, you would need to ask only one person. Now suppose everyone had a slightly different opinion on every issue. If you were to interview just one person, your sampling error would be unacceptably large; one person's opinion could not possibly capture the diversity of thinking within the population. So the greater the diversity of opinion, the more people a researcher needs to survey to be confident of results.

Surveys can contain other sorts of errors. For example, questions can be poorly written or structured to

(continues)

HOW DO WE KNOW?　Can Surveys Accurately Gauge the Opinions of Almost 300 Million Americans? *(continued)*

encourage a particular response. Consider the following questions:

> Given the recent series of murders in our state, some people say the state should reinstate the death penalty. Do you agree or disagree?

> Given the recent cases of police misconduct and the freeing of inmates who had been wrongly convicted, do you agree or disagree that the state should reinstate the death penalty?

The first question is structured to elicit pro–death penalty responses, while the second question is structured to elicit anti–death penalty responses. Even if a question is asked in a straightforward manner—"Do you support or oppose the death penalty for convicted murderers?"—where that question appears in a survey also matters. If, on the one hand, it followed a long series of questions on crime, a pro–death penalty result would be more likely. If, on the other hand, it followed a series of questions on police misconduct, one might expect more anti–death penalty responses.

The demographic characteristics of interviewers can also introduce error. Evidence shows that men reply differently to male interviewers than to females on issues such as abortion and birth control, and answers to questions about race are influenced by the race of the interviewer.

Another source of error is **nonresponse bias**. Even though a researcher may have drawn a reliable sample, not everyone in that sample may agree to participate in the survey. If those who participate have attitudes different from those who decline, the results will be biased. In a survey on Social Security, for example, young workers would be expected to have opinions different from those of older workers and retired individuals. If the refusal rate for the younger group were much higher than for the older group, the survey would contain disproportionate input from older individuals and inadequate input from younger people.

Certain types of surveys also suffer from their own sets of problems. Despite their rising popularity, nonprobability online surveys can be misleading. These online surveys, sometimes also called volunteer or opt-in surveys, have participants sign up

and answer questionnaires on the Internet, usually in exchange for gifts or money. This type of survey has grown into a multibillion dollar business in the last 10 years, mainly due to the low cost and faster survey turnaround time.[24] Yet because of the inherent nature of these surveys, they suffer from many flaws. The majority of these surveys rely solely on individuals who have Internet access, leading to significantly inadequate coverage. As of December 2009, only 74 percent of U.S. adults use the Internet, and Internet usage tends to be positively associated with income and negatively associated with age.[25] Some demographic groups also tend to be online less frequently and are therefore underrepresented in online surveys. There can also be errors associated with the high level of nonresponse, resulting in extensive bias. Despite these problems, nonprobability online surveys continue to be used for market research in such areas as product testing and customer satisfaction. They have even become more commonly used in political polling.[26]

The increased use of online surveys in such applications has led to their heightened scrutiny, specifically from the American Association for Public Opinion Research, whose report in March of 2010 challenged the use of nonprobability surveys. The AAPOR report concludes that "researchers should avoid non-probability online panels when one of the research objectives is to accurately estimate population values." The report goes on to say that "there is currently no generally accepted theoretical basis from which to claim that survey results using samples from non-probability online panels are projectable to the general population." It is the findings of the report, therefore, that claiming "representativeness" should be avoided when using online surveys.[27] Whether these warnings have a discernable influence on the use of online surveys is yet to be seen.

Thinking Critically

1. Suppose you were in charge of designing a survey to gauge public opinion on certain major issues. How would you word your questions, and in what

HOW DO WE KNOW? Can Surveys Accurately Gauge the Opinions of Almost 300 Million Americans?

order would you place your questions? How would you make sure there is little nonresponse bias?

2. What do you need to know about polls in order to properly understand the results? In other words, what would you need to know about a survey before you would trust the results?

3. Do you think polling via the Internet is as trustworthy as other, more established polling techniques? What are some problems Internet polls may have?

The Bottom Line

Surveys can be an incredibly useful tool for journalists, political scientists, and politicians. However, identifying good survey methods and understanding how particular surveys are conducted are highly useful skills for citizens as well. Those skills will serve you well in other courses as well as enabling you to be a good consumer of polls.

---

age, survey respondents are more likely to declare themselves conservative—a classic life cycle effect.[28] Americans also grow more secure in their partisan attachments as they grow older: they are increasingly likely to side with the Democratic or Republican parties and less likely to say that they are politically independent.[29]

Making Public Opinion Work in a Democracy

6-2 Establish how american democracy functions despite the public's low levels of political knowledge.

Although political knowledge and sophistication among Americans may be somewhat lacking, there are certain reassuring regularities in the ebb and flow of public opinion. For example, when a president performs poorly in office, the public usually recognizes this, reduces its collective approval of his job performance, and ultimately denies him reelection. Likewise, when a president performs well in office, the public recognizes this, too, and typically rewards the president with high job approval numbers and another term.

The miracle of aggregation can compensate for low levels of information among the mass public.

Recall the example presented at the beginning of this chapter, when at the country fair in 1906 common men and women accurately guessed the weight of an ox. It illustrates a paradox that has often been referred to as

sampling taking a small fraction of something that is meant to represent a larger whole: for example, a group of people that represents a larger population.

random sample a population sample in which it is equally likely that each member of the population will be included in the sample.

sampling error the difference between the reported characteristics of the sample and the characteristics of the larger population that result from imperfect sampling.

margin of error the range surrounding a sample's response within which researchers are confident the larger population's true response would fall.

nonresponse bias a nonrandom error that occurs when people who choose to participate in a survey have different attitudes from those of people who decline to participate.

miracle of aggregation the phenomenon that occurs when a group consists of individuals who are largely ignorant of a particular issue, but their collective opinion tends to make sense.

the **miracle of aggregation**. The "miracle" is that, even though a group of individuals can be largely ignorant of a particular phenomenon, when their opinions are aggregated, their collective opinion tends to make sense.

Here is how the miracle of aggregation works. Imagine an American public in which only 30 percent of the people paid close attention to politics and the other 70 percent were completely ignorant. Now imagine that politicians are looking for guidance from the public on whether to undertake a dramatic reform of the Social Security program. According to the terms of our example, 70 percent of the public has no real opinion on the matter. But let's assume that, of the other 30 percent, two-thirds want reform and one-third do not. Now we have 20 percent of the electorate that wants reform, 10 percent that does not, and 70 percent that have no idea.

Even completely ignorant members of the public will often give answers to survey questions just to be polite, or perhaps not to seem as ignorant of a particular issue as they really are. Let us assume, then, that the 70 percent split equally on the Social Security question—35 percent for reform and 35 percent for no reform. (There is no reason to believe that individuals essentially inventing their answers to a survey question should favor one side more than the other.)

Now the picture of public opinion on the issue looks like this: 55 percent support reform and 45 percent do not. Notice what has happened: Opinion from the public as a whole, including the great mass of ignorant individuals, conveys the same message to policy makers as opinion from only the informed 30 percent: Americans want Social Security reform. A miracle!

As long as the random opinions of uninformed members of the public cancel each other out, policy makers will get a clear, meaningful signal that accurately reflects the wishes of those who are paying attention. This result may cause some anguish for those who would like the entire public to be aware, interested, and informed. However, the miracle of aggregation at least provides a way for the truly interested and informed to see their policy preferences accurately represented to decision makers.

Opinion leaders shape what the public thinks about and what they think about it.

Studies of public opinion typically divide the American public into three segments: those who pay very close attention to politics, those who are generally indifferent to politics but pay attention sporadically, and those who pay no attention to politics at all. There are debates over the relative size of these different segments, but the most attentive group is likely to be a small one, and on particularly obscure issues, extremely small.

opinion leaders individuals with high levels of interest and expertise in politics who seek to communicate their political beliefs to others.

That this most attentive group is small, however, does not mean that it lacks significant influence. In fact, many of the members of this group can be considered "opinion leaders." **Opinion leaders** are people who can legitimately claim high levels of interest and expertise in politics and seek to communicate their political beliefs to others. This group may include political writers and journalists, politicians, political professionals, bloggers, academic political scientists, community activists, and garden-variety "political junkies." Opinion leaders make it their business to send strong signals to the public regarding which political issues are important and what the public ought to think about them.

You can see an example of opinion leadership by looking at the results of the "most important problem" question over the years. Periodically, polling organizations have asked the American public the following question: "What do you think is the most important problem facing the country today?" In April 2009, only 9 percent of the public identified health care as America's most important problem. A mere four months later, however, in August 2009, that number had risen to 20 percent. Clearly, the health care situation in the United States had not changed in those two months. What had changed, however, was that members of Congress began debating the urgent need for reform in the health care system. The media carried that message, and various opinion leaders continued this "trickle down" process, discussing the issue in town hall meetings and personal conversations. The polling data indicate that at least part of the public ultimately got the message coming out of Congress.

Beyond giving the public cues about what issues it should be thinking about, opinion leaders also help shape how the public thinks about certain issues. In one scholarly study, for example, researchers identified 80 different questions that were asked at least twice on a variety of surveys from 1969 to 1983. In many cases, opinion had changed noticeably between the first time the question was asked and the second. In explaining these changes, the researchers found that changes in public opinion corresponded significantly with television news commentary—in other words, messages from opinion leaders.[30]

Partisanship simplifies political judgments.

Unlike many other aspects of public opinion, most voters have a self-defined, stable affiliation with a political party. In making judgments about the political world, then, they can use partisanship as a cue.[31] The partisan affiliation of a political candidate communicates a tremendous amount of information. If you are a Republican, for example, you know that you are much more likely to agree with the policy preferences of Republicans, without having to sort through each and every position of a particular candidate. If you vote strictly along party lines, you may regret your choice occasionally, but for the most part a vote for your party versus the other party will tend to be consistent with your preferred outcome. The same is true if you are a Democrat. Knowing that your party proposed them provides you with some assurance that the ideas make sense.[32] Similar logic applies to your approval or disapproval of the job performance of policy makers, from the president on down. If they share your partisan affiliation, it is likely that you will agree, on the whole, with the policy choices they are making.[33]

Moderately attentive "scorekeepers" cause most aggregate public opinion change.

One political scientist proposes that the middle stratum of Americans referred to above—the group that is only moderately attentive to politics—serves an important "scorekeeping" function.[34] This group has little passion for politics and does not think about the political world in ideological terms. It pays just enough attention to politics to pick up on signals indicating big changes. When members of this group pick up a signal that a noticeable change has occurred, they change their opinions accordingly. According to this view, those changes account for most of the movement in aggregate public opinion. Furthermore, they are connected to real-world events in a fairly logical, orderly fashion that results in government accountability.

The Unique Role of the American Mass Media

6-3   Evaluate the unique role that the media play in American politics and society.

mass media or media
various modes of communication intended to reach a mass audience, including television, radio, newspapers, news magazines, and the Internet.

The **mass media, or media**, are the various modes of communication designed to reach a mass audience. These include television, radio, newspapers, news magazines, and the Internet. The term also refers to the individuals responsible for producing the content disseminated through various communications media. Thus, "the media" may refer to the actual communications media themselves (newspapers, for example), or to the people who are responsible for their content (such as newspaper reporters and editors).

American mass media are largely privately owned.

The largest media outlets in the United States are owned and operated in the private sector, rather than by the government. Prior to the 1980s, there were government restrictions on how many news and broadcast outlets one company could own. But after these limitations were lifted, the United States saw a wave of takeovers and mergers. The News Corporation, a global media enterprise under the ownership of Rupert Murdoch, added Fox News and the *Wall Street Journal* to its holdings. CNN and Time Warner merged. Disney bought ABC. CBS was purchased by Westinghouse, which was then placed in the hands of Viacom.

The U.S. government does not own any major television networks or cable news outlets. Public broadcasting in the United States receives only a small share of its funding from the government and accounts for about 2 percent of the total television audience share.[35]

Most American newspapers are tied to a particular city, state, or region—the *San Francisco Chronicle*, *New York Post*, *Des Moines Register*, and *Denver Post* are examples. Although *USA Today* attempted to change that, producing a national daily paper in 1982, the majority of Americans continued to rely on their local papers.

American mass media stress objective political coverage.

The American media generally make an effort to be objective and nonpartisan in covering the news. This means that reporters and editors generally seek to present all sides completely, fairly, and accurately. Journalists usually refrain from advocating particular views or suggesting who or what is right and wrong. They have always operated independently of government and the political parties, refusing to become spokespeople for any particular party or government administration.

But the concept that the mainstream media were unbiased was put under question in the 1990s with the advent of cable television and conservative talk radio. Personalities like Rush Limbaugh, Sean Hannity, and Bill O'Reilly argued that the mainstream media (or MSM), which included the *New York Times*, CBS, NBC, and ABC News, may have claimed to be unbiased but showed a penchant for reports that favored liberal viewpoints. This accusation led to a profusion of advocacy journalism. Fox News, with its conservative focus, quickly outpaced the older and established CNN. MSNBC countered with a left of center point of view.

During this timeframe, newspapers, challenged by the growing dominance of the Internet throughout the country, began to lose readers and advertisers. Strapped for cash, many of the once mighty newspapers in major cities were on the verge of bankruptcy by the first decade of the twenty-first century.

Thinking Causally Why were many newspapers in major cities facing bankruptcy by the first decade of the twenty-first century?

Media in other countries have always had different standards than the United States. In Western Europe, for example, newspapers frequently assume an advocacy role, presenting the news in ways that support a particular political party or ideology.[36] In the United States, such open advocacy for a party, candidate, or philosophy by a mainstream newspaper would be unthinkable. But the editorials of papers like the *New York Times,* the *Los Angeles Times*, and the *Washington Post* have been consistently left of center, while the *Wall Street Journal* has advocated a conservative view. There are almost no major newspapers in the United States that are truly centrist in their editorials.

Journalists in other countries also hold different views of the meaning of objectivity. American journalists are more likely than others to see their role as limited to reporting opposing sides' positions. In a multinational survey, for example, only 28 percent of American journalists said that "objectivity" meant "going beyond the statements of the contending sides to the hard facts of a political dispute." In Sweden, this definition was supported by 58 percent of journalists. Moreover, 39 percent of American journalists defined objectivity as "expressing fairly the position of each side in a political dispute," whereas only 21 percent of German journalists said that this definition closely reflected their understanding of objectivity.[37]

These differing views of objectivity have practical implications. Journalists in Sweden and Germany act not only as reporters of information but also as analysts and social critics. Many American journalists would consider this stepping into the middle of a political debate, which would violate their objectivity standard. But foreign journalists see it as delivering a truthful version of events to audiences—a version of events not typically available from politicians.[38]

American mass media play a watchdog role in government and politics.

watch dog the media's role in keeping a close eye on politicians and presenting stories and information that politicians might not willingly reveal to the media on their own.

The job of American journalists is sometimes described as serving in a **watchdog** role. They keep a close eye on government and politics, watching for signs of dishonesty, corruption, unfair dealing, and broken promises, and investigating aggressively when they find such evidence. The most famous example of this approach was the news coverage after the Watergate burglary in 1972 that eventually led to the resignation of President Richard Nixon on August 9, 1974. Had it not been for two dogged reporters with the *Washington Post*, Carl Bernstein and Bob Woodward, the entire account of lies and deceit that went all the way up to the president might have been brushed aside by the media.

American mass media operate largely unfettered by government restriction.

prior restraint government intervention to prevent the publication or utterance of material it finds objectionable.

American media are allowed to publish or broadcast free from the threat of **prior restraint**—that is, government intervention to stop the publication or utterance of material it finds objectionable. This freedom has never been absolute, however. The Supreme Court has ruled that if publication of certain information "will surely result in direct, immediate, and irreparable harm to our nation or its people," then prior restraint can be exercised.[39] For instance, the government often tries and sometimes succeeds in exercising prior restraint in cases involving national security. A broadcast or print outlet could be restrained from publishing the secret locations of U.S. armed forces in enemy territory, or the names and addresses of intelligence agents overseas. Significantly, however, the Supreme Court has made it clear that the burden rests with government to demonstrate that publication would be harmful, rather than with the media to show why the information merits a public airing.

In the second year of the Iraq War, newspapers wanted to publish photographs of the returning caskets of Americans killed in action. The Bush administration did not allow this for reasons of privacy. Those opposed

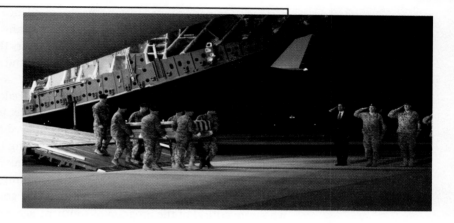

SHOWING THE COST OF WAR

The bodies of American soldiers killed in combat overseas arrive at Dover Air Force Base in Delaware. The Obama administration overturned the Bush administration directive that forbade media coverage of these events.

to the war considered publication of the photographs as a way to remind Americans of the war's high cost in lives lost. When President Obama took office, the ban was reversed and the families of fallen soldiers were given the option of having the return of their sons or daughters photographed and made public.

Constraints on American Media Freedom

6-4 Identify the legal constraints on American media.

The press's ability to publish what it deems appropriate without government restriction has come a long way over the course of American history. Members of the modern media have few of the restraints faced by their earliest forebears. However, contemporary political journalists in the United States do face some significant constraints on what they can air or publish.

The freedom the American press enjoys was not won quickly.

The relative freedom that characterizes U.S. media operations today was not established by the adoption of the First Amendment in 1791. At the time of its passage, the First Amendment was thought to guarantee freedom of the press only from prior restraint by government. Expansions of freedom were won through ongoing battles between the press, the government, and public figures, many of which the press lost.

Early restrictions on the press The most famous early restriction on the press was the Sedition Act, a federal law passed in 1798. The act effectively criminalized criticism of Congress and the president. Ostensibly, the act was designed for national security purposes—to silence American supporters of France, a country with which President John Adams feared the United States might soon be at war.[40] Critics argued, however, that the act was intended instead to quiet the critics of President Adams and his Federalist Party allies in Congress.[41]

When Thomas Jefferson, leader of the Anti-Federalists, was elected president in 1800, he freed those still serving prison sentences because of Sedition Act convictions. The Sedition Act itself was allowed to expire in 1801, but the struggle for a free press was far from over. During the Civil War, the federal government limited telegraph transmissions from Washington, D.C., which it argued might compromise the successful planning and prosecution of the war. During the post–Civil War era, the federal government jailed reporters who were critical of the program of southern Reconstruction.

By the turn of the twentieth century, press outlets were being sued, successfully, for printing photographs of and intimate gossip about figures of interest to the public. The Espionage Act, passed in 1917 and expanded in 1918, made illegal any "seditious expression"—in particular, publications that might undermine military recruitment or weaken support for the military draft during World War I. Nearly 1,000 individuals ultimately were convicted for engaging in such expression.[42]

Establishment of press freedoms in the twentieth century A countervailing trend began to appear during the 1930s, when the Supreme Court started to develop a more expansive interpretation of the First Amendment. The trend took decades to reach maturity, but by the end of the 1970s, the press freedoms that we recognize today had largely been established in case law and federal statute, although restrictions remain.

The media can be both forbidden and compelled to provide certain information.

Laws prevent the media from engaging in defamation, which refers to a false or unsubstantiated attack on someone's good name or reputation. To be considered defamation, an attack must be false. If the press calls the president a liar and a thief and he can be shown to be a liar and a thief, laws against defamation do not apply. As the case law has evolved, the courts have stated that actual malice by the media must be demonstrated in order to prove defamation of a public figure. Given the difficulty of meeting this standard, or surviving the appeals process, public figures must rely on journalists' integrity and self-policing by media outlets, as much as on anti-defamation laws, to protect their reputations.

If the government cannot actively restrain the American media from disseminating content, can the media be compelled to publish or broadcast certain information? With respect to print media, the courts have ruled that no individual or institution has a right to coverage of an opinion or pet issue in the print media. The broadcast media, on the other hand, are treated differently. The broadcast spectrum is considered a public asset; unlike a newspaper or magazine, no one owns it. And whereas the broadcast spectrum can carry only a limited amount of programming, the number of potential print outlets is unlimited.

For both of these reasons, the federal government takes a more active role—through the Federal Communications Commission (FCC)—in regulating broadcasters. One regulation relevant to political programming is the equal time provision. Under this rule, if a television station gives time to a candidate for office, it must give all other candidates for that office equal access. Because national debates, news, and public affairs programming are exempt from this rule, its primary impact is on campaign advertising. If a local television or radio station runs a 30-second advertisement by a candidate for governor, for example, the station must offer to sell the same amount of time to the candidate's opponents at equal cost.

Reporters may be compelled by the federal government to reveal their sources.

Despite their resistance to the idea, reporters can be compelled to reveal the names of confidential sources. This mandate can become an issue when the information provided by a source is germane to a legal matter. In 2003, for example, *Time* magazine published an article revealing the name of CIA officer Valerie Plame. The reporters involved in the story did nothing illegal by revealing Plame's identity, but it is illegal for a government official with authorized access to a covert agent's identity to deliberately reveal that information to a reporter. Accordingly, a federal grand jury was assembled to determine whether any criminal wrongdoing had taken place.

At the heart of the investigation was one question: who revealed Plame's identity to reporters? One of the reporters involved in the story, Judith Miller of the *New York Times*, was called to testify, but she refused to reveal her source in testimony before the grand jury. For her refusal, she was sentenced to remain in jail until the grand jury was dismissed. She eventually revealed her source—Lewis Libby, Vice President Richard Cheney's chief of staff—when he released her from her pledge of confidentiality. But this disclosure happened only after she spent 85 days in jail.

In order to avoid the choice between spending time in jail and revealing a confidential source, reporters have advocated shield laws. These laws grant them certain exemptions from having to testify in legal matters. Just as a priest cannot be compelled to testify against a penitent, or a husband against a wife, shield laws protect journalists from having to reveal the name of a confidential source in a legal proceeding. Most states have adopted shield laws of varying leniency, but the federal government has not.

The Nature of Media Coverage of Politics and Government

6-5 Analyze the nature of media coverage of politics and government.

What kind of information do Americans get from their news sources? Because of the diversity of the media, the kinds of stories they cover, and the high variance in quality of news information, the answer is not simple. Nonetheless, there are a few general trends. Next we'll examine both the subjects that are covered and how the media covers them.

The media devote most of their attention to explaining and interpreting the president's actions.

When covering national politics, the media focus primarily on the president, the White House staff, and the executive branch. Collectively, they are the subject of about 70 percent of government news coverage by national and local newspapers and about 80 percent of the government news coverage on the network news. Congress receives the next highest level of coverage, with about "one-in-four discussions of government in the print press and one-in-six on television."[43] The judiciary receives so little coverage as to be almost an afterthought, except when a new Supreme Court justice is nominated. Then the confirmation hearings can hold the nation's rapt attention.

TALKING TO THEMSELVES
Evidence shows that reporters tend to receive significantly more air time than the subjects they are covering, and that news shows often interview media figures and other talking heads instead of their news subjects.

Reporters receive much more airtime than candidates do.

The second trend in media coverage is that in presidential election coverage on television, reporters tend to get substantially more camera time than the actual candidates. In the 2000 presidential election campaign, for example, reporters accounted for 74 percent of spoken airtime, Al Gore and George W. Bush accounted for 11 percent, and other sources accounted for 15 percent.[44] These numbers indicate that reporters assume a prominent mediating role in election coverage as they report and analyze what candidates say.[45]

Since Vietnam and Watergate, TV coverage of politics has become conspicuously cynical.

The third media trend is that media coverage of politics and government has assumed an increasingly skeptical—even cynical—tone.[46] Most media historians date this trend to the late 1960s and early 1970s, coincident with the Vietnam War and the Watergate scandal.[47] These two events convinced many reporters that government officials were capable of dishonesty and corruption on a scale previously unthinkable, and the media had let them get away with such behavior for too long. To this day, journalists frequently cast politicians in a negative light or quote sources who do. In addition, social media, especially blogs, have allowed journalists to share information and commentary faster than ever before. In real time, they can write a scathing remark about a political figure, which in seconds can be read by anyone.

NEW WAYS TO GET THE MESSAGE OUT
Although campaigns continue to spend millions of dollars putting their ads on television, they can also easily post them on Internet sites like YouTube. Online video sharing sites have also become an easy way for campaigns and their supporters to post other sorts of videos that support their candidate or embarrass an opponent.

TV coverage generally focuses on strategy over substance.

Yet another trend is that television coverage of elections tends to neglect substantive matters, such as the content of policy proposals, candidates' positions on issues, and politicians' voting records. Instead, the focus often is on the **horse race**—who is up or down in the latest polls, what is happening behind the scenes, who has committed the latest gaffe or landed a rhetorical blow, and which candidates are winning a competitive advantage. Such reporting is also referred to as "strategy frame coverage" because it sometimes treats elections purely as a competitive game for power or a contest of political strategies rather than policy ideas.

horse race a focus in election coverage on who and what are up or down in the latest poll numbers.

Why do television reporters prefer this kind of coverage? It may simply be that reporters, and viewers, find such stories more entertaining than the dry stuff of policy papers and voting records.[48] Such coverage may also reflect the cynicism referred to above.[49] Reporters may believe that stories on tactics and behind-the-scenes discussions shed light on what is really driving a campaign (as opposed to what candidates and their handlers say is driving the campaign). Furthermore, candidates' issue positions and policy proposals do not change from day to day, but poll numbers, political tactics, and politicians' behavior can change on a daily basis, so they get reported as news.

Evidence of a media bias is mixed.

bias favorable treatment to certain politicians, policy positions, groups, and political outcomes.

One enduring debate among observers of American politics is whether media coverage of politics and government exhibits **bias**—that is, favorable treatment to certain politicians, policy positions, groups, and political outcomes. Certain aspects of the American media are decidedly and unapologetically partisan, but that is not evidence of media bias. The media's objectivity ethic—its stated commitment to avoid partisan or political bias—applies only to hard news reporting, not to commentaries or editorials.

But what about journalists, television programs, newspapers, news magazines, radio programs, Internet sites, and other news outlets that are supposedly devoted primarily to reporting the basic facts of the news in an objective manner? Do the media favor some political figures and outcomes over others? Some media critics argue that the media favor Republicans and conservatives at the expense of Democrats and liberals, while others argue just the opposite.

In the debate over media bias, much of the evidence is anecdotal—that is, it is based on a few isolated examples that may or may not represent overall media coverage. An organization called Fairness and Accuracy in Reporting (FAIR), for example, has produced studies indicating that conservative think

Case Study

Obama Versus Fox News

As long as there has been a United States president, there has been friction between that office and the press. But there have been times when that long-standing rivalry has taken some unusually mean turns. Newspaper editorials savaged Abraham Lincoln during the Civil War, calling him a "blockhead," a "moron," and a "widow maker." The majority of daily newspapers, led by the powerful *Chicago Tribune*, politically opposed Franklin Roosevelt. Richard Nixon took the *New York Times* and the *Washington Post* all the way to the Supreme Court over the Pentagon Papers, when he tried

OBAMA VERSUS FOX Frustrated with the tone of the network's coverage, the Obama administration picked a fight with Fox News.

and failed to stop those newspapers from publishing the government's secret reports on Vietnam. Later, it was the *Post* that kept up the investigation of the Watergate scandal, which eventually brought down the Nixon presidency.

In the fall of 2009, Barack Obama began his own conflict with Fox News, a cable network started by Republican strategist Roger Ailes in 1996 that focuses on opinion journalism and leans to the conservative side of American politics. Fox News was harshly critical of Obama's young

Case Study Obama Versus Fox News

presidency. After a hugely successful campaign a year earlier, tremendous popularity in the polls, and with a large Democratic majority in both houses of Congress, the administration thought it was in a position to force its opponents in the media to cave in. But the new president would quickly learn what previous administrations had learned before: taking on a free press in the United States in head-to-head combat is rarely a winning proposition. This skirmish also came at a time when the entire landscape of the news media in America was in the midst of a seismic makeover. Newspapers were losing their influence, and alternative media, like the Internet and cable news channels, were changing the basic assumptions about how Americans get their information.

From the beginning of the Obama administration in January 2009, Fox News focused much of its airtime on the new president's policies in a more critical way than the other news outlets, which were accused by conservative critics of being too supportive of the White House. It was Fox News that broke the story that one of the administration's appointees, Van Jones, had a more radical past than many Americans were comfortable with. Jones quickly resigned, but the appointment was an embarrassment to the White House. Similarly, Fox broadcasted a tape of White House Communications Director Anita Dunn singling out Chinese Communist leader Mao Zedong as someone she admired. She would soon be gone as well.

In September 2009, the White House launched a counterattack against Fox. In a direct shot aimed at Fox News, President Obama appeared on every major news channel except Fox. Anita Dunn said that "Fox News often operates as either the research arm or the communications arm of the Republican Party." In an attempt to further cut off Fox, the Fox News White House correspondent was excluded from an interview with an administration economist. In addition, one Democratic consultant who regularly appeared on Fox was even warned by the White House to stay off the network.

By March 2010, Fox News' two major personalities, Bill O'Reilly and Glen Beck, respectively, enjoyed a 28 and 50 percent increase in ratings from a year earlier.[50] The Obama Administration gained nothing, and it came at a time when the president's popularity ratings slipped as well. Clearly, the White House had miscalculated. In the words of the old newspaper maxim, often attributed to Mark Twain: "Never get into a fight with someone who buys ink by the barrel."

Thinking Critically

1. Why is there generally friction between the media and the president? How, if at all, is this friction different from that experienced by legislators and the press?

2. Is it possible for an openly partisan network to cover political officials without bias? Why or why not?

---

tanks are cited more often in the media than left-leaning ones.[51] On the other hand, the Center for Media and Public Affairs found that in the 2008 election, Barack Obama received the most favorable coverage of any general election candidate for the presidency since 1980.[52]

Obviously, by choosing issues, media outlets, and time periods selectively, one can produce evidence of both liberal and conservative media bias. The question, however, is whether a comprehensive analysis across a broad range of issues, a wide variety of media outlets, and a substantial time period would indicate systematic bias. Ultimately, the proof is in the actual content of media reporting.

One way to assess the content is to ask journalists themselves what they think of it. In a survey of more than 1,700 newspaper journalists, the American Society of Newspaper Editors asked the following question: "Thinking about how your newspaper tends to cover particular social or political groups, is that coverage sometimes too favorable or sometimes unfavorable?"

TABLE 6-1 Newspaper Journalists' Self-Assessments

Journalists are more likely than the general public to call themselves liberal.

Ideological Self-Rating	General Public	National Press	Local Press
Liberal	20%	32%	23%
Moderate	35%	53%	58%
Conservative	35%	8%	14%
Don't know	10%	7%	5%
	100%	100%	100%

Note: Figures for general public from August 2008 Pew Media Believability Study (N=1800)
Source: www.stateofthemedia.org.

The reporters indicated that they report less favorably on conservatives than on liberals. However, the same reporters indicated that the military and the wealthy, two groups usually associated with the American right, received overly favorable coverage. Similarly, poor people and labor union members, groups usually associated with the left, appeared to receive disproportionately unfavorable coverage. Still, a series of surveys conducted over more than 40 years has shown journalists to be more liberal than conservative, and to be more liberal than the average American (see Table 6-1 for the results from a 2008 survey).[53]

Advocates of the survey approach argue that reporters' political predispositions inevitably make their way into news stories, leading to biased reporting. Others argue that there is no correlation between journalists' personal beliefs and the content of their reporting. First, they note that journalists are trained to set aside their personal predispositions when reporting on politics and government. Second, they say that the economics of the media industry are designed to drive out biased coverage. Third, they argue that although many reporters may exhibit liberal tendencies, publishers and owners of radio, television, and print media outlets, being businesspeople, are presumed to exhibit more conservative views. Somewhere, then, in the balance between reporters' and owners' politics, the media get the story right.

Media Effects on Public Opinion

6-6   Assess the effect of the media on political attitudes and behaviors.

To what extent does the content of mass media coverage affect public opinion? The early research on this subject was prompted by startling demonstrations of the power of mass media in the 1920s, 1930s, and 1940s. An early instance was the panic following news of the stock market crash in 1929. Next was the rise of fascist dictators Benito Mussolini in Italy and Adolf Hitler in Germany. Both men cultivated popular support through radio addresses and newsreels that carried their fiery speeches to enraptured crowds. Observing these events,

THE POWER OF THE MEDIA

When Orson Welles performed the radio play *War of the Worlds*, millions of Americans heard the broadcast and actually thought the United States was under alien invasion. This event and the massive newspaper coverage that it received suggested that people could be moved by the media to believe just about anything. How much do you think you are influenced by mass media?

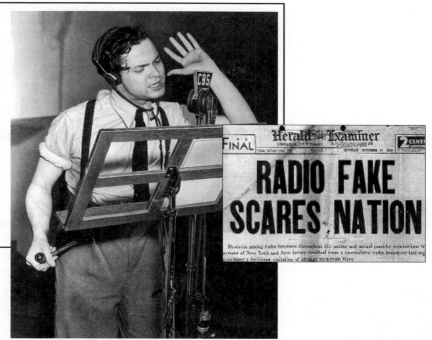

scholars worried that clever use of the mass media could enable leaders to inject the masses with supportive attitudes the way a hypodermic needle injects a patient with medicine.

Early research into the impact of media pointed to minimal effects.

Researchers in the United States first investigated the effects of the mass media on voting behavior. These seminal voting studies conducted in the 1940s and 1950s revealed an electorate surprisingly unaffected by media coverage. The studies found most voters were party loyalists whose votes could not be swayed by media messages. Partisanship and other political predispositions were so strong, in fact, that large majorities of voters in the 1950s and 1960s made their voting decisions before the general election campaign and the related media coverage even began.[54] Thus, changes in voting intent as a result of mass media exposure were relatively rare.

This finding in the early literature came to be referred to as **minimal effect**. For years, media scholars accepted the minimal effect conclusion, although many found it unsatisfying. One researcher explained the scholars' dilemma as follows:

minimal effect the theory that change in voting intent as a result of mass media exposure is relatively rare.

> The mass media have been a source of great frustration to social scientists. On one hand, citizens in modern democracies routinely develop opinions about

political events and personalities far beyond their direct experience. It is hard to imagine where many of these opinions come from if not from the mass media. And yet it has proven maddeningly difficult to demonstrate that the mass media actually produce powerful effects on opinion.[55]

Ultimately, scholars were able to demonstrate that the media's effect is more than minimal. But to do so, they had to overcome certain assumptions about the kinds of effects they should be looking for and how such effects might work.

The media may exert influence through agenda-setting and priming.

Early researchers into media effects focused on persuasion, or changing someone's mind about an issue, person, or group. But the media can also play a role in political socialization; in educating the public with basic information about politics, government, issues, groups, and candidates; in stimulating or discouraging political participation among the public; in helping to crystallize or reinforce existing beliefs and predispositions; and in determining which issues the public and policy makers consider important, or agenda-setting.

Of these topics, **agenda-setting**—determining which issues are considered important—has been highly influential in shaping political scientists' thinking about media effects. The issues that the media cover the most extensively are in turn the issues that the public considers most important. By covering some issues and ignoring others, the media help determine which issues the public considers important.

Researchers have also demonstrated **priming**, a media effect in which the public assesses the performance of politicians and candidates in terms of the issues that the media have emphasized. Imagine, for example, that the media devote extensive coverage to the issue of welfare fraud. If the public begins to evaluate the performance of the president in terms of what he is doing or not doing about welfare fraud, that is evidence of priming.

The media draw the attention of policy makers as well. But, research in this area has not been as thorough, and the conclusions not as strong, as studies of the effect that the media have on what gets on the public's policy agenda. Furthermore, the research often suggests a two-way relationship: media coverage affects policy makers' agendas, but policy makers' agendas also affect what the media cover.[56]

Three primary phenomena may limit the media's influence on attitudes and behaviors.

The early media effects research tended to assume that with enough exposure to a particular media message, individuals would eventually accept it. But this assumption was inconsistent with theories and findings from the fields of communications and psychology. Three phenomena limit the ability of media to influence attitudes and behaviors.

Thinking Causally Why are the effects of media on individuals' beliefs and opinions difficult to determine?

agenda-setting the ability to shape which issues the public considers important, by covering some issues and ignoring others.

priming a media effect in which the public assesses the performance of politicians and candidates in terms of the issues that the media have emphasized.

The first is **selective exposure**, the tendency of people to expose themselves to information that is in accord with their beliefs. The fragmented and increasingly partisan world of cable and Internet coverage of politics enables people to avoid information and arguments that might upset their belief system—and potentially change their opinions. This phenomenon has an important impact on the effect of Web-based communications and talk radio. Individuals have to deliberately expose themselves to or actively seek out information from the Web or from a talk radio station. These sources may mobilize and energize base supporters, but because people probably already agree with the source, the persuasive effects are likely to be severely limited.

selective exposure the tendency of people to expose themselves to information that is in accord with their beliefs.

The second phenomenon is **selective perception**, the tendency of individuals to interpret information in ways consistent with their beliefs. Consider the debates held during presidential election campaigns. Republicans and Democrats watch the very same debates, but Republicans inevitably conclude that the Republican performed better, and Democrats conclude that the Democrat performed better. In part, this is a consequence of selective perception.

Thinking Causally Why do the media seem able to influence the attitudes and opinions of some individuals more than others?

selective perception the tendency of individuals to interpret information in ways consistent with their beliefs.

Finally, there is **selective retention**, the tendency of individuals to recall information that is consistent with existing beliefs and to discard information that runs counter to them. An admirer of President Ronald Reagan and his supply-side economics, for example, would recall the significant tax cuts enacted in Reagan's first and second terms but might well forget the substantial tax increases that were also enacted during Reagan's first term.

selective retention the tendency of individuals to recall information that is consistent with existing beliefs and to discard information that runs counter to them.

Selective exposure, selective perception, and selective retention all limit the impact that the mass media can have on individual attitudes. If people are inclined to see, hear, interpret, and retain only information that reinforces their existing beliefs, it becomes more difficult for the media to produce a large-scale attitude change.

Exposure, comprehension, and receptivity are preconditions for media effects.

Discovering the consequences of selective exposure, perception, and retention led political scientists to approach the study of media effects differently. Rather than simply assuming a direct link between the content of media messages and public opinion, they began studying the necessary preconditions for a message to change opinion. One of these is *exposure*—whether a person actually sees, hears, or reads a particular media message. Another is *comprehension*, understanding a message to which one has been exposed. A third is *receptivity*, which refers to an individual's openness to accepting a message communicated through the media. Without exposure, comprehension, and receptivity, an individual cannot be influenced by a media message.

Moderately attentive and predisposed individuals are most likely to feel media influence.

In *The Nature and Origins of Mass Opinion*, political scientist John Zaller argues that the likelihood of exposure to and comprehension of a media message depends largely on **political attentiveness**, an individual's general attention to and knowledge of politics.[57] An individual who is highly attentive to and knowledgeable about politics is likely to be exposed to, and understand, most politically oriented media messages. On the other hand, someone who pays little attention to politics and understands little of the political world will either miss most political messages in the media or fail to understand them if he or she should happen to come across them.

Receptivity also depends on one's **political predisposition**—the interests, values, and experiences that help organize one's thinking about politics. Someone who has very strong political predispositions is unlikely to be receptive to media messages that contradict those predispositions. For example, someone who is firmly convinced that U.S. troops should be used only to guard America's borders is unlikely to be receptive to media messages indicating the need for a deployment of troops to, say, Libya.

These insights have many interesting implications. Since data indicate that the most politically attentive individuals also tend to have the strongest political predispositions, individuals who are most likely to be exposed to and comprehend media messages (people who are most politically attentive) are least likely to be persuaded by them (because they have the strongest predispositions). The reverse is also true. Figure 6-1 illustrates these relationships.

Who, then, are the most likely candidates for political persuasion by the media? People right in the middle—that is, individuals with a medium level of political attentiveness and political dispositions of medium strength. They

political attentiveness an individual's general attention to and knowledge of politics.

Thinking Causally What factors might influence an individual's ability to receive and process media messages?

political predisposition the interests, values, and experiences that help organize one's thinking about politics.

FIGURE 6-1 Probability of Comprehending and Being Influenced by a Political Message.

Those most likely to be influenced by the media are less likely to be exposed to and understand media messages.

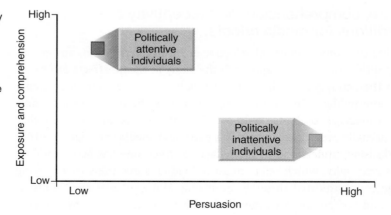

will not be exposed to and comprehend every message that comes through the media, but they will encounter and understand many of them. And when they do, their political predispositions will be flexible enough to accept many of these messages.

Zaller does not argue that this middle group is the only one that can be influenced by the media or that the media always influence this middle group. In some cases, when a message is particularly prominent, even the least attentive person will be unable to miss it. The massive increase in President George W. Bush's job approval ratings after the September 11, 2001, terrorist attacks reflected the fact that everyone—from the most politically attentive to the least—had gotten the message about the attacks and the administration's strong response. If a message is relatively "quiet," opinion change can still take place, but it will bypass all except the most politically attentive.

If we think in these terms, it becomes relatively easy to identify areas in which the media can have a large impact and those in which the impact is likely to be limited. For example, we know now that predispositions limit people's receptivity to media messages. If we want to look for media effects, then, we should look for cases in which predispositions are weak. Think, for example, about primary elections in which no incumbent is running—the 2008 Republican and Democratic presidential primaries, for example. In each primary race, all of the candidates were of the same party. Party identification, therefore, was useless as a tool for judging candidates. Furthermore, many of the candidates were unfamiliar to the public at large when the primary season began. Without partisanship and previous information about the candidates to draw on, voter predispositions toward candidates were weak. Accordingly, the potential for media influence was greatly enhanced. In fact, research has shown that the media do exert a strong influence on voter judgments during the presidential primary process.[58]

On the other hand, consider a case in which policy maker and media discussions of an issue are largely balanced between a "pro" side and a "con" side. The general election between Republican and Democratic candidates for president usually fits this model. The campaigns and their supporters have roughly equal amounts of money to spend on their message, and the mainstream media present broadly balanced coverage of the campaigns. Under these circumstances, even if there were universal exposure to "the message," a balanced message would not challenge anyone's political predispositions because it would not convey a strong point of view. It would be unlikely, therefore, to result in large-scale opinion change.[59] Note, however, that in a country as closely politically divided as the United States, even small shifts in public opinion can have significant consequences.

Media effects can be found if you look in the right places.

Scholars may have failed to find large media effects because they may have been looking in the wrong places.

- First, we now know that to find media effects scholars should look for opinion change among people with moderate levels of political attentiveness and only moderately strong political predispositions.

- Second, opinion change occurs most often when the message is "loud"—that is, when it is covered thoroughly, by a number of media outlets, for a long period of time.

- Third, a media message that carries a largely one-sided point of view is more likely to lead to opinion change than balanced coverage.

- Fourth, opinion change occurs when media messages do not fit neatly with existing political predispositions. Recall the example of media coverage of presidential primary elections, in which partisanship and thorough knowledge of the candidates are generally not available to bolster predispositions.

- Fifth, opinion change results from media messages to which people are most likely to be exposed.

- Sixth, opinion change takes two forms—gross and net. In an extreme example, imagine a society divided into two equal-sized groups—Group A and Group B. One hundred percent of Group A approves of the job the president is doing, while zero percent of Group B approves. This equal split puts the president's overall job approval at 50 percent. Imagine, though, that in a moment of weakness the president reveals to reporters that he finds members of Group A annoying and unattractive but finds members of Group B delightful and easy on the eyes. The media provide blanket coverage of the president's verbal indiscretion and the president's job approval falls to zero in Group A but rises to 100 percent in Group B. The president's overall approval rating remains at 50 percent, so there has been no net change, but there has been massive gross change, that is, change within Group A and Group B. By concentrating solely on net change, researchers can miss large but offsetting gross changes in opinion within subgroups of the population.

- Finally, if a media message is particularly "quiet" or largely balanced between two sides, look for opinion change only among the most politically attentive.

Chapter Summary

In this chapter you have learned to:

6-1   Define public opinion, and outline the process and agents of political socialization.

Public opinion is a subject at the heart of democratic theory, and it has four basic traits: salience, stability, direction, and intensity. Political socialization is the process by which citizens acquire the values and attitudes that shape their thinking about politics. It tends to be governed by two important principles: primacy and persistence, both of which point to the importance of early childhood learning. There are several phases of socialization from early childhood all the way through young adulthood, and the development of ideological thinking demonstrates increased political sophistication. Socialization occurs through specific agents of socialization and socializing events. Although the family is foremost among agents of socialization, socializing events include generational effects, period effects, and life cycle effects.

6-2   Establish how American democracy functions despite the public's low levels of political knowledge.

American public opinion collectively makes sense in many cases. Despite the lack of political knowledge and sophistication at the individual level, collective opinion is often rational, ordered, and predictable. A number of shortcuts and devices enable the American public to communicate to policy makers a collectively ordered, rational set of preferences.

6-3   Evaluate the unique role that the media play in American politics and society.

The U.S. mass media are largely privately owned; there are different views about objectivity and taking sides; and the American media play a watchdog role. The American media also operate with relative freedom, including freedom from prior restraint.

6-4   Identify the legal constraints on American media.

Despite their relative press freedom, the American media do operate under some constraints, including laws against defamation, the "equal time" rule, and the limited protection of shield laws. These limits are minor compared to those faced by American journalists in earlier centuries, when the media operated under much stricter government control. Beginning in the 1930s, this situation changed dramatically with a series of U.S. Supreme Court decisions expanding press freedoms.

6-5   Analyze the nature of media coverage of politics and government.

A few principles govern broadcast media coverage of American politics and government and distinguish broadcast media from other media sources. These include the tendency to focus on the president to the exclusion of Congress and the courts; the mediating role played by reporters in news coverage of elections; the negative tone of much television news coverage; and the tendency of television news to focus on the "horse race" and campaign strategies rather than candidates' policy positions and voting records. An enduring debate among observers of American politics is whether media coverage of politics and government exhibits bias. Much of the evidence is anecdotal.

6-6   Assess the effect of the media on political attitudes and behaviors.

Early studies of media influence focused on voting behavior and produced evidence of only minimal effects. More recent studies of agenda-setting, framing, and priming have revealed more instances of media influence. However, selective exposure, selective perception, and selective retention limit media influence on attitudes and behavior. Research has also shown that individuals who are only moderately attentive to media coverage are likely to be the most influenced.

CHAPTER TEST

1. Explain the four basic traits of public opinion.

2. What is political socialization? And what are the major agents and events that contribute to political socialization?

3. How can surveys accurately reflect the opinions of Americans?

4. What is the miracle of aggregation? How can it provide meaningful information to politicians and others who seek to understand American public opinion?

5. What types of legal constraints are placed on the American media?

6. What are the conditions that make it most likely an individual will be influenced by media messages?

7. Which major institution of government receives the largest amount of media focus? Why?

8. Why do the media often focus on the horse race and strategy over substance?

9. Are the media biased? Why or why not?

10. In what ways do the media serve agenda-setting and priming functions? Which three phenomena may limit the media's influence on attitudes and behaviors?

MyPoliSciLab® POLITICAL OPINION AND THE MEDIA
Apply what you learned in this chapter on MyPoliSciLab.

Read on mypoliscilab.com

eText: Chapter 6

Study and **Review** on mypoliscilab.com

Pre-Test
Post-Test
Chapter Exam
Flashcards

Watch on mypoliscilab.com

Video: Obama Approval Rating
Video: The Pentagon's Media Message
How Do We Know Video: Do people react to coverage of events or to the events themselves?

Explore on mypoliscilab.com

Comparative: Comparing Governments and Public Opinion
Comparative: Comparing News Media
Simulation: You Are a Polling Consultant
Simulation: You Are the News Editor
Timeline: Three Hundred Years of American Mass Media
Timeline: War, Peace and Public Opinion

KEY TERMS

agenda-setting, p. 180
bias, p. 176
direction, p. 157
generational effect, p. 161

horse race, p. 175
ideology, p. 158
intensity, p. 157
life cycle effect, p. 161

margin of error, p. 165
mass media or media, p. 168
minimal effect, p. 179
miracle of aggregation, p. 166

nonresponse bias, p. 165
opinion leaders, p. 166
period effect, p. 161
persistence, p. 158
political attentiveness, p. 182
political predisposition, p. 182
political socialization, p. 158

primacy, p. 158
priming, p. 180
prior restraint, p. 170
public opinion, p. 157
random sample, p. 165
salience, p. 157
sampling, p. 165

sampling error, p. 165
selective exposure, p. 181
selective perception, p. 181
selective retention, p. 181
stability, p. 157
watchdog, p. 170

SUGGESTED READINGS

Robert Erickson and Kent Tedin. 2005. *American Public Opinion: Its Origins, Content, and Impact*. New York: Longman. An excellent text that covers a wide range of information about the measurement, nature, and importance of public opinion.

Shanto Iyengar and Donald R. Kinder. 1989. *News That Matters: Television and American Opinion*. Chicago: University of Chicago Press. The ways in which television news programs set agendas, order priorities, shape opinions, and affect Americans' participation in political life.

Morris Fiorina. 2006. *Culture War? The Myth of a Polarized America*. New York: Longman. Argues that Americans are not nearly as divided on major political issues as many commentators claim.

James Stimson. 2004. *Tides of Consent: How Public Opinion Shapes American Politics*. Cambridge: Cambridge University Press. Although the public rarely engages in politics, when public opinion is aroused, major changes in policy result.

John Zaller. 1992. *The Nature and Origins of Mass Opinion*. New York: Cambridge University Press. Argues that people sample from a mix of political considerations in their head when confronted with the need to make political decisions or share political attitudes.

SUGGESTED WEBSITES

GALLUP
www.gallup.com

Gallup conducts regular public opinion polls on timely topics.

THE PEW RESEARCH CENTER FOR THE PEOPLE AND THE PRESS
people-press.org

The Pew Center is an independent opinion research group that studies attitudes toward the press, politics, and public policy issues. Pew conducts regular national surveys to measure public attentiveness to major news stories. This site provides links to recent surveys.

POLLSTER.COM
www.pollster.com

Taking advantage of the proliferation of publicly released polls, this site aggregates and tracks public opinion across a wide range of issues. It features expert commentary on the practice of polling and clear graphical presentation of data.

ABC NEWS POLITICAL PUNCH
blogs.abcnews.com/politicalpunch/

A political blog by Jake Tapper, ABC News senior White House correspondent, with sometimes controversial remarks on politics and the White House.

BRITISH BROADCASTING CORPORATION
www.bbc.co.uk/info

The BBC, a public service broadcaster established by Royal Charter, is publicly owned and operated.

Political Participation, Voting, and Elections

GORE WINS! Television network executives had to explain to the American people why they made not one but two mistaken calls in Florida before deciding the race was too close to call.

CHAPTER LEARNING OBJECTIVES

After reading this chapter you will be able to:

7-1 Analyze the costs and benefits of political participation for individuals and groups.

7-2 Identify the different kinds of political activities in which Americans participate.

7-3 Explain the main factors that influence political participation.

7-4 Outline election procedures, such as how candidates are nominated and how winners are determined.

7-5 Identify the key factors that determine how voters make electoral choices.

7-6 Assess the key factors that determine the outcome of presidential elections.

When Americans woke up on the day after the 2000 election, they did not know who their next president would be. After all was said and done, a number of people had a lot of explaining to do. Television network executives had to explain why they made not one, but two mistaken calls in Florida (first calling the state for Democratic Vice President Gore, then for George W. Bush) before finally saying it was too close to call. Voting machine manufacturers and election officials had to explain the high number of spoiled (uncountable) ballots across the entire country. The Democratic election supervisor in Palm Beach County, Florida, had to explain the confusing butterfly ballot design, which many voters claimed had caused them to vote unwittingly for the independent candidate Pat Buchanan. Supreme Court justices had to explain their controversial ruling, which ended the Democrats' legal challenges. And Al Gore had to explain why he had not won the election in a landslide, given his association with eight years of peace and prosperity under the Clinton administration.

Lost among the errant network calls, confusing ballots, and novel legal rulings was another embarrassing fact—embarrassing, at least, for political scientists. Using analysis that had proved highly reliable in previous presidential elections, a panel of political scientists at an American Political Science Association conference had uniformly predicted that Gore would beat Bush.[1] "It's not even going to be close," one had confidently proclaimed.[2]

What went wrong in 2000 and right in all those other years? The types of analysis used to predict elections share some basic characteristics. First, they assume that party identification determines individual vote choice. When more voters go into an election identifying with one party more than another, that party will have an advantage. In the 2000 election year, more members of the electorate identified themselves as Democrats than as Republicans.

Second, the models also assume that voters cast their ballots retrospectively, selecting candidates based on their or their party's past performance. The 2000 election came after nearly a decade of robust economic growth, presided over by a Democratic administration. Since voters' retrospective judgment of the Democrats' performance was generally positive, according to the theory, it should have been reflected more widely in the popular vote. In 2008, the economy was in trouble and voters were dissatisfied with the Bush administration. In 2010, voters were holding the Obama administration and the Democrats accountable for high unemployment and difficult economic times.

So, while the results in 2008 and 2010 seem to make sense, what happened in 2000? Did Al Gore blow the election? Or did political scientists blow their predictions? In order to answer these questions, in this chapter we will examine the factors that influence political participation and that also determine individual vote choice and collective election outcomes—not just party identification and incumbent performance, but also the nature of the candidates' campaigns, their issue positions, and voter assessments of them as individuals. ■

The Paradox of Political Participation

7-1 Analyze the costs and benefits of political participation for individuals and groups.

If you have ever voted on Election Day, volunteered for a political campaign, or written a letter to a public official advocating a certain position, you had to make a decision beforehand about whether these actions were worth your time and effort. Many people in America engage in these sorts of activities, but just as many—and usually more—choose not to.[3] Political scientists have studied why some people get involved in politics and others do not. These political scientists believe that decisions about whether or not to participate in politics depend in large part on individual evaluations about the costs and benefits of political activity.

Citizens weigh costs and benefits in deciding whether to vote.

Although we will illustrate the cost/benefit concept with voting, the basic logic we outline here holds for other sorts of political activities. Assume that your decision about whether or not to vote depends on your weighing the relative costs and benefits of voting. First, consider the costs of voting. These costs include the time and effort required for you to register to vote or to update your registration, to travel to a polling place, to wait in line, to cast your vote, and perhaps the most time-consuming aspect, learning enough about the different candidates and issues to make educated choices. Now, consider the benefits. If your vote helps elect your preferred candidate, some or all of his or her policies—policies that you support—will be adopted. The final element in your decision involves a comparison of the costs and benefits of voting. If the benefits to you outweigh the costs, you will vote. If they do not, you will stay at home.

It is unlikely that a single individual will influence an election outcome or political decision.

Initially, it is likely that the potential benefits of voting would seem to outweigh the costs and you would decide to vote. But, what if your candidate could win without your vote? Then you could enjoy all of the benefits of voting—specifically, the policy changes that your candidate will bring about when he or she wins—without experiencing any of the costs. And, if that were true, why would you bother voting?

Looking at the history of elections, even local elections with very few voters involved, it is exceedingly rare that an election is decided by a single vote. In fact, for all intents and purposes, you can assume before any particular election that your vote will not decide the outcome. Whether you stay home or cast your ballot, the election result will be the same. From this perspective it makes no sense for you to vote ever. Yet every Election Day, Americans vote by the millions. That they do so, even though they could enjoy the benefits of voting without bearing the costs of casting a ballot, is the paradox of voting. This paradox applies to other types of political participation, too. For this reason, the paradox of voting really can be considered a paradox of participation.

There are a number of possible solutions to the paradox of participation.

Of course, people do put forward the effort of political participation every day, in all walks of life, and in many different kinds of activities. This effort leaves political scientists to resolve the paradox of participation—the fact that people participate in politics, even though the impact of their individual participation would seem far too small to matter.

Thinking Causally Why do people participate in politics even when their participation is unlikely to be the final decisive difference between success and failure?

One argument is that citizens worry that other individuals will make the same decision they make. If all citizens were to make the same calculation, then democracy would be threatened because no one would participate. Not wanting democracy to collapse, at least some citizens decide to participate.[4]

But there is another possible resolution of the paradox: individuals may think about benefits of voting other than the immediate election. A candidate's victory or defeat is what political scientists call a **collective benefit**—everyone gets to enjoy it, whether they vote or not. But political scientists have also identified what can be called **selective benefits** of voting—benefits that only voters get to enjoy.[5] The most frequently mentioned selective benefit is that only those who vote get to experience the satisfaction of having fulfilled their civic duty. For those who actually show up to vote on Election Day, this benefit is enough to outweigh the costs associated with voting.[6]

collective benefit a benefit everyone enjoys, regardless of whether they contributed to its attainment.

selective benefit benefit that can be accessed only by those who participate in or contribute to group activity.

Cost-benefit analysis can help us understand who participates.

The cost-benefit approach can be extremely useful in understanding why some people participate in politics and others do not. There is evidence that people behave as if they are taking into account, if not making precise calculations about, costs and benefits in their heads, even if political scientists do not quite understand how or why this works. For example, in a large-scale survey of Americans who regularly participate in a variety of political activities, 61 percent said that one of the reasons they vote is "the chance to influence government policy."[7]

People are more likely to participate when expected costs are low. For example, it is easy to register to vote because registration deadlines are now closer to Election Day and opportunities to register are more plentiful. In these circumstances, potential voters need not do much advance planning. People are also more likely to vote when they can easily absorb the costs of voting and afford the cost of the time it takes to become informed: for example, when they can afford to hire a babysitter so they can get to the polls, or can afford to pay for magazines or cable television programming that will help them understand election issues.

As for expected benefits, participation in elections (typically dubbed voter turnout) is likely to be higher when the collective benefits are greater and lower when they are smaller. When, for example, the election is for the county registrar of deeds, then the expected benefit of one candidate or the other winning is unclear to many potential voters. As a result, turnout will likely be lower. If candidates seem very close on many issues, the expected benefit of voting will also be more difficult to discern, because regardless of which candidate wins, the policy outcomes would likely be quite similar. Or, if a particular candidate is running for office unopposed, the selective benefits derived from voting are negligible. Why? The sense of civic duty a voter feels and the satisfaction from doing one's duty are probably not as strong when the election has effectively been decided before Election Day.

HOW DO WE KNOW?

Why Is It So Difficult to Determine How Many People Vote on Election Day?

The Question

The 2008 presidential election is a great example of just how tricky it can be to get a precise figure on voter turnout. The Census Bureau's Current Population Survey, Voting and Registration Supplement, which gives information on voting behavior and trends based on surveys, indicates that the national turnout rate and registration rate decreased from 2004 to 2008, from 63.8 percent to 63.6 percent. These figures contradict aggregate findings that take into account actual voters and estimates of the voting eligible population that suggest that the turnout rate actually increased from 60.1 percent in 2004 to 61.7 percent in 2008.[8] Although both of these methods for determining turnout rates are reliable, they separately settle on different figures for the 2008 general election and come to diverse conclusions about trends in voter turnout. And although the 1.9 percent difference may seem small, it is rather a significant difference that illustrates just how difficult calculating turnout rates can be.

More generally, the success of democracy depends in part on popular participation in politics and government. Knowing how many people vote on Election Day gives an indication of whether the United States is thriving as a democracy or is struggling or even failing to live up to its democratic ideals. Because of the importance of this question, political scientists ask after every national election: How many people voted? How do we know?

Why It Matters

Voting is the most fundamental, most important act of democratic citizenship. Indeed, for government to be truly accountable to its citizens, those citizens must vote. They must express approval for policies and policy makers they like, and disapproval for those they do not. When voter turnout is high, we can be satisfied that this important part of American democracy is working as intended. When turnout is low, we may wish to consider reforms designed to stimulate registration and voting. Before weighing the merits of any of these reforms, however, we need to construct a valid, reliable measure of voter turnout in order to assess our progress—a far more challenging task than it seems.

HOW DO WE KNOW? Why Is It So Difficult to Determine How Many People Vote on Election Day?

Investigating the Answer

We want a measure of turnout that accurately tells us how many people voted on Election Day, that is consistent, and that produces comparable results from one election to the next, regardless of the particular characteristics of each election. Political scientists usually measure not the absolute number of voters who show up on Election Day (e.g., 125 million), but rather the turnout rate (for example, 50 percent). Calculating the turnout rate for an election entails dividing the number of people who voted in the election by the number of people who could have voted:

Turnout Rate = Actual Voters ÷ Potential Voters

So, for example, if 100 people could have voted in an election, but only 50 people actually did vote, the turnout rate would be 50 percent.

Although this is a seemingly straightforward exercise, several problems arise in performing a real-world calculation of turnout based on this formula. We have to decide whether potential voters are: (a) only those people who were registered to vote and therefore could have cast a ballot on Election Day, or (b) this first group, plus those people who failed to register and so were ineligible to vote, but nonetheless met all of the other legal requirements for voting. Most political scientists prefer to use the latter definition. If we were to use the registered voter measure, a situation could arise in which, say, only 30 percent of the eligible voting population was registered to vote, but 90 percent of those who were registered actually showed up on Election Day. In this case, turnout would be 90 percent—the kind of number we would like to see in a democracy. In actuality, though, only 27 percent of individuals eligible to vote would have shown up to cast a ballot (30 percent multiplied by 90 percent)—an unhealthy number. In addition, the population of registered voters has historically been subject to political manipulation. African Americans in particular were denied opportunities to register under the pre-1965 political system in the South because of literacy tests and poll taxes. Thus, if we used a registered-voter measure to calculate turnout in, say, the 1960 presidential election, we would be obscuring the fact that large numbers of Americans were effectively prohibited from turning out.

Finally, using a measure based on registered voters makes it difficult to compare turnout rates in the United States with those in other countries. Why? In the United States, individuals who wish to vote are responsible for registering themselves and then keeping their registration status up-to-date. In most other democracies, however, the government assumes responsibility for registering legal voters. In those countries, therefore, all individuals who are eligible to vote are registered. If we wish to compare turnout in these countries to U.S. turnout, we must make the comparison among equivalent groups. For purposes of comparing U.S. turnout to foreign turnout, therefore, it makes sense to use the entire eligible U.S. voter population.

There are also problems, however, with using the eligible-voter population. How do we know how many members of the U.S. population are eligible to vote? Statisticians estimate the number of eligible voters using census data on the "voting-age population," that is, the number of individuals 18 years of age or older living in the United States. But not everyone who lives in the U.S. is eligible to vote—citizens of other countries, for example, whether living in the United States legally or illegally, cannot vote in American elections. Furthermore, in some states convicted felons are legally prohibited from voting. But these groups, along with others who for one reason or another cannot vote, are all lumped into the pool of the voting-age population. At the same time, legally eligible American citizens living overseas are not counted as members of the voting-age population, because they do not live in the United States.

Despite these problems, many researchers—including most political scientists—typically rely on some measure of the U.S. voting-age population to determine the number of potential voters. In recent years, though, researchers have begun to refine their measures of the legally eligible voting population.[9] The Census Bureau, for example, has prepared an alternate measure that seeks to exclude noncitizens from the pool of potentially eligible voters.

Up to this point, we have addressed only half of the problem—how to measure the number of potential voters. But what about measuring the number of people

(continues)

HOW DO WE KNOW?   Why Is It So Difficult to Determine How Many People Vote on Election Day? *(continued)*

who actually vote? The most common way of doing this is simply to count up all of the ballots that are cast on Election Day. With one ballot per person, the number of ballots cast would represent the number of voters. It is surprisingly difficult, however, to get an accurate count of the number of ballots cast. As we learned from the 2000 presidential election in Florida, not all of the ballots cast are counted. This omission can result from voter error, machine error, mistakes by poll workers, or some combination of those factors. Though Florida attracted most of the attention in 2000, uncounted ballots are a problem nationwide. Across the country in 2000, for example, researchers have estimated that between 4 million and 6 million ballots were uncounted.[10]

Political scientists and assorted media outlets have pursued one other avenue in estimating the number of voters: public opinion surveys. In fact, surveys can be used to determine both parts of the turnout equation. For example, survey researchers could ask a nationally representative sample of voting-age adults: (a) whether they met the legal requirements to vote, and (b) whether they did, in fact, vote. Then, they could estimate turnout on the basis of the survey as follows:

Turnout Rate = Number of Survey Respondents Who Report Having Voted ÷ Number of Survey Respondents Legally Eligible to Vote

Unfortunately, as with all survey data, there are risks in using this approach. First, many surveys fail to draw a representative sample of the voting-age population. For example, if a survey is conducted by telephone, it will not include individuals without phones. Such people are likely to have lower incomes and are less likely to vote. If such individuals are omitted from telephone surveys, the resulting turnout calculations may be inflated. Similarly, surveys typically exclude residents of dormitories and others who exclusively use cell phones, thus excluding younger people, who are less likely to vote. Accordingly, excluding students from a survey sample could result in an overestimate of the turnout rate. Surveys also may overstate the number of people who actually cast a ballot. Studies comparing survey responses to actual voting records show that many survey respondents report having voted when they did not—perhaps because they

were embarrassed to admit to interviewers that they had not done their "civic duty."

The combination of these two problems—excluding low-turnout voters from the denominator and overstating the number of voters in the numerator—tends to result in an inflated turnout estimate. Even so, surveys are still among the best tools for studying turnout. Although turnout rates based on survey data may be inflated, political scientists are able to use even inflated rates to compare behavior among different demographic groups and to compare rates of turnout over time. For example, assume that a standard, nationally representative survey will overstate turnout by roughly 20 percentage points every year. If a turnout calculation based on survey data shows a turnout rate of 70 percent in one year, and then 75 percent four years later, we can be confident that turnout rose by about 5 percentage points. It does not matter that the overall turnout rates are overstated, as long as they are overstated by the same amount in each survey.

WHO COUNTS?
Constructing a valid, reliable measure of voter turnout is a far more challenging task than it seems. Should counts of potential voters include those who have failed to register to vote?

HOW DO WE KNOW? Why Is It So Difficult to Determine How Many People Vote on Election Day?

Thinking Critically

1. Can you think of other reasons, besides the ones stated above, that may account for the difficulty in calculating the actual number of real voters and eligible voters? How would you mitigate these factors?

2. Why might it be easier to calculate turnout rates in other countries?

3. As a political scientist, what steps would you take to ensure that you counted as many voters, or eligible voters, as possible? In other words, what methods best approximate the actual number of voters and eligible voters?

The Bottom Line

Even something as seemingly straightforward as measuring how many people vote in American elections presents difficult methodological issues. Nonetheless, recent work that takes into account the number of eligible voters—the voting-eligible population—makes us more confident that we are assessing the actual proportion of voters who turn-out to vote in any particular election. Furthermore, although surveys almost definitely overstate turnout in any one election, they are a useful way to look at trends over time and assess how particular groups behave, such as the young, old, rich, poor, strong partisans, or weak partisans.

The Nature and Extent of Political Participation in America

7-2   Identify the different kinds of political activities in which americans participate.

How many Americans participate in politics? The answer to that question varies, depending on the type of participation. In any mention of political participation, the activity that first comes to mind is voting. Although voting is the most common type of political activity, there are many other ways that citizens can participate in politics.

Each year, Americans typically participate in a variety of political activities other than voting (see Table 7-1). These include signing petitions, attending demonstrations, organizing or attending community meetings, joining political organizations, contacting government officials, volunteering for political campaigns, and contributing money to political campaigns.

Another form of nonvoting political participation is the social movement. Social movements are made up of informal alliances of groups or individuals for the purpose of enacting or resisting social change. They often include several other types of the nonvoting behavior discussed previously, such as joining and attending meetings of political organizations, contacting government officials, and participating in political protests. The civil rights movement of the 1950s and 1960s and the anti–Vietnam War movement of the 1960s and early 1970s are famously influential social movements.

TABLE 7-1 Participation in Politics Outside the Voting Booth

Type of Activity	Percentage of Americans Who Reported Participation in Politics During Previous Year
Discuss politics with family or friends	77.7
Volunteer	39.2
Work at/join organization to deal with community problem	30.6
Attend community meeting about school or community issue	22.8
Participate in protest	19.1
Contact public officials	18.5
Campaign contributions to party, candidate, or other group	14.9
Campaign-related activities (attend meeting, put up signs, etc.)	8.5
Attend campaign meetings, rallies, speeches, etc.	8

Source: Authors' analysis of 2008 National Election Study, electionstudies.org.

DUELING IMMIGRATION DEMONSTRATIONS

In 2010, the politics of immigration was in the news as Americans demanded more strict enforcement of immigration laws while others protested a new law passed in Arizona. The Arizona law made the failure to carry immigration documents a crime and gave law enforcement officers more broad powers to detain anyone suspected of being in the country illegally.

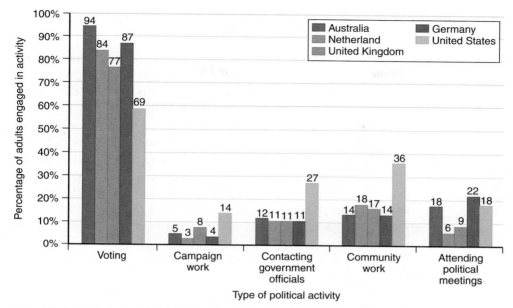

Source: Verba, Sidney, Kay Scholzman, and Henry Brady. 2006. *Voice and Equality*, Boston: Harvard University Press, p. 70.

FIGURE 7-1 Comparative Participation Rates in US and Other Western Democracies
The United States votes at lower rates than other countries but has higher rates of other types of political participation.

Although Americans have the reputation of being relatively inactive in politics, that reputation may be largely undeserved. Figure 7-1 compares levels of participation in various political activities across several countries. Only in voting do Americans lag substantially behind their peers in industrialized democracies. In the remaining four activities, American rates of participation either exceed or are roughly equivalent to those seen in other industrial democracies.

Factors That Influence Participation

7-3 Explain the main factors that influence political participation.

Political scientists have identified a number of factors that affect individuals' perceptions of the costs and benefits of participation, and therefore the likelihood that they will participate when presented with the opportunity. These include personal factors, legal factors, the political environment, and mobilization.

Personal factors have a critical impact on participation.

By a wide margin, the most important personal factor influencing political participation is **socioeconomic status (SES)** or a combination of an individual's occupation, income, and education levels. This factor has turned up as a highly significant predictor of participation in study after study, election after

socioeconomic status (SES) a combination of an individual's occupation, income, and education levels.

election. SES influences participation directly, but also through its impact on other factors that influence participation.

Socioeconomic status   Someone with a high-ranking professional position, a high income, and an advanced education has a high socioeconomic status. Someone who has a low socioeconomic status has a poor education, minimal specialized skills, and a job with low earnings.

Why should occupation level have an impact on political participation? In a high-level professional position, one normally cultivates the skills of writing, speaking, analyzing, and organizing. These **civic skills** translate handily into the political arena, where political activists often have to speak, write, persuade others, think on their feet, and organize events and individuals.

> **civic skills** the skills of writing, speaking, analyzing, and organizing that reduce the cost of political participation.

A large income clearly makes one type of political participation less costly—contributing money to political campaigns. Moreover, a substantial income also may bring one in contact with certain institutions—philanthropies, social clubs, and civic organizations—in which discussion of and participation in politics are common.

Education is not only the most important component of SES; it is one of the most important determinants of political participation generally. For one thing, education tends to give people access to better jobs and to more income. The classroom also provides instruction and practice in the skills critical for taking part in political life—reading, writing, speaking, organizing, and critical thinking. Lastly, a more advanced education level increases the likelihood that an individual has gained enough understanding of politics and government to believe that he or she can influence what happens in the political world, developing a sense of **political efficacy**.[11]

> **political efficacy** an individual's belief that he or she can influence what happens in the political world.

These qualities affect one's perception of the costs and benefits of political participation. Greater interest in politics results in more satisfaction from political activity. A sense of political efficacy also raises an individual's assessment of the benefits of participation. Finally, the knowledge about politics that education brings can help reduce the costs of getting involved.

Personal factors and voting behavior   In addition to socioeconomic status, civic skills, political efficacy, political interest, and political knowledge, a few other personal qualities can affect political participation. These include strength of political partisanship, age, and having intense feelings on particular issues, such as abortion or the death penalty.

Legal factors affect the cost of participation.

> **suffrage** the right to vote.

In the United States, **suffrage**—the right to vote—has become available to all citizens relatively recently. At various points in U.S. history, wealth, gender, race, age, and property ownership have all served as voting qualifications.

Until the 1820s, most men who did not own land, regardless of their race or ethnicity, were prohibited from voting. Although allowed to vote earlier in some states, women were not allowed the right to vote by federal law until ratification of the Nineteenth Amendment in 1920. Many African Americans were effectively barred from voting in a large segment of the country because of literacy tests until passage of the **Voting Rights Act of 1965.** Young people in the 18- through 20-year-old age range were not allowed to vote until passage of the Twenty-sixth Amendment in 1970.[12] Today, convicted felons and noncitizens are the only remaining groups of adults to whom voting rights have been denied.[13]

> **Voting Rights Act of 1965** legislation that abolished literacy tests as a requirement to register to vote.

Even for adults who can vote, however, the United States is rare among democracies in that voting is a two-step process. All states except North Dakota require that citizens register to vote before they cast a ballot. Registration requirements vary from state to state. In some states, citizens can register at the polls on Election Day. In those states, turnout rates tend to be higher. States that allow early voting or make it easier to vote absentee by mail when a voter cannot make it to the polls also tend to see higher turnout.

In general, over time, the movement has been toward a reduction in the legal barriers to registration and voting. For example, thanks to the efforts of political parties, civic groups, and the courts, registration offices are now required to stay open during standard business hours. Also, since the passage of Motor Voter legislation in 1993, citizens are allowed to register by mail and at many different government offices. Furthermore, the maximum number of days before an election that one must register is now 30 days, rather than 60 or 90 days, which had been the deadlines in some states.

The political environment also influences voter turnout decisions.

In addition to personal and legal factors, the nature of the candidates, campaigns, and issues in an election year can also influence who turns out to vote. The 2008 election stands as a watershed event in American political history. The first African American nominee of a major party, Barack Obama, created tremendous pride in African American voters who cast ballots in record numbers and increased their share of the electorate from 11 percent in 2004 to 13 percent in 2008. Hispanics and young voters also voted overwhelmingly for Obama, greatly increasing their turnout by 2.7 percent and 2.1 percent, respectively, in the 2008 election.[14] A powerful image or message of a minority president was the benefit that gave both groups the added incentive to cast their ballots.

Similarly, the presence on the ballot of more interesting or important races and candidates can boost turnout. A race for president, governor,

Case Study

The Tea Party Movement and Conservative Mobilization

In 1773, a group of 200 colonists boarded three ships docked in the Boston harbor and dumped 342 chests of tea overboard. It was a passionate act of defiance against taxation without representation, and it would become the rallying cry of a similar movement 236 years later after CNBC's Rick Santelli voiced outrage at the mortgage relief plan being proposed by the Obama administration. This much-viewed clip, in which Santelli and a group of bond traders talked about a Chicago tea party to protest federal spending, spurred a conservative movement urging fiscal responsibility, a constitutionally limited government, and free markets.

The twenty-first century Tea Party rallies are nationally organized events that specifically and publicly oppose government spending, President Barack Obama, the federal deficit, the stimulus package, and increased taxes. And, despite their conservative base, leaders of the movement are not afraid to lash out against Republicans.

Whether their arguments are correct or not is not as important to us as is the movement's ability to garner a wide range of support and media coverage for their cause. Organizers held rallies and protests all around the country, from Atlanta to Santa Monica to Washington, D.C., bringing thousands into the movement, many of whom had never before participated in politics. They were shown on CNN, Fox News, and MSNBC, and were mocked on shows like *The Daily Show* and *The Colbert Report*. People became interested, and the movement grew. Many were angry, and followers were encouraged to speak out. Spurred on by social media networks like Facebook and Twitter, written about in countless blogs, and discussed on talk radio, the

THE BIRTH OF TEA PARTY POLITICS
CNBC bond analyst Rick Santelli, shown here on Meet the Press in 2011, made headlines for his now famous tirade against the Obama administration's economic and financial policies.

movement reached millions. Skeptics emerged, claiming that many of the protests and rallies were a form of "astro-turfing," a carefully planned and meticulously funded PR campaign to disrupt the Democratic Party and the initiatives of President Obama. The Tea Party organizers countered, claiming that many of the participants were first-time protesters and all were part of purely grassroots activities.

The Tea Party movement has garnered so much attention, and in some cases support, that many mainstream politicians (primarily Republicans) are attempting to latch onto the group's ideals and popularity. Organizers of the Tea Party hope that the same type of community activism that helped elect Obama will work for them, too. We shall see how big an impact, if any, the Tea Party movement will have in the years to come, and whether they can mobilize enough supporters to bring the changes they seek. Are they a viable movement? Or will they wither and fade like many movements before them?

Thinking Critically

1. Do you expect the Tea Party movement to be a big factor in the 2012 elections? How about elections 10 years from now?

2. Do you think the Tea Party movement is good for America? Do you think this type of political participation is healthy?

3. Looking into the future, how do you expect the costs of political participation to change in the next 10, 20, or 30 years? What impact will this have on political participation?

or U.S. Senate would likely motivate greater turnout than a race for, say, state mine inspector (an elective position in Arizona).[15] Having appealing, attractive, or even "star quality" choices on the ballot also appears to elevate turnout.[16]

Some research has shown, too, that elections that are perceived to be close will boost turnout.[17] Close elections stimulate more intense campaign activity and media coverage, which provide voters with more information about the campaign. Furthermore, citizens are more likely to discuss politics among themselves when an election is close. Close elections can also convince voters that their individual vote may influence the outcome and, thus, determine whether they receive benefits.

Mobilization efforts increase turnout.

Mobilization efforts, often dubbed **get-out-the-vote (GOTV)** are activities by candidates, political parties, activists, interest groups, friends, and co-workers to induce others to participate in politics. These efforts can include phone calls, personal visits, mailings, and even transportation to the polls on Election Day. If you have ever been called the night before an election and urged to vote, or had someone stop you outside the library and ask you to sign a petition, you have been the target of mobilization efforts.

get-out-the-vote (GOTV) term used by campaign professionals to describe the various activities that candidates, political parties, activists, and interest groups use to make sure their likely supporters go to the polls on Election Day.

Mobilization can increase participation in three ways. First, mobilization efforts tend to provide information about the relevant candidates and issues, making it easier for people to learn what they need to know in order to make a voting decision. Second, mobilization efforts lower the costs of participation by providing information to individuals on exactly how to carry out the activity—where and when to vote, how to get to the rally, how to sign up to be heard at the committee hearing, and so on. Third, mobilization brings implicit social rewards for those who agree to participate, and possibly negative consequences for those who do not. Individuals who get involved in politics at the behest of others will enjoy the gratitude and esteem of those who asked them to participate—often co-workers, neighbors, or fellow parishioners.[18]

Mobilization is also about the message. Campaigns, parties, and interest groups first select the people most receptive to being contacted, then transmit the specific message to these people in the hopes that they will be motivated to participate. Voter contact and organization do play significant roles in voter turnout, but it is often the message of campaigns or the current political situation that ultimately gets voters to the booth.

One of the big stories of the 2010 election was the enthusiasm gap among Democrats and Republicans. Republicans were simply much more engaged and likely to vote than Democrats were in 2010. Samples of likely voters in

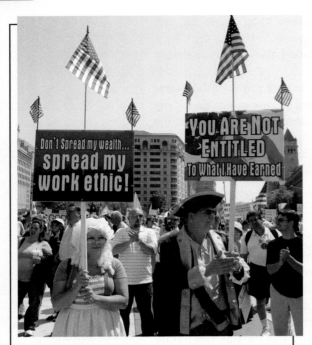

TEA PARTY PROTESTS

Tea party protestors often dressed in colonial garb during their demonstrations.

Thinking Causally Was **Barack Obama's** aggressive use of online media to mobilize supporters the reason for his victory in 2008?

pre-election polls skewed strongly Republican, while surveys that included all registered voters or all adults had the Democrats doing better. Fundamentally, the 2010 electorate was a mirror image of 2008 when Democrats were more energetic, engaged, and likely to vote.

Typically, the mobilization efforts of Democrats and Republicans have taken different directions, based on their assumptions about their voters. Democrats have usually focused efforts on voters with somewhat lower socioeconomic status (SES), whereas Republicans have tended to mobilize suburbanites, church members, and hunters.

In the 2008 election, Barack Obama took advantage of relatively new media and social networking sites like Facebook, Twitter, and MySpace to mobilize millions of supporters. He effectively used online media to raise millions of dollars and generated a type of online activism never seen before. Many political pundits pointed to, and arguably overemphasized, Obama's aggressive utilization of online media as a major reason for his victory. Still, although many who participated in Obama's online outreach were already Obama supporters, it nonetheless gave them an easy medium for communicating and a sense of community not realized in any previous presidential campaign.

Mobilization efforts tend to add to the already substantial influence of socioeconomic status in determining participation. If you wanted to have someone help advance a political issue you cared about, you would be smart to pick someone with developed civic skills and a high-prestige job; someone with substantial amounts of money to give to the cause; someone with access to clubs and charities full of other people with money; and someone with a good education and all of the knowledge, skills, and confidence that education brings with it. In other words, you would ask a high-SES individual. In fact, high-SES individuals are the ones most likely to be asked to participate in political activities. So even though individuals who enjoy high socioeconomic status are more likely to participate in politics in the first place, they are also prime targets for mobilization campaigns.

The Basic Rules Governing American Elections

7-4 Outline election procedures, such as how candidates are nominated and how winners are determined.

The choices available to voters in America, and the decisions voters ultimately make about who they want their leaders to be, are strongly shaped by the rules governing elections. To understand individual vote choice and collective election outcomes, then, we must understand the rules of American elections.

The first objective of a candidate who is running for president is to receive his or her party's nomination.

Only one candidate can be listed on state ballots as the Democratic candidate for president, or a House or Senate seat, and only one can be listed as the Republican candidate.[19] That is the candidate who receives the party nomination. As a result of running under the party label, that candidate will receive "built-in" support from the party's members in the electorate and may also get substantial financial and logistical help from the state and national party organizations.

How does a candidate receive the nomination of his or her party? In the presidential race, he or she does so by successfully accumulating a majority of **delegates**—representatives of the voters—at the party's nominating convention in the summer before the November election. Candidates earn delegates' support primarily by competing in state primaries and caucuses. All of the primaries and caucuses for presidential elections are held during a five-month period of each election year, from late January or early February through June. By tradition, Iowa always holds the country's first caucuses, and New Hampshire always holds the country's first primary.

In a **caucus** system, registered members of each political party are invited to get together in small meetings around their state. At these meetings, party members select delegates to attend regional and state-level conventions. These conventions then choose delegates to send to the national conventions. The delegates who attend the national conventions are usually pledged to specific presidential candidates.

A primary system is considerably simpler. A **primary** election is conducted just like a regular election, with voters casting ballots for the candidate of their choice. However, the voter may choose only from candidates of one party. In some primaries, delegates are assigned to candidates in proportional fashion—that is, a state's delegates are assigned to each candidate based on his or her proportion of the primary vote.

In Republican presidential primaries, by contrast, delegates in some states are allocated according to the **winner-take-all** rule. Coming in second—even

delegates individuals who represent a state's voters in the selection of a political party's presidential candidate.

caucus a small meeting at which registered political party members select delegates to attend the national party convention and nominate a presidential candidate.

primary election in which voters choose the candidate that will represent their political party in the general election.

winner-take-all election in which the candidate who gets the most votes wins, while any other candidate loses and receives nothing.

open primary an election in which a voter can participate in either party's primary (but not both), regardless of party registration.

modified open primary an election in which registered voters who are not affiliated with either party can vote in either party's primary.

closed primary an election in which only registered members of a political party can participate in the party's primary election.

if one loses by only one vote—means that the losing candidate gets no delegates. The choice between proportional and winner-take-all allocation is left up to the party in individual states.[20]

Rules governing primaries may differ from state to state. In an **open primary**, a voter can participate in either party's primary (but not both), regardless of his or her party registration. In a **modified open primary**, registered voters who are not affiliated with either party can vote in either party's primary. A registered Democrat, however, cannot "cross over" and vote in a Republican primary, or vice versa. Finally, in a **closed primary**, only registered Democrats can participate in the Democratic primary, and only registered Republicans can participate in the Republican primary.

Most states have closed primaries and caucuses. The logic of this system is obvious: only registered members of the party should have a voice in selecting the party's nominee. But if party voters have more extreme views than members of the general electorate, they may end up selecting a nominee who will not have broad appeal in the general election. An open primary helps address this problem, by allowing voters outside the party to have a say in choosing the party's nominee.

Most of our discussion here focuses on the presidential nominating process. The process for securing the nomination for a House or Senate seat is different—and much more straightforward—than that for the presidential race. A congressional candidate must win the party's primary election in order to run as the party's candidate in the fall election. But, unlike presidential primary contests, which occur over a series of months as candidates attempt to secure delegates, congressional primaries are conducted like a typical election in which the plurality winner receives his or her party's nomination.

The presidential nomination process has changed significantly in American history.

The allocation of convention delegates by presidential caucuses and primaries is a relatively new phenomenon that has come about in the last 30 years. Until 1972, state delegations were chosen not by voters but by powerful party leaders and elected officials within the states. Some states did have primaries prior to 1972, but they were usually not binding and did not actually choose delegates. Instead, they were "beauty contests," so-called because candidates ran in order to demonstrate to party leaders their appeal to voters.

The watershed year of 1968 Party primaries began to take on much greater importance after the tumultuous Democratic nomination campaign of 1968. In that year, after a weaker-than-expected victory over Minnesota Senator Eugene McCarthy in the New Hampshire primary, incumbent

Democratic President Lyndon Johnson decided not to seek reelection. With the once formidable Johnson out of the way, two other prominent Democrats joined the race—New York Senator Robert Kennedy, younger brother of John F. Kennedy, and Vice President Hubert Humphrey. McCarthy and Kennedy competed in a number of primaries and mobilized many young voters who were adamantly opposed to the ongoing war in Vietnam. After Senator Kennedy was assassinated on the night of his victory in the California primary, the field was left to Humphrey, who supported President Johnson's Vietnam War policy, and McCarthy, who had become the standard-bearer for the anti-war movement.

Even though Humphrey did not campaign in any of the Democratic primaries, party leaders supported his candidacy. Thus, Humphrey arrived at the 1968 Democratic convention in Chicago with a sufficient number of delegates to win the nomination. To anti-war activists and supporters of McCarthy and Kennedy, this meant a continuation of the current Vietnam policy, which they strongly opposed. Their anger boiled over into the streets of Chicago, where violent demonstrations and clashes with the police ensued. All of this unrest during the convention was captured on live television and broadcast to the entire country. Ultimately, Humphrey lost a close election in November to Republican Richard Nixon.

Democratic reforms Aware of the damage that the convention had done to their party's nominee, the Democratic Party appointed a commission to study ways to give rank-and-file party members a greater voice in the choice of the party's nominee. South Dakota Senator George McGovern chaired the commission. The recommendations of the McGovern commission led to the system of delegate selection described above—one in which candidates

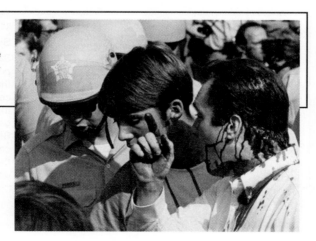

CHAOS AT THE CONVENTION
Police and protesters collide in the streets of Chicago following the 1968 Democratic convention.

accumulate delegates chiefly through primary and caucus votes, rather than through the back-room dealings of party leaders.

The Democratic reforms led to a proliferation of presidential primaries. In 2008, 38 states held Democratic primaries, and 34 states held Republican primaries. In 1968, by contrast, the numbers were 17 and 16, respectively. The remaining delegates in 2008 were chosen in caucuses. All of these delegates chosen by voters in primaries and caucuses are dubbed "pledged delegates" and are committed to voting for the candidate they pledged to on the first ballot at the nominating convention.

Super-delegates and brokered conventions One exception to the trend toward the increasing importance of primaries is the creation of Democratic "super-delegates." Since the 1980s, the Democratic Party—though not the Republican Party—has selected a bloc of about one-fifth of its convention delegates outside the primary and caucus process. These super-delegates include:

- Members of the Democratic National Committee (DNC).

- Democratic members of the U.S. House and Senate.

- Sitting Democratic governors.

- Other distinguished Democratic party leaders, such as former presidents, vice presidents, and DNC chairs.

Super-delegates may vote for whomever they choose at the convention, but they are typically expected to follow the preferences expressed by voters during the primary and caucus season. If a single candidate does not emerge with a majority of the delegates, however, there would be a "brokered convention," in which party leaders would have to choose a candidate to carry their party's banner in the fall election. In such a situation, the super-delegates

THE SUPERPOWERS OF SUPER-DELEGATES
Super-delegates have the power to vote for whomever they choose at the Democratic convention. They often express their support for a particular candidate beforehand. Hillary Clinton and Barack Obama competed for the votes of these all-powerful few throughout the primary season.

would be expected to support the most electable candidate, and would probably induce other convention delegates to follow their lead. This brokered convention scenario, although a perennial favorite of political journalists, political scientists, and other political junkies, has not occurred since the 1968 Democratic reforms were instituted.

More primaries, earlier primaries   As the number of primaries has increased over the past 30 years, they have also occurred earlier in the year. In 1972, for example, the New Hampshire primary took place on March 7. In 2008, the New Hampshire primary was held on January 8. Other states, seeing the attention and money that flow to the early contests in Iowa and New Hampshire, have moved up their contests as well. In 2008, nearly 75 percent of states held earlier primaries. In 2008, the states of Florida and Michigan moved up their primary days to January to get more attention. This change resulted in the Democratic Party's penalizing the two states and taking away their delegates. Ironically, primaries late in the season that few thought would matter—Ohio and Texas on March 3, Pennsylvania on April 22, and North Carolina and Indiana on May 7—became crucial and received immense attention from the campaigns and the media.

Presidential election rules are complicated.

In a presidential election, determining winners and losers tends to be substantially more complicated than in congressional races. In the fall general election for president, the winner of the popular vote may or may not win the presidency. As mentioned at the start of this chapter, in 2000, for example, Al Gore won the national popular vote, but he lost the presidential election to George W. Bush. To win the presidency, a candidate must win a majority in the Electoral College—regardless of the popular vote total—and Gore did not. This scenario had also played out in the highly controversial election of 1876. Despite winning the popular vote by more than 200,000 ballots, Samuel J. Tilden lost the Electoral College and the presidency by one vote, 185 to 184, to more popular Rutherford B. Hayes.

The decision to select the president via the Electoral College rather than by popular vote resulted from a compromise during the Constitutional Convention in Philadelphia in 1787. Delegates at the convention considered two options for selection of the president—popular vote, and selection by members of the House of Representatives. The popular vote was not favored by representatives of smaller states, who imagined that their states' influence in the presidential election would be overwhelmed by the larger states.[21]

The alternative to popular election—selection of the president by the House of Representatives—was more strongly favored by convention members, but it also raised concerns that the president would be beholden to the legislature that had selected him, violating the principles of separation of powers and checks and balances. This scenario might lead to the very tyranny that the new system was intended to prevent.[22]

Electoral College the group of electors from each state and the District of Columbia who cast votes to elect the president.

The convention reached a compromise solution, the **Electoral College**, which addressed a number of these concerns, albeit imperfectly. Small states received disproportionately high representation in the Electoral College relative to their population. Each state was granted an elector for each member it sent to the House of Representatives. But each state, regardless of size, was also granted an elector for each of its two senators.

The electors from each state would meet in their respective states about a month after Election Day and vote for the presidential and vice presidential candidates of their choosing. If no candidate received a majority of the delegates' votes, then the House of Representatives would determine the president.[23] On Election Day, therefore, voters in presidential elections are casting their ballots for a party's slate of electors to the Electoral College, not directly for the president.

With the exception of Maine and Nebraska, states assign their electoral votes on a winner-take-all basis. In Maine and Nebraska, the winner of a state's popular vote as a whole receives two electoral votes. Then, the remainder of the electoral votes is allocated by congressional district, with the popular vote winner in each district receiving one electoral vote.

The modern Electoral College consists of 538 electors, representing the 50 states and the District of Columbia. Each state's number of electors is equivalent to its combined number of House and Senate members. (The District of Columbia does not have voting representatives in the House or Senate, but it receives three electors in the Electoral College.)

The evolution of the modern party system—dominated by two political parties, the Democrats and the Republicans—has changed at least one aspect of the Electoral College in a way America's founders did not envision. Local political parties and the presidential campaigns now select the electors who will participate in the Electoral College vote. Selection is based not necessarily on wisdom or experience, but on service to the party, political contributions, and other demonstrations of party loyalty. Electors are expected to vote for their party's nominee for the presidency—whether or not they believe that nominee is the best-qualified person. In fact, in most states, they are required to do so or they face a fine.

Figuring out the winner in general elections for Congress is easy.

plurality rule rule by which a candidate wins office by getting more votes than his or her opponent, even if that candidate does not receive an absolute majority of the votes.

Congressional and most other U.S. elections are also conducted according to the plurality rule. The **plurality rule** means that a candidate wins office by getting more votes than his or her opponent, even if that candidate does not receive an absolute majority. There are a few isolated exceptions to the plurality rule in the United States, however. Some elections have two rounds of voting. If no candidate receives a majority of the vote in the first round, the contest goes to a second round, or runoff election, in which the top two candidates face off against each other.

Understanding Individual Vote Choice

7-5   Identify the key factors that determine how voters make electoral choices.

In a presidential election, voters generally have two chances to cast a vote for a candidate—once in the primaries, and once in the general election. Once the campaigns are over, the advertisements have been aired, the debates have come and gone, and the media have made their endorsements, the voters must make a choice and cast a ballot. And because there are different processes for the primary election and the general election, the factors that determine those choices may be different.

Primary voting is less studied and understood than general election voting.

No single aspect of political behavior in America has been examined more often or more closely than the individual vote for president. However, political scientists know relatively little about individual decision-making among presidential primary voters. There are two reasons for this discrepancy. First, the general election determines who will be president, and that choice, in turn, usually has major consequences in terms of domestic policy, the economy, and international affairs.

The second reason for political scientists' greater attention to presidential elections is that one critical factor in understanding voting behavior in the general election is not a factor in primary elections—party identification (or party ID). An individual voter's party identification is the single most important influence on vote choice in the general election. In the 2008 general election, for example, 89 percent of Democrats voted for Barack Obama, and 90 percent of Republicans voted for John McCain.[24]

In a primary, though, all of the candidates are of the same party. Political scientists, therefore, cannot explain the primary vote choice as well as they can explain the general election vote. They do, however, have some understanding of why a particular candidate ends up being the party's nominee. Accordingly, we will address primary election results in the section on election outcomes.

Partisanship can both influence and be influenced by the general election vote.

In the 1950s, a pioneering study established enduring theories on the role of partisan identification in the behavior of individual voters. In their seminal work *The American Voter*, Angus Campbell, Philip Converse, Warren Miller, and Donald Stokes argue that in pre-adult years, most voters adopt a partisan affiliation that becomes a psychological attitude akin to the attachment a person has to a religion or racial identity. Therefore, it tends to be highly stable over time, and it is the predominant force in determining most other political attitudes and behaviors—including voting. This view has come to be known as the "traditional" view of partisan affiliation.

Direction and strength of partisan identification *The American Voter* identified two components in an individual's partisan attachment: direction and strength. Direction refers to whether a person identifies more with the Republican Party or with the Democratic Party. Strength refers to the intensity of that attachment. Accordingly, researchers typically measure partisan identification using a series of questions and a 7-point scale that captures both direction and strength, like the one in Figure 7-2.

Differing views of party identification The traditional view of partisanship sensibly emphasized party ID as a factor that determined other beliefs and behaviors—that is, a causal factor. Because the average citizen pays little attention to the fine points of politics, the voter needs some way to simplify and make sense of the political world. Partisan affiliation is a highly effective mechanism for this.

Thinking Causally Does party identification determine other beliefs and choices or are other factors causing individual party ID?

Not all political scientists are completely satisfied with this view of party ID, however. In the "revisionist" view embraced by some scholars, vote choice, issue stands, and evaluations of candidates can influence party identification instead. Ronald Reagan, a Democrat who became a Republican in the 1950s, reflected this aspect of party identification when he stated, "I didn't leave the Democratic Party. The Democratic Party left me."

Which view of partisan attachment makes more sense: the traditional or the revisionist? Consider that each explains some of the puzzle of partisan attachment. Because of political socialization, most voters develop a partisan attachment long before they would be capable of assessing the parties' performance in office. Furthermore, there is little evidence that individuals switch from one party to another in reaction to party performance.

FIGURE 7-2 Partisan Identification on a Seven-Point Scale.

Intensity and direction of partisan attachments are measured by this standard scale.

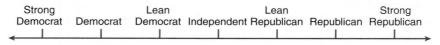

| Strong Democrat | Democrat | Lean Democrat | Independent | Lean Republican | Republican | Strong Republican |

Source: The American National Election Studies (www.electionstudies.org).

Partisan change and instability At the same time, partisan affiliation is not always permanent or perfectly stable, nor need it be seen only as a causal agent. Partisans, especially weaker ones, sometimes do switch sides and affiliate with the other party. Consider the emergence in the 1980s of a group of voters known as "Reagan Democrats." These were generally white, working-class voters who had traditionally considered themselves Democrats but began to identify with the Republican Party on social issues. Accordingly, many of these individuals voted for Ronald Reagan in 1980 and 1984 and ultimately registered as Republicans.

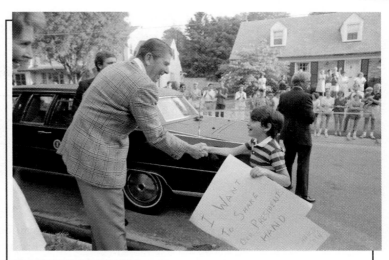

REAGAN DEMOCRATS

Ronald Reagan shakes hands with white working-class voters. Some of these voters followed him as he moved from the Democratic to the Republican Party.

Other scholars have pointed to the weakening of partisan attachments in the electorate as a whole as evidence that partisanship is not as stable as indicated by the traditional view. As Figure 7-3 shows, the direction and intensity of partisan attachments have changed noticeably since the 1960s.

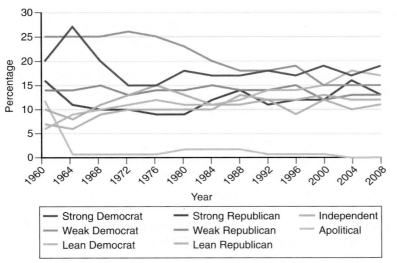

FIGURE 7-3 Partisan Affiliation Among American Adults, 1960–2008.

Party attachments at the aggregate level have fluctuated, but generally Democrats have had the advantage.

Source: American National Election Study, Cumulative File. THE 1948–2004 ANES CUMULATIVE FILE [dataset]. Stanford University and the University of Michigan [producers and distributors], 2005. Any opinions, findings, and conclusions or recommendations expressed in these materials are those of the author(s) and do not necessarily reflect the views of the funding organizations.

FIGURE 7-4 Party Identification from 2004 to 2010.

Party ID has been unusually volatile over the last six years, moving from parity in 2004 to large Democratic advantages in 2006 and 2008, and back to parity in 2010.

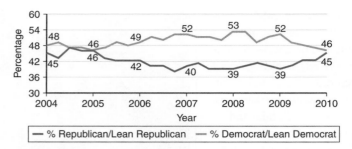

Source: www.gallup.com/poll

One is generally safe in assuming the durability and stability of partisan attachments. That said, change can occur, and one of the big stories of the 2008 election was the change in party attachments. In 2004, most polls showed that there was relative parity in the number of voters identifying themselves as Democrats and Republicans. In 2008, Democrats had a double digit lead in party identification. One of the big stories of 2010 was the pendulum swinging back to a more even distribution of party identification. The swings that we have seen in recent years are some of the most dramatic that scholars have documented in the over 60 years of tracking partisan attachments.

Regardless of one's precise view of partisanship and its durability and predictive value in the long run, there is no question that, in the short term, partisan affiliation remains a singularly important predictor of vote choice (see Figure 7-4). In recent presidential elections, typically 90 percent or more of "strong" Democratic and Republican partisans have voted for their party's candidate. Among individuals who identify themselves as Democrats and Republicans, though not strongly, the loyalty rate is somewhat lower but still impressive—generally in the range of 70 to 85 percent.[25] In 2010, according to the exit polls, 92 percent of Democrats voted for Democratic candidates for Congress and 95 percent of Republicans voted for Republicans for Congress. Thus, knowing voters' partisan affiliations will yield a tremendous insight into their probable vote choice.

Not all partisans are loyal to their party's candidate in every election, however. Furthermore, not every voter considers himself or herself a Democrat or Republican. Two other factors are thought to have an important influence on the individual vote—issue and policy preferences and candidate evaluations.

Thinking Causally Why do voters sometimes make decisions contrary to those we would expect based upon their party ID?

Issue and policy preferences have a complex and uncertain impact on voter choice.

issue voting voting style in which the voter judges candidates based on the voter's and the candidates' opinions on specific issues and preferences for certain policies.

Most political scientists agree that voters' opinions on specific issues and their preferences for certain policies can and do affect their presidential vote. The shorthand phrase for this phenomenon in the research literature is **issue voting**. It makes sense intuitively. For example, if you are a strong supporter of universal, government-paid health care, you will likely be inclined to vote for a candidate who also supports that concept rather than one who opposes it (other things being equal). Political scientists also agree on certain preconditions that must exist in order for a voter to engage in issue voting:

- The voter must be aware of the issue and have an opinion concerning it.

- The issue must be at least minimally important to the voter.

- The voter must be able to identify accurately the candidates' positions on the issue.

- The voter must believe that one party or candidate represents the voter's own position better than the other party or candidate.[26]

Beyond these basics, political scientists disagree about the relative importance of issues in the voting decision, the precise mechanisms by which voters compare their issue positions to those of presidential candidates, the kinds of issues that are relevant to voters, and the best ways to study issue voting.

Consistency between issue preference and voter choice Although the above list of requirements for issue voting seems daunting, V. O. Key argued that on highly salient campaign issues, voters were capable of developing meaningful issue positions and voting in part on the basis of them. Using a body of survey data, Key looked at the behaviors and attitudes of individuals in consecutive presidential elections. The most interesting data came from "party switchers"—individuals who voted for different parties in consecutive elections. In comparison with individuals who voted for the same party in both elections, Key found the party switchers much more likely to have disagreements with their previous party on major campaign issues, such as Social Security or U.S. involvement in World War II. From these data, Key inferred that those issue disagreements were the cause of the party switchers' vote changes.

Key's research methods were not without problems, however. Imagine, for example, that you as a voter find a particular candidate personally appealing for reasons having nothing to do with his issue stances. Because you like the candidate so much, you may also come to embrace his issue positions, seeing them in the "reflected glow" of his personal characteristics. This logic would suggest that your preference for the candidate led to your support of his issue positions, rather than the opposite.

Later generations of political scientists, using much more comprehensive voter databases and sophisticated analytical techniques, have addressed this and other shortcomings in Key's analysis. For example, in a now classic 1979 article, Gregory Markus and Philip Converse found that voters' ultimate evaluations of candidates were significantly affected by their policy preferences in five different issue areas. Voters' evaluation of candidates, in turn, also had a significant effect on their ultimate vote choice. Thus, voters' issue positions affected the vote indirectly, by contributing to voters' evaluation of candidates.

prospective voting voting style in which voters judge a candidate based on their assessment of what the candidate will do in office if elected.

retrospective voting voting style in which voters judge candidates based on the past performance of the candidates or their parties rather than issue stands and assessments of what each candidate would do if elected.

Retrospective and prospective voting Scholars also introduced another insight on issue voting. Voters do not only try to project how candidates will perform on important issues in the future—a process known as **prospective voting**. Rather, issue voting can also be **retrospective**; voters simply assess the performance of the party that has held the presidency for the past four years. If the party has performed well on the issues the voter cares about, she will reward that party's candidate with her vote. According to this logic, presidential elections are considered more of a referendum on the incumbent party's stewardship of the country than a judgment about the relative strengths and weaknesses of two competing candidates. Key summed up the essence of this idea in fairly dramatic terms, describing the voter as "a rational god of vengeance and reward."[27]

Support for Key's argument can be seen in a number of twentieth-century presidential elections. Presidents who presided over periods of recession or slow economic growth, or who found themselves mired in serious scandal or controversy, or who were associated with conspicuous foreign policy failures, did not win reelection—Herbert Hoover, Gerald Ford, and Jimmy Carter, among others. Other presidents have served during eras of peace and general prosperity, and so have been rewarded with reelection—Dwight Eisenhower, Ronald Reagan, and Bill Clinton, for example. This same logic applies even when an incumbent president is not up for reelection. These patterns also hold in midterm elections, as we saw in 2010. Although he was not on the ballot, President Obama's plunging job approval numbers in the months leading up to the elections hurt Democratic congressional candidates.

One reason for the intuitive appeal of the retrospective voting model is that making retrospective judgments about whether a particular party deserves to be rewarded or punished is a much easier, more reasonable task than making prospective judgments based on candidate issue positions. Retrospective voting simply requires the voter to observe the results of the incumbent presidential party's policies.

As noted, voters tend to make retrospective judgments on the basis of "big" issues—for example, the state of the national economy, whether the country is at peace or at war, and if the latter, whether that war is being executed successfully. Furthermore, whether making retrospective or prospective judgments, one should expect issue voting to take place with respect to issues that voters, not researchers, consider important.

Developing positions and making voting decisions Some issues are relatively easy for voters to develop opinions on—and therefore to incorporate into their voting decisions—whereas others are much more technical and complex. For example, compare and contrast two issues: same-sex marriage, and the military action in Iraq after the 9/11 terrorist attacks. With respect to the same-sex marriage issue, there are only two options: for or against.

Developing a well-informed position on this issue might require nothing more than thinking through one's own existing beliefs and values. With respect to the Iraq situation, however, a number of policy options were available:

- Maintain the status quo.
- Attempt to strengthen the existing economic sanctions against Iraq.
- Seek to overthrow Saddam Hussein's regime through covert action.
- Support Iraqi forces seeking to overthrow Hussein.
- Launch a renewed weapons inspection program.
- Seek U.N. approval to invade Iraq.
- Invade Iraq unilaterally, without U.N. approval.
- Some combination of these steps.

Although many Americans had opinions, developing a well-informed position on the appropriate Iraq policy would involve a thorough consideration of all these options and their potential costs and benefits—an expertise beyond the reach of the vast majority of Americans. In general, one should expect a greater incidence of issue voting on issues that are relatively easy for the mass electorate to consider.[28]

Perhaps the "easiest" issues of all are so-called **valence issues**—issues on which virtually everyone agrees. Almost all voters agree, for example, that less crime is better than more, that peace is better than war, and that lower unemployment is better than higher unemployment. On these issues, voters cannot be said to have conflicting positions. However, voters do have distinct beliefs about which party is better able to handle such valence issues.[29] One voter might believe, for example, that the Democratic Party is more likely to help achieve low unemployment than is the Republican Party. Another voter might believe precisely the opposite.

valence issues issues on which virtually everyone agrees.

Beyond these generalities, it is difficult to draw conclusions on the circumstances under which a particular issue will affect a given election outcome. This obstacle does not stop journalists, campaign consultants, and even political scientists from claiming that a specific issue—say, abortion, gun control, or "moral values"—influenced or even determined an election. When assessing such claims, keep in mind the prerequisites for issue voting identified above. When these circumstances do not hold, or when their applicability is open to debate, then any talk about issue voting is just that—talk.

Voters appraise candidates in three big ways.

A final factor that many political scientists consider important in influencing individual vote choice is candidate evaluation. Voters evaluate candidates based on ideology and certain traits that characterize their personalities or policies. Political scientists have measured candidate appraisals through the following methods:

- Open-ended voter comments about aspects they like and dislike about specific candidates.[30]

- Voter assessments of whether particular presidential candidates have "the kind of personality a president ought to have."[31]

- "Feeling thermometer" ratings of presidential candidates, in which voters are asked to assign a number to a candidate on a zero to 100 scale, with zero indicating "very cold or unfavorable" and 100 indicating "very warm or favorable."[32]

Despite many studies regarding the effects of candidate evaluations on vote choice—some large, some very modest—no consensus has evolved on the best ways to measure candidate evaluations, or on the relative importance of candidate evaluations among other factors that influence the vote. Even so, it is reasonable to consider candidate evaluations, along with party ID and issue voting, as one of the "big three" determinants of vote choice.

Party identification, issues, and candidate appraisals come together to produce a vote choice.

How exactly do these three elements combine to produce an individual vote decision? Despite the complexity and degree of randomness inherent in human decision-making, a good, general rule that describes most presidential voting behavior might be:

> The voter canvasses his likes and dislikes of the two candidates involved in the election. He then votes for the candidate for whom he has the greatest net number of favorable attitudes. If no candidate has such an advantage, the voter votes consistently with his partisan affiliation, if he has one.[33]

One can test the accuracy of the rule by generating vote predictions from it using voter survey data. This basic rule, relying on candidate evaluation and party ID, can generate a correct prediction nearly 85 to 90 percent of the time (depending on the election). Thus, it would seem to be a good approximation of the way that voters actually arrive at a final decision.

You may have noticed, however, that the rule includes only two of the "big three" vote determinants: candidate evaluations and party identification. What about voter issue positions? Issue positions influence the vote by way of candidate evaluations. Specifically, the voter's assessment of candidates' issue positions affects the voter's candidate evaluation, which in turn affects the vote. Not surprisingly, party identification also affects voter evaluations of candidates. Because of these relationships, party ID influences the vote through candidate evaluation, and not just as a tie-breaker, as the rule given above would seem to indicate. Finally, party identification also affects voter issue positions, a connection that provides another avenue through which party ID can affect the vote indirectly.[34]

Thinking Causally How might party ID affect a voter's positions on health care or the economy?

Understanding Presidential Election Outcomes

7-6   Assess the key factors that determine the outcome of presidential elections.

The winners and losers of public office in the United States emerge from the interaction of three factors: the laws governing how elections are conducted, the manner in which candidates wage their campaigns, and the ways in which voters decide whom to support. Now we examine how rules and campaigns and choices and decisions all come together to determine election outcomes and the leaders who govern us.

Frontrunners have a great advantage in presidential nomination contests.

Even if political scientists do not understand all the ins and outs of vote choice, they do understand the primary election process and how it produces a particular nominee. This understanding has changed significantly over the past generation, however.

The pre-primary season   A candidate hoping to win the party's nomination needs to be prepared to make a credible run in multiple states before the primary season even begins. The candidates best equipped to do this begin the primary season having raised the most money, having already achieved frontrunner status in pre-primary polls, or both. Candidates who have reached one or both of these success milestones—who have won the **invisible primary**—almost always go on to win their party's nomination. This principle has held over most of the previous 11 contested nomination battles for the presidency, as shown in Table 7-2.

invisible primary the race to raise the most money and achieve frontrunner status before the primary season begins.

Importance of momentum in past primaries   Until the early 1980s, the key to understanding the primary process was one word: **momentum**. Thirty years ago, primary contests were few in number and spaced far enough apart that even long-shot candidates had time to build a credible campaign over the course of a primary season. An early success in Iowa or New Hampshire gave them a coveted shot of momentum, indicated by a boost in media coverage, name recognition, fund-raising, and perceptions of electability. They could convert these assets into a successful campaign in the next primary, and the benefits going forward would compound.[35]

momentum the boost in media coverage, name recognition, fund-raising, and perceptions of electability that accompanies unexpected and repeated primary success.

TABLE 7–2 Pre-Primary Leaders in Fund-Raising and Opinion Poll Preference Among Party Identifiers, 1980–2008.

Year	Party	Candidate with Lead in Last Poll Before Iowa Caucuses	Candidate Raising Most Money Prior to the Year of the Election	Clear Invisible Primary Winner?	Eventual Nominee
1980	Republican	Reagan	Connally	None	Reagan
1980	Democratic	Carter	Carter	Carter	Carter
1984	Democratic	Mondale	Mondale	Mondale	Mondale
1988	Republican	Bush	Bush	Bush	Bush
1988	Democratic	Hart	Dukakis	None	Dukakis
1992	Republican	Bush	Bush	Bush	Bush
1992	Democratic	Clinton	Clinton	Clinton	Clinton
1996	Republican	Dole	Dole	Dole	Dole
2000	Republican	Bush	Bush	Bush	Bush
2000	Democratic	Gore	Gore	Gore	Gore
2004	Democratic	Dean	Dean	Dean	Kerry
2008	Democratic	Clinton	Clinton	None	Obama
2008	Republican	Romney	Giuliani	None	McCain

Still, the crowded primary calendar leaves very little time to raise money, organize local volunteers, attend campaign events, and develop and implement state-specific media strategies while the campaign is in progress. A candidate who attempts to run a credible campaign in only one or two early states, hoping to turn that into success in the next round of contests, probably will not have adequate time to make this strategy work.

Emergence of the frontrunner As demonstrated above, the pre-primary period usually creates a clear frontrunner for the nomination. And in general, that frontrunner is the candidate who has abundant resources and support in place before the primaries begin. Despite the relative accuracy of this claim, there is still something unsatisfying about it. Note that it says nothing about how or why a particular individual comes to win the invisible primary in the first place. The reason we have neglected this topic is that political scientists do not fully understand how one builds momentum in the pre-primary period. They do know that early fund-raising success leads to favorable media coverage, which in turn leads to greater name recognition and a higher standing in the polls, which can then lead to more successful fund-raising, and so on. But these relationships simply raise the question, why are some candidates more successful than others at raising money?[36] And why do some candidates who raise large sums of money not succeed? Even if political scientists could answer these questions, they almost certainly would find it difficult to predict winners of the invisible primary.

Beyond this gap in our understanding of the invisible primary, the evolution of the Internet as a political tool and communications medium may be changing some of the basic logic of the primary process. Candidates can now instantaneously raise and immediately spend large sums of money. Furthermore, websites, Twitter, Facebook, and e-mail make round-the-clock mass communication and campaign coordination possible at an extremely low cost. The Web has also changed the news cycle significantly. Stories that used to be updated once a day, in the morning paper or on the evening news, are now updated continuously, online. Twenty-four-hour news channels and the proliferation of nationwide talk-radio programming have also contributed to this phenomenon. Thus, candidates who need to raise money, communicate with millions of supporters, recruit volunteers, raise media awareness, and get their message out in a hurry now have tools that were not available to them even 15 years ago. Eventually, these factors may change the existing primary season dynamic in which candidates who start behind almost always end behind as well.

Key factors allow political scientists to accurately forecast presidential election results.

In 2008, the American Political Science Association solicited election forecasts from nine different scholars or teams of scholars. These scholars completed their forecasts several months before the fall election. In six out of nine cases, they predicted that Barack Obama would be the new president. On average, the forecasters predicted that Obama would receive 52 percent of the two-party vote.[37] In actuality, Obama received just over 52 percent of the vote. In this instance, the forecasters were amazingly accurate, signifying the reliability and accuracy of these forecasting models.

Factors in forecasting　In predicting presidential election outcomes, the political scientists' models generally take into account four different kinds of factors:

- The partisan orientations of the electorate.
- The job approval rating of the incumbent party president.
- The performance of the economy during the first half of the election year.

- Incumbency, that is, whether an incumbent president is running for reelection, and if so how long his party has held the presidency.

From one election to the next, the factors that are most likely to change sharply, and thus exert decisive effects on election outcomes, are presidential approval ratings and economic performance. Looking at presidential elections since 1952, for example, when the incumbent party's president has an average approval rating of 49 percent or better during April, May, and June of the election year, that party's candidate wins the general election. When that number is 46.7 percent or lower, on the other hand, the incumbent party's candidate loses.[38] In between these two numbers is a sort of "no man's land," an area of uncertainty. George W. Bush was dangerously near this no man's land in 2004, barely achieving an approval rating of 49 percent during the second quarter of the election year. Thus, predictions based solely on his approval ratings would have considered him vulnerable, but with a slightly better chance of winning than losing.

Looking at economic performance as a predictor between 1952 and 2008, when gross domestic product (GDP) grows at an annualized rate of at least 2.6 percent in the second quarter of the election year, the incumbent party wins. When growth is 1.5 percent or less, the incumbent party loses. Growth rates in between are inconclusive. Looking again at 2004, GDP grew by 3 percent during the second quarter of the year. This should have put George W. Bush in a relatively good position to earn reelection, though not as strong as some of his predecessors. Richard Nixon, for example, saw 6.9 percent GDP growth in 1972 and was reelected overwhelmingly. Ronald Reagan and Bill Clinton benefited from growth rates of 5.3 percent and 4.6 percent, respectively, during their reelection years. Both were rewarded with a second term.[39] In 2008, with the country in a recession and GDP growth rates negative, even though George W. Bush was not on the ballot, fellow Republican John McCain faced an almost impossible headwind.

The reward/punishment equation   What all of these voting considerations suggest is that a basic "reward/punishment" or retrospective voting model, combined with a recognition of the importance of partisanship, is a sensible way to think about and understand election outcomes. Every election year starts with the electorate divided into three camps: Republicans, Democrats, and independents. Naturally, the vast majority of strong partisans vote loyally. Some of the weaker partisans, though, and most of the independents will likely decide on the basis of comparative candidate evaluations that are heavily influenced by the performance and leadership of the party in power. In terms of the political scientists' predictive models, if voters are generally pleased with the incumbent party and its president—as indicated in presidential approval ratings—they will be inclined to look favorably on the party's candidate for president. Likewise, if the economy has performed well with the incumbent party in charge, that party's candidate for president is likely to receive favorable voter evaluations and be rewarded with the presidency.

Those who are not political scientists tend to be uncomfortable with this logic, and with political scientists' predictive models, because they seem to omit so much. In 2004, for example, the news was full of stories on the Iraq War. Had George W. Bush misled the country about the presence of weapons of mass destruction in Iraq? Was deposing Saddam Hussein worth the cost in American lives and tax dollars? Although it might seem that the forecasting models do not take into account such important voter concerns, they do—by way of presidential approval. To the extent these concerns were important to voters, they were included in the president's job approval ratings. And, President Bush's second quarter approval ratings were hardly in a comfortable range for him.

Chapter Summary

In this chapter you have learned to:

7-1   Analyze the costs and benefits of political participation for individuals and groups.

People analyze the costs and benefits of voting in any particular election and decide whether or not to vote based on these perceived costs and benefits. Many Americans vote even though a rational analysis suggests they should not—this is the paradox of participation. As the incremental benefit of one vote is often quite small, a confusing situation arises in which the costs seem to outweigh the benefits of voting. Although the paradox of voting remains unresolved, it seems likely that the satisfaction voters receive from performing their civic duty plays some role in encouraging voting.

7-2   Identify the different kinds of political activities in which Americans participate.

There are many different ways in which citizens can participate in politics in America. Although voting is the type of participation that first comes to mind, citizens can participate in politics in many other ways. Signing petitions, attending demonstrations, organizing community meetings, joining political membership organizations, volunteering for political campaigns, and contacting elected officials are examples of other sorts of political activity. Although Americans tend to vote at lower rates than citizens in other countries, they do tend to engage in these other activities at higher rates.

7-3   Explain the main factors that influence political participation.

Personal factors, legal factors, the political environment, and mobilization efforts are key elements that influence political participation. By a wide margin, the most important personal factor influencing political participation is socioeconomic status. The civic skills it implies make the costs of political participation seem lower, and levels of political efficacy are generally higher for those with higher socioeconomic status. Legal factors also play an important role in participation decisions. The twentieth century brought an end to a number of legal barriers that prevented women and African Americans from voting. Further, Motor Voter legislation made voter registration more convenient. The competitiveness of a race, as well as the efficacy of mobilization efforts, also affect participation. The more competitive the race and the more effective the mobilization, the higher the levels of political participation.

7-4 Outline election procedures, such as how candidates are nominated and how winners are determined.

The first objective of a candidate running for office is to receive his or her party's nomination. In the presidential race, the candidate does so by winning a majority of delegates to the party's nominating convention during the state primary elections. The Electoral College and the winner-take-all system do much to define the American political landscape.

7-5 Identify the key factors that determine how voters make electoral choices.

Certain key factors determine how voters make electoral choices. Primary among these are "the big three" determinants: party identification, issue voting (including the retrospective vote), and candidate evaluations. A voter's party ID is the single most important influence on vote choice in the general election. Other influences are voters' opinions on specific issues, and retrospective voting, in which voters judge candidates based on their, or their party's, past performance. Despite idiosyncratic voter behavior and the complex interaction of "the big three," vote prediction forecasting models are highly accurate.

7-6 Assess the key factors that determine the outcome of presidential elections.

In order to succeed in presidential primaries, it is crucial to win the invisible primary. This includes leading the field in public opinion polls, in fund-raising, or in both at the end of the pre-primary period. Candidates who begin the heavily front-loaded primary season in the lead often go on to win. Primaries follow each other too rapidly for underdog candidates to devote resources to multiple races and to build the momentum necessary to win the nomination. In general elections, presidential approval ratings and economic performance are the two variables most often included in election forecasting models—and they have excellent predictive power. The partisan orientations of the electorate, whether there is an incumbent president running for reelection, and how long the party has held the presidency are also significant factors.

CHAPTER TEST

1. What is the paradox of political participation?
2. Explain some of the ways that people participate in politics other than voting.
3. What might explain why Americans vote at lower levels than citizens of other countries but surpass comparative participation in many other political activities?
4. Why is it so difficult to determine how many people vote on Election Day?
5. Which factors have a critical impact on political participation? Why?
6. Are voter mobilization efforts likely to be successful in most cases? Why or why not?
7. How do caucuses and primaries differ? Why are primaries used more often today than caucuses?
8. What dramatic event led to reforms in the way the Democratic Party nominates candidates for presidential elections? Which of the reforms was most significant? Why?
9. Why do frontrunners have a great advantage in presidential nomination contests?
10. Which key factors allow political scientists to accurately forecast presidential election results?

MyPoliSciLab® POLITICAL PARTICIPATION, VOTING, AND ELECTIONS
Apply what you learned in this chapter on MyPoliSciLab.

Read on **mypoliscilab.com**

eText: Chapter 7

Study and **Review** on **mypoliscilab.com**

Pre-Test
Post-Test
Chapter Exam
Flashcards

Watch on **mypoliscilab.com**

Video: L.A. Riots: 15 Years Later
Video: Dissecting Party Primaries
Video: State Primary Race
Video: Who Are the Superdelegates?
How Do We Know Video: Why is it so difficult to determine how many people vote?

Explore on **mypoliscilab.com**

Comparative: Comparing Voting and Elections

Simulation: You Are a Campaign Manager: Countdown to 270!
Simulation: You Are a Campaign Manager: Help McCain Win Swing States and Swing Voters
Simulation: You Are a Campaign Manager: Lead Obama to Battleground State Victory
Timeline: Nominating Process
Timeline: Close Calls in Presidential Elections
Timeline: Television and Presidential Campaigns
Visual Literacy: Iowa Caucuses
Visual Literacy: The Electoral College: Campaign Consequences and Mapping the Results
Visual Literacy: Voting Turnout: Who Votes in The United States?

KEY TERMS

caucus, p. 203
civic skills, p. 198
closed primary, p. 204
collective benefit, p. 191
delegates, p. 203
Electoral College, p. 208
get-out-the-vote (GOTV), p. 201
invisible primary, p. 217

issue voting, p. 212
modified open primary, p. 204
momentum, p. 217
open primary, p. 204
plurality rule, p. 208
political efficacy, p. 198
primary, p. 203
prospective voting, p. 214

retrospective voting, p. 214
selective benefit, p. 191
socioeconomic status (SES), p. 197
suffrage, p. 198
Voting Rights Act of 1965, p. 199
valence issues, p. 215
winner-take-all, p. 203

SUGGESTED READINGS

Steve Rosenstone and Mark Hansen. 2002. *Mobilization, Participation, and Democracy in America*. New York: Longman Classics. Argues that people participate in voting based on the perceived costs and benefits of doing so and because politicians mobilize them, but whether people vote may also depend on their income, education, age, race, efficacy, and social networks.

Paul Abramson, John Aldrich, and David Rohde. 2007. *Change and Continuity in the 2008 Elections*. Washington, DC: CQ Press. Straightforward and accessible analysis of the 2008 election, evaluating campaign strategies and their impact on the outcome of the midterm elections.

Gary Jacobson. 2008. *Politics of Congressional Elections*. New York: Longman. A comprehensive review of the current literature on congressional elections: why people vote as they do, variance in outcomes across districts and states, changes over time in aggregate representation (who has power), and the implications for democratic governance.

Angus Campbell, Philip E. Converse, Warren E. Miller, and Donald E. Stokes. 1960. *The American Voter*. Chicago: University of Chicago Press. Argues that party ID is the major influence on voters' perceptions of political choice and their final vote, that party ID is stable and resistant to outside influence, and that partisanship is adopted early in life.

Jan Leighley. 2010. *The Oxford Handbook of American Elections and Political Behavior*. New York: Oxford University Press. The various approaches and issues in research design, political participation, vote choice, and the influences on individuals' political behavior.

SUGGESTED WEBSITES

ROCK THE VOTE
www.rockthevote.org

Rock the Vote is a nonprofit organization that works to engage young people in the political process by incorporating the entertainment community and youth culture in outreach efforts. This website provides a link to voter registration.

MOVEON.ORG
moveon.org

MoveOn.org aims to help busy but concerned citizens "find their political voice." The organization's website provides links to current campaigns.

DEMOCRATIC NATIONAL COMMITTEE
www.democrats.org

Provides links to the Democratic National Convention, action plans, and agenda as well as opportunities to register to vote and contribute to current campaigns or the party.

REPUBLICAN NATIONAL COMMITTEE
www.rnc.org

Offers links to blogs, calls to action, groups affiliated with the party, party issues, and state parties.

POLITICALMAPS.ORG
politicalmaps.org

The best and most interesting political maps. Site managers update the site regularly during election season.

Political Parties

THE FIGHT IS OVER Delegates at the 2010 Republican convention in Utah rejected Senator Bob Bennett's bid for a fourth term in the U.S. Senate. Bennett was one of a number of Republican politicians nationally who faced serious challenges due to a resurgent conservatism among Republican voters.

CHAPTER LEARNING OBJECTIVES

After reading this chapter you will be able to:

8-1 Analyze the functions of political parties in American politics.

8-2 Determine why American electoral competition is dominated by two political parties rather than multiple parties.

8-3 Trace the evolution of American party organizations and their expanding role in campaigns.

8-4 Explain how parties achieve electoral success by building and maintaining coalitions of supporters.

Connecticut voters elected Joe Lieberman to the U.S. Senate in 1988. Over the years, he compiled a record as a moderate Democrat and won reelection handily in 1994 and 2000. Democratic nominee Al Gore even tapped Lieberman to be his running mate in the 2000 presidential election.

The Iraq War, however, would prove to be Lieberman's undoing among Democratic supporters. Lieberman was a staunch supporter of the war prior to its onset in 2003, as were many other Democrats. Over time Democratic support waned, but Lieberman remained convinced that the war was a key battle in the fight against terrorism. His support for the war earned him public rebukes by Harry Reid and Nancy Pelosi, the leaders of the Senate and House Democrats, respectively at the time. As the coalitional ground shifted beneath him and the party's anti-war activism grew, Lieberman did not change his stance.

In 2006, Ned Lamont, a candidate heavily supported by MoveOn.org, a prominent political group pushing the Democratic Party to move in a more liberal direction, defeated Lieberman in the party primary. Running for reelection to the U.S. Senate as an independent, Lieberman prevailed in a three-way race in November. The man who was 537 votes away from being elected a Democratic vice president in 2000 was, six years later, no longer a Democrat. He campaigned for John McCain, the Republican presidential nominee, in 2008. Although extreme, Lieberman's case is not unique.

Robert Bennett was first elected to the U.S. Senate, representing Utah, in 1992. He won reelection easily in 1998 and 2004 and was part of the Republican leadership team in the Senate. Bennett's ideological record over three terms was similar to that of Orrin Hatch, Utah's other Republican U.S. senator. But in 2010 this track record was not enough. Bennett was rejected by delegates at the state's party convention, where he lost to two political newcomers and failed to receive enough votes to proceed to the party primary.

Although receiving the endorsement of the National Rifle Association and some prominent conservative Republicans, Bennett had disappointed some of the party's key support groups. Sealing Bennett's fate were his vote in late 2008 for the Troubled Assets Relief Program, often referred to as "the Wall Street bailout"; his reintroduction in 2009, along with Democratic Senator Ron Wyden of Oregon, of an ultimately unsuccessful health insurance reform bill that required individuals to obtain coverage; and his history of actively pursuing federal earmarks or "pork" for spending projects in Utah.

Many Americans may appreciate Joe Lieberman's independent streak and the bipartisan gestures of Bob Bennett, but political activists that supported the Democrats and Republicans, respectively, did not. As events change, the issues and positions that energize or enrage party activists can change. The shifting balance of power within a party's coalition can have dramatic causal effects on electoral outcomes, as both Lieberman and Bennett learned. The public often expresses admiration for the politician who goes against the party tide or who casts unpopular votes, but to activists and fellow elected officials, these politicians are often derided as DINOs and RINOs—Democrats and Republicans In Name Only. ■

What Political Parties Do

8-1 Analyze the functions of political parties in American politics.

Americans' views of parties have changed over time from fearful, to supportive, to skeptical. President George Washington, in his farewell address, warned Americans about the dangers of political parties. By the late nineteenth century, however, partisanship was a central aspect of Americans' identity. Today, Americans still have strong attachments to parties, but there is a pervasive skepticism that parties are too polarized and stubborn and refuse to work together. What has provoked these strong reactions? What are political parties and what do they do?

Political parties are organized groups that seek to gain office and exercise political power through legislation, executive action, and control of government agencies, among other means. They aim to elect office holders who identify themselves by the group's common label and who consider themselves associated with that group. Candidates rally voters to their side who share the outlook or background of other supporters of the party.[1] Party activity occurs at all levels in American politics: from the individual voter who feels close to a party, to the public official who tries to rally fellow partisans around a policy proposal.

political parties organized groups with public followings that seek to elect office holders who identify themselves by the group's common label, for the purpose of exercising political power.

Defined narrowly, "the party" usually refers to its elected officials and the individuals working for official party organizations. More broadly, political parties are *networks* of people and groups who share common policy goals. Labor unions, trial lawyers, environmental groups, teachers, pro-choice groups, liberal think tanks, and the liberal blogosphere tend to align with the Democratic Party. Libertarian-leaning groups, business associations, gun rights groups, veterans, pro-life groups, conservative think tanks, and conservative talk radio outlets tend to align with the Republican Party. Dozens of other issue advocacy groups have close ties with one of the two major parties and expect that their voices will be heard as their party debates policy options. The party network thus involves the ongoing dialogue and mutual support between the party organizations, elected officials, party candidates, and political activists. In thinking of "the Republican Party" or "the Democratic Party," it is useful to keep in mind this entire party network of influence and conversation.[2]

Despite the negative attitudes the public often expresses about parties, political scientists generally offer a more positive assessment. Although not discounting parties' shortcomings, scholars see them as a vital part of democratic politics, performing roles that produce benefits for the operation of American government and for the public.

Parties fill gaps left by the Constitution.

The Constitution provided the basic structure for the selection of public officials but left it up to candidates and voters to make the process work. For the system established by the Constitution to gain credibility and legitimacy, some way had to be found to staff the offices of government and involve the public in politics.

Political parties filled this void. They were created by ambitious, hard-headed politicians to solve particular problems of candidate recruitment, to mobilize enough voter support to win elections, to increase the likelihood of winning debates in the legislature, and ultimately to influence the policy-making process.[3]

Parties recruit candidates into the electoral process and nominate them for office.

Nationally and in most states, political parties take an active role in identifying promising individuals and recruiting them to run for office. They assist both first-time and seasoned candidates with the various aspects of running a campaign, including raising money, dealing with the media, identifying potential supporters, developing positions on issues, and putting together a campaign organization to contact citizens and research opponents.

Parties are engaged in finding candidates so that the party can increase its power. The party has the incentive to run as many candidates as it can in order to win control of as many offices as it can. But this self-interest also serves a social interest. Parties provide voters with choices, which are key to generating a sense of legitimacy for American politics. Elections with choices make voters feel empowered.

After recruiting candidates, parties nominate them as the party's standard-bearers and put them on the ballot. Around the world, control of the nomination process is among the most significant powers of political parties: the power to filter who is elected to public office. In the United States, the nomination of candidates was first controlled by party leaders, then expanded to selection by delegates at party conventions, and now is determined in most cases by state-mandated primary elections.

Parties bridge constitutional gaps between institutions.

The Constitution deliberately spread power across institutions and created a governing system that made the abuse of power difficult, but it also made lawmaking difficult. Political parties bridge these institutional gaps by providing incentives for officials to cooperate in policy-making with each other, as shown in Figure 8-1. Officials who share a party label share a "brand name." When a president does well, members of his party in Congress enjoy some of the glow of that success. If he suffers from low approval ratings, the public's critical view can carry over to his fellow partisans in Congress. For example, in 2010, with President Obama's approval low, health care reform unpopular, and the economy struggling, voters flipped over 65 House and Senate seats from Democratic to Republican control, and Republicans also gained big at

A. Institutional walls of separation in the Constitution

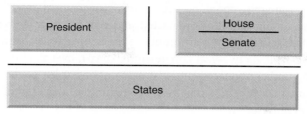

B. The party brand name provides incentives for coordination and cooperation across the constitutional walls

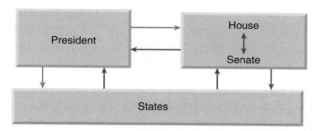

FIGURE 8-1 Political Party Assistance to Policy-Making.

The Constitution created a set of institutions that would be involved in policy-making. It focused on the way these institutions could check each other's use of power. Left unstated was how the individuals in these institutions might work together. A political party provides a common "brand name" that encourages cooperation across institutional boundaries. Politicians know that when other members of their party are successful, the party brand name is enhanced and public approval and the probability of future election victories increase.

the state level. Officials who share a party's brand name have an interest in seeing fellow partisans govern successfully.

This common bond does not undermine the Constitution's separation of powers, checks and balances, or federalism, but it does increase the ability to get things done. Because members of a party will usually share general goals and approaches, they start from a base of support when trying to enact policy. While they may not always agree, the shared party label increases the probability of cooperation.

This logic would seem to suggest that government gets more "big things" done when one party controls both Congress and the presidency—**unified government**—rather than when different parties control each of these branches—**divided government**. Does it? Political scientists have extensively studied the causes and consequences of unified and divided government and the contributing factors to legislative productivity. There is no guarantee that having the presidency and Congress controlled by the same party will result in a burst of significant legislation. A sense of crisis might inspire action; a shortage of revenue might discourage it. A president with high approval ratings might get more support from Congress, regardless of which party controls the House and Senate. A party with unified control of government might accomplish more early in its tenure rather than later. And it matters whether a party is ideologically cohesive—a party can control the presidency and Congress, but if it suffers from internal dissension, legislative action will be difficult.

unified government a situation in which the presidency and both houses of Congress are controlled by the same party.

divided government a situation in which the presidency is held by one party and at least one house of Congress is controlled by a different party.

Thinking Causally Does unified or divided control of government have any impact on the number of significant laws that are enacted?

Studies by political scientists that take these and other factors into account generally conclude that unified government tends to increase the number of important laws enacted and reduces delay in various facets of legislative activity. While the number of enactments may be small (maybe two or three during a two-year congressional term), over time they can add up to a large number of enactments that may not have been possible under divided government.[4] Whether that is a good thing is a matter of one's personal political philosophy.

Parties bring citizens into the electoral process.

Parties seek power to pursue their goals. To gain and assert power, parties need to win offices. To win offices, they need to win elections. And to win elections, they need more votes on Election Day than their opponents. Parties therefore have an incentive to get voters involved, and they do so in a number of ways.

Educate and inform voters Historically, political parties have played a significant role in educating voters about candidates. In the nineteenth century, parties staged parades, festivals, and other events that would attract a crowd to listen to candidates and party supporters deliver speeches. Voters would be entertained and energized by listening to detailed speeches explaining how the party was superior to its opponents.

In addition, political parties controlled much of the mass media of that era, newspapers in particular. Major party figures often urged the creation of newspapers as a means to communicate the party's message and assail the opposition. The positions of the party and its candidates were prominently available for citizens on a daily basis.

Parties today do not have the same kind of monopoly on information about their candidates. Nonetheless, they still attempt to educate voters through campaign advertisements; leaflets and other literature; websites and blogs; e-mail, video, and tweets; and frequent appearances by party officials and important party members on television and radio news and talk shows.

Deliver people to the polls Parties work hard to convince supportive voters to turn out. A party will point out to its supporters not only its positions and candidates, to show them the benefits of voting, but also the positions and candidates of the other party, to show them the dire repercussions of failing to vote. More directly, with their get-out-the-vote (GOTV) efforts, party supporters—or sometimes hired telemarketing firms—make phone calls, send e-mail, and go door to door to remind people to vote and ask if they need assistance getting to the polling place.

Do any of these efforts matter? Studies show that individuals who are contacted by political parties, or by other groups, are more likely to say they voted than individuals who were not contacted. This correlation is not proof of causation, however, because it is also the case that parties target their contacts to those individuals who they have reason to believe are more likely to vote. Spending a significant amount of staff time and financial resources in the midst of a campaign to reach out to perpetual nonvoters or individuals highly uninterested in politics would rarely be a wise use of time and money.[5]

Thinking Causally Does contact from a party or its candidates increase an individual's likelihood of voting?

A better way to think of this relationship between contact and voting is that it is mutually reinforcing. Parties are likely to contact individuals with a higher than average likelihood of voting. The party contact can further increase this probability by stressing the importance of an election and the closeness of a contest. Research controlling for this possible reverse causation suggests that the contacts do indeed have an effect on driving up turnout.[6] Party contact is unlikely to turn a habitual nonvoter into a voter, but it can prompt an occasional voter to turn out.

Integrate new social groups Political parties have an incentive to bring new groups into the political process, but they are selective about which groups they reach out to. In order to win elections, their main goal is to maximize the turnout of people who will vote for them, not to maximize overall turnout. They may even invest resources in keeping a group out of politics, as southern Democrats did with blacks through the mid-1960s. The logic of competition suggests that if one party is pushing a group away, the other major party would have an interest in integrating the group into American politics, especially if it can do so without unduly alarming groups that already support the party.[7]

In recent elections, with the balance of power close in Congress and presidential elections hard fought, both major parties have worked to pull young adults into politics as volunteers and as voters. In the 1990s, the Republican Party was especially effective in reaching out to young adults through its network of support from rural-area church groups. More recently, the Democratic Party and its supporters have made extensive use of new technologies to reach out to young people—the Obama campaign in 2008 was especially effective in doing so. This trend was inaugurated primarily by people in their twenties who launched blogs, political meetup and fund-raising sites, and social networking sites.

The public exerts leverage over public officials through use of the party label.

Parties benefit from the attachments and loyalty of the public. Candidates know they can count on 80 to 90 percent, or more, of their party loyalists to vote for them. They can, therefore, devote more of their resources to appealing to undecided voters who do not have strong partisan leanings.

Voters, in turn, can also use the party label to increase their leverage over public officials.[8] By voting for a Democrat, for example, they are roughly endorsing a particular approach to public policy. A Democratic public official seen as straying from this approach may face vigorous criticism. Thus, voters use the party label to hold officials accountable. Joe Lieberman and Bob Bennett, as described at the beginning of this chapter, learned this the hard way.

All voters can use the party label to sweep one party out of office and put the other party in. In 2006, voters put the Democrats in control. Voters changed course in 2010, giving Republicans big gains in the Senate and control of the House. The party label provides Americans with the simplest and most practical tool they have to make wide-ranging changes in the personnel of government and a possible new direction in public policy. Political scientists have found the party label to be an effective, powerful, and usually accurate information shortcut.

The Two-Party System

8-2   Determine why American electoral competition is dominated by two political parties rather than multiple parties.

American electoral competition usually takes place between two major political parties. A major party has a large following, has endured over time, and is perceived to be electorally competitive by the public, potential candidates, and political observers. Minor parties, or "third parties," lack these features. To say there is a **two-party system** in the United States does not mean that only two parties can compete but, rather, that it is a system of electoral competition in which two parties are consistently seen as the most likely to win office and gain power.

two-party system a system of electoral competition in which two parties are consistently the most likely to win office and gain power.

Across American history, there have been five major political parties: the Federalists (1789–1816); the Democratic-Republicans (1790–1824); the Democrats (1828 to the present); the National Republicans, later Whigs (1824–1854); and the Republicans (1854 to the present). Third parties have included parties organized around ideology (Socialist Party, Progressive Party, Green Party, Libertarian Party), particular issues (Prohibition Party, Greenback Party), defection from a major party (States' Rights, also known as Dixiecrats), and parties built initially around a single presidential candidacy (American Independent Party for George Wallace in 1968; National Unity Party for John Anderson in 1980; United We Stand for Ross Perot in 1992, which led to the Reform Party in 1996). Today, the most significant third parties nationally are the Green Party and the Libertarian Party. These two parties contest a large number of offices, occasionally win elections, and have organizational structures from the local level to the national level that are somewhat similar to but not as extensive as the major parties.[9]

Third parties are rarely successful electorally but may be influential in other ways.

The electoral performance of American third parties can be summed up in one word: dismal. Third-party candidates rarely win elections and usually do not garner a significant share of the vote. Over the past 50 years, they rarely have received more than a few percent of the total national congressional vote.[10]

Similarly, in presidential elections, third-party candidates rarely win states. No state has sided with a third-party candidate since 1968, when five southern states backed Alabama's Democratic governor, George Wallace, who was running as an independent candidate with the newly created American Independent Party.

Although third parties do not often win elections, they can still play significant roles in elections. Probably the most important of these roles is that third-party candidates, or independent candidates more generally, can introduce ideas and issues into the campaign that the major-party candidates might be neglecting or avoiding.[11]

Another possible but controversial role for third parties is to alter the election outcome between the major parties. It was easy for Democrats in 1968 and Republicans in 1992 to blame George Wallace and Ross Perot for the defeat of Democrat Hubert Humphrey and Republican George H. W. Bush, respectively. Wallace and Perot received a large number of votes, and Humphrey and Bush lost; therefore, the argument goes, these third-party candidates cost Humphrey and Bush their elections by diverting votes from these two major party candidates. Many Democrats were likewise angry with Ralph Nader for his run in 2000, believing he cost Al Gore the presidency.

Thinking Causally Are third-party candidates to blame for the defeat of major party presidential candidates?

However, these are usually cases where correlation is mistaken for causality. First, these third-party candidates emerged and did well because of weaknesses in the major parties and their candidates. They may have taken advantage of those weaknesses, but they did not necessarily create them. The leap from correlation to causation also assumes that third-party candidates deliberately employ a spoiler strategy—seeking to cause the defeat of the major party they are ideologically closer to, but this claim is not well supported by political science research.[12]

Single-member districts with plurality elections favor two-party competition.

The Constitution does not mention political parties, and Americans often say in surveys that they would welcome another major party.[13] Why then does America's electoral competition tend to feature only two major parties as serious competitors? Political scientists have identified a number of factors that push American party competition toward a two-party model.

single-member districts electoral districts in which only one person is elected to represent the district in a representative body.

plurality elections elections in which the candidate with the most votes, not necessarily a majority, wins.

In U.S. House elections, as with most American elections, **single-member districts** are the norm: voters elect one candidate to represent each congressional district. In addition, the candidate with the most votes wins: these are **plurality elections**, sometimes referred to by scholars as first-past-the-post elections. Like in a race, the image suggests, what matters in an election is who crosses the finish line first, not how much she wins by or how long it took. Assuming that politicians are ambitious and want to increase their chances of consistently winning office, they are more likely to join a larger party that can potentially obtain majority support.[14]

The idea that single-member districts and plurality elections lead to two-party politics assumes that parties have a way to nominate candidates to be on the November general election ballot. Nearly all states allow for party nominations, usually through a primary election or party convention. Louisiana, Washington, and California, however, employ nonpartisan blanket primaries, in which all the candidates for an office, regardless of party, are in the same primary. Under this system, two candidates from the same party could win the primary and then face off in the next round of elections.

proportional representation an election system in which candidates are elected from multimember districts, with a party's share of seats from a district being roughly proportional to their share of the popular vote.

An alternative to the single-member plurality model is a system of **proportional representation** (PR), common in Europe and in many other democracies around the world. In this system, voters elect many representatives from the same district. Depending on the procedure used, voters may vote for a party but not specific candidates. Or, more commonly, they may be able to vote for specific candidates from a party's list. The number of representatives elected from a particular party will depend on that party's percentage of the vote on Election Day. If a party receives 35 percent of the vote in a district, it will send roughly 35 percent of the legislators from that district.[15] What this means is that the second- or third-place parties, or even more, may also be sending representatives to the legislature. Because there is a significant likelihood that no party will win a majority of the legislative seats, a majority coalition will need to be forged, further empowering smaller parties.

Thinking Causally Is two-party competition a result of rules like single-member-district plurality elections, or does two-party competition lead to those rules?

If single-member districts with plurality elections will generally be found in countries with predominantly two-party competition, a puzzle remains: is the two-party competition a consequence of these election rules or a cause of them? One study of the adoption of proportional representation systems found that the PR system was adopted as a response to what was effectively multiparty competition, rather than being the cause of that competition.[16]

In the United States, on the other hand, political scientists have suggested that early political discourse was strongly oriented around fundamental debates about the proper role of government, and these debates tended to feature two competing views, one advocating a bigger role for the national government and the other a smaller role. A system like single-member districts with plurality elections works well in such an environment, reflecting rather than creating the nature of political competition between two predominant opposing viewpoints.[17]

The winner-take-all system in presidential elections favors two major parties.

Presidential elections pose a similar challenge to third parties. With the exception of Maine and Nebraska, all states allocate their electoral votes on a winner-take-all basis.[18] The popular vote winner of the presidential contest in these 48 states wins all the electoral votes from the state, no matter what the size of the popular vote victory. For a third-party candidate, this system makes it difficult to win electoral votes. Because a third party is not likely to be the leading vote winner in a state, it will win no electoral votes. And with the presidency and national government growing in stature and influence over the course of American political history, politicians throughout the country would want to be affiliated with a party that has a chance to win that powerful office. Voters also would want to have a say in choosing the president by voting for one of the major party candidates who has a plausible chance at victory.[19]

Legal and behavioral features of American elections reinforce two-party competition.

In addition to the basic structural features of American politics already discussed, statutes affecting elections, as well as the behavior of voters, politicians, and the media, reinforce the tendencies toward two-party politics.

fusion a strategy in which third parties endorse a major party candidate but list that candidate separately on the ballot so that voters can vote for the candidate under the third-party label.

Anti-fusion laws Anti-fusion laws prohibit third parties from practicing **fusion** with a major party. Fusion, a common and successful strategy until banned in nearly all states around the turn of the twentieth century, allowed voters to vote for a candidate either under the third-party label or under the major party label. The strategy was to make voters comfortable voting for third-party candidates and to increase the influence the third party could exert on the candidates once they were in office.[20] Currently, only seven states allow fusion in its traditional form, most notably in New York where it is known as *cross-filing*. In 1997, the Supreme Court rejected a challenge to the constitutionality of anti-fusion laws.[21]

Ballot access Prior to the 1880s, ballot access was not an issue. Parties printed their own ballots, which

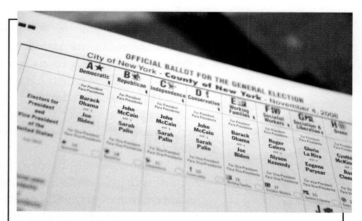

FUSION BALLOT

New York State allows fusion, also known as cross-filing, in which a candidate can appear on a ballot separately as more than one party's nominee. Advocates of third parties hope fusion ballots will make voters comfortable with third-party candidates and that victorious candidates will realize they earned some of their votes as the nominee of a third party.

Australian ballot an official government-produced ballot for elections that lists all offices and all the candidates and parties that have qualified to be on the ballot.

voters took to the polling place and dropped into the ballot box. Over a short period in the 1880s and 1890s, nearly every state adopted the **Australian ballot**, named for its country of origin. This is the ballot as we know it today—an official ballot printed by the government, provided at the polling place, listing all the candidates for every office, and cast secretly. In most states, parties can gain automatic ballot access if they do sufficiently well in prior elections—this rule largely benefits the major parties. Requirements to collect a large number of signatures to earn a spot on the ballot have created a hurdle for minor parties.

Campaign finance Running for office is expensive. Third-party candidates suffer from the fact that donors are usually not interested in contributing money to candidates they perceive as having no chance of winning. The public financing system for presidential candidates is also geared toward the major party candidates. Parties whose candidates received at least 25 percent of the vote in the prior presidential election get a full share of public financing for the general election in the fall. If a candidate received between 5 and 25 percent in the previous election, his or her party is entitled to a proportional share of public financing in the current election. Candidates falling below 5 percent, which is nearly always the case for third-party candidates, do not earn their party any share of public financing.

Voter, media, and candidate behavior The ways in which voters, the media, and candidates respond to the incentives created by these structural and legal aspects of American politics reinforce the tendency toward two-party politics. Voters unhappy with major party candidates often choose not to vote rather than vote for a third-party candidate who is likely to lose.[22] Other voters fear that voting for a third-party candidate amounts to throwing their vote away and implicitly helping their less-favored major party candidate.[23]

Media coverage is also problematic for third parties. Third-party officials often complain that if the media paid more attention to third parties, they would do better electorally. Media representatives respond that if third parties did better electorally, the news media would pay more attention to them. Each side is right. A media outlet that focuses a lot of attention on relatively obscure candidates may well find its readers, viewers, or listeners drifting to other media outlets. But more attention from the media would, overall, be at least marginally helpful for third-party candidates.

Ambitious, qualified candidates are much more likely to run for office as a Democrat or Republican than as a third-party candidate, because most voters are reluctant to vote for third-party candidates. Further, each major party has a network of supporters, consultants, experts, and fund-raisers to draw on.

TABLE 8-1 Most Successful Third-Party Presidential Candidates, 1900–2008

Year	Candidate	Party	Percent of Popular Vote	Number of Electoral Votes
1912	Theodore Roosevelt	Progressive	27.4	88
1992	Ross Perot	Independent/United We Stand	18.9	0
1924	Robert La Follette	Progressive	16.6	13
1968	George Wallace	American Independent	13.5	46
1996	Ross Perot	Reform	8.4	0
1980	John Anderson	Independent/National Unity Party	6.6	0
1912	Eugene Debs	Socialist	6.0	0
1920	Eugene Debs	Socialist	3.4	0
1916	Allan Benson	Socialist	3.2	0
1904	Eugene Debs	Socialist	3.0	0
1908	Eugene Debs	Socialist	2.8	0
1948	Henry Wallace	Progressive	2.8	0
2000	Ralph Nader	Green	2.7	0
1948	Strom Thurmond	States' Rights	2.4	39
1932	Norman Thomas	Socialist	2.2	0

Note: Includes all third-party presidential candidates who received at least 2 percent of the national vote.
Source: Dave Leip's Atlas of U.S. Presidential Elections, www.uselectionatlas.org

Occasionally, third parties overcome these difficulties. Third-party candidates who have already become nationally visible as former members of a major party or in some other way will often be talented and strong candidates (see Table 8-1). Theodore Roosevelt, George Wallace, and Ralph Nader all had significant name recognition. For some wealthy candidates, like Ross Perot in 1992 and 1996, campaign financing is not an obstacle.[24]

Alternative voting rules might assist third-party electoral fortunes.

Supporters of an enhanced role for third parties argue that changes in voting rules could give these parties a better chance of winning elections. Whether this claim is accurate is difficult to determine because these alternative rules are not widely used in the United States. Nonetheless, it seems plausible that preference voting and approval voting would have some minor benefit for third parties.

> **Thinking Causally** Would alternative voting rules lead to more third-party success?

Preference voting In American elections, voters select their favored candidate among those on the ballot. An alternative arrangement would allow voters to rank their choices, indicating which candidate is their first pick, second, third, and so on. The idea is that voters could express support for a third-party candidate but need not indicate support for only that candidate.

INSTANT RUNOFF VOTING BALLOT

Instant runoff voting has voters rank their preferences. If your top-ranked candidate finishes last in the first round of voting, your vote is reallocated to your second choice. This procedure continues until one candidate has received a majority of the votes. The city of Cary, North Carolina, used this sample ballot to help voters become acquainted with IRV. Should more cities and states be encouraged to adopt IRV?

Of the several varieties of preference voting arrangements, instant runoff voting is one that a handful of cities in the United States, including San Francisco and Minneapolis, have adopted. In this system, voters rank their choices. If no candidate receives a majority of the first-place votes, the candidate receiving the fewest first-place votes is eliminated, and the votes cast for him or her are redistributed to other candidates based on the preference ranking indicated by those voters. If a candidate now has a majority, he or she wins. If not, the last-place candidate is again removed and the votes redistributed.

Approval voting   Rather than ranking candidates, approval voting allows voters to indicate all candidates that they approve. The candidate receiving the most votes wins. As with preference voting, voters can vote for a third-party candidate and other candidates of their choosing without worrying about wasting their votes.

Whether promoting multiparty democracy in the United States through alternative voting rules is a good thing or not is a matter of dispute. To some political observers, multiparty democracy is more inclusive and produces higher voter turnout. To other observers, a two-party system produces more focused debates and a greater probability of decisive, majority victories rather than the plurality victories common to multiparty systems.

Party Organization

8-3   Trace the evolution of American party organizations and their expanding role in campaigns.

Scholars sometimes describe American political parties as a three-legged stool. The first leg is the party in the electorate: the party identification of voters, changes in their party attachments over time, and the influence of these attachments on political behavior. The second leg of the stool is party in government: the role of political parties in structuring the behavior, influence, and success of Congress, the president, the courts, and the bureaucracy. The third leg of the stool is party organization, the focus of this section. Party organization generally refers to the formal structure that sets rules for party operations and provides services for various party units and candidates.

Party organization in the nineteenth century was informal.

Political parties in the early nineteenth century did not have large, official organizations. Prominent elected officials like governors or members of Congress usually held great sway over party activities. They would meet informally in small caucuses to select the party's candidates. In later years, parties sent large numbers of delegates to nominating conventions to select candidates, but elected officials still often handpicked the delegates to the convention.

party machine disciplined local party organizations that selected candidates; got out the vote; provided benefits to supporters including government workers, local constituents, and businesses; and served as social service agencies for their followers.

Once candidates were in place, party workers were very involved in organizing parades, rallies, marches, and other events to motivate voters to get involved and support the ticket. These motivational efforts had the feel of "us against them" military campaigns and worked tremendously well. Turnout rates in the nineteenth century, especially its latter decades, were often in the range of 80 percent or more.[25]

Party machines provided organization in urban areas.

The era from 1870 to 1920 was the heyday of the local **party machine**. Machines were disciplined organizations that selected candidates, got out the vote, and provided benefits to loyal constituencies. Usually the leader of the machine was an elected official, typically a mayor, but not always. Machines were hierarchical organizations with a reach all over a city, so that each precinct (usually a few city blocks) had a machine representative in charge, who reported to a ward boss. They were intensely local in focus, but they were willing to offer backing to a state or national politician who could return the favor in some way.

THE "BRAINS"

THAT ACHIEVED THE TAMMANY VICTORY AT THE ROCHESTER DEMOCRATIC CONVENTION.

MONEY MAKES THE MACHINE GO 'ROUND
Cartoonist Thomas Nast was a vigorous critic of party machines. Here he pans them as nothing more than corrupt organizations that bought the support of delegates at nominating conventions in order to get their favored candidates nominated.

The machine spread benefits broadly. As a candidate or office holder, you knew that affiliation with the machine increased your likelihood of victory. Kicking back a portion of your salary to the machine would be an acceptable price to pay and was better than losing. As a worker, the promise of a city job awarded to you for your loyalty, known as **patronage**, made the machine a path to upward mobility. This was especially true for immigrants who might otherwise find it difficult to advance in the American economy. Businesspeople, lawyers, and bankers knew they would prosper through government contracts and favorable regulations if the machine was electorally successful. And individual voters were catered to by precinct captains who would provide them with groceries, financial and legal assistance, job contacts, help renting a facility for a wedding, or any other kind of help that would cement the voter's loyalty to the machine.

patronage awarding jobs in government on the basis of party support and loyalty rather than expertise or experience.

Party organizations were reformed at the beginning of the twentieth century.

With the rise of professions and the middle class at the turn of the twentieth century, machines came under strong attack. Businesses that were not favored by the machines, rival politicians, and middle-class reformers joined forces in what became labeled the Progressive movement, to change civil service laws at the national, state, and local levels. These **Progressive reforms** included the introduction of nonpartisan elections; the development of separate and often appointed rather than elected governing districts for services such as water, transportation, and schooling; and the hiring of city managers to run much of the day-to-day business of the city, taking that job away from elected mayors.

Progressive reforms a set of political and electoral reforms in the early twentieth century that had the combined effect of weakening political parties.

At the state level, reforms included the widespread adoption of personal registration requirements for voting, requirements that primary elections determine party nominations, and the increased use of nonelected boards and commissions to make public policy. Reformers expected these changes to weaken political parties, or at least to weaken the control of their opponents over the parties and government. In this way, reformers and machine politicians were alike: each wanted to make it more difficult for their opponents to hold office and wield power.[26]

Thinking Causally How could a reform like the primary election, which promised to weaken political parties and was advocated vigorously by those opposed to strong parties, be enacted by state legislatures filled with party politicians?

Because it was ardently pursued by reformers, the adoption of the primary election has usually been thought of by political scientists as an assault on a party's most defining power: control over nominations. Certainly, primaries do present challenges, as they create strife within parties and risk the nomination of weak candidates. The correlation between the support of reformers and the adoption of the reform, however, is somewhat misleading. More recent research shows that major party officials welcomed the primaries in part because they had increasingly struggled to maintain control over their growing organizations and the conflicts about who "deserved" a nomination.[27]

The adoption of primaries as the dominant form of party nomination was part of a broader trend of state government regulation of political parties.[28] States established laws and rules concerning party committees, the selection process of party officials, how parties could raise and spend money, in what ways they could assist their candidates, how candidates would qualify for the party primary ballot, and who could vote in the primaries.

Party organizations have become more active in recent decades.

For decades after the introduction of Progressive movement reforms, party organizations were largely ineffective and inactive. Party functions such as recruiting, training, and assisting candidates fell by the wayside as candidates built their own campaign organizations, became less reliant on the resources of the formal party organizations, and deemphasized their link to their political parties. Voter mobilization by parties lagged in many areas. Organizations today have reversed these trends.

State party organizations   State parties challenged their legal status by arguing that they were private associations entitled to set their own rules. In a series of decisions beginning in the late 1980s, the Supreme Court agreed and granted state party organizations more autonomy from government regulations over candidate nominations and party spending.[29] For example, the right of parties to spend unlimited sums on behalf of candidates was upheld, so long as candidates had no say in how the money was spent.[30]

To respond to the competitors for some of their key functions, state party organizations and legislative campaign committees increased their professionalism, hiring new staff and experts to recruit, train, and help finance candidates, and working more closely with the new web of pollsters, consultants, and media advisers.

National party organizations   The national party organizations include the Democratic and Republican national committees and the campaign committees for each party in the House and Senate, referred to as the Hill committees.

Starting in the mid-1970s, both parties began modernizing their operations and becoming more active in presidential campaigning. Both parties expanded their funding and staff. The key to this revival was that parties benefited from the complexity of campaigning in an era of high technology, constant media, large fund-raising demands, and intense demand

PARTY CHIEFS

The national party committee establishes rules by which the party's business is conducted and provides support for recruiting, training, and financing candidates. The party chairs, such as Reince Priebus and Deborah Wasserman Schultz, 2011 chairs of the RNC and DNC, respectively, are usually the most visible spokespersons for the national party organizations.

from issue activists. Some candidates—especially new ones—simply cannot assemble on their own the necessary money and expertise needed to run a modern campaign, thus opening the door to national party organization involvement.[31]

In addition to contributing funds and providing services to their candidates, the national party organizations also acted independently. The national party committees spent anywhere from 3 to 15 times as much money in their independent spending than in their contributions to the party's candidates.[32] In total dollars, independent party expenditures were well over 100 times higher in 2010 than they had been in 2002.[33] In competitive congressional races, it was not unusual for the party organizations to spend more on a campaign than either of the candidates.

national party convention a meeting held over several days at which delegates select the party's presidential nominee, approve the party platform, and consider changes in party rules and policies.

party platform a document expressing the principles, beliefs, and policy positions of the party, as endorsed by delegates at the national party convention.

For most Americans, the most visible activity of the national party organizations is running the **national party convention** held every four years to select the party's presidential and vice presidential nominees. The convention delegates pass the **party platform**, a statement of the party's principles, goals, and plans, and settle rules controversies within the party. Up through the mid-twentieth century, conventions were the place where rival factions within a party battled to select the party's presidential nominee. Multiple ballots were sometimes needed to determine the nominee. Today, however, largely because of the reforms to the nominating process after 1968, the nominee is usually known well in advance of the convention.

Case Study

Getting to Know Voters, One by One

One feature of the party machine praised by political scientists was its tight connection with voters. The machine was, in part, a social service or welfare agency. In exchange for providing help, the machine sought votes. It knew its voters.

Party organizations today also try to know their voters, but they do not have the deep personal connection with voters that the machine did. Nor do they provide social services. However, through microtargeting, they try to understand voters one by one to target messages to each. The hope is to persuade the undecided to support the party's candidate and to motivate the already decided to get out to vote.[34]

Microtargeting consists of building huge databases of information about voters. For each potential voter, party workers enter hundreds of bits of information, ranging from neighborhood characteristics available from the U.S. Census to consumer characteristics, such as purchasing habits, brand of car owned, television networks watched, magazine subscriptions, gun ownership, sports preferred, type of musical preference, and much more. Phone or direct contact from a party staffer or volunteer—known as party canvassing—might extract some additional information for the database. Canvassing is one of the main ways young people become involved in party activity.

Examining voter records and lists, which are readily available from states, provides information on a voter's turnout history, party registration, and possibly which party primary she or he voted in. Voter visits to the party's website or, for example, its Facebook profile, provide additional information.[35] Public opinion data are then merged into the file, allowing data analysts to unearth connections between demographic, consumer, and other information and views on public issues.

These data are then analyzed to produce a specific message tailored to a voter's key interests. The database helps generate sophisticated and narrowly targeted advertising, mailings, phone contact, personal contact, and get-out-the-vote drives on behalf of a range of party candidates.[36] Analysts compute scores for each individual to estimate his or her likelihood of supporting the party's candidates, so the party can target its outreach efforts efficiently.[37]

Republicans in 2002 were the first to use microtargeting in a systematic way, and it was a prominent part of the party's campaign effort in 2004. The Republican National Committee, in coordination with the Bush campaign and Republican state and local party organizations, purchased commercial databases that held hordes of information on individuals. The party also purchased or received from

GETTING OUT THE VOTE Political parties engage in extensive get-out-the-vote (GOTV) activities. Urging individuals to vote on Election Day is the culmination of a long and often precisely targeted effort to appeal to voters' key concerns. Through microtargeting, parties appeal to voters on issues of specific interest to them. The parties consult massive databases to discern what an individual's key issues might be.

(continues)

Case Study   Getting to Know Voters, One by One *(continued)*

supporters the membership information from organizations expected to lean toward the party's positions. All this information was entered into the national Republican database known as the Voter Vault, which holds information on over 170 million voters.

The Democrats microtargeted extensively in 2006 as they regained majorities in the U.S. House and Senate. By 2008, the Democratic National Committee had built a national voter database known as DataMart that matched the Republicans' in size. Volunteers could log into the database over the Web and provide real-time updates to the information collected on potential voters. The Democrats' database benefited from the Obama campaign's heavy use of new media and technology to reach volunteers and supporters.[38]

Creating and analyzing microtargeting databases are examples of jobs usually best performed

by the national party organizations, because of their resource advantages. As a result of these efforts in previous elections, both parties in the 2010 midterm elections and going into the 2012 elections had billions of bits of voter information at their disposal.

Thinking Critically

1. What might be some objections to parties tailoring their messages and appeals to individual voters? What are some virtues?

2. Under what circumstances can you imagine microtargeting not being an effective mobilization technique?

3. Is the advent of microtargeting a plus or a minus for third parties? Why?

A new federalism of the parties is now in place.

Today, the national party organizations have more influence on the state organizations than was true previously. The Democratic and Republican national party organizations provide financing and technical assistance for their state parties. Each national party channels contributions to the state parties with directions about how to employ these funds to benefit candidates for national office.

Both parties, but especially the Democrats, set mandatory rules at the national level. The Democrats have established rules for how delegates are apportioned among candidates in presidential primaries and caucuses, the demographic composition of state delegations to the national convention, and the procedures by which caucuses are run. The Republicans leave more of these matters to the state parties to determine. However, for 2012, the party is imposing rules on states that hold their nomination contest too early to encourage states to move their contests later into the spring.

As part of their increased activity in recent elections, national party organizations have created coordinated campaigns with state party organizations, in which the national party provides financial resources, expertise, and staff to help a state party's effort to win a congressional or other seat. Howard Dean, chair of the Democratic National Committee in 2006, adopted the "50-State Strategy" to signal to state party organizations that this kind of national assistance was possible across the country, not just in traditional Democratic strongholds. Barack Obama in 2008 followed Dean's lead by placing staff across the country, not just in loyal Democratic states and swing states.

The Evolution of Party Competition and Party Coalitions

8-4 Explain how parties achieve electoral success by building and maintaining coalitions of supporters.

Successful American parties are large coalitions that bring together a wide range of groups with varied interests and policy perspectives. Groups benefit by associating with a winning party because it increases the likelihood of action on the groups' key issues. Bringing interests together does pose challenges, however. The larger the party, the more factions it is likely to have. For a while, these factions can reside in peaceful coexistence, but as groups in the coalition begin to believe that the party is marginalizing their issues and concerns, the coalition comes under strain. Coalition management presents a complex challenge for party leaders.

The fact that American party coalitions need to be large has been the basis for a long-standing debate about American parties. Some analysts have called for candidates from a party to run as a team that offers a clear platform of proposals, works in a highly unified, disciplined fashion to enact them, and then runs on its record. This is the **responsible party model**.

Some analysts, however, have said the broad nature of American party coalitions makes this kind of party behavior unlikely over an extended time because parties constantly need to adjust their positions to either become or to maintain a majority. They need to respond to events and to the tactics of the other major party. And because some positions might be more popular in one part of the country than another, candidates of the same party will differ in their views from place to place. The practical reality, these critics say, is that

responsible party model the idea that political parties should run as unified teams, present a clear policy platform, implement that platform when in office, and run on their record in the subsequent election.

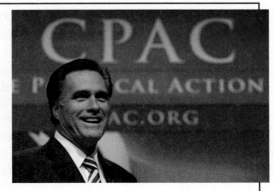

TOUCHING BASE WITH ACTIVISTS

Each party has particular groups whose support is important for candidates. The Conservative Political Action Conference provides a chance for Republican candidates to establish their conservative credentials with an audience of political activists. Here, former Massachusetts governor Mitt Romney, a Republican presidential candidate in 2012, addresses the group at its 2010 conference.

successful parties will usually have to compromise and adjust their positions more than their most fervent supporters would like.[39]

Coalitions are dynamic, not static.

"The party coalition" is a general term that obscures the complicated nature of holding together a coalition. Coalitions come together in a wave of optimism because their members believe that their goals will be better achieved by joining forces.

A victorious party might wish for time to stand still while it revels in its unity—its coalition intact and the party a national majority. This is impossible. Party coalitions are always changing and facing strains. Cracks in the party foundation may appear immediately. At other times they may build up over decades.

If a party knows that its success depends on serving the members of its coalition, what might prevent it from doing so? Media personalities, newspaper columnists, and bloggers often solve this puzzle by pinning the blame on unprincipled and spineless politicians. This explanation ignores the significant difficulty involved in holding together diverse coalitions of dozens of interest groups, hundreds of elected officials, and tens of millions of voters spread coast to coast. There are several strategic factors explaining why a party might not serve all parts of its coalition equally.

Thinking Causally Why would a political party seem to downplay the concerns of some members of its coalition, when it knows it needs the votes of these coalition members to win?

First, a group might be so loyal to the party that it reduces pressure on the party to advance the group's agenda.[40] Second, one group's interests might clash with the interests of other groups in the coalition—someone will have to be disappointed. Third, as the mix of voters supporting a party changes over time, a group may become a smaller share of a party's voters and therefore be less central to the party's electoral strategies. Lastly, a party that has lost recent elections will have conflicting internal interpretations about what lessons to learn from these defeats. The winning interpretation will favor some party groups and their issues more than others.[41]

issue evolution a change in the partisan base of support for an issue over time, such that the positions of Democrats and Republicans switch.

All four of these factors contribute to parties changing their emphasis on particular issues, perhaps to the chagrin of some coalition members. At the extreme, a party might even reverse its position on an issue. Political scientists refer to flips in party positioning as **issue evolution**. Some examples of issue evolution are the support of civil rights by the Democratic Party beginning in the 1960s, a stance previously taken by Republicans; and the move by Republicans to a free trade position in the 1970s, after having been the party more supportive of protectionism since its founding in 1854. Issue evolution is a dramatic illustration of how party coalitions are always evolving. Sometimes party leaders calculate that maintaining and enlarging the party's base of support requires setting aside some groups' concerns or revising or even reversing a long-standing party position.[42]

The Democratic New Deal coalition dominated electoral politics for over 40 years.

Over time, the key issues and relative strength of the two major parties have changed. Political scientists refer to the switch from one period of competition to another as **electoral realignment**—the shifting of support groups between the parties, the addition of new groups, and the rise of a new set of prominent issues. Political scientists dispute the process by which electoral realignment occurs and whether the most important change is sudden and dramatic, in the form of a "critical election," or slow building and gradual.[43] They more widely accept the view, however, that there are some roughly demarcated periods of competition (see Table 8-2).

electoral realignment a shift in the composition of party coalitions that produces a new, relatively durable pattern of party competition.

The coalition brought together by Democratic presidential candidate Franklin Roosevelt in 1932 proved to be remarkably resilient. Galvanized by Roosevelt's promise to respond aggressively to the economic stress of the Great Depression, Democratic supporters agreed that economic recovery through a collection of programs known as the New Deal was the first and most important priority of government. The coalition included southern whites; agricultural workers; unionized labor; lower- to lower-middle-income individuals; big-city public officials and their ethnic group supporters such as the Irish and Poles; Catholics and Jews; and industries pleased by Roosevelt's free trade approach.

TABLE 8-2 Number of Years of Party Control of Congress and the Presidency, 1801–2012

	President		House		Senate	
	Democratic-Republicans	Federalists	Democratic-Republicans	Federalists	Democratic-Republicans	Federalists
1. 1801–1828	28	0	26	2	26	2
	Democrats	National Republicans/ Whigs	Democrats	National Republicans/ Whigs	Democrats	National Republicans/ Whigs
2. 1829–1860	24	8	24	8	28	4
	Democrats	Republicans	Democrats	Republicans	Democrats	Republicans
3. 1861–1896	8	28	6	30	14	22
a. 1861–1876	0	16	2	14	0	16
b. 1877–1896	8	12	4	16	14	6
4. 1897–1932	8	28	10	26	6	30
5. 1933–1968	28	8	32	4	32	4
6. 1969–2012	16	28	30	14	27	17
a. 1969–1992	4	20	24	0	18	6
b. 1993–2012	12	8	6	14	9	11

Source: Marjorie Randon Hershey, *Party Politics in America*, 13th ed. (New York: Pearson Longman, 2009), p. 119, and authors' calculations.

Over time, the Democratic coalition shifted. With the civil rights achievements of Democratic presidents in the 1960s, blacks moved firmly into the Democratic column, support among white southerners fell, and Hispanic voters increased their support for Democrats. The prominence of new issues based on civil rights, women's rights, environmentalism, lifestyle, sexuality, the Vietnam War, and the use of American military power split the party. The 1968 Democratic National Convention descended into televised chaos as pro-war and anti-war factions clashed over the party's internal democracy.

After 1968, upper-middle-class professionals, along with upper-income voters and college graduates, became a larger share of the Democratic Party coalition. Meanwhile, support began to wane among the original members of the New Deal coalition.[44] About 70 percent of Catholics favored Democratic candidates in the 1950s; by the 1980s, a little over 50 percent did. Support among white working-class voters—non-college-educated workers engaged in manual labor—also dropped.[45] And as union membership declined after the 1950s, especially in the private sector, the proportion of Democratic voters who were from union households dropped from nearly 35 percent to less than 15 percent.[46]

The coalition crafted by Ronald Reagan brought the Republicans to national parity.

Ronald Reagan in 1980 built a coalition that brought the Republicans to parity with Democrats nationally. In the wake of bad economic times and struggling U.S. foreign policy, Reagan encouraged new identities for disgruntled groups. He asked middle-class and working-class voters to think of themselves not as the beneficiaries of government programs, but as the taxpayers bearing the heavy cost of supporting these programs. Blue-collar workers were asked to focus not only on their economic concerns but on their patriotic concerns for the United States and their values that were "looked down on" by media and liberal elites. These "Reagan Democrats" joined conservative white southerners, conservative Christians, businesses frustrated by high taxes and regulation, and middle- to high-income individuals and small-town and rural residents.[47]

This coalition of voters produced presidential victories for Republicans Reagan (1980, 1984), George H. W. Bush (1988), and George W. Bush (2000, 2004). In 1994, Republicans gained control of the House and Senate for the first time in 40 years. Representative Newt Gingrich of Georgia played a leading strategic role in this electoral success. The Republican congressional majority lasted until 2006 when the party lost its control of both the House and Senate due to economic concerns, the Iraq War, a series of scandals, and President Bush's low approval ratings.[48]

The Democrats regained unified control of government in 2008.

Whereas the years from 1933 through 1968 consistently featured a Democratic majority, party competition since 1969 has been more complex. Divided government has been common. Rather than a party realignment, some analysts argued the first half of this period featured **dealignment**, with voters splitting tickets, feeling less attachment to the parties, increasingly identifying themselves as independents, and turning out less to vote. These behaviors peaked in the mid-1980s. After that, ticket splitting dropped.[49]

dealignment a substantial reduction in the proportion of the voting population consistently voting for and identifying with one party.

Barack Obama's victory in 2008, coupled with Democratic gains in the House and Senate, had many Democrats hopeful for a realignment and the beginning of a seventh period of party competition. Republicans were distressed by the extent of their defeat in 2008, not only for the presidency but in Congress as well. By 2010, however, Republican gains were sweeping, with the party gaining several governorships and flipping about 20 state legislative chambers to Republican control. Nationally, Republicans gained a majority in the House and improved their vote share in 393 of 435 districts. The party also added a number of seats in the Senate.

How do the parties interpret these results? Republicans differ whether the Tea Party movement led to their success or prevented the party from winning even more seats. Democrats debate whether their policy philosophy is to blame or whether voters were simply expressing dissatisfaction with the pace of economic recovery. These debates will guide the parties' policies and electoral strategies in the run-up to the 2012 elections.[50]

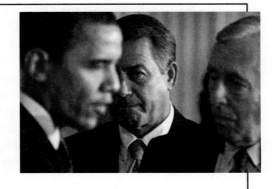

DIVIDED GOVERNMENT
The 2010 midterm elections vaulted Republicans to a majority in the House of Representatives, with John Boehner (center) becoming Speaker of the House. In 2011, split party control led to a dramatic budget showdown that threatened to shut down some government functions and potentially affect federal government debt payments. What might be the advantages and disadvantages of divided control of government?

Democrats and Republicans today have significant differences over public policy.

Despite the common criticism that they are just two peas in a pod, the two major parties do differ significantly on many policy issues. Indeed, if this were not so, it would be difficult to understand why the parties have different voting coalitions, different alliances of interest groups that support them, and different campaign contributors. Presumably, voters support candidates in part for their issue stances. Parties have an incentive to maintain their ideological distance. This distance keeps them attractive to supportive interest groups and voters, so that the party can count on, though not assume, their support in upcoming elections. Like a business, a party wants to have "repeat customers"—it will not achieve this goal by making its "product" a copycat of the other party.

Party differences vary at the national and state levels. Within a particular state, parties may adjust their position to be competitive. Republicans in the Northeast, for example, are generally more liberal than Republicans in the Southwest. Democrats in the South are generally more conservative than Democrats in the Pacific Northwest. Though the parties in a state may offer genuinely different positions, they may not mirror the range of ideological differences present at the national level. Democrats at the national level, for example, are more likely to support stronger gun control regulations, but in many states with widespread gun ownership, that would not be a viable position for Democrats to take.

Nationally, Democrats tend to argue for a more expansive use of government in addressing social and economic problems. Republicans will instead lean toward market-based, private sector solutions to problems and ask whether government policies have created obstacles to individuals and businesses who seek to undertake desired behavior. On social issues such as abortion, however, Democrats are less inclined to involve government in individual decision-making, whereas Republicans are more inclined to support government restrictions.

Although cultural and social issues like abortion or same-sex marriage receive significant attention in public discussion of parties and candidates, the contrasting agendas of the parties focus much more on economic, financial, and regulatory matters, including economic growth, prices, employment, taxes, regulating business, health care, retirement, and other issues such as education that can be defined as having economic significance.[51] In foreign policy, Republicans have generally supported a more aggressive use of military force to obtain desired goals; Democrats have expressed more reluctance in this area.[52]

Voters identify some issues so much with one party that scholars say the party "owns" these issues. For example, the public has long identified Social Security and government assistance programs as Democratic strong suits. The public usually gives the Republicans a similar advantage on foreign policy and keeping taxes low. Prior to the 2010 midterm election, Republicans held more than a 10-point advantage on handling terrorism and the size and power of the federal government. Democrats had leads of about 30 points on the environment and discrimination against minority groups.[53] Not every issue is owned by a party—some bounce back and forth.

These "owned" issues will shape party competition. The party that owns an issue will emphasize the issue to maximize its advantage on it. Republicans during the 2010 campaign hammered away on the issues of the power of the federal government and the size of federal debt, issues that appealed to Republicans, independents, and some Democrats, and on which the Republicans held an advantage. Democrats sought to focus public attention on the benefits of health care and financial reform and the need for legislation to deal with climate change, and portraying Republicans as too cozy with big corporations, all issues owned by Democrats.[54]

In recent years, observers have suggested that party differences have become extreme. They depict this competition as a clash of values and culture between red America and blue America, or red states (Republican) and blue states (Democratic). Some observers, like television commentator Bill O'Reilly, refer to it as a culture war. To other observers, though, the nature of American public opinion and the breadth of party coalitions mean there is at best a culture skirmish rather than a culture war.

HOW DO WE KNOW?

Is America Polarized?

The Question

In the eyes of many Americans, politics in the United States has become nasty, bitter, and rife with conflict. In 2008, presidential candidates Barack Obama and John McCain both criticized the nature of political debate in the United States, with Obama deriding it as "do-anything, say-anything, divisive politics" and McCain labeling it as "mindless, paralyzing rancor."[55] "Two Americas," the "50/50 nation," "red and blue America," and "culture war" are labels said to define current American politics.[56] Is America polarized? How do we know?

Why It Matters

Both for citizens and for politicians looking to influence the policy process, it matters whether Americans are in two different worlds politically or have political differences that are modest in degree. If the country is polarized, then political success will depend on highly charged mobilization based on strong rhetoric. If the country is not, then success will depend more on mobilizing the support of those whose views are relatively moderate. Party differences might also influence one's appraisal of the health of American democracy. Some citizens might consider different viewpoints to be the lifeblood of a healthy democracy. Others might see high degrees of partisan conflict as an obstacle to solving problems and a blot on democracy.

Investigating the Answer

Television election result maps in 2000 and 2004 showing the country divided sharply into regions of Republican

(continues)

HOW DO WE KNOW?   Is America Polarized? *(continued)*

support (colored red) and Democratic support (colored blue) helped popularize the idea that Americans live in polarized worlds politically, with a vast gulf in their cultural values and political preferences.

Closer examination, however, showed that the maps were misleading. Some red states were barely red, and some blue states barely blue. Maps colored at the county level and shaded for their degree of support for the Republican and Democratic presidential candidates in these two elections showed that much of the country was a shade of purple rather than distinctly red or blue. More-over, examination of maps of state legislative party control showed that the red–blue distinction did not carry over very well to that level, and the 2008 presidential election map showed nine states flipping color from red to blue.[57]

Despite the popularity of the red state/blue state language in media reports, it does not appear to get us very far in understanding whether America is polarized. Perhaps the place to look for polarization is not in the state-level pattern of party victories, but in public opinion.

One prominent study examines public opinion on a range of "hot button" issues like abortion and gay rights. The authors find that, when given the option, most Americans place themselves toward the middle of the scale rather than taking a position on the far left or far right. Even where opinion has become more polarized over time, the difference is not that great. For example,

the National Election Study asks survey respondents to place themselves on a series of 7-point issue scales. The average difference between Democrats and Republicans has increased since the early 1970s, when it was half a point, but only to about 1 point.[58]

Another study confirms that differences between Democrats and Republicans have grown—and uniquely so. The authors looked at public opinion on 35 issue areas since 1972. They found that by almost every measure—age, education, race, religious affiliation, region, and gender—there had been convergence rather than divergence of opinion between groups. Only for Democrats versus Republicans had opinion grown further apart.[59] This research suggests that public opinion may not be much more polarized now than previously, but that the political parties more precisely reflect the differences that do exist, making the conflict seem more pronounced. Political scientists refer to this as ideological sorting (see Figure 8-2).[60]

Partisans at the elite level have also moved further apart. Studies of legislative roll call voting show Democrats and Republicans in Congress are more ideologically distinct now than previously, with polarization of party voting patterns in the House and Senate at the highest levels since the end of Reconstruction.[61] Unlike the public, relatively few members of Congress fall in the ideological center. And they are better sorted than previously.

FIGURE 8-2 Partisan and Ideological Sorting in the Public, 1974–2008.

Over time, liberals became more likely to identify with the Democratic Party and conservatives with the Republican Party. Liberal identification with the Democrats rose from 73 percent in 1974 to 95 percent in 2004, a 22 percentage point rise. Conservative identification with the Republicans rose from 54 to 90 percent over the same period, a 36 point increase. Ideological sorting dropped slightly in 2008.

Source: American National Election Studies Cumulative File, 1948–2004, questions VCF0303 and VCF0803; American National Election Studies 2008, questions V083069, V083097, V083098b.

HOW DO WE KNOW? Is America Polarized?

For example, in the U.S. Senate, all Republicans are now more conservative than all Democrats. The opinion of party activists, as measured by a survey of delegates to the two parties' national conventions in 2008, is also strongly divergent, more so than among the public.[62]

So both elites and the public are better sorted ideologically into parties. That is the correlation. But what is the causality—what led to what? Did liberal and conservative voters begin the process by flocking more consistently to the Democratic and Republican parties, respectively, forcing the parties' candidates to respond by taking more extreme views? Or did candidates start the process by taking more extreme views, leading voters to respond by shifting and strengthening their party allegiance?

Political scientists have wrestled with these questions, exploring a number of explanations. Perhaps redistricting created safe partisan districts that encouraged legislators to behave in a more ideological fashion. Or perhaps congressional leaders began emphasizing partisan unity and ideology more after they adopted new leadership tools during congressional reforms in the 1970s and 1980s. Perhaps declining voter turnout signaled to parties that voters wanted stronger choices, and parties noticed that the public responded to fundraising appeals when the ideological lines were drawn sharply. Or perhaps the story is really about the South and its emergence out of a one-party political competition in which nearly every voter, whether liberal or conservative, supported Democratic candidates. Scholars have tested many more possible explanations.[63]

Although the data are mixed, and each of the factors just mentioned likely played a role, overall it appears that elites led and the public followed. As political activists within the party networks—representatives of business groups, advocacy groups, nonprofits, unions—became better organized and more involved, candidates increasingly took the positions that would garner their support. With this relationship between activists and candidates occurring in both parties, the public was faced with candidates taking stronger ideological stances, and individual voters sorted themselves into the party closer to them ideologically. With a more ideologically unified base of support in the public, candidates then had further reason to distance themselves from the candidates in the other party and parties had further reason to recruit more conservative and liberal candidates, rather than moderates.[64] Voters responded by voting even

more consistently for one party. Why? Imagine a voter who is slightly to the right of center. This voter might be open to voting for a mildly conservative Republican at some times and a mildly liberal Democrat at others. He might vote for the mildly liberal candidate over a more strongly conservative candidate. However, if the choices for this voter are now regularly between a strong liberal Democrat and a strong conservative Republican, he will likely vote Republican consistently.[65]

Thinking Critically

1. Is the trend toward greater ideological sorting among voters something to be applauded or feared?

2. If polarization is tied to the activities of party activists and supporters, is there any way to reverse it?

3. Would electoral reforms that increased the possibility for third-party success be likely to exacerbate or reduce polarization?

The Bottom Line

Public opinion overall is not dramatically more polarized now than previously. What has changed is that for both voters and politicians, opinion differences are now more sharply lined up by political party—fewer conservatives are aligned with the Democratic Party and fewer liberals identify with the Republican Party. Ideological sorting has led to a bigger philosophical gap between the typical Democratic and Republican politician and, to a lesser degree, a bigger gap between the typical Democrat and Republican in the public. Because of these trends, the cultural, economic, and other differences among Americans have become a more significant part of political debate. Polarized media rhetoric on high-profile economic and cultural issues attracts an audience. Public evaluations of Barack Obama's job performance are just as polarized along party lines as were those for George W. Bush and Bill Clinton. Congress remains staunchly divided. Because people do see the world differently, ideological sorting is likely to remain. Some observers say these developments in partisanship artificially create more conflict in government and leave moderate voters with unappealing choices. But others counter that ideological sorting has led to party competition that gives voters real choices, provides them with a reason to vote, and encourages fellow partisans in government to work together.[66]

Chapter Summary

In this chapter you have learned to:

8-1   Analyze the functions of political parties in American politics.

Political parties play a variety of roles. The Constitution provided for an electoral system but did not say how a sufficient number of candidates would emerge or how citizens would become engaged in the electoral process. Parties fill these roles. These functions of candidate recruitment and citizen mobilization, intended largely to advance the interests of the parties and their candidates, also enhance the legitimacy of American politics and government by bringing into practice the promise of electoral competition that was implicit in the Constitution. Political parties also contribute to American governance by giving public officials in different institutions and at different levels of government incentives to cooperate with each other to make public policy.

8-2   Determine why American electoral competition is dominated by two political parties rather than multiple parties.

Two-party electoral competition has dominated American politics since the very beginning. The structure of American government, including single-member districts, plurality elections, and winner-take-all electoral votes in presidential elections, pushes electoral competition toward a two-party model. In addition, a number of laws as well as the behavior of voters, the media, and candidates, reinforce the tendency for two parties to be the serious competitors. Third parties are only rarely successful electorally, but they can make a mark in other ways, such as introducing issues to the campaign that the major party candidates have ignored.

8-3   Trace the evolution of American party organizations and their expanding role in campaigns.

Party organization has gone through several phases. In early American history, party organizations were informal and largely implemented the wishes of important political leaders, especially regarding candidate nomination. Party machines emerged in the late nineteenth century. Machines thrived by developing a very personal form of politics but ran afoul of reformers who saw them as bastions of corruption. Progressive reformers passed a series of laws that weakened and regulated political parties in the early twentieth century. In recent decades, party organizations have become more active, especially by providing campaign services to party candidates.

8-4   Explain how parties achieve electoral success by building and maintaining coalitions of supporters.

The broad and diverse nature of coalitions necessary to produce a majority and win elections creates a difficult job of political management for party leaders. They play the balancing act of maintaining the coalition and focusing on the key public policy concerns of coalition members, while also adapting to new circumstances and trying to keep the coalition growing. As they accommodate new issues and new groups, they risk unraveling the coalition by driving current supporters away. Neither party can produce victories today by simply relying on the coalitions of the past. American parties have evolved through six periods of party competition, with different issues and different major parties dominating.

CHAPTER TEST

1. How do political parties bridge the gaps between institutions in American government?

2. In what ways do political parties bring citizens into the political process?

3. How does use of the party label increase voter leverage over the political system?

4. What is the general effect of single-member districts and plurality elections on the number of competitive parties?

5. How does the behavior of voters create challenges for third-party electoral success?

6. What innovations did Progressive reformers add to American politics and how did they affect political parties?

7. What are the major activities of party organizations today?

8. What are the major strategic dilemmas facing party leaders as they attempt to hold their coalition together?

9. In what ways do the policy orientations of Democrats and Republicans differ?

10. Why does the nature of coalition building sometimes frustrate those party supporters with strong ideological points of view?

MyPoliSciLab® POLITICAL PARTIES
Apply what you learned in this chapter on MyPoliSciLab.

[□●┤Read on mypoliscilab.com

eText: Chapter 8

✓●┤Study and Review on mypoliscilab.com

Pre-Test
Post-Test
Chapter Exam
Flashcards

👁┤Watch on mypoliscilab.com

Video: Senator Specter Switches Parties
Video: Tea Party Victories Concern for GOP

How Do We Know Video: Is America a Polarized Red/Blue Country?

✳┤Explore on mypoliscilab.com

Comparative: Comparing Political Parties
Timeline: The Evolution of Political Parties in the United States
Timeline: Third Parties in American History
Visual Literacy: State Control and National Platforms

KEY TERMS

Australian ballot, p. 236
dealignment, p. 249
divided government, p. 229
electoral realignment, p. 247
fusion, p. 235
issue evolution, p. 246

national party convention, p. 242
party machine, p. 239
party platform, p. 242
patronage, p. 240
plurality elections, p. 234
political parties, p. 227

Progressive reforms, p. 240
proportional representation, p. 234
responsible party model, p. 245
single-member districts, p. 234
two-party system, p. 232
unified government, p. 229

SUGGESTED READINGS

Marty Cohen, David Karol, Hans Noel, and John Zaller. 2008. *The Party Decides: Presidential Nominations Before and After Reform*. Chicago: University of Chicago Press. Argues that political parties, conceived as a network of interest groups, activists, and elected officials and members of official party organizations, remain the dominant force in selecting presidential nominees.

Leon D. Epstein. 1986. *Political Parties in the American Mold*. Madison: University of Wisconsin Press. Thorough explanation of the functions and history of American political parties.

Paul Frymer. 1999. *Uneasy Alliances: Race and Party Competition in America*. Princeton, NJ: Princeton University Press. Argues that the American party system was built on racial considerations and inevitably marginalizes the interests of black Americans.

David Karol. 2009. *Party Position Change in American Politics: Coalition Management*. New York: Cambridge University Press. Challenges the idea that parties and politicians maintain persistent issue positions, and contends that parties frequently change issue stances as a means to maintain or expand their coalitions, redefining what liberal and conservative mean in the process.

James Sundquist. 1986. *Dynamics of the Party System: Alignment and Realignment of Political Parties in the United States*. Washington, DC: Brookings Institution Press. Very readable account of the passage of the United States through various periods of party competition, including what might accelerate or stop these passages.

SUGGESTED WEBSITES

FAIRVOTE
www.fairvote.org

Advocacy group for proportional representation and alternative voting systems. Site provides explanation of various voting reforms.

AMERICAN PRESIDENCY PROJECT: POLITICAL PARTY PLATFORMS
www.presidency.ucsb.edu/platforms.php

Full text of platforms of all parties receiving electoral votes since 1840.

CAMPAIGN FINANCE INSTITUTE
www.cfinst.org

Extensive databases and helpful analysis of campaign finance, especially party revenues and spending.

ANES GUIDE TO PUBLIC OPINION AND ELECTORAL BEHAVIOR
www.electionstudies.org/nesguide/nesguide.htm

Collection of tables presenting over 40 years of data on partisanship, evaluation of candidates, participation, and public opinion from the premier academic election survey.

DAVE LEIP'S ATLAS OF U.S. PRESIDENTIAL ELECTIONS
www.uselectionatlas.org

Excellent collection of tables, data, graphs, and maps related to presidential election outcomes throughout American history. Also covers gubernatorial, U.S. Senate, and U.S. House elections.

Interest Groups

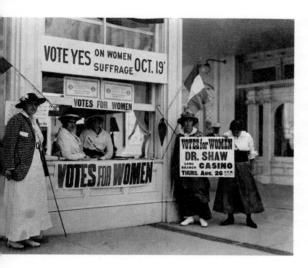

UNITED WE STAND Many women's groups came together to ensure passage of the Nineteenth Amendment to the U.S. Constitution. Their collective action and success in the states culminated in 1920 when they were formally granted the right to vote.

CHAPTER LEARNING OBJECTIVES

After reading this chapter you will be able to:

9-1 Distinguish between pluralist theory's and James Madison's interpretation of the role of interest groups within American politics.

9-2 Describe how critics of pluralist theory view the role of interest groups today.

9-3 Explain how interest groups form and attract members.

9-4 Analyze the strategies and tactics interest groups use to impact elections and public policy.

9-5 Assess how much influence interest groups have over policy outcomes.

First rule of human nature: people will always disagree. Name anything, and people will have different opinions on the matter. This maxim, in essence, is the greatest challenge of a democratic government: how do you come to a consensus allowing the free-flow of ideas without letting the losing side feel cheated, or worse, without people coming to blows? The Founding Fathers gave serious thought to the nature of political conflict and the fact that some groups have more resources and power than others. They specifically put in place rules that would make sure all voices were heard. Consider the examples of women's rights and immigration.

In 1868, no women anywhere in the United States were allowed to vote. By 1920, however, women in every state had the same voting rights as men. How did this change take place? It came primarily through the efforts of an interest group. In 1869, after the Civil War, two organizations promoting women's suffrage were founded: the National Woman Suffrage Association (NWSA) and the American Woman Suffrage Association (AWSA). After two decades of pursuing their agendas separately, the groups merged in 1890 to form the National American Woman Suffrage Association (NAWSA) with Susan B. Anthony as its leader.

The suffrage movement grew as it accumulated legal victories at the state level. NAWSA was soon joined by other women's groups, and this enhanced clout helped secure further victories and more converts, creating a positive momentum for a nationwide policy change. Congress proposed an amendment to the Constitution in 1919 that granted women the right to vote, and the amendment was ratified by the required 36 states in 1920.[1]

Admirers of American democracy look to this story with pride. The success of the women's suffrage movement, they argue, shows the openness of the American political system to influence by groups of all political stripes—regardless of their resources or their previous level of political involvement.

Now consider the immigration issue. The United States of America was established as a land that welcomed and benefited from immigration. But throughout its history laws were set up to control the flow of immigration. In the latter half of the twentieth century, the flow of immigrants entering the country illegally began to expand exponentially, most coming across the southwest borders from Latin America. This change created a highly emotional issue. On one side, the pro-immigration forces argue that the country wants and benefits from the labor and that the vast majority of these immigrants are hard working and law abiding. On the other side, critics say that illegal immigrants strain already overburdened schools and hospitals, and that the growing drug wars and human trafficking have increased problems with crime. However, both sides agree that today's immigration system is not working, and no one seems able to fix it.

These competing narratives lead to a few important questions about the place of organized interests in American politics. Are interest groups active and powerful or passive and ineffective? Are they a positive or negative influence on American democracy? Do they encourage a healthy, broad-based consideration of a variety of interests, or do they promote the pursuit of narrow self-interest? Guided by these questions, in this chapter we examine the role of interest groups in America. ■

The Problem of Factions and the Pluralist Answer

9-1   Distinguish between pluralist theory and James Madison's interpretation of the role of interest groups within American politics.

Almost every discussion of group politics in the United States begins with one of the most famous pieces of political rhetoric ever written by an American—*Federalist 10* by James Madison, one of the nation's founders. This brief essay was part of a broader collection of writings known as *The Federalist Papers*. In *Federalist 10*, Madison noted the capacity of the proposed federal republic "to break and control the violence of faction." In using the word *faction*, Madison was referring to a group of individuals who share a belief that, if acted upon, would jeopardize the rights of individuals outside the group, or the interests of the community as a whole. Madison argued that government—and by extension, Americans as individuals and the country as a whole—must be protected from the influence of factions. But, he also believed that the American system was well designed to mute the influence of such interests.

Political scientists in the 1950s began to reconsider the place of group interests in politics. And they generally referred to factions as "groups," "interests," "organized interests," or "**interest groups**." These scholars viewed the competition for influence in American politics as generally healthy, and a legitimate aspect of democratic governance.

interest groups organizations that seek to influence government decisions.

This thinking on the place of group interests in America came to be known as **pluralism**, referring to the multiple groups and interests making demands on government (even if the demands were to be ignored). Pluralists believed that politics could be considered primarily as an organized effort to resolve conflicts among competing group interests.[2] Furthermore, they viewed political power and resources as being dispersed widely throughout society, with no one group or set of groups achieving long-term supremacy across a significant number of issue areas.

pluralism the theory that all groups are well represented and no single interest controls government decisions.

Pluralists also believed that the political system provides multiple access points for influence. Groups are free to petition government at the local, state, and national levels, and through the offices of the executive, the legislature, and the judiciary. Because of this, almost every group can expect an opportunity to be heard and taken seriously somewhere in the political system.[3] Finally, pluralists argued that, even if not organized into a formal group, individuals with a common interest can still have their needs addressed through politics.

Elected officials have an incentive to take into account the needs of unorganized interests, precisely to keep them from becoming organized.

Critics of Pluralism

9-2   Describe how critics of pluralist theory view the role of interest groups today.

Since at least the 1950s, pluralism has been a highly influential framework for thinking about American politics and government. Along with influence, however, comes scrutiny. Thus, pluralism has also attracted a significant number of criticisms: that the American political system is inherently resistant to change; that political resources are not distributed equally; that many important issues never make it onto the agenda; and that groups do not automatically form.

The American political system is resistant to change.

A fundamental critique of pluralism is that the American political system is resistant to change. The checks and balances designed by the Framers, coupled with the multiple decision points in the system, make it much more difficult to change the status quo than to defend the status quo. As we will see in Chapter 10, on Congress, an individual or group wishing to defeat a new policy proposal can, among other things, stop the proposal from being introduced as a bill; being heard, approved, or reported out of committee; being heard on the House or Senate floors; or being approved by the House or Senate. In addition to the numerous possibilities for defeating a policy proposal, programs and initiatives that make it through the legislative process can also be challenged in the court system, denied necessary funding in the appropriations process, or watered down or ignored by bureaucrats or state and local officials.

Someone wishing to preserve the status quo need only succeed at one point to kill a policy initiative, but someone wishing to change the status quo must succeed at every point. As a result, if a group succeeds in getting its policy preferences adopted, other groups with different preferences will have difficulty coming along later and altering the status quo. Thus, although the complex machinery of American government protects citizens against tyranny and factions, it also makes it hard for organized interests to bring about change.

Political resources are distributed unequally.

Another criticism of pluralism is that it does not account for non-participation that is a result of insurmountable obstacles to political participation, rather than a lack of interest. In the pre–civil rights era, for example, participation in politics by blacks was at strikingly low levels. We should not, however, interpret this as contentment with the status quo, or as a failure to see the relevance of politics to their own interests.[4] Indeed, for much of American history African Americans were deliberately excluded from the political system.

Although the political history of African Americans in America is an unusual case, other less extreme cases of political exclusion are indeed common. According to the most recent data, for example, more than 39 million Americans are in families with incomes below the poverty line.[5] Many of the impoverished are children, a group toward which the public is very sympathetic. Yet, while gun owners, nurses, attorneys, teachers, and the elderly are represented by vocal, highly successful interest groups in Washington, D.C., poor kids are not.

There are many reasons for this inequity. One is that effective political organization requires resources that the poor often do not have in abundance: money, time, knowledge, education, personal relationships, and political experience, among others. Critics of pluralism argue that, since critical political resources are not distributed equally across the population, the interest group system is biased in favor of upper- and middle-class groups, who have relatively easy access to the most important political resources and assets.

> **Thinking Causally** What factors might keep other groups from participating?

HOW DO WE KNOW?

Studying What Doesn't Happen

The Question

Sometimes in politics, things that do not happen are just as important as things that do. However, identifying and studying political fights that did not occur present no easy task. Is it possible to measure the impact of an issue's absence from the policy agenda? How do we know?

Why It Matters

Interest groups wield power by influencing what sorts of issues get talked about. Understanding power in the United States and the influence that interest groups might wield demands that we pay attention to the "dogs that are not barking."

Investigating the Answer

In The *Un-Politics of Air Pollution*, Matthew Crenson examines why some cities take aggressive action against local pollution, while others neglect the is-

sue. First, he uses the results of a 51-city survey of community leaders to identify the extent to which pollution was considered an important public issue in each city. With these results, he identifies cities that have put the pollution problem on their policy agenda and those that have largely ignored the issue. Crenson then seeks to develop explanations for these two different outcomes.

One possible explanation is that the cities that take pollution seriously have particularly bad pollution problems, while the cities that neglect the issue do so because pollution is not a serious problem there. Looking at pollution measures for each city, though, Crenson finds that this is only part of the explanation.

Next, Crenson undertakes an intensive study of two cities that exhibited very different responses to their pollution problems: Gary and East Chicago, both in Indiana. Gary delayed action in tackling a serious pollution problem, while East Chicago acted quickly to address the issue. Why? Crenson's intensive study

(continues)

HOW DO WE KNOW?   Studying What Doesn't Happen *(continued)*

leads him to believe that the failure of industrial interests in Gary, Indiana, either to support or to oppose the city's anti-pollution plans left the pollution issue in limbo.

Based on this finding, Crenson marshals survey data from local public figures to gain their assessment of local business influence and matches it against survey data indicating how seriously the community takes the issue of air pollution. Crenson finds that in high pollution cities, the stronger the perceived influence of the business community, the less likely that city is to elevate the problem of air pollution to the public policy agenda.

In *Power and Powerlessness*, John Gaventa investigates why miners in Middlesboro, Kentucky, did not take action in the face of miserable economic inequalities and poor working conditions. Part of Gaventa's explanation is that the townsfolk internalized a system of beliefs and values advanced by powerful economic and political interests in their town, which were structured to keep the miners quiet and submissive.

Gaventa has no difficulty demonstrating that the town's mining interests sought to cultivate a value system and ideology that would hold at bay any challenge to their power. What is more difficult to demonstrate, however, is that the townsfolk embraced that value system and ideology, and therefore did not seek to improve their situation. Gaventa applies two basic approaches in trying to demonstrate this latter point. First, he considers the behavior of miners in nearby communities that are not as dominated by economic interests as the town of Middlesboro. If his argument about Middlesboro is correct, then he should find greater tendency for protests, strikes, and even insurrections in these nearby communities. He finds precisely that.

However, Gaventa's finding might simply indicate that miners in Middlesboro recognized the unlikelihood of a successful strike, given the pervasive power of the mine owners. Acknowledging this, Gaventa analyzes the response of the Middlesboro townsfolk when the power of the mining interests weakens. We might expect the miners and their supporters to respond to this weakness with an increasing volume of demands. On the other hand, if the townsfolk had internalized the idea of subordination as their "natural" role, as Gaventa suspects, they might remain quiet when the power relationship changes. Gaventa finds the truth somewhere in the middle—there are limited demands for change

THE CAUSES OF INACTION Why didn't miners in Middlesboro, Kentucky, take action in the face of economic adversity? Answers to this question and others like it are often difficult to find, but creativity enables us to study political power, even when we don't see it directly exercised.

when the power of the mine owners weakens, but not as numerous or vocal as we might expect if the miners fully tried to advance their own interests.

Thinking Critically

1. In the two studies outlined above, explain how political power was manifested. How can you explain the direct correlation between wielding political power and action (or lack thereof)?

2. Can you think of any examples of groups that hold little to no power to convince powerful interests to enact change?

3. Explain how a "nonevent" can sometimes be more important than an actual event.

The Bottom Line

By definition, studying non-events or non-decisions is difficult. That said, these two in-depth and creative studies show how it is possible to study political power even when we do not see it wielded directly. This is crucial because if we study only the winners and losers in battles that we can see, we miss two fundamental ways that power is wielded: through inaction and through the internalization of powerlessness by groups that fail to organize.

Many important issues never make it onto the agenda.

An additional critique of pluralism begins with the observation that pluralists tend to study issue areas in which policy makers are debating solutions, but some issues are not actually considered issues by political elites.[6] Consider poverty as a political issue. In the Great Depression of the 1930s, and then again with Lyndon Johnson's declaration of a War on Poverty in 1964, the plight of the country's poor occupied center stage on the national agenda. But between these two periods—in the 1940s and 1950s—poverty virtually disappeared as a topic on the public policy agenda. Policy makers simply assumed (wrongly, as it turns out) that with the nation's return to prosperity in the 1940s, poverty had been largely vanquished. Thus, the attention of government decision makers turned to other issues.

This example illustrates the importance of what political scientists call **nondecisions**.[7] A nondecision can be defined as a decision not to put a particular issue on the **policy agenda**, which is the set of issues actively under consideration and discussion by policy makers. When government shunts some issues aside, the pluralist model breaks down. Group preferences on a particular issue cannot be taken into account if policy makers have chosen not to address that issue.

nondecisions decisions not to consider particular issues or incorporate them into the policy agenda.

policy agenda the set of issues under consideration by policy makers.

Groups do not automatically form.

In order for the pluralist model of democracy to work in optimal fashion, collections of individuals with interests that can be addressed by government need to come together to form groups. Pluralists explain the formation of groups through the **disturbance theory**, which holds that when social, political, and economic relationships are upset by some outside force, affected individuals often form a group in response.[8] Groups do not always form, however, when there is a disturbance. In 1965, economist Mancur Olson argued that "rational, self-interested individuals will not act to achieve their common or group interests."[9] Why? Because an individual's own efforts "will not have a noticeable effect on the situation of his organization, and he or she can enjoy any improvements brought about by others whether or not he has worked in support of his organization."[10]

disturbance theory the theory that when social, political, and economic relationships change, individuals form groups in response.

Olson's argument is a statement of what is known, variously, as the public goods problem, the **free rider problem**, the collective action problem, the prisoner's dilemma, and the tragedy of the commons. Imagine that you and your fellow students wish to have the school year shortened by two weeks. This requires a decision by school administrators. The best way of getting the decision you want is to form a group, organize rallies and e-mail campaigns, and lobby the relevant decision makers. From your perspective as an individual, however, it would be ideal if other students did all of the work and

free rider problem a barrier to collective action because people can reap the benefits of group efforts without participating.

Thinking Causally What other factors inhibit participation and lead to the "collective action problem"?

left you in peace. If the group consisted of, say, 500 active participants, your individual effort probably would not be missed anyway. Furthermore, if you failed to participate and the group succeeded without you, you would reap all of the benefits without having to give up any of your own time, money, or energy. What a great deal for you!

The obvious problem is that if everyone were to think this way, then everyone would leave it to others to do the work and the group would never form, get organized, bring attention to the issue, and lobby decision makers. This is a simple statement of the free rider problem, but the free rider problem is a shot right at the heart of pluralism. If individuals with a common interest fail to organize to pursue that interest, they can hardly join in the competition for government attention that defines pluralism. If this happens often enough, the pluralist model collapses.

Solving the Collective Action Problem: Group Formation and Maintenance

9-3   Explain how interest groups form and attract members.

We know, of course, that groups do form, get organized for political action, and participate in politics. Political scientists have identified a variety of ways groups can overcome the collective action problem. These include (a) selective benefits provided to group members, typically material or monetary, but also social or ideological; (b) individual entrepreneurship, which can motivate individuals to get involved in a group's activities and stay involved; and (c) patronage from outsiders who support the group's mission.[11]

Selective benefits are only available to those who contribute.

selective benefit benefit that can be accessed only by those who participate in or contribute to group activity.

Groups often provide contributors with **selective benefits**— benefits that can be accessed only by those who contribute to group activity. Providing selective benefits is a way for groups to get around the free rider problem.

material benefit a good or service offered to encourage participation in group activity.

Material benefits   The most obvious kind of benefit that groups may provide is a **material benefit**. Benefits of this type can include publications, goods and services, discounts on products, and professional advice. For example, individuals who join the American Association of Retired Persons (AARP) become eligible for scores of benefits, including discounts on hundreds of consumer products; members-only insurance plans; a subscription to AARP's monthly magazine; exclusive investment products, credit cards, and financial advice; and dozens of others. The cost of all this? Anyone 50 years old or older can join AARP for as little as $16 per year. Considering the low cost of membership, there are undoubtedly millions of AARP members who join the group for the benefits alone.

Associations of professionals—doctors, lawyers, teachers, nurses, accountants, social workers, and so on—provide similar material benefits, as well as professional certification and credentialing, which have a direct bearing on various professionals' ability to earn a living. Attorneys, for example, cannot practice law without first being admitted to their state bar, and they must meet continuing legal education requirements to remain bar members in good standing. State bar associations regulate these processes and charge members a fee for these services. The fees help subsidize the bar organizations' government-relations activities, which tend to be considerable. An attorney who does not wish to subsidize group political action can refuse to pay the fee, but the bar will deny him or her the ability to practice law.

Social benefits A group also can provide its members with **social benefits**. Imagine, for example, that you are an avid environmentalist. Joining the Sierra Club, Greenpeace, or the Nature Conservancy would allow you to interact with people who are just as passionate about the environment as you are. If you were the owner of a small business, joining the National Federation of Independent Businesses could put you in touch with individuals who share many of the same challenges and successes.

> **social benefit** benefit that encourages individuals to join a group in order to enjoy the company of those who share similar opinions and interests.

Such group participation creates opportunities for you to socialize with people who have similar interests. Moreover, you may have a sense of camaraderie from associating with others who are like you and a sense of status from affiliating with people who share certain beliefs or values.

Purposive benefits Finally, and perhaps most importantly, millions of people join groups because they believe in what a group stands for. In this way, a group may provide a **purposive benefit** to its members. Purposive benefits are so called because they are connected to a group's stated purpose. Consider the following testimonial from a volunteer with Compassionate Action for Animals (CAA), an animal rights advocacy group:

> **purposive benefit** benefit that encourages group participation by connecting individuals to an organization's political purpose.

> Through CAA I've come to realize that every little bit I do to end the suffering of animals makes a difference. But my efforts combined with others sets an example for a whole new generation, offering knowledgeable support in everything from raising positive awareness of farming to maintaining nutrition as a vegan. Through CAA I believe people give animals and our society a brighter, more socially responsible future. CAA has definitely given me hope for a better tomorrow.[12]

This person clearly derives satisfaction from helping promote animal rights. Of course, individuals need not volunteer or join a group in order to promote a cause that they believe in. Groups, however, make that process easier by creating, structuring, and supporting specific participation opportunities for members and volunteers.

Individual entrepreneurship can motivate individuals to get and stay involved in a group's activities.

Selective benefits are an important mechanism for overcoming the collective action problem, but before a group can offer selective benefits, someone has to do significant organizational work to create the group. How do groups get started in the first place? One strain of the interest group literature points to the **interest group entrepreneur**. This term refers to someone who launches and manages an interest group.[13]

interest group entrepreneur an individual who overcomes the costs of collective action by launching and managing an interest group.

Consider one of the most effective and well-known interest groups in America, the National Rifle Association (NRA). Though its primary interest today is in promoting and protecting the rights of gun owners, the NRA began with a very different agenda. Two Civil War veterans had been alarmed by the poor shooting skills of Union troops. To address this perceived problem, they sought a charter from the New York legislature, along with $25,000 with which to purchase land and develop shooting ranges. They also urged New York's "citizen soldiers" to write their legislators and encourage approval of the charter and funding (a strategy the NRA follows to this day). The legislature ultimately obliged, and the NRA was born.[14]

The interest group entrepreneurs in this story were the two Civil War veterans. They invested the initial time and energy (and some cash) to get the NRA off the ground. Like business entrepreneurs, they gambled that their efforts would pay off, and that their initial investment would be returned, along with some "profit." Had they not done so, an NRA-style organization probably would have emerged at some point. But it would not have happened when it did, or in the form that it did.

AIM HIGH
Interest group entrepreneurs like the late actor Charlton Heston, former president of the NRA, help to launch or manage interest groups.

Patrons provide the resources groups need to organize and flourish.

The decision by the New York state legislature to give the NRA $25,000 in start-up funds was critical. It may very well have made the difference between the NRA's sinking or swimming. This is why **patrons** are so important. Patrons provide groups with the resources they need to get established. Patrons may work with an interest group entrepreneur to get a group started or may launch the group themselves but leave its management to others. Either way, they eliminate the need for groups to try to cobble together small contributions from potential members, all of whom are susceptible to free rider thinking.

> **patron** an individual who supports an interest group by providing the resources needed to organize and flourish.

Sometimes a patron is a single individual with a passion for an issue, and with resources to share. Other times, corporations, units of government, foundations, and even other interest groups can act as patrons, founding new groups or helping start-ups get off the ground. Consider the United States Chamber of Commerce, a membership group of businesses, associations, and state, local, and international chambers of commerce. The U.S. Chamber was created in 1912, in part as a result of the patronage of Secretary of Commerce and Labor Charles Nagel. Nagel had brought the idea of a national business organization to the attention of President William Howard Taft. At Nagel's encouragement, Taft publicly expressed his interest in the creation of a commercial group that could speak to Washington policy makers with a single voice. But how would it be possible to bring together diverse businesses from all over the country? Nagel provided the answer through an important act of patronage. He used the resources of his department to convene a national business conference to which approximately 1,000 associations were invited. Nagel and President Taft both spoke at the conference, once again promoting the idea of a consolidated national business group. By the time the conference was adjourned, a new, nationwide business organization had been born.[15] The Chamber of Commerce would grow into a very influential group, and it was a major player in the 2010 mid-term elections.

Even the casual observer of American politics knows that one way or another, tens of thousands of groups have succeeded in overcoming the collective action problem and have fended off threats to their survival (see Figure 9-1). The challenges inherent in this are not the same for all groups, however. Some groups have

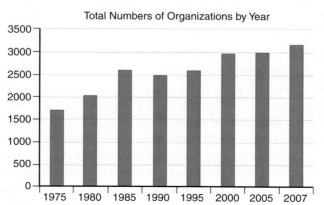

Total Numbers of Organizations by Year

FIGURE 9-1 Rise in the Number of Interest Groups over Last 40 Years.

In spite of the collective action problem, the number of interest groups in Washington has nearly doubled in the last 40 years.

Source: Washington Representatives 32 ed. 2007. Columbia Books: Bethesda, MD and authors' analysis.

ready access to desirable selective benefits, or to dynamic entrepreneurs, or to re-source-rich patrons, while others have access to none. Some groups are very small and therefore do not have to struggle with the free rider problem, while others are so large they must continually work to keep their members engaged. In short, different groups face different challenges and have strengths and weaknesses in different areas. Thus, groups must choose among various potential strategies and tactics to achieve their ends.

What Groups Do, and Why They Do It

9-4   Analyze the strategies and tactics interest groups use to impact elections and public policy.

The ultimate goal of most politically oriented interest groups is to shape public policy in ways consistent with the group's interests, values, and beliefs. In general, groups use two primary strategies to do this. They attempt to influence either the selection of public officials (an electoral strategy) or the decisions of elected officials, bureaucrats, or members of the judiciary who have already been elected or appointed (a legislative strategy). Of course, groups can pursue both strategies at once. Furthermore, the two strategies often intertwine.

An electoral strategy consists of a variety of tactics.

In pursuing an electoral strategy, interest groups and their members may employ a number of tactics. The most familiar, and controversial, tactics involve spending money in an effort to get certain candidates elected. Less controversial tactics include endorsements, voter mobilization efforts, voter education, and volunteering.

political action committee (PAC) a group that collects money from individuals and makes donations to political parties and candidates.

Political action committees Many groups interested in election outcomes form **political action committees** (PACs), or encourage group members to donate to a PAC created by someone else. A PAC is an organization funded by 50 or more people, usually affiliated with a corporation, labor union, or some other special interest group. The PAC collects donations from individuals and then turns those donations into contributions to political parties and candidates for election (Table 9-1).

Groups form PACs, rather than contributing directly to a campaign or party, for several reasons. Federal law prohibits labor unions and corporations from contributing directly to political parties or candidates for federal office, but these groups may form a PAC and collect and distribute money from individuals sympathetic to their interests. PACs also allow individuals to multiply the effect of a campaign contribution. If you were to contribute $50 directly to a Senate campaign, you might feel that your contribution didn't amount to much. But if you were to donate that same $50 to a PAC and that PAC in turn

TABLE 9-1 Top 10 PAC Contributors to Federal Candidates in 2010

PAC	Amount Contributed
National Assn of Realtors	$ 3,773,296
Honeywell International	$ 3,645,200
AT&T Inc	$ 3,251,375
National Beer Wholesalers Assn	$ 3,001,000
Intl Brotherhood of Electrical Workers	$ 2,988,373
American Assn for Justice	$ 2,806,000
American Bankers Assn	$ 2,773,154
Operating Engineers Union	$ 2,766,720
National Auto Dealers Assn	$ 2,440,900
International Assn of Fire Fighters	$ 2,368,500

Source: From www.opensecrets.org/pacs/toppacs.php?cycle=2010&party=A. Based on data released by the FEC on February 7, 2011

donated $10,000 to the candidate by combining your contribution with many others, you might feel that you had gotten more bang for your buck.

Like individuals, PACs are limited in the amounts of money they can contribute to a political campaign (Table 9-2). PACs may give a maximum of $15,000 per year to a political party and a maximum of $5,000 per election to any federal election candidate. Because primaries and general elections are considered separate elections, however, a PAC may actually give a total of $10,000 to each federal candidate per election cycle. In the 2010 election,

TABLE 9-2 Summary of Campaign Donation Limits

2010 Contribution limits	
Individuals can give	
To candidate	$2,400
To national party committee	$30,400
To PAC/state or local party	$10,000 to state or local party $5,000 to each PAC
Aggregate total	$115,500 per two-year election cycle $45,600 to candidates $69,900 to all national party committees of which no more than $45,600 per cycle can go to PACs
Multicandidate PACs can give	
To candidate	$5,000
To national party committee	$15,000
To PAC/state or local party	$5,000
Aggregate total	No limit

PACs contributed almost $375 million to candidates running for the House and Senate.[16] This represents about one-fourth of the funds that candidates for Congress raised during the 2009–2010 election cycle.

Other spending options Groups can be involved in elections in ways other than PAC contributions. For example, rather than contributing directly to a political campaign, a PAC can make unlimited **independent expenditures**, which are made with the explicit intent of advocating for the election or defeat of a candidate. By law, such expenditures may not be coordinated with the candidate's campaign. Aside from that, however, they may serve exactly the same purpose as advertisements placed by candidates themselves.

independent expenditures funds spent to elect or defeat candidates that are not coordinated with any candidate's campaign.

Groups can also request that members write checks directly to a candidate's campaign. The group can then collect the individual checks and present them to the candidate all at once, a practice known as **bundling**. Considering that individuals can write candidate checks for up to $2,400 each, a bundle of checks from dozens of well-heeled donors can make quite an impression.

bundling the practice of collecting individual checks and presenting them to a candidate at one time.

527 committee an independent, nonparty group that raises and spends money on political activities.

Groups may also form and raise funds for **527 committees**, also called "527s," named for the relevant section of the Internal Revenue Code. A 527 is a tax-exempt, nonparty group that can raise and spend money on political activities and advertising with no effective limits.

In 2010, the Supreme Court decided in *Citizens United* v. *FEC* to permit corporations and unions to have a much more direct role in campaigns. Among other things, the Supreme Court allowed corporations or unions to engage in direct advocacy (explicit electioneering that uses "magic words" such as "vote for," "defeat," or "support" as defined in the 1976 case *Buckley v. Valeo*) using money from their corporate or union treasuries. Although the decision was harshly criticized by President Obama, during the 2010 elections there were no television commercials that said "Defeat Jones, paid for by Gillette Shaving Cream." On the other hand, corporations such as News Corporation, among others, sent large checks to advocacy groups that aired ads praising or attacking candidates. Moreover, much of this was funded by groups who do not disclose their donors, making it hard to track the true extent of corporate activity.

In many ways, the *Citizens United* case did not transform the overall look of campaigns. For years, organized interests had searched for loopholes to invest unregulated money into the electoral process, and no matter what the Court had decided, competitive races would still have cost lots of money, interest groups would have found ways to invest in their preferred candidate, and voters would have seen lots of political ads on television.

Other electoral tactics Although campaign spending is probably the most high-profile and controversial tactic that interest groups use to pursue their electoral goals, it is just the beginning. Groups interested in electoral outcomes have a number of other tactics at their disposal. These include:

- *Endorsements*: Groups often publicize their support for a candidate, providing a valuable voting cue to group members, and to nonmembers who are sympathetic to the group's mission.

- *Voter mobilization*: Groups often dedicate themselves to increasing voter registration and turnout in competitive congressional races and presidential elections.

- *Voter education*: Sometimes groups seek to influence elections by disseminating educational materials to prospective voters. These materials may discuss a candidate's background, beliefs, or record; compare and contrast competing candidates; or rate a whole slate of candidates according to their votes or positions on various issues.

- *Volunteer work*: Groups may provide volunteers to do some of the necessary day-to-day work on behalf of candidates they favor. This can include answering phones, preparing campaign mailers, coordinating local meetings, reminding voters to do their civic duty on Election Day, and even driving voters to the polls.

Lobbying is the key ingredient in a legislative strategy.

As with the electoral strategy, groups that pursue a legislative strategy have a variety of tactics at their disposal. The most familiar of these is **lobbying**: communicating with government officials to persuade them toward a particular policy decision. Lobbying and lobbyists are sometimes stigmatized as sleazy, unseemly, and even undemocratic. But when pursued legally and ethically, lobbying is a legitimate tactic used to achieve a legitimate democratic end: influencing the deliberations, decisions, and actions of government officials. In fact, the right to lobby is guaranteed by the First Amendment, which prohibits Congress from interfering with the right of the people "to petition the government for a redress of grievances." Lobbying takes two general forms, inside lobbying and grassroots lobbying.

lobbying communicating with government officials to persuade them toward a particular policy decision.

Inside lobbying and Congress What most people think of as lobbying is technically called **inside lobbying**; it occurs when group representatives meet with public officials or their staff members. The lobbyist's job in these meetings is generally twofold: to present specific, evaluative information to the public official, and to request an action or a decision based on that information.

inside lobbying meeting directly with public officials to influence political decisions.

The lobbyist does not simply say, "We want you to know that our group is pro-environment, and we hope you will be, too." Instead, the lobbyist presents the group's position on a specific bill, amendment, nomination, budget item, or issue along with the reasons for that position: "The Sierra Club is opposed to this amendment because we think it will undercut some major provisions of the Clean Air Act that have nearly universal public support." To this statement, the lobbyist adds his or her request for action by the public official: "Because of that, we are asking that you vote against the amendment."

There are, of course, dozens of variations on this basic information/request-for-action two-step. Lobbyists recognize that public officials have a variety of goals, including good policy, reelection, and advancement within the institution. The information that lobbyists provide to legislators, then, is presented with these goals in mind.

The type and amount of information that lobbyists provide will vary from situation to situation. Some policy makers want to see detailed studies supporting a group's position. Others are more interested in expressly political information on the issue: polling data, communications from voters, and activities of opposing groups. Some legislators want to know what recognized experts think. Some simply want a short list of talking points they can use to explain their vote. Others want to know what kind of media coverage the issue has received in national and home-town newspapers.

The lobbyist must be prepared to answer all such questions and provide supporting information. Lobbyists' ability to do so makes them immensely helpful to members of Congress. Faced with dozens of high-profile issues, representatives and senators cannot become experts in more than two or three issue areas. Having lobbyists available to provide information on other issues is like having a public policy encyclopedia at the ready.

Unlike an encyclopedia, however, a lobbyist has a point of view and often a broad philosophical orientation on issues of a certain type ("pro-labor," for example, or "pro-business"). This is actually helpful to public officials. They can hear the strongest arguments from the most passionate, well-informed advocates on both sides. These may help them evaluate an issue in ways that they otherwise could not because they lack the lobbyists' information, expertise, and familiarity with the most salient arguments.

The nature of the request for action by a lobbyist can also vary tremendously from situation to situation. Among other things, the lobbyist might ask a member of Congress to vote for or against a piece of legislation, talk to colleagues, hold hearings, or support or oppose a nominee.

Members of Congress may agree to do such work on behalf of an interest group because it is consistent with their goals, they are grateful for the lobbyist's or group's support in the past, or they are trying to build goodwill in anticipation of a request for support in the future. Whatever the case, by helping the lobbyist that comes to visit—and by extension, the group the lobbyist represents—members of Congress generally help themselves.

This kind of help is not a one-way street. A lobbyist who asks a member to sponsor a piece of legislation often provides a draft bill that the member can use as a starting point. The lobbyist might also volunteer to answer any questions on the legislation from the member's colleagues. Furthermore, once a lobbyist has established a trusted relationship with a public official, that official may seek out the lobbyist for help. Lobbyists are normally happy to oblige, knowing that a close, trusting, and mutually supportive relationship will benefit the groups they represent.

Inside lobbying and the executive branch Although inside lobbying is most often thought of in relation to members of Congress and their staff, interest group lobbyists also devote resources to the executive branch. In some cases this focus means the president and White House personnel, but more often lobbying efforts focus on executive branch agencies, which issue regulations, statutory interpretations, and quasi-legal decisions on issues as diverse as endangered species protection, the content of television and radio advertising, and interstate speed limits. They also participate in the executive branch budget process and are responsible for administration of major federal programs and tax credits. Finally, they pursue policy agendas of their own, encouraging the president to promote and fund certain policy initiatives and to abandon others.

Obviously, interest groups and their members can have a significant stake in these executive agency decisions and activities. Some groups, therefore, devote major lobbying resources to the executive branch.

Inside lobbying and the judiciary Inside lobbying of the judicial branch takes two primary forms. In one, an interest group may file *amicus curiae* briefs on cases that involve an issue in which it has an interest. Such briefs present the group's analysis of legal or factual questions in the hope that judges, justices, or their clerks will take their arguments into account when deciding the case. The other judiciary-related tactic available to interest groups is litigation. Although this is not lobbying per se, it can have important policy implications.

Grassroots lobbying Another major tactic that groups use in support of a decision strategy is known as **grassroots lobbying** (also called outside lobbying). In this form of lobbying, rather than communicating directly with decision makers in government, interest groups and their lobbyists seek to influence opinion and stimulate action by the general public, specific groups, and the media. The goal is that public officials will be swayed by what they hear from influenced individuals, groups, and media outlets.

grassroots lobbying efforts to persuade citizens to contact their elected officials regarding a particular issue or piece of legislation.

Groups generally begin a grassroots lobbying effort with their own members. Group leaders have established communication channels with their members, and they know that most agree on the issues and many will also take action if asked. Thus, leaders bring new issues to members' attention, try to shape opinions on existing issues, and request phone calls, e-mails, and letters to policy makers in positions of influence.

However, interest groups know that government officials respond to public opinion broadly, not just to opinions expressed by group members with an interest in a particular issue. They know, too, that policy makers react to what they see, hear, and read in the media. Because of these strengths, a grassroots lobbying campaign may be both extensive and multifaceted.

Case Study

Health Care Lobbying

The cases of two different attempts at national health care reform—one by the Clinton White House and the other by the Obama administration—offer very different methods of dealing with this issue with very different results.

In 1993, a new president made health care for all Americans his first signature piece of legislation. The concept of national health insurance had been in debate since the New Deal, but in 1993 a particularly intense grassroots lobbying campaign emerged around President Clinton's proposal. The campaign was focused on three committees responsible for deciding whether any health care reform would pass, and if so, what shape it would take. Within these committees, lobbying efforts focused on those members who were undecided, and also on a group of moderate Republican and Democratic senators that were seeking a broadly acceptable compromise.

One crucial element in the grassroots lobbying effort against the Clinton proposal was a television commercial financed by the Health Insurance Association of America, a trade organization of health insurance providers. The commercial showed a typical married couple, Harry and Louise, sitting in their kitchen, seemingly loaded down with piles of papers. They worried aloud about some of the Clinton plan's features, trying to figure out if this bill would create a government monopoly over the health industry. Would health care involve a huge, intrusive, impersonal federal bureaucracy? Would government bureaucrats have the power to deny health care to some? The commercial ended by exhorting people to get in touch with their congressional representative if they, too, were worried about the Clinton plan. "Harry and Louise" proved enormously effective. The producers claimed that the campaign "prompted 500,000 phone calls to a toll-free number, turned 50,000 of those

callers into activists, and resulted in one-quarter million contacts with members of Congress."

The ad also led to a tremendous amount of media coverage in newspapers, on television, and on the radio. Thus, it received much wider exposure than it would have received from paid placements alone. As a result, policy makers and opinion shapers were forced to address the arguments in the Harry and Louise campaign.

Other radio and TV ads were directed not at Congress as a whole, but at the districts and states of members of Congress who were expected to be influential or persuadable in the health care debate. Groups also worked to identify constituents who were most likely to influence members of Congress.

Unlike a political activity such as voting, the letters or phone calls from different individuals are not equally influential. Interest groups seek to mobilize individuals with the most potential influence with their elected representatives—an approach sometimes referred to as a "grass tops" strategy.

Data indicate that such a strategy was at work during the Clinton health care debate. The National Federation of Independent Businesses, a key player in defeating the proposed legislation, created Guardian Advisory Council teams consisting of influential business people, college friends, neighbors, and former colleagues of targeted legislators—people who were thought to have extraordinary influence with those legislators. The Clinton bill went down to a humiliating defeat for the new president, setting back his entire legislative agenda and hurting him in the polls.

Sixteen years later, the outcome would be considerably different when another new president used health care as his first signature piece of legislation. Most Americans had not changed their view

Case Study   Health Care Lobbying

of national health care, but the political landscape had changed in that time. First, Barack Obama had a super majority in the Senate (60 Democrats) along with a strong Democratic control of the House. Second, President Obama learned a lot from President Clinton's earlier defeat. And yet, even with those numbers in his favor, passing health care was no slam-dunk.

HARRY AND LOUISE RETURN Harry Johnson and Louise Clark, who appeared in health industry advertisements in 1993 that were critical of the Clinton health care reform proposal, announced in 2009 that they would appear in a spot that encouraged Congress to pass comprehensive health care reform.

The bill itself—well over 2,000 pages long—was so complicated that few members could read the entire piece of legislation. Polls showed a majority of Americans opposed the bill, so politicians understood that voting for it could have a huge impact on their futures.

When the final vote came, it was strictly across party lines. Not one Republican supported the measure, and 34 Democrats opposed it. But in the end, the bill passed in the House by 7 votes, 219 to 212. President Obama had his first significant victory at a time when his approval numbers were falling. And Harry and Louise went back to their kitchen, awaiting the next significant controversy that might use their talents.

Early on, the Obama administration co-opted the adversaries who defeated the Clinton bill. They quickly struck a deal with the large and powerful pharmaceutical industry, making sure their worries (financial compensation) were not a problem. They struck a deal with the American Medical Association (AMA), making it look as though all of the country's doctors were behind it. And, in perhaps the most brilliant and visible turn-around, Harry and Louise came back to the television screens, looking a bit older. The couple was still concerned about the bill, but—lo and behold—now they were more concerned for all of their fellow Americans out there who did not have health insurance.

Not taking any chances, there were also tremendous giveaways. The president promised individual members of Congress special deals—extra money for their states, pet projects, and even a ride in Air Force One seemed to be enough to sway one congressman.

Thinking Critically

1. Compare the tactics employed by both Clinton and Obama in their attempts to pass health care legislation. Why was Obama successful while Clinton failed? What lessons did Obama learn from Clinton's failed attempt?

2. Now compare the role that public interest groups played in both examples. How did interest groups help Obama and hurt Clinton? Do you think that their role was instrumental in getting a health care bill passed a second time around?

The electoral strategy and the legislative strategy intertwine.

Groups need not choose between an electoral strategy and a legislative strategy. Many pursue both strategies at once, and one often reinforces the other. A member of Congress who has been elected with the support of a particular group, for example, may be more open to entertaining that group's viewpoints on policy issues. He or she knows that maintaining a friendly relationship will likely ensure the group's support in the next campaign and so may feel obligated to meet with them. Thus, the group's electoral strategy can support its legislative strategy.

The reverse can be true as well. A group that wants a member of Congress to vote its way on a bill will often note the political appeal of that vote (or the political damage of opposition) in the next election. A group that engages in an outside lobbying strategy by encouraging communications to a legislator is, of course, registering its viewpoints on issues. At the same time, it is showing the kind of muscle it can flex—on behalf of the legislator or an opponent—in the next election.

Interest groups have a wide variety of tactics in their toolkits.

As the preceding discussion indicates, interest groups have a wide variety of tactics that they can choose from to try to influence the policy process. Their choice of tactics depends on the goals they are pursuing. All the various tactics try to convey some sort of information to policy makers—either on the substantive merits of their position or on the political consequences of a particular course of action. Table 9-3 summarizes the various tactics and how often they tend to be used.

TABLE 9-3 Lobbying Techniques and Their Prevalence

Legislative Branch	
Doing favors or providing gifts for legislators	–
Meeting personally with legislators or their aides	very often
Testifying at legislative hearings	very often
Executive Branch	
Interacting with special agencies that advise the chief executive	–
Interacting with special liaison offices within the chief executive's office	–
Meeting personally with chief executive or aides	seldom
Meeting personally with executive agency personnel	very often
Serving on executive agency advisory boards or committees	occasionally
Submitting written comments on proposed rules or regulations	very often
Testifying at executive agency hearings	–
Judicial Branch	
Attempting to influence judicial selections	–
Engaging in litigation	occasionally
Submitting *amicus curiae* ("friends of the court") briefs	occasionally

(continues)

TABLE 9-3 *(continued)*

Grassroots

Arranging face-to-face meetings between group members/supporters and government officials	–
Dispatching a spokesperson to the media	–
Engaging in e-mail, letter, or telephone campaigns	very often
Engaging in demonstrations or protests	seldom
Running advertisements in the media	seldom

Direct Democracy

Attempting to place an initiative or referendum on the ballot	–
Campaigning for or against an initiative or referendum	–

Electoral

Campaigning for or against candidates	seldom
Endorsing candidates	seldom
Engaging in election issue advocacy	seldom
Making in-kind contributions to candidates	seldom
Making monetary contributions to political parties	seldom
Making monetary contributions to candidates	occasionally
Mobilizing activists to work on a candidate's behalf	–
Issuing voter guides	seldom

Other

Joining coalitions with other organizations or lobbyists	very often

Note: Dashes (–) indicate that there is little evidence with which to judge the frequency of such activities.

Do Groups Matter?

9-5 Assess how much influence interest groups have over policy outcomes.

High-profile corruption cases have received significant media attention over the last few years. In these cases, some interest groups went well beyond the sorts of activities we have outlined here and attempted outright to bribe members of Congress. Randy Cunningham, a former representative from California, received a Rolls Royce and a yacht for steering Defense Department business toward a particular contract. Cunningham is currently biding his time in prison. Jack Abramoff, a well-known lobbyist in D.C. for many years, also earned prison time for his role in orchestrating bribes to members of Congress.

These sorts of blatant and illegal activities are rare, and as we have argued, interest groups and lobbyists have an important role in our political system as they engage in various legitimate strategies to influence the policy process. That said, and having examined what groups do and why they do it, we are left with a final question: do groups matter? The answer to that question is surprisingly murky.

It is difficult to prove the impact of campaign contributions.

Few researchers doubt that if interest groups were to disappear from the American political landscape, different public officials would be elected and appointed, different issues would appear on the public agenda, different pieces of legislation would be approved, and budget items would be funded at different levels. For political scientists, however, the challenge comes in providing clear evidence that group activity caused a particular political outcome. Consider, for example, the case of interest-group spending on federal campaigns. The hundreds of millions of dollars that interest groups spend supporting and opposing candidates must surely have some impact, but political scientists cannot say as a general proposition that the more money a candidate spends, the more votes he or she gets.

Why this indecision? For one thing, candidates facing a highly competitive race tend to raise and spend more money, whereas candidates who are shoo-ins for reelection typically spend less. This paradox produces counterintuitive results: candidates who spend a lot of money often end up in very close races, and candidates who spend very little money often end up winning big. Unfortunately, political scientists have not yet found their way out of this methodological thicket and therefore do not have a complete understanding of the impact of interest-group spending on election outcomes.

We find similar problems, but somewhat more satisfying answers, when we look at the impact of political action committee contributions on legislator behavior. Journalistic accounts of legislator voting sometimes note that legislators who receive large PAC contributions often vote as their donors wish. Members who receive large campaign contributions from tobacco PACs, for example, often cast votes in support of legislation advocated by the tobacco lobby. From this, we might infer that "big tobacco" is buying votes. Political scientists, however, have suggested an alternative explanation: tobacco PACs take note of legislators who support tobacco interests and distribute campaign dollars accordingly.

Thinking Causally How much influence do PAC campaign contributions have on the voting behavior of members of Congress?

Which explanation is the right one? Most research finds that PAC contributions do not buy the votes of legislators. First, a floor vote on a piece of legislation comes at the end of the legislative process. Important decisions, hearings, committee votes, negotiations, and coalition-building have to take place before a bill makes it this far. An interest group trying to buy influence after all of these steps have occurred would be like a football fan who pays full price for a Super Bowl ticket with only two minutes left in the game.

Second, members of Congress face other influences on their vote in addition to campaign contributions. These include their own policy preferences, the preferences of their constituents, the dictates of party leaders, and their voting records. These influences tend to be so strong that most political scientists consider it unlikely that an interest-group contribution could override them, turning a "yea" vote into a "nay," or vice versa.

Group influence may be strongest where it is hardest to observe.

If not floor votes, then what sorts of legislative outcomes might interest groups be buying? One insightful study of this question concluded that money buys time—that is, time the targeted legislator might spend working to incorporate an interest group's preferences into new legislation. Political scientists Richard Hall and Frank Wayman found that legislators who received campaign funds from an interest group were more likely to engage in the following activities on the group's behalf: "authoring or blocking a legislative vehicle; negotiating compromises behind the scenes, especially at the staff level; offering friendly amendments or actively opposing unfriendly ones; lobbying colleagues; planning strategy; and last and sometimes least, showing up to vote in favor of the interest group's position."[17] Hall and Wayman argued that such activities, rather than floor votes, were most likely to show evidence of group influence.

These activities can result not just in broad pieces of legislation that interest groups favor but in the provision of "private goods" for specific groups: government contracts, price increases, tax breaks, "earmarked" funds, exemptions from certain statutory provisions, and so on.[18] Private goods of this sort are typically distributed to groups behind the scenes, away from reporters, in private meetings and committee mark-up sessions, and without a formal vote. They are often buried in the fine print of massive appropriations bills and are therefore easily missed—even by political scientists.

In part, the challenge in finding effects is because political scientists tend to study highly contested issues in which the conflict is in plain view.[19] The politics surrounding these issues can be very dramatic. Accordingly, they seem interesting and important, and they generate readily available data, which makes them attractive subjects for study.

But groups probably have their greatest influence when the outcomes they seek are not contested by anyone; are negotiated or decided in low-profile settings; do not have a significant impact outside of the groups immediately affected; and cannot easily be observed or exposed by casual observers of politics. For obvious reasons, interest group influence is much harder to study in these situations.

In summary, political scientists clearly need to spend more time looking for group influence in less obvious settings, on lower-profile issues, in obscure but consequential legislative provisions, on decisions that do not require a vote, in discussions that typically take place behind closed doors, and in the marginal cases that tend to be decisive in determining an electoral or policy outcome. Reorienting interest group research in this way would undoubtedly demonstrate group influence in virtually every aspect of executive, legislative, judicial, and electoral activity.

Chapter Summary

In this chapter, you have learned to:

9-1 Distinguish between pluralist theory's and James Madison's interpretation of the role of interest groups within American politics.

Founder James Madison was concerned about the negative influence of interest groups, what he termed *factions,* on individual rights and the collective good. However, he concluded that the American system was well designed to mute the influence of interest groups. The pluralists viewed politics as an organized effort to resolve conflicts among competing group interests, and they attempted to demonstrate empirically what Madison had argued theoretically. They concluded that political power and resources in the United States were dispersed widely, with some interest groups being influential and resource rich in some issue areas, and a completely different set being influential and resource rich in other issue areas.

9-2 Describe how critics of pluralist theory view the role of interest groups today.

Critics of pluralism argue that the American system is resistant to change and prevents certain issues from getting on the agenda. Furthermore, the free rider or collective action problem questions the assumption that groups automatically form and suggests some types of groups are more able to form than others.

9-3 Explain how interest groups form and attract members.

Groups pursue a variety of strategies to get around the collective action problem. They provide selective benefits and material benefits, which members receive in return for joining. They also provide social benefits, in which members enjoy the camaraderie of being part of a group. In addition, they provide purposive benefits, in which those who join get satisfaction from being involved in an important political struggle.

9-4 Analyze the strategies and tactics interest groups use to impact elections and public policy.

Groups try to influence public policy in two ways. In an election strategy, groups try to influence which leaders achieve power and make public policy. In a legislative strategy, groups try to influence the behavior of elected officials, bureaucrats, and judges who are already in power.

9-5 Assess how much influence interest groups have over policy outcomes.

Media coverage and public opinion suggest that interest groups are too powerful and often malevolent. They are neither. While particular lobbyists and legislators sometimes cross the line, groups in general play an important role in American politics, even though they are more likely to influence policy-making in small and subtle ways.

CHAPTER TEST

1. Why did James Madison believe the country must be protected from the influence of factions?
2. Explain pluralism theory. How does pluralism compare with James Madison's beliefs about the role of organized interests?
3. What are the four criticisms of pluralism?
4. What is the free rider problem?

5. Explain three ways that groups can overcome collective action problems.

6. Of the three different types of selective benefits, which is likely to be most influential? Why?

7. Why do groups form political action committees?

8. Distinguish between the two types of lobbying.

9. Why is it difficult to prove the impact of campaign contributions on policy outcomes?

10. The authors propose that interest group influence may be strongest where it is hardest to observe. What does this mean?

MyPoliSciLab® INTEREST GROUPS
Apply what you learned in this chapter on MyPoliSciLab.

Read on mypoliscilab.com

eText: Chapter 9

Study and Review on mypoliscilab.com

Pre-Test
Post-Test
Chapter Exam
Flashcards

Watch on mypoliscilab.com

Video: California Teachers Stage Sit-Ins

Video: Murtha and the PMA Lobbyists
How Do We Know Video: Studying What Doesn't Happen

Explore on mypoliscilab.com

Comparative: Comparing Interest Groups
Simulation: You Are a Lobbyist
Timeline: Interest Groups and Campaign Finance

KEY TERMS

527 committee, p. 270
bundling, p. 270
disturbance theory, p. 263
free rider problem, p. 263
grassroots lobbying, p. 273
independent expenditures, p. 270
inside lobbying, p. 271

interest group entrepreneur, p. 266
interest groups, p. 259
lobbying, p. 271
material benefit, p. 264
nondecisions, p. 263
patron, p. 267
political action committee (PAC), p. 268

pluralism, p. 259
policy agenda, p. 263
purposive benefit, p. 265
selective benefit, p. 264
social benefit, p. 265

SUGGESTED READINGS

Frank Baumgartner and Beth Leech. 1998. *Basic Interests: The Importance of Groups in Politics and in Political Science.* Princeton, NJ: Princeton University Press. Reviews decades of political science research on interest groups, arguing for more large-scale empirical studies and that group behavior should be studied in tandem with Congress and other institutions that groups try to influence.

Jeffrey Berry and Clyde Wilcox. 2008. *Interest Group Society*, 5th ed. New York: Longman. A comprehensive summary of what scholars know about the role of interest groups in American politics, putting interest groups into context and discussing their strategies and tactics.

Michael Franz. 2008. *Choice and Changes*. Philadelphia, PA: Temple University Press. The impact of interest groups on electoral politics, with a particular focus on "soft money" contributions, issue ads, and "527s."

Mancur Olson. 1971. *The Logic of Collective Action*. Cambridge, MA: Harvard University Press. Discusses the hurdles that groups with collective goals face in forming and maintaining themselves, what sorts of groups are likely to form, and who in politics is advantaged by the collective action problem.

Jack L. Walker. 1991. *Mobilizing Interest Groups in America: Patrons, Professionals, and Social Movements*. Ann Arbor: University of Michigan Press. One of the most important empirical studies in interest group behavior, using a systematic survey of interest groups to outline the characteristics of the interest group world and identify what sorts of organizational factors influence the strategies that groups pursue.

SUGGESTED WEBSITES

AARP
www.aarp.org

The AARP website offers members tips on managing money, health care, family, and leisure and links to various resources related to these and other concerns of the retirement-age population.

SIERRA CLUB
www.sierraclub.org

The Sierra Club is dedicated to protecting communities and the environment. It is America's oldest, largest, and most influential grassroots environmental organization.

EMILY'S LIST
www.emilyslist.org

An acronym for "Early Money Is Like Yeast" (it makes the dough rise), EMILY's List has become the nation's biggest political action committee. Members work to elect pro-choice Democratic women to office by recruiting and funding viable women candidates, helping these women to build effective campaigns, and mobilizing women voters.

NATIONAL RIFLE ASSOCIATION
www.nra.org

The NRA represents millions of Americans who "believe in the Constitution" and "actively pursue some of the country's finest traditions—Hunting and Sports Shooting."

NATIONAL FEDERATION OF INDEPENDENT BUSINESSES
www.nfib.com

The National Federation of Independent Businesses is a network of grassroots activists who send their views directly to state and federal lawmakers through member ballots.

Congress

OUTFITTING STATES TO FIGHT TERRORISM
In the aftermath of September 11, 2001, Congress began to redistribute funds to every state in the country to combat terrorism. A decade later, funds still are not allotted strictly according to assessed risk of a terrorist attack. In your opinion, how should these funds be distributed around the nation?

CHAPTER LEARNING OBJECTIVES

After reading this chapter you will be able to:

10-1 Describe the basic structure of Congress.

10-2 Analyze the relationships of members of Congress to their constituencies, and distinguish between the trustee and delegate models of representation.

10-3 Assess the challenges that emerge when members of Congress set about working together.

10-4 Identify the resources and the committee and party structures that help Congress address its challenges.

10-5 Outline the lawmaking process in Congress.

10-6 Explain the appropriations process.

In fiscal year 2010, the federal government spent $842 million on domestic counterterrorism.[1] Wyoming, not generally considered to be a terrorist target, secured funds amounting to $12.15 for each of its half-million residents from the Homeland Security Grant Program. New York, by contrast, received just $5.80 per resident, in spite of the fact that it was a site of the September 11, 2001, terrorist attacks.[2]

How did Wyoming manage to secure such a large chunk of federal funds to fight terrorism? The answer lies in the USA PATRIOT Act, which Congress passed in the aftermath of September 11, 2001. Among other things, the Patriot Act established a federal grant system to help state and local governments prepare for and respond to terrorist attacks. However, it required the State Homeland Security Program (SHSP) to distribute almost 40 percent of its funds evenly among the 50 states, regardless of their population, size, or risk of being targeted by terrorists.[3]

The Patriot Act met little resistance in Congress. It was introduced in the House of Representatives on October 23, 2001, and passed the very next day by a vote of 357 to 66. Although some senators opposed other provisions of the bill, no one spoke out against the formula for distributing anti-terrorism funds to states. The Senate approved the bill with all but one vote in favor, and President George W. Bush signed it into law on October 26, 2001.

As the Department of Homeland Security devoted increasingly large sums of money to helping state and local governments prepare for possible terrorist attacks, the wastefulness of the Patriot Act's fund distribution formula became apparent. Common sense probably tells you that helping North Dakota buy a $200,000 remote-control bomb-disposal robot is not the most effective way of preparing the nation for a terrorist attack. Thomas H. Kean, chair of the September 11 Commission, agreed: "We've had some of this money spent to air condition garbage trucks. We've had some of the money spent for armor for dogs. This money is being distributed as if it's general revenue sharing."[4] Michael Chertoff, homeland security secretary at the time, further acknowledged that a uniform distribution of funds across states was not good policy.[5]

Yet when Representative Christopher Cox of California tried to craft a new law in 2005 that would have distributed anti-terrorism funds on the basis of threat and risk, he could not get enough support from members of the Senate. Senators from smaller, less populous states lined up against the proposed measure, hoping to preserve the funding going to their states under the existing law. Senator Leahy argued that distribution based on the degree of terrorist threat would "shortchange rural states."[6]

The failure of Congress to address clear inefficiencies in the distribution of federal anti-terrorism funds makes sense only when we think about the incentives that motivate individual members of Congress. Opponents of the Cox proposal were representing the interests of the voters who put them into office. By arguing that Vermont *did* need to protect itself from terrorist attacks, Leahy hoped to secure federal funds for improving Vermont's police and fire protection services. Other members of Congress also wanted to secure funding to please voters who had the power to reelect them, even if it was not best for the country as a whole.

Neither irrationality nor happenstance is primarily responsible for the existing distribution of federal anti-terrorism funds. Rather, its origins lie in the strategic negotiations that occur every day on Capitol Hill. The individual members who serve in Congress work hardest on behalf of those who elected them. The laws they write represent compromises among hundreds of individuals fighting on behalf of districts and states. Sometimes, the final result is legislation that serves the interests of the country as a whole. Often, though, the pressure of pleasing voters results in laws that do not address problems as effectively or efficiently as many would like. To understand why these inefficiencies occur, and what might be done about them, we need to think about the structure of Congress and the incentives it creates for those who work within it. ∎

An Institution with Two Chambers and Shared Powers

10-1   Describe the basic structure of Congress.

Congress is a **bicameral** institution—that is, it consists of two chambers, a House of Representatives and a Senate. In the House, the 435 voting members (and the five nonvoting delegates) are elected every two years and represent state districts, which are remade every decade to reflect changes in the number of people living in different regions of the country. On average, each member of the House represents roughly 600,000 voters.[7] In the Senate, the 100 members are elected every six years and represent entire states.[8] Obviously, the sizes of states vary tremendously. As a consequence, senators from larger states like New York, Texas, and California represent tens of millions of voters, whereas senators from smaller states like North Dakota, Wyoming, and Montana represent far fewer.

bicameral an institution consisting of two chambers.

Most powers enumerated in Article I of the Constitution, which concerns Congress, do not differentiate between the Senate and House. Both chambers have the responsibility of overseeing the bureaucracy, declaring war, regulating interstate commerce, raising and supporting armies, and most importantly, writing "all Laws which shall be necessary and proper for carrying into Execution the foregoing power." However, there are some important differences. In terms of duties, the Senate has the responsibility of ratifying foreign treaties. Additionally, senators are charged with approving presidential appointments to the federal judiciary and the executive branch.

As part of the nation's system of checks and balances, Congress has the power to remove from office the president, vice president, and others

impeachment performed by the House of Representatives, the act of charging government officials with "treason, bribery, or other high crimes and misdemeanors." The Senate then decides whether to convict and remove the official from office.

immediately under their command. Members of the House must first decide whether to **impeach** the president—that is, determine that the charges against him or her are sufficiently credible and meet the standards laid out in the Constitution of "treason, bribery, or other high crimes and misdemeanors." Should the House impeach the president, the case goes before the Senate, where the chief justice of the Supreme Court then presides. For a conviction, two-thirds of the senators must vote against the president. In the nation's history, two presidents (Andrew Johnson in 1868 and Bill Clinton in 1998) have been impeached. The Senate, however, refused to convict either president.

Members of the House and Senate also have different kinds of relationships with the people they represent. Because representatives are elected every two years and usually face a smaller (and typically more homogenous) group of voters than do senators, they tend to maintain closer relationships with the voters and work on behalf of a narrower band of interests. Senators, by contrast, hold office for six-year terms and represent larger (and typically more heterogeneous) populations. Senators, therefore, have more freedom to exercise their own judgment on policy matters, and are less beholden to a small group of people.

This difference is no accident. The Framers of the Constitution envisioned the House to be the "People's Chamber," where the interests of specific groups would be aired. The Senate was intended to be more deliberative than the House, allowing elected officials to reflect upon issues with national implications.

Principles and Dilemmas of Representation

10-2   Analyze the relationships of members of Congress to their constituencies, and distinguish between the trustee and delegate models of representation.

By design, the two chambers of Congress represent the people like no other branch of government. The public has more opportunities to evaluate members of Congress than any other group of politicians in the federal government. It should come as little surprise, then, that members of Congress are always focused on the next election.

Members of Congress share one objective: getting reelected.

Members of Congress are a diverse bunch, coming from all walks of life. But they have one thing in common. According to David Mayhew, a political scientist who wrote one of the most influential books on Congress, members are "single-minded seekers of reelection."[9] Every vote they cast, speech they write, argument they advance, favor they offer, and bill they sponsor is with an eye toward the next election—and the one after that.

Of course, members of Congress have other objectives as well. Some want to make a difference by reforming health care or cracking down on illegal immigration. Others want to direct government benefits to a particular population. Still others just enjoy sitting in a position of power. The mix of policy and personal objectives in Congress is as varied as the members. To attain their individual goals, though, members must first win a seat and then hold onto it, both of which require money. As a consequence, members carefully calibrate their every action according to their assessments of the next election.[10]

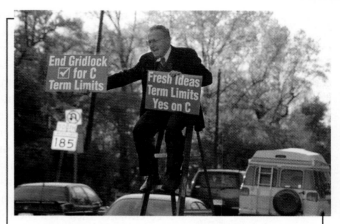

TERM LIMITS, BRINGING THE ELECTED CLOSER TO THE PUBLIC?

Often, members of Congress are criticized for being out of touch with the interests of everyday citizens. In this regard, members of Congress are not unique. Here, a protester calls for the imposition of term limits in order to "end gridlock" in Montgomery County, Maryland.

To improve their reelection prospects, members serve their constituents.

More than anything else, successful members of Congress work hard on behalf of their **constituents**—that is, the individuals who reside within their political jurisdictions. To convince these people to vote for them, members generally support legislation that is popular in their home states or districts. Thus, members from the Midwest stand up for farm subsidies, and representatives in Florida attend to the elderly.

constituents the people who reside within an elected official's political jurisdiction.

Political scientists have shown that members' electoral fortunes critically depend on how well they represent their constituents. Members who represent liberal populations but who support conservative bills, and vice versa, are more likely to lose the next election than members who faithfully represent the interests of their constituents. The basic lesson: "out of step, out of office."[11]

It stands to reason that **incumbents**—individuals who currently hold office—have more freedom to do as they please. It turns out that over 90 percent of Congressional members are reelected, and they are usually reelected by large margins. In 2010, 86 percent of incumbents in the House and 84 percent of incumbents in the Senate were reelected. Incumbents who are confident of reelection might feel less bound by their constituents' views. We need to be careful, however, about the causal interpretations we draw from incumbent

incumbent the individual in an election who currently holds the contested office; as distinct from the challenger, who seeks to remove the incumbent from power.

Thinking Causally Do large election victories entice political actors to do as they choose once in office?

casework the direct assistance that members of Congress give to individuals and groups within a district or state.

reelection rates. After all, does the fact that voters overwhelmingly approve of their representatives free them to do as they please, or are representatives reelected because they reflect the voters' views?

Beyond the positions they take on the issues of the day, members of Congress also serve their constituents through **casework**—direct assistance to individuals and groups within a district or state. The staffs that work for members of Congress will help constituents locate missing Social Security checks, direct constituents to federal agencies, and provide procedural support for dealing with these agencies, among other things. Obviously, members of Congress cannot address the individual needs of every constituent. Still, by performing casework for at least some of these constituents, members can hope to secure their votes at the next election.

To enhance their reelection prospects, members of Congress also direct federal benefits to their home districts and states. When new legislation is being considered that is intended to clean up the nation's streams, reduce poverty, or provide health insurance to children, members of Congress work hard to ensure that their own constituents reap the benefits of these initiatives.

Serving constituents can mean different things.

delegate model of representation the type of representation by which representatives are elected to do the bidding of the people who elected them; representatives are "delegates" in that they share the same policy positions as the voters and promise to act upon them.

trustee model of representation the type of representation by which representatives are elected to do what they think is best for their constituents.

The structural differences between the House and Senate reflect two broader conceptions of representation. According to the **delegate model of representation**, successful members of Congress share the same interests as the voters and promise to act upon them, even when their conscience or personal preferences dictate otherwise. In contrast, according to the **trustee model of representation**, members of Congress are chosen for their judgment, experience, and skill. Rather than simply mirroring their constituents' opinions, trustees reflect deeply on the arguments for and against different policies before taking a position. Trustees still represent their constituents, but they do so by thinking about the longer-term implications that policies have both for their constituents and for the nation as a whole.

Roughly speaking, members of the House tend to act more like delegates, and members of the Senate behave more like trustees. They do so because of the electoral incentives they face. Because they face more homogenous constituents at more frequent intervals, members of the House have stronger incentives to act on behalf of their public's current preferences. But senators, because they face more heterogeneous constituents over longer periods of time, can reflect on the deeper interests of a citizenry.

Not all constituents are represented equally well.

While all members have powerful incentives to represent their constituents, not all constituents are represented equally well. Instead, constituent groups who are likely to have a greater impact on a member's reelection bid tend to receive greater consideration on Capitol Hill.

Some constituents are less important because they cannot vote and therefore have fewer opportunities to influence the outcome of an election. Consider, for instance, the differences between the elderly and children. Older Americans tend to monitor the behavior of members of Congress quite closely and to vote in high numbers. Children, by contrast, pay little attention to politics. And even if they wanted to, children cannot vote until they officially become adults at age 18. Thus, it is not surprising that members of Congress tend to work harder on behalf of the elderly than they do on behalf of children. For every federal dollar spent to reduce poverty and poor health among children, four dollars are spent to accomplish the same objectives among the elderly.[12]

The citizens who organize, fund, and participate in interest groups also figure prominently in members' reelection strategies.[13] Through financial contributions and endorsements, interest groups can influence both the number of people who come out on Election Day and the candidates they choose. In 1998, lobbyists spent $1.4 billion in their efforts to court members of Congress. A decade later that number jumped to $3.5 billion. During this period, the number of congressional lobbyists also increased by roughly 30 percent.[14]

Members of Congress also have strong incentives to listen to their core supporters and those who can be persuaded to vote on their behalf. By contrast, members have less incentive to work on behalf of those individuals who would not, under any circumstances, vote for them. Consequentially, a Republican would likely support different kinds of policy proposals than a Democrat who came from the same district two years earlier, despite the fact that they both technically represented the same people.[15]

Political scientists have also examined the ways in which people of different genders, races, ethnicities, and incomes are represented by members of Congress. Some argue that citizens are best represented by members who have much in common with them: women are best represented by women members, African Americans by African American members, and so forth.[16]

If the findings from these studies apply more generally, then recent Congresses should be doing a better job than past ones of representing the full spectrum of interests around the country. As Figure 10-1 shows, members of Congress are reasonably diverse and are getting more so over time. The 112th Congress had a total of 91 women, two fewer than in the previous Congress. Seventeen of these women served in the Senate, and 74 served in the House of Representatives.

How Members Make Group Decisions

10-3 Assess the challenges that emerge when members of Congress set about working together.

Members of Congress do not work alone. To stand with confidence before their constituents, they must find ways to work together. For a variety of reasons, however, working together can be immensely challenging.

FIGURE 10-1 African Americans, Women, and Hispanic Americans in Congress, 1951–2011.

In 1951, there were just 2 African Americans, 3 Hispanics, and 11 women serving in Congress. Two decades later, 11 African Americans, 6 Hispanics, and 11 women were serving. By 2011, in the 112th Congress, there were 44 African Americans, 31 Hispanics, and 91 women in the House and Senate.

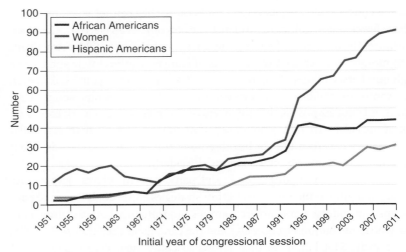

Note: Numbers include delegates, such as those from Washington, D.C., who do not have formal voting rights.
Source: Jennifer Manning, "Membership of the 112th Congress." A Congressional Research Service Report available online at www.fas.org/sgp/crs/misc/R41647.pdf.

Members of Congress often disagree with one another.

Members of Congress hail from different regions of the country. They have wildly different views about the purposes of government. They represent different genders and ethnicities. They even follow different electoral calendars. To understand how Congress functions, it is vital to recognize the diversity of its membership.

Members' different views reflect in part the districts they serve. The set of issues on which Barbara Boxer (a Democratic senator from California) and Tom Coburn (a Republican senator from Oklahoma) agree is small indeed. But even members who represent the same state and come from the same party regularly disagree about all sorts of issues. For example, Lindsey Graham and Jim DeMint, both Republican senators from South Carolina, differ on issues ranging from immigration to the maintenance of the Guantanamo Bay detention facility.

There are even differences in members' concerns about reelection—the core issue that supposedly unites them. Some members come from less competitive states and districts, whereas others expect to face stiffer competition at the next election. In addition, members of Congress come up for reelection at different times. Every two years, all House members must face the electorate, making it easier for them to coordinate their activities with one another. Senators, however, serve six-year, staggered terms, with one-third up for election in each election year. Every other year, one-third of the Senate's members are distracted by an election, while the other two-thirds can afford to focus on the obligations of governance.

Members of Congress confront basic challenges.

Members of Congress must find ways of sorting through their differences in order to satisfy their different constituents and thereby retain their seats. Unfortunately, members of Congress—like members of any collective decision-making body—confront a set of problems that makes it difficult to work together.

Collecting information Imagine the challenges facing members of Congress each session. They must keep track of changes in everything from the domestic economy to crime to international trade to transportation networks to wars around the world. Having canvassed all of these and many more policy domains, members then must identify the biggest problems facing the country and the best solutions. To do this, they need information—and lots of it.

Take, for example, the minimum wage. Minimum wage legislation consists of much more than a single line identifying the smallest hourly wage that employers can pay their workers around the nation. It is filled with exemptions and qualifications.[17] To complete the legislation, members must address all kinds of questions: Should there be a different minimum for teenagers and for adults? What about for those who rely on tips for much of their earnings? What about for noncitizens? Should the government provide financial assistance to industries, such as hotels and restaurants, which rely on large numbers of low-wage workers? If so, then how much and for how long? Should new rates take effect immediately or be phased in? What kinds of penalties should apply to employers who fail to pay at least a minimum wage?

Lawmakers must consider myriad issues when they do something seemingly as simple as changing the minimum wage. Imagine, then, the challenges of writing laws that address U.S. trade relations with China, immigration reform with Mexico, or urban redevelopment. Though they may have some expertise in a handful of issues, members often know very little about most substantive issues they confront. They must first collect the information they need to write the nation's laws.[18]

Having collected the relevant information, members must then convince one another about the benefits of their preferred policies. They must learn about each other's

SETTING A MINIMUM WAGE
For many, minimum wage legislation strictly defines the hourly earnings they can expect to receive. The legislation itself, though, is extraordinarily complex, requiring members of Congress to develop and analyze lots of information about different industries.

preferences and anticipate what others will accept, what they will reject, and what they are willing to compromise over. Lacking this additional information, members of Congress would find it virtually impossible to legislate.

Acting collectively It takes time and money to collect the information needed to write laws. Though the benefits of lawmaking generalize to all members of Congress, the costs do not. Specifically, the costs fall disproportionately on those who devote their own resources to researching an issue, devising possible solutions, and then building the coalitions needed to enact a policy. This, though, creates a basic **collective action problem**, which arises from the mismatch of individual and group incentives. As a group, members of Congress want to devise solutions for the nation's problems; individually, though, members would prefer that others pay the costs of formulating these solutions. And, because every member, individually, would prefer that other members pay these costs, there is a substantial risk of inaction.

collective action problem a problem that arises when individuals' incentives lead them to avoid taking actions that are best for the group as a whole, and that they themselves would like to see accomplished.

Cycling Members have very different ideas about what constitutes good public policy. A majority of members—that is, a group of at least 50 percent—would prefer some alternative to the existing policy. A second majority—that is, a different group that contains at least some members from the first majority—will then prefer a different alternative to the one first proposed. Yet a third majority will prefer still another alternative to the one proposed second. The result, which political scientists refer to as **cycling**, is that members cannot settle on a single change to existing policy.

cycling a phenomenon that occurs when multiple decision makers must decide among multiple options and cannot agree on a single course of action.

In the world of lawmaking, the list of possible policy alternatives is seemingly limitless. And because it is almost always possible to identify another version of a policy that a majority might prefer, debate could go on and on without a decision ever being reached. Members, therefore, must figure out a way to conclude debates so laws can be written and enacted.

Imposing Structure on Congress

10-4   Identify the resources and the committee and party structures that help Congress address its challenges.

To effectively do their jobs, members of Congress must find ways of collecting information, making sure everyone does their part, and resolving differences. They have devised structural solutions to make Congress in many ways ideally designed to deal with the problems of information, collective action, and cycling.

Committees establish a division of labor.

In both the House and Senate, members are assigned to different committees that oversee distinct policy areas. These committees draft versions of bills, hold hearings about policy issues, and investigate activities in the executive branch.

Types of committees In the 112th Congress, there were 16 standing committees in the Senate and 23 in the House. **Standing committees** have well-defined policy jurisdictions, which do not change markedly from Congress to Congress. Standing committees also are the real workhorses of Congress, developing, writing, and updating the most important legislation. **Select committees**, by contrast, are designed to address specific issues over shorter periods of time. Typically, they cease to exist once their members have completed their assigned task. So, for instance, in 2005 the House created the Select Bipartisan Committee to Investigate the Preparation for and Response to Hurricane Katrina. The committee was to conduct "a full and complete investigation" of the responses of local, state, and federal governments to Hurricane Katrina. One month after filing its report, the select committee was disbanded.

Whereas separate standing and select committees operate in the House and Senate, **joint committees** draw members from both chambers. Similar to select committees, joint committees focus on fairly narrow issue areas, but unlike select committees, joint committees are permanent. Rather than develop bills that either the House or Senate subsequently considers, joint committees typically act as fact-finding entities, addressing Congress's need to collect information.

Committees consist of smaller, and more specialized, **subcommittees**. Subcommittees allow for an even greater division of labor, which encourages the production of still more information. Because of their small size, it is easier to monitor members' behavior within subcommittees, improving the chances that all members do their share of the work.

Legislatures in other countries are organized much the same way. The organization of Britain's Parliament, in fact, looks quite like Congress. Parliament consists of two chambers, the House of Commons (akin to the House of Representatives) and the House of Lords (akin to the Senate). Within each chamber are a variety of standing and select committees, whose purposes are defined by the types of policies that they write and oversee. Like Congress, Parliament has committees that focus on education, health, foreign affairs, and public works. But, Parliament also has committees devoted to issues

standing committee a permanent committee with a well-defined, relatively fixed policy jurisdiction that develops, writes, and updates important legislation.

select committee a temporary committee created to serve a specific purpose.

joint committee a committee made up of members of both chambers of Congress to conduct a special investigation or study.

subcommittee a smaller organizational unit within a committee that specializes in a particular segment of the committee's responsibilities.

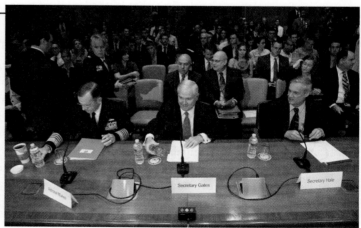

COLLECTING INFORMATION IN HEARINGS
In the summer of 2010, Joint Chiefs Chairman Admiral Mike Mullen, Defense Secretary Robert Gates, and Pentagon Comptroller Robert Hale testified before the Senate Appropriations Committee hearing on the Defense Department's fiscal 2011 budget.

that are particularly important to the United Kingdom, such as the Northern Ireland Affairs Select Committee and the European Union Select Committee.

Committee membership On average, senators serve on four committees and representatives serve on two. Committee members develop expertise in a handful of policy areas that they can share with their colleagues. With such a division of labor, Congress as an institution is able to collect more and better information.

Members of Congress try to serve on committees that oversee policies that their constituents care the most about. For instance, members who have large concentrations of veterans and active military personnel in their districts will often serve on the Veterans' Affairs or Armed Services committees.[19]

Other committees attract members not because of the policies that they oversee, but rather because of the power that they wield. The appropriations committees—Ways and Means in the House and Finance in the Senate—deal with tax and spending issues, which concern all sorts of government programs. Similarly, the Commerce Committee in the House provides members with opportunities to influence a broad array of public policies. Joining these committees gives members prestige and influence that can serve them well at the next election.

A chair, who is always from the party with a majority of seats in his or her chamber, oversees each committee and subcommittee. Because they set the agenda, schedule hearings, and call meetings, chairs often exert special influence. For much of the twentieth century, chairs were selected on the basis of **seniority**—that is, the length of time that they had served in office.

seniority the length of time a legislator has served in office.

Parties impose order on their members.

The two major parties in the United States, Democratic and Republican, provide still more order to Congress. The parties determine who will control the various committees and subcommittees, and thus determine which core issues Congress will consider, which it will disregard, and how the debate will proceed. Through parties, coalitions in favor of one policy or another are formed. And within parties, strategies are developed to promote the policies that best serve their members' reelection prospects. Parties, in short, help to overcome the collective action and cycling problems that otherwise would cripple Congress.

party caucus the gathering of all Democratic members of the House or Senate.

party conference the gathering of all Republican members of the House or Senate.

Speaker of the House the person who presides over the House and serves as the chamber's official spokesperson.

Party leadership At the beginning of each term, congressional Democrats and Republicans gather to select their leadership. For Democrats, the gathering is called the **party caucus**; for Republicans, it is the **party conference**. In the House, the party with the most seats elects the **Speaker of the House**, which is the only position in the House that the Constitution specifically mentions. In the Senate, the majority party selects the **majority leader**. In both chambers, the party with fewer seats selects the **minority leader**.

The Speaker of the House and the majority leader of the Senate perform many of the same functions. They preside over their chambers when they are in session, communicate with the White House about the progress of different bills, and act as congressional spokespersons. Because they decide which committees will consider which legislative proposals, they also help set the legislative agenda. If they strongly oppose a particular proposal, they often find ways of delaying its consideration by Congress as a whole.

For the most part, the Speaker of the House plays a more important role in overseeing affairs in the House than the majority leader does in the Senate. The reason has to do with the differences in the size and culture of the two chambers. Because the House has 435 voting members whereas the Senate has just 100, it is much more important to have a stronger leader in the House overseeing the business of the day.

Party discipline Second in command in the House is the House majority leader, whose responsibility it is to unify the party caucus and help deliver the party's message to the public. The majority and minority party leaders of both parties also have **whips** who deliver messages from the leaders to the rank-and-file members, keep track of their votes, and encourage them to stand together on key issues.

The efforts of the House majority leader and whips to get party members to vote together are generally successful (see Figure 10-2). Over the last half-century, less than 30 percent of Republicans and Democrats have voted against their parties on issues that are especially important to their leaders. And the percentage continues to drop.

majority leader the individual in each chamber who manages the floor; in the Senate, he or she is the most powerful member in the chamber; in the House, he or she is the chief lieutenant of the Speaker.

minority leader the individual who speaks on behalf of the party that controls the smaller number of seats in each chamber.

whips designated members of Congress who deliver messages from the party leaders, keep track of members' votes, and encourage members to stand together on key issues.

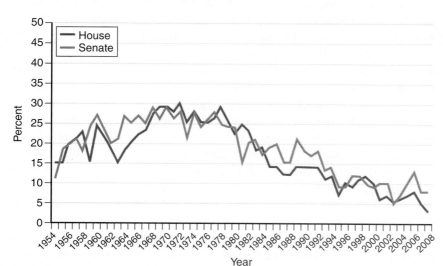

FIGURE 10-2 Defections Among Majority Party Members on "Party Votes," 1954–2008.

Since about 1970, both Democrats and Republicans in Congress vote with their party with increasing regularity.

Note: Southern Democrats not included in the analysis.

Political scientists debate how party discipline is achieved. Some emphasize the powers of the party leadership to direct their members to vote in certain ways.[20] Leaders have a variety of means by which to punish members for defecting, such as cutting off financial aid to reelection campaigns. And, by controlling the legislative agenda, party leaders can keep divisive issues from ever coming up for a vote. Moreover, these scholars argue, members benefit from party discipline, since it helps them achieve their goal of enacting laws that will satisfy constituents.

Thinking Causally Do parties force members of Congress to behave differently from the way they would prefer?

Other scholars suggest that party leaders have very little to do with the decline of party defections.[21] Instead, party members vote together because they agree with one another. These scholars argue that there is little evidence that members of Congress systematically vote against their constituents' interests in order to toe the party line. Nor should members vote this way. After all, to vote against one's constituents is to reduce one's chances of being reelected. By this account, the correlation between party positions and individual voting behavior is not causal but simply reflects the shared views of members of the same party.

There has been a recent increase in party polarization.

One of the most striking trends in Congress during the past 30 years has been the increase in party polarization. As members have increased their tendency to vote together with their partisans, they in turn vote less frequently with members of the opposition party. Congressional Republicans in 2009 were significantly more conservative than they were in 1970.[22]

Why are Republican members of Congress more conservative and Democratic members more liberal than they were a generation ago? The question is especially puzzling because there is very little evidence that citizens today are any more conservative or liberal than they were in 1970. According to one recent study, the root cause of this phenomenon is the rise in inequality across America.[23] Over the last century, partisan polarization has increased along with income inequality. It remains less clear, though, if inequality and polarization are causally related. The authors of this study, in fact, recognize that the opposite might be true—polarization might generate inequality.

Thinking Causally Why have Democrats and Republicans become more polarized over the past 30 years?

It is not clear whether party polarization strengthens or weakens democratic governance. On the one hand, polarized parties present voters with clear choices about different policy issues. With these clear choices, voters can more easily hold members of a party accountable for their performance in office. If they do not like the policies advanced by an incumbent, voters can shift their support to a challenger with reliably different policy positions. On the other hand, polarized parties can impede legislative processes. As William Galston laments, under conditions of rising polarization "Congress can become a haven for obstruction and gridlock rather than deliberation and compromise."[24] Moreover, as the two majorities drift to the extremes of the

HOW DO WE KNOW?

Has Congress Abdicated Its War-Making Authority?

The Question

The Constitution gives most war-making powers to Congress. Article I says that Congress shall have the power to declare war, raise and support armies, appropriate funds for war, and regulate the conduct of ongoing wars. By contrast, the war powers granted to the president are much shorter. Indeed, those Article II passages that refer explicitly to foreign policy merely identify the president as the commander in chief and authorize him to "receive ambassadors and other public ministers." Today, though, most decisions about war are made by the president. And rarely does Congress formally restrict the president's ability to wage war abroad. Has Congress abdicated its war-making powers? How do we know?

Why It Matters

There is no greater government power than the ability to send citizens abroad to fight, kill, and perhaps die. For precisely this reason, the Founders worried a great deal about which branch of government would have the authority to wage war. If they vested too much authority in the president, the Founders worried that the system of checks and balances might one day collapse. And so they looked to the legislative branch, which could be expected to better represent the will of the people in making decisions about war. For much of U.S. history, this is exactly how decisions about whether to go to war were made. In the last half-century, though, the president has made most decisions involving war, and Congress has been pushed to the sidelines.

Investigating the Answer

One way to determine whether Congress has abdicated its war-making powers is to examine the declarations and actions of presidents and members of Congress. Who sets the agenda, and who follows?

Not since World War II has Congress formally declared war. It has authorized some wars (including the Vietnam, Persian Gulf, and Iraq wars) but not others (including the Korean War and conflicts in Panama, Kosovo, Bosnia, and Haiti).[25] Congress also has been reluctant to exercise its formal legislative

and appropriations powers to influence wars that are under way. Though it has the constitutional authority to cut funding for a war, issue regular reports about a war's progress, and demand a withdrawal, Congress rarely takes advantage of these options—even when wars are unpopular.

In 1973, frustrated with the progress of the Vietnam War, members of Congress attempted to reassert their authority by passing the War Powers Resolution, which gave the president 60 to 90 days to secure formal authorization of a military deployment before troops would have to be withdrawn. Advocates believed the resolution would stop presidential incursions on congressional war powers and put members of Congress back in charge of decisions involving the use of military force. Instead, every president since the resolution was passed has refused to recognize its constitutionality. These presidents have launched one military initiative after another without securing congressional authorization.

More recently, political scientists have begun to examine subtle ways in which Congress nonetheless influences decisions about war. During the first three years of the Iraq War, for instance, members gave 5,000 speeches on the floors of the House and Senate. Such

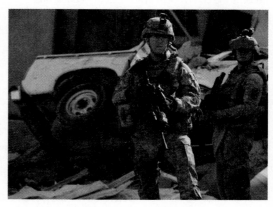

CONGRESS'S WARS? U.S. soldiers stand watch at the site of a bomb attack in Baghdad, Iraq, in January 2010. Article I of the Constitution grants members of Congress considerable authority over issues relating to war, including the funding of troops conducting ground-level operations. In overseeing the Iraq War, has Congress met its constitutional obligations?

(continues)

HOW DO WE KNOW? Has Congress Abdicated Its War-Making Authority?

(continued)

speeches, political scientists have shown, can have a profound impact on the ways in which the media cover a war, influencing the tone and content of news stories. By influencing the media, these speeches also can affect public opinion. And, over time, changes in public opinion can yield new governing majorities.

Recent research also demonstrates that the partisan composition of Congress has implications for the president's ability to wage war. Political scientists have observed the following patterns in military deployments since World War II: presidents whose party holds a large number of seats in the House and Senate tend to wage war more often than those whose party holds relatively few seats; presidents who enjoy lots of support within Congress tend to take military action more quickly.[26] The checks that Congress places on the president, then, are not constant. Rather, they vary according to the level of partisan support that the president has.

Of course, partisan politics can be even more complicated when a war is passed off to a president of a different party. President Obama, a Democrat, inherited wars in Iraq and Afghanistan from former President Bush, a Republican. When these wars began, congressional Republicans almost uniformly supported them, while Democrats remained divided. However, once Obama became the commander in chief, both Republicans and Democrats appeared torn between the positions they had staked out under an earlier president and their current partisan allegiances. Hence, Republicans who called for more troops when Bush was president now went out of their way to criticize Obama's handling of the war, while Democrats who had previously contested the

expansion of war made a point of complimenting Obama for the care and deliberation he exhibited in office.

Thinking Critically

1. Has the emergent threat of terrorism made it more or less difficult for Congress to influence national decisions about the U.S. military?

2. What kinds of members of Congress are likely to become most involved in debates about war?

3. What types of evidence might demonstrate whether the work of members of Congress influences the content of U.S. foreign policy?

The Bottom Line

The president's power to make decisions involving war has expanded dramatically during the past half-century, and congressional involvement in decisions involving war has declined. Congress, however, still represents an important check on presidential war powers. The fact that military deployments tend to vary with the strength of the president's party in Congress says two important things about the domestic politics of war. First, Congress is a collection of diverse individuals with different assessments of the national interest and the value of war. Second, when evaluating how presidents conduct war or any other public policy, one must carefully monitor the ways in which they anticipate, and attempt to ward off, efforts by members of Congress to limit their authority.

ideological spectrum, a rising share of the American public refuses to affiliate with either of them. Whereas 28 percent of the American public self-identified as independent in 1970, fully 35 percent did so in January of 2011.[27]

Staff and support agencies help collect and analyze information.

Members of Congress are assisted by roughly 11,000 staffers who perform all sorts of tasks, many of which concern the collection and analysis of information. On average, each senator has about 40 staffers working for him or her, and each House member has 17.[28] Some staffers work in a member's Washington, D.C., office, and others work back in the member's district or state. Those in D.C. tend to research public policies, write briefs, draft proposals, organize hearings, and interact with lobbyists. They also communicate with staffers for other members, helping to build coalitions in support of various policy initiatives. Staffers back home, meanwhile, interact with constituents about their concerns, their interests, and their ideas. These staffers then communicate this information back to the D.C. office.

Members also have access to several administrative agencies that provide vital information about public policy matters. The Congressional Research Service (CRS), established in 1914, handles hundreds of thousands of requests each year from members seeking information. Employees at CRS also take inventory of all the bills introduced in Congress and track their progress through the legislative process. The Government Accountability Office (GAO) also studies policy issues upon congressional request. Established in 1921, the GAO acts as an investigatory body for members who wish to know more about the programs and activities of bureaucratic agencies. The Congressional Budget Office (CBO), established in 1974, provides members with information about the costs of policies that they are considering, the economic implications of different budget proposals, and the general state of the economy.

Lawmaking

10-5 Outline the lawmaking process in Congress.

Members of Congress perform a variety of functions. They hold hearings and launch investigations. They help educate the public about the major issues of the day. They communicate with constituents and help resolve their problems. The single most important function that Congress serves, however, is to write the nation's laws.

The legislative process is long.

To become a law, a bill must travel a long road, which is outlined in Figure 10-3. To begin the process, a **sponsor** introduces a bill into either the House or Senate. Any member of Congress can serve as a bill's sponsor. A bill can originate in either chamber, and sometimes equivalent bills are introduced simultaneously to both.

sponsor a member of Congress who introduces a bill.

Subsequently, the bill must be referred to the appropriate committee for consideration. In the House, the Speaker decides which committee will take up the bill. In the Senate, the bill is assigned to a committee by the chamber's presiding officer, either the vice president or, more commonly, the president pro tempore. The president pro tempore is the most senior member of the majority party.

Bills typically are assigned to the committees that oversee the relevant policy domain. For example, bills on foreign conflicts are generally assigned

FIGURE 10-3 How a Bill Becomes a Law (or Not).

The lawmaking process is long, and most introduced bills fail to become laws.

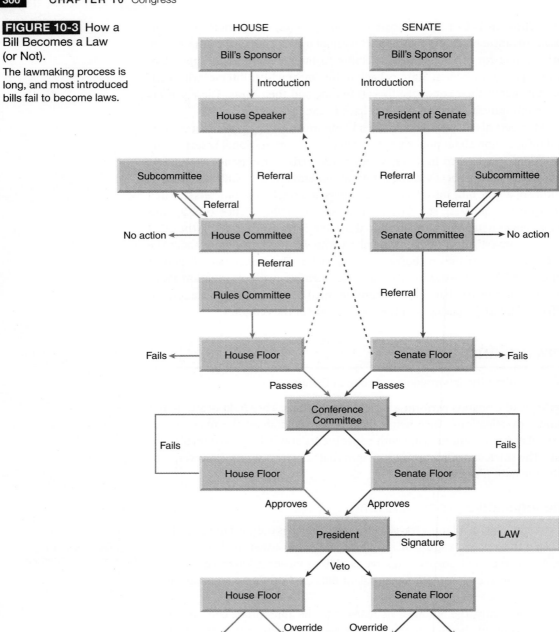

to the Foreign Relations committee in the Senate and the Foreign Affairs committee in the House. Some bills are assigned to more than one committee—a practice called multiple referral.[29] After assignment to one or more committees, a bill then is assigned to one or more subcommittees. The substance of a bill is typically first considered at the subcommittee level. Members of subcommittees carefully review the bill, holding hearings and conducting research on how it will likely affect their constituents and the nation as a whole. In a process called **markup,** members rewrite portions of the bill, delete others, and add still more. Once satisfied, the members then report the bill back to the full committee, whose members review the subcommittee's work and offer revisions of their own.

markup the process by which the members of a committee or subcommittee rewrite, delete, and add portions of a bill.

What happens next depends on which chamber is considering the bill. In the Senate, bills move straight from the committee of origin to the Senate floor, where the entire assembly of senators is given an opportunity to debate the merits of the proposed legislation. In the House, though, most bills coming out of committee are referred to the Rules Committee.[30] The Rules Committee decides how a bill will be debated on the floor by the entire membership of the House. It decides when the bill will go to the floor, how long members will debate the bill, and what kinds of amendments (if any) can be offered. When assigning an **open rule** to a bill, the Rules Committee allows for a wide range of amendments. Under a **closed rule**, the number and types of possible amendments are more restricted. Having completed its business, the Rules Committee then refers the bill to the House floor.

open rule the terms and conditions applied to a particular bill that allow members of Congress to make a wide range of amendments to it.

closed rule the terms and conditions applied to a particular bill that restrict the types of amendments that can be made to it.

On the floors of both the House and Senate, members typically give speeches about the bill, offer amendments, and eventually vote. To pass the House, a bill must receive the support of a majority of voting members. In the Senate, however, the threshold is somewhat higher. Technically, only a majority is needed to pass a bill. Any senator, though, may choose to **filibuster** a bill, which allows for indefinite debate. To end a filibuster—a process called invoking **cloture**—a supermajority of 60 votes is needed. If a majority of senators, but less than 60, support a filibustered bill, the bill will die.[31]

filibuster a procedure by which senators delay or prevent action on a bill by making long speeches and engaging in unlimited debate.

cloture a mechanism by which 60 or more senators can end a filibuster and cut off debate.

To become law, a bill must pass both chambers of Congress. But having gone through markups in subcommittees and committees and then having been subject to further amendments on the floor, Senate and House versions of the same bill often look quite different from one another at this stage. Such differences must be resolved before a bill becomes a law. Often, senators and representatives reconcile their differences informally. Party leaders play an important role in such negotiations, recommending elements of a bill to keep, to discard, and to amend. More formally, appointed members of each chamber serve on a **conference committee,** which has the job of producing a compromise version of the bill. If conference committee members can come to an agreement—and sometimes they cannot—they send a revised version of the bill to the floors of the House and Senate, where it is subsequently voted on.

conference committee a committee made up of members of both chambers that is responsible for ironing out the differences between House and Senate versions of a bill.

If the bill passes the House and Senate, it travels down Pennsylvania Avenue to the White House. The president can sign the bill, in which case it automatically becomes law. Alternatively, the president may **veto,** or reject, the legislation. Members can respond to a veto in three ways. First, they can refuse to reconsider the bill, in which case it dies. Second, they can make concessions to win over the president. In this case, both the House and Senate then vote on a new version of the bill, which is sent back to the president. Third, members can try to override the president's veto by securing the support of two-thirds of both houses. If they fail, the veto is sustained.

veto the president's rejection of a bill passed by both chambers of Congress, which prevents the bill from becoming law. Congress can override a veto with a two-thirds vote in both the House and Senate.

Most bills are not enacted into law.

Traveling down this long legislative road, it is not surprising that bills often hit a pothole and veer onto an embankment. There are, after all, plenty of opportunities for a strategic politician, either working alone or with others, to derail a bill. Committees, minority factions in either the House or the Senate, and the president, too, can undermine the prospects of even those bills that enjoy the support of congressional majorities.

Let's begin with committees. Committee members who are assigned a bill they oppose could try to tailor the bill more to their liking or could refuse to do anything at all and "table" the bill indefinitely. This **gate-keeping authority** can give committees substantial power over the kinds of bills that come before the floor of either chamber. Despite the fact that a majority of either the House or the Senate, presumably, would like to see at least some of these bills enacted, in most congresses, upwards of 80 percent of all introduced bills never make it out of committee.[32]

gate-keeping authority the power to decide whether a particular proposal or policy change will be considered.

Using a filibuster, just 41 opponents in the Senate can kill a bill—even if the other 59 senators and all 435 members of the House prefer to see it enacted. The filibuster is a powerful tool for minorities within Congress to check the powers of majorities, and minorities are making increasing use of it. During the first half of the twentieth century, only a handful of bills in each congressional session were subject to a filibuster. Beginning in the early 1970s, however, the average number increased to 22; during the 1990s, it increased to over 40.[33] And, in the 111th Congress, a whopping 87 filibusters were made.[34]

The president can often thwart the general interests of majorities in both chambers of Congress. If either chamber fails to override a presidential veto, a proposed bill fails to become law. During the nation's history, presidents have used this power with greater and greater frequency to influence the content of legislation. During the first half of the nineteenth century, presidents tended to use the veto power sparingly, and then only to ward off congressional efforts to usurp executive powers. By the middle of the twentieth century, however, presidents were not at all shy about vetoing bills they objected to on policy grounds. Not surprisingly, the vast majority of these vetoes were sustained.

Almost every president has succeeded in having more than 75 percent of his vetoes upheld in Congress.[35]

Because lawmaking is so difficult, most bills are not enacted into law. Between 1981 and 2008, roughly 10 percent of the bills introduced to the House made it through that chamber. Even fewer became laws. In the 110th Congress, which operated from 2007 to 2009, less than four percent of bills were enacted into law.[36] In addition, not all bills that are enacted into law follow the traditional path outlined in Figure 10-3. Indeed, a variety of parliamentary procedures enable members to occasionally circumvent the conventional approach. One such procedure is the "self-executing rule," which is a way of indirectly passing a bill through Congress without ever actually voting on it. If prior to the consideration of a bill the House votes in favor of a rule containing a self-executing provision, then passage of that rule ensures passage of the bill that it references. Since the 1930s, Republicans and Democrats alike have employed the self-executing rule. Although it was initially used as a way to make minor modifications to bills, it soon became a partisan tool to promote specific policies concerning immigration, smoking regulation, and the Internal Revenue Service.[37] Since the 95th Congress, over 200 self-executing rules have been used.[38]

Altogether different parliamentary procedures and political machinations were needed to enact health care reform in 2010. Senate Democrats lacked the votes they needed to overcome a threatened filibuster. To enact health care reform, therefore, Democrats decided that rather than hammering out differences in the House and Senate versions of the bill in conference committee and then revoting in each chamber, as is typically done, the House would simply pass the Senate's version of the bill, which would then go to the president for signature.

To deal with a variety of objections to this law, meanwhile, Congress voted a separate set of "fixes" under a budget reconciliation, which requires only a majority of votes in both chambers and thereby avoids the threat of a Senate filibuster. Furthermore, to placate a handful of pro-life Democrats in the House, President Obama issued a separate executive order that reiterated language in the statute prohibiting the use of federal funds to pay for abortions.

Laws, nonetheless, are enacted.

Just because lawmaking is difficult does not mean that it is impossible. In a typical year, Congress enacts several hundred laws. Though most of these laws concern rather mundane affairs, at least some have profound policy consequences. According to one study that categorized legislation into four different categories of significance, each year Congress enacts roughly 5 "landmark" laws, 6 "major" laws, 36 "ordinary" ones, and no less than 314 "minor" laws.

Political scientists have tried to determine the mix of political factors most likely to result in successful legislation. One of the most powerful predictors

Case Study

Immigration Reform

Today the Census Bureau reports more foreign-born residents—38.5 million—than ever before in its history. Some estimate that 12 million are in the country illegally, with that number growing by an average of 400,000 per year. Moreover, over 7 million of these illegal immigrants are employed, accounting for nearly 5 percent of the country's civilian labor force and constituting substantial portions of such industries as construction and agriculture.[39]

More than once, Barack Obama expressed his intention to address the various problems associated with illegal immigration and undocumented workers. As a candidate in 2008, Obama pledged to make immigration reform one of his top priorities during his first term as president. "Well, I don't know about you," he said, "but I think it's time for a president who won't walk away from comprehensive immigration reform when it becomes politically unpopular."[40] In a Cinco de Mayo speech in 2010, President Obama reiterated his commitment to enacting immigration reform: "I want to begin work this year, and I want Democrats and Republicans to work with me—because we've got to stay true to who we are, a nation of laws and a nation of immigrants."[41] To date, however, Congress has not cooperated.

This was not the first time that a president had proposed immigration reform. In his 2007 State of the Union Address, President George W. Bush proposed an overhaul of immigration rules, "without amnesty and without animosity," as one of four domestic policy priorities for the remainder of his second term.

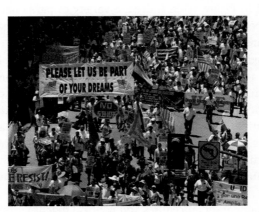

FAILING TO ACT To date, Congress has failed to pass comprehensive immigration reform of any kind. As a result, some states have taken it upon themselves to do so. Arizona's action on the matter in 2010 evoked widespread protests from supporters of immigration. In your view, how should Congress address the issue of immigration? And should the states have any say in the matter?

In the 2006 midterm elections, control of the House and Senate switched to the Democrats, who looked more favorably upon the kinds of immigration reforms that Bush supported. After three months of deliberation, members of Congress produced a draft bill. The proposed Comprehensive Immigration Reform Act of 2007 downplayed deportation and instead offered a path to citizenship for illegal immigrants.

Senate Majority Leader Harry Reid agreed to introduce the bill directly to the Senate floor, bypassing the Judiciary Committee. Supporters mustered 66 votes in favor of the most controversial portion of the bill, which offered legal status to most illegal immigrants. But Reid pulled the bill from the floor on June 7, after three successive votes for cloture failed and only seven Republicans agreed to close debate. On June 26, the Senate voted 64–35 to reconsider the proposal, but two days later another cloture motion fell short, killing the bill.

Experts generally agree that the current immigration system is broken. Why, then, did the president's and Congress's reform efforts falter? For starters, the bill's opponents expressed their views more forcefully than did its proponents. As one researcher put it, the bill was "born an orphan in terms of popular support."[42] A substantial portion of Americans did not feel strongly about the issue. Illegal immigrants could not vote, and their American employers, afraid of calling attention to their employment of undocumented workers, tended not to trumpet their support for amnesty. Opponents, by contrast, let their voices be heard, making well over 250,000 contacts with U.S. senators during the run-up to the June 28 vote.[43]

Case Study Immigration Reform

Disagreements between Democrats and Republicans about the immigration issue also made it difficult for Congress to enact needed reform. Both sides agreed to help employers fill jobs with government approved temporary laborers. However, many Republicans insisted that those workers eventually must leave, while many Democrats wanted to allow them to stay and become citizens.[44]

The immigration debates also revealed divisions within the two major parties. The desire of most Democrats to naturalize immigrants put them at odds with labor unions, while the inclination of most Republicans to send workers home pitted them against business owners.

A weakened presidency may also have contributed to the bill's failure. With low approval ratings, a controversial war in Iraq, and poor results in the 2006 midterm elections, President Bush could not overcome the objections of Republican members of Congress.

Immigration reform, then, ended in collapse rather than compromise. Members of both parties, as well as the executive and legislative branches, bemoaned the failure but were unable to prevent it. Without highlighting his own party's role in killing the bill, President Bush expressed disappointment in Congress's "failure to act."[45] But Senate Majority Leader Harry Reid may have summarized it best: "The big winner today was obstruction; the big winner today was inaction."[46]

Thinking Critically

1. How does the fact that illegal immigrants cannot vote figure into the politics of immigration reform?

2. Why were some of President Bush's strongest critics members of his own party?

---

is the strength of the majority party's control in the House and Senate. When Democrats or Republicans control both chambers of Congress by wide margins, they find it much easier to overcome the various institutional challenges that derail so many bills.

Though most laws live on indefinitely, laws with **sunset provisions** must be reauthorized after a specified number of years. The 2001 No Child Left Behind Act was a reauthorization of the 1965 ESEA Act, which must be reconsidered by Congress every seven years. Given that existing laws maintain programs that are already up and running, that they have received political support in the past, and that they come up for formal consideration in a specified year, they are more likely to pass than other legislation.

sunset provision a condition of a law that requires it to be reauthorized after a certain number of years.

The Appropriations Process

10-6 Explain the appropriations process.

The work of Congress is not complete after it enacts a law. Congress subsequently must commit funds so that the law can be set in motion. Every year, Congress uses money from the Treasury Department to fund federal agencies and programs.[47] According to Article I, section 9, of the Constitution, "no money shall be drawn from the treasury, but in consequence of appropriations made by law." But besides stipulating that "a regular statement and account of receipts and expenditures of all public monies shall be published from time to time," the Constitution has left most of the specifics to the legislature itself.

Spending is a two-step process.

authorization the granting of legal authority to operate federal programs and agencies.

appropriations the granting of funds to operate authorized federal programs and agencies.

Two steps must be taken for monies to make their way to different agencies and programs. First, these programs and agencies must receive **authorization** by the legislation that serves as the legal basis for their continued operation. The second step is **appropriations**, the actual granting of funds to federal agencies and programs. Authorization committees help determine the kinds of programs within their legislative jurisdiction that will be funded; appropriations committees determine the exact amounts of monies to be disbursed.

In principle, authorizations and appropriations are kept separate in order to reduce the chances that members of Congress will use federal monies to alter the actual operations of federal agencies and programs. In practice, though, the distinction between authorizations and appropriations often blurs—in part, because appropriations committee members make quite a habit of using limitations on the use of funds as a way to legislate indirectly.[48]

Nonappropriations committees also use authorizing legislation to grant permanent budget authority to programs and agencies. As a result, a sizable fraction of each year's federal budget is dedicated to mandatory spending (often called entitlements) on these past obligations. The largest entitlements include such massive programs as Social Security, Medicare, and Medicaid. The remainder of the budget—the portion not already promised elsewhere and therefore available for discretionary spending on new obligations—is the subject of deliberations within the appropriations committees.[49]

earmarks federal funds that support specific local projects.

Members also use **earmarks** to bypass executive agencies altogether and direct funds straight to their constituents. According to one watch-dog organization, Congress disclosed over 11,000 earmarks worth almost $15 billion in the 2008 fiscal year.[50] Responding to public concerns about deficit spending, Congress and the president in early 2011 adopted a two-year moratorium on all earmarks. The general practice of directing funds to special projects, however, is unlikely to disappear in the near future. These projects enable members of Congress to deliver benefits directly to their constituents, to take decisions out of the hands of executive officials, and to make bills more popular and passable.

Appropriations come in three forms.

regular appropriations the standard mode by which federal moneys are allotted to programs.

There are three main types of appropriations. **Regular appropriations** are the main source of revenues that are disbursed to agencies and programs. Regular appropriations contain three standard features: an enacting clause that designates the fiscal year for which funds are given, a breakdown of budget authority by accounts, and general provisions that apply to all of the accounts.

Small agencies might possess only one account, but larger ones usually are financed by several distinct accounts, designated with names such as "procurement" or "salaries and expenses."

A second type of appropriations is a **continuing resolution**, which disburses funding when regular appropriations have not been set by the close of the fiscal year on October 1. Continuing resolutions have become quite common. Traditionally, continuing resolutions were brief measures listing the agencies that had not yet received their regular funding and providing temporary assistance at the previous year's level or the president's budget request, whichever was lower. Today, however, continuing resolutions increasingly include measures that cover several of the regular appropriations bills at once.

continuing resolution funds used to keep programs up and running when regular appropriations have not been approved by the end of the fiscal year.

Congress also provides **supplemental appropriations**, the third type, when regular appropriations do not cover certain activities or are deemed insufficient. In order to evade spending caps, Congress sometimes designates supplements as emergency funds. Franklin D. Roosevelt's New Deal used supplemental appropriations to create new government agencies and create new jobs. In 2009, President Obama's economic stimulus package contained supplemental appropriations to stabilize the economy and preserve jobs. Much of the Iraq War has been funded not through regular defense appropriations but through a series of supplemental appropriations.

supplemental appropriations the process by which Congress and the president can provide temporary funding for government activities and programs when funds fall short due to unforeseen circumstances.

The appropriations process differs from the legislative process.

The process of appropriating federal funds looks quite a bit like the legislative process. Suggested appropriations are debated and marked up within committees, considered on the floors of the House and Senate, reconciled across chambers, and eventually sent to the president. In two important respects, however, the appropriations process differs from the lawmaking process.

First, appropriations are purposefully streamlined. Whereas a failure to legislate may disappoint key constituencies, a failure to appropriate funds can bring the federal government to a grinding halt. And, because appropriations are required every year, members of Congress have a vested interest in minimizing the procedural roadblocks—such as the Senate filibuster—that they are likely to encounter.

Second, the appropriations process is supposed to follow a strict timetable. The president initiates the process by submitting his annual budget proposal to Congress on or before the first Monday in February. The full House and Senate appropriations committees then have the option of conducting overview hearings to discuss the proposal with the Office of Management and Budget. From February to April, agencies meet with the relevant appropriations subcommittees to justify the difference between their newly requested amounts and the previous year's allotments. By April 15, Congress passes a resolution that determines the federal budget for the next five fiscal years and allocates that year's budget among all of its committees.

In May and June, the House chair, subcommittees, and the full appropriations committee mark up the proposals, reporting regular bills to the entire House by July. The House debates, considers amendments, passes the bills, and sends them to the Senate, which passes the bills (perhaps with amendments) before the August congressional recess. In September, members of both chambers' appropriations committees hold conferences to resolve any remaining differences. Usually the House considers the conference report first, and the Senate decides whether to accept or reject the House's report. Once the two chambers have settled on the final appropriations bills, they are sent to the president, who has 10 days to sign or veto them in their entirety.

In practice, Congress and the president rarely abide by this strict schedule. In some years, the legislature does not pass the budget resolution by the April 15 deadline, delaying transmittal of explicit spending ceilings to the appropriations committees. In fact, in fiscal years 1999, 2003, 2006, and 2010, Congress did not complete the resolution at all. And, in December 1995, Bill Clinton vetoed the reconciliation bill that would have enacted Republican-backed tax cuts and curtailed spending on social programs. When Congress failed to override the president's veto, portions of the federal government temporarily shut down.

Chapter Summary

In this chapter you have learned to:

10-1   Describe the basic structure of Congress.

As a bicameral institution, the U.S. Congress has two chambers: the House of Representatives and the Senate. Members in the House serve for two years, and senators serve for six. Whereas members of the House represent congressional districts, senators represent entire states. The Senate also has some duties (such as the ratification of treaties and approval of Supreme Court nominees) that members of the House do not have.

10-2   Analyze the relationships of members of Congress to their constituencies, and distinguish between the trustee and delegate models of representation.

Congress represents the interests of some citizens more than others. Above all, members of Congress want to be reelected, and to be reelected they must adequately represent the interests of their constituents. Depending on whether members follow a trustee or delegate model of representation, their relationship with their constituents will differ dramatically. Moreover, members do not represent all constituents equally. Depending on whether they vote, are organized, are Democrats or Republicans, or fit a certain demographic profile, some constituents receive more or less representation by the member of Congress who serves their district or state.

10-3   Assess the challenges that emerge when members of Congress set about working together.

Members of Congress face important challenges when working together. They have different interests, priorities, and worldviews. To build a record of accomplishments that will serve them well at the next election, members of

Congress must effectively navigate these differences. Additionally, they must overcome problems of information, collective action, and cycling that emerge when decisions require the participation of multiple members.

10-4   Identify the resources and the committee and party structures that help Congress address its challenges.

The resources and structures that define Congress as an institution alleviate the challenges. Members of Congress have staffs that help collect information. They serve on committees and subcommittees that establish a division of labor. And most members belong to one of the two dominant parties, which provide further structure.

10-5   Outline the lawmaking process in Congress.

The lawmaking process is long and difficult. To become a law, a bill must pass through multiple committees and sub-committees in both the House and Senate, the floors of both chambers, and a conference committee, before it lands on the president's desk for signature. Even then, though, the president may veto the bill, in which case it returns to Congress for reconsideration. Not surprisingly, most proposed bills fail to become laws. Nonetheless, Congress does manage to enact laws on a regular basis—sometimes because its members agree about the solution to a particular problem, and sometimes because the business of the day (appropriations and reauthorizations) requires them to set about finishing the task.

10-6   Explain the appropriations process.

The appropriations process differs from the lawmaking process. Because budgets must be approved every year, appropriations usually are easier to set than laws are to enact. Some of the roadblocks to lawmaking are eliminated, the budget has a permanent place on the congressional agenda, and the processes themselves are routinized. Still, delays are common. Increasingly, Congress has had to rely on continuing and supplemental appropriations to keep the government running.

CHAPTER TEST

1. How do structural differences between the Senate and House explain differences in behavior of those people who work in the two chambers of Congress?

2. What kinds of things can members of Congress do to increase their chances of being reelected?

3. When members of Congress challenge the president over matters involving war, are they behaving more consistently with the delegate model of representation or the trustee model? Why?

4. How do congressional committees help address the challenges of collecting information?

5. How do parties reduce collective action problems in Congress?

6. As long as a bill retains the support of a majority of members of Congress, will it necessarily be enacted into law?

7. How can the president influence the content of legislation?

8. Why do members of the same party typically vote the same way on legislative initiatives?

9. Through what mechanism does Congress direct funds to relief efforts for unforeseen emergencies?

10. In what ways is the appropriations process easier to navigate than the legislative process?

MyPoliSciLab® CONGRESS
Apply what you learned in this chapter on MyPoliSciLab.

Read on mypoliscilab.com

eText: Chapter 10

Study and **Review** on mypoliscilab.com

Pre-Test
Post-Test
Chapter Exam
Flashcards

Watch on mypoliscilab.com

Video: Kagan Hearing
Video: Unknown Wins South Carolina Senate Primary
How Do We Know Video: Has Congress Abdicated its War-Making Authority?

Explore on mypoliscilab.com

Comparative: Comparing Legislatures
Simulation: How a Bill Becomes a Law
Simulation: You Are a Member of Congress
Timeline: The Power of the Speaker of the House
Visual Literacy: Congressional Redistricting
Visual Literacy: Why Is It So Hard to Defeat an Incumbent?

KEY TERMS

appropriations, p. 306
authorization, p. 306
bicameral, p. 285
casework, p. 288
closed rule, p. 301
cloture, p. 301
collective action problem, p. 292
conference committee, p. 301
constituents, p. 287
continuing resolution, p. 307
cycling, p. 292
delegate model of representation, p. 288
earmarks, p. 306

filibuster, p. 301
gate-keeping authority, p. 302
impeachment, p. 286
incumbent, p. 287
joint committee, p. 293
majority leader, p. 295
markup, p. 301
minority leader, p. 295
open rule, p. 301
party caucus, p. 294
party conference, p. 294
regular appropriations, p. 306
select committee, p. 293

seniority, p. 294
Speaker of the House, p. 294
sponsor, p. 299
standing committee, p. 293
subcommittee, p. 293
sunset provision, p. 305
supplemental appropriations, p. 307
trustee model of representation, p. 288
veto, p. 302
whips, p. 295

SUGGESTED READINGS

Richard Fenno. 2002. *Homestyle: House Members in Their Districts*, new ed. New York: Longman. A classic examination of the relationship between members of Congress and their constituents.

David Mayhew. 2004. *Congress: The Electoral Connection*, 2nd ed. New Haven: Yale University Press. The classic statement on how members' concerns about reelection help explain their behavior in Congress.

Walter Oleszek. 2007. *Congressional Procedures and the Policy Process*, 7th ed. Washington, DC: CQ Press. Summarizes the rules and institutions that make up Congress.

Allen Schick. 2007. *The Federal Budget: Politics, Policy, Process*, 3rd ed. Washington, DC: Brookings Institution. Provides a comprehensive overview of the appropriations process.

Charles Stewart. 2001. *Analyzing Congress*. New York: Norton. Surveys the ways in which individual members act strategically to accomplish their objectives within Congress.

SUGGESTED WEBSITES

LIBRARY OF CONGRESS, THOMAS

thomas.loc.gov

Includes a tremendous amount of information about the legislative process, including a searchable database of bills introduced to the House or Senate in recent congresses.

U.S. SENATE
www.senate.gov

Official website of the U.S. Senate.

U.S. HOUSE
www.house.gov

Official website of the U.S. House of Representatives.

C-SPAN
www.c-span.org

Includes a rich array of video footage of congressional debates, hearings, and investigations.

CONGRESSIONAL RESEARCH SERVICE
opencrs.com

Access reports on a wide range of policy and political issues that are produced for members of Congress.

The Presidency

A DELUGE OF CHALLENGES Presidents are expected to identify and then offer solutions to every conceivable social problem. Here in June 2010, President Barack Obama spoke with Governor Charlie Crist of Florida about the environmental damage wrought by the British Petroleum oil spill.

"It has been a long time coming, but tonight, because of what we did on this date, in this election, at this defining moment, change has come to America."[1]

President-elect Barack Obama's words soared out to the crowd of 125,000 people gathered in Grant Park, Chicago, to celebrate the election of the new president of the United States.

As Obama concluded a campaign whose signature theme was "change," the nation remained mired in two wars and confronted a domestic economy in freefall. Much as he might have liked, he could not turn immediately to the domestic policy reforms that had figured so prominently in his campaign. In politics, the urgent often trumps the favored.

Presidents must manage an agenda in an uncooperative political world. They are responsible for setting and striving to meet the goals they campaigned on, while dealing with all the other issues that emerge when they are in office. Presidents are judged by both today's public and tomorrow's historians on how they balance their promises with their obligations.

In his inaugural address, President Obama outlined his plan for the nation. America, he promised, would rise from the ashes of the previous presidency and return to the world scene with a renewed image and reputation. By reducing troop commitments in Iraq, reaching out to the Muslim world, and increasing aid to the world's poorest, the United States would usher in a new era of peace. Domestically, Obama promised a drastic shift toward alternate forms of energy as well as a restructuring of the educational system with a renewed emphasis on science and technology.

Before he could do any of this, though, Obama had to stabilize a domestic economy in freefall. In February 2009, he pushed the Recovery and Reinvestment Act through Congress in an attempt to stimulate the depressed economy. The stimulus package was the largest in U.S. history, injecting $787 billion into the economy in the form of tax breaks, subsidies, and investments.

Obama's ability to immediately deliver on his earlier campaign promises was further limited by the paucity of formal powers granted to the president. The Constitution merely gives the president the power to veto legislation and appoint bureaucrats and judges, subject to the Senate's confirmation. For the most part, individuals outside the White House hold the responsibilities for writing, interpreting, and implementing laws. Thus, to get things done, the president must curry their favor.

Realizing the promise of change is made all the more difficult by the intense and interminable scrutiny cast upon the president. Every appointment, speech, veto, executive order, and official visit attracts attention and debate. Like it or not, the president is the figurehead of the federal government—and no matter how much praise he may garner for one decision, he always is at risk of shouldering blame the moment things go wrong. As we will learn in this chapter, successful leadership and the realization of change depend upon the president's ability to rally support among the public and political actors that themselves have their own, independent bases of authority. ■

Presidential Authority and Leadership

11-1 Trace the Constitutional origins and historical expansion of presidential power.

Americans project their hopes on the presidency. They expect their president to develop a legislative program and convince others to enact it. They expect the president to have, articulate, and defend policy ideas, all while unifying the country. They expect him (someday her), in the most general sense, to provide peace, prosperity, stability, and security.

In the last half-century, an avalanche of expectations has fallen at the White House doorstep. When the *Challenger* space shuttle exploded in 1986, when terrorists attacked on September 11, 2001, when Hurricane Katrina devastated New Orleans and the Gulf Coast in 2005, and when hundreds of thousands of gallons of crude oil poured out of a busted British Petroleum rig in the Gulf of Mexico in 2010, the country turned to the president for reassuring words, for due expressions of outrage, for signs that the country was strong and would persevere. And in calmer times, citizens look to the president, more than anyone else, for guidance on the basic policy priorities that are needed to address the challenges of the day.

The Constitution created the office of the presidency.

How do presidents meet the extraordinary expectations laid before them? To begin to answer this question, we must first consult the document that created the presidency: the U.S. Constitution.

Creating the presidency Wary of giving too much power to any single officeholder, the Framers wrestled with whether one person should hold the office of president or whether an executive committee or council was more appropriate. Some delegates to the Constitutional Convention initially called for a congressionally appointed executive council that would not have any specific powers granted in the Constitution. Other delegates argued that accountability would be stronger and more focused if a single individual held the office. These delegates, however, differed among themselves about the relationship between the president and Congress. Some wanted the president to be selected by Congress and have no independent authority. Others believed the presidency needed to have its own set of constitutionally enumerated powers. There was, however, general agreement among the delegates that the president would need to be able to check Congress, primarily through the veto power.

Selecting the president After deciding that one person would hold the position, the Framers debated how to select that person. Direct election by the public had little support. Instead, indirect election, whereby the public selects other individuals who, in turn, elect the president, dominated the discussion.

The indirect election plan that prevailed was the **Electoral College**. In the Electoral College system, electors in each state vote for the president. In some states, the state legislatures choose the electors; in others the people vote for them. Regardless of how they are chosen, the electors hold the responsibility of selecting the president. This plan increased the president's independence from the legislature. If no individual received a majority of the electoral vote, only then would Congress have a say, with the House of Representatives choosing the president.

The Electoral College was initially thought of as a way for the country's leaders in each state to meet, deliberate, and vote for the president. The people or the state legislature would be voting for "wise men" who would use their knowledge and wisdom to cast a vote for president. Today, this distinction between the electors and the people is meaningless—electors almost always are required by state law to vote for the candidate who wins the presidential popular vote in that state.

Reaching compromise over the presidency The American presidency that ultimately took form was a compromise that left no one at the Constitutional Convention entirely satisfied, but it contained elements that appealed to most delegates. The Constitution limited the presidency to individuals at least 35 years of age, born in the United States (or born abroad as the child of American citizens), and a resident of the United States for at least 14 years. Indirectly elected by the people via the Electoral College, the president would serve a four-year term with the possibility of reelection.

Table 11-1 identifies the president's powers that are enumerated in Article II of the Constitution. Some constitutional powers, such as making treaties and appointing ambassadors and judges, are shared with the Senate. In these cases, the Senate must approve treaties negotiated by the president or confirm his nominees. Other powers, meanwhile, are reserved for the president alone. These include the power to commission officers in the military, to grant pardons to those convicted of crimes (or, preemptively, to those who might be charged with a crime), to receive foreign ambassadors, and to convene sessions of Congress.

The Constitution also includes some open-ended and potentially power-enhancing clauses. One clause directs the president to "from time to time give to the Congress information of the State of the Union, and recommend to their Consideration such Measures as he shall judge necessary and expedient" (Article II, section 3). The **necessary and expedient clause**, which echoes the "necessary and proper" clause related to Congress, validates the president as a significant legislator—not merely an executive who is implementing and enforcing the law.[2]

The Constitution also requires that the president "take care that the laws be faithfully executed." The vagueness of this **take care clause** allows strong

Electoral College the group of electors from each state and the District of Columbia who cast votes to elect the president.

necessary and expedient clause a clause in Article II, section 3, of the Constitution that authorizes the president to recommend legislation to Congress.

take care clause the constitutional clause that grants the president the authority and leeway to determine if laws are being "faithfully executed" and to take action if in his judgment they are not.

TABLE 11-1 Important Presidential Powers Enumerated in the Constitution.

With the exception of the veto power, which is located in Article I of the Constitution, all important sources of presidential authority are found in Article II.

EXCLUSIVE POWERS OF THE PRESIDENT

Pardon

The president can personally exonerate any individual from criminal charges or judicial pursuit. "He Shall have the Power to grant Reprieves and Pardons for Offenses against the United States."

Commander in Chief

The president is the ranking officer of the U.S. Armed Forces. He directs the military and is responsible for military strategy. "The President shall be the Commander in Chief of the Army and Navy of the United States, and of the Militia of the several States."

Implement Laws

The Constitution gives the president the power and responsibility to oversee the execution of laws passed by the Congress. He does so through his cabinet and its bureaucracy. "He [the president] shall take care that the laws be faithfully executed."

Executive Power (the Vesting Clause)

The president holds the "executive power," the exact meaning of which continues to be debated to this day. "The executive Power shall be vested in a President of the United States of America."

POWERS SHARED WITH CONGRESS

Veto

The president can send a bill he is unsatisfied with back to Congress for reconsideration. "Every Bill which shall have passed the House of Representatives and the Senate, shall, before it becomes a Law, be presented to the President of the United States; If he approve he shall sign it, but if not he shall return it, with his Objections to the House in which it shall have originated."

Treaties

Through the State Department, the president can negotiate treaties with other countries. However, they only take effect once they are ratified by a two-thirds vote of the Senate. "He shall have Power, by and with the Advice and Consent of the Senate to make Treaties."

Appointments

The president has the power to nominate and appoint U.S. officials, subject to Senate approval. "He shall nominate, and by and with the Advice and Consent of the Senate, appoint Ambassadors, other public Ministers and Consuls, Judges of the Supreme Court, and all other Officers of the United States."

independent action, if the president believes laws are being ignored.[3] The clause also invites the president to interpret exactly what would be necessary to "faithfully execute" a law passed by Congress, which means he might take much bolder, or much less bold, action than Congress would like.

Finally, the Constitution gives the president "executive power." Debates continue about the exact meaning of this clause. Advocates of the unitary theory of the executive, for instance, suggest that this clause gives the president complete control over the departments and agencies that operate in the executive branch.[4] Others argue that this clause merely recognizes the president's responsibility to execute those laws enacted by Congress.[5]

Presidents have stretched the language of the Constitution to expand their influence in American government.

In addition to the authority granted to the president in the Constitution, presidents have experimented to define and, in some cases, enlarge the powers and responsibilities of the office. Presidents have had to stretch a few constitutional clauses to see what Congress, the courts, and the public would accept as legitimate exercises of presidential authority. Does being commander in chief, for instance, mean that the president can take the country into war? Does the power to appoint bureaucrats also imply the power to fire them? Can presidents refuse to implement laws that they think are unconstitutional? Does the power to "execute" laws include the power to interpret them?

Presidents pushed, other institutions responded, and over time the office became more clearly defined and what some early Americans feared: a powerful seat of executive authority. What some in Congress and the public might see as an expansion of presidential power, presidents are inclined to see as a practice of the office's inherent power—the chief executive inherently has certain authority that need not be spelled out explicitly in the Constitution.

The early presidency When George Washington, who served from 1789 to 1797, took the oath of office as president, he was determined to protect the president's independence. He immediately established the president's key role as head of state—that is, the individual who represents the face of the federal

MILITARY ENGAGEMENT IN LIBYA, 2011
When President Obama announced his decision to launch a military offensive against the Libyan government, he did so without securing a congressional authorization, raising questions among some about the constitutionality of his actions.

government in diplomatic relations with other countries. Indeed, selected for the office primarily because of his enormous reputation throughout the country, his establishment of the symbolic importance of the office as a representative of the nation was highly significant. Washington also began the tradition of the two-term presidency, to establish the practice of shifting power and to reassure Americans that no concentrated monarchical powers were contained in the presidency. Until 1951, the Constitution did not require a president to step down after a maximum of two terms, but all presidents except one (Franklin Roosevelt) did.[6]

The stamp of other early presidents on the office also established the president's independence and made clear that the president would not simply be implementing congressional legislation. Thomas Jefferson (1801–1809) arranged the Louisiana Purchase, which vastly expanded the geographical reach of the United States, with no prior congressional consultation. Andrew Jackson (1829–1837) employed aggressive use of vetoes on such politically explosive issues as the rechartering of the Bank of the United States. In doing so, he established the use of the veto as a key tool of presidential power.

During the Civil War, Abraham Lincoln (1861–1865) took an expansive view of the authority of the presidency. In an emergency, Lincoln argued, Article II clauses concerning "executive power," "necessary and expedient," and "take care" had to be given very broad interpretation. Therefore, Lincoln initiated measures restricting civil liberties, including eavesdropping on telegraph lines and allowing prisoners to be held without charge.[7] To support the war effort, he launched the first national income tax not only in the absence of any constitutional language allowing such a policy but, in the eyes of many, directly contrary to constitutional language that seemed to prohibit this tax. Lincoln also created a national army that exceeded the size previously approved by Congress, helped found the state of West Virginia, declared a boycott of southern ports, and authorized the construction of warships, all without prior congressional approval. In most instances, though, Congress ultimately granted its approval of these actions.

Creation of the modern presidency Theodore Roosevelt (1901–1909) was the first president to travel abroad during his term in office, establishing the president's role as the nation's chief diplomat. Roosevelt also was a pioneer of the tradition of the president's communicating directly to the public in easy-to-understand speeches about specific policy and legislative goals. In the nineteenth century, presidents presented themselves primarily as the head of state in their speaking tours around the country. Roosevelt, however, wanted to influence public opinion, which he believed would pressure members of Congress to enact his legislative agenda.

In the 1930s, crisis again dramatically reshaped the presidency—this time the economic crisis of the Great Depression. "This country wants action, and action now," new President Franklin Roosevelt declared in 1933, and many saw the president's determination to act as a welcome change from previous presidents' cautious responses to the problems of the day.

Roosevelt (1933–1945) initiated a vast array of federal programs to deal with the collapse of the economy. In his inaugural address in 1933, he declared that he was willing to work with Congress, but that if Congress failed to act, he would seek "broad executive power" to address the emergency. Roosevelt put the nation on notice that he intended to experiment in bold ways to re-define the presidency. He would accomplish these goals, in part, through the creation of supporting institutions in the Executive Office of the President. With a much larger staff at his disposal, the president could be even more active in policy-making.

Roosevelt also revolutionized the relationship between presidents and the people they represent. Roosevelt made a habit of speaking directly to his constituents. Through his weekly radio addresses, commonly referred to as "fireside chats," the president's voice entered the living rooms of citizens across the nation, speaking to their everyday concerns and the government efforts to fix them.

Roosevelt's presidency, though, was not without its share of controversy. Several of the laws that he pushed through Congress were later declared unconstitutional by the Supreme Court. In response, Roosevelt (in his second term) proposed a plan to increase the size of the Supreme Court, a plan that would allow him to appoint justices who would look more favorably upon his domestic policy agenda. Neither the public nor Congress supported this perceived power grab.[8] Despite the setback, the Court promptly shifted course and supported Roosevelt's policy agenda.

The postwar presidency As the United States emerged from World War II as a world superpower, the president's power grew accordingly. During the Cold War between the United States and the Soviet Union, the president not only was the single most important person in American government but was commonly seen as the most powerful person in the world. Domestic policy became entwined with foreign policy—as the world's economic leader, actions of the U.S. government could have significant repercussions for allies and potential allies.

One area in which all presidents have expanded the boundaries of the office is the control of information. The administration of Dwight Eisenhower (1953–1961) was the first to use the now common phrase **executive privilege** to refer to the idea that executive branch officials need to be able to advise the president in confidence, and that the president has a right to prevent that advice from becoming public. When invoking executive privilege, the president usually argues that, if members of Congress have access to private discussions, he and his staff are less likely to be fully forthcoming and that members of Congress are prone to requesting information merely out of a desire to discredit the president.

executive privilege the idea that executive branch officials need to be able to advise the president in confidence, and that the president has a right to prevent that advice from becoming public.

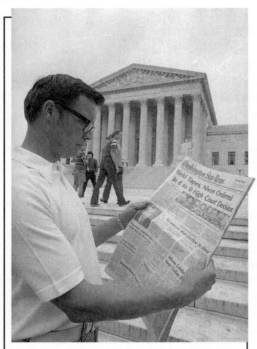

SUPREME COURT RULES AGAINST PRESIDENT NIXON, 1974

The Supreme Court ruled unanimously that Richard Nixon's executive privilege did not allow him to withhold recordings of his conversations in the Oval Office. Two weeks later, Nixon became the only president to resign his position.

The most famous, or infamous, proponent of executive privilege was Richard Nixon (1969–1974). During the investigation of the scandal that became known as Watergate, Nixon claimed that he had the right to withhold from the public his notes, papers, and tapes of discussions in the White House.[9] In *U.S. v. Nixon* (1974), the Supreme Court rejected Nixon's claim of executive privilege. In this first judicial test of executive privilege, however, the Court agreed that presidents had such a privilege, but that it was not absolute and needed to be weighed against the public interest.

Despite these signs of increased strength, postwar presidents have faced significant obstacles to exercising power. The country has grown in population and complexity. The political environment contains powerful organized groups with diverse policy concerns. Numerous governmental programs are already in place, and attempts to remove them generate howls of protest. The federal budget is not limitless, nor is the public's willingness to tolerate increasing tax burdens. Presidents, therefore, often find themselves shackled by preexisting policy commitments that they inherit upon taking office. They cannot simply erase decades of history and start fresh. And as members of Congress forge their own power during long careers, presidents confront congressional challenges to their leadership.

Congress delegates authority to the president.

Beyond the Constitution, Congress yields additional authority to the president, either explicitly granting specific policy-making tasks to him or looking to him to take the initiative in some policy sphere. Through **delegation** of this sort, the president acquires discretion to act in a particular area, typically within broad parameters of what is acceptable to Congress. If the president goes beyond these boundaries, Congress can find ways to indicate its displeasure, by either refusing to fund the implementation of the president's plan, setting stricter boundaries around future presidential action in this area, or being less cooperative in considering and passing a bill that is important to the president.

Congress has delegated especially vast powers in foreign affairs. For instance, Congress has delegated to the president the authority to negotiate foreign trade agreements, limiting itself to a single vote without the possibility of amending its language or engaging in a filibuster. Known as fast-track authority, this is a significant concession of congressional power. Fast-track

delegation the granting of authority by Congress to the president to be the first or main actor in a policy area, usually with implicit or explicit limits on actions that Congress would find acceptable.

authority began in 1975, expired in 1994, was renewed in 2002, but expired once again in 2007.

What would cause legislators to give up their ability to amend trade agreements? Political scientists have offered several possible explanatory factors. Legislators may believe that negotiation with other countries works better when the United States presents a unified voice. Perhaps some of them fear that other members of Congress would be eager to protect industries in their districts, and the negotiations would unravel if the president then had to go back to other countries with a revised version of the treaty. Other legislators might consider trade to be a controversial subject and want the president to take the criticism.

Thinking Causally Considering that trade agreements potentially provide benefits to some constituents while imposing losses on others, why would reelection-minded legislators give up the power to amend these bills?

Importantly, Congress also delegated to the president significant powers in the federal budget process. Partly to help the president control executive branch agencies more effectively, Congress after 1921 required the president to submit an annual overall budget as a framework for congressional deliberation. The overall budget, as passed by Congress in a series of separate spending bills, typically looked very much like the president's original plan. In 1974, Congress passed the Congressional Budget and Impoundment Control Act to return some of the leverage to Congress. From then on, Congress passed budget resolutions that established targets for revenue and spending across all policy areas. But even the budget resolutions were a response to the president's plan.

Successful leadership entails convincing people to do what the president wants them to do.

Broadening interpretations of the president's constitutional authority, coupled with the growth in Congress's delegation of power to the president, have increased public expectations about the president's ability to lead. These expectations can be a burden for the president: a president seen as falling short may find that a growing proportion of the public disapproves of his performance in office. But higher expectations may also enhance the president's political influence by forcing the president to pressure Congress for cooperation. The president can appeal directly to the public, indicating he wants to meet their expectations but that Congress is obstructing him. Such appeals might generate public pressure on Congress to act and contribute to successful presidential leadership.

Leadership can be evaluated in terms of outcome (Did the president succeed in getting Congress to pass his plan to reduce crime?) or in terms of impact (Did the plan actually reduce the crime rate?).[10] Political scientists tend to focus more on the outcome side of leadership. Thought of this way, leadership involves convincing the public that action is needed and getting a favored piece of legislation passed in Congress. It can also involve stopping action in Congress or influencing the content of legislation. Thus, to political scientists, **leadership** means the ability of a president to influence and guide others to achieve some desired policy or action.

leadership the ability to influence and guvide others to achieve some desired policy or action.

HOW DO WE KNOW?

Was President George W. Bush a Successful Leader?

The Question

In the tense hours after the terrorist attacks on September 11, 2001, Americans waited to hear from President George W. Bush. How would the country respond to the devastation in New York, at the Pentagon, and in Pennsylvania? On September 20, the president delivered a solemn, forthright speech to the nation. Soon after, with congressional support, he forged a coalition of allies to attack the Taliban regime in Afghanistan, believed to be a prime sponsor of terrorism and a haven for the perpetrators of the September 11 attacks. To most Americans at that time, Bush's actions after September 11 were the work of a strong, successful leader, someone who took charge of a situation and got things done. By the end of his second term in office, however, the president's public approval ratings were among the lowest of any modern administration. Was George W. Bush a successful leader? How do we know?

Why It Matters

Most Americans consider the election of the president to be among their most significant political acts. If we as citizens say we want strong and successful leadership, it helps to have standards by which to predict who will be the better leader or to determine whether a president has been a successful leader.

Investigating the Answer

Before researchers can determine whether a president is a strong leader, they first have to determine how to define and measure successful leadership. The public often thinks about presidential leadership in terms of impact: did the president's action alleviate a problem, have no impact, or make things worse?

To political scientists, however, measuring success by impact is problematic for several reasons. First, whether the impact of a policy has been positive or negative can take a long time to determine and may change over time. Second, drawing the line between success and failure can seem arbitrary. What if the economic growth rate increases by 0.1 percent? By 1 percent? By 4 percent? Where does a researcher draw the line between success and failure, and why?

Third, measuring presidential leadership by impact can be unreliable because the evaluation may be biased by political ideology. Lastly, the impact you see may not be the result of presidential action: the correlation of the president's action with a particular outcome does not prove causation. Instead, it may result from others' coincidental actions, or from altogether different historical events.

Therefore, political scientists tend to define presidential leadership in terms of outcome rather than impact. They look at what the president has attempted to accomplish and they evaluate his success in those areas. Some researchers have compared the president's campaign promises with his actual performance. Others have studied the president's State of the Union Address as a measure of his highest priorities and tracked what he accomplished legislatively in those areas. Other researchers have compared the president's preferences on roll-call votes taken in Congress and calculated how often Congress agreed with the president's position. The focus in these outcome-oriented studies of leadership is whether the president was able to persuade Congress to side with him.

The most common political science measure of successful presidential leadership is the frequency with which Congress votes in accord with the president's preferences. The measure is not a perfect indicator of leadership success—the president might not have done much to produce the outcome in Congress, and the final outcome on a vote does not tell us whether the president had to abandon major aspects of his policy in the days or months leading up to the vote. One especially attractive feature of this measure, though, is that there are typically hundreds of congressional roll-call votes on which the president takes a position; thus, the frequency of presidential success can be calculated across time, across issue areas, and across different presidents.

If we look at how often Congress voted the way the president wanted on roll-call votes, President Bush was a successful leader (see Figure 11-1). In 2005 and 2006, his success rate was higher than that of any other president in his fifth and sixth year since the Eisenhower administration (1953–1961).[11] His

HOW DO WE KNOW? Was President George W. Bush a Successful Leader?

FIGURE 11-1 Presidential Victories on Roll-Call Votes, House and Senate, 1953–2008.

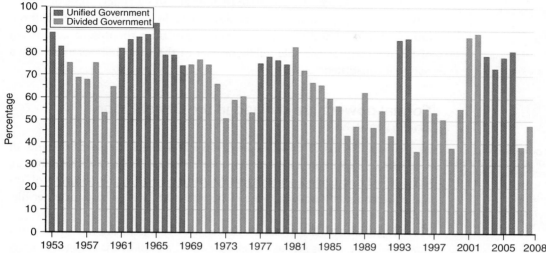

Presidential success in Congress is generally higher when the president's party has a majority in both houses of Congress. This graph shows the percentage of time members of Congress voted with the president on the subset of bills that the president took a clear position on.

Source: Harold W. Stanley and Richard G. Niemi, VITAL STATISTICS ON AMERICAN POLITICS 2009–2010 (Washington, DC: CQ Press, 2009), pp. 258–59. Copyright © 2009 CQ Press, a division of SAGE Publications. Reprinted with permission.

overall success rate from 2001 to 2005 rivaled that of Lyndon Johnson (1964–1968) and John Kennedy (1961–1963). But, unlike those two presidents, Bush achieved this result while facing a Senate narrowly controlled by the opposition party for 18 months of his first term. Bush's first-term success rate with the opposition party was substantially higher than that of any president since Richard Nixon, particularly within the Senate. In his second term in office, however, it declined substantially.[12]

Thinking Critically

1. How should we compare the success rates of two presidents, one of whom has an aggressive and far-reaching domestic policy agenda, and the other of whom has only a modest set of proposals that he would like Congress to enact?

2. When trying to assess Bush's success in Congress over time, how should we factor in the Democratic takeover of Congress in the 2006 elections?

3. How would you compare the legislative accomplishments of Bush's last year in office with Obama's first year? What accounts for the differences you observe?

The Bottom Line

When assessing presidential leadership, political scientists focus on tangible outcomes. This method avoids the ideological bias that influences the assessments made by political activists and zealous partisans. George W. Bush took a position on fewer congressional votes than did any other president since Dwight Eisenhower (1953–1961), but overall he was highly successful on those votes. By this measure, Bush can be considered a successful leader, despite his very low approval ratings. Focusing on other outcomes, such as his inability to get Congress to act on his Social Security reform initiative, supports different conclusions.

Powers of the President

11-2   Distinguish between the formal and informal powers
of contemporary presidents.

Presidents invoke various powers in their efforts to set policy. Some of these—
formal and expressed powers—are designated by law or the Constitution.
Others—informal and inherent powers—derive from the unique advantages
of the president as the sole public official in the United States elected by a
national constituency.

Formal powers are defined in the Constitution and in law.

formal powers specific
grants of authority defined in
the Constitution or in law.

As we have discussed, the president's **formal powers** are specific grants of
authority defined in the Constitution or delegated by Congress. Others, though,
were created through independent presidential initiative. The resulting mix of formal powers currently available to presidents establishes the first basis for leadership.

New legislation   The president shares with Congress the role of enacting
new legislation. In his role as "chief legislator," a president is engaged in every
part of the legislative process. He and his staff can draft bills, although a
member of Congress must introduce the bill on the president's behalf. During
deliberations over the bill, the president and his staff typically contact members of Congress and also the media, interest groups, and the public itself to
apply pressure on Congress. If the bill passes, the president almost always will
need to sign it before it becomes law.[13]

veto the president's rejection of a bill passed by both
chambers of Congress,
which prevents the bill from
becoming law. Congress
can override a veto with a
two-thirds vote in both the
House and Senate.

pocket veto the president's
veto of a bill without the
opportunity for Congress to
override the veto. It occurs
if the president does not act
on a bill within 10 days after
passage by Congress and
Congress adjourns during
that time.

Presidential veto   One of the most important formal powers is the **veto**,
which allows the president to reject bills enacted by Congress. When the president vetoes a bill, Congress can override the veto with a two-thirds vote of
each chamber, but this step typically proves very difficult to do. In the case of a
pocket veto, Congress does not even have that opportunity. The Constitution
gives the president 10 days either to sign or to reject a bill. If he does neither,
the bill becomes law. If, however, Congress has adjourned (i.e., is not in session) during those 10 days and the president does not act, the bill is rejected—
the president kills the bill by keeping it in his pocket. Presidents can use their
veto power to extract legislation more to their liking from Congress.[14]

The veto is also powerful when the president threatens its use. Members of
Congress, particularly those who are not in the president's party, must decide
whether they want to revise the bill according to the president's preferences.
If the bill is unchanged, the president will reject it. If they agree to revise the
bill, members may be dissatisfied with the compromised version. If they decide
to allow the president to veto the bill, they are hoping that the public opinion
backlash will force the president to reevaluate his stance or, if an election is

near, that the president's position might hurt him or his fellow partisans running for office. The president's threat of using the veto does not necessarily mean that he opposes a bill in that particular policy area, but rather that he does not like some provisions of the particular bill that Congress is considering.

Presidents from John Kennedy through Bill Clinton vetoed legislation an average of nine times per year, but President George W. Bush made rare use of the veto power, issuing only 11 vetoes during his two terms in office. President Obama pocket vetoed a stop-gap spending bill in 2009, and in October 2010, he formally vetoed a bank foreclosure bill.

A veto is a big knife, but sometimes what the president really wants is a scalpel. Presidents have long sought a more delicate device for fine-tuning bills in the form of the **line-item veto,** which would allow them to veto portions of bills rather than entire bills. A 1996 law gave this power to presidents, but President Clinton held it for only a short time. In 1998, the U.S. Supreme Court ruled that the line-item veto unconstitutionally added to the president's powers by, in effect, allowing him to amend proposed legislation—a task limited to Congress in the Constitution. The president could only approve or reject proposed legislation in its entirety: if he wanted the power to approve legislation in part, the Court ruled, a constitutional amendment would be needed.

line-item veto the authority of a chief executive to reject part of a bill passed by the legislature.

Commander in chief The president serves as the commander in chief of all the military services—the Army, Navy, Marines, Air Force, and Coast Guard. Being commander in chief requires the president to work in concert with Congress, but in this role the president tends to lead while Congress follows.

As commander in chief, presidents have argued that they have inherent powers to respond to emergencies and protect the safety of Americans and the security of the United States. The George W. Bush administration took controversial actions in response to terrorism, including indefinite detention of enemy combatants, denial of civilian court review of cases involving detainees, and surveillance of communications without prior judicial authorization. In defending these actions, President Bush and his spokespeople frequently argued that they fell squarely within the inherent powers of the president as commander in chief. Since taking office, President Obama has taken a similarly expansive interpretation of the commander-in-chief clause.

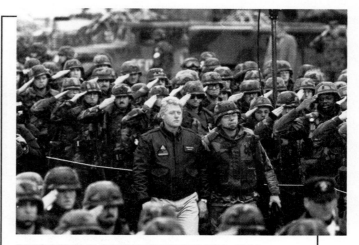

PRESIDENT CLINTON VISITS TROOPS, 1996
The president's commander-in-chief role over the world's largest military is a major part of his constitutional authority.

Executive agreements and executive orders Two other formal powers available to presidents—the executive agreement and the executive order—enable them to enact public policy without the direct cooperation of Congress. These powers are not found in the Constitution but instead arise out of presidents' entrepreneurial efforts to expand their base of authority.

executive agreement an international agreement in which the United States becomes a party once the president has signed it, without requiring approval from two-thirds of the Senate.

With an **executive agreement**, a president can negotiate an arrangement with a foreign government without formal approval by Congress. These agreements cannot require changes in U.S. law; in those instances, Congress must sign off on the change through a treaty. But many subjects of international diplomacy do not require such changes. Hence, as Figure 11-2 makes clear, presidents often substitute executive agreements for treaties.

Executive agreements are not intended to be hidden from Congress and the public, although sometimes presidents have used them that way. A series of executive agreements between the United States and South Vietnam drew the United States more heavily into military involvement in Vietnam beginning in the late 1950s. Congress was unaware of the agreements until 1969. To forestall secret use of executive agreements in the future, Congress passed the Case Act in 1972 to require presidents to inform Congress of an executive agreement within 60 days of its inception (amended to 20 days in 1977).

executive order a presidential directive or proclamation that has the force of law.

Executive orders (as well as proclamations, memoranda, and other directives) are presidential commands that have the force of law. They do not require Congress's approval or involve a foreign government. Executive

FIGURE 11-2

Executive Agreements and Treaties, Annual Average, 1789–2008.

Presidents make much more extensive use of executive agreements than of treaties.

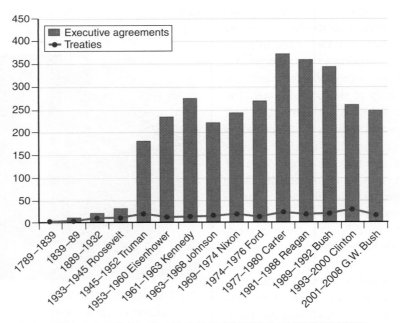

Source: Harold W. Stanley and Richard G. Niemi, VITAL STATISTICS ON AMERICAN POLITICS 2009–2010 (Washington, DC: CQ Press, 2009), p 339. Copyright © 2009 CQ Press, a division of SAGE Publications. Reprinted with permission.

orders apply to the executive branch and its employees. But, they can affect the private sector because private organizations interact with government, usually through contracts. For example, an executive order might state that companies wishing to provide goods or services to the government must have certain equal opportunity hiring policies in place. Although most orders are fairly routine matters of administrative procedure, the president can also use this tool to implement a wide range of policies, some of which aid constituencies important for the president's political success (see Table 11-2).[15]

The president's power to use executive orders can be limited by Congress or by the U.S. Supreme Court. The Supreme Court can declare an executive order void if it finds that the president's action exceeded his statutory authority or is contrary to the Constitution. As with executive agreements, Congress can weaken executive orders by cutting off their funding. Congress can also define areas in which prior congressional approval is required, thus negating the possibility of an executive order. A future president also can overturn a prior executive order.

TABLE 11-2 Examples of Policy Initiatives Implemented Using Executive Orders.

Executive Order	Date	Subject	Issued By
9066	February 19, 1942	Internment of Japanese-American citizens	F. Roosevelt
9981	July 26, 1948	Segregation in the armed forces ended	Truman
10730	September 23, 1957	Enforcement of school desegregation using National Guard	Eisenhower
10925	March 6, 1961	Affirmative action to be used by government agencies and contractors to ensure nondiscriminatory hiring practices	Kennedy
11615	August 15, 1971	Wage and price controls	Nixon
13158	May 26, 2000	Development of national environmental system of marine protected areas	Clinton
13379	December 12, 2002	More participation by faith-based organizations in federal social programs	G. W. Bush
13507	April 8, 2009	Creation of a White House Office of Health Reform	Obama

Informal powers include the power to persuade.

Presidents also have informal powers that derive from a president's personal experience, leadership style, reputation, or prestige. Most famously in the category of informal powers, presidents have the "power to persuade." Presidents devote considerable resources (financial and otherwise) toward persuading elected officials and the public about the merits of their policy positions. Some presidents, like Lyndon Johnson and Franklin Roosevelt, had legendary bargaining skills. Others, like Jimmy Carter, struggled to understand the political pressures faced by members of Congress, and failed to compromise with them.

Presidents often need the cooperation of members of Congress, aides and advisers, officials in federal agencies, and fellow politicians on the state and local levels. On some issues, presidents will be more passionate and involved and less willing to see their plans thwarted.[16] A president may trade success on more peripheral issues to defend his position on the key issue. To secure cooperation, a president also tries to persuade other policy makers that his position is right and may even appeal directly to a congressional member's constituents.[17]

Signing statements, which presidents can issue when they sign legislation, are one manner of persuading bureaucrats and judges. Increasingly, presidents have used these statements to reinterpret legislation in meaningful ways. For example, President George W. Bush argued in signing statements that he retained the option to ignore certain provisions of laws if he concluded they unduly infringed on his constitutional role as commander in chief. The statements do not afford the president an opportunity to actually rewrite the content of the law. They are attempts to persuade the bureaucrats who implement laws and the judges who may someday be called upon to interpret them.

Do signing statements cause bureaucrats to change their behavior? A congressional investigation in 2007 found some correlation between concerns raised in presidential signing statements and portions of legislation not implemented by federal agencies.[18] Although critics quickly asserted a direct causal relationship between statements and bureaucratic inaction, it is not clear whether agencies ignored provisions of laws because of the signing statements or whether the statements were simply a convenient justification after the fact. It might also be that the president was more likely to issue a signing statement when an agency had already signaled its predisposition to ignore some aspect of a law. In that case, it would be the agency's planned behavior that caused the signing statement, rather than the other way around.

Thinking Causally Do presidential signing statements change bureaucratic behavior?

Congress and the courts can check presidential power.

Both Congress and the courts serve as a check on presidents who try to expand their authority too aggressively. When someone challenges a policy, ruling, or other action taken by the executive branch, the courts might declare it illegal or unconstitutional and therefore void. For example, in June 2004, the Supreme Court ruled in three cases that President Bush had exceeded his constitutional authority by indefinitely detaining noncitizens captured in Afghanistan as part of the U.S. campaign against terrorism. The detainees were held at the U.S. military base at Guantanamo Bay, Cuba, and were prohibited access to attorneys or the courts. The Supreme Court concluded that the detainees had the right to access the federal courts to challenge their incarceration.[19]

Congress can check the president's power through the normal legislative process by not acting on legislation he desires, refusing to approve judicial and other nominees, designing agencies to have some independence from presidential control, and withholding funding. The threat of these actions often leads presidents to adjust their plans and soothe congressional objections.

The most severe congressional check on presidential power is **impeachment**, a process through which the House of Representatives can vote to initiate a trial conducted by the Senate that can lead to the removal of the president from office.[20] Under the Constitution, impeachment is the appropriate remedy for presidents who have committed "high crimes and misdemeanors," treason, or bribery. The exact meaning of "high crimes and misdemeanors" is left for members of Congress to decide.

> **impeachment** performed by the House of Representatives, the act of charging government officials with "treason, bribery, or other high crimes and misdemeanors." The Senate then decides whether to convict and remove the official from office.

The process of impeachment begins in the House of Representatives, based on "articles of impeachment" that describe the charges against the president. The case against the president is first heard in the House Judiciary Committee. If that committee votes that there is a credible case against the president on all or some of the charges, it sends those articles to the full House to vote whether to proceed with impeachment. The impeachment trial is then held in the Senate, and senators vote whether the president is guilty and must be removed from office. Conviction in the Senate, not impeachment in the House, removes the president from office.

Two presidents, Andrew Johnson in 1868 and Bill Clinton in 1998, have been impeached. In both cases, the Senate acquitted them. Johnson had antagonized congressional Republicans with his too lenient (in their view) approach toward the former Confederate states and with his attempts to derail Republican plans for reconstruction of the South. The case against Clinton was based largely on the charge that he had lied to a federal grand jury about his sexual involvement with White House aide Monica Lewinsky, and that he had obstructed justice by stonewalling the case.

Public, Electoral, and Contextual Resources for Presidential Leadership

11-3 Analyze how presidents use public support, electoral victories, and congressional allies to push through their policies.

American presidents have varying degrees of success in leading the country, dealing with Congress, and achieving their goals. What explains these differing levels of success? Popular accounts often focus on a single factor—a president

Thinking Causally What factors explain the differing levels of success achieved by presidents in leading the country, dealing with Congress, and reaching their goals?

speaks well on television, or he is fortunate to have a growing economy, or he receives overwhelming support from "mindless partisans" in Congress. Political science research, in contrast, shows that multiple factors contribute to presidential leadership success. Pointing to just one factor can generate misleading interpretations.

Successful leadership often depends on the resources available to the president. These resources include the president's relationship with the public, electoral factors such as the strength of the president's victory and the size and support of his party in Congress, and historical and policy contexts such as presidential advantages in foreign policy. A president who has an abundant supply of these resources should be more successful with Congress than a president who does not.[21] But a president with a favorable political environment must still manage that environment with skill.

The president's approval ratings are carefully and continually monitored.

One of the president's most important resources is his relationship with the public. Since the late 1930s, the public's assessment of the president's job performance has been measured by his public **approval rating**. Public opinion firms conduct surveys and ask respondents whether they approve or disapprove of the job the president is doing. The percentage of the respondents saying they approve of the president's job performance is the president's approval rating.

approval rating the percentage of the public that approves of the job the president is doing overall.

Trends in approval ratings Approval ratings tend to start high and drift down over time. During the early "honeymoon" period of a president's term, opposition to the president's plans has not yet solidified, and the public is still likely to give him the benefit of the doubt. He will not likely be blamed, at least not immediately, for problems inherited from his predecessor. And, usually, he has not had time to make any major mistakes. As these mistakes happen, and as it gets harder to blame the predecessor, people find reasons to criticize the president's performance. When Barack Obama first took office in January 2009, he enjoyed approval ratings of 68 percent. A year later, amid an oil spill, persistently high unemployment rates, and opposition by large segments of the American public to the 2009 economic stimulus package and health care reform, the president's approval ratings registered at just 50 percent.[22]

Party identification is a key factor in approval ratings. Democrats are reliably more likely to approve of President Obama's job performance, Republicans less likely, and independents somewhere in between. This pattern does not mean that Democrats will blindly approve of President Obama because of the party label, but rather that Democrats are more likely to agree philosophically with actions taken by a Democratic president than are Republicans.[23]

Approval ratings and the economy The economy is the most important determinant of a president's job approval rating. Though political scientists disagree about which economic indicator is paramount—unemployment, inflation, growth, or something else—virtually all concede that the economy's recent performance has a profound bearing on public assessments of the president, as well as important implications for people's vote choices on Election Day. When the national economy declines in the year before a presidential election, the incumbent president's vote share predictably declines. A flagging national economy also can have important implications for the electoral prospects of a presidential candidate from the same party as the incumbent. In 2008, already facing long odds, John McCain's chances of winning the presidency were all but dashed when the economy spiraled downward in early October.

Approval ratings and rally events Another factor in approval ratings are **rally events**—short-term international events or military actions that boost approval ratings. John F. Kennedy's rating surged 13 points in 1962 when the United States set up a blockade around Cuba after it was revealed that Soviet bases were being installed there. President George W. Bush's approval rating rose enormously after the terrorist attacks in 2001. And, in 2011, President Barack Obama's approval ratings surged after the raid in which Osama bin Laden was killed.

rally event short-term international event or military action that boosts presidential approval ratings temporarily.

Scandal and approval ratings One would expect scandals to depress presidential approval ratings, and in most cases they do. However, Bill Clinton's approval ratings actually went up during the investigation of the Monica Lewinsky matter and his subsequent impeachment. Did scandal cause higher approval? Not really. Many people, especially Democrats, saw the investigation as a partisan effort to weaken the president rather than a serious scandal, so the investigation and impeachment had little effect on their approval of Clinton. In addition, at the same time the impeachment drama was unfolding, the economy—a powerful predictor of presidential approval—was growing rapidly. The public rewarded Clinton primarily for the economy, not for being impeached.

Thinking Causally Did scandal and impeachment lead paradoxically to higher approval ratings for President Clinton?

Presidents seek popular support by "going public."

When **going public**, a president engages in a highly visible campaign of trips, press conferences, interviews, speeches, and appearances designed to galvanize support around his agenda. These campaigns are precisely plotted, scripted, choreographed, and timed to elicit a favorable response from the public and the media. Every symbol and prop on the platform from which the president speaks is carefully chosen.

going public activities of presidents such as highly visible trips, press conferences, interviews, speeches, and public appearances in an attempt to raise public support for a policy agenda.

Since World War II, presidents have gone public at an increasing rate. Dwight Eisenhower, in the 1950s, engaged in these activities about four times per month. The number 40 years later, during Bill Clinton's presidency, was nearly 30 times per month.

In these public appeals, the president has strong advantages over Congress. Simply put, he is more likely to attract media attention than are members of Congress. In part, the inherent significance of the presidency leads journalists to focus on this office. It is also due to the power of one—the president provides a single focal point that simplifies the task of presenting the news. Unlike 535 voting members of Congress, the president gives a journalist one story to tell.[24]

Sizable election victories lead presidents to claim they have a mandate.

Presidents elected to office with sizable victories, and who ran on a clear policy platform, are often in an advantageous position when dealing with Congress. These presidents can claim that they have received a **mandate** from the American people; that is, the public spoke clearly in the election about the direction in which it wanted the country to move. The more consistent the election results are nationally, the stronger the president's case for a mandate, although it is really a matter of perception: Can the president convince the country, or more immediately, Congress, that he has a mandate? Most will try.[25]

mandate the idea that the public provided clear policy guidance in the results of the prior election.

Barack Obama could make a compelling case for having received a popular mandate. Not only did he carry 28 states for a total of 365 electoral votes and 52.9 percent of the popular vote, he did so by winning states that had traditionally gone to Republicans. Furthermore, on Obama's coattails, the Democratic Party strengthened its hold in both the House and Senate in the 2008 elections. When he assumed office, Obama's approval rating was 68 percent, second only to John F. Kennedy among newly elected presidents. Having campaigned expressly on the theme of change, Obama was poised to claim a mandate and tackle important elements of his policy agenda.[26] He quickly orchestrated the single largest stimulus package in the nation's history that collectively carried a price tag of nearly $1 trillion. Later in the year, the president advanced a variety of education, stem cell research, and most dramatically, health care, initiatives.

Presidents rely on fellow partisans to promote their policies.

Normally, the president can count on the members of his party in Congress to help him enact his policy ideas. The more members of the president's party elected to Congress, the better his chances are for legislative victories. The president still needs to persuade his fellow partisans to go along with him, but that task will usually be simpler than convincing members of the other party.

unified government a situation in which the presidency and both houses of Congress are controlled by the same party.

Presidents, of course, do not choose the partisan balance in Congress, so they need to figure out how to work with the situation they face. When Democrat Barack Obama became president, his party held a majority of seats in both the House and Senate, a situation known as **unified government**.

The president thus was in a strong position to pass legislation to his liking, although success was not certain. In most years since 1953, fellow party members in the House voted against the president's position just 20 to 30 percent of the time (see Figure 11-3). And when they did, it usually had something to do with constituency pressure, district economic interests, public opinion, or personal philosophy differences.

In **divided government**, the opposition party holds a majority of seats in one or both houses of Congress. If his party controls neither chamber, the president will typically face his most difficult challenges.[27] To succeed, the president needs to gain the support of a larger share of the opposition party by moving closer to their position, but without moving so far that he loses the support of his own partisans. The president's success will be influenced by several factors, including how cohesive his party is, how cohesive the opposition party is, and the relative size of the two parties. The larger and more cohesive the opposition party is, the more difficult the president's legislative challenge will be.

> **divided government** a situation in which the presidency is held by one party and at least one house of Congress is controlled by a different party.

Political scientists have found that party control of Congress complicates their analysis of presidential leadership. Politicians are strategic. In divided government, the president may have plans that he does not present to Congress because he believes they will have little chance at success. Or the president might offer a plan that he believes has as much or even more support in the opposition party than in his own. This was true for welfare reform during Bill Clinton's presidency and immigration reform during George W. Bush's. Similarly, during unified government, the president might offer bold legislative proposals that do not initially have strong support in the hope he can coax fellow party members to support him.

> **Thinking Causally** How do unified and divided government affect the likelihood of successful presidential leadership?

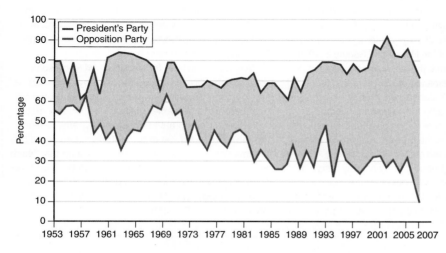

FIGURE 11-3 Percentage of House Roll-Call Votes on Which Party Members Supported the President's Position, 1953–2007.

Presidents get the greatest support from their fellow partisans in Congress. The growing gap in support between the president's party and the opposition party, represented by the shaded area, means presidents have increasingly had to rely on support from their own party.

Source: Harold W. Stanley and Richard G. Niemi, VITAL STATISTICS ON AMERICAN POLITICS 2005–2006 (Washington, DC: CQ Press, 2006), pp. 260–61. Copyright © 2006 CQ Press, a division of SAGE Publications. Reprinted with permission.

Case Study

Passing Health Care Reform

During the 2008 presidential election, Barack Obama promised sweeping changes to the American health care system. Once in office, Obama set health care reform at the top of his domestic policy agenda. To succeed, Obama would need to deploy virtually all the tools of leadership that were available to him.

Earlier U.S. presidents had tried, and usually failed, to reform health care.[28] In the 1912 presidential elections, Theodore Roosevelt campaigned on a promise for national health insurance, but he lost the election to Woodrow Wilson. In 1945, President Harry Truman called on Congress to enact health care reform, including increasing the number of hospitals and doctors. His reform ideas, however, were never put into legislation. In his first term, Bill Clinton famously tried and failed to overhaul the nation's health care system, which led to a Republican takeover of the House and Senate in 1994. Before President Obama, the last major successful reform effort was the creation of Medicare and Medicaid by President Lyndon B. Johnson in 1965.[29]

In March 2009, Obama formally announced his intention to seek health care reform as a top domestic priority.[30] He articulated some broad guidelines for reform but left Congress with the responsibility of filling in the details. The president hoped that by actively currying Congress's involvement, he would rally the support of its members and thereby avoid the perceived mistakes of Bill Clinton's previous efforts at health care reform.

2010 PROTEST AGAINST HEALTH CARE BILL Though he ultimately prevailed, the president evoked widespread opposition when he tried to enact health care reform during 2009 and 2010. Here, Tea Party protestors rallied outside of Congress to the chant of "Kill the Bill."

To build public support for reform, Obama employed many of the grassroots organizing strategies from his 2008 presidential campaign. He held small rallies around the country and spoke at length about the responsibility that members of Congress had to their constituents to bring about real change.[31]

However, Obama also faced significant grassroots opposition from conservatives. The Tea Party movement emerged in 2009 as a series of locally and nationally organized protests directed against what it saw as the administration's more intrusive policies. In response to the White House's push for universal health care, Tea Party members organized rallies throughout the country. Tea Party activists also rallied outside the White House and Congress members' offices in Washington, D.C. By pressuring local representatives and actively participating in political campaigns, the Tea Party hoped to defeat the bill.

When it came time for the House of Representatives to vote, Obama visited the chamber and made a rare personal appeal for lawmakers to support the bill. Just before the bill came up for a vote, Obama met with House Democrats to energize the party, reminding the representatives of the historic nature of the bill. Obama concluded his pep talk by declaring that "each and every one of you will be able to look back and say, 'This was my finest moment in politics.'"[32] President Obama's lobbying paid off, as the bill narrowly passed with a vote of 220 to 215.

Case Study Passing Health Care Reform

The president faced an even tougher battle in the Senate, which was more divided than the House over the bill's details. In an effort to rally the caucus, Obama met with Democratic senators behind closed doors and stressed the urgency of the issue. After heated debate in the late fall of 2009, the senators still had not settled on many contentious issues, such as how the new health care systems would cover abortions. The final vote, 60–39, fell along party lines. The House and Senate versions of the bill now had to be reconciled.

In the weeks following the Senate's vote, Obama increased his campaign of personal appeals, this time enlisting the help of Democratic leaders Nancy Pelosi and Harry Reid. The three leaders met nonstop with the members of their caucus, sometimes issuing direct appeals to the constituents of swing voters within Congress. On March 23, 2010, the president finally signed health care reform into law. Passage would not have been possible absent the president's vigorous support.

Obama's work, however, was not finished. Having passed health care reform, the president sought to convince a skeptical American public of the value of the new law. To stave off a wave of attacks by conservative media outlets and attorneys general seeking to undo as many provisions of the law as possible, the White House launched a multifaceted public relations campaign. The president created a new tax-exempt group to coordinate millions of dollars worth of publicity outreach both in the form of television advertisements and an interactive website comparing insurance plans. And Obama traveled the country, giving speeches and hosting nationally televised question-and-answer sessions on health care. These efforts continued well into the 2010 midterm congressional elections.

Thinking Critically

1. Why did Obama's effort to enact comprehensive health care reform succeed when previous attempts had failed?

2. Did Obama's formal or informal powers play a more distinctive role in the effort to enact health care reform?

3. Will the enactment of health care reform strengthen or weaken the Tea Party movement? Why?

Presidents have advantages in foreign policy.

The context of policy-making differs between foreign and domestic policy. In foreign policy, there are fewer interest groups, journalists, voters, and members of Congress who deeply care about these issues—a climate that gives the president a somewhat freer hand at advancing his agenda.[33] Because of this difference, the "two presidencies" theory argues that presidents exert significantly more influence over the writing and implementation of foreign policy than they do over domestic policy.

Does the different nature of the foreign policy-making environment lead to greater presidential success? Presidential success on foreign policy votes in Congress has not been consistently better than in domestic policy votes. But one analysis found that presidents are better able to secure funding that matches their budget priorities in foreign policy than they are in domestic policy. And when going public, presidents can sway public opinion more easily in foreign affairs than domestic affairs.

Thinking Causally Does the nature of the foreign policy-making environment lead to greater presidential success in that policy area than in domestic policy?

Institutional Resources for Presidential Leadership

11-4   Assess the role of the Cabinet, the Executive Office of the President, and the White House staff in assisting the president.

To improve their chances at leading successfully, presidents rely on the established agencies and offices of the executive branch. They may also create an array of new supporting institutions. Think of these institutions as concentric circles, with the president in the center. The outer ring consists of the Cabinet departments. Closer to the president is the Executive Office of the President. Closest to the president is the White House Staff. These institutions provide different kinds of resources for presidential leadership efforts. All have grown in size over time, especially since World War II.[34]

The Cabinet departments implement federal programs.

Cabinet a group of the top-ranking officials of every major federal department, plus other officials included by the president, who meet periodically with the president to discuss major administration priorities and policies.

The outer ring of institutional resources, furthest away from the president, is the **Cabinet**, which includes departments that implement nearly all government programs and provide the vast majority of government services (see Figure 11-4). The Senate must approve the president's appointments to leadership positions in the 15 Cabinet departments. The heads of these departments are known as "secretaries" except for the Department of Justice, the head of which is the attorney general. These individuals are appointed, first, to run the major departments of the government and, second, to provide advice to the president and help him implement his agenda. Though the president often meets with the Cabinet as a group, he can also call on its members' individual expertise. Treasury, State, Defense, and Justice are generally considered the most important and powerful departments.

All department secretaries are permanent members of the Cabinet, but the president may also include other agencies that are not under the organizational control of any of the major departments. Presidents will add these agencies to the Cabinet primarily because they want to hear the input of these agencies at Cabinet meetings, they want to make a symbolic show of support for a particular issue, or both.

From the president's point of view, there is always a risk that a department secretary will become so closely attached to the interests and perspectives of his or her department that, rather than communicating the president's viewpoint to the department, the secretary may push the department's views onto the president. When the president's ideas meet resistance from department personnel, will the secretary support the president or will he or she obstruct the president's agenda? One notable case during the George W. Bush presidency concerned Christine Todd Whitman, the administrator of the Environmental Protection Agency (who had Cabinet status). She resigned

The Cabinet

Department Secretaries

State
Treasury
Defense
Justice
Health and Human Services
Labor
Commerce
Transportation
Energy
Housing and Urban Development
Veterans Affairs
Agriculture
Interior
Education
Homeland Security

Others Granted Cabinet Rank

Vice President
Administrator, Environmental
   Protection Agency
Director, Office of Management
   and Budget
U.S. Trade Representative
Director, Office of National Drug
   Control Policy

White House Staff

Chief of Staff
Press Secretary
Legislative Affairs
Political Affairs
Public Liaison
Communications Director
White House Counsel
Intergovernmental Affairs
Policy Planning and
   Development
Cabinet Liaison
Domestic and Economic Affairs
Science and Technology Policy
National Security Affairs
Strategic Initiatives

Executive Office of the President

Council of Economic Advisors
Office of Management and Budget
Office of National AIDS Policy
Office of National Drug Control Policy
United States Trade Representative
Council on Environmental Quality
National Security Council
Domestic Policy Council
National Economic Council
Office of Administration
Office of Science and
   Technology Policy
President's Foreign Intelligence
   Advisory Board
Office of Faith-Based and Community
   Initiatives
Homeland Security Council
Privacy and Civil Liberties Oversight
   Board
USA Freedom Corps
White House Fellows Office
White House Military Office
Office of the First Lady
White House Office of Health Reform

FIGURE 11-4 The Institutional Presidency, 2011.

The president relies on the Cabinet departments to implement programs, the Executive Office of the President to provide policy advice, and the White House Staff to provide political advice.

after a series of policy disagreements with the president and his closest advisers out of concern that the opinions of agency scientists were being overruled.

One sign of the strain between presidents and the Cabinet is the large turnover of Cabinet officials in presidents' second terms. Although sometimes a Cabinet official simply wants to move on to a new challenge, obtain a more lucrative job in the private sector, or have a less hectic lifestyle, other times Cabinet turnover results from presidential displeasure with the official's performance. In the twentieth century, an average of about two Cabinet department heads served for both terms of a two-term presidency.[35]

To avoid some of the challenges of working with Cabinet secretaries, some recent presidents have turned to policy "czars" for advice. These czars report directly to the president, do not require Senate confirmation, and assist in the coordination of policies across different departments. The use of the term "czar" dates back to the Franklin D. Roosevelt administration, but Richard M. Nixon was the first president to actually appoint one—a drug czar. Every president since has appointed multiple special advisers. During his tenure in office, President George W. Bush had 36 czars. And depending on the source, President Obama has had anywhere from 18 to 32 czars charged with policy responsibilities ranging from oversight of the car industry to executive compensation, Afghanistan, and climate change.[36]

Some members of Congress, however, complain about the lack of oversight for these positions. Republican Susan Collins of Maine has said, "Little information is available concerning their responsibilities and authorities. There is no careful Senate examination of their character and qualifications. And we are speaking here of some of the most senior positions within our government."[37] Collins has pursued an initiative to curb the amount of government spending on czars and to increase congressional oversight for the positions.

The Executive Office of the President provides policy advice to the president.

Executive Office of the President a group of agencies in the executive branch that primarily generate policy alternatives for the president's consideration.

The next closest concentric ring to the president is the **Executive Office of the President** (EOP), which consists of a number of policy-related groups that aid the president. Officials in the EOP generate policy alternatives and suggestions that are more faithful to the president's political agenda.[38] Their primary responsibility is to provide the president with trusted policy advice.

The single most important EOP agency is the Office of Management and Budget (OMB). The OMB serves as a gateway through which departments must pass in making their budgetary requests, and it approves proposed regulations and testimony that a department wants to bring before Congress. In effect, the OMB serves as a filter to make sure that departments are not seeking funds or regulations that are contrary to the president's program. Other especially important EOP agencies are the Central Intelligence Agency, the Council of Economic Advisers, and the National Security Council.

The vice president is officially part of the EOP. Most vice presidents, however, are selected to provide the president with electoral advantages. A president with no Washington experience, for example, might select a vice president who has held office in the nation's capital. Or a vice president might be chosen because he or she increases the president's chances of winning a key state or region. The vice presidency is an often maligned institution, mostly because it has only two defined duties: to break tie votes in the Senate and to succeed the president in case of the death, incapacity, or removal of the president from office. In some administrations, however, vice presidents have played a greater role in policy-making. Bill Clinton delegated several significant policy tasks to Al Gore, and George W. Bush relied on the foreign policy advice of Vice President Dick Cheney, a former secretary of defense. The current vice president, Joe Biden, offers extensive foreign policy recommendations to President Obama.

The offices of the White House Staff provide political advice to the president.

The institutional circle closest to the president is the **White House Staff** (WHS), sometimes referred to as the White House Office. The WHS provides the president with political advice, promotes the president's program with legislators and interest groups, and handles the president's public relations. With only about 480 employees in the Obama administration, the WHS is relatively small compared to the EOP, which has more than 1,800 employees, and the Cabinet departments, which total nearly 1.9 million civilian employees. The WHS consists of small units such as the offices of the press secretary, legislative affairs, public liaison, and intergovernmental affairs, to name a few. Whereas the EOP provides the president with policy advice and might be thought of as the president's policy filter, the White House Staff is the political filter. Figure 11-5 provides examples of the issues raised by the WHS when

White House Staff a group of offices in the executive branch that provides the president with political advice, promotes the president's program with legislators and interest groups, and handles the president's public relations.

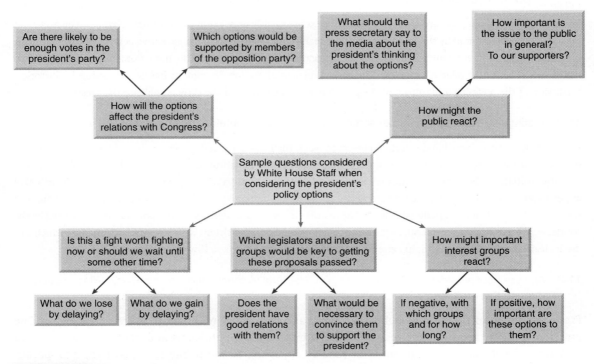

FIGURE 11-5 Types of Questions Asked by the White House Staff.
The White House Staff provides the president with an analysis of the political environment.

it considers policy proposals that emerge either from executive departments or Congress.

When he named Illinois Congressman Rahm Emanuel as his chief of staff, President Obama tapped an accomplished political strategist for a leading WHS role. Emanuel was a senior adviser to President Clinton for seven years, led the Democratic Congressional Campaign Committee in 2006 when Democrats won a majority in the U.S. House, and as chair of the Democratic Congressional Caucus in 2007–2008, was instrumental in setting party strategy on policy positions and communications. Emanuel's time in the White House, however, would prove short lived. In 2010, Emanuel left the White House and successfully ran for mayor of Chicago.

Chapter Summary

In this chapter you have learned to:

11-1   Trace the Constitutional origins and historical expansion of presidential power.

The Constitution created the presidency, but the office subsequently underwent extraordinary changes. The American presidency was an attempt by the Framers to balance many competing ideas about executive power. As a compromise, it contains some inherent contradictions. It is the office that Americans demand the most from, but its constitutional list of specific duties is relatively meager. The very vagueness of the job description has accommodated a historical expansion of the meaning and impact of the presidency from the time of the early republic to the present.

11-2   Distinguish between the formal and informal powers of contemporary presidents.

Presidents have both formal and informal powers to reach their goals. Formal powers such as the veto, executive orders, and the role of commander in chief are specified in law or the Constitution, or are realized through independent executive initiative. The origins of informal powers are less easily identified. These powers include the president's skill at persuading others to do what he wants and the ability to tap into and strategically exploit the reservoir of support for basic values in American political culture. The manner in which presidents use their powers can be checked by the courts, which can declare presidential actions unconstitutional or inconsistent with law, and by Congress, which can use its legislative, budgeting, and, in extreme cases, impeachment powers to thwart presidents.

11-3   Analyze how presidents use public support, electoral victories, and Congressional allies to push through their policies.

Presidents draw on a variety of public, electoral, and contextual resources to exercise leadership. The president's public approval receives substantial attention from politicians and political observers, and presidents devote significant amounts of time to appealing to the public to support their proposals. A president with a convincing election victory and his party in the majority in the House and Senate is in a strong position for successful leadership. Other factors that affect a president's success are the support for existing policies as well as differences between foreign and domestic policy.

11-4 Assess the role of the Cabinet, the Executive Office of the President, and the White House staff in assisting the president.

Presidents also rely on institutional resources to advance their policy agenda. The Cabinet departments implement nearly all federal programs and are therefore crucial to the president's agenda. The Executive Office of the President provides the president with policy advice. The White House Staff specializes in providing the president with political advice and services.

CHAPTER TEST

1. Among the nation's Founders, what were the major points of disagreement about the design of the presidency?

2. What, in your view, was the most significant constitutional power granted to the president? Why?

3. How have presidents exploited the ambiguities of Article II in order to expand the powers of their office?

4. In what ways does the president play a formal role in the legislative process?

5. Do the president's formal and informal powers complement one another, or are they mutually exclusive?

6. Why would Congress delegate authority to the president?

7. Why do presidents tend to exert more influence over foreign policy than they do over domestic policy?

8. When is the American public most amenable to public appeals by the president?

9. Who provides presidents with the information they need in order to lead the country?

10. When formulating their policy agendas, why might presidents prefer to appoint policy "czars" rather than depend on Cabinet secretaries?

MyPoliSciLab® THE PRESIDENCY
Apply what you learned in this chapter on MyPoliSciLab.

Read on mypoliscilab.com

eText: Chapter 11

Study and Review on mypoliscilab.com

Pre-Test
Post-Test
Chapter Exam
Flashcards

Watch on mypoliscilab.com

Video: Bush and the Congress
Video: The Government Bails Out Automakers

Explore on mypoliscilab.com

Comparative: Comparing Chief Executives
Simulation: Presidential Leadership: Which Hat Do You Wear?
Timeline: The Executive Order Over Time
Visual Literacy: Presidential Success in Polls and Congress

KEY TERMS

approval rating, p. 330

Cabinet, p. 336

delegation, p. 320

divided government, p. 333

Electoral College, p. 315

executive agreement, p. 326

Executive Office of the President, p. 338

executive order, p. 326

executive privilege, p. 319

formal powers, p. 324

going public, p. 331

impeachment, p. 329

leadership, p. 321

line-item veto, p. 325

mandate, p. 332

necessary and expedient clause, p. 315

pocket veto, p. 324

take care clause, p. 315

rally event, p. 331

unified government, p. 332

veto, p. 324

White House Staff, p. 339

SUGGESTED READINGS

Edward Corwin. 1948. *The President, Office and Powers, 1787–1948: History and Analysis of Practice and Opinion.* New York: New York University Press. Classic treatment of the president's constitutional powers.

Sidney Milkis and Michael Nelson. 2003. *The American Presidency: Origins and Development, 1776–2002.* Washington, DC: CQ Press. Thorough history of the evolution of the office of the presidency since the nation's founding.

Richard Neustadt. 1990. *Presidential Power and the Modern Presidents.* New York: Free Press. A highly influential analysis of the informal powers that presidents utilize to achieve their policy objectives in the modern era.

Arthur M. Schlesinger, Jr. 2004. *The Imperial Presidency,* reprint ed. New York: Mariner. A popular exploration of the growth of presidential power across American history.

Stephen Skowronek. 2007. *The Politics Presidents Make: Leadership from John Adams to Bill Clinton.* Cambridge, MA: Harvard University Press. A rich account of the various political environments facing presidents when they assume office and the limits and opportunities for leadership in those environments.

SUGGESTED WEBSITES

WHITE HOUSE
www.whitehouse.gov

Provides overviews of the president's initiatives, text of presidential statements, and links to executive branch agencies and offices.

AMERICAN PRESIDENT: AN ONLINE REFERENCE RESOURCE
www.millercenter.org/academic/americanpresident

Detailed biographical information on each president and key administration officials, with links to audio files of major presidential speeches and interviews with major figures from the presidencies of Jimmy Carter through Barack Obama.

AMERICAN PRESIDENCY PROJECT
www.presidency.ucsb.edu

Outstanding collection of resources of nearly 80,000 documents related to the presidency, campaigns, and presidential activities in office.

NATIONAL ARCHIVES: PRESIDENTIAL LIBRARIES AND MUSEUMS
www.archives.gov/presidential-libraries

Guide to the presidential library system, including links to online archival documents.

U.S. PRESIDENCY LINKS
http://cstl-cla.semo.edu/renka/presidencylinks.htm

Comprehensive and helpful A-to-Z guide to presidential information maintained by Russell Renka at Southeast Missouri State University.

The Federal Court System

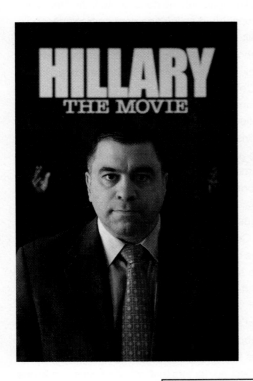

HILLARY THE MOVIE At the center of *Citizens United v. Federal Elections Commission*, a 2009 Supreme Court case involving the funding of political advertising was a documentary, produced by Citizens United leader David Bossie, which was critical of Hillary Clinton. In your view, should campaign finance regulations extend to documentaries, the Internet, and other forms of communication?

CHAPTER LEARNING OBJECTIVES

After reading this chapter you will be able to:

12-1 Determine the role of the judiciary as established by the Framers of the U.S. Constitution.

12-2 Outline the structure of the U.S. judiciary branch.

12-3 Distinguish between civil and criminal cases, and describe methods used to manage the judicial caseload.

12-4 Explain how judges decide cases that involve public policy.

12-5 Analyze the process of judicial appointment and selection.

On January 21, 2009, a deeply divided Supreme Court struck down limits on campaign funding by corporations, nonprofits, and labor unions. The groundbreaking 5–4 decision allows businesses and unions to spend millions on political campaigns.

The case, *Citizens United v. Federal Election Commission*, centered on a dispute over whether the Federal Election Commission could regulate the communications of a documentary called *Hillary: The Movie*, which attacked 2008 presidential candidate Hillary Clinton and was produced by a conservative nonprofit organization. The Court ruled that regulating the documentary, and the funds used to create and disseminate it, constituted an infringement on free speech.[1]

Reaction to the ruling was split along partisan and ideological lines. Republicans praised the Court for upholding free speech.[2] Democrats, however, depicted the decision as a setback for fair elections. And, President Barack Obama condemned the Supreme Court in his first State of the Union Address: "With all due deference to separation of powers, last week, the Supreme Court reversed a century of law that I believe will open the floodgates for special interests, including foreign corporations, to spend without limit in our elections."[3]

The Court's rationale for ruling as it did focused on free speech and anti-regulation. Referencing the First Amendment of the Constitution, the majority claimed that the regulation of corporate spending in elections inhibited political dialogue and debate.

Before President George W. Bush's two appointments, John Roberts and Samuel Alito, swung the Supreme Court in a conservative direction, the Court had ruled differently on similar cases on election spending. Former Justice John Paul Stevens cited this factor in his scathing dissenting opinion: "The only relevant thing that has changed since *Austin* and *McConnell* [a past case on election spending] is the composition of this Court."

The tangible effects of the Court's ruling remain to be seen. The case itself, though, reveals two important facts about the Supreme Court. First, and most obviously, the Court adjudicates disputes that have extremely important political, and by extension policy, consequences. Second, factors that cause justices to rule one way or another often go beyond the legal and constitutional and into the ideological. Rather than being shielded from politics, as the Framers had hoped, the judiciary directly engages and often fuels some of the deepest ideological controversies. ∎

The Constitutional Design of the Federal Judiciary

12-1   Determine the role of the judiciary as established by the Framers of the U.S. Constitution.

At the nation's founding, the Framers sought to build a federal judiciary that would perform the core functions of: (1) interpreting the laws that Congress and the president enacted; (2) issuing rulings over disputes where no guiding legislation previously existed; (3) ensuring that individuals who violated these laws and rulings were appropriately punished; and (4) compensating (where possible) the victims of these violations.

Article III, which lays out the powers and responsibilities of the judiciary, is shorter than the articles covering Congress (Article I) and the president (Article II). It establishes a "supreme Court" and "inferior Courts" operating under its jurisdiction; it recognizes a "judicial power" that applies to laws, treaties, and other formal acts of government; and it offers some brief guidelines about the prosecution of cases involving criminal behavior and treason. And that is all.

A complete system of courts did not appear until 1789, when Congress enacted the Judiciary Act to ease the workload of the one Supreme Court. It should not come as a surprise, then, that most of the Framers expected the judiciary would be the weakest, and according to Alexander Hamilton, the "least dangerous" branch. Whereas Congress had the power of the purse (that is, the power to levy taxes) and the president had the power of the sword (that is, control over the military), the judiciary had only its judgment. Recognizing its original design, the political scientist Robert Dahl concluded that the judiciary's "most important [base of power] is the unique legitimacy attributed to its interpretations of the Constitution."[4]

Consequentially, from the nation's beginning, judicial proceedings were structured to foster notions of respect and legitimacy. When judges enter courtrooms, parties to a case are required to stand. Judges are referred to as "your honor" and wear robes when serving on the bench. All of this symbolic imagery is meant to increase the chances that citizens and other political actors will accept court rulings as binding.

Perhaps most importantly, judges do everything possible to exude the qualities of a trustworthy and independent arbiter of justice who rises above rather than engaging in politics. For the most part, such efforts of successive generations of judges seem to have borne fruit. Today, citizens hold the courts in higher regard than any other branch of government. According to national public opinion polls conducted in the summer of 2010, 69 percent of Americans expressed favorable views of the Supreme Court. By comparison, roughly 45 percent of Americans approved of the job Barack Obama was doing as president, and only 21 percent had a favorable perception of Congress.[5] Even when public approval of the Supreme Court dips, it usually remains at least as high as that for the other branches.[6]

With such strong public support, the courts stand at the center of some of the most pressing national controversies. Failing to advance their preferred political reforms in the legislative and executive branches, interest groups often turn to the courts. Both state and federal law enforcement agencies prosecute criminal activities through the courts. And when individuals believe that their constitutional rights have been violated, they regularly seek redress in the judiciary.

In this chapter, we examine how the federal court system is structured, and how federal judges make decisions about cases. We also analyze the integral role politics plays in both the selection of judges and in judicial decision-making itself.

The Organization of the Federal Judiciary

12-2   Outline the structure of the U.S. judiciary branch.

The core elements of the federal judiciary consist of district courts, appellate courts, and the Supreme Court. These courts accept three kinds of cases: those in which the federal government is a party; those that involve a question about the U.S. Constitution, a federal law, or a federal treaty; and those involving a large civil suit between two parties from different states. In terms of sheer volume, district courts, appellate courts, and the Supreme Court collectively decide the vast majority of cases that come before the federal judiciary.

The federal judiciary is hierarchical.

district courts the first tier of the federal judiciary, in which most cases are decided.

Figure 12-1 shows the three tiers of the federal judiciary. The bottom tier consists of 94 **district courts** (often called trial courts). Every state contains at least one district court, and the most populous states contain as many

FIGURE 12-1 The Federal Judiciary Is Hierarchical.

Most federal cases are decided in district courts. A portion of them are then appealed to appellate courts. A tiny fraction of these make it to the Supreme Court, which has final say over the outcome.

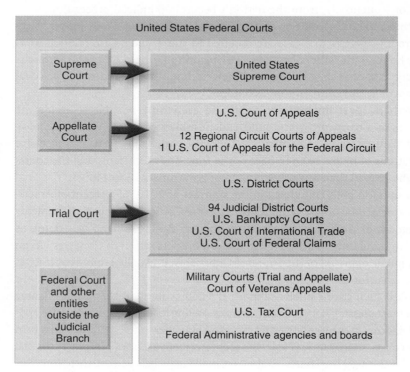

United States Federal Courts

Supreme Court → United States Supreme Court

Appellate Court → U.S. Court of Appeals

12 Regional Circuit Courts of Appeals
1 U.S. Court of Appeals for the Federal Circuit

Trial Court → U.S. District Courts

94 Judicial District Courts
U.S. Bankruptcy Courts
U.S. Court of International Trade
U.S. Court of Federal Claims

Federal Court and other entities outside the Judicial Branch → Military Courts (Trial and Appellate)
Court of Veterans Appeals

U.S. Tax Court

Federal Administrative agencies and boards

Source: Administrative Office of the U.S. Courts, uscourts.govoutreach/structure.jpg.

as four. Federal judges are appointed by the president and can hold office for as long as they are alive. These life-term judges then have the power to appoint **magistrate judges**, who serve either four- or eight-year terms. By hearing and deciding minor cases, and by overseeing the early stages of major cases, magistrate judges help reduce the caseload of district court judges.[7]

The second tier of the federal judiciary consists of **appellate courts**. Appellate courts primarily consider challenges to cases that have already been decided at the district level. Appellate courts are organized into 13 circuits. As shown in Figure 12-2, 12 circuits have regional jurisdictions; that is, the rulings of courts within these circuits are legally binding within a specified geographic area. Eleven of these circuits are referred to by number, and one is referred to as the "District of Columbia Circuit." There is also a federal circuit, which accepts cases based on subject matter rather than regional location. Typically, panels of three judges hear cases at the appellate level. To win a case, therefore, a party must secure the support of either two or three of the judges.

Standing atop the federal judiciary is the **Supreme Court**, which is the only court that is explicitly identified in Article III of the Constitution. In any given year, the Supreme Court, which is located in Washington, D.C., considers only a small fraction of the cases that have proceeded through the district and appellate courts. Between 2004 and 2009, the Supreme Court never heard more than 92 cases per year, and it never offered a decision on more than 85.[8]

magistrate judges judges who support federal district judges by hearing and deciding minor cases at the district court level.

appellate courts the second tier of the federal judiciary, primarily responsible for reviewing decisions rendered by the first tier of district courts.

Supreme Court the highest court in the land, where all decisions are final.

FIGURE 12-2 U.S. Federal Courts are Divided into Circuits.

Circuits serve different geographic regions, which vary dramatically in size. The first circuit includes only the northeastern portion of the country. The ninth, by contrast, includes the entire West, along with Alaska and Hawaii.

Source: Administrative Office of the U.S. Courts, www.uscourts.gov/courtlinks.

Although the Supreme Court decides far fewer cases than the other courts, those that it does decide tend to have the biggest impact on society.

In the United States, the three tiers of state-level courts mirror (in name and function) the three tiers of federal-level courts. Other countries, however, have structured their systems rather differently. In Israel, for example, religious courts—which deal with disputes about Jewish dietary laws, the necessary qualifications to become a rabbi, and other matters relating to religious law and custom—co-exist with secular magistrate, district, and supreme courts that focus on civil and criminal proceedings.

District and appellate rulings can be appealed to the next level.

Almost all federal court cases start at the district level. However, the losing side always has the option of appealing to the appellate court, which can either affirm the district court's ruling, overturn it in part, or overturn it completely. Whatever the outcome at the appellate level, the losing side has yet another opportunity to appeal—this time to the Supreme Court.

writ of certiorari a formal acceptance by the Supreme Court to review a decision of a lower court.

The Supreme Court is especially choosy about which cases it will hear. Historically, the Supreme Court has accepted—or, to use the technical term, granted a **writ of certiorari** to—around 5 percent of petitions for appeals. Given the astronomical rise of cases filed with the Supreme Court in the last half-century, this number has dwindled down to about 1 percent. In 1945, just over 1,000 cases were appealed to the Supreme Court. By 2000, the number surpassed 9,000 cases, but it declined to 8,159 in 2009.[9]

The Supreme Court is the only judicial body that grants "cert," short for writ of certiorari. Doing so requires the support of four Supreme Court justices, the so-called "rule of four." Typically, the Court grants cert when either an important legal or constitutional issue is at stake, or when lower courts in different circuits come to different conclusions about a particular issue.[10]

original jurisdiction the right of a court to be the first to hear a case rather than simply review the decision of a lower court.

Though most cases start at the district level, some go straight to the Supreme Court. Article III of the Constitution, for instance, stipulates that "all Cases affecting Ambassadors, other public Ministers and Consuls, and those in which a State shall be Party" shall be decided by the Supreme Court. When the Supreme Court has **original jurisdiction**, it is the first and last court to hear a federal case. The most common instance of original jurisdiction is when two states are in conflict with one another. North Carolina and South Carolina, for instance, have been fighting over the water from the Catawba River. The river originates in the mountains of North Carolina but then flows into South Carolina through Lake Wylie. South Carolina complained that North Carolina's use of more than its fair share of water was threatening the state's power and agriculture. In *South Carolina v. North Carolina* (2010), the Supreme Court ruled that a third-party private entity would be responsible for the fair distribution of the Catawba's water.

Supreme Court proceedings are highly scripted.

Once the Supreme Court has agreed to hear a case, both sides of the dispute submit **briefs** that contain legal arguments about the dispute at hand. These briefs discuss relevant case law, outline the case's key facts, and present additional research that might bear on a particular policy issue. After they and their clerks have reviewed these briefs, the nine justices meet to hear **oral arguments** directly from the lawyers. During these sessions, the two lead lawyers are granted a half-hour each to make their arguments. Typically, though, the justices interrupt them long before their time is up to ask pointed questions.

Following oral arguments, the justices gather for **conference**, where they discuss their current thinking on the case and cast preliminary votes. This meeting provides each justice with some sense of where the other justices stand on the case. Conferences are completely confidential, however, and no formal record is kept of what is said or done during them.

The **chief justice**, currently John Roberts, presides over the conference. If he is part of the majority, he then selects which justice will write the majority opinion of the Court.[11] As its name implies, the **majority opinion** reflects the collective judgment of those justices—typically five or more—who are on the majority side of the vote.[12] The majority opinion represents the final determination of the Court. It is not uncommon for justices to compose multiple drafts of an opinion.

briefs documents that contain the legal arguments of a dispute.

oral argument a lawyer's spoken presentation to the court of the legal reasons that his or her side should prevail.

conference the confidential gathering of justices in which they discuss their thoughts about the case and cast preliminary votes.

chief justice the presiding member of the Supreme Court who serves as chair of the conference and, if in the majority, selects the justice who will write the majority opinion.

majority opinion the written document that reflects the collective judgment of the justices who are on the majority side of a ruling.

THE CURRENT SUPREME COURT

Current members of the Supreme Court are, beginning in the top row at left, Sonia Sotomayor, Stephen Breyer, Samuel Alito, and Elena Kagan. In the bottom row are Clarence Thomas, Antonin Scalia, John Roberts (the chief justice), Anthony Kennedy, and Ruth Ginsburg.

concurring opinion a document written by one or more justices on the majority side of a ruling that outlines additional considerations he or she thinks are important.

dissenting opinion a document written by one or more justices on the minority side of a ruling that outlines his or her own reasoning on the case and identifies perceived flaws in the majority opinion.

In addition to the majority opinion, some members of the majority may decide to write **concurring opinions**, which provide alternative rationales for the majority opinion. Members of the minority typically write **dissenting opinions**, which outline their reasoning on the case and often identify the flaws that they perceive in the majority or concurring opinions. Concurring and dissenting opinions are elements of the final record of the Court, but only the majority opinion is officially binding. Lawyers and judges in subsequent court cases, nonetheless, may cite elements of concurring and dissenting opinions to justify their positions.

Having issued its decision, the Supreme Court typically sends a case back to a lower court for implementation. The justices tend to see their job as establishing broad principles that are meant to guide judicial decision-making at the district and appellate levels.

The Types and Number of Cases That Courts Process

12-3   Distinguish between civil and criminal cases, and describe methods used to manage the judicial caseload.

As should now be clear, the primary responsibility of judges is to resolve disputes. Judges play the role of referee both in society and in politics. They identify when an individual, a group of individuals, or an organization has suffered because of actions that either are unlawful or violate established agreements; judges then determine the appropriate course of action.

In an adversarial system, judges decide criminal and civil cases.

U.S. courts encourage the two parties in a dispute to behave adversarially. The legal counsel of each side independently decides what arguments and evidence to put forward. They do so, moreover, in an explicit effort to advance their own interests and undermine those of their adversary. This system sharply differs from the approach used in some European countries. In Germany and France, for example, judges, rather than lawyers, lead the investigation, unearthing evidence and questioning witnesses.[13]

plaintiff the party who initiates a lawsuit by filing a complaint.

defendant the party being sued or accused of a crime.

In U.S. court cases, the **plaintiff** brings the case before the court and, usually, makes accusations of wrongdoing. The **defendant** is the person or institution against whom the complaint is made. In a trial, both sides offer arguments and evidence to support their positions. A judge presides over the deliberations, deciding what kinds of evidence and arguments can be presented.

At the end of a trial, a court ruling is rendered about which side made the stronger case and what should happen as a consequence.

The power to issue a court ruling is given to judges and juries. **Juries** typically decide whether the facts of a case best support one party or another, and judges then determine the appropriate outcome of the case. Juries consist of private citizens who are selected to listen to the trial and as a group offer a final verdict. In the lead-up to a trial, lawyers for both the plaintiff and defendant select members of the jury by questioning candidates to ascertain which are most free from any bias or prejudice that may impair the jury's judgment. Lawyers tend to reject those who they think will rule unfavorably. Juries are meant to provide an impartial judgment about a defendant's actions by his or her peers. Whether the practice of jury trials reaches this objective, though, is the subject of considerable controversy.[14]

> **jury** a group of private citizens selected to listen to a trial and issue a final verdict.

Judges issue rulings on two kinds of cases: criminal and civil. **Criminal cases**, as the name implies, involve violations of the criminal code—that is, those statutes that are intended to protect the public's health, order, safety, and morality. In criminal cases, the plaintiff (also called the prosecutor) is always the government, and the defendant is the individual accused of committing a crime—whether it involves using illegal drugs or robbing a store or conducting fraudulent business practices. If the evidence suggests "beyond a reasonable doubt" that the defendant is guilty of committing a crime, then he or she faces punishments ranging from fines or probation to imprisonment or even execution. The severity of the punishment, which is the purview of the judge, depends on the seriousness of the crime.

> **criminal case** a case that involves a violation of the statutes that are intended to protect the public's health, order, safety, and morality.

Civil cases concern violations of the civil code, which summarizes the legal rights and obligations that individuals have toward one another. When an individual slips and falls in a grocery store, he might sue the owner for negligence; when a husband and wife get divorced, they might fight over the fair division of belongings; or when a stock holder loses money from an investment, she might sue the corporation for bad business practices. In civil cases, the plaintiff is not the government, but instead a private individual, group of individuals, or institution. To win a case, the plaintiff in a civil trial need only show that most—or more technically, a "preponderance"—of the evidence supports his or her position. If a jury finds in favor of the plaintiff, the defendant has to pay damages (typically monetary in nature) to the plaintiff.

> **civil case** a case that concerns a violation of the legal rights or obligations of one individual toward another.

In some instances, multiple individuals come together to bring a civil case to trial. In these **class action suits**, the plaintiff typically consists of a group that suffered a common injury. Examples might include residents of a small town whose water is polluted, members of a minority group who have been discriminated against, or parents of children who have been injured by a dangerous toy. If successful, the financial rewards of a class action suit are divided among the members of the group.

> **class action suit** a lawsuit in which the plaintiff is a group of individuals who have suffered a common injury.

Courts do not resolve all disputes.

standing the requirement establishing that for a plaintiff to bring a case to court, he or she must have suffered a well-defined injury that is a result of violation of the civil code.

Not everyone can bring a civil case to trial. To do so, one must have **standing**—that is, one must personally have suffered a well-defined injury because of actions that violate the civil code. A pedestrian who watches two cars crash into one another from the safety of a nearby restaurant cannot sue the owners of the vehicles for reckless driving, and citizens who are outraged but personally unaffected by a business's hiring and firing decisions cannot sue for discrimination. To bring a case, the plaintiff must have experienced personal harm.

ripeness doctrine principle by which the courts will accept only cases in which the actual harm has already taken place.

Even if an individual has standing, a judge may decide to dismiss a case if an actual harm has not yet arisen. The **ripeness doctrine** is intended to "prevent the courts . . . from entangling themselves in abstract disagreements over administrative policies."[15] Before agreeing to accept a case, the ripeness doctrine says, judges must determine that a tangible harm has been inflicted on an individual or group. So, for example, a citizen cannot sue a city for a poorly drafted law if that law has not been enforced.

plea bargain an agreement between the prosecutor and the defendant in a criminal case through which the parties agree to a specified crime and punishment.

Many civil cases do not make it to trial because the two parties resolve their differences out of court. In these instances, the two parties are not required to disclose the terms of the settlement to either the court or the public. Most criminal cases are also decided without going to trial because the prosecutor and the defendant's lawyer reach a deal outside the court. In such **plea bargains**, both parties agree to a specified crime and punishment. A judge must approve the terms of plea bargains, which are then put into the public record. The prosecutor benefits from plea bargains by locking in a conviction; the defendant benefits by typically receiving a lesser punishment; and the court system benefits by avoiding the considerable costs of holding a trial. Today, the vast majority of criminal cases are resolved through plea bargains. In 1989, according to one report, 84 percent of federal criminal cases were settled via plea bargains. By 2001, the figure had risen to 94 percent.[16]

Federal courts process hundreds of thousands of cases each year.

Even though many cases do not make it to court, federal judges around the nation face massive caseloads. In FY 2010, nearly 80,000 criminal cases were filed. Meanwhile, litigants filed 282,895 civil cases in federal district courts.[17] In an average year, these cases came before just over 1,000 full-time and magistrate federal district judges. As a consequence, each judge processed an average of several hundred criminal and civil cases each year.

The total number of federal court cases was not always so large. In fact, caseloads have trended steadily upward in recent decades. From 1960 to 1995, federal district court filings more than tripled, and appeals to higher courts grew by more than 13 times over.[18] These trends have multiplied court costs and delayed the implementation of government policy.[19]

Federal appeals judges now must read 1,500 to 2,000 new opinions per year to remain up-to-date with legal developments.[20] Facing such a heavy workload, judges often have a difficult time keeping track of goings-on within their own courtrooms. Consider the experience of appellate judge Donald Lay: "A few months ago I was reading an opinion from our court; after reading several pages on a certain point, I wondered who wrote it. I was amazed to find that I had authored the opinion some 10 years before. The point is we read so much that we can no longer even recognize—let alone remember—our own opinions."[21] The "litigation explosion" has led some observers to assert that "litigation has become the nation's secular religion."[22]

THE ANNALS OF LAW
The sheer volume of existing case law requires lawyers and judges to conduct a tremendous amount of research in preparation for trial. What challenges does this expansion of case law present for lawyers and litigants?

The Judiciary Makes and Interprets the Law

12-4   Explain how judges decide cases that involve public policy.

There are two ways that judges can influence public policy. The first is through actually making law. When no legislation exists, judges can develop rules that dictate how certain disputes are to be resolved. In these instances, judges create **common law** that becomes binding in future cases.

Judges also resolve political disputes about **public law**, which deals with the statutes that presidents and Congress write and that bureaucrats implement. Sometimes judges help interpret the correct meaning of a statute; other times they determine whether statutes are consistent with basic constitutional provisions, or intervene because bureaucrats failed to implement congressional statutes. Collectively, these cases provide judges with considerable influence over the policy-making process.

Through the power of **judicial review**, judges also interpret and, when necessary, overturn actions taken by the legislative and executive branches of government. Unlike many of the court's other powers, however, this one cannot be found in Article III of the Constitution. It is a power, instead, that the judiciary claimed for itself in a landmark 1803 court case called *Marbury v. Madison*. After losing the 1800 election, President John Adams appointed 42 individuals to the federal judiciary before his term expired. In the confusion of changing presidential administrations, however, the official commissions were never delivered to the new appointees. When the newly elected president, Thomas Jefferson, took office, he refused to deliver the commissions. As a consequence, these individuals could not assume their new posts in the judiciary.

common law law made by judges when no legislation currently exists.

public law those laws enacted by presidents and Congress that define the relationship between individuals (and organizations) and the state.

judicial review the power of the judiciary to interpret and overturn actions taken by the legislative and executive branches of government.

One of the appointees, William Marbury, requested that the federal courts issue an order forcing Jefferson and his secretary of state, James Madison, to finalize the appointments. This put the newly formed federal judiciary in a difficult spot. On the one hand, the Supreme Court was being asked to take on a popularly elected president who might well ignore a court order that he opposed. On the other hand, if it did not force the president to deliver the commissions, the Court might appear weak and ineffectual.

In a brilliant move, the Supreme Court managed to assert its own power without offending the new presidential administration. The Court ruled that portions of the Judiciary Act itself were unconstitutional. In so doing, the judiciary claimed the power of deciding which laws were constitutional and which were not—transforming it from the weakest of the three branches of government to, perhaps, one on equal footing with the other branches. As Chief Justice John Marshall stated in the Supreme Court's opinion, "it is emphatically the province and duty of the judicial department to say what the law is."

With the power of judicial review, the judiciary established a place for itself in the policy debates that would preoccupy the national government over time. But how would it use this power? How, exactly, would judges determine when a law was unconstitutional? Political scientists have identified three models of judicial decision-making: legal, attitudinal, and strategic. Each model casts the courts in a very different light.

Judges develop and apply legal principles in the legal model.

legal model a theory of judicial decision-making in which judges make decisions by deciphering the correct interpretation of the law and the relevant portion of the Constitution, and determining whether there is a conflict between the two.

According to the **legal model** of judicial decision-making, to which most constitutional law scholars adhere, judges rely on their judgment and expertise to decipher the correct interpretation of a law, the relevant portion of the Constitution, and whether there is any conflict between the two.

Different judges interpret the Constitution in different ways. Some pay careful attention to the intentions of those who wrote and ratified the document. For these judges, the Constitution can only be understood by reference to its historical record. Other judges think of the Constitution as a document that changes over time. For these judges, the correct meaning of the Constitution depends on the context in which it is applied. Still other judges prefer to concentrate on a literal reading of the Constitution's text. For them, neither the intentions of the Constitution's authors nor changing historical norms are relevant. Instead, they focus on the actual words of the Constitution and what implications they have for the dispute at hand.

stare decisis the principle that judges deciding a case must carefully weigh the decisions of their predecessors in similar cases and come to the same decision if the basic elements of the case before them are the same.

Although judges may rely on different ways of interpreting the Constitution, they all try to apply basic principles of jurisprudence. The most important of these is **stare decisis**, which literally translates into "to stand by things already decided." According to this principle, judges deciding cases today must carefully weigh the decisions made by their predecessors in similar cases. And if the basic elements of the case are the same, they should come to the same decision about a law's constitutionality.

Advocates of **judicial restraint** insist that judges should almost never overturn past decisions; when they must, they should do so on the narrowest possible grounds. Advocates of **judicial activism**, by contrast, suggest that judges have considerably more leeway when deciding whether to abide by past court decisions. They suggest that the principle of *stare decisis* should not force judges to repeat mistakes from the past or apply the Constitution in ways that plainly are at odds with the dominant political culture at the time.

Evidence in support of the legal model would appear plentiful. Judges, after all, routinely cite legal principles and the relevant case law when making their arguments. It is extremely difficult, though, to show that such principles and precedents alone cause judges to rule as they do. Judges, after all, have a tremendous amount of discretion to choose which cases they want to cite, and how they want to cite them. Perhaps judges first figure out how they want to rule on a case, and then search existing case law for cases that best support their position.

Judges have their own policy preferences in the attitudinal model.

According to the **attitudinal model** of judicial decision-making, courts "are not importantly different than legislatures and judges are no different than elected politicians."[23] Although judges may try to project an image of neutrality, this model holds that judges still use their powers to advance their policy preferences.

To justify their claims, political scientists have developed a variety of ways to measure judges' policy preferences. The most common of these is the party identification of the president who appointed the judge. Judges appointed by Republicans tend to be conservative, and judges appointed by Democrats tend to be liberal. The great majority of judicial appointees identify with the same political party as the president who nominated them. These judicial nominees, moreover, are not passive party members. Most of them have actively supported their political parties in the past.[24]

Political scientists also have found an extremely strong relationship between judges' ideologies and the decisions they make. According to one study, judges rule on civil liberties cases in ways that are consistent with their ideological preferences roughly 80 percent of the time. Even after accounting for a wide range of other influences on judicial decision-making, judges' personal ideologies appear to be far and away the most important determinant of case outcomes.[25]

The fact that judges' ideology is such a powerful predictor of case outcomes does not mean that ideology is the only, or even the most important,

judicial restraint the practice judges engage in when they limit the exercise of their own power by overturning past decisions only when they are clearly unconstitutional.

judicial activism the tendency of judges to give themselves leeway in deciding whether to abide by past court decisions, which allows them to consider possible outcomes, public opinion, and their own preferences before issuing a ruling.

Thinking Causally Does past court precedence force current judges and justices to issue rulings with which they actually disagree?

attitudinal model the theory of judicial decision-making in which judges use their own policy preferences in deciding cases.

causal factor in the outcome of every case. For instance, if public opinion strongly leans in one direction or another, or if the nation is at war, or if the president indicates that he will ignore an objectionable court ruling, then judges may be persuaded to set aside their own policy preferences when formulating their decision.

Thinking Causally Under what conditions is a judge's ideology likely to play a bigger role in informing the decisions he or she renders?

Just the same, it is worth underscoring how radical the attitudinal model really is. In law schools, students spend years learning about the principles that are supposed to guide judicial decision-making; law journals are filled with articles about how the Constitution is appropriately interpreted; and when advancing arguments, both lawyers and judges constantly pay tribute to the relevant case law at hand. If the attitudinal model is correct, then these principles amount to little more than theater; they are dressing up what are, at heart, political motivations and interests.

Judges pay attention to politics in the strategic model.

strategic model the theory of judicial decision-making in which judges consider their own policy preferences as well as the possible actions of the other branches of government when making decisions.

Most political scientists agree that judges issue rulings that are consistent with their policy preferences. Advocates of the **strategic model** of judicial decision-making, however, argue that judges also keep an eye to the long-term integrity of their rulings. Justices are strategic actors who recognize that their own ability to advance their policy preferences depends on the larger political environment in which they work.[26] Justices understand that other political institutions (most notably Congress) may subsequently amend or overturn their rulings. When a reversal is imminent, therefore, justices may craft opinions that do not perfectly reflect their policy preferences in order to avoid a clash with either adjoining branch of government.

Judges must also think about how their rulings will be implemented. Different administrative units in federal, state, and local governments may choose to interpret court orders either narrowly or broadly, depending on their own views about a policy dispute. When the court rulings appear entirely out of step with public opinion, administrative agencies and state governments may actively resist a court order.

solicitor general the individual who represents the federal government in the Supreme Court.

Not surprisingly, then, judges often monitor the political views of key political actors outside the judiciary. Consider, for instance, the impact of the **solicitor general**, who is appointed by the president and who represents the interests of the executive branch in the Supreme Court. The solicitor general's influence with the Supreme Court is so great that the position is sometimes referred to as "the tenth justice." The Court accepts only about 5 percent of all cases, but it accepts over 70 percent of the cases in which the solicitor general's office is the petitioning party.[27] And among those accepted cases, the office maintains an impressive record.[28]

amicus curiae a brief written by someone who is not a party to a case but who submits information or an argument related to the dispute at hand.

Courts also pay attention to the arguments made by relevant interest groups. Individuals and organizations that are not party to a court case may nonetheless express their opinions through *amicus curiae* ("friend of the

HOW DO WE KNOW?

Was *Bush v. Gore* a Political Decision?

The Question

A full month after the 2000 presidential election, the United States still had not declared a new president. The race between George W. Bush and Al Gore had been so close that determination of a winner rested entirely on which candidate was to receive Florida's 25 electoral votes. The day after the election, Florida announced that Bush had won by a mere 1,784 votes out of almost 6 million ballots cast. A statewide machine recount revealed that Bush's victory margin was even smaller.[29]

With the presidency hanging by a thread, Gore requested manual recounts of ballots in four Florida counties. Two of the four counties, however, did not complete the recounts by the deadline established under Florida state law. Moreover, each of the counties used different procedures to process ballots that the machines had failed to read. Despite the fact that the recounts turned up a few hundred additional votes for Gore, Florida Secretary of State Katherine Harris rejected the new figures from the two tardy counties. She declared Bush the winner on November 26, 2000.[30]

Gore next contested the election in the Florida state court system. The Florida Supreme Court ruled in his favor: the recount votes for Gore from the two tardy counties were to be added to his total, and all Florida counties were to conduct their own manual recounts. Bush immediately appealed this decision to the U.S. Supreme Court. Within days, a five-member majority of the Court ruled that the manual recounts were unconstitutional. The vote tallies announced by Harris on November 26 therefore became final.[31]

As a direct result of the Court's decision, George W. Bush became president of the United States. Unsurprisingly, Bush followers praised the Court, while Gore supporters were outraged. In *Bush v. Gore*, were the justices primarily motivated by political commitments? How do we know?

Why It Matters

Judges' decisions can have extremely important consequences. In *Bush v. Gore*, justices decided who would be president for the next four years. Because of their immense importance to society, we expect judges to be neutral and open-minded, free of all the influences of political bargaining and allegiance. But politics often seems to intrude. It is important, then, to understand how judges make decisions that give shape, meaning, and force to the nation's law and politics.

Investigating the Answer

The legal underpinnings of any Supreme Court decision can readily be found in the arguments made, the *amicus* briefs filed, and the opinions written in a case. A political scientist applying the legal model to a case would therefore want to determine whether the precedent the Court used was appropriate and whether the Court's interpretation of the law made sense. In deciding *Bush v. Gore*, the Supreme Court relied on the equal protection clause of the Fourteenth Amendment. Seven of the nine justices agreed that the use of different standards to recount votes violated Floridians' right to have their votes count equally. Two of these seven wanted to give the counties a chance to come up with a uniform method of recounting that would guarantee voters equal and fair treatment. The remaining five, however, opted to stop the recounting entirely. They cited the Florida Supreme Court's earlier decision that the state would abide by a federal law that required presidential election disputes to be settled by December 12, 2000. The U.S. Supreme Court decision was handed down that very day, leaving no time for additional recounts.

A political scientist applying the attitudinal model would argue that these legal explanations simply provided cover for the real reasons justices voted the way they did. Rather than analyzing the written opinions for a particular case, an attitudinalist typically uses data on many court decisions to show how often conservative judges make conservative choices, how often liberal judges make liberal choices, and how closely judges adhere to precedent. Jeffrey Segal and Harold Spaeth, for example, analyzed 40 years of Supreme Court justices' votes and found that justices who dissented in important cases rarely changed their stance when the same issue came up in later cases. If those justices had truly been abiding by *stare decisis*, Segal and Spaeth argued,

(continues)

HOW DO WE KNOW?   Was *Bush v. Gore* a Political Decision? *(continued)*

they would have changed their stance in respect for precedent.[32] Segal and Spaeth later said of the *Bush v. Gore* decision, "Never in its history has a majority of the Court behaved in such a blatant politically partisan fashion."[33] The five most conservative justices, all appointed to the Court by Republican presidents, joined together in a decision that handed the presidency to the Republican candidate, while the Court's most liberal members dissented.[34]

The strategic model highlights the political context in which justices consider a case. The Supreme Court was under a great deal of pressure to hear and decide the case of *Bush v. Gore*. Many Americans worried that the impasse would raise doubts about the legitimacy of American government.[35] At the time, outgoing President Clinton felt the need to assure world leaders that there was "nothing to worry about."[36] In deciding the case, was the Court responding to a nationwide desire to have the matter resolved? The issue was so politically charged that the majority decided to hand down a *per curiam* decision, one that is not signed by any justice, suggesting that no justice wanted to be associated with its authorship, perhaps for fear the author would be a target for intense personal criticism.

Which view of the courts is correct? In a researcher's ideal world, a political scientist would be able to interview the justices and ask them directly. She or he might even conduct a survey of federal judges to ask about their true motivations in deciding cases. In the American political system, however, judges tend to stay out of the public eye. They conduct their deliberations in secret. When they finally reveal a decision, it is always grounded in legal reasoning. The legitimacy of the entire federal court system rests on the neutrality of the judges, and most judges would not admit to being influenced by politics.

Although conservative judges consistently vote conservatively and liberal judges vote liberally, this trend may not reveal political motivation. Perhaps conservative and liberal judges just use different methods of interpreting the Constitution. In other words, maybe judges divide not on political lines but on beliefs about interpreting the law. To test this proposition, one would ideally like to replay history and allow Gore to have a slight lead in Florida and Bush to call for a manual recount. If the attitudinal model is correct, this basic

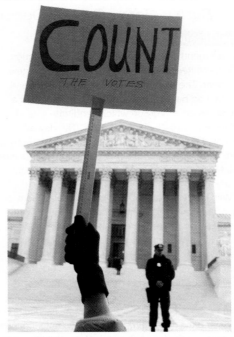

A PRESIDENTIAL ELECTION IN THE BALANCE Protesters gathered outside the Supreme Court as the Justices heard arguments for *Bush v. Gore*. This case, which many claim yielded a blatantly political decision, resolved the 2000 election disputes in Florida and put George W. Bush into the White House. Was it right, in your view, for the Supreme Court to intervene and settle the 2000 election dispute?

fact would cause the justices to rethink their positions. If the legal model is right, the underlying principles would stand and the votes would remain the same.

Thinking Critically

1. Had Bush, rather than Gore, stood to benefit from a recount of the Florida votes, do you think the Supreme Court would have ruled the same way?

2. Does carefully crafted legal reasoning in the Court opinions for *Bush v. Gore* rule out the possibility that the justices ultimately decided on the basis of political considerations?

HOW DO WE KNOW? Was *Bush v. Gore* a Political Decision?

3. In your view, are the political divisions in *Bush v. Gore* evident in the preponderance of cases that come before the Supreme Court? Or is *Bush v. Gore* exceptional?

The Bottom Line

Though judges go to great lengths to justify their opinions, it is extremely difficult to identify their true motivations. Taken at face value, the written record that judges leave behind suggests that legal and constitutional issues are paramount. But the inescapable fact is that judges' partisan identification is a powerful predictor of the votes they cast. This is abundantly clear in *Bush v. Gore*, in which the selection of the next president was at stake. The conservative justices sided with the Republican candidate, and the liberal justices sided with the Democratic candidate. On this case in particular, then, judges' political views probably did influence the court's ruling.

court") briefs. The practice of *amicus curiae* allows arguments to be presented by groups that may not have standing, and hence may not be able to bring a case forward themselves.

Political scientists have generated a substantial body of evidence suggesting that judges are sensitive to public opinion. There probably is no starker example of the Supreme Court's setting aside legal and constitutional principles in order to cater to public opinion than the 1944 case *Korematsu v. United States*. During World War II, President Franklin Roosevelt unilaterally decided to place 120,000 Japanese Americans into internment camps. In the aftermath of the Japanese attack on Pearl Harbor, Roosevelt argued, Japanese Americans represented an imminent security threat. The president's only cause of action, however, was their national origin. The Supreme Court nonetheless ruled in favor of Roosevelt's policy. When the nation stood on a war footing, and the public stood squarely behind its president, the justices dared not intervene, even though most would agree that the president's actions were unconstitutional.[37]

Studies of public opinion, in particular, require special sensitivity to issues of causation. It is not always clear, after all, whether the

CHALLENGING THE JAPANESE INTERNMENT IN WORLD WAR II
Fred Korematsu, shown here in 1983, was the subject of one of the most important wartime cases ever decided by the Supreme Court. In a case that bore Korematsu's name, the Supreme Court upheld the internment of Japanese Americans during World War II.

Thinking Causally Does public opinion influence judicial decisions, or do judicial decisions shape public opinion?

courts are following the public, or the public is following the courts. A number of scholars have shown that public opinion changed in the direction of court rulings in the aftermath of important desegregation and abortion cases.[38] It is possible, though, that judges sensed or anticipated these shifts in public opinion, in which case the public may have influenced the court ruling.

Judicial Appointments

12-5   Analyze the process of judicial appointment and selection.

The Constitution gives the president the power to appoint judges and justices with "the advice and consent" of the Senate. Because judges hold office for life, these appointments enable presidents to have a lasting impact on the workings of government long after they have left office. And because of the stakes involved, presidents take great care when selecting individuals for federal judgeships.

Over the last half-century, each president has appointed scores of individuals to the federal judiciary. Recent presidents have had the opportunity to appoint hundreds more.[39] The power to appoint so many federal judges gives presidents some control over the policy preferences and priorities of those individuals who wield the extraordinary power of judicial review.

In terms of race and gender, judges look more and more like a cross section of America. Among President Obama's nominations during his first two years in office, 45 percent were women, 21 percent were African American, 10 percent were Hispanic, and 8 percent were Asian American. In terms of other demographics, however, nominees to the federal judiciary continue to look very different from the rest of the population. Over 50 percent of both Bill Clinton's and George W. Bush's nominees, for instance, had a net worth over $1 million. The average age of a nominee has remained steady at about 50 years. And not surprisingly, almost all nominees worked in politics as either elected or appointed officials or as lawyers before being nominated to a judgeship.[40]

Confirmation hearings for district and federal courts are political.

Presidents try to appoint individuals who are competent at what they do, have legal expertise, and have strong records of accomplishment. But politics also looms large in judicial appointments. Presidents regularly appoint judges who share their partisan affiliation. No less than 91 percent of Carter's appointments were Democrats, as were 88 percent of Bill Clinton's. Similarly, 92 percent of Ronald Reagan's appointments were Republicans, as were 89 percent of George H.W. Bush's and 83 percent of George W. Bush's during his first term in office.[41]

Despite this political favoritism, most lower-court nominees are confirmed. In the 1980s and early 1990s, Congress confirmed the appointments of roughly four in five district and appellate nominees. With the Republican takeover of the 104th Congress (1995–96), however, and the advent of divided government, nominees for appellate courts were significantly less likely to be confirmed than nominees for district courts. Indeed, in every subsequent Congress, confirmation rates among appellate court nominees have been significantly lower than those among district court nominees.

Part of the reason most district nominees are confirmed is that senators play an important role in their selection. When choosing a judicial nominee for a district court, the president will often seek the approval of the senior senator who represents the state where the court is located. This norm, known as **senatorial courtesy**, tends to hasten the process of selecting and confirming district court judges around the nation.

senatorial courtesy the custom by which the senior senator from the state in which there is a district court vacancy assists the president in selecting a replacement for that seat.

Things get more complicated, however, at the appellate levels. For starters, senatorial courtesy applies only to district court appointments. Moreover, appellate court judges tend to be subject to greater scrutiny by both the president and the Senate. As a consequence, some individuals are easily confirmed at the district level but are denied assignment to an appellate judgeship.

In this confirmation process, it is difficult to figure out just how much influence the president and the Senate wield. On the one hand, the fact that most presidential nominees are appointed would appear to be a clear testament to the president's influence. If the president were weak, the Senate might decide to block a greater number of his nominees. On the other hand, the fact that most nominees are confirmed might instead indicate congressional influence. Fearing that the Senate will refuse to confirm them, the president might not even nominate certain individuals—even though he would like them to serve on the bench. Instead, the president might nominate only those individuals who he thinks stand a good chance of being confirmed. As a consequence, senators may approve nominees not because the president is strong, but because the president has chosen candidates that are to the senators' liking.

Thinking Causally Does the Senate or the president wield more influence over the composition of the federal judiciary?

Confirmation hearings for the Supreme Court are extremely political.

If the stakes involved in district and appellate court nominations are high, those in Supreme Court nominations are off the charts. Norms of senatorial courtesy play no role in Supreme Court appointments. Instead, presidents consult directly with their closest advisers and heed the demands of different political constituencies. The trick is to find an individual with just the right mix of judicial experience, expertise, and policy preferences. Occasionally, presidents also find it advantageous to select a candidate with a particular socioeconomic background. For example, George H.W. Bush in 1991 nominated Clarence Thomas to the Court. Thomas was a strong conservative who

CONFIRMING THOMAS

Clarence Thomas' Supreme Court confirmation hearing was among the most politically charged in recent memory. During the hearings, the media and politicians fixated on accusations that Thomas had sexually harassed former co-worker Anita Hill.

did not have a wealth of judicial experience.[42] Some political observers argued, however, that by selecting an African American, Bush managed to mute some liberals' criticisms of the nomination.

Once he comes up with a potential Supreme Court nominee, the president asks the Federal Bureau of Investigation to conduct a full background check on the individual. This check is intended to identify any evidence of unlawful behavior that a nominee might have engaged in. Some recent presidents also have sent the names of prospective nominees to the American Bar Association (ABA), an interest group that represents the legal profession and that provides ratings of the qualifications of candidates. The ABA's Standing Committee on the Federal Judiciary typically rates nominees as either "well qualified," "qualified," or "not qualified."

If a presidential nominee survives these background checks, he or she then must face the public. From the moment the president announces a name, a torrent of media scrutiny follows. Interest groups take out radio and television advertisements to highlight the candidate's strengths and foibles. Legal scholars write opinion pieces about the candidate's qualifications and judicial philosophies. Journalists investigate the candidate's personal and professional histories. When an individual is being considered for appointment to the Supreme Court, no element of his or her past is considered off-limits.[43]

The real action of the judicial appointment process occurs during the confirmation hearings, which are open to the public. Members of the Senate Judiciary Committee have the opportunity to directly interrogate a nominee about decisions he or she made as a lawyer or lower court judge. They may ask about his or her views on issues ranging from abortion to the legal status of enemy combatants. Given that they may eventually issue rulings that fundamentally alter these public policies, it is perfectly appropriate that these nominees be interrogated on their views. Whether the nominees are completely forthcoming in their answers, however, is another matter.

In general, the Senate is less likely to confirm Supreme Court nominees than appellate or district court nominees. Since the nation's founding in 1789, presidents have formally submitted 158 nominations to the Court, including those for chief justice. Of these, the Senate confirmed 122, and 115 actually took office.[44] As Table 12-1 shows, dissenters can be found in all of the recent Supreme Court confirmation hearings. Of late, however, nothing compares to the confirmation hearings of Robert Bork, whom Reagan nominated to the Supreme Court in 1987. No fewer than 86 different interest groups testified at his confirmation hearings.[45]

TABLE 12.1 Supreme Court Nominations Since World War II

President	Nominee	Senate Vote Date	Vote Count	Confirmation
Obama	Elena Kagan	August 5, 2010	63–37	Yes
	Sonia Sotomayor	August 6, 2009	68–31	Yes
G. W. Bush	Samuel Alito	January 31, 2006	58–42	Yes
	John Roberts	September 29, 2005	78–22	Yes
	Harriet Miers	None	None	No
Clinton	Stephen Breyer	July 29, 1994	87–9	Yes
	Ruth Bader Ginsburg	August 3, 1994	96–3	Yes
G. H. W. Bush	Clarence Thomas	October 15, 1991	52–48	Yes
	David Souter	October 2, 1990	90–9	Yes
Reagan	Anthony Kennedy	February 3, 1988	97–0	Yes
	Robert Bork	October 23, 1987	42–58	No
	Antonin Scalia	September 17, 1986	98–0	Yes
	Sandra Day O'Connor	September 21, 1981	99–0	Yes
Ford	John Paul Stevens	December 17, 1975	98–0	Yes
Nixon	William Rehnquist	December 10, 1971	68–26	Yes
	Lewis Franklin Powell Jr.	December 6, 1972	89–1	Yes
	Harry Blackmun	May 12, 1970	94–0	Yes
	G. Harrold Carswell	April 8, 1970	45–51	No
	Clement Haynesworth	November 21, 1969	45–55	No
	Warren E. Burger	June 9, 1969	74–3	Yes
L. Johnson	Homer Thornberry	None	None	No
	Thurgood Marshall	August 30, 1967	69–11	Yes
	Abe Fortas*	August 11, 1965	—	Yes
Kennedy	Arthur Goldberg	September 25, 1962	—	Yes
	Byron White	April 11, 1962	—	Yes
Eisenhower	Potter Stewart	May 5, 1959	70–17	Yes
	Charles E. Whittaker	March 19, 1957	—	Yes
	William J. Brennan Jr.	March 19, 1957	—	Yes
	John M. Harlan	March 16, 1955	71–11	Yes
	Earl Warren	March 1, 1954	—	Yes
Truman	Sherman Minton	October 4, 1949	48–16	Yes
	Tom C. Clark	August 18, 1949	73–8	Yes
	Fred M. Vinson	June 20, 1946	—	Yes
	Harold H. Burton	September 19, 1945	—	Yes

*Sitting justice also nominated in 1968 to be chief justice, but nomination was withdrawn. Where no vote count is listed, confirmation was by voice or otherwise unrecorded.

Source: David G. Savage, *Guide to the U.S. Supreme Court*, 4th ed., vol. 2 (Washington, DC: CQ Press, 2004), 1186–89. Updated by authors.

Case Study

The Appointment of Sonia Sotomayor

Justice David Souter's decision to retire from the Supreme Court presented President Barack Obama with his first opportunity to appoint a justice to the Court. Souter was a member of the court's liberal wing. If the president wanted to maintain the Court's ideological balance, he would need to replace him with another liberal. On May 26, 2009, the president chose federal appellate Judge Sonia Sotomayor. Upon her confirmation, Sotomayor became the first Hispanic and the third woman to serve on the Supreme Court.

Sotomayor, a child of Puerto Rican immigrants, grew up in a Bronx housing project. Her father, a factory worker with no education past third grade, died when she was nine years old. Thereafter, her mother worked two jobs to support the family. Sotomayor excelled in school, graduated from Princeton, and then attended Yale Law School. As a professional lawyer, she served for many years as a prosecutor and a corporate litigator. In 1991, President George H.W. Bush tapped her to serve on New York's U.S. District Court. President Bill Clinton nominated her for the 2nd Circuit in 1997, a position that she held until Obama nominated her for the Supreme Court. Obama recognized that her background was different from that of most Supreme Court justices when he announced her nomination: "What Sonia will bring to the Court, then, is not only the knowledge and experience acquired over a course of a brilliant legal career, but the wisdom accumulated from an inspiring life's journey."[46]

Because Democrats held a strong majority in the Senate, Republicans were not likely to successfully

A NEW SUPREME COURT JUSTICE President Obama's first Supreme Court appointment, Sonia Sotomayor, smiles as she concludes her testimony before the Senate Judiciary Committee in July of 2009. One year later, the Senate would confirm Obama's second nominee to the nation's highest Court, Elena Kagan.

block the appointment of a liberal justice. But that did not keep them from trying. Typical of an appointment hearing, the nominee's past was scrutinized to determine whether she was qualified to serve on the nation's highest court. And Sotomayor's critics seized on two items from her past: a "wise Latina" comment and her ruling in a controversial court case over New Haven firefighters.

The controversial comment was from a lecture Sotomayor delivered at the University of California at Berkeley in 2001. Reflecting on her experience as a Latina judge, Sotomayor said, "I would hope that a wise Latina woman with the richness of her experiences would more often than not reach a better conclusion than a white male who hasn't lived that life."[47] The quote was repeated many times by the press, and some Republican members of Congress expressed concern that she believed that race and gender figured prominently in the capacity of justices to perform their duties in office.

The second controversy centered on her decision to uphold New Haven's actions to disregard the results of a firefighter's promotion exam out of concern that it was biased against lower-scoring minorities. The case eventually made its way to the Supreme Court, and Sotomayor's lower court decision was overturned. Critics argued that her written decision on the case was too short and did not fully explain her opinion. These claims raised concerns over whether she would be an adequate and fair Supreme Court justice.[48]

Like most Supreme Court nominees, Sotomayor deflected accusations made about her ideological views. Her record as a district and appellate judge,

Case Study   The Appointment of Sonia Sotomayor

she claimed, reflected her impartiality. She refused to answer a host of specific legal questions on the grounds that a similar case might soon come before the Supreme Court, and that therefore it would be inappropriate to stake out a position one way or another. With the successful navigation of these two challenges, and then the careful avoidance of controversial issues such as abortion, Sonia Sotomayor's appointment appeared secure. On August 6, 2009, by a 68–31 vote, the Senate confirmed the nation's first Hispanic Supreme Court justice.

Thinking Critically

1. Was Sotomayor's "wise Latina" comment relevant to her appointment to the Supreme Court? How much should a nominee's race, ethnicity, or gender matter?

2. Do you think Sotomayor would have had a more difficult time being confirmed if she were replacing a conservative member of the Supreme Court? Why or why not?

Critics focused not on Bork's knowledge of the law—the ABA rated him "well qualified"—but on his political views on abortion, civil rights, and civil liberties. Less than an hour after Reagan announced Bork's nomination, Senator Edward Kennedy declared, "Robert Bork's America is a land in which women would be forced into back alley abortions, blacks would sit in segregated lunch counters, rogue police could break down citizens' doors in midnight raids."[49] For the next three and a half months, an avalanche of criticism fell upon the nominee. On October 23, 1987, the Senate rejected Bork's confirmation by a vote of 58–42.

Chapter Summary

In this chapter you have learned to:

12-1   Determine the role of the judiciary as established by the Framers of the U.S. Constitution.

Many of the original Framers of the Constitution anticipated that the federal judiciary would be the weakest of the three branches. Lacking the powers of both the sword and the purse, judges were left merely with the persuasive appeal of their judgment. From the nation's beginning, therefore, judges worked hard to promote the legitimacy of their institution. Over time, the public learned to hold the courts in high regard.

12-2   Outline the structure of the U.S. judiciary branch.

The federal judiciary is organized hierarchically, with district courts at the bottom, appellate courts in the middle, and a Supreme Court on top. Most cases are decided at the district court level. The losing party to a case, however, has the option of appealing the decision to appellate courts and the Supreme Court. Decisions made by higher courts are binding for lower courts.

12-3   Distinguish between civil and criminal cases, and describe methods used to manage the judicial caseload.

In civil and criminal cases, the judiciary resolves disputes among individuals, organizations, and the government. Though many cases are settled before ever going to trial, federal courts nonetheless process hundreds of thousands of cases each year.

12-4   Explain how judges decide cases that involve public policy.

With the power of judicial review, judges exert considerable influence over the interpretation and implementation of laws. When deciding a case, judges rely on a variety of different considerations. They attempt to correctly interpret the Constitution and apply legal principles to the case at hand. They turn to their own political preferences and ideas about what constitutes good public policy. They also pay attention to politics more generally, trying to steer clear of certain decisions that are likely to evoke widespread opposition.

12-5   Analyze the process of judicial appointment and selection.

Politics, in varying degrees, intrudes on the process of appointing judges to the federal judiciary. Presidents have strong incentives to select individuals who share their views and will advocate on behalf of these views long after the president has left office. As a consequence, the Senate confirmation process can be highly contentious. Nominees to the Supreme Court, in particular, face an extraordinary amount of public scrutiny. Occasionally, these nominees fail to be confirmed, either because the Senate votes against them or because the president withdraws the nominee.

CHAPTER TEST

1. What about Article III of the Constitution makes "legitimacy" so important to the judiciary?

2. What are the three levels of the federal judiciary? At what level are most court cases decided?

3. Must the Supreme Court accept all appeals?

4. Do most cases that come before a federal judge ultimately go to trial?

5. Do "plaintiffs" and "defendants" always consist of just one person or organization?

6. In what ways might judges rely on political considerations when interpreting the meaning of a congressional statute or constitutional provision?

7. Would the strategic model of judicial decision-making predict that the Supreme Court is more or less likely to overturn a policy issued by Barack Obama when Democrats hold a majority of seats within Congress?

8. What role, if any, do partisanship and ideology play in judicial appointments?

9. How do presidents go about selecting a nominee to a federal judgeship? How do these criteria differ, if at all, for Supreme Court nominees?

10. Are high rates of senatorial confirmation evidence that presidents are free to choose whomever they would like to serve on the federal judiciary? Why or why not?

MyPoliSciLab® THE FEDERAL COURT SYSTEM
Apply what you learned in this chapter on MyPoliSciLab.

Read on mypoliscilab.com

eText: Chapter 12

Study and Review on mypoliscilab.com

Pre-Test
Post-Test
Chapter Exam
Flashcards

Watch on mypoliscilab.com

Video: Prosecuting Cyber Crime
Video: Most Significant Abortion Ruling in 30 Years

Explore on mypoliscilab.com

Comparative: Comparing Judiciaries
Simulation: You Are a Clerk to Supreme Court Justice Judith Gray
Simulation: You Are the President and Need to Appoint a Supreme Court Justice
Timeline: Chief Justices of the Supreme Court
Visual Literacy: Case Overload

KEY TERMS

amicus curiae, p. 356
appellate courts, p. 347
attitudinal model, p. 355
briefs, p. 349
chief justice, p. 349
civil case, p. 351
class action suit, p. 351
common law, p. 353
concurring opinion, p. 350
conference, p. 349
criminal case, p. 351
defendant, p. 350

dissenting opinion, p. 350
district courts, p. 346
judicial activism, p. 355
judicial restraint, p. 355
judicial review, p. 353
jury, p. 351
legal model, p. 354
magistrate judges, p. 347
majority opinion, p. 349
oral argument, p. 349
original jurisdiction, p. 348
plaintiff, p. 350

plea bargain, p. 352
public law, p. 353
ripeness doctrine, p. 352
senatorial courtesy, p. 361
solicitor general, p. 356
standing, p. 352
stare decisis, p. 354
strategic model, p. 356
Supreme Court, p. 347
writ of certiorari, p. 348

SUGGESTED READINGS

Cornell Clayton and Howard Gillman, eds. 1999. *Supreme Court Decision-Making: New Institutionalist Approaches*. Chicago: University of Chicago Press. A collection of essays on different aspects of the strategic model of judicial decision-making.

Lee Epstein and Jeffrey Segal. 2005. *Advice and Consent: The Politics of Judicial Appointments*. New York: Oxford University Press. A contemporary look at the politics of judicial appointments.

Herbert McCloskey. 2000. *The American Supreme Court*, 3rd ed. Chicago: University of Chicago Press. A careful analysis of the relationship between Supreme Court rulings and public opinion.

Shep Melnick. 1994. *Between the Lines: Interpreting Welfare Rights*. Washington, DC: Brookings Institution. Analysis of the ways in which judges interpret (and reinterpret) congressionally enacted laws.

Jeffrey Segal and Harold Spaeth. 2002. *The Supreme Court and the Attitudinal Model Revisited*. New York: Cambridge University Press. A thorough examination of the attitudinal model of judicial decision-making.

SUGGESTED WEBSITES

OFFICIAL WEBSITE OF THE FEDERAL JUDICIARY
www.uscourts.gov

At this site, it is possible to track information about all courts and look up case rulings throughout the federal judiciary.

FEDERAL JUDICIAL CENTER
www.fjc.gov

This site houses research reports on a wide range of issues involving the federal judiciary and the law.

AMERICAN BAR ASSOCIATION
www.abanet.org

This is the oldest and most prominent organization representing the interests of the legal profession.

FEDERALIST SOCIETY
www.fed-soc.org

A conservative organization that professes to fight the "liberal orthodoxy" that pervades law schools and the legal profession.

THE OYEZ PROJECT
www.oyez.org

A multimedia archive devoted to the U.S. Supreme Court.

The Bureaucracy

TRACKING SECURITY THREATS In the spring of 2010, onlookers watch after parts of New York's Times Square were closed off. The sport utility vehicle that triggered the evacuation contained a large stash of explosive materials. How, in your opinion, might the federal bureaucracy better respond to the threat of domestic terrorism?

CHAPTER LEARNING OBJECTIVES

After reading this chapter you will be able to:

13-1 Identify the functions of the federal bureaucracy.

13-2 Outline the organization and the expansion of the bureaucracy.

13-3 Assess the role of the bureaucracy in public policymaking.

13-4 Evaluate the different approaches to overseeing and reforming the bureaucracy.

Less than a month after the terrorist attacks of September 11, 2001, newly appointed presidential adviser Tom Ridge reminded fellow Homeland Security Council members about the dangers of political infighting. "The only turf we should be worried about protecting is the turf we stand on," he warned.[1] Ridge was rightly concerned, for observers increasingly suspected that certain departments of the federal government had jealously guarded information that might have prevented the attacks. Initiatives to prevent such turf battles included coordinating various agencies under a single homeland security umbrella, while also expanding the federal government's efforts to protect the country against terrorism. Ironically, however, early efforts not only failed to eliminate interagency squabbles but in fact fueled even more infighting—between the executive and legislative branches, and between Republicans and Democrats.

The seeds of the controversy were sown on September 21, when Senate Intelligence Committee Chair Bob Graham (D-FL) and several other Democrats introduced a proposal to create a National Office for Combating Terrorism. The new body would be lodged within the Executive Office of the President. The office's director, however, would require Senate confirmation, and its activities would be subject to congressional oversight.

White House officials balked at this perceived intrusion by lawmakers. On October 8, President Bush preempted congressional action by issuing an executive order that created an Office of Homeland Security (OHS) within the Executive Office of the President. Its director would be a special assistant to the president and thus would not be subject to Senate confirmation. In addition, its activities would not require congressional oversight. A few days later, however, Senators Arlen Specter (R-PA) and Joseph Lieberman (D-CT) issued a counter-proposal. They introduced in the Senate a bipartisan bill that would establish a Cabinet-level position, subject to congressional confirmation and oversight.

After months of resisting congressional efforts to create a Cabinet-level position, on June 7 the administration blindsided legislators from both political parties by announcing a plan to create a Department of Homeland Security (DHS). The proposed DHS would have four divisions responsible for border security, emergency preparedness, weapons of mass destruction, and intelligence. It would combine 22 federal agencies, programs, and research centers into a single organization.

For the most part, Capitol Hill welcomed the White House proposal. But because the new DHS would incorporate portions of eight current Cabinet-level departments, the proposal was soon mired in yet another political battle. The Bush administration wanted to be able to reorganize departmental operations without congressional approval, while Democrats were intent on limiting further the president's control over personnel matters.

After losing control of the Senate after the 2002 mid-term elections, however, Democrats quickly saw fit to give the president most of what he wanted. On November 25, President Bush signed into law a bill that created the DHS, and he nominated Tom Ridge as its first secretary. The Senate confirmed the appointment, and Ridge took office in January 2003. The DHS would take the lead in investigating all of the major terrorist threats that would follow.

The power struggles surrounding the birth of the DHS reveal the stumbling efforts of a federal government to more effectively address a pressing social need—in this case, the development of new, and the consolidation of existing, antiterrorism initiatives. Almost everyone agreed on the importance of creating a federal organization that would serve this goal. Nonetheless, deep concerns about how the organization would be structured and who would control it fueled drawn out and highly charged political battles between the president and Congress, Republicans and Democrats.

This is the stuff of bureaucratic politics. On the one hand, people recognize the extraordinary importance of experts who perform vital tasks, such as protecting our nation against terrorist attacks. On the other hand, serious disputes can rage over who is charged with overseeing the agencies that perform these activities and the amount of independence that is granted to them. ■

What Bureaucrats Do

13-1   Identify the functions of the federal bureaucracy.

What do bureaucrats do? The staggering number of functions that government bureaucracies perform might instead raise the question: What *don't* bureaucrats do? Bureaucrats—the individuals who work within a **bureaucracy**—run the nation's prisons and schools, collect garbage, maintain job training programs, write Social Security checks, monitor the pollution of our rivers, pave highways, patrol streets, regulate industries, put out fires, issue drivers' licenses, and so much more. When we experience government in our daily lives, we typically interact with employees of the local, state, or federal bureaucracy. Such interactions, however, reflect just a small portion of the things that bureaucrats actually do.

bureaucracy a group of departments, agencies, and other institutions that for the most part are located in the executive branch of government and that develop and implement public policy.

Bureaucrats interpret and implement laws.

When Congress enacts a law, when the president issues a unilateral directive, or when a court issues a decree of one sort or another, somebody must figure out what exactly these policies require in practice, and then they must ensure that the government actually takes the steps needed to realize them. Both of these tasks fall to bureaucrats. And both are remarkably difficult.

When the language of a statute is vague, or when Congress expressly delegates the responsibility to them, bureaucrats must decipher the exact meaning of broad legislative pronouncements. They must determine the exact amount of various pollutants that an industry can release into the air, the precise number of questions that students must answer correctly on standardized tests, the particular design of highway exit signs, and the regularity with which such signs must be replaced.

In the summer of 2010, bureaucrats were charged with making sense of the extraordinarily complex overhaul of the financial industries. Earlier in the year, Congress enacted legislation that increased regulations of various financial services in an attempt to guard against the economic meltdown associated

AFTER THE STORM

To uphold the law and ensure their own safety, police officers must make all sorts of decisions on the ground. Every day, they must discern when laws have been violated, who the likely perpetrators are, and what should be done about it. In the aftermath of Hurricane Katrina, basic law and order broke down in the streets of New Orleans. Here, police officers arrest a man who was found with stolen beer in his bags. How should police officers, sometimes called "street-level bureaucrats," go about assessing the threat posed by suspected criminals?

implementation the process by which policy is executed.

rules administrative determinations about how laws will be interpreted and implemented.

with the housing crash of 2008. The law, however, is short on details. The legislation, for instance, calls for caps on the amount of fees that banks can charge for ATM transactions, but it leaves it up to bureaucrats to set the exact level. As the *New York Times* reported, the law "is basically a 2,000-page missive to federal agencies, instructing regulators to address subjects ranging from derivatives trading to document retention. But it is notably short on specifics, giving regulators significant power to determine its impact."[2]

Having deciphered the meanings of laws, bureaucrats then are charged with putting them into practice. The **implementation** of public policy constitutes the single biggest task assigned to bureaucrats. Laws, after all, constitute nothing more than words on paper until bureaucrats put them into practice.

Just as bureaucrats have considerable discretion to interpret laws, they also have considerable discretion when implementing them. Imagine, for example, a hypothetical agent working for the U.S. Drug Enforcement Administration (DEA) whose job is to enforce the nation's drug laws. This agent receives a tip that drugs are being sold out of an abandoned house on the outskirts of town. When he goes to investigate, he finds a teenage girl selling small amounts of cocaine. After arresting her, though, he learns that this teenager works for a well-known drug dealer in the region. To capture this dealer, the DEA agent will need the teenager's cooperation. To secure her cooperation, can the DEA promise not to prosecute her? Or must he enforce the law every time that he observes a violation?

The laws that DEA agents are sworn to uphold provide little guidance on the matter. Instead, DEA agents—and bureaucrats everywhere—must draw on their expertise, their common sense, and whatever recommendations their superiors provide in order to determine the best way to enforce the laws of the land.

Bureaucrats make rules.

One of the principal ways in which bureaucrats flesh out the meaning of congressional statutes, presidential directives, and court orders is by issuing **rules**. Rules typically provide more specific directions about how policy is to be interpreted and implemented. Moreover, once rules are issued, they take on the weight of law. For this reason, political scientists refer to bureaucratic rules as "quasi-legislation."[3]

Rules have a dramatic effect on a vast array of policies—environmental, worker safety, food safety, to name only a few. They also influence the kinds of things we watch on television almost every day. Consider, for example, the efforts of the Federal Communications Commission (FCC) to regulate television and radio under the Communications Acts of 1934, the Communications Satellite Act of 1962, and the Telecommunications Act of 1996. Under these laws, the FCC is charged with "promoting safety of life and property and for strengthening the national defense." Part of this duty is the oversight of "obscene" and "indecent" programming. But what kind of programming qualifies as obscene or indecent? Does it matter whether the programming is aired when children are likely to be watching television? None of the three acts listed above provides clear answers to these questions. The FCC, therefore, has had to issue rules that clarify the original laws enacted by Congress. Through such rules, the FCC forbids the airing of "obscene" programming at any time and the airing of "indecent programming" or "profane language" during certain hours. After the FCC develops guidelines, it must then ensure that media outlets abide by the rules. The FCC does so by monitoring the content of programming and then punishing infractions by issuing warnings, imposing fines, or revoking station licenses.

The 1946 Administrative Procedures Act lays out the specific steps that agencies must follow when they issue rules. To begin, rules are offered as proposals, allowing interested parties an opportunity to express their opinions. Agencies then must respond to each of the issues raised during the public comment period, which varies in length depending on the complexity of the rule. Further, the agency may be required to issue formal reports to Congress and the president to identify how, for instance, a rule will impact the economy. Final rules then are published in the *Federal Register*, a compendium of government rules, proposed rules, and notices. As agencies have issued increasing numbers of rules over the last 60 years, the *Federal Register* has grown longer and longer. Whereas rules, notices of rules, and other executive branch policies required fewer than 8,000 pages in 1949, they now take up about 80,000 pages each year.[4]

Bureaucrats provide expert advice.

Bureaucrats in a particular area typically know a great deal more about the specifics of public policy than do members of Congress or the president. This know-how should come as no surprise, for bureaucrats usually are experts who have devoted their professional lives to a specific policy issue, while paying considerably less attention to most other issues.

When determining which public policies are most in need of change, and then figuring out how best to change them, members of Congress and presidents regularly consult bureaucrats. The main responsibility of the Government Accountability Office (GAO), for example, is to provide formal reports to members of Congress about specific policy issues. Often, though, members of Congress and presidents consult with bureaucrats through less formal means. Through either testimony in congressional hearings, advisory meetings, or simple conversations, bureaucrats provide lawmakers with vital information about how policies are affecting citizens, which policies seem to be working, which are not, and what should be done about it.

Bureaucrats resolve disputes.

Just as bureaucrats serve core executive functions by implementing laws and core legislative functions by issuing rules and providing expertise, so too do they serve core judicial functions by resolving disputes. The Social Security Administration has, for instance, a well-established process by which citizens who are denied disability payments can appeal their cases. In this process, the agency acts very much like a court, holding formal hearings, listening to testimony, evaluating evidence, and ultimately rendering a decision.

Growth and Organization of the Bureaucracy

13-2   Outline the organization and the expansion of the bureaucracy.

Most of the federal bureaucracy is located within the executive branch of government. But the bureaucracy is not a unitary body operating in a single building down the street from Congress and the president. Rather, it is spread out all over the country and consists of many different units, some more independent than others. The type and number of those units, as well as the kinds of people who work within them, have evolved over time.

The bureaucracy has changed dramatically over the nation's history.

In most of Western Europe, national political systems were bureaucratized long before they were democratized. Particularly in France and Germany, bureaucracies served kings and emperors before they did presidents and prime ministers. With bureaucratic organizations already in place when these countries became democracies, elected officials merely had to redirect administrative activities to serve popular ends. Today, civil servants hold much more prominent positions in European governments, regularly serving in the British prime minister's office and the cabinet office, the French president's Secretariat and the prime minister's cabinet office, and the office of the German chancellor.[5]

In the United States, by contrast, democratic political institutions were in place prior to the development of a fully fledged bureaucracy. In fact, America's

Founders, disgusted by the British government's abuse of the colonies, intentionally restricted the size and powers of the bureaucracy. In the early years of the Republic, the federal government produced and implemented far fewer policies than today. It provided little or no regulation of business practices. It also assumed very little responsibility for the welfare of average citizens.

Nineteenth-century federal bureaucrats, therefore, had relatively little to do. Furthermore, they tended to be hired not for their expertise, but for their political allegiance to the party in power. The **spoils system**, as it came to be known, defined the common practice of handing out government jobs, contracts, and other favors not on the basis of merit, but on the basis of political friendships and alliances. When a new president was elected and a different political party assumed control of the executive branch, it would promptly fire most bureaucrats then in office and replace them with its own loyalists.

> **spoils system** a system of government in which a presidential administration awards jobs to party loyalists.

The spoils system served the political needs of people in power. Most obviously, it provided a basis on which to reward individuals for their political support. But, because bureaucrats tended to be employed only as long as their party remained in office, turnover tended to be quite high. This turnover, in combination with the fact that bureaucrats were selected on the basis of their party support rather than their skills, education, or experience, meant that agencies were less professional and often less capable of furnishing much-needed expertise about public policy.

During the latter half of the nineteenth century, increasing pressure emerged to replace the spoils system with a **civil service system**, which awarded jobs primarily on the basis of merit. When President James Garfield was assassinated by a disgruntled (and mentally ill) office seeker in 1881, Congress finally saw fit to address their concerns. In 1883, Congress enacted the Pendleton Act, which established the Civil Service Commission (later the Office of Personnel Management). The Civil Service Commission oversaw the hiring and firing of federal bureaucrats on the basis of new procedures, examinations, and qualifications. Merit, rather than party allegiances, constituted the employment qualification that mattered most.

> **civil service system** a system of government in which decisions about hiring, promotion, and firing are based on individuals' work experience, skills, and expertise.

During the same time period that the management of federal bureaucracy personnel experienced dramatic reform, the size of the federal bureaucracy began to grow rapidly. Figure 13-1 tracks the growth in the number of executive branch employees from 1816 to 2008. As the government took on greater and greater responsibility, it needed more agencies and employees to administer public policy.[6] In 1871, the entire executive branch had only about 50,000 employees. Fifty years later, it had more than 400,000 employees. In the 1930s, Franklin D. Roosevelt created several new agencies through his "New Deal" program in an effort to lift the nation out of the Great Depression. The size of the bureaucracy skyrocketed when the United States became involved in World War II.

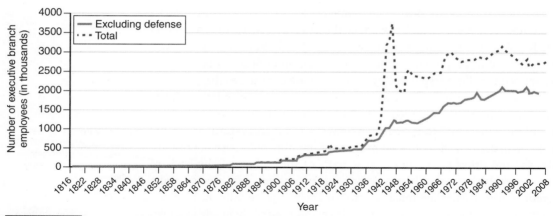

FIGURE 13-1 The Size of the Federal Bureaucracy.

During the past century, the number of employees in the federal bureaucracy has increased dramatically. The dotted line includes all civilian executive branch employees. The solid line represents that total minus the number of civilian defense employees.

Source: US Bureau of Census, *Historical Statistics of the United States: Colonial Times to 1970* (Washington, DC: Government Printing Office, 1975), 1102–1103, series 312–314. US Bureau of the Census, *Statistical Abstract of the United States: 2008,* (Washington, DC: Government Printing Office, 2006).

The bureaucracy today consists of many different units.

Since the end of World War II, the size of the federal bureaucracy has leveled off. In 1946, roughly the same number of bureaucrats worked for the federal government as today—slightly over 2 million.[7] These bureaucrats work within very different kinds of governing structures: departments, independent agencies and regulatory commissions, and government corporations.

department a major administrative unit that is composed of many agencies serving many policy functions, and that is headed by a secretary, who serves in the president's Cabinet.

Departments   Most bureaucratic agencies are housed in a **department**, which is the largest organizational unit in the federal bureaucracy. Departments address broad areas of government responsibility, and the head of each department is appointed by the president to serve in his cabinet.

Today, there are 15 departments. As Table 13-1 shows, at the nation's founding George Washington oversaw only three departments: Treasury, War (now Defense), and State. During the nineteenth century, three more departments were added: Interior, Justice, and Agriculture. But during the twentieth century, especially during the latter half, as citizens expected the federal government to do more and more on their behalf, departments were created to help write and implement policy. Health and Human Services, Housing and Urban Development, Transportation, Energy, Education, Veterans Affairs, and finally Homeland Security were all created to confront concerns ranging from the mental and physical health of citizens to the looming threat of terrorism.

Now take a look at Figure 13-2, which shows the amount of money spent by each of the departments in fiscal year 2009. Among the groups, the department that spends the most annually is Health and Human Services, whose

TABLE 13-1 Founding Date and Purpose of Federal Departments

Department	Year Founded	Responsibilities
War Department, renamed Department of Defense in 1949	1789	Coordinates and oversees the U.S. Army, Navy, and Air Force as well as smaller agencies that are responsible for national security.
Department of the Treasury	1789	Manages the government's money; prints paper currency, mints coins, and collects taxes through the Internal Revenue Service.
Department of State	1789	Develops and executes the president's foreign policy agenda. The department head, the secretary of state, is the chief foreign policy adviser to the president.
Department of the Interior	1849	Conserves land owned by the federal government; manages cultural and natural resources like national parks, dams, wildlife refuges, and monuments.
Department of Justice	1870	The U.S. legal department that houses several law enforcement agencies, including the Federal Bureau of Investigation, Drug Enforcement Administration, and Federal Bureau of Prisons. Its lawyers represent the government in court. The chief lawyer of the federal government is the attorney general.
Department of Agriculture	1889	Develops policy to protect farmers, promote agricultural trade, and alleviate hunger in the U.S. and abroad. It also inspects food to ensure that it is safe to consume.
Department of Labor, reconstituted in 1913	1903	Oversees labor practices in the U.S.; makes sure that workplaces are safe, enforces a minimum wage, and provides unemployment insurance.
Department of Commerce, reconstituted in 1913	1903	Works to maintain the health of the U.S. economy; supports businesses, promotes the creation of jobs, gathers and provides economic data, and issues patents and trademarks.
Department of Health and Human Services	1953	Administers more than 300 federal programs to protect the health and safety of Americans; provides health insurance to the elderly and disabled, offers immunization services and treatment for substance abuse, and inspects drugs to ensure their safety.
Department of Housing and Urban Development	1965	Works to increase home ownership in the U.S.; helps low-income individuals secure affordable housing.
Department of Transportation	1966	Ensures the safety, accessibility, and efficiency of air travel, the national highway network, railroads, and public transportation systems.
Department of Energy	1977	Oversees domestic energy production and conservation; manages the nation's nuclear weapons and reactors as well as the disposal of radioactive waste.
Department of Education	1980	Provides funding to education programs and enforces federal education laws such as No Child Left Behind.
Department of Veterans Affairs	1988	Provides a wide array of benefits to war veterans, including general compensation, health care, education, life insurance, and home loans.
Department of Homeland Security	2002	Responsible for protecting the U.S. from terrorist attacks and responding to natural disasters.

FIGURE 13-2 Department Spending.

The amounts of money spent by the departments that make up the federal bureaucracy vary dramatically.

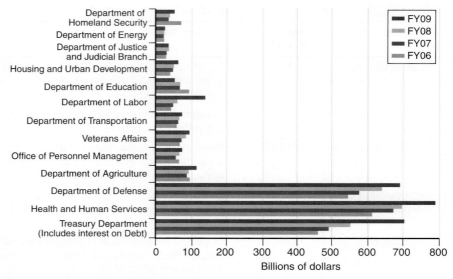

Source: US Bureau of the Census, (Washington, DC: Government Printing Office).

budget approached $800 billion in 2009. Education, Housing and Urban Development, and Energy, by contrast, spent roughly $150 billion combined.

Independent agencies and regulatory commissions   Not all agencies operate within a department. Many **independent agencies and commissions** are directed by administrators or boards who are appointed by the president, subject to Senate confirmation. The heads of these organizations, however, do not serve in the president's Cabinet. Unlike department heads, whom the president can select freely and who can be fired at any time, heads of independent agencies and regulatory commissions must meet well-defined qualifications, and they hold office for fixed periods.

> **independent agencies and commissions** bureaucratic organizations that operate outside of Cabinet-level departments and are less subject to congressional or presidential influence.

Independent agencies, like those listed in Table 13-2, perform all sorts of functions. They manage national museums like the Smithsonian Institution. Through the Peace Corps, they send college graduates to volunteer in countries all over the globe. And recently, still more agencies have been created that serve an equally diverse array of responsibilities.

The first regulatory commission was the Interstate Commerce Commission, created in 1887 to regulate railroads. The nation subsequently experienced a rapid rise of commissions with the Administrative Procedures Act. These commissions regulate all kinds of industries and organizations, ranging from toy manufacturers to stock markets to television stations.

One of the newest independent agencies is the Financial Crisis Inquiry Commission, which was created in response to the national economic collapse of 2007 and 2008. The commission was a stipulation of the Fraud Enforcement and Recovery Act of 2009.[8] The scope of the agency's inquiries went from fraud and abuse in the financial sector to the legal and regulatory

TABLE 13-2 Founding Date and Purpose of Select Independent Agencies, Regulatory Commissions, and Government Corporations.

The federal bureaucracy contains over 100 independent agencies and government corporations. The lists here contain some highlights.

	Year Founded	Responsibilities
Independent Agencies and Regulatory Commissions		
United States Postal Service (USPS), became an independent agency in 1971	1775	Delivers all first and third class mail. It is the only organization that can deliver mail to private mailboxes.
Board of Governors of the Federal Reserve System	1913	Governing body of the Federal Reserve System, which is the central bank of the United States. Manages the nation's money supply, working to control inflation and maintain economic growth.
Federal Trade Commission (FTC)	1914	Created to protect consumers from deceptive and anti-competitive business practices; ensures that businesses advertise truthfully and provide buyers with adequate information about their products and services.
Securities and Exchange Commission (SEC)	1934	Enforces laws against insider trading and accounting fraud; created to regulate the stock market after the stock market crash of 1929 that led to the Great Depression.
Federal Communications Commission (FCC)	1934	Regulates radio and television broadcasting as well as interstate wire, satellite, and cable telecommunications.
Social Security Administration, reinstated as an independent Agency in 1995	1935	Manages Social Security, the nation's social insurance program that delivers benefits to the elderly and disabled.
Central Intelligence Agency (CIA)	1947	Provides national security information on foreign governments, people, and corporations to senior officials in the federal government.
National Aeronautics and Space Administration (NASA)	1958	Responsible for the nation's space program, including space exploration and scientific research.
Environmental Protection Agency (EPA)	1970	Protects Americans from the harmful health effects of air, water, and land pollution.
Privacy and Civil Liberties Oversight Board	2007	Previously housed in the Executive Office of the President, this board was reconstituted in 2007 as an independent commission. It offers advice regarding civil liberties and privacy concerns in all matters involving anti-terrorism policies.
Government Corporations		
Federal Deposit Insurance Corporation (FDIC)	1933	Created during the Great Depression to promote confidence in the U.S. banking system; insures the money people deposit into checking and savings accounts in banks.
Corporation for Public Broadcasting (CPB)	1967	Private, nonprofit corporation that distributes funding for public television and radio programming, including programming made available through the Public Broadcasting Service (PBS) and National Public Radio (NPR).
Millennium Challenge Corporation (MCC)	2004	Provides funding to poverty-stricken countries in order to promote economic growth, infrastructure investment, and good government.

structure of the U.S. housing market. Unlike some other commissions, the FCIC was granted subpoena power for witness testimony and the acquisition of documents.

Government corporations   Even more removed from presidential and congressional control are **government corporations**.[9] These organizations most closely resemble private companies. Unlike private companies, however, government corporations receive steady streams of government funding and are subject to modest oversight. In most cases, Congress or the president has decided that the private marketplace does not provide sufficient monetary incentives to provide these services (especially to low-income individuals). Prominent examples of government corporations include the National Railroad Passenger Corporation (Amtrak), which provides public transportation and the Federal Deposit Insurance Corporation, which ensures the safety of bank deposits.

government corporation a corporation created and funded by the government to provide some public service that would be insufficiently provided by the private sector.

Challenges of Bureaucracy

13-3   Assess the role of the bureaucracy in public policymaking.

Bureaucrats provide vital services in an increasing number of policy areas. But bureaucracy is not without its problems. Sometimes bureaucrats attend to their own private interests or those of a narrow band of citizens rather than to the interests of the broader public. Other times, the organizations in which bureaucrats work are extraordinarily inefficient, providing services that are often more expensive and less effective than we might like.

Bureaucrats have their own interests.

In principle, bureaucrats are supposed to implement the policies written by their political superiors. When needed, bureaucrats are also supposed to clarify the meaning of laws. In practice, though, bureaucrats have their own interests, which may or may not align with those of the president or Congress. Because bureaucrats tend to have more expertise than the president or Congress, they enjoy considerable discretion to pursue these ends, sometimes at a cost to the larger public.

To understand the problem of different interests, imagine that while you are driving home one day, your car suddenly breaks down. What do you do? If you are like most Americans, you have the car towed to the local mechanic. At this point, the interests of two people become involved. You need the mechanic's expertise, and the mechanic needs your money. The mechanic fixes your car in exchange for a mutually agreed upon price.

But therein lies the rub. Precisely because you do not understand what is wrong with your car, you have little ability to determine how much it ought to cost to fix it. The mechanic's interests are different from yours. You want to pay the least amount of money for the most amount of work using the best possible parts. The mechanic, by contrast, wants to receive the most amount of money for the least amount of work using the least expensive parts. And because the mechanic knows more than you about what is wrong with your car and what is needed to fix it, the mechanic is often able to win out in this exchange.

The resulting inefficiencies are an example of what is commonly referred to as a **principal–agent problem**. In this example, you are the principal, and the mechanic is the agent. Both individuals are made better off by having the work done to the car at a fair price. But because the mechanic, as the agent, has private information that you, as the principal, cannot know, the mechanic is made even better off, and you worse off.

principal–agent problem the problem that occurs when one person (the principal) contracts with another person (the agent) to provide a service and yet cannot directly observe what the agent is actually doing; the agent, meanwhile, is motivated to take advantage of the principal.

This principal–agent problem fundamentally defines the relationship between Congress and the president (the principals), on the one hand, and the bureaucracy (the agent), on the other. Congress and the president, as policy generalists, need bureaucrats for their expertise. Bureaucrats, however, do not necessarily share the same interests as Congress and the president.[10] Bureaucrats may not want to work as hard as Congress and the president would like them to, generating what political scientists refer to as **slack**. Alternatively, bureaucrats may be perfectly willing to work hard, but they choose to do so in the service of objectives that Congress and the president oppose, generating what political scientists refer to as **drift**. Examples of drift include the district attorney who, contrary to his superior's wishes, aggressively pursues white-collar criminals but prefers not to prosecute minor drug offenses, or the teacher who decides to stick with her tried and true lesson plans rather than teach a new state-mandated curriculum.

slack a situation in which bureaucrats do not work as hard as Congress or the president would like.

drift a situation in which bureaucrats create policy that does not match the policy preferences of Congress or the president.

An essential element of what makes slack and drift possible is the principal's difficulty of monitoring the agent. Congress and the president cannot personally watch every decision of a district attorney or a teacher. Moreover, outcomes are often hard to measure. Because all of the available measures of criminal activity are imperfect, it is difficult for Congress and the president to know for sure whether bureaucrats are working as effectively as they can in the service of their formal goals and responsibilities. Moreover, because there are so many contributors to each of these outcomes, bureaucrats can often explain away any observed failures to achieve stated objectives as being beyond their control.

The troubles, though, do not end there. In the example of the broken car, there is but one agent and one principal. In government, by contrast, at any given moment there are many principals and many agents. And when Congress and the president disagree about a policy issue, agents may be able to play one principal against the other or blame others when failures are observed.

Compounding the principal–agent problem is the fact that in government the preferences of the principals change every two or four years. A coalition within Congress may set a bureaucratic agency's official mandate one year, but following an election the individuals who comprised this coalition may no longer be in power. Those individuals who replaced them, meanwhile, may have very different ideas about what bureaucrats ought to be doing. For obvious reasons, such changes can place incredible burdens on those bureaucrats charged with interpreting and implementing a continually changing legislative mandate.

Bureaucrats sometimes serve the interests of unelected groups.

Bureaucrats occasionally stray from their mandate not in the pursuit of their own interests, but rather in the pursuit of someone else's. Sometimes it is a well-funded special interest group. At other times it is a highly mobilized segment of the population, or it might be the industry that a bureaucratic agency is supposed to be regulating. In any one of these instances, bureaucrats would appear to be taking their cues not from their political superiors, but instead from individuals and organizations that operate outside of government entirely.

agency capture the condition under which an agency primarily serves the interests of a nongovernmental group rather than those of elected officials.

Political scientists use the term **agency capture** to describe the situation when an agency primarily serves the interests of a nongovernmental group rather than those of elected officials. The possibility of agency capture is especially high under two conditions.[11] The first is when the benefits of agency actions are concentrated on a few individuals or organizations, while the costs are spread more or less evenly throughout society. The second is when the costs of policy implementation fall on a small group of individuals or organizations, but the social benefits are more diffuse.

Some critics have argued that the Food and Drug Administration (FDA) has been captured by pharmaceutical companies, which help fund FDA activities, lobby members of Congress, and launch major public relations campaigns.[12] Pharmaceutical companies stand to make massive amounts of money when a drug is approved for public consumption. As a result, companies with existing drugs sometimes encourage raising the standards of evaluations, thereby reducing the opportunities for new treatments to enter the market. At other times companies pressure the FDA to approve drugs before the safety of those drugs has been conclusively established.

It is worth noting, though, that the FDA often is placed in an impossible position. If they do not approve drugs fast enough, they appear to be ignoring the needs of citizens in need of new treatments. But if they approve drugs hastily, they risk exposing the public to unsafe drugs. It often is difficult, therefore, to know whether the actions that the FDA takes are an attempt to balance these competing considerations, or whether the agency is ultimately guided by the very drug companies it is supposed to regulate.

Bureaucrats can be inefficient.

The most common complaint about bureaucrats is not that they serve their own interests or those of a narrow band of the U.S. public. Rather, it is that they do not do a good job of serving anyone's interest. For some, the very word *bureaucracy* has come to imply inefficiency, waste, and **red tape**.

Every few months, it seems, a story breaks in the news about a $1,000 hammer purchased by the federal government, a half-built bridge that never seems to be completed, a dozen agencies that are all supposed to be doing the same thing, or bureaucrats being paid large amounts of money to do little but sit. A predictable set of charges follows: bureaucrats waste public funds, fail to complete their tasks, ignore pressing public needs, and live off the public's dole without any apparent justification.

> **red tape** the inefficiency and waste that result from excessive regulation and overly formal procedures.

Boston's "Big Dig" project stands out as one of the more alarming examples of bureaucratic waste and mismanagement. Intended to reduce traffic in the downtown area and to clear space for parks, the public works project was officially launched in 1991, when Congress appropriated funds for the project over a presidential veto. Early plans for the project suggested an official price of $2.5 billion. In less than a decade, though, costs rose to $7.5 billion, and by 2006 costs reached an astronomical $14.6 billion. For all the money spent, the project was awash (literally) in scandal. After the tunnels opened in January 2006, hundreds of water leaks sprung; multiple investigations uncovered the use of faulty materials; falling ceiling tiles killed a commuter; and charges of corruption and waste were leveled against both the companies who undertook the work and the government agencies charged with overseeing them.[13] In 2008, three of the private contractors involved in the Big Dig collectively paid almost half a billion dollars to the city of Boston and the state of Massachusetts for these various blunders and catastrophes.

Although the waste and mismanagement of the Big Dig were extreme, smaller versions of such failures are common. Moreover, they are entirely predictable. The bureaucracy, after all, is supposed to promote notions of fairness and equity. To ensure that individual bureaucrats follow these directives, politicians have insisted that bureaucrats follow painstaking procedures for even the simplest of tasks.

Take, for example, the job of purchasing a new computer. In a government agency, bureaucrats must solicit bids from government-approved vendors, choose from a select group of machines, and maintain careful documentation of all transactions. In this way, the public can rest assured that the companies that supply computers to the federal government do not discriminate against their workers, that bureaucrats are not spending lavish amounts of money, and that all monies are accounted for. The process is long and costly, but it exists to promote the important goals of fairness and equality.

Moreover, there are political explanations for certain bureaucratic failures or inefficiencies. Congress and the president often oversee agencies whose activities they would just as soon reduce, or even eliminate. So rather than appoint individuals who will vigorously pursue an agency's mission, they choose people who will take a more lax approach to regulatory enforcement.[14]

Some political scientists argue that the very design of our system of governance undermines opportunities for effective bureaucracy. They claim that regular elections, multiple principals, and political compromise lend themselves to inefficiencies, mismanagement, and redundancies, even in domains that everyone agrees are essential to the nation's well-being, such as intelligence gathering and defense.

The redundancy that pervades so much of the federal bureaucracy has a certain inherent political logic. Imagine the challenge faced by a president who assumes office after a long stretch of control by the opposition party. Should the newly elected president rely on individuals appointed under the former administrations to formulate his policy agenda? Or, after recognizing the awesome challenges of dismantling existing agencies, might he instead construct altogether new ones? Both options have advantages and disadvantages. Hence, when advancing a new policy initiative, presidents often spread out responsibilities across multiple agencies while also creating new ones.

Controlling and Reforming the Bureaucracy

13-4   Evaluate the different approaches to overseeing and reforming the bureaucracy.

Reformers have long sought solutions to the various problems of bureaucratic drift, slack, agency capture, and inefficiency. These reforms generally fit into one of three categories: those that focus on the bureaucrats who work within agencies; those that focus on the structural relationships between agencies and their political superiors; and those that attempt to promote market forces of competition.

The president and Congress exercise control through appointments.

The secretaries of all Cabinet-level departments are appointed by the president, subject to Senate confirmation. The president is free to choose whomever he likes to fill these positions. The president also can select the individuals and boards that govern independent agencies, regulatory commissions, and government corporations, though these appointees often must satisfy various rules and restrictions.

When making their selections, what criteria might Congress and the president consider? Both want to appoint individuals who are well qualified, who have expertise and experience in the given policy arena, and who are likely to inspire their workforce. The appointment process, however, remains deeply political. Precisely because bureaucrats have a tendency to drift away from their given mandate, Congress and the president have strong incentives to choose leaders on the basis of their expressed ideological views and policy commitments.

Political scientists call this phenomenon the **politicization** of the bureaucracy.[15] Presidents and Congress select individuals they can trust to implement their wishes and ensure that their staff will follow suit. What is the point, after all, of appointing someone who is highly skilled and experienced but has no interest in following your wishes?

politicization a phenomenon that occurs when Congress and the president select bureaucracy leaders who share their political views.

Politicization, though, can come at a cost. By emphasizing loyalty, presidents may undermine an agency's ability to perform as well as its institutional memory. When political appointees replace policy experts, and when agency turnover increases, bureaucratic operations may founder. According to one recent study, agencies with larger proportions of political appointees were systematically less effective than agencies with fewer political appointees.[16]

Of course, presidents and members of Congress themselves may disagree about the kinds of policies that bureaucratic agencies should implement. In these instances, the appointment process can be highly controversial. When the Senate will not confirm a president's appointment, the president has two choices. He can withdraw the nomination and offer up an entirely new candidate. Or he can issue what is known as a **recess appointment**. Historically, presidents relied on recess appointments to ensure that the government continued to function when the Senate adjourned for longer periods of time. Increasingly, though, presidents have relied on recess appointments to circumvent political opposition within Congress.[17] In December of 2010, President Obama made six such appointments to positions including the ambassador to Syria and the deputy attorney general in the Department of Justice. Recess appointments can be used only under very specific conditions. Each year after the Senate term ends, the president may appoint individuals who immediately assume their positions of leadership in the federal bureaucracy. When Congress reconvenes, the Senate may choose whether to formally confirm these candidates. If a confirmation vote is not held, the candidate can remain in office at least until the end of Congress's session.

recess appointment the means by which the president fills a vacant position in the bureaucracy when Congress is not in session, thus avoiding the need for prior congressional approval.

Whether the result of presidents acting on their own or with Congress, the politicization of the bureaucracy has invited much criticism. Grumblings turned to heated condemnations when President George W. Bush selected Michael Brown to help run the Federal Emergency Management Agency. Brown had no prior experience running a major disaster relief organization. Many argued that Brown was selected because of his political allegiance to the

HOW DO WE KNOW?

Did the Federal Bureaucracy Fail to Protect the City of New Orleans After Hurricane Katrina?

The Question

In August 2005, Hurricane Katrina tore through the Gulf Coast, devastating the city of New Orleans and other coastal areas in Louisiana, Mississippi, and Alabama. The collapse of several levees in New Orleans submerged much of the city under water. Survivors in the most ravaged sections of the city had no electricity, no way to communicate by telephone or radio, no roads or bridges on which to escape, and no functioning law enforcement to protect them from theft and violence. The disaster overwhelmed the response systems of the federal, state, and local bureaucracies. Thousands of residents who had not evacuated were left stranded on their rooftops for days without food or water, waiting to be rescued. More than 1,300 people died in the storm and its aftermath.

Americans were appalled by the slowness and inadequacy of the government's response to the disaster. In the months following, many questioned the effectiveness of multiple government agencies, especially the Federal Emergency Management Agency (FEMA). Did the federal bureaucracy fail to protect the city of New Orleans after Hurricane Katrina? How do we know?

STRANDED Hurricane Katrina completely overwhelmed the capacities of local and state bureaucratic agencies. Following the hurricane, many residents of New Orleans were stuck on rooftops for days. Here, a woman is rescued from a school rooftop after she and dozens of others had been trapped by the rising waters.

Why It Matters

By objectively analyzing the effectiveness of the federal bureaucracy, we may contribute to policy discussions about what could be done better. These discussions shape decisions that affect us every time we take a prescription drug approved by the FDA or send a piece of mail through the U.S. Postal Service. Because we both consume those services and pay for them through taxes, we must think critically about whether our money is being spent well and whether the services provided by the bureaucracy meet our expectations.

Investigating the Answer

In the U.S. federalist system, state governments bear a great deal of responsibility for designing and implementing policy, and the executive branches of the state governments have their own bureaucracies. Moreover, within the states, city and county governments have their own responsibilities. To evaluate the performance of the federal government, then, it is also important to account for the performance of state and local governments. Cities, states, and the federal government share the responsibility of responding to natural disasters. Technically, it is the job of counties and cities to respond first. Only after local resources have been exhausted do the governor and the state bureaucracies provide further disaster assistance. The governor can call in the federal government to help if the state cannot handle the situation. Even when federal assistance is called for, however, federal agents must work with state and local agents to carry out relief. The shared nature of disaster relief makes it extremely difficult to sort out which level of government is most to blame for a poorly conducted relief effort.

Almost immediately after Hurricane Katrina struck New Orleans, local relief agencies realized that they could not possibly handle the crisis on their own. Nor was it clear that federal agencies were up for the task. In a statement to the American

HOW DO WE KNOW?   Did the Federal Bureaucracy Fail to Protect the City of New Orleans After Hurricane Katrina?

people, President Bush admitted, "It was not a normal hurricane, and the normal disaster relief system was not equal to it. . . . The system at every level of government, was not well coordinated and was overwhelmed in the first few days."[18]

The U.S. Army Corps of Engineers was singled out for failing to detect a flaw in the design of the levees that ultimately led to their collapse. In addition, FEMA came under heavy fire for its failure to respond to the crisis speedily and effectively. The competence and credentials of then-FEMA director Michael Brown were called sharply into question, and in a hefty report issued several months after the disaster, Inspector General Richard Skinner concluded, "Much of the criticism [of FEMA] is warranted."[19] The report cited a lack in manpower, a decline in preparation for natural disasters, and confusion over the roles and responsibilities of FEMA officials as reasons why the agency's response was so slow and inefficient.

Even the federal courts entered the business of trying to assess blame. On November 18, 2009, a federal judge ruled that the Army Corps of Engineers had not exercised due care in maintaining the channel of levees that ran through the city. In the court's opinion, "the negligence of the corps, in this instance by failing to maintain the MR-GO properly, was not policy, but insouciance, myopia and shortsightedness." The judge granted six plaintiffs over $750,000 in reparations, opening the door for billions more to be given out. The case is currently on appeal.

It is not altogether clear, though, that the federal bureaucracy should bear the full brunt of criticism. The magnitude of the hurricane was so great that arguably even an efficient and effective organization would have

had difficulty dealing with the aftermath. In addition, by most accounts, some federal agencies performed quite well—in particular, the Coast Guard, the National Guard, and the military were instrumental in rescuing tens of thousands of people from their rooftops and their flooded homes.

Thinking Critically

1. Who, in your opinion, bore primary responsibility for responding to the devastation wrought by Hurricane Katrina?

2. When bureaucratic agencies have overlapping responsibilities, how can the American public best evaluate their individual performances?

3. Do the administrative failures associated with Hurricane Katrina have any resemblance to the problems associated with the oil spill in the Gulf of Mexico in the summer of 2010?

The Bottom Line

The devastation wrought by Hurricane Katrina would seem to speak for itself. Clearly the government failed to protect its citizens from the consequences of a natural disaster. Assigning blame, though, is complicated by the fact that multiple levels of government, and multiple agencies within any given level, are responsible for disaster relief. Furthermore, it is difficult to assess blame and prescribe structural reforms in the aftermath of atypical events. Given the inherent challenges of a bureaucratic system, the response of the government as a whole may not have been as bad as the horrifying images of the hurricane's aftermath would imply.

president rather than on the basis of merit. When he failed to demonstrate clear leadership during the lead-up to and aftermath of Hurricane Katrina, many called for his resignation and attacked the Bush administration for having placed a purely political appointee in a position of such responsibility.

The politicization of the bureaucracy also relates to the decision to fire individuals. Again, the Bush administration is illustrative. When it came to light in 2006 that Attorney General Alberto Gonzales had dismissed eight U.S. attorneys for political reasons, a firestorm erupted in Washington, D.C., with Democrats leading the charge.[20] The attorneys had solid reputations and positive job evaluations. They purportedly clashed with the administration, however, on such issues as immigration and capital punishment. Because the attorney general was seen to be politicizing the Justice Department—a charge he vehemently denied—Democrats and even some Republicans called for his resignation.[21]

The election of each new president brings an entirely new set of appointments. Though the vast majority of workers within the bureaucracy enjoy strong job protection—the core result of the switch from the spoils system to the civil service system—many agency heads leave office at the end of a presidential term.[22] Such short tenures can diminish their ability to learn the culture of their agencies, secure the trust of their subordinates, and implement lasting policy changes.

In other countries, by contrast, a much more stable supply of policy experts runs the administrative apparatus. Take, for example, Canada. Whereas about 20 percent of American public servants leave their jobs in a typical year, only 4 percent of Canadian bureaucrats do so.[23] One reason for this difference may be that the Canadian bureaucracy is comprised almost entirely of career civil servants (who serve for decades) rather than political appointees (who tend to serve shorter terms). In Canada, nonpartisan career civil servants occupy all Canadian bureaucratic positions from the rank of deputy minister down the chain.[24] By contrast, in the United States, the president chooses roughly 3,000 political appointees to serve in the bureaucracy.[25] Moreover, more than half of the 2.5 million American civil servants are "excepted" from the traditional merit-based guidelines, serving instead under agency-specific personnel systems.[26] As a result, agency-based personnel systems "blur the line between appointees and careerists."[27] For all of these reasons, the U.S. civil service may not possess the same level of stability, independence, and expertise found in Canada and elsewhere.

Presidents and Congress use money, rules, and structure to control bureaucracies.

Agencies do not run on their own. They require money to pay their employees; they must regularly report to their political superiors; they are situated within a larger bureaucratic structure; and their very survival often depends on continued political support. Each of these facts allows for even further control over the federal bureaucracy.

Budgets   Every year, the president must propose a budget, and Congress must enact one. The budget process affords opportunities to reflect on the performance of each bureaucratic agency, and to punish or reward it accordingly. When agencies are doing well, Congress can reward them with higher budgets; when agencies are not performing effectively, Congress may decide to slash their budgets. With control of the purse strings, Congress can create strong incentives for agencies to abide by their interests.

Beyond adjusting the amount of money granted to different agencies, Congress can attach any number of stipulations on how these monies are to be spent. In 2006, for instance, Congress required NASA to allocate $568.5 million of its budget for 198 special-interest items. A decade earlier, Congress had required that NASA devote just $74 million for six items.[28]

Oversight In a principal–agent relationship, you will recall, the agent's most valued advantages are information and expertise. Bureaucratic agencies are great reservoirs of expertise about a vast array of public policies. As policy generalists, the principals (Congress and the president) to some extent must rely on that knowledge for their decisions and directives. To make sure that bureaucratic agencies use this information and expertise in ways that conform to the wishes of their political superiors, **oversight** is crucial. Through oversight, presidents and members of Congress monitor and supervise goings-on within the federal bureaucracy.

One of the best oversight mechanisms is **hearings**. Should an issue or a problem come to light, committees and subcommittees can call upon bureaucrats to testify in formal settings. Though members of Congress often use these opportunities to show off before the television cameras, they also direct pointed questions about agency actions, policies, and procedures. With the information they gather, members of Congress are in a better position to decide whether agency budgets need to be adjusted, whether their legislative mandates need to be revised, and sometimes whether criminal charges need to be brought forward.

oversight congressional and presidential efforts to monitor and supervise the actions of bureaucratic agencies.

hearing a formal process in which committees in Congress call upon bureaucrats and other experts to help them understand and oversee a particular agency.

MONITORING THE BUREAUCRACY

Through hearings, members of Congress can monitor what is happening within the federal bureaucracy. In 2007, Representative Christopher Shays (R-CT) questioned witnesses at a congressional hearing on the treatment of wounded veterans at the Walter Reed Medical Center. What impact do you think these kinds of hearings have on actual public policy, if any?

In addition to hearings, members of Congress can launch their own investigations into perceived abuses of power. The Government Accountability Office, the Congressional Research Service, and the Congressional Budget Office all provide independent sources of information about public policy and agency behavior. With this information, members of Congress can further influence agency behavior and reduce problems that might arise from principal–agent relations.

Congress also has enacted a number of laws intended to make bureaucratic behavior more transparent. The 1976 Sunshine Law, for instance, requires that agency meetings be held in public, unless classified information is being discussed. Similarly, the 1967 Freedom of Information Act enables members of Congress (as well as all citizens) to inspect a wide variety of government documents. Both of these laws are designed to open to public scrutiny the federal government in general, and the bureaucracy in particular.

whistleblower a bureaucrat who witnesses and publicly exposes wrongdoing by either contacting his or her political superiors or tipping off the press.

Finally, members of Congress depend on **whistleblowers** to expose bureaucratic waste, mismanagement, and illegal behavior. The term refers to bureaucrats who witness and publicly expose wrongdoing by either contacting their political superiors or tipping off the press. To encourage these individuals to come forward, Congress passed a number of laws making it illegal to demote, fire, or otherwise punish whistle-blowing bureaucrats.[29] In addition, Congress supports toll-free lines for bureaucrats working in different agencies to call and report problems that they witness. Congress has also created an independent agency, the Office of Special Counsel, which is charged with investigating complaints about whistleblowers who have been punished by their immediate superiors.

Centralization   Left to their own devices, bureaucrats may wander from their policy mandate, especially when their agencies are shielded from media scrutiny, and when Washington elites have few ways of directly monitoring their activity. What are political superiors to do when these bureaucrats resist their orders? One solution: round them up and bring them closer to home.

centralization the method of increasing the president's power by moving key administrative functions from the departments to the Executive Office of the President.

Political scientists have made much of presidents' use of **centralization**—that is, moving key functions from the departments to the Executive Office of the President (EOP), sometimes referred to as the "presidential branch." The core administrative structures in the EOP consist of the White House, the Office of Management and Budget, and the Council of Economic Advisors. It also contains the Office of National Drug Control Policy, the Office of Science and Technology Policy, the United States Trade Representative, the President's Foreign Intelligence Advisory Board, and many other units. In fact, throughout the EOP are people working on every imaginable policy. By relying on these individuals, the president can more easily monitor their behavior and ensure that they are advancing his core interests.[30]

When do presidents rely on individuals within the EOP for policy advice, and when do they turn to bureaucrats employed in the departments? The choice, some analysts argue, comes down to the perceived costs and benefits of loyalty and expertise. According to one study, presidents tend to worry more about the importance of expertise when an issue is either new or very complex; in these instances, the president turns to department bureaucrats when developing his policy agenda.[31] When large numbers of people from the opposition party hold seats in Congress, however, presidents worry more about loyalty; under these conditions, presidents are more likely to depend on EOP staffers.

This same study finds that the president's legislative initiatives are less likely to be enacted when the president centralizes authority. Why? Perhaps members of Congress are less likely to trust the president when he forsakes the expertise located in the departments in favor of the judgments of loyalists in the EOP. Alternatively, presidents may choose to centralize when they anticipate a difficult legislative road ahead. If so, then causality would appear to be reversed—expectations about legislative failure promote centralization, rather than centralization's leading to legislative breakdown.

Thinking Causally Do presidential efforts to centralize authority in the Executive Office of the President improve the chances of enacting the president's policy agenda?

Beyond its impact on the likelihood of enacting presidential initiatives, centralization creates other problems. With increasing numbers of individuals and organizations working on any particular policy issue, lines of responsibility begin to blur. As the EOP grows, critics argue that there emerges "an unwieldy, tower hierarchy in which accountability is diffuse at best and the president is sometimes the last to know."[32]

Agency eliminations If all else fails, Congress and the president can eliminate an agency outright. According to one analysis, fully 60 percent of all agencies created between 1946 and 1997 had been eliminated by 2000. When President Nixon assumed office after eight years of Democratic control, for instance, he eliminated the Office of Economic Opportunity, which was then responsible for administering many of the social welfare programs created under President Johnson.

Different kinds of agencies tend to survive for different amounts of time. Government corporations and independent agencies and commissions, which are intentionally given more autonomy, tend to live longer than do agencies located within the Executive Office of the President, which are subject to more presidential control.

Politics also appears to contribute to the lifespan of different agencies. Agencies are more likely to be eliminated when the current president is of the opposite party of the president who was in power when the agency was created. Perhaps presidents tend to kill programs that they oppose, and these programs tend to be created by predecessors from the opposition party. On the other hand, a switch from one party to another in the presidency may reflect

Thinking Causally Why do some agencies live longer than others?

Case Study

Tying the Hands of the Environmental Protection Agency

Sometimes, efforts by presidents and Congress to control the bureaucracy undermine the work of an agency that is, by all accounts, faithfully attending to its mandate. The resulting problem has less to do with slack or drift, and more to do with political interference. The recent history of the Environmental Protection Agency (EPA) is a case in point.

Upon signing the first act of Congress of his administration, Republican President Richard Nixon in 1969 declared that the 1970s would be the "environmental decade." The new law, the National Environmental Policy Act, was the first of several to dramatically expand the role of the federal government in protecting the environment. At the time, the president and Congress were eager to respond to a widely publicized environmental movement and a growing number of powerful environmental interest groups.[33]

In 1970, Congress established the EPA, whose most important responsibility was implementing the Clean Air Act. Under the act, EPA officials were charged with setting limits for the amount of pollution that could be emitted by steel mills, chemical plants, motor vehicles, and other sources. During the first 10 years of its existence, emissions of the five major air pollutants—particulates, nitrogen oxides, sulfur oxides, carbon monoxide, and hydrocarbons—decreased by 21 percent. By 1980, the EPA had 10,600 full-time employees who were committed to strict enforcement of the nation's clean air laws.[34]

During Ronald Reagan's 1980 presidential campaign, he had promised to address the nation's economic problems and drastically reduce the size of the federal government. He interpreted his victory as a mandate to cut domestic program budgets and push business-friendly policies. One of his first targets was the EPA, an agency not well liked by business and industry leaders.[35]

Reagan started by filling EPA leadership positions with loyalists. He appointed lobbyists, lawyers, and scientists who were closely tied to the very business interests the EPA was supposed to regulate.[36] In May 1981, he appointed Anne Gorsuch who did not try to conceal her plan to ease enforcement of the Clean Air Act.[37] She assured small oil refineries that they did not have to worry about her enforcing the EPA's lead-in-gasoline regulations.[38] She disbanded the agency's Office of Enforcement and then recreated it with a smaller staff.[39] The decisions she made in the name of "administrative efficiency" outraged environmentalists, who accused her and Reagan of intentionally sabotaging the EPA.

Reagan also pursued an aggressive legislative strategy through proposed budget cuts. The EPA operating budget was reduced by 24 percent in 1982. Funding for air pollution enforcement alone dropped by 42 percent between 1980 and 1983, and the number of EPA employees assigned to clean air responsibilities fell by 31 percent.[40]

In the short run, Reagan's budget cuts produced the desired result—not a stronger, more effective organization, but a weaker, less effective one. The EPA conducted 41 percent fewer inspections and compliance tests of air pollution sources in 1982 than it had in 1981, and it took 69 percent fewer enforcement actions to rein in overpolluters. His initial personnel changes, however, did not appear to affect the enforcement activity of the EPA. When Gorsuch was first appointed, the agency's monitoring activities actually *increased*. EPA employees continued to do their jobs as they had before Reagan came into office. If anything, they increased the intensity of their enforcement activity.[41]

By the end of 1982, it had become clear that the public did not want federal clean air regulations to be relaxed: 48 percent of Americans thought the EPA's old air pollution policies were fine as they were, and 38 percent wanted the Clean Air Act to be made stricter.[42] In another blow to Reagan's agenda, the 1982 congressional elections brought more pro-environment Democrats to the House. They cited Gorsuch for contempt of Congress for her mismanagement of the EPA hazardous waste program, which ultimately resulted in her resignation in March 1983.[43]

Immediately after, EPA employees renewed their previous levels of enforcement activity. Even before its budget was restored, the EPA's pollution monitoring and abatement activity recovered to levels *higher* than during the Carter administration of the late 1970s.

Case Study   Tying the Hands of the Environmental Protection Agency

Reagan was not the last president to attempt to curb the EPA. President George W. Bush attempted to ease air pollution restrictions, relax enforcement of emissions standards, reduce requirements for industries' capital maintenance and upgrades, and roll back wilderness and wildlife regulations. His proposed policies led to clashes with EPA leaders—even with his own appointee, former EPA Administrator Christine Todd Whitman.[44]

The election of Barack Obama revitalized the federal government's efforts to protect the environment. Soon after he took office, Obama proposed a $10.5 billion budget for the EPA—the largest in the agency's history—signaling that environmental protection and enforcement would be a priority. During the president's first year in office, the EPA reversed numerous pro-industry rules from the prior Bush administration.[45] In the aftermath of one of the nation's greatest environmental disasters—the oil spill in the Gulf of Mexico in 2010—Obama imposed a six-month moratorium on deep-well, offshore drilling, pressured British

Petroleum to set aside $20 billion to begin compensating U.S. citizens whose livelihoods were affected by the spill, and renamed the Minerals Management Service (the federal agency charged with overseeing offshore drilling) the Bureau of Ocean Energy Management, Regulation, and Enforcement, an act that many viewed as a precursor to even more vigorous regulations of the oil industry.

Thinking Critically

1. From the perspective of President Reagan, were the EPA's activities examples of slack, drift, or something else entirely?

2. Is it necessarily a bad thing when bureaucrats do things that Congress and the president oppose?

3. How should lifetime bureaucrats respond to the ideological and policy changes that accompany transitions in presidential administrations, such as the one from Bush to Obama?

broader changes in the public's spending priorities. If true, then the fact that agencies tend to die when a new party takes control of the White House has less to do with the independent policy agenda of the president and more to do with the efforts of elected officials to keep pace with public opinion.

Reformers seek to introduce market forces.

All of the methods that presidents and Congress use to control the bureaucracy represent efforts to reform the existing system of bureaucratic governance. Increasingly, though, reformers are suggesting that increased effectiveness and efficiency can only come about through deregulation or privatization.

Deregulation   Claiming that government regulations cripple the entrepreneurial spirit of private industries, reformers argue that rather than restructuring these agencies or introducing better oversight mechanisms, political leaders ought to scale back their activities altogether.

Through **deregulation**, the government reduces the workload of bureaucrats. It cordons off certain areas of business activity, insisting that bureaucrats not interfere with market forces of supply and demand. During the 1970s and 1980s, substantial efforts were made to deregulate the airline, trucking, telecommunications, and financial services industries. Through these efforts, the

deregulation the process of decreasing the number of agency rules that apply to a particular industry or group of industries so as to introduce market forces to their operations.

government encouraged new companies to form, providing more choices and cheaper services to consumers. For example, the deregulation of the telecommunications industry made possible the emergence of companies like Sprint and MCI (and later, Verizon, T-Mobile, and others).

Occasionally, though, deregulation can backfire. When the government deregulated the financial services industry in the early 1980s, savings and loan companies suddenly had many of the powers of traditional banks, without their regulations. With their new powers, savings and loan companies began to invest large amounts of money in highly risky ventures. Not surprisingly, many of these ventures failed, and savings and loan companies were left without the money needed to pay back their investors. In total, these defaults cost the federal government (and the taxpayers) over $100 billion.

privatization the transfer of government functions from the federal government to private companies.

Privatization Whereas deregulation concerns the relaxation of bureaucratic oversight of different industries, **privatization** concerns the transfer of government functions from the federal government to private companies. In communities around the country, private contractors have replaced government agencies to run prisons, provide security services, and manage hospitals.

Note that privatization is not an all-or-nothing arrangement. Many bureaucratic agencies turn to private companies to perform selected tasks. The military, for instance, pays billions of dollars each year to private contractors that build parts, conduct research, and provide strategic advice. Even when it decides to hand over complete responsibility for a certain public service to private companies, the government may continue to fund their work. When writing contracts with these companies, moreover, the government may introduce any number of requirements about how they conduct their business. The key question, then, is not whether a government service has been privatized, but how much it has been privatized.

Chapter Summary

In this chapter you have learned to:

13-1   Identify the functions of the federal bureaucracy.

Bureaucrats serve a wide variety of vital functions for the American public. They implement the policies that Congress and the president write; they write rules that clarify these policies; they provide expert advice to their political superiors; and they help resolve disputes. Thus the bureaucracy serves quasi-legislative, executive, and judicial functions.

13-2   Outline the organization and the expansion of the bureaucracy.

During much of the nineteenth century, the bureaucracy was quite small and tended to employ individuals better known for their political ties than for their experience or expertise. At the turn of the twentieth century, however, the nation witnessed the transformation of the spoils system into a merit-based system. During this period, the federal bureaucracy also expanded dramatically. Today, the bureaucracy consists of Cabinet departments, independent agencies, regulatory commissions, and government corporations.

13-3   Assess the role of the bureaucracy in public policymaking.

Though the bureaucracy serves important functions, it also presents serious challenges. Because bureaucrats know more about the policy issues that they oversee, they can act in ways that do not always represent the interests of Congress, the president, the courts, or the American public. Sometimes bureaucrats act on behalf of their own policy interests, sometimes they serve the interests of other unelected officials, sometimes they do not work especially hard, and often they are less efficient than the public would like.

13-4   Evaluate the different approaches to overseeing and reforming the bureaucracy.

Congress and the president have devised a number of ways to address the problems of bureaucracy. Through appointments, they put like-minded individuals in charge of federal agencies. Through budgets, oversight hearings, and centralization efforts, Congress and the president reshape the incentives of bureaucrats and monitor their actions. When all else fails, Congress and the president can eliminate agencies, substantially reduce their regulatory powers, or turn to the private marketplace for help in providing public services.

CHAPTER TEST

1. Is it possible to implement laws without first interpreting them? And if not, how can agencies figure out the meaning of different statutes?

2. In what ways are bureaucratic agencies' responsibilities similar to those of members of Congress?

3. In what ways are bureaucratic agencies' responsibilities similar to those of judges?

4. What were the essential features of the spoils system?

5. What are the most important advantages of a civil service system?

6. Why is bureaucracy often equated with inefficiency?

7. In what ways does the relationship between Congress and the federal bureaucracy resemble a principal–agent problem?

8. In what ways do appointments enable members of Congress and the president to gain control over administrative units?

9. How can members of Congress find out what bureaucratic agencies are doing?

10. Why might presidents want to rely on officials within the Executive Office of the President rather than departmental bureaucrats for policy advice?

MyPoliSciLab® THE BUREAUCRACY
Apply what you learned in this chapter on MyPoliSciLab.

Read on **mypoliscilab.com**

eText: Chapter 13

Study and **Review** on **mypoliscilab.com**

Pre-Test
Post-Test
Chapter Exam
Flashcards

Watch on **mypoliscilab.com**

Video: Internal Problems at the FDA
Video: Making Environmental Policy

Explore on **mypoliscilab.com**

Comparative: Comparing Bureaucracies
Simulation: You Are a Deputy Director of the Census Bureau
Simulation: You Are a Federal Administrator
Simulation: You Are the Head of FEMA
Timeline: The Evolution of the Federal Bureaucracy

KEY TERMS

agency capture, p. 382
bureaucracy, p. 371
centralization, p. 390
civil service system, p. 375
department, p. 376
deregulation, p. 393
drift, p. 381
government corporation, p. 380

hearing, p. 389
implementation, p. 372
independent agencies and commissions, p. 378
oversight, p. 389
politicization, p. 385
principal–agent problem, p. 381
privatization, p. 394

recess appointment, p. 385
red tape, p. 383
rules, p. 372
slack, p. 381
spoils system, p. 375
whistleblower, p. 390

SUGGESTED READINGS

Peri Arnold. 1998. *Making the Managerial Presidency: Comprehensive Reorganization Planning, 1905–1996*, 2nd ed. Lawrence: University Press of Kansas. A comprehensive summary of presidents' efforts to reorganize the federal bureaucracy during the twentieth century.

Herbert Kaufman. 2006. *The Forest Ranger: A Study in Administrative Behavior*, special reprint ed. Washington, DC: Resources for the Future. A classic study of how top-level managers within the bureaucracy maintain control over lower-level bureaucrats whose day-to-day activities are not easily monitored.

David Lewis. 2008. *The Politics of Presidential Appointments: Political Control and Bureaucratic Performance*. Princeton, NJ: Princeton University Press. Provides a detailed empirical account of the politicization of the bureaucracy.

Michael Lipsky. 1983. *Street Level Bureaucracy*. New York: Russell Sage. A bottom-up approach to studying the bureaucracy, with special attention to lower-level bureaucrats.

James Q. Wilson. 1991. *Bureaucracy: What Government Agencies Do and Why They Do It*. New York: Basic Books. A contemporary classic that examines how politics contributes to bureaucratic organization and behavior.

SUGGESTED WEBSITES

ENVIRONMENTAL PROTECTION AGENCY
www.epa.gov

This organization oversees the implementation of environmental and energy legislation.

GOVERNMENT ACCOUNTABILITY OFFICE
www.gao.gov

This agency monitors goings-on within the federal bureaucracy.

EXECUTIVE OFFICE OF THE PRESIDENCY
www.whitehouse.gov/government

This bureaucracy houses, among other units, the Council of Economic Advisors, the Domestic Policy Council, and the National Security Council.

OMB WATCH
www.ombwatch.org

A nonpartisan watchdog organization that pays particular attention to regulatory and budgetary processes in the federal bureaucracy.

USA.GOV
www.usa.gov/Agencies/Federal/Executive.shtml

A listing of all the major departments, agencies, and commissions in the federal bureaucracy.

Domestic and Foreign Policy

RECESSION Many Americans lost their homes in the recent economic recession. Here, a sheriff supervises as a landlord removes furniture from a home in Lafayette, Colorado, after the tenants were evicted. In your opinion, what, if anything, should be done on behalf on those individuals who have been displaced from their homes?

CHAPTER LEARNING OBJECTIVES

After reading this chapter you will be able to:

14-1 Assess efforts by the federal government to manage the domestic economy.

14-2 Trace the development of the largest federal social program, which assists the elderly.

14-3 Describe federal health care programs.

14-4 Explain the powers of the president to direct foreign policy, and identify the executive agencies that support the president.

14-5 Understand congressional efforts to shape foreign policy.

14-6 Assess the policy challenges that face the United States today.

Over the course of 2008, the U.S. economy stumbled, gasped, and then collapsed. In September, the government assumed control of two of the nation's largest mortgage finance companies, Fannie Mae and Freddie Mac. Lehman Brothers filed for bankruptcy shortly thereafter, marking the largest bankruptcy filing in U.S. history. Washington Mutual then went under, the biggest bank failure in history. In October, the stock market fell 22 percent in just eight days.[1]

The effects of the financial meltdown rippled across the country. Housing foreclosures skyrocketed, and millions of Americans lost their jobs. Those banks that did not shut down nonetheless cut way back on their credit, making it extraordinarily difficult for students to secure education loans and entrepreneurs to acquire business loans. In October 2008, the unemployment rate was 6.2 percent. A year later, unemployment shot up to 9.8 percent, the highest in 26 years. Across the nation, local governments were forced to cut basic services.[2]

According to many economists, the downturn began with a housing crisis. As a result of large inflows of foreign investment and government regulations that were designed to increase home ownership rates among the poor, the housing market in the early 2000s experienced rapid and widespread growth. Banks went out of their way to extend loans to an ever increasing proportion of the American public, some of whom were ill equipped to make the mortgage payments. The lenders then sold these mortgage loans to investors such as Fannie Mae and Freddie Mac for huge profits. Still more investment firms sold complex insurance packages on these loans—tying vast swaths of the domestic and international economy to the U.S. housing market.

The housing growth proved to be unsustainable. Beginning in 2006, housing prices nationwide began to fall as people defaulted on loans that they could no longer afford. Then the "housing bubble" popped and housing prices dropped precipitously.[3] The domino effect continued as banks and their investors experienced huge losses and stopped lending money, throwing the entire economy into chaos.[4] Retailers such as Linens 'n Things were forced into bankruptcy as lenders stopped giving out more credit.[5]

As the crisis grew, many Americans called for the indictment of top hedge fund managers and for new regulations to oversee the incredibly complex financial arrangements that supported the housing boom. Others wanted new stimulus funding for small businesses and bailout funds for major banks. But some Americans protested against any major governmental intervention.

In a major national address in the fall of 2008, President George W. Bush proposed a $700 billion bank bailout to prevent an economic collapse. Although typically a champion of free enterprise, the Bush administration now emphasized that in these extraordinary circumstances, government intervention was essential. In October 2008, Congress approved the bailout, which purchased unwanted assets that were clogging the financial system. Soon after he became president in 2009, Barack Obama proposed the American Recovery and Reinvestment Plan, which aimed to create jobs and encourage long-term growth. Approved by Congress, the plan included a $787 billion stimulus to the economy and tax cuts for working families. In addition, Obama sought to jumpstart the economy by repairing schools, creating a clean energy program, and improving the quality of health care. Obama also underscored the need to rebuild the nation's financial regulatory framework.[6] It was not until the summer of 2010, however, that Congress enacted regulatory reform for the nation's financial institutions.

The hubbub over the financial meltdown reveals a basic fact about domestic policy-making: the wheels of policy-making whirl fastest during periods of crisis. Spurred by pressing social needs, politicians entertain all sorts of economic and social reforms and programs. And as we shall soon see, these kinds of social programs almost always live longer than the crises that created them.

This chapter examines a host of domestic and foreign policies. We start by surveying economic policy, Social Security, and health care. We then provide a brief overview of the major political actors who influence foreign policy. The chapter concludes with a careful examination of three policy challenges that are likely to remain on the agenda for the foreseeable future. ∎

Economic Policy

14-1   Assess efforts by the federal government to manage the domestic economy.

One of the government's greatest responsibilities involves regulating the domestic economy. The ability of manufacturers to sell their goods at a profit, the ability of consumers to purchase them, and the willingness of intermediaries to facilitate the exchange critically depend on a healthy domestic economy.

Economists monitor different aspects of the domestic economy.

When gauging the health of the economy, economists tend to monitor three main indicators. First, they focus on unemployment trends, which reveal the percentage of people who would like to work but do not have jobs. The unemployment rate typically has been 4 to 6 percent. In the early 1990s, though, it reached 8 percent, and in both the early 1980s and in late 2009, it reached double digits.[7]

Second, economists monitor inflationary trends, which concern how the costs of basic goods and services change over time. When inflation is high, the costs increase at a rapid rate; when inflation is low, costs increase at a more moderate pace. The government tends to measure inflation through the Consumer Price Index (CPI), which tracks the costs of food, clothing, medical services, and other essential items from year to year. For all goods and services, the annual CPI in December 2010 was 1.5 percent, which is somewhat lower than the annual average of 2.8 percent recorded between 1913 and 2007.[8]

Third, analysts monitor the overall growth of the economy. A prime indicator is the **gross domestic product (GDP)**, a statistic that measures all

gross domestic product (GDP) a statistic that measures all goods and services produced by a nation's economy.

goods and services produced by individuals and businesses within the United States.[9] Between 2003 and 2005 the GDP hovered around $13 trillion, and it topped $14 trillion in 2010, surpassing that of any other country.[10]

Economists have different ideas about how to improve the economy.

How might the government respond to fluctuations in the economy, as reflected in changes in unemployment, inflation, or GDP? Economists, like all social scientists, regularly disagree about the best course of action. The first option is to do nothing—or at least very little. This is the governing philosophy of **laissez-faire economics**. According to this theory, the private marketplace experiences natural periods of expansion and decline, and the best thing for the government to do, by and large, is to stay out of the way.

laissez-faire economics a theory that discourages the government from becoming involved in the economy.

Most economists, however, admit that a vibrant economy requires at least some government intervention. The government, for instance, might alter the supply of money in the marketplace, which is the central objective of **monetary policy**. The national bank system, called the Federal Reserve, retains the power to set interest rates, which affect the flow of money in the domestic economy. By increasing interest rates, the Federal Reserve can restrain economic growth and inflationary pressures. By decreasing interest rates, the Federal Reserve can stimulate economic activity, though at the risk of increasing inflation rates. The president has the power to appoint the chair of the Federal Reserve (currently Ben Bernanke). For the most part, though, the Federal Reserve is kept independent from political pressures.

monetary policy policy designed to improve the economy by controlling the supply of available money.

The government also can directly intervene in the economy through taxing and spending, the central elements of **fiscal policy**. The government can attempt to stimulate economic activity either by spending in the marketplace (as Obama did in 2009) or by decreasing taxes (as George W. Bush did over the course of his presidency). Conversely, in more prosperous times, when inflationary trends may need to be curbed, the government may opt to cut spending or increase taxes.

fiscal policy policy designed to improve the economy through spending and taxation.

When the government spends less than it recovers through taxes, it incurs a surplus. More commonly, though, the government spends more than it recovers through taxes. In so doing, it contributes to the annual **deficit**, which represents the total amount of money that the federal government had to borrow from U.S. citizens and foreign governments in order to meet its spending obligations.

deficit the amount of money a government spends in a year, above and beyond what it brings in through taxation and other means.

Over time, of course, these deficits mount. The **public debt** refers to the total amount of money that the federal government owes. As of 2011, the public debt surpassed a whopping $14 trillion. The federal government must pay hundreds of billions of dollars each year just to finance the interest on the debt.[11]

public debt the total amount of money that the federal government owes.

With the U.S. economy increasingly dependent on foreign sources of revenue, particularly from China, some scholars have raised concerns about the impact of rising national debt on U.S. foreign policy. China currently holds $1.2 trillion in U.S. Treasury securities, making it the second largest foreign investor in the United States, just behind Japan.[12] As long as the United States remains beholden to Chinese debtors, some worry, the U.S. government lacks the necessary leverage to press for a variety of human rights reforms.[13] Others, however, insist that just as the United States needs China, China also needs the United States. Should they divest from the United States, China would suffer substantial economic losses.[14]

The total amount of U.S. debt is higher now than it has ever been. As a percentage of GDP, it is quickly approaching the historical highs witnessed in the 1940s. By international standards, however, the current U.S. debt appears more moderate. Although some countries such as South Korea and Luxemburg have much lower debt levels, other countries such as Switzerland, Japan, Greece, Belgium, France, and Italy hold debt levels that, as a percentage of their GDP, surpass that of the United States.

Economists have long debated the relative benefits of fiscal and monetary policy.[15] However, the federal government does not have to choose between the two, and regularly implements both. In early 2008, economists worried about the onset of a **recession**, which exists when the GDP declines for two successive quarters. To encourage economic growth, the Federal Reserve decreased interest rates. Shortly thereafter, Congress enacted an economic stimulus package that disbursed funds to individuals and families around the country in the hopes of jumpstarting the economy.[16]

Different people are affected by the economy in different ways. In the pages that follow, we examine a variety of social programs that are designed to address the specific challenges facing different populations within the United States.

> **Thinking Causally** How does the U.S. debt affect the government's domestic and foreign policy?

> **recession** an economic downturn, which technically exists when the gross domestic product drops in size for two successive quarters.

Social Security

14-2 Trace the development of the largest federal social program, which assists the elderly.

Think what it must have been like for the elderly during the Great Depression. After working for decades and putting money aside for their eventual retirement, they watched as their savings vanished overnight. Unlike younger people, the elderly could not readily start over again and recover what they had lost, and many spent their last years in poverty.

The **Social Security Act**, enacted in 1935, attempted to correct this state of affairs. The act established the framework for the Social Security

> **Social Security Act** a 1935 law that established Social Security, an entitlement program providing retirees with a monthly income in order to reduce poverty among the elderly.

Administration (SSA), charged with providing a reliable income stream for the elderly.[17] Today, most individuals qualify for Social Security benefits either when they turn 67 or when they become disabled and cannot work.[18] The benefits come in the form of a monthly check, the size of which varies according to the amount of money that the individual paid into the Social Security fund during years of employment.

During the course of their working lives, employees pay a portion of their income into a fund, which the SSA maintains. These payments, however, are not like deposits in a bank. Rather, most of the contributions made today are promptly paid out to today's beneficiaries. This "pay as you go" system means that funds flow into and out of the Social Security fund at a continual rate.

THE BIRTH OF SOCIAL SECURITY
Several members of the House and Senate look on as President Franklin Roosevelt signs the Social Security Act in August 1935.

Social Security benefits are **entitlements**—benefits that all qualifying individuals have a legal right to obtain. Thus, to receive Social Security benefits, one does not need to demonstrate financial need. Indeed, the size of the payments is unrelated to the amount of private savings an individual has. With this design, Social Security checks are an essential form of income for some people, and a welcome supplementary income for others.

entitlements benefits that all qualifying individuals have a legal right to obtain.

Social Security benefits have steadily expanded.

Since its enactment in 1935, Social Security has grown from a modestly sized government program to a massive one. Originally, the Social Security Act excluded roughly one-half of the civilian labor force, including farm workers, government employees, the self-employed, and individuals working for small businesses. In 1950, farmers qualified for Social Security, and since then virtually all industry restrictions have been lifted. In 2010, nearly 55 million individuals received Social Security benefits in the United States.[19]

The size of the benefits has also increased. In part, this reflects the natural maturation of the program. During the program's early years, retired workers had paid into the system for relatively short periods of time. As their total contributions increased, however, workers stood to receive larger benefits when they retired. And workers who have contributed into the system over their entire working lives can expect to receive, on average, around $1,000 each month.[20]

The government itself also contributed to increases in Social Security benefits. The most important action occurred in 1975, when Congress revised the act to account for changes in the cost of living. Automatic increases in the size of benefits were mandated, but they eventually exceeded inflation. Therefore, the average benefits in 2010 were roughly 41 percent larger than they were in 1975, even after accounting for inflation.[21]

Obviously, total Social Security outlays have increased dramatically over the past 70 years. In 1935, Social Security expenditures hovered at around $1 million. They broke the $1 billion mark in 1950, and the $100 billion mark in 1980. In 2010, the Social Security system paid out over $584 billion in benefits.[22]

Health Care

14-3 Describe federal health care programs.

In addition to attending to the elderly, the poor, and the young, the federal government also assists the infirm. Many U.S. citizens receive private health insurance for themselves and their families through their employers. However, millions rely on the two largest government insurance programs: Medicare, which assists the elderly, and Medicaid, which assists the poor.

Medicare and medicaid provide coverage to the elderly, poor, and disabled.

Although Lyndon Johnson's Great Society legislation tackled poverty, education, and discrimination, its most sweeping achievements were reserved for the infirm. Through two programs enacted in 1965, Johnson put the government firmly into the health care business. **Medicare** provided government health insurance to the elderly, and **Medicaid** did so for the poor and disabled.[23]

Medicare a federally funded entitlement program that offers health insurance to the elderly.

Medicaid a means-tested program, funded by federal and state governments, that extends health insurance to the poor and disabled.

When originally enacted, Medicare covered physicians' fees and the costs of compulsory hospitalization for citizens over the age of 65. Over time, though, the program expanded dramatically. Today it allows the elderly to secure a wide range of services, including inpatient hospital care, certain kinds of home health care, hospice assistance, outpatient hospital care, and prescription drug benefits.

Medicare is a massive government program financed through a variety of means. As with Social Security, workers must pay a Medicare-specific tax. In 2010, Medicare assisted 47 million people. After figuring in total state and federal expenditures, along with the added costs of the 2009 American Recovery and Reinvestment Act, expenditures ran about $330 billion in 2010, which amounts to roughly two-thirds of the total expenditures on Medicare.[24]

In some ways, Medicaid is even bigger than Medicare. Medicaid provides health insurance to more than 58 million low-income and disabled citizens.[25] Medicaid expenditures, however, are quite a bit lower than those of Medicare. In 2010, Medicaid cost federal and state governments a total of $275 billion, roughly $170 billion less than Medicare.[26] Two primary reasons explain why Medicaid is less expensive than Medicare, even though it provides more services to more people. First, Medicaid does not offer as generous a prescription drug benefit program. Second, the costs of caring for the elderly have steadily increased over time. Today, the elderly are living an average of eight years longer than they did when Medicare began. The elderly, moreover, typically require more expensive medical procedures than does the rest of the citizenry. Medicare is picking up most of these extra costs.

Comprehensive health care reform was eventually achieved in 2010.

Almost everyone agrees that something needs to be done about the state of U.S. health care. It is too costly. For many, the quality of care is unacceptable. And, despite massive government programs like Medicare and Medicaid, as well as the patchwork of private insurance plans, many Americans lack health insurance. In every year between 1995 and 2005, more than 15 percent of U.S. citizens lacked any health insurance. Every other major industrialized nation in the world, by comparison, has some form of universal health care.

What people cannot agree about is the right way to go about improving this state of affairs. Some suggest that allowing U.S. citizens to purchase prescription drugs from foreign countries might drastically reduce costs. Others push for closer regulation of the pharmaceutical industry. The most ambitious, however, advocate government-provided health insurance that covers every U.S. citizen.

In the fall of 2009 and spring of 2010, a national debate evoked long-standing disputes about the effect of government-provided health insurance on private insurance markets. Proponents of a vigorous government intervention advocated for a single-payer system, which would pay for all medical fees from a single government source. Others advocated for a two-tier system in which the government would provide for basic health services, and people could purchase other health care coverage in the private marketplace. Still others argued for nonprofit, health care co-ops, which would constitute something of a compromise between a genuine government insurance option and purely private providers.

Thinking Causally Does increased government involvement in health insurance markets help or hurt private providers?

Ultimately, Democrats in Congress and President Obama managed to overcome nearly unanimous Republican opposition and enact sweeping health care reform. The Patient Protection and Affordable Care Act (PPACA) extends health care coverage to 32 million uninsured Americans and expands Medicaid to cover families of four that earn less than roughly $29,327 per year.[27]

HEALTH CARE REFORM

Flanked by members of Congress and his cabinet, President Barack Obama signs the health care bill in the East Room of the White House on March 23, 2010.

Uninsured and self-employed citizens, as well as small businesses, will be able to buy into state-based insurance plans. By 2014, the act mandates that every American have health insurance, else they pay a yearly fine of $695. Similarly, employers with more than 50 workers will have to provide insurance or pay a yearly fine of $2,000 per worker. The legislation also regulates the practices of insurance companies. Under the PPACA, starting in 2014, insurance companies can no longer deny patients coverage because of preexisting conditions. Moreover, insurance companies are obligated to allow children to stay under their parent's plan until the age of 26.

Just after the president signed the bill into law on March 23, 2010, Senate Majority Leader Harry Reid proclaimed, "We have worked and waited for this moment for over a century. This, of course, was a health bill. But it was also a jobs bill. It was also an economic recovery bill. It was a deficit reduction bill. It was truly a bill of rights. And now it is the law of the land."[28] Others, though, were not nearly so effusive. Republican opposition remains strong and is increasingly vocal. Raising concerns about its costs and the expansion of government involvement in health care, some opponents began calling for the legislation's repeal just hours after its enactment. The legislation's fate, though, surely depends on its ability to deliver on its promises to reform the U.S. health care system—an eventuality we have yet to witness.

The Foreign Policy Bureaucracy

14-4   Explain the powers of the president to direct foreign policy, and identify the executive agencies that support the president.

foreign policy the mix of military, diplomatic, and economic policies that define U.S. relations with other nations around the world.

Although the federal government shares responsibility over domestic policy with state governments, it holds complete control over **foreign policy**—that is, the policies that define the relationships between the United States and other nations. No other individual dominates U.S. foreign policy-making as much as the president. As commander in chief, the president regularly decides when troops will be deployed, for how long, and what their mission will be. As chief diplomat, the president often holds summits with foreign heads of state about the major issues of the day. As chief administrator, the president appoints many of the individuals who are charged with developing and implementing foreign policy. Serving the president in these various roles is a massive foreign policy bureaucracy.

The National Security Council advises the president.

Thousands of individuals within the executive branch oversee foreign affairs. In many ways, the executive agency closest to the president on issues of foreign policy is the **National Security Council (NSC)**. Formed in 1947, the NSC coordinates the activities of the armed forces and other executive agencies (e.g., the Departments of State and Defense and the CIA) to increase national security cooperation.

National Security Council (NSC) an advisory body, formed in 1947 by the National Security Act, which assists the president in gathering information from military services and other security-related executive agencies.

By law, the NSC must include the vice president, the national security advisor, the secretaries of state and defense, and the chair of the Joint Chiefs of Staff. In practice, most presidents have chosen to include more individuals than these. In addition to the formal council, the NSC also includes staff assistants whose roles have grown in size and importance over the years.

The State Department oversees U.S. diplomacy.

At its core, foreign policy is about **diplomacy**—the ongoing negotiation of economic and political relationships between different countries. Historically, the State Department has held primary responsibility for U.S. diplomacy. The **State Department** is the agency home of diplomats, embassies, and most foreign aid programs run by the U.S. government. The primary job of the State Department is to represent U.S. interests overseas and in various international organizations. In so doing, it communicates with foreign governments and publics, and it provides analysis on events abroad and their implications for American foreign policy. The State Department also negotiates treaties and agreements, makes policy recommendations, and takes steps to implement them. Finally, the department coordinates with the Agency for International Development (USAID) to oversee American foreign aid.

diplomacy the peaceful negotiation of economic and political relationships between different countries.

State Department the agency home of diplomats, embassies, treaty negotiators, and most foreign aid programs run by the U.S. government.

The State Department operates hundreds of foreign embassies and consulates all over the globe. Roughly 30,000 employees, of which 3,500 are foreign service officers (FSOs), work in these outposts. These FSOs work alongside personnel from other federal departments and agencies, including Defense, Commerce, Agriculture, Homeland Security, USAID, and the Peace Corps.[29]

The Defense Department focuses on the military.

The primary responsibility of the **Defense Department** is to defend the nation from external attack. Increasingly, though, the United States also has relied on the Defense Department to pursue a wide variety of other objectives, including counterterrorism efforts in the Middle East, provision of assistance

Defense Department the agency created by the National Security Act in 1947 that replaced the Department of War.

to war-torn areas in Africa, training of other militaries for anti-drug operations in South America, and maintaining stability in Afghanistan. This expansive set of missions has increased the importance of the American military and raised conflicts between the military and its civilian leaders over the appropriate uses of American military personnel.

As shown in Figure 14-1, expenditures by the Department of Defense eclipse expenditures by the Department of State. Although defense spending has varied with historical events such as the escalation of the Vietnam War in the mid-1960s and the Reagan buildup of the 1980s, it trends clearly upward. State Department spending has also grown over time, but at a much slower rate.

Despite its size, the Defense Department is relatively young. It was created in 1947 to replace the Department of War, a weak institution that did not include the U.S. Navy and was usually dormant until a major conflict arose. In the Cold War era, when the United States sought to meet any threat presented by the Soviet Union, a more permanent military establishment was needed. Thus began the growth of the Department of Defense into the largest executive branch agency.[30]

Numerous executive agencies provide intelligence services.

To formulate U.S. foreign policy, the government needs reliable information about goings-on around the globe—about the activities and objectives of other states, the creation of new alliances between states and the dissolution of old ones, possible threats to U.S. economic and political interests, and many

FIGURE 14-1 The Defense Department Has Always Been Bigger Than the State Department.

Shown here are the annual Defense and State Department outlays between 1962 and 2010. The Defense Department has always had a larger budget than the State Department, but the discrepancy between the two increased substantially beginning in the Reagan administration.

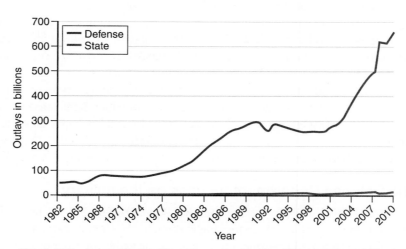

Source: Historical Tables: Budget of the United States Government: Fiscal Year 2008, pp. 73–78. Available online from: www. gpoaccess.gov/usbudget/fy08/browse.html. Accessed February 8, 2008.

HOW DO WE KNOW?

Do Economic Sanctions Work?

The Question

Effective diplomacy includes the right blend of carrots and sticks. Carrots typically consist of things like foreign aid, preferential trade agreements, and promises of military assistance that are meant to reward other governments for doing things that the United States supports. Sticks, by contrast, consist of various forms of punishment that are meant to discourage certain kinds of behaviors and policies.

In foreign affairs, economic sanctions are some of the most frequent sticks employed by the U.S. government against other countries. Through sanctions, the State Department can pursue objectives ranging from signaling its displeasure toward other countries to undermining domestic support for another government. Although sanctions have a long history, do they achieve their intended goals? How do we know?

Why It Matters

During the 1990s and 2000s, the United States levied sanctions against countries ranging from Iran to Cuba to Iraq to India. In addition, in 2002 the George W. Bush administration imposed tariffs on imported goods from China and India, leading the World Trade Organization to organize sanctions of its own against the United States. If sanctions are ineffective, though, then other more aggressive tactics might be called for, at the possible expense of U.S. lives and treasure. However, a primary goal of sanctions is to avoid military action.

Investigating the Answer

How might we determine whether sanctions are effective tools of foreign policy? Scholars began to assess the effectiveness of sanctions by building a large data set that cataloged incidents of sanctions, their goals, and their effects. This initial work, by Gary Hufbauer, Jeffrey Schott, and Kimberly Elliot, found 116 episodes of economic sanctions placed by all states in the world from World War I to 1990.[31] These scholars concluded that sanctions could be effective as long as the goals were modest, such as changing aspects of a foreign government's

trade policies. But sanctions put in place to achieve more difficult goals, such as unseating powerful and entrenched regimes, have not performed as well. Moreover, Hufbauer and his colleagues argued that more recent sanctions have been less successful overall.

Numerous scholars, however, have questioned these conclusions. Daniel Drezner has argued that the key to success is the threat of future conflict between the sanctioner and the sanctioned.[32] If sanctions are part of a larger pattern of conflict between states (that is, they are placed after a war or years of disagreement), they are unlikely to work.

Later, Dean Lacy and Emerson Niou challenged the earlier scholars, claiming the sanctions data were incomplete.[33] They argued that potential targets of sanctions, hoping to prevent damage to their economy, may give in to international pressure prior to sanctions taking effect. If unneeded sanctions are never levied, they are not cataloged in the sanctions data set; therefore, scholars did not account for those instances when the threat of sanctions is sufficient to cause change.

Even if a complete data set of sanctions were assembled, though, it would remain difficult to systematically evaluate their success. How, after all, should analysts go about determining whether sanctions

NOT TO BE PUSHED AROUND While addressing the United Nations General Assembly in 1979, Cuban Premier Fidel Castro points his finger in defiance of a U.S. trade embargo against his country.

(continues)

HOW DO WE KNOW? Do Economic Sanctions Work? *(continued)*

achieved their stated goals? On the one hand, states adopt sanctions to force other states to change their behavior in reasonably clear ways, and scholars observe whether target states change their behavior or not. But, sanctions, it bears emphasizing, are often multilateral—that is, they are levied by multiple states, frequently with different goals. This fact makes it all the more difficult to assess whether sanctions have succeeded. Much of the existing scholarship on sanctions has not dealt with this complication. Rather, most scholars continue to use the Hufbauer data, which treats each sanction episode as one unified sender and target, even if multiple states are senders or targets.

Thinking Critically

1. When trying to assess whether sanctions work, how should we compare historical cases when sanctions were merely threatened with cases in which they were actually imposed?

2. Other than sanctions, what foreign policy options are available to the United States when another country behaves in ways that are objectionable? How might we go about evaluating the effectiveness of sanctions vis-à-vis these other options?

The Bottom Line

The debate over the effectiveness of economic sanctions is complex, but it is important. Given the frequent use of sanctions by foreign policy makers, it is crucial to be able to evaluate their effectiveness. The general conclusion is that, under certain circumstances, sanctions can be effective: namely, when the goals are modest, when the sanctions are against an ally, and when the costs to the sanctioned state are very high. Future studies will no doubt further refine our knowledge of the conditions under which economic sanctions are likely to be successful.[34]

---

other things. This "intelligence" crucially facilitates the State Department's diplomatic efforts and the Defense Department's war planning.

Central Intelligence Agency (CIA) the cornerstone of U.S. efforts to gather and analyze data in order to confront America's real and potential enemies.

Since World War II, the **Central Intelligence Agency (CIA)** has had primary responsibility for collecting and analyzing foreign intelligence. The CIA is a fairly large organization, although the exact size of its budget and staff is classified. The popular conception of the CIA depicts the agency's employees as shadowy figures staging cloak-and-dagger operations to overthrow foreign governments. This reputation is not altogether undeserved. In the immediate aftermath of World War II, for instance, the CIA engaged in activities as diverse as influencing election outcomes, sponsoring coups, and assassinating foreign leaders. The CIA's success in these endeavors led to its increased use as an operational foreign policy tool, sometimes replacing traditional military forces.

For the most part, though, CIA employees undertake far more mundane operations: monitoring overseas news for signs of crises, reading and analyzing reports from field offices abroad, briefing executive branch members or Congress on looming threats to American interests, or simply distilling the massive amounts of information it gathers. Historically, the CIA has enjoyed tremendous power and latitude to conduct such operations, yet it is subject to considerable scrutiny and occupies a challenging role. When a surprise event occurs, Congress often holds the CIA accountable for neglecting to anticipate it. If the CIA fails, all Americans see the outcome—a revolution, bombing, or other incident that harms American interests. Yet when the agency succeeds in thwarting secret threats, it receives no public accolades. The CIA must walk a fine line between "crying wolf" and keeping the White House prepared for potential problems.

The CIA, however, is not the only agency charged with collecting and analyzing national security intelligence. The National Security Agency (NSA), formed in 1952, monitors communications coming into and out of the United States. The NSA also specializes in cryptography—the making and breaking of secret codes.[35] For decades, denial of the agency's existence by the U.S. government led many to quip that NSA stood for "No Such Agency." The Departments of State and Defense and each military service branch also include their own intelligence arms. Even the Federal Bureau of Investigation (FBI), which is supposed to focus on domestic security issues, is involved in intelligence. The FBI tracks international terrorism suspects who travel to the United States and keeps tabs on any terrorist group that may attempt to find resources in America.

With so many different agencies pursuing overlapping mandates, the foreign policy bureaucracy is neither as efficient nor as effective as many would like it to be. In the aftermath of September 11, therefore, the Office of National Intelligence (ONI) was created to oversee the many intelligence agencies in the federal government. In theory, the ONI coordinates the analysis of intelligence from *all* sectors of the intelligence community and all Defense Department agencies. In practice, this goal is difficult because each agency attempts to protect its turf (and thereby its budget). Although the Office of National Intelligence has worked hard to coordinate the activities of all these executive branch agencies, it continues to encounter significant resistance.

The **Department of Homeland Security (DHS)** was also created in the aftermath of September 11. Like the ONI, the DHS coordinates the work of agencies involved in preventing and responding to attacks on the United States. The director of homeland security is a Cabinet-level official who, in theory, has the power to coordinate intelligence, analysis, and response to strikes against the United States. Creation of the DHS merged 22 agencies with over 177,000 employees. It combined agencies as varied as the Secret Service, U.S. Customs, the Immigration and Naturalization Service (INS), the Federal Emergency Management Agency (FEMA), and the Coast Guard. It has yet to be seen whether the ONI and the DHS, in combination, can effectively coordinate the efforts of their respective agencies charged with collecting the information needed to protect the country.

Department of Homeland Security (DHS) the agency created in the aftermath of September 11 to coordinate the work of agencies involved in preventing and responding to attacks on the United States.

The Role of Congress in Foreign Affairs

14-5   Understand congressional efforts to shape foreign policy.

Presidents stand front and center in debates about foreign policy. Congress, nonetheless, often appears as a worthy adversary. As we survey the various foreign policy powers of Congress, we will highlight historical examples in which Congress attempted to check presidential influence over foreign policy.

Congress enacts foreign policy statutes.

Congress legislates on a variety of foreign policy topics: weapons programs, foreign aid, environmental standards, and numerous other issues. Sometimes Congress wields influence by crafting legislation. At other times, Congress uses appropriations bills to provide more or less funding than the president has requested for specific projects.

tariff a tax on goods exchanged between nations.

Members of Congress tend to pay special attention to foreign trade, for it has immediate implications for the nation's economic growth, unemployment, and the cost of goods to the average citizen. The key issue in trade policy concerns **tariffs**, which are taxes on goods exchanged between nations. High tariffs tend to discourage trade, whereas lower tariffs tend to promote it.

North American Free Trade Agreement (NAFTA) an agreement, signed in 1992, to reduce tariff and non-tariff barriers to trade and investment among Canada, Mexico, and the United States.

The most significant trade agreement in recent history is the **North American Free Trade Agreement (NAFTA)**. In the early 1990s, Mexican President Carlos Salinas, U.S. President George H. W. Bush, and Canadian Prime Minister Brian Mulroney signed an agreement to reduce barriers to trade and investment among Canada, Mexico, and the United States. In November 1993, NAFTA passed in both the House and the Senate.[36]

How has NAFTA affected the U.S. economy? Some areas of the country benefit from freer trade because their industries produce goods that are export oriented—that is, most of the goods made are sold overseas. Given that free trade agreements also mean that the other countries in the agreement will cut their own tariffs, this step decreases the price of American goods overseas and leads to more sales, which can increase revenue, create jobs, and cut the costs of goods to consumers. Other industries, though, may suffer from free trade. The increased competition inspired by NAFTA means that domestic factories that are less efficient may close, jobs may be lost, and economic growth may falter. Further, different countries and districts have different specializations, which NAFTA also stands to disrupt. Thus, free trade can be seen as good or as bad, depending on the particular district in question and the country with which the United States is signing the agreement.

Thinking Causally How does international trade affect the domestic U.S. economy?

Congress also influences the foreign policy-making process through procedural legislation—legislation that changes how institutions in the executive branch are structured or operate on a day-to-day basis. In addition, Congress occasionally enacts symbolic resolutions that have implications for foreign policy. On March 4, 2010, for instance, the House Foreign Affairs Committee passed a resolution labeling the mass killings of Armenians in Turkey in 1915 as a "genocide." Despite last-minute pressure by the Obama administration, the nonbinding resolution passed the committee by a vote of 23–22. Turkey reacted negatively to the vote, endangering the normalization of relations between the two countries.[37]

Congress retains the power to declare war.

Perhaps no area of congressional–presidential politics has received more attention than the question of who has the ultimate authority to initiate and oversee the conduct of war.[38] One reason for the pitched debate is that the Constitution is vague by design: whereas Congress is given the power to declare war, the president is the commander in chief of the military. Consequently, Congress and the president must share the power to initiate and sustain armed conflict.

Undoubtedly, the president maintains important advantages over Congress in the realm of military policy. For example, Congress can call hearings to gather information about a potential or actual military conflict; however, a president has the NSC, including all the major military and civilian figures, at his beck and call. As a result, the president is able to respond to foreign crises more quickly—and with more information—than Congress.

Congress, however, occasionally challenges the president's war powers. In response to what many critics argued was a failed deployment in Vietnam, Congress passed the War Powers Act in 1973. The law, passed over President Nixon's veto, placed several legal constraints on the executive's ability to initiate international conflict. First, the president must consult with Congress *before* committing armed forces into hostile situations. Second, the president must report to Congress within 48 hours after troops are introduced into an area where hostilities exist or are imminent. Third, and most important, the troops must be withdrawn within 60 days unless Congress authorizes them to stay longer.[39] In practice, though, the act has constrained presidents less than its designers had hoped. Never has the act been used to end a military venture.[40]

> **Thinking Causally** Has the War Powers Act aided Congress's efforts to constrain the president's use of the U.S. military on the international stage?

Congress provides advice and consent on international treaties.

The Senate also has the power to ratify **treaties** signed by the president. There have been several high-profile instances of the Senate rejecting treaties signed by a president, thus dealing a blow to the ongoing conduct of foreign policy. In the most famous instance, the Senate rejection of American involvement in the League of Nations after World War I returned the United States to a course of isolationism for another two decades.

> **treaty** an international agreement in which the United States becomes a party once the president has signed it and two-thirds of the Senate have ratified it.

Rejection is rare, however. In fact, the Senate itself reports that it rejected only 21 of the approximately 1,500 treaties it has considered since 1789.[41] Still, if they are worried about Congress's reaction, presidents can bypass the treaty ratification process by signing an **executive agreement**, which automatically is binding on state signatories.

executive agreement an international agreement in which the United States becomes a party once the president has signed it, without requiring approval from two-thirds of the Senate.

Executive agreements, however, do not allow presidents to do exactly as they please. Congress may pass a law that rescinds an executive agreement, or it may refuse to appropriate the funds needed to implement it. In addition, executive agreements tend to survive for shorter periods of time, as future presidents are free to overturn them unilaterally.

Case Study

Interest Groups Call for Funds to Combat AIDS in Africa

In early 2003, President George W. Bush announced a major effort to fight AIDS overseas. The president's Emergency Plan for AIDS Relief focused on 15 developing countries and called for $15 billion over five years to fund prevention, treatment, and orphan care.[42]

Congress is not always so eager to provide such generous allotments of foreign aid. Only a few years earlier, the Clinton administration fought with Congress to secure just $225 million in global AIDS spending.[43] What explains such a remarkable turn of events? Interest groups, it seems, put pressure on the president and congressional leaders to do something about the spread of AIDS in developing countries. The most prominent of these interest groups, however, consisted of Christian organizations and an especially entrepreneurial rock star.

WALK ON, AFRICA Bono is greeted at a school in South Africa. In May 2006, the Irish rock star toured six African nations in an attempt to draw attention to the issues of HIV and AIDS. In your view, how successful are celebrities in drawing attention to global issues?

In February 2002, Franklin Graham—the son of evangelist Billy Graham and founder of the charity Samaritan's Purse—sponsored the first "international Christian conference on HIV/AIDS." Graham announced that it was his Christian duty to "bring healing, to bring love, to bring compassion" to the sick and dying.[44]

Bono, the lead singer of the Irish rock band U2, subsequently advocated for combating AIDS, framing the issue as a moral imperative for Christians. In a meeting with conservative Senator Jesse Helms (R-SC), Bono pointed out that 2,103 verses of Scripture pertain to the poor, but Jesus mentions judgment only once.[45] Helms was moved by such arguments. In March, the influential senator published an op-ed piece in the *Washington Post* renouncing his lifelong skepticism of foreign aid and arguing for increased federal

---

Case Study   Interest Groups Call for Funds to Combat AIDS in Africa

government spending on programs to combat AIDS abroad.[46]

Other conservative politicians also played instrumental roles. Senator Jeff Sessions (R-AL) held two congressional hearings about the role of unsafe health care in spreading the disease.[47] Senator Bill Frist (R-TN), a physician, co-sponsored a bill offering millions of dollars to prevent mother-to-child transmissions. In addition, key members of the Bush administration embraced the issue.[48] President Bush himself compared AIDS to genocide, implying that fighting it was a moral imperative.[49] Expressing solidarity with his religious constituents, he declared that "everybody has worth, everybody matters, everybody was created by the Almighty."[50]

The president also had strategic reasons for backing the policy. In 2002, Bush highlighted the danger of allowing Africa to become a haven for terrorists.[51] Bush further hoped that AIDS relief would improve America's tarnished international reputation. Among members of the Organization for Economic Cooperation and Development, the United States had ranked last or near last in terms of foreign development aid as a percentage of gross national income (GNI) for many years. Whereas countries such as Denmark, the

Netherlands, Sweden, Norway, and Luxembourg donated around 1 percent of their GNI, the United States contributed only about *one-tenth of* 1 percent.[52]

The administration and its congressional allies brought more than rhetoric to the table. Republican leaders introduced an ambitious five-year, $15 billion plan known as the U.S. Leadership Against HIV/AIDS, Tuberculosis, and Malaria Act of 2003.[53] It aimed to treat 2 million people, provide care for 10 million, and prevent 7 million new infections.[54]

The increase in foreign assistance to combat AIDS shows how the preferences of an interest group can align with broader strategic goals held by the executive or legislative branch. Would AIDS have become a major priority without pressure from religious organizations? Possibly, but this pressure certainly helped.

Thinking Critically

1. What other opportunities are there for religious organizations to join forces with interest groups in order to further influence U.S. commitments of foreign aid?

2. What are some other ways in which religious organizations affect U.S. foreign policy?

Contemporary Policy Challenges

14-6   Assess the policy challenges that face the United States today.

The United States continues to face extraordinary domestic and foreign policy challenges. This section highlights three contemporary ones: how to protect Social Security over the long term; how to reduce the threats of a North Korean nuclear program; and how to balance the costs and benefits of free trade.

The future of Social Security is uncertain.

Changing demographics in the United States have introduced new challenges to the Social Security system. Recall that the program critically depends on the ability of today's workers to fund the payments to today's elderly. The balance of workers to beneficiaries, however, has changed markedly over time. When the Social Security Act went into effect, roughly nine workers supported each elderly beneficiary. Today, just over three workers support each beneficiary.

By some projections, this number will drop to only two workers per beneficiary by 2030.[55]

Because workers dramatically outnumbered the elderly for so long, Social Security built up substantial reserves, known as Old-Age, Survivors, and Disability Insurance (OASDI) trust funds. Figure 14-2 shows these reserves will soon begin to fall. By some economists' projections, Social Security expenditures will exceed both receipts and available reserves by as soon as 2037. The effects of a large Baby Boom generation entering retirement, cost of living adustments (COLAs) that mandate higher payments each year, and longer life expectancies are straining the Social Security system.[56]

What can the government do about these dwindling reserves? For starters, it can reduce the size of Social Security benefits doled out each year. To do this, it could raise the age at which individuals qualify for benefits, thereby reducing the number of beneficiaries. Alternatively, the government could decrease the benefits that it gives to each individual. Neither option, though, is especially attractive. Having paid into the Social Security system throughout their working lives, the elderly rightly expect to receive their due. And should they feel slighted, they will likely punish the offending politicians in the next election.

Although cutting Social Security benefits is difficult, it is not impossible. In 1983, after several years of stagflation—periods of high unemployment and high inflation—the federal government decided to reduce Social Security outlays. To ensure the program's solvency, the government for the first time began to tax Social Security benefits, increased the eligible age for full benefits

FIGURE 14-2 Social Security Reserves Are Predicted to Decline.

Based on the current policy and the best available information about the size of the contributing workforce and the number of retired individuals, Social Security reserves will continue to increase until approximately 2028, at which time they will begin to rapidly decline.

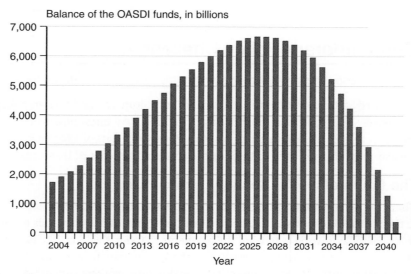

Balance of the OASDI funds, in billions

Source: Sidor, Gary. "Social Security: Brief Facts and Statistics" CRS Report for Congress. January 26, 2006. price.house.gov/issues/uploadedfiles/socialsecurity2.pdf.

from 65 to 67, and added federal civil employees to the workers who could contribute to Social Security.

Another way to protect Social Security would be to increase taxes. Historically, this has been the approach most commonly adopted. When the Social Security Act was enacted in 1935, the Social Security tax was set at 1 percent of the first $3,000 earned. Over the next 65 years, both the tax rate and the maximum taxable earning were increased 20 times. In 2011, the rate for individuals who are not self-employed was 4.2 percent of the first $106,800 earned.[57] Of course, there are political costs associated with increasing taxes.

Finally, a number of politicians have recommended the adoption of private investment accounts. Rather than depositing funds into a general reserve account, which typically receives a low yield, workers under this scheme could invest a portion of their Social Security contributions into government-approved stocks and bonds. This reform represented the core innovation in President George W. Bush's 2005 effort to shore up Social Security. Ultimately, however, Bush's plan flopped. Worried about the risks of private investments, members of Congress proved unwilling to fundamentally restructure the largest and most popular domestic social program.

Diplomatic efforts to halt North Korea's nuclear program have not proceeded smoothly.

On August 6, 1945, during World War II, a U.S. military plane dropped an atomic bomb code-named "Little Boy" that leveled the Japanese city of Hiroshima, killing tens of thousands almost immediately. Three days later, another U.S. plane dropped the atomic bomb code-named "Fat Man" on the Japanese city of Nagasaki. The United States thereby became the first—and to date the only—country to use a nuclear weapon against another country. The demonstration of such weapons' devastating strength, coupled with the crystalizing Cold War, fueled an international race for nuclear weapons. In 1949, the Soviet Union tested bombs of its own. By 1964, the United Kingdom, France, and China had acquired nuclear capabilities. Developments in rocket science made the specter of nuclear-armed states, able to project their power to far corners of the globe, much more real. And U.S. foreign policy needed to contend not only with the ramifications of America's own nuclear capability but also with that of its allies and rivals.

Some observers saw this dilemma as a benefit for U.S. foreign policy. Perhaps the overwhelming might of nuclear weapons actually made them integral for *deterring* open hostilities between the East and West. By pursuing certain tactics—such as dividing up arsenals and placing warheads in underground facilities—nuclear powers could maintain second-strike capabilities. Thus, states would think hard about offensive moves, for while the instigator might wreak havoc on its enemy, it would bring similarly devastating retaliation upon itself.

Thinking Causally Does the proliferation of nuclear weapons stabilize relations between nations?

This notion of "mutually assured destruction" may be one of the key reasons why the Cold War remained cold.

Diplomatic efforts to stem the proliferation of nuclear weapons were codified in the Nuclear Non-Proliferation Treaty, which opened for signature in 1968. The United States, the United Kingdom, and the Soviet Union signed almost immediately. The treaty stipulates that nonnuclear countries will not seek nuclear capabilities, pre-existing nuclear states will not facilitate proliferation to more states, countries can acquire nuclear technology for peaceful uses such as energy, and all will work toward a somewhat vague disarmament goal.[58]

Still, considerable uncertainties persisted. Miscalculations, laxity, or accidents in *any* of the five nuclear-capable states promised dire consequences. Moreover, although some nonnuclear countries called for total disarmament, others were eager to obtain nuclear power for themselves. During the 1970s, 1980s, and 1990s, countries such as South Africa, Libya, and Iraq launched, and then subsequently abandoned, efforts to acquire nuclear weapons. More recently, other countries, such as Iran and North Korea, have been accused of concealing weapons development behind civilian energy programs.

North Korea represents a key challenge for U.S. efforts to hinder the proliferation of nuclear weapons. Since the Korean War, relations between the United States and North Korea have fluctuated between strained and nonexistent. In the aftermath of the terrorist attacks of September 11, 2001, new intelligence indicated that North Korea was still pursuing a nuclear weapons program. In his 2002 State of the Union Address, President Bush denounced the developments and designated North Korea (as well as Iraq and Iran, which also were suspected of developing nuclear weapons) as a lynchpin of the "Axis of Evil."[59] A year later, North Korea announced its withdrawal from the Nuclear Non-Proliferation Treaty, declaring that it absolutely needed nuclear weapons to protect itself from U.S. "hostility."[60]

In 2007, North Korea detonated a nuclear bomb in an underground test. The following year, in return for fuel oil, North Korea agreed to dismantle its facilities and disclose its nuclear programs, and President Bush held out the prospect of open trade and political engagement if North Korea

TENSIONS RISE AGAIN

On July 2, 2009, North Korea test launched two short-range missiles, further heightening tensions in the region. Here, two South Koreans watch a televised broadcast of the event.

upheld its obligations under the agreement. Further signs of progress surfaced in June 2008, as the cooling tower at the country's main nuclear weapons plant was destroyed. President Bush called the event "a moment of opportunity for North Korea," and presumably the United States as well.

Tensions between North Korea and the United States resurfaced in April 2009, however, when North Korea test-launched a long-range ballistic missile. But, the United States failed to rally the United Nations to punish North Korea for its actions. In May 2009, news broke that North Korea successfully tested its second nuclear weapon. This time, the international response was much stronger as many nations condemned the test. President Obama used the event to strengthen ties with South Korea and other international allies. The United Nations Security Council tightened sanctions on North Korea, and Japan enacted additional economic sanctions on exports to the country.[61] If past is prologue, the rest of Obama's presidency is likely to witness a continued rocky relationship between North Korea and the United States.

Domestic lobbying groups push for protective tariffs.

The United States has been a vocal advocate of "free trade," which involves lowering or eliminating tariffs and other mechanisms that impede the movement of goods and services. In his 1776 book *The Wealth of Nations*, the economist Adam Smith argued that countries should export according to their relative advantage. Thus, if Britain was the lowest-cost producer of wool while Portugal was the lowest-cost producer of port wine, then the former should export wool in exchange for the latter's wine, and both parties would be better for it.

As Smith makes clear, free trade has a powerful economic justification. But political realities complicate matters. Some sectors, most obviously weapons producers, raise important security concerns that can prompt governments to entertain less-efficient domestic production in order to avoid such dependence.[62] Furthermore, even when gains from trade outweigh losses, those gains and losses may not be equally distributed across different populations. And when politically connected groups sustain significant losses, they make sure that politicians take notice.

As a result, even countries that advocate free trade may pursue selective **protectionism**—that is, the imposition of specific tariffs to protect the interests of domestic industries. The case of U.S. steel tariffs illustrates this point well. In the late 1990s, a number of countries in Asia and elsewhere suffered financial crises that diminished the value of their currencies. The devaluation made exports from those countries relatively cheap and encouraged companies to sell their products quickly before their home currencies fell even further. Many tried to sell to the world's largest economy, the United States, which relies on steel to manufacture all sorts of products. This abundance caused a drop in steel prices, benefiting steel consumers

protectionism the practice of imposing selective tariffs on trade in an effort to protect specific domestic industries from international competition.

but hurting U.S. steel producers. Labor (represented by unions) and capital (represented by producers' associations) in the steel sector teamed up to petition the Clinton administration for help.[63] President Clinton, however, remained unconvinced that the steel producers had a strong legal case, and he declined to take action.

In the spring of 2001, just months after George W. Bush took office, steel lobbyists launched another political offensive.[64] This time, the lobbyists met with greater success. The Bush administration anticipated political payoffs from siding with steel producers, and President Bush initiated a move that gave the International Trade Commission, an independent American panel, six months to investigate the allegations and provide recommendations to the White House.[65] The International Trade Commission, having determined that imports had injured the U.S. industry, recommended that the president impose import quotas, as well as tariffs ranging from 15 to 40 percent.[66]

In March 2002, President Bush finally decided on three-year tariffs as high as 30 percent (depending on the type of steel) against countries such as Japan, China, South Korea, Russia, Ukraine, and Brazil. He asserted that the action was within the World Trade Organization (WTO) allowance for temporary "safeguard provisions" and exempted many developing nations, in addition to NAFTA trading partners Canada and Mexico.[67]

Almost immediately, China—the world's largest steel producer—filed a complaint with the World Trade Organization. Then the European Union, Japan, and China threatened to impose tariffs on other U.S. goods without waiting for the WTO's ruling, accurately pointing out that U.S. steel imports had in fact declined rather than risen over the past three years. Russia hinted that the tariffs would reduce its willingness to cooperate in the war on terror.[68]

In November 2002, the WTO rejected the U.S. government's protectionist policies, authorizing other countries to impose countervailing tariffs as punishment. The following month, facing a full-blown trade war, Bush repealed the tariffs 15 months before their scheduled expiration.[69]

This episode reveals important lessons about the politics of trade. Despite the economic rationality of free trade, political realities may lead to selective protectionism. As Gary Hufbauer of the Institute for International Economics points out, a free trade president who seeks quotas and tariffs may be uncharacteristic, "but it's a way of trying to keep moving on the bigger goal while dealing with the truly squeaky wheels—and steel is truly a squeaky wheel."[70]

Chapter Summary

In this chapter you have learned to:

14-1   Assess efforts by the federal government to manage the domestic economy.

The government regularly monitors the health of the economy, paying particular attention to unemployment rates, inflation trends, and the gross domestic product. Depending on how well the economy is performing, the government may alter fiscal or monetary policy. Some economists recommend that the government intervene in the economy as little as possible, so as to allow markets to adjust to new economic realities.

14-2   Trace the development of the largest federal social program, which assists the elderly.

As the backbone of the modern welfare state, Social Security provides a steady income stream to the nation's elderly. During their working lives, individuals pay into the system with the expectation that they can draw from it when they retire. Over the past 70 years, the number of people paying into the system has increased markedly, but so has the amount of the benefits paid out.

14-3   Describe federal health care programs.

More money is spent on health care than any other social program. Run exclusively by the federal government, Medicare provides medical insurance to the elderly. A joint venture of federal and state governments, Medicaid assists the poor and disabled. In 2010, Congress passed and President Barack Obama signed the Patient Protection and Affordable Care Act, the most important health care bill to pass in the last half-century.

14-4   Explain the powers of the president to direct foreign policy, and identify the executive agencies that support the president.

As commander in chief, chief diplomat, and chief administrator, the president has extraordinary powers and responsibilities in foreign policy. Moreover, a vast network of agencies and departments assists the president in formulating and implementing his foreign policy agenda.

14-5   Understand congressional efforts to shape foreign policy.

Congress has a variety of means at its disposal to influence U.S. foreign policy-making. By enacting statutes, retaining the power to declare war, confirming bureaucratic nominees, and ratifying treaties, Congress can influence U.S. foreign policy in important ways.

14-6   Assess the policy challenges that face the United States today.

Presidents, officials in the State and Defense Departments, Congress, a wide variety of interest groups, and the courts all participate in ongoing domestic and foreign policy debates. Issues range from the future of Social Security, to the spread of nuclear weapons, to the protection of U.S. industries against foreign competition.

CHAPTER TEST

1. What role for government intervention in the economy do advocates of fiscal and monetary policy envision?

2. What is the difference between the national deficit and national debt?

3. Why are at least some political analysts worried about the future of Social Security?

4. What were the most significant elements of the health care reforms enacted into law in March 2010?

5. How do the responsibilities of the State Department and Defense Department differ from one another?

6. Short of military action, what kinds of things can the United States do in response to objectionable behavior by other nations?

7. In the aftermath of the September 11 terrorist attacks, what kinds of changes were made to the U.S. foreign policy bureaucracy?

8. What is the difference between a treaty and an executive agreement?

9. How can Congress influence the conduct of U.S. military policy?

10. In what ways does U.S. trade policy pit the interests of consumers and U.S. industries against one another?

MyPoliSciLab® DOMESTIC AND FOREIGN POLICY
Apply what you learned in this chapter on MyPoliSciLab.

Read on mypoliscilab.com

eText: Chapter 14

Study and Review on mypoliscilab.com

Pre-Test
Post-Test
Chapter Exam
Flashcards

Watch on mypoliscilab.com

Video: Economic Policy Debate at the G20
Video: America's Aging Population
Video: Health Care Plan
Video: Sanctions on Iran

Explore on mypoliscilab.com

Comparative: Comparing Social Welfare Systems
Comparative: Comparing Foreign and Security Policy
Simulation: Making Economic Policy
Simulation: You Are President John F. Kennedy
Timeline: The Evolution of Social Welfare Policy
Timeline: The Growth of the Budget and Federal Spending
Visual Literacy: Where the Money Goes

KEY TERMS

Central Intelligence Agency (CIA), p. 410
Defense Department, p. 407
deficit, p. 401
Department of Homeland Security (DHS), p. 411
diplomacy, p. 407
entitlements, p. 403
executive agreement, p. 414
fiscal policy, p. 401

foreign policy, p. 406
gross domestic product (GDP), p. 400
laissez-faire economics, p. 401
Medicaid, p. 404
Medicare, p. 404
monetary policy, p. 401
National Security Council (NSC), p. 407
North American Free Trade Agreement (NAFTA), p. 412

protectionism, p. 419
public debt, p. 401
recession, p. 402
Social Security Act, p. 402
State Department, p. 407
tariff, p. 412
treaty, p. 413

SUGGESTED READINGS

Nancy Altman. 2005. *The Battle for Social Security: From FDR's Vision to Bush's Gamble*. Hoboken, NJ: Wiley. Reviews the history of Social Security while offering a spirited critique of recent efforts to privatize the program.

Staff of the Washington Post. 2010. *Landmark: The Inside Story of America's New Health Care Law and What It Means for Us All*. New York: Public Affairs. A blow-by-blow account of the legislative history and contents of the single most important health care bill to pass in nearly a half century.

Stephen Hook and John Spanier. 2007. *American Foreign Policy Since World War II*, 17th ed. Washington, DC: CQ Press. A classic book tracing the major phases of American foreign policy since World War II through September 11, with special attention to the political process and context in which decisions were made.

William Howell and Jon Pevehouse. 2007. *While Dangers Gather: Congressional Checks on Presidential War Powers*. Princeton, NJ: Princeton University Press. Examines the proposition that the president has become all-powerful in formation of policies concerning use of military force, and shows that Congress has a definite, if circumscribed, influence over decisions involving troop deployments abroad.

Amy Zegart. 1999. *Flawed by Design: The Evolution of the CIA, JCS, and NSC*. Stanford, CA: Stanford University Press. Reviews the creation and evolution of several executive branch agencies, and argues that pressures from Congress, the White House, and the voting public have undermined effective operation of certain security institutions, while bureaucratic politics limit the sharing of expertise and coordination of actions across agencies.

SUGGESTED WEBSITES

SOCIAL SECURITY ADMINISTRATION
www.ssa.gov

This organization governs the single largest entitlement program run by the federal government.

BOARD OF GOVERNORS OF THE FEDERAL RESERVE SYSTEM
www.federalreserve.gov

This agency oversees U.S. monetary policy.

ECONOMICS AND STATISTICS ADMINISTRATION
www.economicindicators.gov

A vast array of statistics on the state of the U.S. economy is available at this site.

STATE DEPARTMENT
www.state.gov

Assumes primary responsibility for U.S. diplomatic relations with foreign countries.

SENATE FOREIGN RELATIONS COMMITTEE
www.foreign.senate.gov

Primarily responsible for overseeing the foreign policy apparatus within the executive branch.

APPENDIX 1

Annotated Declaration of Independence[*]

In Congress, July 4, 1776
The Unanimous Declaration of the Thirteen United States of America

The Declaration of Independence marked the break of the 13 American colonies away from Great Britain. After decades of disputes, the colonists announced to the world the beginning of a new country. The chief goals of the Declaration were to announce and provide the reasons for separating the colonies from the British Empire and to cement support in the colonies for independence. Ensuring this support was not an easy task. Historians' estimates place the proportion of colonists returning to Britain following the start of the Revolutionary War as somewhere between one-quarter and one-third. The writers of the Declaration sought to build a sense of national identity among the colonists as Americans. The document has four sections: a preamble, a statement of principles that should guide a political system, a list of grievances against the British government, and a statement that the states are now independent.

The preamble is the introduction to the Declaration. The writers explain that they wish to detail why the colonies are separating from Britain.

When in the Course of human events it becomes necessary for one people to dissolve the political bands which have connected them with another, and to assume among the powers of the earth, the separate and equal station to which the Laws of Nature and of Nature's God entitle them, a decent respect to the opinions of mankind requires that they should declare the causes which impel them to the separation.

The Declaration in its second section provides a statement of the principles that should guide a political system. In this section, the Declaration quickly makes the claim that some rights are natural, they are inherent in people and cannot be given away (they are "unalien-

able"); that there is a social contract between the governed and the rulers (governments derive their power from the peoples' consent); that the people are sovereign, have a right to revolution, and have the right to self determination—to create a new system that reflects their principles when the contract is broken. The authors then explain that the colonists were patient and suffered many abuses before taking the step of independence.

We hold these truths to be self-evident, that all men are created equal, that they are endowed by their Creator with certain unalienable Rights, that among these are Life, Liberty and the pursuit of Happiness.—That to secure these rights, Governments are instituted among Men, deriving their just powers from the consent of the governed,—That whenever any Form of Government becomes destructive of these ends, it is the Right of the People to alter or to abolish it, and to institute new Government, laying its foundation on such principles and organizing its powers in such form, as to them shall seem most likely to effect their Safety and Happiness. Prudence, indeed, will dictate that Governments long established should not be changed for light and transient causes; and accordingly all experience hath shewn that mankind are more disposed to suffer, while evils are sufferable, than to right themselves by abolishing the forms to which they are accustomed. But when a long train of abuses and usurpations, pursuing invariably the same Object evinces a design to reduce them under absolute Despotism, it is their right, it is their duty, to throw off such Government, and to provide new Guards for their future security.

Such has been the patient sufferance of these Colonies; and such is now the necessity which constrains them to alter their former Systems of Government. The history of the present King of Great Britain is a history of repeated injuries and usurpations, all having in direct object the establishment of an absolute Tyranny over these States. To prove this, let Facts be submitted to a candid world.

The Declaration now provides a lengthy list of grievances against the British king and Parliament.

---

[*]Annotations by the authors. This text retains the spelling, capitalization, and punctuation of the original.

The charges it lodges are serious. The king has trivialized any notion that the consent of the governed should be taken into account. He has interfered with all branches of government in the colonies, and even shut some down. He has elevated military power over the people's power. Despite the colonists' attempts to manage their affairs, he has frequently revised or overthrown their decisions. The theme that legitimate government must be based on the consent of the governed runs strongly throughout the 27 charges. The first 12 charges are directed toward the king.

He has refused his Assent to Laws, the most wholesome and necessary for the public good.

He has forbidden his Governors to pass Laws of immediate and pressing importance, unless suspended in their operation till his Assent should be obtained; and when so suspended, he has utterly neglected to attend to them.

He has refused to pass other Laws for the accommodation of large districts of people, unless those people would relinquish the right of Representation in the Legislature, a right inestimable to them and formidable to tyrants only.

He has called together legislative bodies at places unusual, uncomfortable, and distant from the depository of their Public Records, for the sole purpose of fatiguing them into compliance with his measures.

He has dissolved Representative Houses repeatedly, for opposing with manly firmness his invasions on the rights of the people.

He has refused for a long time, after such dissolutions, to cause others to be elected; whereby the Legislative Powers, incapable of Annihilation, have returned to the People at large for their exercise; the State remaining in the mean time exposed to all the dangers of invasion from without, and convulsions within.

He has endeavored to prevent the population of these States; for that purpose obstructing the Laws for Naturalization of Foreigners; refusing to pass others to encourage their migration hither, and raising the conditions of new Appropriations of Lands.

He has obstructed the Administration of Justice, by refusing his Assent to Laws for establishing Judiciary powers.

He has made Judges dependent on his Will alone, for the tenure of their offices, and the amount and payment of their salaries.

He has erected a multitude of New Offices, and sent hither swarms of Officers to harass our people, and eat out their substance.

He has kept among us, in times of peace, Standing Armies without the Consent of our legislatures.

He has affected to render the Military independent of and superior to the Civil power.

The next set of charges are leveled against the king and Parliament ("he has combined with others"). The first paragraph establishes the colonists' view that Parliament's actions are not binding on the colonies. "Their acts of pretended legislation" refers to laws passed by Parliament, to which the king gave his approval. The colonists had no representation in Parliament and, since government depends on the consent of the governed, any actions of Parliament are but "pretend" legislation. The long list of complaints includes, among many others, the famous charge that the king and Parliament imposed taxes on the colonists without their consent. "No taxation without representation" soon became a symbolic reference for generations of Americans to understand the principles that led to Revolution.

He has combined with others to subject us to a jurisdiction foreign to our constitution, and unacknowledged by our laws; giving his Assent to their Acts of pretended Legislation:

For quartering large bodies of armed troops among us:

For protecting them, by a mock Trial, from punishment for any Murders which they should commit on the Inhabitants of these States:

For cutting off our Trade with all parts of the world:

For imposing Taxes on us without our Consent:

For depriving us in many cases, of the benefits of Trial by Jury:

For transporting us beyond Seas to be tried for pretended offences:

For abolishing the free System of English Laws in a neighboring Province, establishing therein an Arbitrary government, and enlarging its Boundaries so as to render it at once an example and fit instrument for introducing the same absolute rule into these Colonies:

For taking away our Charters, abolishing our most valuable Laws, and altering fundamentally the Forms of our Governments:

For suspending our own Legislatures, and declaring themselves invested with power to legislate for us in all cases whatsoever.

The next five charges address the king's conduct of war and violence against the colonists.

He has abdicated Government here, by declaring us out of his Protection and waging War against us.

He has plundered our seas, ravaged our Coasts, burnt our towns, and destroyed the lives of our people.

He is at this time transporting large Armies of foreign Mercenaries to compleat the works of death, desolation and tyranny, already begun with circumstances of Cruelty & perfidy scarcely paralleled in the most barbarous ages, and totally unworthy the Head of a civilized nation.

He has constrained our fellow Citizens taken Captive on the high Seas to bear Arms against their Country, to become the executioners of their friends and Brethren, or to fall themselves by their Hands.

He has excited domestic insurrections amongst us, and has endeavored to bring on the inhabitants of our frontiers, the merciless Indian Savages, whose known rule of warfare, is an undistinguished destruction of all ages, sexes and conditions.

> The writers end the section on grievances by noting that the colonists have tried to make the arrangement with Britain work, but they have been rejected. They have petitioned the king and conveyed to their fellow Britons the unique nature of the colonies. The authors note that neither the British ruler nor the British people have been responsive to these pleas.

In every stage of these Oppressions We have Petitioned for Redress in the most humble terms: Our repeated Petitions have been answered only by repeated injury. A Prince, whose character is thus marked by every act which may define a Tyrant, is unfit to be the ruler of a free people.

Nor have We been wanting in attention to our British brethren. We have warned them from time to time of attempts by their legislature to extend an unwarrantable jurisdiction over us. We have reminded them of the circumstances of our emigration and settlement here. We have appealed to their native justice and magnanimity, and we have conjured them by the ties of our common kindred to disavow these usurpations, which would inevitably interrupt our connections and correspondence. They too have been deaf to the voice of justice and consanguinity. We must, therefore, acquiesce in the necessity, which de-nounces our Separation, and hold them, as we hold the rest of mankind, Enemies in War, in Peace Friends.

> The Declaration concludes in its fourth section by establishing American independence. On behalf of the American people and as representatives of the United States, the writers declare the colonies are now free and independent states, with all political connection between them and Great Britain dissolved. They pledge to each other to join in the battle to achieve independence.

We, therefore, the Representatives of the United States of America, in General Congress, Assembled, appealing to the Supreme Judge of the world for the rectitude of our intentions, do, in the Name, and by Authority of the good People of these Colonies, solemnly publish and declare, That these United Colonies are, and of Right ought to be Free and Independent States; that they are Absolved from all Allegiance to the British Crown, and that all political connection between them and the State of Great Britain, is and ought to be totally dissolved; and that as Free and Independent States, they have full Power to levy War, conclude Peace, contract Alliances, establish Commerce, and to do all other Acts and Things which Independent States may of right do. And for the support of this Declaration, with a firm reliance on the protection of divine Providence, we mutually pledge to each other our Lives, our Fortunes and our sacred Honor.

JOHN HANCOCK,
President of the Congress

NEW HAMPSHIRE
Josiah Bartlett,
Wm. Whipple,
Matthew Thornton.

MASSACHUSETTS BAY
Saml. Adams,
John Adams,
Robt. Treat Paine,
Elbridge Gerry.

RHODE ISLAND
Step. Hopkins,
William Ellery.

CONNECTICUT
Roger Sherman,
Samuel Huntington,
Wm. Williams,
Oliver Wolcott.

NEW YORK
Wm. Floyd,
Phil. Livingston,
Frans. Lewis,
Lewis Morris.

NEW JERSEY
Richd. Stockton,
Jno. Witherspoon,
Fras. Hopkinson,
John Hart,
Abra. Clark.

PENNSYLVANIA
Robt. Morris,
Benjamin Rush,
Benjamin Franklin,
John Morton,
Geo. Clymer,
Jas. Smith,
Geo. Taylor,
James Wilson,
Geo. Ross.

DELAWARE
Caesar Rodney,
Geo. Read,
Tho. M'kean.

MARYLAND
Samuel Chase,
Wm. Paca,
Thos. Stone,
Charles Caroll of Carrollton.

VIRGINIA
George Wythe,
Richard Henry Lee,
Th. Jefferson,
Benjamin Harrison,
Thos. Nelson, Jr.,
Francis Lightfoot Lee,
Carter Braxton.

NORTH CAROLINA
Wm. Hooper,
Joseph Hewes,
John Penn.

SOUTH CAROLINA
Edward Rutledge,
Thos. Heyward, Jr.,
Thomas Lynch, Jr.,
Arthur Middleton.

GEORGIA
Button Gwinnett,
Lyman Hall,
Geo. Walton.

The Constitution of the United States of America[*]

The Preamble

We the People of the United States, in Order to form a more perfect Union, establish Justice, insure domestic Tranquility, provide for the common defense, promote the general Welfare, and secure the Blessings of Liberty to ourselves and our Posterity, do ordain and establish this Constitution for the United States of America.

> "We, the people." Three simple words, yet of profound importance and contentious origin. Every national government in the world at the time of the Constitutional Convention was some type of monarchy in which sovereign power flowed from the top. The Framers of the Constitution rejected monarchy as a form of government and proposed instead a republic, which would draw its sovereignty from the people.
>
> The remainder of the preamble describes the generic functions of government.

Article I—The Legislative Article
Legislative Power

> The very first article in the Constitution established the legislative branch of the new national government. Why did the Framers start with the legislative branch instead of the executive branch? Under the Articles of Confederation, the legislature was the only functional instrument of government. The Framers believed it was the most important component of a government, where sovereignty rested directly or indirectly with the people.

Section 1 All legislative Powers herein granted shall be vested in a Congress of the United States, which shall consist of a Senate and House of Representatives.

> Section 1 established a bicameral (two-chamber) legislature including an upper (Senate) and lower (House of Representatives) chamber.

House of Representatives: Composition; Qualifications; Apportionment; Impeachment Power

Section 2 *Clause 1.* The House of Representatives shall be composed of Members chosen every second Year by the People of the several States, and the Electors in each State shall have the Qualifications requisite for Electors of the most numerous Branch of the State Legislature.

> This section sets the term of office for House members (2 years) and indicates that those voting for Congress will have the same qualifications as those voting for the state legislatures. Originally, states limited voters to white property owners. Some states had religious disqualifications, such as prohibition of voting by Catholics or Jews. Most property and religious qualifications for voting were removed by the 1840s, but race and gender restrictions remained until the 15th and 19th Amendments were passed.

Clause 2. No Person shall be a Representative who shall not have attained to the Age of twenty five Years, and been seven Years a Citizen of the United States, and who shall not, when elected, be an inhabitant of that State in which he shall be chosen.

> This section sets forth the basic qualifications of a representative: at least 25 years of age, a U.S. citizen for at least 7 years, and a resident of a state. Note that the Constitution does not require a person to be a resident of the district he or she represents, nor does it require that each district be represented by only one representative. Despite some earlier legislative actions, it was not until 1967 that states with more than one representative were prohibited from electing the representatives at large (representing the entire state) or electing multiple representatives in a district.

[*]Annotations by the authors, based on annotations originally written by James Corey, previously of High Point University.

Clause 2 does not specify how many terms a representative can serve in Congress. Some states passed legislation to limit the terms of their U.S. representatives. Because of the specificity of the qualifications for office, however, the Supreme Court ruled in *U.S. Term Limits, Inc. v. Thornton* (1995) that term limits for U.S. legislators could not be imposed by any state but would instead require a constitutional amendment.

Clause 3. Representatives and direct Taxes[1] shall be apportioned among the several States which may be included within this Union, according to their respective Numbers, which shall be determined by adding to the whole Number of free Persons, including those bound to Service for a Term of Years, and excluding Indians not taxed, three fifths of all other Persons.[2] The actual Enumeration shall be made within three Years after the first Meeting of the Congress of the United States, and within every subsequent Term of ten Years in such Manner as they shall by Law direct. The Number of Representatives shall not exceed one for every thirty Thousand, but each State shall have at Least one Representative, and until such enumeration shall be made, the State of New Hampshire shall be entitled to chuse three, Massachusetts eight, Rhode Island and Providence Plantations one, Connecticut five, New York six, New Jersey four, Pennsylvania eight, Delaware one, Maryland six, Virginia ten, North Carolina five, South Carolina five, and Georgia three.

This clause contains the Three-fifths Compromise in which 60 percent of a state's number of slaves was counted to compute a state's population for congressional representation purposes. This clause also addresses the question of congressional reapportionment every 10 years, which requires a census. Since the 1911 Reapportionment Act, the size of the House of Representatives has been set at 435. This is the designated size that is reapportioned every 10 years. Based on changes of population, some states gain and some states lose representatives. This clause also provides that every state, regardless of population, will have at least one representative. Currently, seven states have only one representative.

Clause 4. When vacancies happen in the Representation from any State, the Executive Authority thereof shall issue Writs of Election to fill such Vacancies.

This clause provides a procedure for replacing a U.S. representative in the case of death, resignation, or expulsion from the House. Generally, if less than half a term is left, the governor will appoint a successor. If more than half a term is remaining, most states require a special election to fill the vacancy.

Clause 5. The House of Representatives shall chuse their Speaker and other Officers, and shall have the sole Power of Impeachment.

Only one officer of the House is specified—the Speaker. All other officers are decided by the House. This clause also gives the House authority for impeachments (accusations) against officials of the executive and judicial branches. Thus, it is the House that determines whether there are charges against the official that are worthy of trial in the Senate.

Senate Composition: Qualifications, Impeachment Trials

Section 3 *Clause 1.* The Senate of the United States shall be composed of two Senators from each State, chosen by the Legislature thereof,[3] for six Years and each Senator shall have one Vote.

This clause treats each state equally—all have two senators each. Originally, senators were chosen by state legislatures, but since the ratification of the Seventeenth Amendment, they are now elected by popular vote. This clause also establishes the term of a senator—6 years—to be three times longer than that of a House member.

Clause 2. Immediately after they shall be assembled in Consequence of the first Election, they shall be divided as equally as may be into three Classes. The Seats of the Senators of the first Class shall be vacated at the Expiration of the second Year, of the second Class at the Expiration of the fourth Year, and of the third Class at the Expiration of the sixth Year, so that one third may be chosen every second Year and if Vacancies happen by Resignation, or otherwise, during the Recess of the Legislature of any State, the Executive thereof may make temporary Appointments until the next Meeting of the Legislature which shall then fill such Vacancies.[4]

This clause provides that one-third of the Senate will be elected every two years. Senate vacancies are

---

[1]Modified by the Sixteenth Amendment.
[2]Replaced by Section 2, Fourteenth Amendment.

[3]Repealed by the Seventeenth Amendment.
[4]Modified by the Seventeenth Amendment.

filled similar to those in the House—either by appointment by the governor or by a special election.

Clause 3. No person shall be a Senator who shall not have attained to the Age of thirty Years, and been nine Years a Citizen of the United States, and who shall not, when elected, be an Inhabitant of that State for which he shall be chosen.

> This clause sets forth the qualifications for U.S. senator: at least 30 years old, a U.S. citizen for at least nine years, and a resident of the state he or she represents.

Clause 4. The Vice President of the United States shall be President of the Senate but shall have no Vote, unless they be equally divided.

> The only constitutional duty of the vice president is specified in this clause—president of the Senate. The Senate president has a vote only when there is a tie vote in the Senate; then the vice president's vote breaks the tie.

Clause 5. The Senate shall chuse their other Officers, and also a President pro tempore, in the Absence of the Vice President, or when he shall exercise the Office of President of the United States.

> One official office in the U.S. Senate is specified—temporary president, who fills in during the vice president's absence (which is normally the case). All other Senate officers are designated and selected by the Senate.

Clause 6. The Senate shall have the sole Power to try all Impeachments. When sitting for that Purpose, they shall be on Oath or Affirmation. When the President of the United States is tried, the Chief Justice shall preside. And no Person shall be convicted without the Concurrence of two thirds of the Members present.

Judgment in Cases of impeachment shall not extend further than to removal from Office, and disqualification to hold and enjoy any Office of honor, Trust or Profit under the United States, but the Party convicted shall nevertheless be liable and subject to Indictment, Trial, Judgment and Punishment according to Law.

> The Senate acts as a trial court for impeached federal officials. If the accused is the president, the chief justice of the U.S. Supreme Court presides. Otherwise, the vice president normally presides. Conviction of the

charges requires a two-thirds majority vote of those senators present at the time of the vote. Conviction results in the federal official's removal from office and, at the Senate's discretion, disqualification to hold any other appointed federal office. Removal from office does not bar further prosecution under applicable criminal or civil laws.

Congressional Elections: Times, Places, Manner

Section 4 The Times, Places and Manner of holding Elections for Senators and Representatives, shall be prescribed in each State by the Legislature thereof, but the Congress may at any time by Law make or alter such Regulations, except as to the Places of chusing Senators.

The Congress shall assemble at least once in every Year, and such Meeting shall be on the first Monday in December, unless they shall by Law appoint a different Day.[5]

> The states determine the place and manner of electing representatives and senators, but Congress has the right to make or change these laws or regulations, except for the election sites. Congress is required to meet annually, and now, by law, annual meetings begin in January.

Powers and Duties of the Houses

Section 5 *Clause 1.* Each House shall be the Judge of the Elections, Returns and Qualifications of its own Members, and a Majority of each shall constitute a Quorum to do Business, but a smaller Number may adjourn from day to day, and may be authorized to compel the Attendance of absent Members, in such Manner, and under the Penalties as each House may provide.

> This clause enables each legislative branch to make its own rules. Normally, to take a vote, a quorum is necessary. But if no votes are scheduled, fewer than a quorum can convene a session.

Clause 2. Each House may determine the Rules of its Proceedings, punish its Members for disorderly Behaviour, and with the Concurrence of two thirds, expel a Member.

> Each branch promulgates its own rules and punishes its own members. The ultimate punishment is expulsion of the member, which requires a two-thirds vote. Expulsion does not prevent the member from running again.

[5]Changed by the Twentieth Amendment.

Clause 3. Each House shall keep a Journal of its Proceedings, and from time to time publish the same, excepting such Parts as may in their Judgment require Secrecy, and the Yeas and Nays of the Members of either House on any question shall, at the Desire of one fifth of those Present, be entered on the Journal.

> An official record called the *Congressional Record* or *House Journal* is kept for all sessions. It is a daily account of Senate and House floor debates, votes, and members' remarks. However, a record is not printed if a proceeding is closed to the public for security reasons. Many votes are by voice vote, but if at least one-fifth of the members request a recorded vote of Yeas and Nays, the members will vote individually and their votes will be recorded. This procedure permits analysis of congressional roll-call votes.

Clause 4. Neither House, during the Session of Congress shall, without the Consent of the other, adjourn for more than three days, nor to any other Place than that in which the two Houses shall be sitting.

> This clause prevents one branch from adjourning for a long period or to some other location without the consent of the other branch.

Rights of Members

Section 6 *Clause 1.* The Senators and Representatives shall receive a Compensation for their Services, to be ascertained by Law, and paid out of the Treasury of the United States. They shall in all Cases, except Treason, Felony and Breach of the Peace, be privileged from Arrest during their Attendance at the Session of their respective Houses, and in going to and returning from the same, and for any Speech or Debate in either House, they shall not be questioned in any other Place.

> This section ensures that senators and congressional representatives will be paid a salary from the U.S. Treasury. This salary is determined by the legislature. The salary for members of Congress in 2011 was $174,000. The Speaker of the House and the Majority Leader and Minority Leader in both the House and Senate receive higher salaries. Under current law, legislators receive a cost-of-living-adjustment to their salary annually. Members of Congress receive many other benefits as part of their compensation, including health care, a pension, access to athletic facilities, and travel to their home state or district. This section also provides immunity from arrest or prosecution for congressional actions on the floor or in travel to and from the Congress.

Clause 2. No Senator or Representative, shall, during the Time for which he was elected, be appointed to any civil Office under the Authority of the United States, which shall have been created, or the Emoluments whereof shall have been encreased during such time; and no Person holding any Office under the United States, shall be a Member of either House during his Continuance in Office.

> This section prevents the United States from adopting a parliamentary democracy, since congressional members cannot hold executive offices and members of the executive branch cannot be members of Congress.

Legislative Powers: Bills and Resolutions

Section 7 *Clause 1.* All Bills for raising Revenue shall originate in the House of Representatives; but the Senate may propose or concur with Amendments as on other Bills.

> This clause specifies one of the few powers specific to the U.S. House—revenue bills.

Clause 2. Every Bill which shall have passed the House of Representatives and the Senate, shall, before it becomes a Law, be presented to the President of the United States; If he approve he shall sign it, but if not he shall return it, with his Objections to that House in which it shall have originated, who shall enter the Objections at large on their Journal, and proceed to reconsider it. If after such Reconsideration two thirds of that House shall agree to pass the Bill, it shall be sent, together with the Objections, to the other House, by which it shall likewise be reconsidered, and if approved by two thirds of that House, it shall become a Law. But in all such Cases the Votes of both Houses shall be determined by yeas and Nays, and the Names of the Persons voting for and against the Bill shall be entered on the Journal of each House respectively. If any Bill shall not be returned by the President within ten Days (Sundays excepted) after it shall have been presented to him, the Same shall be a Law, in like Manner as if he had signed it, unless the Congress by their Adjournment prevent its Return, in which Case it shall not be a Law.

> The heart of the checks and balances system is contained in this clause. Both the House and Senate must pass a bill and present it to the president. If the president fails to act on the bill within 10 days (not including Sundays), the bill will automatically become law. If the president signs the bill, it becomes law. If the president vetoes the bill and sends it back to Congress, this body may override the veto by a

two-thirds vote in each house. This vote must be a recorded vote.

Clause 3. Every Order, Resolution, or Vote to which the Concurrence of the Senate and House of Representatives may be necessary (except on a question of Adjournment) shall be presented to the President of the United States; and before the Same shall take Effect, shall be approved by him, or being disapproved by him, shall be repassed by two thirds of the Senate and House of Representatives, according to the Rules and Limitations prescribed in the Case of a Bill.

This clause covers every other type of legislative action other than a bill. The same procedures apply in most cases.

Powers of Congress

Section 8 *Clause 1.* The Congress shall have Power to lay and collect Taxes, Duties, Imposts and Excises, to pay the Debts and provide for the common Defence and general Welfare of the United States, but all Duties, Imposts and Excises shall be uniform throughout the United States.

To borrow Money on the credit of the United States;

To regulate Commerce with foreign Nations, and among the several States, and with the Indian Tribes;

To establish an uniform Rule of Naturalization, and uniform Laws on the subject of Bankruptcies throughout the United States;

To coin Money, regulate the Value thereof, and of foreign Coin, and fix the Standard of Weights and Measures;

To provide for the Punishment of counterfeiting the Securities and current Coin of the United States;

To establish Post Offices and post Roads;

To promote the Progress of Science and useful Arts, by securing for limited Times to Authors and Inventors the exclusive Right to their respective Writings and Discoveries;

To constitute Tribunals inferior to the supreme Court;

To define and punish Piracies and Felonies committed on the high Seas, and Offences against the Law of Nations;

To declare War, grant Letters of Marque and Reprisal, and make Rules concerning Captures on Land and Water;

To raise and support Armies, but no Appropriation of Money to that Use shall be for a longer Term than two Years;

To provide and maintain a Navy;

To make Rules for the Government and Regulation of the land and naval Forces;

To provide for calling for the Militia to execute the Laws of the Union, suppress Insurrections and repel Invasions;

To provide for organizing, arming, and disciplining, the Militia, and for governing such Part of them as may be employed in the Service of the United States, reserving to the States respectively, the Appointment of the Officers, and the Authority of training the Militia according to the discipline prescribed by Congress;

This extensive clause establishes what are known as the "expressed" or "enumerated" powers of Congress. In theory, this clause serves as a limit or brake on congressional power. Among the many important powers listed in this clause, that of regulating commerce between the states has been highly consequential. As the Supreme Court revised its interpretation of interstate commerce, it expanded the policy areas where the federal government could act. The most recent major debate concerned whether, as a part of Congress's regulation of interstate commerce, the federal government could require individuals to purchase health insurance.

Clause 2. To exercise exclusive Legislation in all Cases whatsoever, over such District (not exceeding ten Miles square) as may, by Cession of particular States, and the Acceptance of Congress, become the Seat of the Government of the United States, and to exercise like Authority over all Places purchased by the Consent of the Legislature of the State in which the Same shall be, for the Erection of Forts, Magazines, Arsenals, dock Yards, and other needful Buildings—And

This clause establishes the seat of the federal government, which was first located in New York but eventually was moved to Washington, D.C., when both Maryland and Virginia ceded land to the new national government, which then established the District of Columbia.

Clause 3. To make all Laws which shall be necessary and proper for carrying into Execution the foregoing Powers, and all other Powers vested by this Constitution in the Government of the United States, or in any Department or Officer thereof.

This clause, known as the "elastic clause" or the "necessary and proper clause," provides the basis for the concept of "implied" congressional powers, which was first introduced in the U.S. Supreme Court decision in *McCulloch v. Maryland* (1819). This concept greatly expanded the range of legislative and regulatory actions Congress could take. Even if an action was not explicitly enumerated in Section 8, Clause 1, Congress could now assert that it had the authority to take the action in order to implement one of the enumerated powers.

Powers Denied to Congress

Section 9 *Clause 1.* The Migration or Importation of such Persons as any of the States now existing shall think proper to admit, shall not be prohibited by the Congress prior to the Year one thousand eight hundred and eight, but a Tax or duty may be imposed on such Importation, not exceeding ten dollars for each Person.

> The new Congress was prohibited from stopping the importation of slaves until 1808, but it could impose a head tax, not to exceed ten dollars for each slave.

Clause 2. The Privilege of the Writ of Habeas Corpus shall not be suspended, unless when in Cases of Rebellion or Invasion the public Safety may require it.

> Congress cannot suspend the writ of habeas corpus except in cases of rebellion or invasion. The writ of habeas corpus permits a judge to inquire about the legality of detention or deprivation of liberty of any citizen.

Clause 3. No Bill of Attainder or ex post facto Law shall be passed.

> This provision prohibits Congress from passing either a bill of attainder (forfeiture of property in capital cases) or ex post facto laws (making an earlier action criminal retroactively). Similar restrictions were enshrined in many state constitutions.

Clause 4. No Capitation, or other direct Tax shall be laid, unless in Proportion to the Census or Enumeration herein before directed to be taken.[6]

> This clause prevented Congress from passing an income tax. Only with passage of the Sixteenth Amendment in 1913 did Congress gain this power.

Clause 5. No Tax or Duty shall be laid on Articles exported from any State.

> This section establishes free trade within the United States. The federal government cannot tax state exports.

Clause 6. No Preference shall be given by any Regulation of Commerce or Revenue to the Ports of one State over those of another; nor shall Vessels bound to, or from one State, be obliged to enter, clear, or pay Duties in another.

---

[6]Modified by the Sixteenth Amendment.

> This clause also applies to free trade within the United States. The national government cannot show any preference to any state or maritime movements among the states.

Clause 7. No Money shall be drawn from the Treasury, but in Consequence of Appropriations made by Law, and a regular Statement and Account of the Receipts and Expenditures of all public Money shall be published from time to time.

> This provision prevents any expenditure unless it has been specifically provided for in an appropriations bill. If Congress has not completed work on the budget at the beginning of the fiscal year, it will pass a "continuing resolution" providing temporary authority to continue to spend money until the new appropriations bill is approved and signed into law.

Clause 8. No Title of Nobility shall be granted by the United States. And no Person holding any Office of Profit or Trust under them, shall, without the Consent of Congress, accept of any present, Emolument, Office, or Title, of any kind whatever, from any King, Prince, or foreign State.

> Feudalism would not be established in the new country. There would be no nobles. No federal official can even accept a title of nobility (even honorary) without permission of Congress.

Powers Denied to the States

> This section sets out the prohibitions on state actions.

Section 10 *Clause 1.* No State shall enter into any Treaty, Alliance, or Confederation, grant Letters of Marque and Reprisal, coin Money, emit Bills of Credit, make any Thing but gold and silver Coin a Tender in Payment of Debts, pass any Bill of Attainder, ex post facto Law, or Law impairing the Obligation of Contracts or grant any Title of Nobility.

> This particular clause provides a list of denied powers. Note that these restrictions cannot even be waived by Congress. States are not to engage in foreign relations nor acts of war. A "letter of marque and reprisal" was used during these times to provide legal cover for privateers. The federal government's currency monopoly is established. The sanctity of contracts is specified. State prohibitions are specified for bills of attainder and ex post facto laws.

Clause 2. No State shall, without the Consent of the Congress, lay any Imposts or Duties on Imports or Exports, except what may be absolutely necessary for executing its inspection Laws: and the net Produce of all Duties and Imposts, laid by any State on Imports or Exports, shall be for the Use of the Treasury of the United States, and all such Laws shall be subject to the Revision and Control of the Congress.

> This section establishes the monopoly control of the national government in matters of both national and international trade. The only concession to states is health and safety inspections.

Clause 3. No State shall, without the Consent of Congress, lay any Duty of Tonnage, keep Troops, or Ships of War in time of Peace, enter into any Agreement or Compact with another State, or with a foreign Power, or engage in War, unless actually invaded, or in such imminent Danger as will not admit of delay.

> This final section of the legislative article establishes the war power to be held exclusively by the national government. The only exception to state action is actual invasion or threat of imminent danger.

Article II—The Executive Article

> This article establishes an entirely new concept in government—an elected executive power.

Nature and Scope of Presidential Power

Section 1 *Clause 1.* The executive Power shall be vested in a President of the United States of America. He shall hold his Office during the Term of four Years and, together with the Vice President, chosen for the same Term, be elected, as follows.

> This clause establishes the executive power in the office of the president of the United States of America. It also establishes a second office—vice president. A four-year term was established, but no limit on the number of terms. A limit was later established by the Twenty-second Amendment.

Clause 2. Each State shall appoint, in such Manner as the Legislature thereof may direct, a Number of Electors, equal to the whole Number of Senators and Representatives to which the State may be entitled in the Congress: but no Senator or Representative, or Person holding an Office of Trust or Profit under the United States, shall be appointed an Elector.

> This paragraph establishes the Electoral College to choose the president and vice president.

Clause 3. The Electors shall meet in their respective States, and vote by Ballot for two Persons, of whom one at least shall not be an Inhabitant of the same State with themselves. And they shall make a List of all the Persons voted for, and of the Number of Votes for each; which List they shall sign and certify, and transmit sealed to the Seat of the Government of the United States, directed to the President of the Senate. The President of the Senate shall, in the Presence of the Senate and House of Representatives, open all the Certificates, and the Votes shall then be counted. The Person having the greatest Number of Votes shall be the President, if such Number be a Majority of the whole Number of Electors appointed; and if there be more than one who have such Majority and have an equal Number of Votes, then the House of Representatives shall immediately chuse by Ballot one of them for President; and if no Person have a Majority, then from the five highest on the List the said House shall in like Manner chuse the President. But in chusing the President, the Votes shall be taken by States, the Representation from each State having one Vote; a quorum for this Purpose shall consist of a Member or Members from two thirds of the States, and a Majority of all the States shall be necessary to a Choice. In every Case, after the Choice of the President, the Person having the greatest Number of Votes of the Electors shall be the Vice President. But if there should remain two or more who have equal Votes, the Senate shall chuse from them by Ballot the Vice President.[7]

> This paragraph has been superseded by the Twelfth Amendment. The original language did not require a separate vote for president and vice president. Instead, each elector cast two votes. Only one of the two can be from the state of the elector. When one candidate received a majority of the electoral votes cast and there was no tie, the second-place finisher became the vice president. Thus, two candidates who had just opposed each other could now find themselves as president and vice president. The Twelfth Amendment requires a separate vote for each office.

> The original language provided for the House to elect the president in the case where two candidates both received an equal number of electoral votes and had a majority—it was possible for two candidates to receive a majority because each elector cast two votes and the "majority" being referred to here was a majority of the number of electors casting votes, not the number of votes. There would also be a House election among the top five candidates if no candidate received a majority. The Twelfth Amendment lowered the number of candidates to the top three.

> In both these instances, each state delegation in the House casts a single vote. The Senate is to select the

---

[7]Changed by the Twelfth and Twentieth Amendments.

vice president if a candidate does not have an electoral majority or in the case of a tie vote. The Senate considers only the top two candidates. The Twelfth Amendment later clarified that the age, citizenship, and residency requirements of the vice president are the same as those for president.

Clause 4. The Congress may determine the Time of chusing the Electors, and the Day on which they shall give their Votes; which Day shall be the same throughout the United States.

Congress is given the power to establish a uniform day and time for the state selection of electors.

Clause 5. No Person except a natural born Citizen, or a Citizen of the United States, at the time of the Adoption of this Constitution, shall be eligible to the Office of President, neither shall any Person be eligible to that Office who shall not have attained to the Age of thirty five Years, and been fourteen Years a Resident within the United States.

The qualifications for the office of president (and, as the Twelfth Amendment made clear, by implication the vice president) is specified here—at least 35 years old, 14 years' resident in the United States, and born in the United States (or a citizen of the United States when the Constitution was adopted). Congress has addressed by statute—as early as 1790—that someone born to American parents while in a foreign country is a citizen and effectively considered to have been born in the United States. The rules concerning children born to one American citizen in a foreign country have varied over time.

Clause 6. In Case of the Removal of the President from Office, or of his Death, Resignation, or Inability to discharge the Powers and Duties of the said Office, the Same shall devolve on the Vice President, and the Congress may by Law provide for the Case of Removal, Death, Resignation, or Inability, both of the President and Vice President, declaring what Officer shall then act as president, and such Officer shall act accordingly, until the Disability be removed, or a President shall be elected.[8]

This clause has been modified by the Twenty-fifth Amendment. Upon the death, resignation, or impeachment and conviction of the president, the vice president becomes president. The new president nominates a new vice president, who assumes the office, if approved by a majority vote in both congressional houses. The president is also now able to notify the Congress of his inability to perform his office.

[8]Modified by the Twenty-fifth Amendment.

Clause 7. The President shall, at stated Times, receive for his Services, a Compensation which shall neither be encreased nor diminished during the Period of which he shall have been elected, and he shall not receive within that Period any other Emolument from the United States, or any of them.

This section covers the compensation of the president, which cannot be increased or decreased during the term in office. The current salary is $400,000 per year. Unlike legislators, judges, and the heads of federal agencies, the president's salary does not receive an annual cost-of-living adjustment.

Clause 8. Before he enter on the Execution of his Office, he shall take the following Oath or Affirmation—"I do solemnly swear (or affirm) that I will faithfully execute the Office of President of the United States, and will to the best of my Ability, preserve, protect and defend the Constitution of the United States."

This final clause in Section 1 is the oath of office administered to the new president.

Powers and Duties of the President

Section 2 Clause 1. The President shall be the Commander in Chief of the Army and Navy of the United States, and of the Militia of the several States; when called into the actual Service of the United States, he may require the Opinion, in writing, of the principal Officer in each of the executive Departments, upon any Subject relating to the Duties of their respective Offices, and he shall have the Power to grant Reprieves and Pardons for Offences against the United States, except in Cases of Impeachment.

This clause establishes the president as commander in chief of the U.S. armed forces. The second provision provides the basis for Cabinet meetings that are used to acquire the opinions of executive department heads. The last provision provides an absolute pardon or reprieve power to the president.

Clause 2. He shall have Power, by and with the Advice and Consent of the Senate to make Treaties, provided two thirds of the Senators present concur, and he shall nominate, and by and with the Advice and Consent of the Senate, shall appoint Ambassadors, other public Ministers and Consuls, Judges of the supreme Court, and all other Officers of the United States, whose Appointments are not herein otherwise provided for, and which shall be established by Law but the Congress may by Law vest the

Appointment of such inferior Officers, as they think proper in the President alone, in the Courts of Law, or in the Heads of Departments.

This clause covers two important presidential powers, treaty making and appointments. The president (via the State Department) can negotiate treaties with other nations, but these do not become official until ratified by a two-thirds vote of the U.S. Senate. The president is empowered to appoint judges, ambassadors, and other U.S. officials (such as Cabinet officers, military officers, and agency heads), subject to Senate approval. The Congress can and does delegate this approval to the president in the case of inferior officers. For example, junior military officer promotions are not submitted to the Senate, but senior officer promotions are.

Clause 3. The President shall have Power to fill up all Vacancies that may happen during the Recess of the Senate, by granting Commissions which shall expire at the End of their next Session.

This provision allows recess appointments of the officials listed in clause 2 above. These commissions automatically expire unless approved by the Senate by the end of the next session. Presidents have used this provision, sometimes controversially, to fill jobs when the nomination process is stalled.

Section 3 He shall from time to time give to the Congress Information of the State of the Union, and recommend to their Consideration such Measures as he shall judge necessary and expedient, he may, on extraordinary Occasions convene both Houses, or either of them and in Case of Disagreement between them, with Respect to the Time of Adjournment, he may adjourn them to such Time as he shall think proper, he shall receive Ambassadors and other public Ministers, he shall take Care that the Laws be faithfully executed, and shall Commission all the Officers of the United States.

This section provides for a report on the state of the union during the president's term. Although today this report is delivered in person in the form of the televised State of the Union Address, presidents can also simply submit a report to Congress. "From time to time" has come to mean annual, but in some years, usually a transition year to a new president, there has been no report. The "necessary and expedient" clause indicates that the Framers expected that presidents would have some role in prodding the legislature to act. The president is also authorized to call special meetings of either the House or Senate. If there is disagreement

between the House and Senate regarding adjournment, the president is empowered to adjourn them. This would be extremely rare. The president formally receives other nations' ambassadors. The next to last provision, to faithfully execute laws, provides the constitutional basis for the whole administrative apparatus of the presidency. All officers of the United States receive a formal commission from the president.

Section 4 The President, Vice President and all civil Officers of the United States, shall be removed from Office on Impeachment for, and Conviction of, Treason, Bribery, or other high Crimes and Misdemeanors.

This section provides the constitutional authority for the impeachment and trial of the president, vice president, and all civil officers of the United States for treason, bribery, or other high crimes and misdemeanors. In practice, precisely what constitutes a high crime or misdemeanor has been a matter of great debate.

Article III—The Judicial Article

Judicial Power, Courts, Judges

Section 1 The judicial Power of the United States, shall be vested in one supreme Court, and in such inferior Courts as the Congress may from time to time ordain and establish. The Judges, both of the supreme and inferior Courts, shall hold their Offices during good Behaviour, and shall, at stated Times, receive for their Services, a Compensation, which shall not be diminished during their Continuance in Office.

This section establishes the judicial branch in very general terms. It specifically provides only for the Supreme Court. Congress is given the responsibility to develop the remainder of the court system. It initially did so in the Judiciary Act of 1789, when it established 13 district courts (one for each state), and 3 appellate courts. All federal judges hold their offices for life and can be removed only for breaches of good behavior; judges have been removed for drunkenness, accepting bribes, and other offenses. To date, no justice of the U.S. Supreme Court has ever been removed. The number of Supreme Court justices is not set by the Constitution but is instead determined by statute.

The salary of federal judges is set by Congress and can not be cut while the judge serves. Federal district judges earned $174,000 in 2011, appellate judges $184,500, and Supreme Court justices $213,900. The chief justice was paid $223,500.

Jurisdiction

Section 2 The judicial Power shall extend to all Cases, in Law and Equity, arising under this Constitution, the Laws of the United States, and Treaties made, or which shall be made, under their Authority,—to all Cases affecting Ambassadors, other public Ministers and Consuls;—to all Cases of admiralty and maritime Jurisdiction;—to Controversies to which the United States shall be a Party;—to Controversies between two or more States; between a State and Citizens of another State[9];—between Citizens of different States;—between Citizens of the same State claiming Lands under Grants of different States, and between a State, or the Citizens thereof, and foreign States, Citizens, or Subjects.

In all Cases affecting Ambassadors, other public Ministers and Consuls, and those in which a State shall be Party, the supreme Court shall have original Jurisdiction. In all the other Cases before mentioned, the supreme Court shall have appellate Jurisdiction, both as to Law and Fact, with such Exceptions, and under such Regulations as Congress shall make.

The Trial of all Crimes, except in Cases of Impeachment, shall be by Jury; and such Trial shall be held in the State where the said Crimes shall have been committed, but when not committed within any State, the Trial shall be at such Place or Places as the Congress may by Law have directed.

> This section establishes the Supreme Court's original jurisdiction (the Supreme Court alone hears the case) and appellate jurisdiction (the Court hears the case on appeal from another court). With the Congress of Vienna's 1815 establishment of "diplomatic immunity," the U.S. Supreme Court no longer hears cases involving ambassadors. Since 1925, the Supreme Court no longer hears every case on appeal but can select which cases it will accept, which is now about 100 cases per year. This section also establishes the right of trial by jury for federal crimes.

Treason

Section 3 Treason against the United States, shall consist only in levying War against them, or in adhering to their Enemies, giving them Aid and Comfort. No Person shall be convicted of Treason unless on the Testimony of two Witnesses to the same overt Act, or on Confession in open Court.

The Congress shall have Power to declare the Punishment of Treason, but no Attainder of Treason shall work Corruption of Blood, or Forfeiture except during the Life of the Person attainted.

> Treason is the only crime defined in the U.S. Constitution. Congress established the penalty of death for treason convictions. Note that two witnesses are required to convict anyone of treason. Even in cases of treasonable conduct, seizure of estates is prohibited.

Article IV—Interstate Relations

Full Faith and Credit Clause

Section 1 Full Faith and Credit shall be given in each State to the public Acts, Records, and judicial Proceedings of every other State. And the Congress may by general Laws prescribe the Manner in which such Acts, Records and Proceedings shall be proved, and the Effect thereof.

> This section provides that the official acts and records of one state will be recognized and given credence by other states—for example, marriages and divorces.

Privileges and Immunities, Interstate Extradition

Section 2 *Clause 1.* The Citizens of each State shall be entitled to all Privileges and Immunities of Citizens in the several States.

> This clause requires states to treat citizens of other states equally. For example, when driving in another state, one's driver's license is recognized and the traffic laws apply equally to state citizens and visitors from other states.

Clause 2. A person charged in any State with Treason, Felony or other Crime, who shall flee from Justice, and be found in another State, shall on Demand of the executive Authority of the State from which he fled, be delivered up, to be removed to the State having Jurisdiction of the Crime.

> This clause refers to the concept of extradition—a criminal fleeing to another state, if captured, can be returned to the state where the crime was committed. But this is not an absolute. A state's governor can refuse to extradite someone to another state.

Clause 3. No person held to Service or Labour in one State, under the Laws thereof, escaping into another, shall, in Consequence of any Law or Regulation therein, be discharged from such Service or Labour, but shall be delivered up on Claim of the Party to whom such Service or Labour may be due.[10]

---

[9]Modified by the Twelfth Amendment.

[10]Repealed by the Thirteenth Amendment.

This clause was included to cover runaway slaves and provide for their return. It was overruled by the Thirteenth Amendment, which abolished slavery.

Admission of States

Section 3 New States may be admitted by the Congress into this Union but no new State shall be formed or erected within the Jurisdiction of any other State, nor any State to be formed by the Junction of two or more States, or Parts of States, without the Consent of the Legislatures of the States concerned as well as of the Congress.

The Congress shall have Power to dispose of and make all needful Rules and Regulations respecting the Territory or other Property belonging to the United States, and nothing in this Constitution shall be so construed as to Prejudice any Claims of the United States, or of any particular State.

This section concerns the admission of new states to the Union. Although no new state can be created from part of another state without permission of the state legislature, there is one historical exception: West Virginia was formed from Virginia during the Civil War without the permission of Virginia, which was part of the Confederacy.

Republican Form of Government

Section 4 The United States shall guarantee to every State in this Union a Republican Form of Government, and shall protect each of them against Invasion, and on Application of the Legislature, or of the Executive (when the Legislature cannot be convened) against domestic Violence.

This section commits the federal government to guarantee a republican form of government to each state and protect the state against foreign invasion or domestic insurrection.

Article V—The Amending Power

The Congress, whenever two thirds of both Houses shall deem it necessary, shall propose Amendments to this Constitution, or, on the Application of the Legislatures of two thirds of the several States, shall call a Convention for proposing Amendments, which, in either Case, shall be valid to all Intents and Purposes, as Part of this Constitution, when ratified by the Legislatures of three fourths of the several States, or by Conventions in three fourths thereof, as the one or the other Mode of Ratification may be proposed by the Congress; Provided that no Amendment which may be made prior to the Year One thousand eight hundred and eight shall in any Manner affect the first and fourth Clauses in the Ninth Section of the first Article; and that no State, without its Consent, shall be deprived of its equal Suffrage in the Senate.

Amendments to the U.S. Constitution can be originated by a two-thirds vote in both the U.S. House and the Senate or by two-thirds of the state legislatures asking for a convention to propose amendments. Proposed amendments, by either route, must be approved by three-fourths of state legislatures or by three-fourths of conventions convened in the states for purposes of ratification. Only one amendment has been ratified by the convention method: the Twenty-first Amendment, to repeal the Eighteenth Amendment establishing prohibition of alcohol. There have only been 27 successful amendments to the U.S. Constitution.

Article VI—National Supremacy

Clause 1. All Debts contracted and Engagements entered into, before the Adoption of this Constitution, shall be as valid against the United States under the Constitution, as under the Confederation.

This clause made the new national government responsible for all debts incurred during the Revolutionary War. This provision was very important to those interests concerned that debts and contracts might be discarded in the transition from the Articles of Confederation to the Constitution.

Clause 2. This Constitution, and the Laws of the United States which shall be made in Pursuance thereof, and all Treaties made, or which shall be made, under the Authority of the United States, shall be the supreme Law of the Land, and the Judges in every State shall be bound thereby any Thing in the Constitution or Laws of any State to the Contrary notwithstanding.

The national supremacy clause provides the basis for the supremacy of the national government over the states in policy areas where the national government has constitutional authority to act.

Clause 3. The Senators and Representatives before mentioned, and the Members of the several State Legislatures, and all executive and judicial Officers, both of the United States and of the several States, shall be bound by Oath or Affirmation, to support this Constitution, but no religious Test shall ever be required as a Qualification to any Office or public Trust under the United States.

This clause requires all federal and state officials to swear or affirm their allegiance to and support of the U.S. Constitution. A religious test was prohibited for federal office. However, some states used religious affiliation as a criterion for state office until the 1830s.

Article VII—Ratification

The Ratification of the Conventions of nine States, shall be sufficient for the Establishment of this Constitution between the States so ratifying the Same.

Done in Convention by the Unanimous Consent of the States present the Seventeenth Day of September in the Year of our Lord one thousand seven hundred and Eighty seven and of the Independence of the United States of America the Twelfth. In Witness whereof We have hereunto subscribed our Names.

Realizing the unanimous ratification of the 13 states of the new Constitution might never have occurred, the Framers specified that only 9 states would be needed for ratification. The ratification campaign posed the Federalists, who supported the Constitution, against the Anti-Federalists, who opposed it.

AMENDMENTS

The Bill of Rights

The first 10 amendments were ratified on December 15, 1791, and form what is known as the Bill of Rights. The Bill of Rights applied initially only to the federal government and not to state or local governments. Beginning in 1897 in the case of *Chicago, Burlington and Quincy Railroad v. City of Chicago*, the Supreme Court began to selectively and gradually make the provisions of the Bill of Rights applicable to state and local governments. There are only a few exceptions, which will be discussed at the appropriate amendment.

Amendment 1—Religion, Speech, Assembly, and Politics

Congress shall make no law respecting an establishment of religion, or prohibiting the free exercise thereof; or abridging the freedom of speech, or of the press; or the right of the people peaceably to assemble, and to petition the Government for a redress of grievances.

This amendment has vast range, in that it protects five fundamental freedoms: religion, speech, press, assembly, and petition.

Amendment 2—Militia and the Right to Bear Arms

A well-regulated Militia, being necessary to the security of a free State, the right of the people to keep and bear Arms, shall not be infringed.

In 2010, the Supreme Court determined that this amendment applied to the actions of state and local governments in addition to the federal government. The Court had, one year earlier, established that the amendment protected an individual's right to possess firearms. Previously, the Court had seen this amendment as protecting a collective right of the people as organized in official militias, not an individual right.

Amendment 3—Quartering of Soldiers

No Soldier shall, in time of peace be quartered in any house, without the consent of the Owner, nor in time of war, but in manner to be prescribed by law.

It was the practice of the British government to insist that colonists provide room and board to British troops. This amendment was designed to prohibit this practice. Today, military and naval bases provide the necessary quarters. The Supreme Court has not said that this amendment applies to state and local governments.

Amendment 4—Searches and Seizures

The right of the people to be secure in their persons, houses, papers, and effects, against unreasonable searches and seizures, shall not be violated, and no Warrants shall issue, but upon probable cause, supported by Oath or affirmation, and particularly describing the place to be searched, and the persons or things to be seized.

This amendment provides protection for individuals subject to investigation. Searches or seizures of homes, persons, or property cannot be undertaken without probable cause or a warrant that specifically describes the place to be searched, the person involved, and suspicious things to be seized.

Amendment 5—Grand Juries, Self-Incrimination, Double Jeopardy, Due Process, and Eminent Domain

No person shall be held to answer for a capital, or otherwise infamous crime, unless on a presentment or indictment of a Grand jury, except in cases arising in the land or naval forces, or in the Militia, when in actual service in time of War or public danger; nor shall any person be subject for the same offence to be twice put in jeopardy of life or limb, nor shall be compelled in any criminal case to be a witness against himself, nor be deprived of life, liberty, or property, without due process of law, nor shall private property be taken for public use, without just compensation.

> Only a grand jury can indict a person for a federal crime. This provision does not apply to state or local governments. This amendment also covers double jeopardy: being tried twice for the same crime in the same jurisdiction. However, because the federal government and state governments are different jurisdictions, an individual could be tried in each jurisdiction for the same act. For example, it is a federal crime to kill a congressperson. It is also a state crime to murder anyone. Further, this amendment also covers the prohibition of self-incrimination. "Pleading the Fifth Amendment" is common among defendants. The deprivation of life, liberty, or property is prohibited unless due process of law is applied. Finally, private property may not be taken under the doctrine of "eminent domain" unless the government provides just compensation and the taking is for public purposes.

Amendment 6—Criminal Court Procedures

In all criminal prosecutions, the accused shall enjoy the right to a speedy and public trial, by an impartial jury of the State and district wherein the crime shall have been committed, which district shall have been previously ascertained by law, and to be informed of the nature and cause of the accusation, to be confronted with the witnesses against him, to have compulsory process for obtaining witnesses in his favor, and to have the Assistance of Counsel for his defence.

> This amendment requires public trials by jury for criminal prosecutions. Anyone accused of a crime is guaranteed the right to be informed of the charges, to confront witnesses, to subpoena witnesses for his or her defense, and to have a lawyer for his or her defense. The government must provide a lawyer for a defendant unable to afford one.

Amendment 7—Trial by Jury in Common Law Cases

In Suits at common law, where the value in controversy shall exceed twenty dollars, the right of trial by jury shall be preserved, and no fact tried by a jury shall be otherwise re-examined in any Court of the United States, than according to the rules of the common law.

> Federal civil lawsuits with a guaranteed jury are now restricted to cases that exceed $50,000. The Supreme Court has not required that trial by jury be applied to the states: some state and local governments have trials by judges, not by juries.

Amendment 8—Bail, Cruel and Unusual Punishment

Excessive bail shall not be required, nor excessive fines imposed, nor cruel and unusual punishments inflicted.

> Capital punishment is covered by this amendment, which also prohibits excessive bail. The Supreme Court has outlawed capital punishment for minors and those with severe mental development disabilities as being inherently cruel and unusual.

Amendment 9—Rights Retained by the People

The enumeration in the Constitution of certain rights, shall not be construed to deny or disparage others retained by the people.

> This amendment implies that there may be other rights of the people not specified by the previous amendments. For the most part, the Supreme Court has established that the people have additional rights through other provisions of the Constitution, especially the Fourteenth Amendment. The Ninth Amendment is often mentioned in these decisions but is usually not at the root of the Court's decision.

Amendment 10—Reserved Powers of the States

The powers not delegated to the United States by the Constitution, nor prohibited by it to the States, are reserved to the States respectively, or to the people.

> The Tenth Amendment was seen as the reservoir of reserved powers for state governments and is frequently cited today by individuals concerned that the federal government is involved in too many areas that should be the responsibility of the states. The doctrine of implied national government powers, established by the Supreme Court in *McCulloch v. Maryland* (1819), complicates to some degree the

application of this amendment. The amendment refers to "powers not delegated," yet the Court validated as constitutional the federal government taking actions that were not specifically delegated to it. The meaning and application of the Tenth Amendment are battlegrounds for those involved in politics who are wrestling over the appropriate reach of and limits on federal government power.

Amendment 11—Suits Against the States

[Ratified February 7, 1795]

The Judicial power of the United States shall not be construed to extend to any suit in law or equity, commenced or prosecuted against one of the United States by Citizens of another State, or by Citizens or Subjects of any Foreign State.

Article III of the U.S. Constitution originally allowed federal jurisdiction in cases of one state citizen against another state citizen or state. This amendment removes federal jurisdiction in this area. States may not be sued in federal court by citizens of another state or country.

Amendment 12—Election of the President

[Ratified June 15, 1804]

The Electors shall meet in their respective states, and vote by ballot for President and Vice-President, one of whom, at least, shall not be an inhabitant of the same state with themselves; they shall name in their ballots the person voted for as President, and in distinct ballots the person voted for as Vice-President, and they shall make distinct lists of all persons voted for as President, and of all persons voted for as Vice-President, and of the number of votes for each, which lists they shall sign and certify, and transmit sealed to the seat of the government of the United States, directed to the President of the Senate;—The President of the Senate shall, in presence of the Senate and House of Representatives, open all the certificates and the votes shall then be counted;—The person having the greatest number of votes for President, shall be the President, if such number be a majority of the whole number of Electors appointed; and if no person have such majority, then from the persons having the highest numbers not exceeding three on the list of those voted for as President, the House of Representatives shall choose immediately, by ballot, the President. But in choosing the President, the votes shall be taken by states, the representation from each state having one vote; a quorum for this purpose shall consist of a member or members from two-thirds of the states, and a majority of all states shall be necessary to a choice. And if the House of Representatives shall not choose a President whenever the

right of choice shall devolve upon them, before the fourth day of March next following, then the Vice-President shall act as President, as in the case of the death or other constitutional disability of the President.[11] The person having the greatest number of votes as Vice-President, shall be the Vice-President, if such a number be a majority of the whole numbers of Electors appointed, and if no person have a majority, then from the two highest numbers on the list, the Senate shall choose the Vice-President, a quorum for the purpose shall consist of two-thirds of the whole number of Senators, and a majority of the whole number shall be necessary to a choice. But no person constitutionally ineligible to the office of President shall be eligible to that of Vice-President of the United States.

Article II of the original Constitution specified that each elector would cast two ballots. It did not specify for whom. This amendment clarifies that the electoral vote must be specific for president and vice president. The original Constitution provided that if no candidate received a majority of electoral votes, the House would decide from the candidates with the top five vote totals. This amendment reduces the candidate field to the top three vote totals. If the House delays in this selection past the fourth day of March, the elected vice president will act as president until the House selects the president. The original Constitution provided that the candidate with the second highest number of electoral votes would become vice president; this provision is superseded by this amendment's requirement that there be a separate vote tally for the position of vice president.

The amendment provides for selection by the U.S. Senate if no vice presidential candidate receives an electoral vote majority.

Amendment 13—Prohibition of Slavery

[Ratified December 6, 1865]

Section 1 Neither slavery nor involuntary servitude, except as a punishment for crime whereof the party shall have been duly convicted, shall exist within the United States, or any place subject to their jurisdiction.

Section 2 Congress shall have power to enforce this article by appropriate legislation.

This is the first of the three Civil War amendments. Slavery is prohibited under all circumstances. Involuntary servitude is also prohibited unless it is a punishment for a convicted crime.

---

[11]Changed by the Twentieth Amendment.

Amendment 14—Citizenship, Due Process, and Equal Protection of the Laws

[Ratified July 9, 1868]

Section 1 All persons born or naturalized in the United States, and subject to the jurisdiction thereof, are citizens of the United States and of the State wherein they reside. No State shall make or enforce any law which shall abridge the privileges or immunities of citizens of the United States; nor shall any State deprive any person of life, liberty, or property, without due process of law; nor deny to any person within its jurisdiction the equal protection of the laws.

> This section defines the meaning of U.S. citizenship and protection of these citizenship rights. It also establishes that each state must guarantee the equal protection of the laws. It extended the provisions of the Fifth Amendment of due process and protection of life, liberty, and property and made these applicable to the states.

Section 2 Representatives shall be apportioned among the several States according to their respective numbers, counting the whole number of persons in each State, excluding Indians not taxed. But when the right to vote at any election for the choice of electors for President and Vice President of the United States, Representatives in Congress, the Executive and Judicial officers of a State, or the members of the Legislature thereof, is denied to any of the male inhabitants of such State, being twenty-one[12] years of age, and citizens of the United States, or in any way abridged, except for participation in rebellion, or other crime, the basis of representation therein shall be reduced in the proportion which the number of such male citizens shall bear to the whole number of male citizens twenty-one years of age in such State.

> This section changes the three-fifths clause of the original Constitution. Now all persons in the state, excluding certain Indians, will be included in the population count used to calculate representation in the House of Representatives. If a state denies the right to vote to any male 21 or older, the number of denied citizens will be deducted from the overall state total to determine representation.

Section 3 No person shall be a Senator or Representative in Congress, or elector of President and Vice President, or hold any office, civil or military under the United States, or under any State, who, having previously taken an oath, as a member of Congress, or as an officer of the United States, or as a member of any State legislature, or as an executive or judicial officer of any State, to support the Constitution of the United States, shall have engaged in insurrection or rebellion against the same, or given aid or comfort to the enemies thereof. But Congress may by a vote of two-thirds of each House, remove such disability.

> This section disqualifies from federal office or elector for president or vice president anyone who rebelled or participated in an insurrection against the Constitution. This was specifically directed against citizens of southern states. Congress by a two-thirds vote could override this provision.

Section 4 The validity of the public debt of the United States, authorized by law, including debts incurred for payment of pensions and bounties for services in suppressing insurrection or rebellion, shall not be questioned. But neither the United States nor any State shall assume or pay any debt or obligation incurred in aid of insurrection or rebellion against the United States or any claim for the loss or emancipation of any slave, but all such debts, obligations and claims shall be held illegal and void.

> This section guarantees payment of Civil War debts incurred by the U.S. government but declares void any debts incurred by the Confederacy.

Section 5 The Congress shall have power to enforce, by appropriate legislation, the provisions of this article.

Amendment 15—The Right to Vote

[Ratified February 3, 1870]

Section 1 The right of citizens of the United States to vote shall not be denied or abridged by the United States or by any State on account of race, color, or previous condition of servitude.

Section 2 The Congress shall have power to enforce this article by appropriate legislation.

> This final Civil War amendment guarantees that voting rights cannot be denied by any state on account of race, color, or previous servitude. Gender and age would be addressed in future amendments.

Amendment 16—Income Taxes

[Ratified February 3, 1913]

The Congress shall have power to lay and collect taxes on incomes, from whatever source derived, without apportionment among the several States, and without regard to any census or enumeration.

[12]Changed by the Twenty-sixth Amendment.

Article I, Section 9, of the original Constitution prohibited Congress from enacting a direct tax (head tax) unless in proportion to population as indicated by a census. Congress in 1894 passed an income tax law, levying a 2 percent tax on incomes over $4,000. In 1895, the Supreme Court found that this income tax was a direct tax not apportioned among the states and was thus unconstitutional. This amendment gave Congress the power to enact an income tax without the revenues needing to be proportional among the states.

Amendment 17—Direct Election of Senators

[Ratified April 8, 1913]

The Senate of the United States shall be composed of two Senators from each State, elected by the people thereof, for six years and each Senator shall have one vote. The electors in each State shall have the qualifications requisite for electors of the most numerous branch of the State legislatures.

When vacancies happen in the representation of any State in the Senate, the executive authority of such State shall issue writs of election to fill such vacancies: Provided, That the legislature of any State may empower the executive thereof to make temporary appointment until the people fill the vacancies by election as the legislature may direct.

This amendment shall not be so construed as to affect the election or term of any Senator chosen before it becomes valid as part of the Constitution.

Prior to this amendment, U.S. senators were selected by state legislatures. Now U.S. senators would be selected by popular vote in each state. Further, the governor of each state may fill vacancies, subject to state laws.

Amendment 18—Prohibition

[Ratified January 16, 1919, Repealed December 5, 1933, by Amendment 21]

Section 1 After one year from the ratification of this article the manufacture, sale, or transportation of intoxicating liquors within, the importation thereof into, or the exportation thereof from the United States and all territory subject to the jurisdiction thereof for beverage purposes is hereby prohibited.

Section 2 The Congress and the several States shall have concurrent power to enforce this article by appropriate legislation.

Section 3 This article shall be inoperative unless it shall have been ratified as an amendment to the Constitution by the legislatures of the several States, as provided in the Constitution, within seven years from the date of the submission hereof to the States by the Congress.[13]

This amendment banned the manufacture, sale, or transportation of alcoholic beverages. The amendment was repealed 14 years later by the Twenty-first Amendment. The Eighteenth Amendment is the first for which Congress set a time limit for ratification.

Amendment 19—Women's Suffrage

[Ratified August 18, 1920]

The right of the citizens of the United States to vote shall not be denied or abridged by the United States or by any State on account of sex.

Congress shall have power to enforce this article by appropriate legislation.

This amendment provides that the right of a citizen to vote cannot be denied on account of sex. Women in some states had the right to vote prior to 1920. This amendment applied that right nationwide.

Amendment 20—Ending Lame Duck Sessions

[Ratified January 23, 1933]

Section 1 The terms of the President and Vice President shall end at noon on the 20th day of January, and the terms of the Senators and Representatives at noon on the 3d day of January, of the years in which such terms would have ended if this article had not been ratified, and the terms of their successors shall then begin.

Section 2 The Congress shall assemble at least once in every year, and such meeting shall begin at noon on the 3d day of January, unless they shall by law appoint a different day.

Section 3 If, at the time fixed for the beginning of the term of the President, the President elect shall have died, the Vice President elect shall become President. If a President shall not have been chosen before the time fixed for the beginning of his term, or if the President elect shall have failed to qualify, then the Vice President elect shall act as President until a President shall have qualified, and the Congress may by law provide for the case wherein neither a President elect nor a Vice President elect shall have qualified, declaring who shall then act as President, or the manner in which one who is to act shall be selected, and such person shall act accordingly until a President or Vice President shall have qualified.

---

[13]Repealed by the Twenty-first Amendment.

Section 4 The Congress may by law provide for the case of the death of any of the persons from whom the House of Representatives may choose a President whenever the right of choice shall have devolved upon them, and for the case of the death of any of the persons from whom the Senate may choose a Vice President whenever the right of choice shall have devolved upon them.

Section 5 Sections 1 and 2 shall take effect on the 15th day of October following the ratification of this article.

Section 6 This article shall be inoperative unless it shall have been ratified as an amendment to the Constitution by the legislatures of three-fourths of the several States within seven years from the date of its submission.

> Prior to this amendment, the term of the new Congress and president did not begin until March of an odd-numbered year, which was four months following the November elections. And the actual congressional session often did not start until December of the odd-numbered year, another eight months after March. Thus, elected officials might not begin a legislative session until 13 months after their election, and "lame-duck" sessions of Congress ran from December of the even-numbered year through March when the new term started. This amendment sets the dates for the end and beginning of presidential and legislative terms to end these lame-duck sessions, and requires the new Congress to assemble on January 3, just two months after the elections. The president's term begins a little over two weeks later, on January 20. The amendment also makes provisions for situations where the president-elect dies prior to taking office.

Amendment 21—Repeal of Prohibition

[Ratified December 5, 1933]

Section 1 The eighteenth article of amendment to the Constitution of the United States is hereby repealed.

Section 2 The transportation or importation into any State, Territory, or possession of the United States for delivery or use therein of intoxicating liquors, in violation of the laws thereof, is hereby prohibited.

Section 3 This article shall be inoperative unless it shall have been ratified as an amendment to the Constitution by conventions in the several States, as provided in the Constitution, within seven years from the date of the submission hereof to the States by the Congress.

> This amendment nullified the Eighteenth Amendment. It ended federal Prohibition and placed regulation of liquor at the state level.

Amendment 22—Number of Presidential Terms

[Ratified February 27, 1951]

Section 1 No person shall be elected to the office of the President more than twice, and no person who has held the office of President, or acted as President, for more than two years of a term to which some other person was elected President shall be elected to the office of the President more than once. But this article shall not apply to any person holding the office of President when this article was proposed by the Congress, and shall not prevent any person who may be holding the office of President, or acting as President, during the term within which this article becomes operative from holding the office of President or acting as President during the remainder of such term.

Section 2 This article shall be inoperative unless it shall have been ratified as an amendment to the Constitution by the legislatures of three-fourths of the several states within seven years from the date of its submission to the states by the Congress.

> Franklin D. Roosevelt won an unprecedented four terms as president. All previous presidents had adhered to a maximum of two terms in office, though the Constitution had no such requirement. This amendment limits presidents to two terms.

Amendment 23—Presidential Electors for the District of Columbia

[Ratified March 29, 1961]

Section 1 The District constituting the seat of government of the United States shall appoint in such manner as the Congress may direct:

A number of electors of President and Vice President equal to the whole number of Senators and Representatives in Congress to which the District would be entitled if it were a state, but in no event more than the least populous state, they shall be in addition to those appointed by the states, but they shall be considered for the purposes of the election of President and Vice President, to be electors appointed by a state, and they shall meet in the District and perform such duties as provided by the twelfth article of amendment.

Section 2 The Congress shall have power to enforce this article by appropriate legislation.

> This amendment gave electoral votes in presidential elections to the citizens of Washington, D.C., which

is not a state and thus not included in the original arrangement of state electoral votes. Currently, Washington, D.C., has three electoral votes, bringing the total of presidential electoral votes to 538. Each state has electoral votes equal in number to the sum of the state's members of Congress in the House and Senate.

Amendment 24—Elimination of the Poll Tax

[Ratified January 23, 1964]

Section 1 The right of citizens of the United States to vote in any primary or other election for President or Vice President, for electors for President or Vice President or for Senator or Representative in Congress, shall not be denied or abridged by the United States or any state by reason of failure to pay any poll tax or other tax.

Section 2 The Congress shall have power to enforce this article by appropriate legislation.

The poll tax was a procedure used mostly in southern states to discourage poor white and black voters from registering to vote. An individual would have to pay a tax to register to vote, and in some places one would have to pay the cumulative back taxes for elections in which the individual did not register. The tax was usually not much but might still be enough to deter a potential voter, especially if back taxes were involved. Literacy tests, another device to disqualify voters, were abolished by the Voting Rights Act of 1965.

Amendment 25—Presidential Disability, Vice Presidential Vacancies

[Ratified February 10, 1967]

Section 1 In case of the removal of the President from office or his death or resignation, the Vice President shall become President.

Section 2 Whenever there is a vacancy in the office of the Vice President, the President shall nominate a Vice President who shall take the office upon confirmation by a majority vote of both Houses of Congress.

Section 3 Whenever the President transmits to the President pro tempore of the Senate and the Speaker of the House of Representatives his written declaration that he is unable to discharge the powers and duties of his office, and until he transmits to them a written declaration to the contrary, such powers and duties shall be discharged by the Vice President as Acting President.

Section 4 Whenever the Vice President and a majority of either the principal officers of the executive departments or of such other body as Congress may by law provide, transmit to the President pro tempore of the Senate and the Speaker of the House of Representatives their written declaration that the President is unable to discharge the powers and duties of his office, the Vice President shall immediately assume the powers and duties of the office as Acting President.

Thereafter, when the President transmits to the President pro tempore of the Senate and the Speaker of the House of Representatives his written declaration that no inability exists, he shall resume the powers and duties of his office unless the Vice President and a majority of either the principal officers of the executive departments, or of such other body as Congress may by law provide, transmit within four days to the President pro tempore of the Senate and the Speaker of the House of Representatives their written declaration that the President is unable to discharge the powers and duties of his office. Thereupon Congress shall decide the issue, assembling within forty-eight hours for that purpose if not in session. If the Congress, within twenty-one days after receipt of the latter written declaration, or, if Congress is not in session, within twenty-one days after Congress is required to assemble, determines by two-thirds vote of both Houses that the President is unable to discharge the powers and duties of his office, the Vice President shall continue to discharge the same as Acting President; otherwise the President shall resume the powers and duties of his office.

This amendment provides procedures for handling an incapacitating illness of a president. One path is that the president informs congressional leaders of incapacitation and the vice president takes over. On recovery, the president can so inform congressional leaders and resume office. A second path recognizes that the president may not be able or wish to indicate this debilitation, so the vice president and a majority of Cabinet members can inform congressional leaders. Again, the vice president would assume the presidency temporarily. On recovery, the president so informs congressional leadership and resumes the presidency, unless the vice president and a majority of the cabinet disagree. Then Congress must decide.

The most immediate importance of this amendment concerned the office of vice president. The original Constitution did not address the issue of a vacancy in this office. Six years after ratification, in 1973, the sitting vice president, Spiro Agnew, resigned his office. Under the provisions of this amendment, President Nixon nominated Gerald Ford as vice president. When Nixon resigned in 1974, Ford became president and he in turn nominated a new vice president, Nelson Rockefeller.

Amendment 26—Eighteen-Year-Old Vote

[Ratified July 1, 1971]

Section 1 The right of citizens of the United States, who are 18 years of age or older, to vote, shall not be denied or abridged by the United States or by any state on account of age.

Section 2 The Congress shall have power to enforce this article by appropriate legislation.

The Twenty-sixth Amendment prohibited denying citizens 18 years or older the right to vote because of their age.

Amendment 27—Congressional Salaries

[Ratified May 7, 1992]

No law varying the compensation for the services of the Senators and Representatives shall take effect until an election of Representatives shall be intervened.

This amendment was part of 12 amendments originally submitted by the first Congress to the states for ratification. The states in short order ratified 10 of the 12, which collectively became known as the Bill of Rights. Because Congress did not set a time limit for ratification, the other two amendments remained alive, though largely forgotten until the 1980s. By 1992, three-fourths of the states had ratified this amendment, thus adding it to the Constitution. The amendment delays any increase of compensation for at least one election cycle.

Annotated *Federalist* No. 10*

The Utility of the Union as a Safeguard Against Domestic Faction and Insurrection (continued)

Daily Advertiser

Thursday, November 22, 1787

[James Madison]

TO THE PEOPLE OF THE STATE OF NEW YORK

> *Federalist* No. 10 is often regarded as offering the Framers' clearest theoretical defense of the Constitution. James Madison's writing contains some of the most important and often quoted sections of the *Federalist Papers*. Relying upon a view that suggests the natural imperfections of people, Madison, in *Federalist* No. 10, addresses how the core concepts of a republican form of government and federalism partially remedy those imperfections.

Among the numerous advantages promised by a well constructed Union, none deserves to be more accurately developed than its tendency to break and control the violence of faction. The friend of popular governments never finds himself so much alarmed for their character and fate, as when he contemplates their propensity to this dangerous vice. He will not fail, therefore, to set a due value on any plan which, without violating the principles to which he is attached, provides a proper cure for it. The instability, injustice, and confusion introduced into the public councils, have, in truth, been the mortal diseases under which popular governments have everywhere perished; as they continue to be the favorite and fruitful topics from which the adversaries to liberty derive their most specious declamations. The valuable improvements made by the American constitutions on the popular models, both ancient and modern, cannot certainly be too much admired; but it would be an unwarrantable partiality, to contend that they have as effectually obviated the danger on this side, as was wished and expected. Complaints are everywhere heard from our most considerate and virtuous citizens, equally the friends of public and private faith, and of public and personal liberty, that our governments are too unstable, that the public good is disregarded in the conflicts of rival parties, and that measures are too often decided, not according to the rules of justice and the rights of the minor party, but by the superior force of an interested and overbearing majority. However anxiously we may wish that these complaints had no foundation, the evidence, of known facts will not permit us to deny that they are in some degree true. It will be found, indeed, on a candid review of our situation, that some of the distresses under which we labor have been erroneously charged on the operation of our governments; but it will be found, at the same time, that other causes will not alone account for many of our heaviest misfortunes; and, particularly, for that prevailing and increasing distrust of public engagements, and alarm for private rights, which are echoed from one end of the continent to the other. These must be chiefly, if not wholly, effects of the unsteadiness and injustice with which a factious spirit has tainted our public administrations.

> The proposed United States Constitution, then awaiting ratification, would, according to Madison, address three central problems that had plagued most governments, including the then existing state constitutions. Those problems were (1) instability in governments, by which he chiefly means governments failing to function effectively and being replaced by a new set of governing institutions, (2) rulers who legislate against the

*Annotations by Martin Sweet, Northwestern University, and the authors.

common good, and (3) majority interests that trample the rights of the minority. Madison casts blame almost entirely at the feet of factions. Madison, in the next sentence below, provides his definition of faction.

By a faction, I understand a number of citizens, whether amounting to a majority or a minority of the whole, who are united and actuated by some common impulse of passion, or of interest, adversed to the rights of other citizens, or to the permanent and aggregate interests of the community.

A faction can be either a minority or a majority of the population. The key is that a faction is motivated by a passion or self-interest that negatively affects the rights of other citizens or the public interest in general.

There are two methods of curing the mischiefs of faction: the one, by removing its causes; the other, by controlling its effects.

If factions are dangerous, what is to be done about them? The dangers of factions can be addressed either by removing the causes of factions, or by making sure the effects of factions are not destructive. Madison first considers how the causes of factions could be eliminated.

There are again two methods of removing the causes of faction: the one, by destroying the liberty which is essential to its existence; the other, by giving to every citizen the same opinions, the same passions, and the same interests. It could never be more truly said than of the first remedy, that it was worse than the disease. Liberty is to faction what air is to fire, an aliment without which it instantly expires. But it could not be less folly to abolish liberty, which is essential to political life, because it nourishes faction, than it would be to wish the annihilation of air, which is essential to animal life, because it imparts to fire its destructive agency.

Just as one might wish to eliminate air because it has the potentially dangerous effect of feeding fire, one might wish to eliminate factions by abolishing personal liberty. But, according to Madison, the destructive powers of faction are far less severe than what would happen should the government abolish personal liberty. "Liberty is to faction what air is to fire" may be one of the best lines in all of the *Federalist Papers*. To abolish liberty in order to remove factions is, he says, a cure worse than the disease. Madison next considers the second way of removing the causes of factions—giving all people the same opinions and interests.

The second expedient is as impracticable as the first would be unwise. As long as the reason of man continues fallible, and he is at liberty to exercise it, different opinions will be formed. As long as the connection subsists between his reason and his self-love, his opinions and his passions will have a reciprocal influence on each other; and the former will be objects to which the latter will attach themselves. The diversity in the faculties of men, from which the rights of property originate, is not less an insuperable obstacle to a uniformity of interests. The protection of these faculties is the first object of government. From the protection of different and unequal faculties of acquiring property, the possession of different degrees and kinds of property immediately results; and from the influence of these on the sentiments and views of the respective proprietors, ensues a division of the society into different interests and parties.

Here Madison states that factions are, in fact, natural. They are part and parcel of what makes us human. People cannot be given the same opinions and interests. We are all born with different talents and abilities, and those differences will manifest themselves in different ways—including how much money one makes, how much property one might accumulate, or what one's opinions might be. According to Madison, the government must, chief among all of its myriad responsibilities, protect property rights. In doing so, government protects the individual differences that inevitably lead to different abilities to acquiring that property. Madison continues exploring how factions are a natural outcome of our humanness.

The latent causes of faction are thus sown in the nature of man; and we see them everywhere brought into different degrees of activity, according to the different circumstances of civil society. A zeal for different opinions concerning religion, concerning government, and many other points, as well of speculation as of practice; an attachment to different leaders ambitiously contending for pre-eminence and power; or to persons of other descriptions whose fortunes have been interesting to the human passions, have, in turn, divided mankind into parties, inflamed them with mutual animosity, and rendered them much more disposed to vex and oppress each other than to co-operate for their common good. So strong is this propensity of mankind to fall into mutual animosities, that where no substantial occasion presents itself, the most frivolous and fanciful distinctions have been sufficient to kindle their unfriendly passions and excite their most violent conflicts. But the most common and durable source of factions has been the various and unequal distribution of property. Those who hold and those who are without property have ever formed distinct interests in society. Those who are creditors, and those who are debtors, fall under a like discrimination. A landed interest, a manufacturing interest, a mercantile interest, a moneyed interest, with many lesser interests, grow up of necessity in civilized nations, and divide them into different classes, actuated by different sentiments and views. The regulation of these various and interfering interests forms the principal task of modern legislation, and involves the spirit of party and faction in the necessary and ordinary operations of the government.

> People are bound to fall into disputes, Madison explains in the preceding paragraph. He again notes that the unequal distribution of property has been especially likely to lead to factions—"those who hold and those who are without property have ever formed distinct interests in society." Managing the disputes between these factions is one of government's chief activities.

No man is allowed to be a judge in his own cause, because his interest would certainly bias his judgment, and, not improbably, corrupt his integrity. With equal, nay with greater reason, a body of men are unfit to be both judges and parties at the same time; yet what are many of the most important acts of legislation, but so many judicial determinations, not indeed concerning the rights of single persons, but concerning the rights of large bodies of citizens? And what are the different classes of legislators but advocates and parties to the causes which they determine? Is a law proposed concerning private debts? It is a question to which the creditors are parties on one side and the debtors on the other. Justice ought to hold the balance between them. Yet the parties are, and must be, themselves the judges; and the most numerous party, or, in other words, the most powerful faction must be expected to prevail. Shall domestic manufactures be encouraged, and in what degree, by restrictions on foreign manufactures? are questions which would be differently decided by the landed and the manufacturing classes, and probably by neither with a sole regard to justice and the public good. The apportionment of taxes on the various descriptions of property is an act which seems to require the most exact impartiality; yet there is, perhaps, no legislative act in which greater opportunity and temptation are given to a predominant party to trample on the rules of justice. Every shilling with which they overburden the inferior number, is a shilling saved to their own pockets.

It is in vain to say that enlightened statesmen will be able to adjust these clashing interests, and render them all subservient to the public good. Enlightened statesmen will not always be at the helm. Nor, in many cases, can such an adjustment be made at all without taking into view indirect and remote considerations, which will rarely prevail over the immediate interest which one party may find in disregarding the rights of another or the good of the whole.

> Key in the three preceding paragraphs is the premise that the natural differences among people will result

in wide variety of factions—sometimes divided by occupation, other times by wealth, religion, or a belief in the role of government—and that those same factions will find their way into the government. Therefore, it is natural that our representatives themselves will be influenced and divided by their own interests—the same interests that are readily apparent among the people. Even the most well-intentioned rulers cannot be relied upon to stamp out their own natural inclinations, and we cannot always be sure a well-intentioned ruler is in charge.

The inference to which we are brought is, that the causes of faction cannot be removed, and that relief is only to be sought in the means of controlling its effects.

> Recall that Madison had written above that there are two ways to deal with factions: eliminating their causes or reducing their bad effects. He concludes in this paragraph that there is no desirable way to eliminate the causes of factions. Our attention should instead, he says, be focused on making sure they do not have dangerous effects.

If a faction consists of less than a majority, relief is supplied by the republican principle, which enables the majority to defeat its sinister views by regular vote. It may clog the administration, it may convulse the society; but it will be unable to execute and mask its violence under the forms of the Constitution. When a majority is included in a faction, the form of popular government, on the other hand, enables it to sacrifice to its ruling passion or interest both the public good and the rights of other citizens. To secure the public good and private rights against the danger of such a faction, and at the same time to preserve the spirit and the form of popular government, is then the great object to which our inquiries are directed. Let me add that it is the great desideratum by which this form of government can be rescued from the opprobrium under which it has so long labored, and be recommended to the esteem and adoption of mankind.

> Madison suggests that minority factions can be thwarted in governments based on popular rule, because they can be outvoted. He is more concerned with what happens when a majority faction forms under such a government. His goal, he writes, is to find a way that popular rule can exist without producing majority factions that will harm the minority or the public good.

By what means is this object attainable? Evidently by one of two only. Either the existence of the same passion or interest in a majority at the same time must be prevented, or the majority, having such coexistent passion or interest, must be rendered, by their number and local situation, unable to concert and carry into effect schemes of oppression. If the impulse and the opportunity be suffered to coincide, we well know that neither moral nor religious motives can be relied on as an adequate control. They are not found to be such on the injustice and violence of individuals, and lose their efficacy in proportion to the number combined together, that is, in proportion as their efficacy becomes needful.

> A way needs to be found to make majority factions less likely to come together and execute their "schemes of oppression." Hoping that moral or religious values will stop a majority faction is inadequate.

From this view of the subject it may be concluded that a pure democracy, by which I mean a society consisting of a small number of citizens, who assemble and administer the government in person, can admit of no cure for the mischiefs of faction. A common passion or interest will, in almost every case, be felt by a majority of the whole; a communication and concert result from the form of government itself; and there is nothing to check the inducements to sacrifice the weaker party or an obnoxious individual. Hence it is that such democracies have ever been spectacles of turbulence and contention; have ever been found incompatible with personal security or the rights of property; and have in general been as short in their lives as they have been violent in their deaths. Theoretic politicians, who have patronized this species of government, have erroneously supposed that by reducing mankind to a perfect equality in their political rights, they would, at the same time, be perfectly equalized and assimilated in their possessions, their opinions, and their passions.

> A pure democracy, or a system in which all of the people share ruling power by voting on all laws, provides no safeguard to check the power of majority factions. This form of government makes it easy for majority factions to form and easy for them to win.

A republic, by which I mean a government in which the scheme of representation takes place, opens a different prospect, and promises the cure for which we are seeking. Let us examine the points in which it varies from pure democracy, and we shall comprehend both the nature of the cure and the efficacy which it must derive from the Union.

> A republic, on the other hand, or what we might today label a representative democracy, offers a greater hope of deterring the negative effects of majority factions. Madison in the following paragraphs explains how republics differ from democracies and

why these differences are helpful in deterring majority factions.

The two great points of difference between a democracy and a republic are: first, the delegation of the government, in the latter, to a small number of citizens elected by the rest; secondly, the greater number of citizens, and greater sphere of country, over which the latter may be extended.

> The differences are: (1) instead of voting directly on public matters as in a pure democracy, citizens in a republic elect representatives to vote for them on public matters, and (2) the population and geographical size of a republic can be larger than in a pure democracy.

The effect of the first difference is, on the one hand, to refine and enlarge the public views, by passing them through the medium of a chosen body of citizens, whose wisdom may best discern the true interest of their country, and whose patriotism and love of justice will be least likely to sacrifice it to temporary or partial considerations. Under such a regulation, it may well happen that the public voice, pronounced by the representatives of the people, will be more consonant to the public good than if pronounced by the people themselves, convened for the purpose. On the other hand, the effect may be inverted. Men of factious tempers, of local prejudices, or of sinister designs, may, by intrigue, by corruption, or by other means, first obtain the suffrages, and then betray the interests, of the people. The question resulting is, whether small or extensive republics are more favorable to the election of proper guardians of the public weal; and it is clearly decided in favor of the latter by two obvious considerations:

In the first place, it is to be remarked that, however small the republic may be, the representatives must be raised to a certain number, in order to guard against the cabals of a few; and that, however large it may be, they must be limited to a certain number, in order to guard against the confusion of a multitude. Hence, the number of representatives in the two cases not being in proportion to that of the two constituents, and being proportionally greater in the small republic, it follows that, if the proportion of fit characters be not less in the large than in the small republic, the former will present a greater option, and consequently a greater probability of a fit choice.

In the next place, as each representative will be chosen by a greater number of citizens in the large than in the small republic, it will be more difficult for unworthy candidates to practice with success the vicious arts by which elections are too often carried; and the suffrages of the people being more free, will be more likely to centre in men who possess the most attractive merit and the most diffusive and established characters.

In the preceding three paragraphs, Madison discusses the first difference between a republic and a democracy: the presence of representatives. He argues that in a republic, representatives offer a filter to weed out dangerous and unwise ideas. The result may be more consistent with the public good than, ironically, if the people made the laws themselves in a pure democracy. He then asks whether small or large republics make the election of representatives who will make wise and just decisions more likely. He argues that there is a happy medium between too few representatives—which might be susceptible to corruption or other vices—and too many representatives—which might lead to confusion or chaos. Madison suggests that a larger republic in terms of population and size is more desirable than a smaller republic. First, there will be a greater number of wise candidates in a large republic than in a small one. The likelihood that unfit individuals will be elected is thus lower in a large republic. Second, because there are more voters and proportionally fewer representatives in a large republic—in other words, each district is larger than in a small republic and each representative will have to represent a larger number of people—such a republic is better suited to withstand the deception and sometimes ugliness that can mar elections. It is easier for candidates to be deceptive when appealing to small groups of people in a small area.

It must be confessed that in this, as in most other cases, there is a mean, on both sides of which inconveniences will be found to lie. By enlarging too much the number of electors, you render the representatives too little acquainted with all their local circumstances and lesser interests; as by reducing it too much, you render him unduly attached to these, and too little fit to comprehend and pursue great and national objects. The federal Constitution forms a happy combination in this respect; the great and aggregate interests being referred to the national, the local and particular to the State legislatures.

Madison again notes it is important that the ratio of voters to representatives be neither too large nor too small. The proposed Constitution provides an admirable compromise: national government will address broad issues of general importance, while state governments will focus on the more narrow concerns of their respective states.

The other point of difference is, the greater number of citizens and extent of territory which may be brought within the compass of republican than of democratic government; and it is this circumstance principally which renders factious combinations less to be dreaded in the former than in the latter. The smaller the society, the fewer probably will be the distinct parties and interests composing it; the fewer the distinct parties and interests, the more frequently will a majority be found of the same party; and the smaller the number of individuals composing a majority, and the smaller the compass within which they are placed, the more easily will they concert and execute their plans of oppression. Extend the sphere, and you take in a greater variety of parties and interests; you make it less probable that a majority of the whole will have a common motive to invade the rights of other citizens; or if such a common motive exists, it will be more difficult for all who feel it to discover their own strength, and to act in unison with each other. Besides other impediments, it may be remarked that, where there is a consciousness of unjust or dishonorable purposes, communication is always checked by distrust in proportion to the number whose concurrence is necessary.

Madison now discusses the second difference between a republic and a democracy: a republic can govern a larger geographical area. Why is this a good thing? The larger the area, Madison argues, the less likely majority factions will exist. As a country expands, so does the diversity of its citizens—"extend the sphere, and you take in a wider variety of parties and interests." This expanding diversity means a diffusion of interests and an expansion of the number of factions and a lower likelihood of a common interest uniting a majority of the population. Moreover, even if a majority faction were to emerge, the vast land mass of a large republic would make it harder for citizens to realize that they shared this interest and to come together to impose their will on the minority. He then applies this logic to the proposed national government and the states in the following two paragraphs.

Hence, it clearly appears, that the same advantage which a republic has over a democracy, in controlling the effects of faction, is enjoyed by a large over a small republic,—is enjoyed by the Union over the States composing it. Does the advantage consist in the substitution of representatives whose enlightened views and virtuous sentiments render them superior to local prejudices and schemes of injustice? It will not be denied that the representation of the Union will be most likely to possess these requisite endowments. Does it consist in the greater security afforded by a greater variety of parties, against the event of any one party being able to outnumber and oppress the rest? In an equal degree does the increased variety of parties comprised within the Union, increase this security. Does it, in fine, consist in the greater obstacles opposed to the concert and accomplishment of the secret wishes of an unjust and interested majority? Here, again, the extent of the Union gives it the most palpable advantage.

The influence of factious leaders may kindle a flame within their particular States, but will be unable to spread a general conflagration through the other States. A religious sect may degenerate into a political faction in a part of the Confederacy; but the variety of sects dispersed over the entire face of it must secure the national councils against any danger from that source. A rage for paper money, for an abolition of debts, for an equal division of property, or for any other improper or wicked project, will be less apt to pervade the whole body of the Union than a particular member of it; in the same proportion as such a malady is more likely to taint a particular county or district, than an entire State.

Madison summarizes that republics are better at controlling the effects of factions than are pure democracies, that larger republics are preferable to smaller republics, and that a federal system—with government at both the state and the national level—is superior to the alternative of a single central government (which would be insensitive to local needs) and to a diffused system of state governments (which would be insensitive to broad, national needs). For those who were concerned about the concentration of power in this new national government, Madison provides an argument that suggests this new large government will actually better protect individual rights and the common good than would governments like the states that are smaller and close to the people. An "improper or wicked project"—Madison references some examples that would be familiar to his audience, including the issuance of worthless paper money and the dismissal of debts—is more likely to take hold and inflame in people's passions in one state than it is in an entire country, just as it is more likely in a single district or county within a state. The bigger the area, the more difficult for factious leaders to succeed. Under the proposed Constitution, the ability of factions to succeed would be dim.

In the extent and proper structure of the Union, therefore, we behold a republican remedy for the diseases most incident to republican government. And according to the degree of pleasure and pride we feel in being republicans, ought to be our zeal in cherishing the spirit and supporting the character of Federalists.

PUBLIUS

APPENDIX 4

Annotated *Federalist* No. 51*

The Structure of the Government Must Furnish the Proper Checks and Balances Between the Different Departments

Independent Journal

Wednesday, February 6, 1788

[James Madison]

TO THE PEOPLE OF THE STATE OF NEW YORK

Federalist No. 51 revolves around the key concept of power. One of the primary reservations about the proposed United States Constitution, particularly from the Anti-Federalists, was the fear of the power of a centralized government. James Madison in *Federalist* No. 51 continues an argument that had begun in earlier essays, especially Nos. 47 and 48. One of the complaints against the Constitution was that it was providing not a true separation of powers but a blended system in which each major branch of government interfered with the other. Critics saw this as a threat to liberty, but Madison in this essay emphasizes the benefits of this arrangement for protecting the peoples' rights. He argues that the separation of powers among the three branches of the national government, the checks and balances built into the structure of each branch and their relationship to the other branches of government, federalism (two distinct levels of government, each with some sovereign authority), and pluralism (the proliferation of and competition among interest groups) will each and together refute the criticism that the government proposed in the Constitution threatens liberty by centralizing power.

To what expedient, then, shall we finally resort, for maintaining in practice the necessary partition of power among the several departments, as laid down in the Constitution? The only answer that can be given is, that as all these exterior provisions are found to be inadequate, the defect must be supplied, by so contriving the interior structure of the government as that its several constituent parts may, by their mutual relations, be the means of keeping each other in their proper places. Without presuming to undertake a full development of this important idea, I will hazard a few general observations, which may perhaps place it in a clearer light, and enable us to form a more correct judgment of the principles and structure of the government planned by the convention.

How can the distinction between the executive, legislative, and judicial branches be preserved? Madison says that neither merely writing down the distinctions on paper nor holding elections—"the exterior provisions"—will be sufficient. In addition, the government must be designed so that each branch is "keeping each other in their proper places"—that is, through checks and balances.

In order to lay a due foundation for that separate and distinct exercise of the different powers of government, which to a certain extent is admitted on all hands to be essential to the preservation of liberty, it is evident that each department should have a will of its own; and consequently should be so constituted that the members of each should have as little agency as possible in the appointment of the members of the others. Were this principle rigorously adhered to, it would require that all the appointments for the supreme executive, legislative, and judiciary magistracies should be drawn from the same fountain of authority, the people, through channels having no communication what-

*Annotations by Martin Sweet, Northwestern University, and the authors.

ever with one another. Perhaps such a plan of constructing the several departments would be less difficult in practice than it may in contemplation appear. Some difficulties, however, and some additional expense would attend the execution of it. Some deviations, therefore, from the principle must be admitted. In the constitution of the judiciary department in particular, it might be inexpedient to insist rigorously on the principle: first, because peculiar qualifications being essential in the members, the primary consideration ought to be to select that mode of choice which best secures these qualifications; secondly, because the permanent tenure by which the appointments are held in that department, must soon destroy all sense of dependence on the authority conferring them.

It is equally evident, that the members of each department should be as little dependent as possible on those of the others, for the emoluments annexed to their offices. Were the executive magistrate, or the judges, not independent of the legislature in this particular, their independence in every other would be merely nominal.

One of the primary reasons that Madison and the Federalists favored the new Constitution was the need for strong national government power. The Framers, however, realized that such power would be ripe for abuse, and they made a concerted effort to create structures within the Constitution that would limit the opportunity for such abuse. One of those structural limitations on the abuse of power would later come to be known as the "separation of powers" doctrine. Under separation of powers, each branch of government has its own unique powers and is limited in its ability to absorb the functions of the other branches of government. How can each branch resist the encroachment of the other branches of government? Madison explores the defense against encroachment in the following paragraph. Checks and balances provide the methods of this interinstitutional defense and a strong security that no single branch will gradually take on all the major functions—executive, legislative, judicial—of government.

But the great security against a gradual concentration of the several powers in the same department, consists in giving to those who administer each department the necessary constitutional means and personal motives to resist encroachments of the others. The provision for defense must in this, as in all other cases, be made commensurate to the danger of attack. Ambition must be made to counteract ambition. The interest of the man must be connected with the constitutional rights of the place. It may be a reflection on human nature, that such devices should be necessary to control the abuses of government. But what is government itself, but the greatest of all reflections on

human nature? If men were angels, no government would be necessary. If angels were to govern men, neither external nor internal controls on government would be necessary. In framing a government which is to be administered by men over men, the great difficulty lies in this: you must first enable the government to control the governed; and in the next place oblige it to control itself. A dependence on the people is, no doubt, the primary control on the government; but experience has taught mankind the necessity of auxiliary precautions.

This paragraph has two key quotes. First, "Ambition must be made to counteract ambition." One of the aims of the Constitution was to craft a healthy competition among the branches of government—such that the very natural human impulses contained within individuals in one branch of government would limit those very natural human impulses contained within individuals in another branch of government. Government is only an aggregation of fallible individuals and thus needs limitations. This precept led Madison to remark in the second key quote, "If men were angels, no government would be necessary." Because people are not angels, a government of mortal humans needs to be controlled. Elections and the sovereignty of the people provide the greatest control, but others are necessary as well.

This policy of supplying, by opposite and rival interests, the defect of better motives, might be traced through the whole system of human affairs, private as well as public. We see it particularly displayed in all the subordinate distributions of power, where the constant aim is to divide and arrange the several offices in such a manner as that each may be a check on the other—that the private interest of every individual may be a sentinel over the public rights. These inventions of prudence cannot be less requisite in the distribution of the supreme powers of the State.

But it is not possible to give to each department an equal power of self-defense. In republican government, the legislative authority necessarily predominates. The remedy for this inconveniency is to divide the legislature into different branches; and to render them, by different modes of election and different principles of action, as little connected with each other as the nature of their common functions and their common dependence on the society will admit. It may even be necessary to guard against dangerous encroachments by still further precautions. As the weight of the legislative authority requires that it should be thus divided, the weakness of the executive may require, on the other hand, that it should be fortified. An absolute negative on the legislature appears, at first view, to be the natural defense with which the executive magistrate should be armed. But perhaps it would be neither altogether safe nor alone sufficient. On ordinary occasions it might not be exerted with the requisite firmness, and on extraordinary occasions it might be perfidiously abused. May not this defect of an absolute negative be supplied by some qualified connection between this weaker department and the weaker branch of the stronger department, by which the latter may be led to support the constitutional rights of the former, without being too much detached from the rights of its own department?

If the principles on which these observations are founded be just, as I persuade myself they are, and they be applied as a criterion to the several State constitutions, and to the federal Constitution it will be found that if the latter does not perfectly correspond with them, the former are infinitely less able to bear such a test.

> Today we often think of the three branches of government as "co-equal" branches. Yet Madison writes that in a republic—a representative democracy—the legislative branch must be dominant. But to make sure the legislative branch does not exert too great a power, special constraints would be imposed on it. It will consist of two different legislative bodies (the House of Representatives and the Senate), each elected by different means and with some difference in function. To prevent the executive branch from being too weak compared to the legislative branch, the president should be given a veto power (an "absolute negative"). The executive branch and the Senate ("the weaker branch of the stronger department") should also have an arrangement that protects the power of the executive while also allowing the Senate to honor its legislative function. Madison does not mention these examples, but this relationship appears in the treaty approval process and executive branch appointments, both of which require Senate but not House approval. To the critics of the Constitution, Madison notes in the previous paragraph that although the systems of checks and balances proposed in the new system to protect the separation of powers may not be perfect, it is superior to that found in the state constitutions.

There are, moreover, two considerations particularly applicable to the federal system of America, which place that system in a very interesting point of view.

First. In a single republic, all the power surrendered by the people is submitted to the administration of a single government; and the usurpations are guarded against by a division of the government into distinct and separate departments. In the compound republic of America, the power surrendered by the people is first divided between two distinct governments, and then the portion allotted to each subdivided among distinct and separate departments.

Hence a double security arises to the rights of the people. The different governments will control each other, at the same time that each will be controlled by itself.

> The separation of powers in the American system is twofold. First, powers are to be separated horizontally—among the executive, legislative, and judicial branches. Second, powers are to be separated vertically—between the federal government and the state governments. The American federal system, the "compound republic" with two distinct sovereigns at the national and state levels, serves to further diffuse government power. And just as the competition among the national branches of government serves to counteract the power of any one branch, so will the competition between the federal and state governments serve to counteract the concentration of power in one location. Madison refers to this as a "double security" that will protect the rights of the people.

Second. It is of great importance in a republic not only to guard the society against the oppression of its rulers, but to guard one part of the society against the injustice of the other part. Different interests necessarily exist in different classes of citizens. If a majority be united by a common interest, the rights of the minority will be insecure. There are but two methods of providing against this evil: the one by creating a will in the community independent of the majority—that is, of the society itself; the other, by comprehending in the society so many separate descriptions of citizens as will render an unjust combination of a majority of the whole very improbable, if not impracticable. The first method prevails in all governments possessing an hereditary or self-appointed authority. This, at best, is but a precarious security; because a power independent of the society may as well espouse the unjust views of the major, as the rightful interests of the minor party, and may possibly be turned against both parties.

> Madison begins his long concluding paragraph by noting that the people need to be protected from each other just as much as they need to be protected from their rulers. How can this be accomplished? One way is for an independent "will" in the society that represents the society's interests but is independent of it. Systems based on hereditary rule are one example but, Madison writes, such a solution is unsatisfactory. Such a ruler might still promote the unjust views of the majority rather than do what is best for all, or such a ruler might turn against both the majority and minority, not in the interests of society but in the ruler's own self-interest. Madison continues, in the remainder of the paragraph, by asserting the advantages of

the second method to protect the people from each other—making it difficult for a majority faction to form. Madison summarizes some of his conclusions from *Federalist* No. 10.

The second method will be exemplified in the federal republic of the United States. Whilst all authority in it will be derived from and dependent on the society, the society itself will be broken into so many parts, interests, and classes of citizens, that the rights of individuals, or of the minority, will be in little danger from interested combinations of the majority. In a free government the security for civil rights must be the same as that for religious rights. It consists in the one case in the multiplicity of interests, and in the other in the multiplicity of sects. The degree of security in both cases will depend on the number of interests and sects; and this may be presumed to depend on the extent of country and number of people comprehended under the same government. This view of the subject must particularly recommend a proper federal system to all the sincere and considerate friends of republican government, since it shows that in exact proportion as the territory of the Union may be formed into more circumscribed Confederacies, or States oppressive combinations of a majority will be facilitated: the best security, under the republican forms, for the rights of every class of citizens, will be diminished: and consequently the stability and independence of some member of the government, the only other security, must be proportionately increased. Justice is the end of government. It is the end of civil society. It ever has been and ever will be pursued until it be obtained, or until liberty be lost in the pursuit. In a society under the forms of which the stronger faction can readily unite and oppress the weaker, anarchy may as truly be said to reign as in a state of nature, where the weaker individual is not secured against the violence of the stronger; and as, in the latter state, even the stronger individuals are prompted, by the uncertainty of their condition, to submit to a government which may protect the weak as well as themselves; so, in the former state, will the more powerful factions or parties be gradually induced, by a like motive, to wish for a government which will protect all parties, the weaker as well as the more powerful. It can be little doubted that if the State of Rhode Island was separated from the Confederacy and left to itself, the insecurity of rights under the popular form of government within such narrow limits would be displayed by such reiterated oppressions of factious majorities that some power altogether independent of the people would soon be called for by the voice of the very factions whose misrule had proved the necessity of it. In the extended republic of the United States, and among the great variety of interests, parties, and sects which it embraces, a coalition of a majority of the whole society could seldom take place on any other principles than those of justice and the general good; whilst there being thus less danger to a minor from the will of a major party, there must be less pretext, also, to provide for the security of the former, by introducing into the government a will not dependent on the latter, or, in other words, a will independent of the society itself. It is no less certain than it is important, notwithstanding the contrary opinions which have been entertained, that the larger the society, provided it lie within a practical sphere, the more duly capable it will be of self-government. And happily for the republican cause, the practicable sphere may be carried to a very great extent, by a judicious modification and mixture of the federal principle.

> Madison defends what we label today as "pluralism" or the division of society into such a large number of varied interest groups that the concept of "majority" is rendered suspect. If most individuals are part of these smaller interest groups, these divided interests are difficult to combine into any single organized majority. Without a single organized majority, power cannot concentrate in a centralized location and factions among the people are less likely to threaten fellow citizens. Madison intends for his earlier argument in this essay concerning separation of powers and checks and balances to combine with these points about pluralism, leading the reader to conclude that the proposed Constitution is desirable. A federal system ensures that power does not concentrate within the national or state governments. Separation of powers ensures that power does not concentrate within any single branch of government. Without centralization of power, with this double security, the opportunity is maximized for the government to achieve justice, and, according to Madison, "Justice is the end [goal] of government. It is the end [goal] of civil society."

PUBLIUS

APPENDIX 5

Party Control of the Presidency, Senate, and House of Representatives

Congress	Years	President	Senate* D	Senate* R	Senate* Other	House* D	House* R	House* Other
57th	1901–03	McKinley	29	56	3	153	198	5
		T. Roosevelt						
58th	1903–05	T. Roosevelt	32	58	—	178	207	—
59th	1905–07	T. Roosevelt	32	58	—	136	250	—
60th	1907–09	T. Roosevelt	29	61	—	164	222	—
61st	1909–11	Taft	32	59	—	172	219	—
62nd	1911–13	Taft	42	49	—	228†	162	1
63rd	1913–15	Wilson	51	44	1	290	127	18
64th	1915–17	Wilson	56	39	1	230	193	8
65th	1917–19	Wilson	53	42	1	200	216	9
66th	1919–21	Wilson	48	48†	1	191	237†	7
67th	1921–23	Harding	37	59	—	132	300	1
68th	1923–25	Coolidge	43	51	2	207	225	3
69th	1925–27	Coolidge	40	54	1	183	247	5
70th	1927–29	Coolidge	47	48	1	195	237	3
71st	1929–31	Hoover	39	56	1	163	267	1
72nd	1931–33	Hoover	47	48	1	216††	218	1
73rd	1933–35	F. Roosevelt	59	36	1	313	117	5
74th	1935–37	F. Roosevelt	69	25	2	322	103	10
75th	1937–39	F. Roosevelt	75	17	4	333	89	13
76th	1939–41	F. Roosevelt	69	23	4	262	169	4
77th	1941–43	F. Roosevelt	66	28	2	267	162	6
78th	1943–45	F. Roosevelt	57	38	1	222	209	4
79th	1945–47	Truman	57	38	1	243	190	2
80th	1947–49	Truman	45	51†	—	188	246†	1
81st	1949–51	Truman	54	42	—	263	171	1
82nd	1951–53	Truman	48	47	1	234	199	2
83nd	1953–55	Eisenhower	47	48	1	213	221	1
84th	1955–57	Eisenhower	48†	47	1	232†	203	—
85th	1957–59	Eisenhower	49†	47	—	234†	201	—
86th‡‡‡	1959–61	Eisenhower	64†	34	—	283†	154	—
87th‡‡‡	1961–63	Kennedy	64	36	—	263	174	—

Congress	Years	President	Senate* D	Senate* R	Senate* Other	House* D	House* R	House* Other
88th	1963–65	Kennedy Johnson	67	33	—	258	176	—
89th	1965–67	Johnson	68	32	—	295	140	—
90th	1967–69	Johnson	64	36	—	248	187	—
91st	1969–71	Nixon	58†	42	—	243†	192	—
92nd	1971–73	Nixon	55†	45	—	255†	180	—
93rd	1973–75	Nixon Ford	57†	43	—	243†	192	—
94th	1975–77	Ford	61†	38	—	291†	144	—
95th	1977–79	Carter	62	38	—	292	143	—
96th	1979–81	Carter	59	41	—	277	158	—
97th	1981–83	Reagan	47	53	—	243†	192	—
98th	1983–85	Reagan	46	54	—	269†	166	—
99th	1985–87	Reagan	47	53	—	253†	182	—
100th	1987–89	Reagan	55†	45	—	258†	177	—
101st	1989–91	G. H.W. Bush	55†	45	—	260†	175	—
102nd	1991–93	G. H.W. Bush	56†	44	—	267†	167	1
103rd	1993–95	Clinton	57	43	—	258	176	1
104th	1995–97	Clinton	46	54†	—	202	232†	1
105th	1997–99	Clinton	45	55†	—	206	228†	1
106th	1999–01	Clinton	45	55†	—	211	223†	1
107th	2001–03	G. W. Bush	50#	50	—	212	221	2
108th	2003–05	G. W. Bush	48	51	1	205	229	1
109th	2005–07	G. W. Bush	44	55	1	202	232	1
110th	2007–09	G. W. Bush	50†	49	1	233†	202	—
111th	2009–11	Obama	57	41	2	257	178	—
112th	2011–13	Obama	51	47	2	193	242†	—

*Excludes vacancies at beginning of each session. Party balance immediately following election.

†Chamber controlled by party other than that of the president.

††Republicans won a majority of seats in the 1930 election, but because of deaths and subsequent special elections, Democrats held a majority by the time the 72nd Congress was seated.

†††The 437 members of the House in the 86th and 87th Congresses are attributable to the at-large representative given to both Alaska (January 3, 1959) and Hawaii (August 21, 1959) prior to redistricting in 1962.

#Republicans controlled the Senate until mid-2001. Party control switched to the Democrats when Republican Senator James Jeffords became an independent and began caucusing with the Democrats, making the party balance 50 Democrats, 49 Republicans, and 1 independent.

D = Democrat

R = Republican

APPENDIX 6

Supreme Court Justices

Name	Nominated by	Service
John M. Harlan	Hayes	1877–1911
Horace Gray	Arthur	1882–1902
Melville W. Fuller*	Cleveland	1888–1910
David J. Brewer	Harrison	1890–1910
Henry B. Brown	Harrison	1890–1906
George Shiras Jr.	Harrison	1892–1903
Edward D. White	Cleveland	1894–1910
Rufus W. Peckham	Cleveland	1895–1909
Joseph McKenna	McKinley	1898–1925
Oliver W. Holmes	T. Roosevelt	1902–1932
William R. Day	T. Roosevelt	1903–1922
William H. Moody	T. Roosevelt	1906–1910
Horace H. Lurton	Taft	1910–1914
Edward D. White	Taft	1910–1921
Charles E. Hughes	Taft	1910–1916
Willis Van Devanter	Taft	1911–1937
Joseph R. Lamar	Taft	1911–1916
Mahlon Pitney	Taft	1912–1922
James C. McReynolds	Wilson	1914–1941
Louis D. Brandeis	Wilson	1916–1939
John H. Clarke	Wilson	1916–1922
William H. Taft	Harding	1921–1930
George Sutherland	Harding	1922–1938
Pierce Butler	Harding	1922–1939
Edward T. Sanford	Harding	1923–1930
Harlan F. Stone	Coolidge	1925–1941
Charles E. Hughes	Hoover	1930–1941
Owen J. Roberts	Hoover	1930–1945
Benjamin N. Cardozo	Hoover	1932–1938
Hugo L. Black	F. Roosevelt	1937–1971
Stanley F. Reed	F. Roosevelt	1938–1957
Felix Frankfurter	F. Roosevelt	1939–1962

Name	Nominated by	Service
William O. Douglas	F. Roosevelt	1939–1975
Frank Murphy	F. Roosevelt	1940–1949
Harlan F. Stone	F. Roosevelt	1941–1946
James F. Byrnes	F. Roosevelt	1941–1942
Robert H. Jackson	F. Roosevelt	1941–1954
Wiley B. Rutledge	F. Roosevelt	1943–1949
Harold H. Burton	Truman	1945–1958
Fred M. Vinson	Truman	1946–1953
Tom C. Clark	Truman	1949–1967
Sherman Minton	Truman	1949–1956
Earl Warren	Eisenhower	1953–1969
John M. Harlan	Eisenhower	1955–1971
William J. Brennan Jr.	Eisenhower	1956–1990
Charles E. Whittaker	Eisenhower	1957–1962
Potter Stewart	Eisenhower	1958–1981
Byron R. White	Kennedy	1962–1993
Arthur J. Goldberg	Kennedy	1962–1965
Abe Fortas	Johnson	1965–1969
Thurgood Marshall	Johnson	1967–1991
Warren E. Burger	Nixon	1969–1986
Harry A. Blackmun	Nixon	1970–1994
Lewis F. Powell Jr.	Nixon	1971–1987
William H. Rehnquist	Nixon	1971–1986
John Paul Stevens	Ford	1975–2010
Sandra Day O'Connor	Reagan	1981–2006
William H. Rehnquist	Reagan	1986–2005
Antonin Scalia	Reagan	1986–
Anthony M. Kennedy	Reagan	1988–
David H. Souter	G. H.W. Bush	1990–2009
Clarence Thomas	G. H.W. Bush	1991–
Ruth Bader Ginsburg	Clinton	1993–
Stephen G. Breyer	Clinton	1994–
John G. Roberts Jr.	G. W. Bush	2005–
Samuel A. Alito Jr.	G. W. Bush	2006–
Sonia Sotomayor	Obama	2009–
Elena Kagan	Obama	2010–

*Boldface type indicates service as chief justice.

GLOSSARY

affirmative action efforts to reach and attract applicants for jobs, college admissions, and business contracts from traditionally underrepresented groups, ranging from extensive publicity and outreach to quota plans.

agency capture the condition under which an agency primarily serves the interests of a nongovernmental group rather than those of elected officials.

agenda-setting the ability to shape which issues the public considers important, by covering some issues and ignoring others.

American creed the dominant political culture in the United States, marked by a set of beliefs in individualism, democracy, liberty, property, and religion, tied together by the value of equality.

amicus curiae a brief written by someone who is not a party to a case but who submits information or an argument related to the dispute at hand.

Anti-Federalists individuals opposed to the proposed Constitution, fearing it concentrated too much power in the national government.

appellate courts the second tier of the federal judiciary, primarily responsible for reviewing decisions rendered by the first tier of district courts.

appropriations the granting of funds to operate authorized federal programs and agencies.

approval rating the percentage of the public that approves of the job the president is doing overall.

Articles of Confederation the first constitution of the United States, which based most power in the states.

attitudinal model the theory of judicial decision-making in which judges use their own policy preferences in deciding cases.

Australian ballot an official government-produced ballot for elections that lists all offices and all the candidates and parties that have qualified to be on the ballot.

authoritarian (or totalitarian) system a political system in which one person or group has absolute control over the apparatus of government, and in which popular input in government is minimal or nonexistent.

authorization the granting of legal authority to operate federal programs and agencies.

autocracy a form of government in which a single person rules with effectively unlimited power.

balancing test used by the Supreme Court in free exercise of religion cases, this two-part test first determined whether a government action or law was a burden on religious practice and, if it was, whether a compelling government interest was at stake that would make the burden constitutionally acceptable.

bias favorable treatment to certain politicians, policy positions, groups, and political outcomes.

bicameral an institution consisting of two chambers.

Bill of Rights the first 10 amendments to the U.S. Constitution, intended to protect individual liberties from federal government intrusion.

block grant funds provided by the federal government to a state or local government in general support of a broad government function such as education or transportation.

briefs documents that contain the legal arguments of a dispute.

Brown v. Board of Education Supreme Court ruling in 1954 that in public education, mandatory separation of children by race leads to inherently unequal education. The decision overturned the separate but equal doctrine.

bundling the practice of collecting individual checks and presenting them to a candidate at one time.

bureaucracy a group of departments, agencies, and other institutions that for the most part are located in the executive branch of government and that develop and implement public policy.

Cabinet a group of the top-ranking officials of every major federal department, plus other officials included by the president, who meet periodically with the president to discuss major administration priorities and policies.

casework the direct assistance that members of Congress give to individuals and groups within a district or state.

categorical grant funds provided by the federal government to a state or local government for a specific, defined purpose.

caucus a small meeting at which registered political party members select delegates to attend the national party convention and nominate a presidential candidate.

causal question a question regarding the factors responsible for a particular outcome.

causation a relationship between variables such that change in the value of one is directly responsible for change in the value of the other.

Central Intelligence Agency (CIA) the cornerstone of U.S. efforts to gather and analyze data in order to confront America's real and potential enemies.

centralization the method of increasing the president's power by moving key administrative functions from the departments to the Executive Office of the President.

checks and balances the principle that each branch of the federal government has the means to thwart or influence actions by other branches of government.

chief justice the presiding member of the Supreme Court who serves as chair of the conference and, if in the majority, selects the justice who will write the majority opinion.

civic skills the skills of writing, speaking, analyzing, and organizing that reduce the cost of political participation.

civil case a case that concerns a violation of the legal rights or obligations of one individual toward another.

civil disobedience strategy of breaking a law nonviolently, risking arrest, in order to draw attention to the injustice of the law.

civil liberties individual rights and freedoms that government is obliged to protect, normally by not interfering in the exercise of these rights and freedoms.

civil rights guarantees of equal opportunities, privileges, and treatment under the law that allow individuals to participate fully and equally in American society.

civil service system a system of government in which decisions about hiring, promotion, and firing are based on individuals' work experience, skills, and expertise.

class action suit a lawsuit in which the plaintiff is a group of individuals who have suffered a common injury.

closed primary an election in which only registered members of a political party can participate in the party's primary election.

closed rule the terms and conditions applied to a particular bill that restrict the types of amendments that can be made to it.

cloture a mechanism by which 60 or more senators can end a filibuster and cut off debate.

collective action problem a problem that arises when individuals' incentives lead them to avoid taking actions that are best for the group as a whole, and that they themselves would like to see accomplished.

collective benefit a benefit everyone enjoys, regardless of whether they contributed to its attainment.

commerce clause a provision in the U.S. Constitution that gives Congress the power to regulate commerce with other countries, among the states, and with Indian tribes.

527 committee an independent, nonparty group that raises and spends money on political activities.

common law law made by judges when no legislation currently exists.

communitarianism the view that the needs of the community are of higher priority in government than the needs of the individual, even if the result is a restriction of individual liberties.

compact theory a theory of the founding of the American government that argues states were sovereign units that joined together in the new national government but did not give up their status as sovereign, independent governments.

concurring opinion a document written by one or more justices on the majority side of a ruling that outlines additional considerations he or she thinks are important.

confederation a loose grouping of independent political units, such as states or countries, whose main purpose is to govern the relationship between those units.

conference the confidential gathering of justices in which they discuss their thoughts about the case and cast preliminary votes.

conference committee a committee made up of members of both chambers that is responsible for ironing out the differences between House and Senate versions of a bill.

constituents the people who reside within an elected official's political jurisdiction.

constitutional democracy a form of democracy in which there is a foundational document (such as the U.S. Constitution) that describes the structure, powers, and limits of government.

continuing resolution funds used to keep programs up and running when regular appropriations have not been approved by the end of the fiscal year.

cooperative federalism a form of federalism in which the national and state governments share many functions and areas of authority.

correlation a relationship between factors such that change in one is accompanied by change in the other.

criminal case a case that involves a violation of the statutes that are intended to protect the public's health, order, safety, and morality.

cycling a phenomenon that occurs when multiple decision makers must choose among multiple options and cannot agree on a single course of action.

dealignment a substantial reduction in the proportion of the voting population consistently voting for and identifying with one party.

Declaration of Independence document announcing the intention of the colonies to separate from Great Britain based on shared grievances about the treatment of the colonists by the British government.

de facto segregation racial segregation that results not from explicit laws, policies, or procedures, but from patterns of behavior that have the effect of segregating the races.

defendant the party being sued or accused of a crime.

Defense Department the agency created by the National Security Act in 1947 that replaced the Department of War.

deficit the amount of money a government spends in a year, above and beyond what it brings in through taxation and other means.

de jure segregation racial segregation that occurs because it is written into law, policy, or government procedures.

delegate model of representation the type of representation by which representatives are elected to do the bidding of the people who elected them; representatives are "delegates" in that they share the same policy positions as the voters and promise to act upon them.

delegates individuals who represent a state's voters in the selection of a political party's presidential candidate.

delegation the granting of authority by Congress to the president to be the first or main actor in a policy area, usually with implicit or explicit limits on actions that Congress would find acceptable.

democracy a form of government in which the people rule. This can take place directly, through participation by the people in actual lawmaking, or indirectly, through free elections in which the people choose representatives to make laws on their behalf.

department a major administrative unit that is composed of many agencies serving many policy functions, and that is headed by a secretary, who serves in the president's Cabinet.

Department of Homeland Security (DHS) the agency created in the aftermath of September 11 to coordinate the work of agencies involved in preventing and responding to attacks on the United States.

deregulation the process of decreasing the number of agency rules that apply to a particular industry or group of industries so as to introduce market forces to their operations.

devolution a process in which the authority over a government program's rules and implementation is largely transferred from a higher-level government to a lower-level government.

diplomacy the peaceful negotiation of economic and political relationships between different countries.

direct democracy a form of democracy in which the people themselves make the laws and set the policies adopted by the government.

direction in public opinion, the tendency for or against some phenomenon.

discrimination the view that not all groups in society are deserving of equal rights and opportunities.

dissenting opinion a document written by one or more justices on the minority side of a ruling that outlines his or her own reasoning on the case and identifies perceived flaws in the majority opinion.

district courts the first tier of the federal judiciary, in which most cases are decided.

disturbance theory the theory that when social, political, and economic relationships change, individuals form groups in response.

divided government a situation in which the presidency is held by one party and at least one house of Congress is controlled by a different party.

Dred Scott v. Sandford Supreme Court decision in 1857 declaring that neither slaves nor the descendants of slaves could be U.S. citizens.

drift a situation in which bureaucrats create policy that does not match the policy preferences of Congress or the president.

dual citizenship the idea that an individual is a citizen of both his or her state and the United States. Rights and responsibilities can vary from state to state and can be different on the state and national levels.

dual federalism a form of federalism in which the national and state governments have distinct areas of authority and power, and individuals have rights as both citizens of states and citizens of the United States.

dual sovereignty the idea that both the national and state governments have sovereignty, but over different policy areas and functions.

due process procedural safeguards that government officials are obligated to follow prior to restricting rights of life, liberty, and property.

earmarks federal funds that support specific local projects.

Electoral College the group of electors from each state and the District of Columbia who cast votes to elect the president.

electoral realignment a shift in the composition of party coalitions that produces a new, relatively durable pattern of party competition.

entitlements benefits that all qualifying individuals have a legal right to obtain.

enumerated powers the specifically listed duties that the U.S. Constitution assigns to Congress.

equality the value that all Americans should be treated the same under the law, be able to influence government, and have equal opportunity to succeed in life.

equal privileges and immunities clause a clause in the Constitution stating that states are to treat equally their citizens and the citizens of other states.

equal protection clause clause in the Fourteenth Amendment stating that states are not to deny any person equal treatment under the law.

establishment clause a clause in the First Amendment that prevents government from establishing an official religion, treating one religion preferably to another, proselytizing, or promoting religion over nonreligion.

exclusionary rule principle established by the Supreme Court, according to which evidence gathered illegally cannot be introduced into trial, and convictions cannot be based on this evidence.

executive agreement an international agreement in which the United States becomes a party once the president has signed it, without requiring approval from two-thirds of the Senate.

Executive Office of the President a group of agencies in the executive branch that primarily generate policy alternatives for the president's consideration.

executive order a presidential directive or proclamation that has the force of law.

executive privilege the idea that executive branch officials need to be able to advise the president in confidence, and that the president has a right to prevent that advice from becoming public.

federalism a form of government that distributes power across a national government and subnational governments and ensures the existence of the subnational governments.

Federalists individuals who supported the proposed Constitution and favored its ratification.

filibuster a procedure by which senators delay or prevent action on a bill by making long speeches and engaging in unlimited debate.

fiscal federalism a technique of persuasion in which the federal government offers resources to states that agree to take certain actions.

fiscal policy policy designed to improve the economy through spending and taxation.

foreign policy the mix of military, diplomatic, and economic policies that define U.S. relations with other nations around the world.

formal powers specific grants of authority defined in the Constitution or in law.

free exercise clause a clause in the First Amendment that prohibits government from interfering with individuals' practice of their religion.

free rider problem a barrier to collective action because people can reap the benefits of group efforts without participating.

full faith and credit clause a clause in the Constitution stating that states are to honor the official acts of other states.

fusion a strategy in which third parties endorse a major party candidate but list that candidate separately on the ballot so that voters can vote for the candidate under the third-party label.

gate-keeping authority the power to decide whether a particular proposal or policy change will be considered.

generational effect the situation in which younger citizens are influenced by events in such a fashion that their attitudes and beliefs are forever rendered distinct from those of older generations.

get-out-the-vote (GOTV) term used by campaign professionals to describe the various activities that candidates, political parties, activists, and interest groups use to make sure their likely supporters go to the polls on Election Day.

going public activities of politicians such as highly visible trips, press conferences, interviews, speeches, and public appearances in an attempt to raise public support for a policy agenda.

government the institutions that have the authority and capacity to create and enforce public policies (rules) for a specific territory and people.

government corporation a corporation created and funded by the government to provide some public service that would be insufficiently provided by the private sector.

grassroots lobbying efforts to persuade citizens to contact their elected officials regarding a particular issue or piece of legislation.

Great Compromise the agreement between small states and large states that representation in the Senate would be equal for each state, as small states preferred, and representation in the House would be based on population, as large states preferred.

gross domestic product (GDP) a statistic that measures all goods and services produced by a nation's economy.

hearing a formal process in which committees in Congress call upon bureaucrats and other experts to help them understand and oversee a particular agency.

horse race a focus in election coverage on who and what are up or down in the latest poll numbers.

ideology a consistent set of ideas about a given set of issues.

impeachment performed by the House of Representatives, the act of charging government officials with "treason, bribery, or other high crimes and misdemeanors." The Senate then decides whether to convict and remove the official from office.

implementation the process by which policy is executed.

implied powers functions and actions that Congress or the president could perform in order to implement and exercise their enumerated powers.

incorporation process the application, through the Fourteenth Amendment, of the civil liberties protections in the Bill of Rights to state governments.

incumbent the individual in an election who currently holds the contested office; as distinct from the challenger, who seeks to remove the incumbent from power.

independent agencies and commissions bureaucratic organizations that operate outside of Cabinet-level departments and are less subject to congressional or presidential influence.

independent expenditures funds spent to elect or defeat candidates that are not coordinated with any candidate's campaign.

indirect election an election in which voters select other individuals who directly vote for candidates for a particular office; U.S. Senate and presidential elections were of this type in the Constitution, but Senate elections are now direct elections.

individualism a belief that all individuals should be able to succeed to the maximum extent possible given their talents and abilities, regardless of race, religion, or other group characteristics.

inside lobbying meeting directly with public officials to influence political decisions.

intensity the strength of the direction of public opinion.

interest groups organizations that seek to influence government decisions.

interest group entrepreneur an individual who overcomes the costs of collective action by launching and managing an interest group.

invisible primary the race to raise the most money and achieve frontrunner status before the primary season begins.

issue evolution a change in the partisan base of support for an issue over time, such that the positions of Democrats and Republicans switch.

issue voting voting style in which the voter judges candidates based on the voter's and the candidates' opinions on specific issues and preferences for certain policies.

Jim Crow laws system of laws that separated the races in schools, public accommodations, and other aspects of daily life.

joint committee a committee made up of members of both chambers of Congress to conduct a special investigation or study.

judicial activism the tendency of judges to give themselves leeway in deciding whether to abide by past court decisions, which allows them to consider possible outcomes, public opinion, and their own preferences before issuing a ruling.

judicial restraint the practice judges engage in when they limit the exercise of their own power by overturning past decisions only when they are clearly unconstitutional.

judicial review the power of the judiciary to interpret and overturn actions taken by the legislative and executive branches of government.

jury a group of private citizens selected to listen to a trial and issue a final verdict.

laissez-faire economics a theory that discourages the government from becoming involved in the economy.

leadership the ability to influence and guide others to achieve some desired policy or action.

legal model a theory of judicial decision-making in which judges make decisions by deciphering the correct interpretation of the law and the relevant portion of the Constitution, and determining whether there is a conflict between the two.

Lemon test a three-part establishment clause test used by the Supreme Court that states that, to be constitutional, a government action must have a plausible nonreligious purpose; its primary or principal effect must be to neither advance nor inhibit religion; and it must not foster excessive government entanglement with religion.

libertarianism a view that emphasizes the importance of individual choice and responsibility, the private sector, and the free market, in which government's primary obligations are to defend the country militarily, protect individuals from crime, and ensure that people fulfill contracts entered into freely.

liberty the belief that government should leave people free to do as they please and exercise their natural rights to the maximum extent possible.

life cycle effect attitudes or physical characteristics that change as one ages, no matter the time period or generation. The graying of one's hair is a life cycle effect.

limited government the idea that the scope of government activities should be narrow and that government should act only when the need is great and other sectors of society are unable to meet the need.

line-item veto the authority of a chief executive to reject part of a bill passed by the legislature.

lobbying communicating with government officials to persuade them toward a particular policy decision.

magistrate judges judges who support federal district judges by hearing and deciding minor cases at the district court level.

majority leader the individual in each chamber who manages the floor; in the Senate, he or she is the most powerful member in the chamber; in the House, he or she is the chief lieutenant of the Speaker.

majority-minority districts legislative districts in which boundaries are drawn in a manner to ensure that a majority of the district residents are members of minority groups, intended to increase the probability of minorities being elected.

majority opinion the written document that reflects the collective judgment of the justices who are on the majority side of a ruling.

mandate an order from the federal government that requires state governments to take a certain action. Also, the idea that the public provided clear policy guidance in the results of the prior election.

margin of error the range surrounding a sample's response within which researchers are confident the larger population's true response would fall.

markup the process by which the members of a committee or subcommittee rewrite, delete, and add portions of a bill.

mass media or media various modes of communication intended to reach a mass audience, including television, radio, newspapers, news magazines, and the Internet.

material benefit a good or service offered to encourage participation in group activity.

Medicaid a means-tested program, funded by federal and state governments, that extends health insurance to the poor and disabled.

Medicare a federally funded entitlement program that offers health insurance to the elderly.

minimal effect the theory that change in voting intent as a result of mass media exposure is relatively rare.

minority leader the individual who speaks on behalf of the party that controls the smaller number of seats in each chamber.

miracle of aggregation the phenomenon that occurs when a group consists of individuals who are largely ignorant of a particular issue, but their collective opinion tends to make sense.

Miranda warning ruling that requires police, when arresting suspects, to inform them of their rights, including the right to remain silent and have an attorney present during questioning.

modified open primary an election in which registered voters who are not affiliated with either party can vote in either party's primary.

momentum the boost in media coverage, name recognition, fund-raising, and perceptions of electability that accompanies unexpected and repeated primary success.

monetary policy policy designed to improve the economy by controlling the supply of available money.

multiculturalism the view that group identity influences political beliefs and that, because groups are naturally diverse in their beliefs, the idea of a shared or dominant political culture merely reflects the imposition of a dominant group's beliefs on subordinate groups.

nation a shared sense of understanding and belonging among a people, that they are different and separate from other peoples with particular characteristics and that they have a right to self-government over a defined territory.

national party convention a meeting held over several days at which delegates select the party's presidential nominee, approve the party platform, and consider changes in party rules and policies.

National Security Council (NSC) an advisory body, formed in 1947 by the National Security Act, which assists the president in gathering information from military services and other security-related executive agencies.

nationalist theory a theory of the founding of the American government that sees the Constitution more as the joining together of the people than the joining together of the states.

natural rights rights inherent in the essence of people as human beings; government does not provide these rights but can restrict the exercise of them.

necessary and expedient clause a clause in Article II, section 3, of the Constitution that authorizes the president to recommend legislation to Congress.

necessary and proper clause a provision in the U.S. Constitution that gives Congress the authority to make the laws needed to carry out the specific duties assigned to Congress by the Constitution.

neutrality test the Supreme Court's most recent approach to deciding free exercise of religion cases, this test declares that a government law or action with a neutral intent and application is constitutional, even if it burdens religion and there is no compelling government interest at stake.

New Jersey Plan one of the rival plans at the Constitutional Convention, it called for, among other things, equal representation of the states in a single-house legislature.

nondecisions decisions not to consider particular issues or incorporate them into the policy agenda.

nonresponse bias a nonrandom error that occurs when people who choose to participate in a survey have different attitudes from those of people who decline to participate.

North American Free Trade Agreement (NAFTA) an agreement, signed in 1992, to reduce tariff and nontariff barriers to trade and investment among Canada, Mexico, and the United States.

nullification the theory that states have the right to nullify national laws to which they object and believe violate the U.S. Constitution.

open primary an election in which a voter can participate in either party's primary (but not both), regardless of party registration.

open rule the terms and conditions applied to a particular bill that allow members of Congress to make a wide range of amendments to it.

opinion leaders individuals with high levels of interest and expertise in politics who seek to communicate their political beliefs to others.

oral argument a lawyer's spoken presentation to the court of the legal reasons that his or her side should prevail.

original jurisdiction the right of a court to be the first to hear a case rather than simply review the decision of a lower court.

oversight congressional and presidential efforts to monitor and supervise the actions of bureaucratic agencies.

parliamentary system a political system in which the head of the executive branch is selected by members of the legislature rather than by popular vote.

party caucus the gathering of all Democratic members of the House or Senate.

party conference the gathering of all Republican members of the House or Senate.

party machine disciplined local party organizations that selected candidates; got out the vote; provided benefits to supporters including government workers, local constituents, and businesses; and served as social service agencies for their followers.

party platform a document expressing the principles, beliefs, and policy positions of the party, as endorsed by delegates at the national party convention.

patron an individual who supports an interest group by providing the resources needed to organize and flourish.

patronage awarding jobs in government on the basis of party support and loyalty rather than expertise or experience.

period effect an event that influences the attitudes and beliefs of people of all ages.

persistence the principle that political lessons, values, and attitudes learned early in life tend to structure political learning later on in life.

plaintiff the party who initiates a lawsuit by filing a complaint.

plea bargain an agreement between the prosecutor and the defendant in a criminal case through which the parties agree to a specified crime and punishment.

Plessy v. Ferguson Supreme Court decision in 1896 upholding the constitutionality of laws and government policies that required segregated facilities for blacks and whites.

pluralism the theory that all groups are well represented and no single interest controls government decisions.

plurality elections elections in which the candidate with the most votes, not necessarily a majority, wins.

plurality rule rule by which a candidate wins office by getting more votes than his or her opponent, even if that candidate does not receive an absolute majority of the votes.

pocket veto the president's veto of a bill without the opportunity for Congress to override the veto. It occurs if the president does not act on a bill within 10 days after passage by Congress and Congress adjourns during that time.

police power the protection of public safety, health, welfare, and morality by a government.

policy agenda the set of issues under consideration by policy makers.

political action committee (PAC) a group that collects money from individuals and makes donations to political parties and candidates.

political attentiveness an individual's general attention to and knowledge of politics.

political culture the values and beliefs of citizens toward the political system and toward themselves as actors in it.

political efficacy an individual's belief that he or she can influence what happens in the political world.

political parties organized groups with public followings that seek to elect office holders who identify themselves by the group's common label, for the purpose of exercising political power.

political predisposition the interests, values, and experiences that help organize one's thinking about politics.

political socialization the learning process in which individuals absorb information and selectively add it to their knowledge and understanding of politics and government.

politicization a phenomenon that occurs when Congress and the president select bureaucracy leaders who share their political views.

politics individual and collective efforts to influence the workings of government.

poll tax fee assessed on each person who wishes to vote; prohibited by the Twenty-fourth Amendment in 1964.

preemption legislation legislation that declares, or mandates, certain actions off-limits for state governments.

preferred position the idea, endorsed by the Supreme Court, that protection of First Amendment rights predominates over other rights.

presidential system a political system in which the head of the executive branch is selected by some form of popular vote and serves a fixed term of office. The United States has a presidential system.

primacy the principle that what is learned first is learned best and lodged most firmly in one's mind.

primary election in which voters choose the candidate that will represent their political party in the general election.

priming a media effect in which the public assesses the performance of politicians and candidates in terms of the issues that the media have emphasized.

principal–agent problem the problem that occurs when one person (the principal) contracts with another person (the agent) to provide a service and yet cannot directly observe what the agent is actually doing; the agent, meanwhile, is motivated to take advantage of the principal.

prior restraint government intervention to prevent the publication of material it finds objectionable.

privatization the transfer of government functions from the federal government to private companies.

Progressive reforms a set of political and electoral reforms in the early twentieth century that had the combined effect of weakening political parties.

property rights the belief that people should be able to acquire, own, and use goods and assets free from government constraints, as long as their acquisition and use does not interfere with the rights of other individuals.

proportional representation an election system in which candidates are elected from multimember districts, with a party's share of seats from a district being roughly proportional to their share of the popular vote.

prospective voting voting style in which voters judge a candidate based on their assessment of what the candidate will do in office if elected.

protectionism the practice of imposing selective tariffs on trade in an effort to protect specific domestic industries from international competition.

public debt the total amount of money that the federal government owes.

public goods goods (and services) that are enjoyed by all citizens and unlikely to be provided by any organization other than the government.

public law those laws enacted by presidents and Congress that define the relationship between individuals (and organizations) and the state.

public opinion the collective political beliefs and attitudes of the public, or groups within the public, on matters of relevance to government.

purposive benefit benefit that encourages group participation by connecting individuals to an organization's political purpose.

rally event short-term international event or military action that boosts presidential approval ratings temporarily.

random sample a population sample in which it is equally likely that each member of the population will be included in the sample.

recess appointment the means by which the president fills a vacant position in the bureaucracy when Congress is not in session, thus avoiding the need for prior congressional approval.

recession an economic downturn, which technically exists when the gross domestic product drops in size for two successive quarters.

red tape the inefficiency and waste that result from excessive regulation and overly formal procedures.

Regents of the University of California v. Bakke Supreme Court decision in 1978 that a rigid quota plan for admissions violates the Constitution's equal protection guarantee, but race could be considered a "plus factor" in college admissions to increase student body diversity.

regular appropriations the standard mode by which federal moneys are allotted to programs.

religious freedom a belief that individuals should be free to choose and practice their religious faith and that government should not establish any particular religion as the official or preferred religion.

representative democracy a form of democracy in which the people, through free elections, select representatives to make laws on their behalf and set policies adopted by the government; also known as a republic.

republic a system in which people elect representatives to make policy and write laws; also known as a representative democracy.

reserved powers Tenth Amendment guarantee to state governments of any powers other than those granted to the national government or those specifically prohibited for the states.

responsible party model the idea that political parties should run as unified teams, present a clear policy platform, implement that platform when in office, and run on their record in the subsequent election.

retrospective voting voting style in which voters judge candidates based on the past performance of the candidates or their parties rather than issue stands and assessments of what each candidate would do if elected.

ripeness doctrine principle by which the courts will accept only cases in which the actual harm has already taken place.

rules administrative determinations about how laws will be interpreted and implemented.

salience an issue's importance to a person or to the public in general.

sampling taking a small fraction of something that is meant to represent a larger whole: for example, a group of people that represents a larger population.

sampling error the difference between the reported characteristics of the sample and the characteristics of the larger population that result from imperfect sampling.

select committee a temporary committee created to serve a specific purpose.

selective benefit benefit that can be accessed only by those who participate in or contribute to group activity.

selective exposure the tendency of people to expose themselves to information that is in accord with their beliefs.

selective incorporation the process by which protections in the Bill of Rights were gradually applied to the states, as the Supreme Court issued decisions on specific aspects of the Bill of Rights.

selective perception the tendency of individuals to interpret information in ways consistent with their beliefs.

selective retention the tendency of individuals to recall information that is consistent with existing beliefs and to discard information that runs counter to them.

senatorial courtesy the custom by which the senior senator from the state in which there is a district court vacancy assists the president in selecting a replacement for that seat.

seniority the length of time a legislator has served in office.

separate but equal doctrine Supreme Court doctrine that laws or policies requiring segregated facilities for the races are constitutionally acceptable as long as the facilities are of equal quality.

separation of powers the principle that the executive, legislative, and judicial functions of government should be primarily performed by different institutions in government.

Shays's Rebellion a protest by farmers in western Massachusetts in 1786–1787 to stop foreclosures on property by state courts; it convinced many political leaders that the Articles of Confederation were insufficient to govern the United States.

single-member districts electoral districts in which only one person is elected to represent the district in a representative body.

slack a situation in which bureaucrats do not work as hard as Congress or the president would like.

social benefit benefit that encourages individuals to join a group in order to enjoy the company of those who share similar opinions and interests.

social contract an agreement among members of a society to form and recognize the authority of a centralized government that is empowered to make and enforce laws governing the members of that society.

Social Security Act a 1935 law that established Social Security, an entitlement program providing retirees with a monthly income in order to reduce poverty among the elderly.

socioeconomic status (SES) a combination of an individual's occupation, income, and education levels.

solicitor general the individual who represents the federal government in the Supreme Court.

sovereign immunity the principle that state governments cannot be sued by private parties in federal court unless they consent to the suits or Congress has constitutionally provided an exemption that allows suits to be filed.

sovereign power the individual or institution in a political system whose decisions are binding and unable to be overturned by other individuals or institutions.

sovereignty having the ultimate authority to make decisions within one's borders, without interference by other governments.

Speaker of the House the person who presides over the House and serves as the chamber's official spokesperson.

spoils system a system of government in which a presidential administration awards jobs to party loyalists.

sponsor a member of Congress who introduces a bill.

spurious relationship a relationship between variables that reflects correlation but not causation.

stability the speed with which the change will occur, and the likelihood that the new opinion will endure.

standing the requirement establishing that for a plaintiff to bring a case to court, he or she must have suffered a well-defined injury that is a result of violation of the civil code.

standing committee a permanent committee with a well-defined, relatively fixed policy jurisdiction that develops, writes, and updates important legislation.

stare decisis the principle that judges deciding a case must carefully weigh the decisions of their predecessors in similar cases and come to the same decision if the basic elements of the case before them are the same.

state action Supreme Court interpretation of the equal protection clause that holds the clause prohibited unfair discriminatory actions by government, not by private individuals.

State Department the agency home of diplomats, embassies, treaty negotiators, and most foreign aid programs run by the U.S. government.

strategic model the theory of judicial decision-making in which judges consider their own policy preferences as well as the possible actions of the other branches of government when making decisions.

subcommittee a smaller organizational unit within a committee that specializes in a particular segment of the committee's responsibilities.

suffrage the right to vote.

sunset provision a condition of a law that requires it to be reauthorized after a certain number of years.

supplemental appropriations the process by which Congress and the president can provide temporary funding for government activities and programs when funds fall short due to unforeseen circumstances.

supremacy clause a clause in the Constitution that declares that national laws and treaties have supremacy over state laws and treaties.

Supreme Court the highest court in the land, where all decisions are final.

take care clause the constitutional clause that grants the president the authority and leeway to determine if laws are being "faithfully executed" and to take action if in his judgment they are not.

tariff a tax on goods exchanged between nations.

Three-fifths Compromise an agreement between slave states and free states that a state's slave population would be counted at 60 percent for purposes of determining a state's representation in the House of Representatives.

treaty an international agreement in which the United States becomes a party once the president has signed it and two-thirds of the Senate have ratified it.

trustee model of representation the type of representation by which representatives are elected to do what they think is best for their constituents.

two-party system a system of electoral competition in which two parties are consistently the most likely to win office and gain power.

unfunded mandate a law requiring certain actions without appropriating the necessary funds to carry them out.

unified government a situation in which the presidency and both houses of Congress are controlled by the same party.

unitary system a form of government in which government at the highest level has the power to create, combine, or disband lower-level governments and determine what powers will be allowed at the lower levels.

valence issues issues on which virtually everyone agrees.

veto the president's rejection of a bill passed by both chambers of Congress, which prevents the bill from becoming law. Congress can override a veto with a two-thirds vote in both the House and Senate.

Virginia Plan one of the rival plans at the Constitutional Convention, it argued for a two-house legislature with representation based on a state's population; the lower house would be elected directly by the people, and that house would then select the members of the upper house.

Voting Rights Act of 1965 legislation that abolished literacy tests as a requirement to register to vote.

watch dog the media's role in keeping a close eye on politicians and presenting stories and information that politicians might not willingly reveal to the media on their own.

whips designated members of Congress who deliver messages from the party leaders, keep track of members' votes, and encourage members to stand together on key issues.

whistleblower a bureaucrat who witnesses and publicly exposes wrongdoing by either contacting his or her political superiors or tipping off the press.

White House Staff a group of offices in the executive branch that provides the president with political advice, promotes the president's program with legislators and interest groups, and handles the president's public relations.

winner-take-all election in which the candidate who gets the most votes wins, while any other candidate loses and receives nothing.

writ of certiorari a formal acceptance by the Supreme Court to review a decision of a lower court.

ENDNOTES

Chapter 1

1. Thomas Hobbes, *Leviathan*, Richard Tuck, ed. (New York: Cambridge University Press, 1996).

2. See Hobbes, *Leviathan*; John Locke, *Second Treatise on Government*, C. B. Macpherson, ed. (Indianapolis: Hackett, 1980); and Jean-Jacques Rousseau, *Basic Political Writings*, Donald A. Cress, ed. (Indianapolis: Hackett, 1987).

Chapter 2

1. Steven Erlanger, "France Debates Its Identity, but Some Question Why," *New York Times*, November 29, 2009: A16.

2. The creed is grounded in the "classical liberal" political theory of the seventeenth and eighteenth centuries. See Louis Hartz, *The Liberal Tradition in America: An Interpretation of American Political Thought Since the Revolution* (New York: Harcourt Brace, 1955); David F. Ericson and Louisa Bertch Green, eds., *The Liberal Tradition in American Politics: Reassessing the Legacy of American Liberalism* (New York: Routledge, 1999); Seymour Martin Lipset, *American Exceptionalism: A Double-Edged Sword* (New York: W. W. Norton, 1997).

3. Peter A. Morrison, "A Demographic Perspective on Our Nation's Future," RAND Report, 2001, www.rand.org/publications/DB/DB320/. See also Laura B. Shrestha, "The Changing Demographic Profile of the United States," Congressional Research Service, May 5, 2006, www.fas.org/sgp/crs/misc/RL32701.pdf; and Jeffrey S. Passel and D'Vera Cohn, "U.S. Population Projections: 2005–2050," Pew Research Center, February 11, 2008, pewhispanic.org/files/reports/85.pdf.

4. Werner Sombart's argument was published in German in 1905. It appears in English as *Why Is There No Socialism in the United States?* trans. Patricia M. Hocking (Armonk, NY: M. E. Sharpe, 1976).

5. See Theda Skocpol, "The Origins of Social Policy in the United States: A Polity-Centered Analysis," in Lawrence C. Dodd and Calvin Jillson, eds., *The Dynamics of American Politics: Approaches and Interpretations* (Boulder, CO: Westview 1994); Adam Przeworski, "The Material Bases of Consent," in Adam Przeworski, *Capitalism and Social Democracy* (New York: Cambridge University Press, 1985).

6. Edward S. Herman and Noam Chomsky, *Manufacturing Consent: The Political Economy of the Mass Media* (Pantheon, 2002); Robert Justin Goldstein, *Political Repression in Modern America: From 1870 to 1976* (Champaign: University of Illinois Press, 2001); Victoria Hattam, *Labor Visions and State Power: The Origins of Business Unionism in the United States* (Princeton, NJ: Princeton University Press, 1992).

7. See Michael Lind, "The American Creed: Does It Matter? Should It Change?" *Foreign Affairs*, March/April 1996; and

Forrest Church, "The American Creed," *The Nation*, September 16, 2002.

8. See James Morone, *The Democratic Wish: Popular Participation and the Limits of American Government*, revised edition (New Haven, CT: Yale University Press, 1998).

9. John Locke, *Two Treatises of Government*, originally published in 1689.

10. See Jeffrey A. Winters and Benjamin I. Page, "Oligarchy in the United States?" *Perspectives on Politics* 7, no. 4 (2009): 731–752; and Martin Gilens, "Preference Gaps and Inequality in Representation," PS 42, no. 2 (2009): 335–342.

11. A classic articulation of this view is by Milton Friedman, *Capitalism and Freedom* (Chicago: University of Chicago Press, 1962).

12. Anne Norton, *Republic of Signs: Liberal Theory and American Popular Culture* (Chicago: University of Chicago Press, 1993).

13. James T. Kloppenberg, "The Virtues of Liberalism: Christianity, Republicanism, and Ethics in Early American Political Discourse," *Journal of American History* 74 (1987): 9–33.

14. Pew Center for the People and the Press, 2009 Values Survey, people-press.org/reports/questionnaires/517.pdf.

15. Pew Research Center for the People and the Press and Pew Forum on Religion and Public Life, Religion and Public Life Survey, August 2008, people-press.org/reports/questionnaires/445.pdf.

16. Critics argue that individualist beliefs obscure perceptions of structural problems in the economy and society. See Jack Turner, "American Individualism and Structural Injustice: Tocqueville, Gender, and Race," *Polity* 40, no. 2 (2008): 197–215.

17. See Benjamin I. Page and Lawrence R. Jacobs, *Class War? What Americans Really Think About Economic Inequality* (Chicago: University of Chicago Press, 2009).

18. Pew Center for the People and the Press surveys in 2009 for spending preferences; Pew 2009 Values Survey for evaluations of government effectiveness, people-press.org/reports/questionnaires/517.pdf.

19. See Steven Rathgeb Smith and Michael Lipsky, *Nonprofits for Hire: The Welfare State in the Age of Contracting* (Cambridge, MA: Harvard University Press, 1995); Irwin Garfinkel, Lee Rainwater, and Timothy Smeeding, *Wealth and Welfare States: Is America a Laggard or Leader?* (New York: Oxford University Press, 2010).

20. CNN/Opinion Research Corporation Poll, February 2010; Quinnipiac University Poll, March 2010.

21. Joseph S. Nye, Jr., Philip D. Zelikow, and David C. King, eds., *Why People Don't Trust Government* (Cambridge,

MA: Harvard University Press, 1997); Pew Research Center for the People and the Press, "How Americans View Government: Deconstructing Distrust," March 10, 1998, people-press.org/reports/print.php3?ReportID=95; Russell J. Dalton, "The Social Transformation of Trust in Government," unpublished manuscript: 5, www.worldvaluessurvey.org.

22. Marc J. Hetherington, "The Political Relevance of Political Trust," *American Political Science Review* 92, no. 4 (December 1998): 791–808.

23. Richard J. Ellis, *American Political Cultures* (New York: Oxford University Press, 1993).

24. Daniel T. Rodgers, *Contested Truths: Keywords in American Politics Since Independence* (Cambridge, MA: Harvard University Press, 1998).

25. There have been multi-legislator districts in some states at some times, but they have been a very small share of the total.

26. *Wesberry v. Sanders* and *Reynolds v. Sims.*

27. Matthew Hayes, Matthew V. Hibbing, and Tracy Sulkin, "Redistricting, Responsiveness, and Issue Attention," *Legislative Studies Quarterly* 35, no. 1 (2010): 91–116.

28. Four cases were consolidated as *League of United Latin American Citizens v. Perry.*

29. Daniel J. Elazar, *American Federalism: A View from the States*, 3rd ed. (New York: HarperCollins, 1984). A map is available at www.valpo.edu/geomet/pics/geo200/politics/elazar.gif.

30. Communitarianism is a modern version of a political philosophy known as classical republicanism. Although there are some distinctions between communitarianism and classical republicanism, they are similar enough for us to use the single label in this discussion.

31. Gordon S. Wood, *The Creation of the American Republic, 1776–1787* (New York: W. W. Norton, 1969); Bernard Bailyn, *The Ideological Origins of the American Revolution* (Cambridge, MA: Harvard University Press, 1992).

32. In the words of a colonist in 1776, "No man is a true republican that will not give up his single voice to that of the public." Cited in Wood, *The Creation of the American Republic, 1776–1787*: 61.

33. One of the best-known popularizers of communitarian ideas is Amitai Etzioni. See, for example, his *The Spirit of Community: The Reinvention of American Society* (New York: Touchstone, 1993).

34. Karl Polanyi, *The Great Transformation: The Political and Economic Origins of Our Times*, 2nd ed. (Boston: Beacon Press, 2001); Andrew Stark, "The Consensus School, Its Critics, and Welfare Policy: A Study of American Political Discourse," *Journal of Politics* 71, no. 2 (2009): 627–643.

35. Francesca Colombo and Nicole Tapay, "Private Health Insurance in OECD Countries: The Benefits and Costs for Individuals and Health Systems," *OECD Health Working Paper* no. 15 (2004): 11–12.

36. CBS News/*New York Times* Poll, April 22–26, 2009; CNN/Opinion Research Corporation Poll, March 12–15, 2009.

37. See John T. Scott and Brian H. Bornstein, "What's Fair in Foul Weather and Fair? Distributive Justice across Different Allocation Contexts and Goods," *Journal of Politics* 71, no. 3 (2009): 831–846.

38. See Sven Steinmo and Jon Watts, "It's the Institutions, Stupid! Why Comprehensive National Health Insurance Fails in America," *Journal of Health Politics, Policy and Law* 20, no. 2 (1995): 329–372.

39. See Colin Gordon, *Dead on Arrival: The Politics of Health Care in Twentieth-Century America* (Princeton, NJ: Princeton University Press, 2003); Jacob S. Hacker, "The Historical Logic of National Health Insurance: Structure and Sequence in the Development of British, Canadian, and U.S. Medical Policy," *Studies in American Political Development* 12, no. 1 (1998): 57–130.

40. See Chapter 9 for a discussion of the interest group politics surrounding President Bill Clinton's health care plan.

41. Victor R. Fuchs and M. Kate Bunford, "Who Favors National Health Insurance? Who Opposes It? And Why?" talk delivered at the Center for Health Policy and Center for Primary Care and Outcomes Research, Stanford University, March 8, 2006, chppcor.stanford.edu/events/4436.

42. Pew Values Survey 2009, people-press.org/reports/questionnaires/517.pdf.

43. Rogers M. Smith, "Beyond Tocqueville, Myrdal, and Hartz: The Multiple Traditions in America," *American Political Science Review* 87, no. 3 (1993): 549–566. Survey data in this paragraph are from the General Social Survey.

44. See the 2009 survey data in "A Place to Call Home: What Immigrants Say Now About Life in America," Public Agenda, www.publicagenda.org/pages/immigrants; and Maria Hsia Chang, "Multiculturalism, Immigration and Aztlan," paper presented at the Second Alliance for Stabilizing America's Population Action Conference, Breckenridge, Colorado, August 6, 1999, www.diversityalliance.org/docs/Chang-aztlan.html.

45. Doriane Lambelet Coleman, "Individualizing Justice Through Multiculturalism: The Liberals' Dilemma," *Columbia Law Review* 96, no. 5 (1996): 1093–1167.

46. Susan Moller Okin, "Is Multiculturalism Bad for Women?" in Joshua Cohen and Matthew Howard, eds., *Is Multiculturalism Bad for Women?* (Princeton, NJ: Princeton University Press, 1999). See also Cynthia Lee, "Cultural Convergence: Interest Convergence Theory Meets the Cultural Defense?" *Arizona Law Review* 49, no. 4 (2007).

Chapter 3

1. In a 2006 legislative compromise, President Bush agreed to submit the program to the FISA Court for a one-time review on its constitutionality, but he did not agree to obtain warrants for each individual target of surveillance. A 2008 revision of FISA reaffirmed this procedure. See Eric Lichtblau, "Bush Would Let Secret Court Sift Wiretap Process," *New York Times*, July 14, 2006; Charles Babington and Peter Baker, "Bush Compromises On Spying Program," *Washington Post*, July 14, 2006.

2. Declan McCullagh, "Feds Push for Tracking Cell Phones," *CNet News*, February 11, 2010. news.cnet.com/.

3. See Gordon S. Wood, *The Creation of the American Republic, 1776-1787* (New York: W. W. Norton, 1969): 7-8.

4. Bailyn, *Ideological Origins*, 173.

5. All colonies except Georgia sent representatives to the Congress.

6. Social scientists label this the "state," but that terminology is complicated by the fact that in the United States the word "state" is most often used in reference to state governments.

7. See Merrill Jensen, *The Articles of Confederation* (Madison: University of Wisconsin Press, 1970).

8. Michael Kammen, *The Origins of the American Constitution: A Documentary History* (New York: Penguin Books, 1986); Catherine Bowen, *Miracle at Philadelphia: The Story of the Constitutional Convention, May-September 1787* (Boston: Little, Brown, 1966); Jack Rakove, *Original Meanings: Politics and Ideas in the Making of the Constitution* (New York: Alfred A. Knopf, 1996).

9. Some historians believe that the Framers were influenced by the governing practices of the Six Nations, known more commonly as the Iroquois Confederacy, which included the Cayuga, Mohawk, Oneida, Onondaga, Seneca, and Tuscarora tribes. Certainly many of the features of U.S. government were present in the Confederacy: checks and balances, federalism, participation, and civil liberties protections. The preamble to the Constitution echoes the language in a 1520 Iroquois treaty: "We the people, to form a union, to establish peace, equity, and order." The Iroquois occupied territory now in New York State. Members of the Iroquois visited the Continental Congress in June 1776. See Bruce E. Johansen, *Forgotten Founders: Benjamin Franklin, the Iroquois and the Rationale for the American Revolution* (Ipswich, MA: Gambit, 1982).

10. Randolph presented a resolution at the outset of the Convention that served, in effect, as a draft for a new system of government.

11. The three-fifths calculation would also apply for federal taxation purposes.

12. See Mark A. Graber, *Dred Scott and the Problem of Constitutional Evil* (New York: Cambridge University Press, 2008); Justin Buckley Dyer, "After the Revolution: *Somerset* and the Antislavery Tradition in Anglo-American Constitutional Development," *Journal of Politics* 71, no. 4 (2009): 1422-1434.

13. See Bryan D. Jones, Heather Larsen-Price, and John Wilkerson, "Representation and American Governing Institutions," *Journal of Politics* 71, no. 1 (2009): 277-290.

14. In everyday language, when people think "democracy" they are thinking along the lines of republican government. "Direct democracy" is often used to describe democracy in which the people themselves make law.

15. Nolan McCarty, "Presidential Vetoes in the Early Republic: Changing Constitutional Norms or Electoral Reform?" *Journal of Politics* 71, no. 2 (2009): 369-384.

16. Mark A. Graber, "Establishing Judicial Review? *Schooner Peggy* and the Early Marshall Court," *Political Research Quarterly* 51, no. 1 (1998): 221-239. For judicial review and its relationship to democracy, see J. Mitchell Pickerill, *Constitutional Deliberation in Congress: The Impact of Judicial Review in a Separated System* (Durham, NC: Duke University Press, 2004); Annabelle Lever, "Democracy and Judicial Review: Are They Really Incompatible?" *Perspectives on Politics* 7, no. 4 (2009): 805-822.

17. In *Federalist 51*, Madison notes that the legislature predominates, but its power can be moderated by creating two houses with different modes of election.

18. *Federalist 51*.

19. *Federalist 51*.

20. The Supreme Court verified national supremacy on this issue in its decision in *Lorillard Tobacco Company v. Reilly* (2001).

21. See David J. Siemers, *Ratifying the Republic: Antifederalists and Federalists in Constitutional Time* (Stanford, CA: Stanford University Press, 2002).

22. William Riker, *Federalism: Origin, Operation, Significance* (Boston: Little, Brown, 1964).

23. These names are misnomers. Federalism connotes a sharing of power across the national and state governments, and the Anti-Federalists ardently advocated this position.

24. Charles A. Beard, *An Economic Interpretation of the Constitution of the United States* (New York: Macmillan, 1913); Jerry Fresia, *Toward an American Revolution: Exposing the Constitution and Other Illusions* (Boston: South End Press, 1988).

25. Karen Orren and Stephen Skowronek, *The Search for American Political Development* (New York: Cambridge University Press, 2004): 53-54.

26. John P. Roche, "The Founding Fathers: A Reform Caucus in Action," *American Political Science Review* 55, no. 4 (1961): 799-816; Calvin C. Jillson and Cecil L. Eubanks, "The Political Structure of Constitution Making: The Federal Convention of 1787," *American Journal of Political Science* 28, no. 3 (1984): 435-458.

27. Robert E. Brown, *Charles Beard and the Constitution: A Critical Analysis of "An Economic Interpretation of the Constitution"* (Princeton, NJ: Princeton University Press, 1956).

28. Colleen A. Sheehan, "Madison v. Hamilton: The Battle Over Republicanism and the Role of Public Opinion," *American Political Science Review* 98, no. 3 (2004): 405–420.

29. David Brian Robertson, "Madison's Opponents and Constitutional Design," *American Political Science Review* 99, no. 2 (2005): 405–420.

30. See Robert W. T. Martin, "James Madison and Popular Government: The Neglected Case of the 'Memorial,'" *Polity* 42, no. 2 (2010): 185–209; Tiffany Jones Miller, "James Madison's Republic of 'Mean Extent' Theory: Avoiding the Scylla and Charybdis of Republican Government," *Polity* 39, no. 4 (2007): 545–569.

31. John R. Vile, "The Long Legacy of Proposals to Rewrite the U.S. Constitution," *PS: Political Science and Politics*, June 1993: 208–211.

32. Christopher P. Manfredi, "Institutional Design and the Politics of Constitutional Modification: Understanding Amendment Failure in the United States and Canada," *Law & Society Review* 31, no. 1 (1997): 111–136.

33. The discussion in this case study draws extensively on Alexander Keyssar, *The Right to Vote: The Contested History of Democracy in the United States* (New York: Basic Books, 2000).

34. Caldeira, "Constitutional Change in America: Dynamics of Ratification under Article V."

35. See Gregory A. Caldeira, "Constitutional Change in America: Dynamics of Ratification under Article V," *Publius* 15, no. 4 (1985): 29–49.

36. The average length of state constitutions is about three times that of the federal document, and the average number of amendments is over four times that of the U.S. Constitution.

Chapter 4

1. They charge that same-sex marriage is not consistent with the traditional conceptual understanding of marriage.

2. See National Conference of State Legislatures, www.ncsl.org/IssuesResearch/HumanServices/SameSexMarriage/tabid/16430/Default.aspx#DOMA); the Pew Forum on Religion and Public Life, pewforum.org/Gay-Marriage-and-Homosexuality/Gay-Marriage-Around-the-World.aspx.

3. Nullification made its first appearance in 1798 when Virginia and Kentucky nullified the Alien and Sedition Acts.

4. Stefan Voigt, "Explaining Constitutional Garrulity," *International Review of Law and Economics* 29 (2009): 290–303.

5. The District has been given some state-like features, such as votes in the Electoral College, but it does not have formal voting representation in the House and Senate.

6. *United States v. E. C. Knight Co. et al.* (1895).

7. The Court's language is clearly that of dual federalism: "The relief of the citizens of each state from the burden of monopoly and the evils resulting from the restraint of trade among such citizens was left with the states to deal with, and this court has recognized their possession of that power. . . . On the other hand, the power of Congress to regulate commerce among the several states is also exclusive."

8. See Suzanne Mettler, *Dividing Citizens: Gender and Federalism in New Deal Public Policy* (Ithaca, NY: Cornell University Press, 1998).

9. See also the Marshall Court decisions in *Martin v. Hunter's Lessee* (1816) and *Cohens v. Virginia* (1821).

10. See all the Court's decision in *Wickard v. Filburn* (1942).

11. *United States v. Darby* (1941). See also Donald F. Kettl, "Real-Life Federalism," *Governing Magazine*, August 2001.

12. See www.bia.gov for information and statistics on Indian tribes.

13. www.nigc.gov/Gaming_Revenue_Reports.aspx. See also Kim Isaac Eisler, *Revenge of the Pequots: How a Small Native American Tribe Created the World's Most Profitable Casino* (New York: Simon and Schuster, 2001).

14. Generally speaking, state criminal law is considered binding on the reservations, but gambling law is considered to be regulatory rather than criminal. The exception to this rule is the Organized Crime Control Act of 1970, which provides federal criminal prosecution against certain gambling activity.

15. *Washington v. Confederated Tribes of Colville Indian Reservation* (1980).

16. See Steven Andrew Light and Kathryn R. L. Rand, *Indian Gaming and Tribal Sovereignty: The Casino Compromise* (Lawrence: University Press of Kansas, 2007).

17. Paul Rogers, "Increase in National Gas Mileage Standards Announced; California Drove Obama Policy," *Silicon Valley Mercury News*, April 1, 2010.

18. The National Conference of State Legislatures tracks immigration law, www.ncsl.org. See also Lina Newton and Brian E. Adams, "State Immigration Policies: Innovation, Cooperation or Conflict?" *Publius* 39 (2009): 408–431.

19. Angela Antonelli, "Promises Unfulfilled: Unfunded Mandates Reform Act of 1995," *Regulation* 19, no. 2 (1996): 44–54; David S. Broder, "Those Unfunded Mandates," *Washington Post*, March 17, 2005, A25.

20. U.S. Government Accountability Office, *Unfunded Mandates: Views Vary About Reform Act's Strengths, Weaknesses, and Options for Improvement*, GAO-05-454, March 31, 2005, www.gao.gov/products/GAO-05-454. See also U.S. Government Accountability Office, *Unfunded Mandates: Analysis of Reform Act Coverage*, GAO-04-637, May 2004, www.gao.gov/new.items/d04637.pdf.

21. United States House of Representatives, Committee on Government Reform, Minority Staff Special Investigations

Division, "Congressional Preemption of State Laws And Regulations," June 2006. See also the Preemption Monitor published regularly by the National Conference of State Legislatures, www ncsl.org.

22. U.S. Government Accountability Office, *Formula Grants: Funding for the Largest Federal Assistance Programs Is Based on Census-Related Data and Other Factors,* December 2009, GAO-10-263, www.gao.gov/new.items/d10263.pdf.

23. U.S. Census Bureau, *Statistical Abstract of the United States 2010,* Table 419, www.census.gov/compendia/statab/cats/state_local_govt_finances_employment/federal_aid_to_state_and_local_governments.html.

24. Budget of the United States Government: Historical Tables Fiscal Year 2011, Table 12-2, www.gpoaccess.gov/usbudget/fy11/hist.html.

25. Within each region, states vary in whether they receive more than they pay, or pay more than they receive.

26. Under revenue sharing, the federal government provided funds to the states based on a formula that considered population, per capita income, and the property tax base. States were dropped from the program in 1981, and revenue sharing was completely eliminated in 1987.

27. Wisconsin officials, for instance, have expressed concerns that the state was becoming a magnet for out-of-state parents seeking educational and medical services for their autistic children.

28. Michael A. Bailey and Mark Carl Rom, "A Wider Race? Interstate Competition Across Health and Welfare Programs," *Journal of Politics* 66, no. 2 (2004): 326–347, find that in basic welfare programs, there is a race to the bottom on benefits and access; on Medicaid, on overall costs; and on supplemental security income (for individuals with medical or other disabilities), on benefits, access, and overall costs.

29. Race-to-the-bottom research and findings are discussed in William D. Berry, Richard C. Fording, and Russell L. Hanson, "Reassessing the 'Race to the Bottom' in State Welfare Policy," *Journal of Politics* 65, no. 2 (2003): 327–349; Michael A. Bailey, "Depressing Federalism: Re-Assessing Theory and Evidence on the 'Race to the Bottom,'" manuscript, April 2002; John Kennan and James R. Walker, "Wages, Welfare Benefits, and Migration," *Journal of Econometrics* 156, no. 1 (2010): 229–238.

30. Stephen C. Fehr, "The United Regions of America," Pew Center on the States, Stateline.org, April 22, 2010, www.stateline.org/live/details/story?contentId=478959. See also Rebecca M. Blank, *It Takes a Nation: A New Agenda for Fighting Poverty* (Princeton, NJ: Princeton University Press, 1997).

31. Paul Peterson, *The Price of Federalism* (Washington, DC: Brookings Institution Press, 1998); Kevin M. Esterling, "Does the Federal Government Learn from the States? Medicaid and the Limits of Expertise in the Intergovernmental Lobby," *Publius* 39 (2009): 1–21.

32. The *Federal Register* lists pending regulations and also the period for public comment on them.

33. The case concerned Alfonso Lopez, Jr., a grade 12 student at Edison High School in San Antonio who brought a concealed handgun and ammunition to school and was charged with violating the Gun-Free School Zone Act.

34. Section 5 of the Fourteenth Amendment provides the authority to override this immunity.

35. See www.ncsl.org/realid/.

36. Priscilla M. Regan and Christopher J. Deering, "State Opposition to REAL ID," *Publius* 39, no. 3 (2009): 476–505.

37. Paul Posner, "The Politics of Coercive Federalism in the Bush Era," *Publius* 37, no. 3 (2007): 390–412.

38. www2.ed.gov/programs/racetothetop/index.html.

39. See, for example, Barry Rabe, "Environmental Policy and the Bush Era: The Collision Between the Administrative Presidency and State Experimentation," *Publius* 37, no. 3 (2007): 413–431; Posner, "The Politics of Coercive Federalism in the Bush Era."

40. In *Nevada Department of Human Resources v. Hibbs* (2003).

41. Marci Hamilton, "The Supreme Court's Federalism Cases This Term: A String of Decisions Upholding Federal Power Show the Portrayal of the Court as Extreme Is a Caricature," FindLaw, June 3, 2004, writ.news.findlaw.com/hamilton/20040603.html.

Chapter 5

1. John J. Coleman, "*Citizens United* and Political Outcomes," manuscript, February 2, 2010, users.polisci.wisc.edu/coleman; Timothy Werner, "The Sound, the Fury, and the Non-event: Business Power and Market Reactions to the *Citizens United* Decision," *American Politics Review,* forthcoming; Carol D. Leonnig, "Political Ads Are Tough Sell For Image-Conscious Corporations," *Washington Post,* June 1, 2010.

2. We discuss freedom of the press later in this chapter.

3. Where rights come from is a matter of philosophical dispute.

4. See also the twin studies by Robert Barro, "Determinants of Democracy," *Journal of Political Economy* 107, no. 6 (1999): 158–183; and *Determinants of Economic Growth: A Cross-Country Empirical Study* (Cambridge, MA: MIT Press, 1997).

5. Seventeen amendments had been adopted in the House of Representatives; 12 of these were accepted by the Senate. Ten were ratified by the states in December 1791.

6. Two cases kicked off the incorporation process: *Chicago, Burlington, and Quincy Railroad Company v. Chicago* (1897) and *Gitlow v. New York* (1925).

7. *Chicago, Burlington, and Quincy Railroad v. Chicago* (1897); *Gitlow v. New York* (1925).

8. *McDonald v. Chicago* (2010).

9. See Philippa Strum, *Privacy: The Debate in the United States Since 1945* (New York: Harcourt Brace, 1998); Ken I. Kersch, "The Right to Privacy," in James W. Ely, Jr., and David Bodenhamer, eds., *The Bill of Rights in Modern America*, 2nd edition (Bloomington: Indiana University Press, 2008).

10. *Eisenstadt v. Baird* (1972).

11. The Court's opinion famously stated that "specific guarantees in the Bill of Rights have penumbras, formed by emanations from those guarantees that help give them life and substance." Penumbras are partial shadings or shadows that are cast on outlying regions or peripheries.

12. The Court did not rule whether a fetus is a person, but stated that throughout the early nineteenth century, "prevailing legal abortion practices were far freer than they are today, persuad[ing] us that the word 'person,' as used in the Fourteenth Amendment, does not include the unborn."

13. In *Webster v. Reproductive Health Services* (1989), the Court declared constitutional a Missouri law outlawing abortions in public hospitals and prohibiting public employees from being involved in abortion services.

14. Lance Whitney, "Consumer Groups: Online Tracking at "Alarming Levels,'" CNet, May 4, 2010, news.cnet.com; Julia Angwin and Tom McGinty, "Sites Feed Personal Details to New Tracking Industry," Wall Street Journal, July 30, 2010, online.wsj.com.

15. *City of Ontario v. Quon* (2010).

16. Federal courts only rarely agree to prior restraint.

17. *Murdock v. Pennsylvania* (1943).

18. *Chaplinsky v. New Hampshire* (1942).

19. *Beauharnais v. Illinois* (1952).

20. *New York Times Co. v. Sullivan* (1964); *Gertz v. Robert Welch, Inc.* (1974); *Milkovich v. Lorain Journal Co.* (1990).

21. *Valentine v. Chrestensen* (1942); *Greater New Orleans Broadcasting Association v. United States* (1999); *Lorillard Tobacco v. Reilly* (2001).

22. *Roth v. United States* (1957).

23. In 2002, the Supreme Court overturned the Child Pornography Prevention Act of 1996, concluding that the act attempted to restrict materials that were not necessarily obscene as defined in previous court decisions.

24. *Jacobellis v. Ohio* (1964).

25. *Reno v. American Civil Liberties Union* (1997).

26. *Ashcroft v. American Civil Liberties Union* (2004).

27. *United States et al. v. American Library Association, Inc., et al.* (2003).

28. *Engale v. Vitale* (1962); *Abington School District v. Schempp* (1963); *Lee v. Weisman* (1992); *Wallace v. Jaffrie* (1985); *Santa Fe Independent School District v. Doe* (2000).

29. *County of Allegheny v. ACLU Greater Pittsburgh Chapter* (1989). The Texas case is *Van Orden v. Perry* (2005); the Kentucky case is *McCreary County v. A.C.L.U. of Kentucky* (2005).

30. In *Wisconsin v. Yoder* (1971), the Supreme Court determined that Amish religious exercise was burdened by Wisconsin's requirement that students remain in school until age 16, and that the state's interest was not compelling enough to justify the burden.

31. *City of Boerne v. Flores* (1997).

32. *Christian Legal Society v. Martinez* (2010). See Jonathan Turley, "Inequality, in the Name of Equality," *Washington Post*, April 18, 2010, for a discussion of the issues in the case. See also Stanley Fish, "Being Neutral is Oh So Hard to Do," *New York Times*, July 29, 2010, opinionator.blogs.nytimes.com.

33. *Mapp v. Ohio* (1961).

34. www.nytimes.com/2008/07/19/us/19exclude.html?_r=1.

35. *Kentucky v. King* (2011).

36. *Davis v. United States* (1994). See also *Arizona v. Fulminante* (1991) and *Dickerson v. United States* (2000).

37. *Coker v. Georgia* (1977); *Kennedy v. Louisiana* (2008).

38. *Atkins v. Virginia* (2002) concerns the mentally retarded. *Roper v. Simmons* (2005) overturned the Court's *Stanford v. Kentucky* (1989) decision on capital punishment for minors.

39. *Graham v. Florida* (2010).

40. *Rompilla v. Beard* (2005).

41. George E. Marcus, John L. Sullivan, and Elizabeth Theiss-Morse, *With Malice Toward Some: How People Make Civil Liberties Judgments* (New York: Cambridge University Press, 1995).

42. This position was consistent with the stance of the northern states that considered slaves to become free when they traveled in free states.

43. The act was a response to so-called Black Codes passed by southern states in 1865 and 1866.

44. Fearing that the act might be declared unconstitutional, supporters moved quickly to include its major provisions in the Fourteenth Amendment.

45. The Thirteenth Amendment was particular to slavery, not private racial discrimination in general, the Court ruled, so it could not be pointed to as justification for the act.

46. To free blacks prior to the Thirteenth Amendment, the Court argued, "[m]ere discriminations on account of race or color were not regarded as badges of slavery."

47. Seventeen states required segregation; another four allowed it as a local option.

48. The timetable applied to the District of Columbia also. On the same day as *Brown I*, the Court ruled that segregated schools in the District, a federal entity, violated the Fifth Amendment's guarantee of due process in *Bolling v. Sharpe* (1954).

49. Gary Orfield and Chungmei Lee, "Racial Transformation and the Changing Nature of Segregation," The Civil Rights

Project at Harvard University, January 2006, www.civilright-sproject.ucla.edu/research/deseg/Racial_Transformation.pdf.

50. *Milliken v. Bradley* (1974).

51. The use of Congress's commerce clause and spending powers in the Civil Rights Act of 1964 was upheld by the Supreme Court in *Heart of Atlanta Motel v. United States* (1964) and *Katzenbach v. McClung* (1964).

52. The Voting Rights Act of 1965 was upheld by the Supreme Court in *South Carolina v. Katzenbach* (1965).

53. *Harper v. Virginia Board of Elections* (1966).

54. Executive Orders 10925 (Kennedy), 11246 and 11375 (Johnson), 12106 (Carter), 13087 and 13152 (Clinton).

55. Executive Orders 10925 (Kennedy), 11246 and 11375 (Johnson), and 11478 (Nixon).

56. See Richard M. Valelly, *The Two Reconstructions: The Struggle for Black Enfranchisement* (Chicago: University of Chicago Press, 2004).

57. Edward G. Carmines and James A. Stimson, *Issue Evolution: Race and the Transformation of American Politics* (Princeton, NJ: Princeton University Press, 1990).

58. Robert C. Lieberman, *Shaping Race Policy: The United States in Comparative Perspective* (Princeton, NJ: Princeton University Press, 2007).

59. *Shaw v. Reno* (1993); *Miller v. Johnson* (1995); *Hunt v. Cromartie* (2001).

60. David Epstein and Sharyn O'Halloran, Columbia University, "The Voting Rights Act: Here Today, Gone Tomorrow?" manuscript, 2005. See also Hutchings and Valentino, "The Centrality of Race in American Politics" *Annual Review of Political Science* 7 (2004): 383–408.

61. See John D. Griffin and Brian Newman, *Minority Report: Evaluating Political Equality in America* (Chicago: University of Chicago Press, 2008).

62. *Bartlett v. Strickland* (2009).

63. *United States v. Carolene Products* (1938), footnote 4.

64. *Reed v. Reed* (1971); *Craig v. Boren* (1976).

65. See *Nordinger v. Hahn* (1992).

66. *Yick Wo v. Hopkins* (1886).

67. Hutchings and Valentino, "The Centrality of Race in American Politics."

68. Hutchings and Valentino, "The Centrality of Race in American Politics," 389.

69. Two pivotal figures in the debate have been Paul Sniderman and Donald Kinder. See Paul M. Sniderman and Edward G. Carmines, *Reaching Beyond Race* (Cambridge: Harvard University Press, 1997); Sniderman and Thomas Piazza, *The Scar of Race* (Cambridge, MA: Harvard University Press, 1993); and Donald

R. Kinder and Lynn M. Sanders, *Divided by Color: Racial Politics and Democratic Ideals* (Chicago: University of Chicago Press, 1996).

70. A number of alternative terms have been employed, including new racism, symbolic racism, and covert racism.

71. See Stanley Feldman and Leonie Huddy, "Racial Resentment and White Opposition to Race-Conscious Programs: Principles or Prejudice?" *American Journal of Political Science* 49, no. (2005): 168–183; Christopher Tarman and David O. Sears, "The Conceptualization and Measurement of Symbolic Racism," *Journal of Politics* 67, no. 3 (2005): 731–761.

72. Paul M. Kellstedt, "Media Framing and the Dynamics of Racial Policy Preferences," *American Journal of Political Science* 44, 2 (2000): 258; Kenneth Prewitt, "When Social Inequality Maps to Demographic Diversity, What Then for Liberal Democracies?" *Social Research* 77, no. (2010): 1–20.

73. A related area of study is whether diversity and interracial trust are connected. See Thomas J. Rudolph and Elizabeth Popp, "Race, Environment, and Interracial Trust," *Journal of Politics* 72, no. (2010): 74–89.

74. Paul M. Kellstedt, *The Mass Media and the Dynamics of American Racial Attitudes* (New York: Cambridge University Press, 2003); Rene P. Rocha and Rodolfo Espino, "Racial Threat, Residential Segregation, and the Policy Attitudes of Anglos," *Political Research Quarterly* 62, no. 2 (2009): 415–426.

75. Jason Barabas and Jennifer Jerit, "Are Survey Experiments Externally Valid?" *American Political Science Review* 104, no. 2 (2010): 226–242.

76. Gary M. Segura and Helena Alves Rodrigues, "Comparative Ethnic Politics in the United States: Beyond Black and White," *Annual Review of Political Science* 9 (2006): 375–395; Rodney E. Hero and Robert R. Preuhs, "Beyond (the Scope of) Conflict: National Black and Latino Advocacy Group Relations in the Congressional and Legal Arenas," *Perspectives on Politics* 7, no. 3 (2009): 501–518.

77. *Elks v. Wilkins* (1884).

78. In 1961, the Supreme Court ruled in *Hoyt v. Florida* that Florida could exclude women from jury service.

79. Mark R. Daniels and Robert E. Darcy, "As Time Goes By: The Arrested Diffusion of the Equal Rights Amendment," *Publius* 15, no. 4, (1985): 51–60.

80. *Gregory v. Ashcroft* (1991).

81. A Supreme Court decision in 2000 (*Kimel v. Florida Board of Regents*) narrowed the law by stating that it did not apply to state government employees.

82. *Oncale v. Sundowner Offshore Services* (1998).

83. *Boy Scouts of America v. Dale* (2000).

84. *Wong Wing v. U.S.* (1896); *Yick Wo v. Hopkins* (1886).

85. See Section 8 of Department of Defense Instruction 1332.14, March 29, 2010, www.dtic.mil/whs/directives/corres/pdf/133214p.pdf.

86. *Plyler v. Doe* (1982).

Chapter 6

1. Excerpted, with edits, from James Surowiecki, *The Wisdom of Crowds* (New York: Random House, 2004).

2. Pew Research Center for People and the Press, "Unabated Economic Gloom, Divides on Afghanistan and Health Care," December 16, 2009, people-press.org./reports/pdf/572.pdf

3. David Easton and Jack Dennis, *Children in the Political System* (Chicago: University of Chicago Press, 1969): 236.

4. Easton and Dennis, *Children in the Political System*: 115.

5. Edward Greenberg, "Black Children in the Political System," *Public Opinion Quarterly* 34 (1970): 335–348; Chris F. Garcia, *Political Socialization of Chicano Children* (New York: Praeger, 1973); Dean Jaros, Herbert Hirsch, and Frederick Fleron, "The Malevolent Leader: Political Socialization in an American Sub-Culture," *American Political Science Review* 62 (June 1968): 564–575; and Robert Erikson and Kent Tedin, *American Public Opinion: Its Origins, Content, and Impact* (New York: Longman, 2005), 121, but see also 122.

6. Erikson and Tedin, *American Public Opinion*: 146; and Fred Greenstein, *Children and Politics* (New Haven, CT: Yale University Press, 1965): 58–59.

7. Greenstein, *Children and Politics*: 58–59; and Easton and Dennis, *Children in the Political System*: 138.

8. Easton and Dennis, *Children in the Political System*: 254–70.

9. Easton and Dennis, *Children in the Political System*: 256.

10. M. Kent Jennings and Richard G. Niemi, *The Political Character of Adolescence* (Princeton, NJ: Princeton University Press, 1974): 274; and Greenstein, *Children and Politics*: 55.

11. Robert W. Connell, *The Child's Construction of Politics* (Melbourne: Melbourne University Press, 1971): 46–49, 59, 62.

12. Robert D. Hess and Judith V. Torney, *The Development of Political Attitudes in Children* (Chicago: Aldine, 1967): 215.

13. Greenstein, *Children and Politics*: 68, 73.

14. Connell, *The Child's Construction of Politics*: 50.

15. Jennings and Niemi, *The Political Character of Adolescence*: 266.

16. Jennings and Niemi, *The Political Character of Adolescence*: 271.

17. Jennings and Niemi, *The Political Character of Adolescence*: 275–276.

18. Roberta S. Sigel, *Learning About Politics* (New York: Random House, 1970): 103.

19. Kenneth P. Langton, *Political Socialization* (New York: Oxford University Press, 1969): 53.

20. M. Kent Jennings and Richard Niemi, *Generations and Politics* (Princeton, NJ: Princeton University Press, 1981): 90.

21. Hess and Torney, *Development*: 134–137; Frank J. Sorauf and Paul Allen Beck, *Party Politics in America* (New York: Harper Collins Publishers, 1988): 180–182.

22. Sigel, *Learning*: 412.

23. William G. Mayer, *The Changing American Mind* (Ann Arbor: University of Michigan Press, 1992): 252–254.

24. "U.S. Online MR Gains Drop," *Inside Research* 20, no. 1 (2009): 11–134, blogs.abcnews.com/thenumbers/2010/04/study-group-issues-a-warning-on-optin-online-surveys.html.

25. L. Rainie, "Internet, Broadband, and Cell Phone Statistics," Pew Internet and American Life Project, Pew Research Center, 2010.

26. AAPOR Report on Online Panels, 2010, aapor.org/AM/Template.cfm?Section=AAPOR_Committee_and_Task_Force_Reports&Template=/CM/ContentDisplay.cfm&ContentID=2223.

27. AAPOR Report on Online Panels.

28. Erikson and Tedin, *American Public Opinion*: 142.

29. Erikson and Tedin, *American Public Opinion*: 140.

30. Benjamin I. Page and Robert Y. Shapiro, *The Rational Public* (Chicago: University of Chicago Press, 1992): 341–348.

31. One of the most important and influential discussions of the role of party identification in shaping Americans' thinking about politics appears in Angus Campbell, Philip E. Converse, et al., *The American Voter* (New York: Wiley, 1960). See especially Chapter 6.

32. Campbell, Converse, et al., *The American Voter*: 201. Reference is to 1980 reprint.

33. For a discussion of this phenomenon as applied to presidential economic performance, see Campbell, Converse, et al., *The American Voter*, Chapter 14.

34. James A. Stimson, *Tides of Consent: How Public Opinion Shapes American Politics* (Cambridge: Cambridge University Press, 2004): 163.

35. D. C. Hallin and R. Giles, "Presses and Democracies," in G. Overholser and K. Hall Jamieson, eds., *The Press* (New York: Oxford University Press, 2005): 7.

36. T. Patterson, "Political Roles of the Journalist," in D. A. Graber, D. McQuail, and P. Norris, eds., *The Politics of News: The News of Politics* (Washington, DC: CQ Press, 2007); R. E. Horn, *Visual Language: Global Communication for the 21st Century* (Bainbridge, WA: MacroVU, 1999).

37. Patterson, "Political Roles of the Journalist": 22, Table 1.1.

38. Patterson, "Political Roles of the Journalist": 23.

39. *New York Times Co. v. United States*, 403 U.S. 713 (1971).

40. Margaret A. Blanchard, "Freedom of the Press," in W. David Sloan and Lisa Mullikin Parcell, eds., *American Journalism: History, Principles, Practices* (Jefferson, NC: McFarland, 2002): 127.

41. Richard W.T. Martin, *The Free and Open Press* (New York: New York University Press, 2001): 132.

42. W. Overbeck, *Major Principles of Media Law* (Belmont, CA: Wadsworth, 2007).

43. Lichter and McGinnis, "Government in and out of the News": 48–49.

44. Schudson and Tifft, "American Journalism in Historical Perspective," in Overholser and Jamieson's *The Press*: 33.

45. Schudson and Tifft, "American Journalism in Historical Perspective."

46. J. N. Cappella and K. H. Jamieson, *Spiral of Cynicism: The Press and the Public Good* (New York: Oxford University Press, 1997).

47. J. T. Hamilton, "The Market and the Media," in Overholser and Hall, eds., *The Press*: 358.

48. T. Patterson and P. Seib, "Informing the Public," in Overholser and Hall, eds., *The Press*: 194.

49. Patterson and Seib, "Informing the Public": 195; Patterson, *Out of Order*.

50. Bill Carter, "CNN Fails to Stop Fall in Ratings," *New York Times*, March 29, 2010.

51. R. Coen, "New Study: Center/Right Think Tanks Dominate News," 2000, FAIR Press Release, www.fair.org/index.php?page=1888.

52. The Center for Media and Public Affairs, "Election Watch: Campaign 2008 Final: How TV News Covered the General Election Campaign," *Media Monitor* XXIII, no. 1 (Winter 2009), www.cmpa.com/pdf/media_monitor_jan_2009.pdf.

53. S. Tiner, "Why Editors Are Dumber than Mules," 1999, www.asne.org.

54. Angus Campbell, Philip E. Converse, Warren E. Miller, and Donald Stokes, *The American Voter* (New York: Wiley, 1960).

55. John Zaller, "The Myth of Massive Media Impact Revived: New Support for a Discredited Idea," in Diana C. Mutz, Paul M. Sniderman, and Richard A. Brody, eds., *Political Persuasion and Attitude Change* (Ann Arbor: University of Michigan Press, 1996): 17.

56. Time of Presidential Election Vote Decision 1948–2004, 2005, www.electionstudies.org.

57. John Zaller, *The Nature and Origins of Mass Opinion* (New York: Cambridge University Press, 1992). Zaller's work forms the basis for much of the discussion in this section.

58. Bartels, "Politicians and the Press"; T. Patterson, *Mass Media Election* (New York: Praeger, 1980); S. J. Farnsworth and S. R. Lichter, "No Small Town Poll: Network Coverage of the 1992 New Hampshire Primary," *Harvard International Journal of Press/Politics* 4 (1999): 51–61.

59. Bartels, "Politicians and the Press"; Zaller, *The Nature and Origins of Mass Opinion*: 23, 37, 48.

Chapter 7

1. D. W. Miller, "Election Results Leave Political Scientists Red-Faced over Their Forecasting Models," *Chronicle of Higher Education*, November 8, 2000.

2. Robert G. Kaiser, "Gore to Win Election?" *Washington Post*, May 26, 2000: A1.

3. Sidney Verba, Kay Shlozman, and Henry Brady, *Voice and Equality* (Boston: Harvard University Press, 2006): 127.

4. Anthony Downs, *An Economic Theory of Democracy* (New York: Harper, 1957): 267–268.

5. It was political scientist Mancur Olson who introduced the idea of selective benefits, which he called "selective incentives," in a classic work: *The Logic of Collective Action*. We have much more to say about this book in Chapter 9 on interest groups.

6. Riker and Ordeshook elaborated on this article in a 1973 book entitled *Introduction to Positive Political Theory*. Their logic does not apply as well to other forms of political behavior—writing a letter to a member of Congress, for example, or gathering signatures on a petition. The concept of "civic duty" does not apply as well to such activities. To cover these other kinds of participation, therefore, political scientists have tended to talk about their "psychic benefits." "Psychic benefits" is just another way of saying that people derive satisfaction from participating in politics, regardless of whether their participation has any effect on relevant political outcomes.

7. Verba et al., *Voice and Equality*: 115, 550.

8. United States Election Project, "2008 Current Population Survey Voting and Registration Supplement," November 20, 2009, elections.gmu.edu/CPS_2008.html.

9. Michael McDonald and Samuel Popkin, "The Myth of the Vanishing Voter," *American Political Science Review* 95 (2001).

10. Shirley Zilberstein, "Ballot, Machine Problems to Blame for Uncounted Votes in 2000 Election," CNN, July 17 2001, archives.cnn.com/2001/ALLPOLITICS/07/16/voting.problems/index.html.

11. Verba et al., *Voice and Equality*: 349.

12. Some states allowed women and those aged 18 to 20 to vote prior to these amendments.

13. Roger Clegg, "Felon Disenfranchisement Is Constitutional, and Justified," National Constitution Center, www.constitutioncenter.org/education/ForEducators/Viewpoints/FelonDisenfranchisementIsConstitutional,AndJustified.shtml.

14. United States Election Project, "2008 Current Population Survey Voting and Registration Supplement," November 20, 2009, elections.gmu.edu/CPS_2008.html.

15. Robert A. Jackson, "The Mobilization of State Electorates in the 1988 and 1990 Elections," *Journal of Politics* 59 (1999): 520–537; Richard W. Boyd, "The Effects of Primaries and Statewide Races on Voter Turnout," *Journal of Politics* 51 (1989): 730–739.

16. Priscilla L. Southwell, "Voter Turnout in the 1986 Congressional Elections: The Media as a Demobilizer?" *American Politics Quarterly* 19 (1991): 96–108; Dean Lacy and Barry C. Burden, "The Vote-Stealing and Turnout Effects of Ross Perot in the 1992 U.S. Presidential Election," *American Journal of Political Science* 43 (1999): 233–255.

17. Gary W. Cox and Michael C. Munger, "Closeness, Expenditures, and Turnout in the 1982 U.S. House Elections," *American Political Science Review* 83 (1989): 217–231; Mark N. Franklin and Wolfgang P. Hirczy de Mino, "Separated Powers, Divided Government, and Turnout in U.S. Presidential Elections," *American Journal of Political Science* 42 (January 1998): 316–326; Gregory A. Caldeira and Samuel C. Patterson, "Getting Out the Vote: Participation in Gubernatorial Elections," *American Political Science Review* 77 (1982): 675–689.

18. Steven J. Rosenstone and John M. Hansen, *Mobilization, Participation, and Democracy in America* (New York: Macmillan, 1993): 29.

19. This isn't so in two states: Louisiana and Washington both use a "top two" system in which the two final candidates (if no candidate receives over 50 percent in the first round) could both be Democrats or both be Republicans.

20. Ron Gunzburger, "Presidency 2000: Arizona Primary Results," Politics 1, www.politics1.com/vote-az.htm.

21. Lawrence D. Longley and Neal R. Peirce, *The Electoral College Primer 2000* (New Haven: Yale University Press, 1999): 18–19.

22. Gary L. Gregg II, *Securing Democracy: Why We Have an Electoral College* (Wilmington, DE: ISI Books, 2001), 7, 8.

23. Gregg, *Securing Democracy*, 27–29. Originally the second-place finisher became the vice president. This was changed by constitutional amendment in 1804 so that electors cast votes separately for president and vice president. By awarding the vice presidency to the second-place finisher, the previous system set up the possibility for severe disharmony in the executive branch.

24. "U.S. Electoral College," Wikipedia, en.wikipedia.org/wiki/U.S._Electoral_College#Maine-Nebraska_method.

25. Michael Gant and Norman Luttbeg, "The Cognitive Utility of Partisanship," *Western Political Quarterly* 40 (1987): 499–517.

26. William H. Flanigan and Nancy H. Zingale, *Political Behavior of the American Electorate* (Washington, DC: CQ Press, 2002), 78.

27. Michael R. Alvarez, *Information and Elections* (Ann Arbor: University of Michigan Press, 1998): 8.

28. V.O. Key, *The Responsible Electorate, Rationality in Presidential Voting, 1936-1960* (Cambridge, MA: Belknap Press, 1966); Gregory B. Markus and Philip Converse, "A Dynamic Simultaneous Equation Model of Electoral Choice," *American Political Science Review* 73 (1979).

29. Edward G. Carmines and James A. Stimson, *Issue Evolution: Race and the Transformation of American Politics* (Princeton, NJ: Princeton University Press, 1989).

30. Larry M. Bartels, "Impact of Candidate Traits in American Presidential Elections," in *Leaders' Personalities and the Outcomes of Democratic Elections*, Anthony King, ed. (New York: Oxford University Press, 2002): 46.

31. Angus Campbell et al., *The American Voter* (Chicago: University of Chicago Press, 1980): 44–45.

32. Markus and Converse, "A Dynamic Simultaneous Equation Model of Electoral Choice."

33. Campbell et al., *The American Voter*; Stanley Kelley, Jr., and Thad W. Mirer, "The Simple Act of Voting," *American Political Science Review* 68 (1974): 572–591; Markus and Converse, "A Dynamic Simultaneous Equation Model of Electoral Choice"; Warren E. Miller and J. Merrill Shanks, *The New American Voter* (Cambridge, MA: Harvard University Press, 1996): Chapter 17.

34. Kelley and Mirer, "The Simple Act of Voting"; Markus and Converse, "A Dynamic Simultaneous Equation Model of Electoral Choice."

35. Markus and Converse, "A Dynamic Simultaneous Equation Model of Electoral Choice."

36. Larry M. Bartels, *Presidential Primaries and the Dynamics of Public Choice* (Princeton, NJ: Princeton University Press, 1998).

37. American Political Science Association, "6 of 9 Presidential Election Forecasts Predict Obama Will Win 2008 Popular Vote," October 16, 2008, www.apsanet.org/content_58969.cfm.

38. James E. Campbell, "Forecasting the Presidential Vote in the States," *American Journal of Political Science* 36 (1992): 386–407.

39. Randall J. Jones, Jr., *Who Will Be in the White House: Predicting Presidential Elections* (New York: Longman, 2002): 31.

Chapter 8

1. The definition here is based on William N. Chambers, "Party Development and the American Mainstream," in William N. Chambers and Walter Dean Burnham, eds., *The American Party Systems: Stages of Political Development*, 2nd ed. (New York: Oxford University Press, 1975): 5; and Leon D. Epstein, *Political Parties in the American Mold* (Madison: University of Wisconsin Press, 1986): 18–19.

2. See Gregory Koger, Seth Masket, and Hans Noel, "Partisan Webs: Information Exchange and Party Networks," *British Journal of Political Science* 39 (2009): 633–53; Paul S. Herrnson, "The Roles of Party Organizations, Party-Connected Committees, and Party Allies in Elections," *Journal of Politics* 71, no. 4 (2009): 1207–24.

3. John H. Aldrich, *Why Parties? The Origin and Transformation of Political Parties in America* (Chicago: University of Chicago Press, 1995). See also Seth E. Masket, "It Takes an Outsider: Extralegislative Organization and Partisanship in

the California Assembly, 1849–2006," *American Journal of Political Science* 51, no. 3 (2007): 482–97.

4. John J. Coleman, "Unified Government, Divided Government, and Party Responsiveness," *American Political Science Review* 93, no. 4 (1999): 821–35; Sarah A. Binder, "The Dynamics of Legislative Gridlock, 1947–96," *American Political Science Review* 93, no. 3 (1999): 519–33; William G. Howell, E. Scott Adler, Charles Cameron, and Charles Riemann, "Divided Government and the Legislative Productivity of Congress, 1945–1994," *Legislative Studies Quarterly* 25, no. 2 (2000): 285–312. See David R. Mayhew, *Divided We Govern: Party Control, Lawmaking, and Investigations, 1946–2002,* 2nd ed. (New Haven, CT: Yale University Press, 2005), for a contrary view.

5. Seth E. Masket, "Did Obama's Ground Game Matter? The Influence of Local Field Offices During the 2008 Presidential Election," *Public Opinion Quarterly* 73, no. 5 (2009): 1023–39.

6. Kenneth M. Goldstein and Travis Ridout, "The Politics of Participation: Mobilization and Turnout over Time," *Political Behavior* 24, no. 1 (2002): 3–29; R. Michael Alvarez, Asa Hopkins, and Betsy Sinclair, "Mobilizing Pasadena Democrats: Measuring the Effects of Partisan Campaign Contacts," *Journal of Politics* 72, no. 1 (2010): 31–44.

7. Anna Harvey, *Votes Without Leverage: Women in American Electoral Politics, 1920–1970* (New York: Cambridge University Press, 1998).

8. Alan S. Gerber and Gregory A. Huber, "Partisanship, Political Control, and Economic Assessments," *American Journal of Political Science* 54, no. 1 (2010): 153–73.

9. For overviews, see Alan Ware, *Political Parties and Party Systems* (New York: Oxford University Press, 1996); and Steven J. Rosenstone, Roy L. Behr, and Edward H. Lazarus, *Third Parties in America: Citizen Response to Major Party Failure,* 2nd ed. (Princeton, NJ: Princeton University Press, 1996).

10. Harold W. Stanley and Richard G. Niemi, *Vital Statistics on American Politics, 2007–08* (Washington, DC: CQ Press, 2008): 43.

11. Candidates of third parties that are relatively large, such as the People's Party of the 1890s or the Progressive Party of the early twentieth century, may eventually absorb back into the major parties and can work to change the major parties' positions from within.

12. Barry C. Burden: "Minor Parties and Strategic Voting in Recent U.S. Presidential Elections," *Electoral Studies* 24, no. 4 (2005): 603–18; and "Ralph Nader's Campaign Strategy in the 2000 U.S. Presidential Election," *American Politics Research* 33, no. 5 (2005): 672–99.

13. Pew Research Center for the People and the Press, people-press.org/reports/questionnaires/630.pdf, question 22.

14. William H. Riker, "The Two-Party System and Duverger's Law: An Essay on the History of Political Science," *American Political Science Review* 76 (1982): 753–66; William Roberts Clark and Matt Golder, "Rehabilitating Duverger's Theory: Testing the Mechanical and Strategic Modifying Effects

of Electoral Laws," *Comparative Political Studies* 39, no. 6 (2006): 679–708.

15. Most systems employ a threshold and deny seats to very small parties.

16. Josep M. Colomer, "It's Parties That Choose Electoral Systems (Or, Duverger's Laws Upside Down)," *Political Studies* 53, no. 1 (2005): 1–21; Kenneth Benoit, "Electoral Laws as Political Consequences: Explaining the Origins and Change of Electoral Institutions," *Annual Review of Political Science* 10 (2007): 363–90.

17. Aldrich, *Why Parties?* See also Anthony Downs, *An Economic Theory of Democracy* (New York: Harper, 1957).

18. Maine and Nebraska award two electoral votes to the presidential candidate who wins the state, and one electoral vote for winning a congressional district.

19. Pradeep Chhibber and Ken Kollman, "Party Aggregation and the Number of Parties in India and the United States," *American Political Science Review* 92, no. 2 (1998): 329–42.

20. Lisa Disch, *The Tyranny of the Two-Party System* (New York: Columbia University Press, 2002).

21. *Timmons v. Twin Cities Area New Party* (1997). The seven states are Connecticut, Delaware, Idaho, Mississippi, New York, South Carolina, and Vermont.

22. See Rosenstone et al., *Third Parties in America: Citizen Response to Major Party Failure,* 254–6.

23. John Zaller and Mark Hunt, "The Rise and Fall of Candidate Perot: Unmediated Versus Mediated Politics—Part I," *Political Communication* 11, no. 4 (1994): 357–90; Paul R. Abramson, John H. Aldrich, Philip Paolino, and David W. Rohde, "Challenges to the American Two-Party System: Evidence from the 1968, 1980, 1992, and 1996 Presidential Elections," *Political Research Quarterly* 53, no. 3 (2000): 495–522.

24. Rosenstone, Behr, and Lazarus, *Third Parties in America.*

25. Ronald P. Formisano, "The 'Party Period' Revisited," *Journal of American History* 86, no. 1 (1999): 93–120.

26. Jessica Trounstine, *Political Monopolies in American Cities: The Rise and Fall of Bosses and Reformers* (Chicago: University of Chicago Press, 2008).

27. Alan Ware, *The American Direct Primary: Party Institutionalization and Transformation in the North* (New York: Cambridge University Press, 2002); and "Anti-partism and Party Control of Political Reform in the United States: The Case of the Australian Ballot," *British Journal of Political Science* 30, no. 1 (2000): 1–29.

28. Epstein, *Political Parties in the American Mold*; Amy Bridges, *Morning Glories: Municipal Reform in the Southwest* (Princeton, NJ: Princeton University Press, 1997); Byron E. Shafer, *Quiet Revolution: The Struggle for the Democratic Party and the Shaping of Post-Reform Politics* (New York: Russell Sage Foundation, 1983).

29. See Cornelius P. Cotter, James L. Gibson, John F. Bibby, and Robert J. Huckshorn, *Party Organizations in American Politics*

(New York: Praeger, 1984); Paul S. Herrnson, "The Revitalization of National Party Organizations," in L. Sandy Maisel, ed., *The Parties Respond* (Boulder, CO: Westview Press, 1994).

30. *California Democratic Party v. Jones* (2000); *Tashjian v. Connecticut* (1986).

31. Paul S. Herrnson, *Party Campaigning in the 1980s* (Cambridge, MA: Harvard University Press, 1988); John J. Coleman, "Party Organizational Strength and Public Support for Parties," *American Journal of Political Science* 40, no. 3 (1996): 805–24.

32. Marjorie Randon Hershey, *Party Politics in America*, 13th ed. (New York: Longman, 2009), 76.

33. Campaign Finance Institute, www.cfinst.org/data/pdf/Vital-Stats_t12.pdf.

34. Matthew J. Burbank, Ronald J. Hrebenar, and Robert C. Benedict, *Parties, Interest Groups, and Political Campaigns* (Boulder, CO: Westview Press, 1999): 149.

35. The discussion in this case study relies extensively on Hershey, *Party Politics in America*, 205–06; and Matthew J. Burbank et al., *Parties, Interest Groups, and Political Campaigns*, 148–49.

36. David Paul Kuhn, "DNC Blunts GOP Microtargeting Lead," May 23, 2008, www.politico.com. See also: Hershey, *Party Politics in America*, 205; Peter Wallsten and Tom Hamburger, "The GOP Knows You Don't Like Anchovies," *Los Angeles Times*, June 25, 2006.

37. Hershey, *Party Politics in America*, 205; Peter Wallsten and Tom Hamburger, "The GOP Knows You Don't Like Anchovies," *Los Angeles Times*, June 25, 2006.

38. David Talbot, "The Democrats' New Weapon," *Technology Review*, December 18, 2008; Jim Rutenberg and Christopher Drew, "National Push by Obama on Ads and Turnout," *New York Times*, June 22, 2008.

39. Nicol C. Rae, "Be Careful What You Wish For: The Rise of Responsible Parties in American National Politics," *Annual Review of Political Science*10 (2007): 169–91.

40. Paul Frymer, *Uneasy Alliances: Race and Party Competition in America* (Princeton, NJ: Princeton University Press, 1999).

41. Philip A. Klinkner, *The Losing Parties: Out-Party National Committees, 1956–1993* (New Haven: Yale University Press, 1994); Zeynep Somer-Topcu, "Timely Decisions: The Effects of Past National Elections on Party Policy Change," *Journal of Politics* 71, no. 1 (2009): 238–48.

42. Edward G. Carmines and Michael W. Wagner, "Political Issues and Party Alignments: Assessing the Issue Evolution Perspective," *Annual Review of Political Science* 9 (2006): 67–81; David Karol, *Partisan Position Change in American Politics: Coalition Maintenance* (New York: Cambridge University Press, 2009).

43. For an overview and critique, see David R. Mayhew, *Electoral Realignments: A Critique of an American Genre* (New Haven, CT: Yale University Press, 2002).

44. See James L. Sundquist, *Politics and Policy: The Eisenhower, Kennedy, and Johnson Years* (Washington, DC: Brookings Institution Press, 1968); and Donald Green, Bradley Palmquist, and Eric Schickler, *Partisan Hearts and Minds: Political Parties and the Social Identities of Voters* (New Haven, CT: Yale University Press, 2002).

45. William G. Mayer, *The Divided Democrats: Ideological Unity, Party Reform, and Presidential Elections* (Boulder, CO: Westview Press, 1996), chap. 5; Paul R. Abramson, John H. Aldrich, and David W. Rohde, *Change and Continuity in the 2004 Elections* (Washington, DC: CQ Press, 2006), chap. 5.

46. Larry M. Bartels, "Where the Ducks Are: Voting Power in a Party System," in John G. Geer, ed., *Politicians and Party Politics* (Baltimore: Johns Hopkins University Press, 1998); Alan I. Abramowitz and Kyle L. Saunders, "Ideological Realignment in the U.S. Electorate," *Journal of Politics* 60, no. 3 (1998): 634–52; Abramson, Aldrich, and Rohde, *Change and Continuity in the 2004 Elections*.

47. Walter Dean Burnham, "The 1980 Election: Realignment, Reaction, or What?" in Thomas Ferguson and Joel Rogers, eds., *The Hidden Election: Politics and Economics in the 1980 Presidential Campaign* (New York: Pantheon, 1981). See also Brett M. Clifton, "Romancing the GOP: Assessing the Strategies Used by the Christian Coalition to Influence the Republican Party," *Party Politics* 10, no. 5 (2004): 475–98.

48. Democrats controlled the Senate from mid-2001 until the end of 2002 after James Jeffords, a Republican senator from Vermont, declared himself an independent and aligned with the Democrats.

49. Larry M. Bartels, "Partisanship and Voting Behavior, 1952–1996," *American Journal of Political Science* 44, no. 1 (2000): 35–50; Joseph Barfumi and Robert Y. Shapiro, "A New Partisan Voter," *Journal of Politics* 71, no. 1 (2009): 1–24; David A. Hopkins, "The 2008 Election and the Political Geography of the New Democratic Majority," *Polity* 41, no. 3 (2009): 368–87.

50. Robert S. Erikson, Michael B. MacKuen, and James A. Stimson argue that public opinion tends to push against the ideological grain of current policy. See *The Macro Polity* (New York: Cambridge University Press, 2002).

51. www.voteview.com/polarized_america. htm#Politicalpolarization.

52. CBS News/New York Times Poll, August 31, 2008, www.cbsnews.com/htdocs/pdf/RNCDelegates_issues.pdf. See also Hershey, *Party Politics in America*, 187.

53. Morris P. Fiorina, "Parties and Partisanship: A 40-Year Retrospective," *Political Behavior* 24, no. 2 (2002): 93–115.

54. David R. Jones, "Partisan Polarization and Congressional Accountability in House Elections," *American Journal of Political Science* 54, no. 2 (2010): 323–37.

55. Edward G. Carmines and Geoffrey Layman, "Issue Evolution in Postwar American Politics: Old Certainties and Fresh

Tensions," in Byron E. Shafer, ed., *Present Discontents: American Politics in the Very Late Twentieth Century* (Chatham, NJ: Chatham House, 1997).

56. See John Gerring, *Party Ideologies in America, 1828–1996* (New York: Cambridge University Press, 1998).

57. Analysis based on percentage of the population rating these issues as a "top priority" in the Pew Research Center's January 2010 survey; cited in "Public's Priorities for 2010: Economy, Jobs, Terrorism," January 25, 2010, people-press.org/report/584/policy-priorities-2010.

58. Lydia Saad, "Federal Debt, Terrorism Considered Top Threats to U.S.," Gallup Poll, June 4, 2010, www.gallup.com/poll/139385/Federal-Debt-Terrorism-Considered-Top-Threats.aspx.

59. Saad, "Federal Debt, Terrorism Considered Top Threats to U.S."

60. John R. Petrocik, William L. Benoit, and Glenn J. Hansen, "Issue Ownership and Presidential Campaigning, 1952–2000," *Political Science Quarterly* 118, no. 4 (2003–04): 599–626.

61. David Wright, Andy Fies, and Sunlen Miller, "Obama: 'Old Politics Just Won't Do'—Democratic Contender Frames Race Against Clinton as 'Past Versus the Future,'" January 30, 2008, www.abcnews.go.com; Associated Press, "McCain Outlines Vision of Iraq Victory, Reduced Partisanship," May 15, 2008, elections.foxnews.com.

62. The "two Americas" label was used by Democratic presidential candidate John Edwards in 2004 and 2008 and "culture war" by 1992 Republican presidential candidate Patrick Buchanan.

63. Pietro S. Nivola and David W. Brady: *Red and Blue Nation? Characteristics and Causes of America's Polarized Politics* (Washington, DC: Brookings Institution Press, 2006); and *Red and Blue Nation? Consequences and Correction of America's Polarized Politics* (Washington, DC: Brookings Institution Press, 2008).

64. Morris P. Fiorina, Samuel J. Abrams, and Jeremy C. Pope, *Culture War? The Myth of a Polarized America*, 2nd ed. (New York: Longman, 2005).

65. Paul DiMaggio, John Evans, and Bethany Bryson, "Have Americans' Social Attitudes Become More Polarized?" *American Journal of Sociology* 102, no. 3 (1996): 690–755.

66. Matthew Levendusky, *The Partisan Sort: How Liberals Became Democrats and Conservatives Became Republicans* (Chicago: University of Chicago Press, 2009).

Chapter 9

1. Adapted from M. Margaret Conway, *Political Participation in the United States,* 3rd ed. (Washington, DC: CQ Press, 2000): 108–111; and Nancy E. McGlen and Karen O'Connor, *Women, Politics, and American Society* (Englewood Cliffs, NJ: Prentice Hall, 1995): Chapter 1.

2. Earl Latham, *The Group Basis of Politics: A Study in Basing-Point Legislation* (New York: Octagon, 1965): 221.

3. David B. Truman, *The Governmental Process: Political Interests and Public Opinion* (New York: Knopf, 1951): 507.

4. Truman, *The Governmental Process:* 289.

5. U.S. Census Bureau News, "Household Income Rises, Poverty Rate Declines, Number of Uninsured Up," August 28, 2007, www.census.gov/Press-Release/www/releases/archives/income_wealth/010583.html (accessed August 11, 2008).

6. Peter Bachrach and Morton S. Baratz, "Two Faces of Power," *American Political Science Review* 56, no. 4 (1962): 947–952.

7. Peter Bachrach and Morton S. Baratz, "Decisions and Nondecisions: An Analytical Framework," *American Political Science Review* 57, no. 3 (1963): 632–642.

8. Truman, *The Governmental Process.*

9. Mancur Olson, *The Logic of Collective Action: Public Goods and the Theory of Groups* (Cambridge, MA: Harvard University Press, 1965): 2.

10. Olson, *The Logic of Collective Action:* 16.

11. Olson, *The Logic of Collective Action:* 51. Olson coined "selective incentives."

12. Compassionate Action for Animals, "Volunteer Testimonials," www.exploreveg.org/help/volunteer-testimonials (accessed August 11, 2008).

13. Robert H. Salisbury, "An Exchange Theory of Interest Groups," *Midwest Journal of Political Science* 13, no. 1 (1969): 1–32.

14. Violence Policy Center, "National Rifle Association Information," www.vpc.org/nrainfo/chapter1.html (accessed August 11, 2008).

15. Richard Hume Werking, "Bureaucrats, Businessmen, and Foreign Trade: The Origins of the United States Chamber of Commerce," *Business History Review* 52, no. 3, *Corporate Liberalism* (Autumn 1978): 321–341.

16. Opensecrets.org, Center for Responsible Politics, "Stats at a Glance," www.opensecrets.org/overview/index.php.

17. Richard L. Hall and Frank W. Wayman, "Buying Time: Moneyed Interests and the Mobilization of Bias in Congressional Committees," American Political Science Review 84, no. 3 (1990): 802.

18. R. Kenneth Godwin and Barry J. Seldon, "What Corporations Really Want from Government," www.politicalscience.uncc.edu/godwink/RecentPublications/What%20Corporations%20Really%20Want%20from%20Government.pdf (accessed August 11, 2008).

19. Godwin and Seldon, "What Corporations Really Want from Government."

Chapter 10

1. Shawn Reese, Congressional Research Service Report for Congress, *Fiscal Year 2005 Homeland Security Grant Program: State Allocations and Issues for Congressional Oversight* (Washington, DC: Congressional Research Service, 2004). See also "FY 2010 Homeland Security Grant Program," Federal Emergency Management Agency, www.fema.gov.

2. These figures are based on spending figures found in "Homeland Security and Grant Program, Guidance and Application Kit," Department of Homeland Security, 27; and population figures found in "Annual Estimates of the Resident Population for the United States, Regions, and Puerto Rico," U.S. Census Bureau, January 26, 2009. See also Kathleen Hunter, "Per Capita, New Anti-terror Funds Still Favor Wyoming," Pew Research Center, December 16, 2004, www.stateline.org.

3. The remaining 60 percent of the funds are distributed by formula according to population.

4. "U.S. Not 'Well-prepared' for Terrorism," December 5, 2005, www.cnn.com.

5. Kathleen Hunter, "Budget Would Revise Anti-terrorism Funding," Pew Research Center, February 8, 2005, www.stateline.org.

6. Veronique de Rugy, "Homeland-Security Scuffle," *National Review*, October 15, 2004, www.nationalreview.com/comment/rugy200410150840.asp.

7. Nonvoting members come from the District of Columbia, American Samoa, Guam, Puerto Rico, and the Virgin Islands.

8. At the nation's founding, state legislatures appointed senators to office. In 1913, however, the states ratified the Seventeenth Amendment, which required the direct election of senators. Representatives in the House have always been popularly elected.

9. David Mayhew, *The Electoral Connection* (New Haven: Yale University Press, 1974).

10. "Lobbying: Top Spenders," Open Secrets: Center for Responsive Politics, www.opensecrets.org/lobby/top.php?showYear=2010&indexType=s.

11. Brandice Canes-Wrone, David Brady, and John Cogan, "Out of Step, Out of Office: Electoral Accountability and House Members' Voting," *American Political Science Review* 96, no. 1 (2002): 127–140.

12. Based on figures from fiscal year 2000. Congressional Budget Office, "Federal Spending on the Elderly and Children," July 2000, cbo.gov/ftpdocs/23xx/doc2300/fsec.pdf.

13. Gary Jacobson, *The Politics of Congressional Elections*, 6th ed. (New York: Longman, 2003).

14. Brody Mullins, "Growing Role for Lobbyists: Raising Funds for Lawmakers," *Wall Street Journal*, January 27, 2006: 1. In 2010 alone, in terms of spending, the top 10 interest groups contributed between $20 million and $132 million each to the reelection campaigns of representatives.

15. Keith T. Poole and Thomas Romer, "Ideology, 'Shirking,' and Representation," *Public Choice* 77 (1993): 185–196.

16. For more on descriptive or numerical representation, see Jane Mansbridge, "Should Blacks Represent Blacks and Women Represent Women? A Contingent 'Yes,'" *Journal of Politics* 61, no. 3 (August 1999): 628–657.

17. Daniel Gitterman, *Boosting Paychecks: The Politics of Supporting America's Working Poor* (Washington, DC: Brookings Institution, 2009).

18. For one study of the role of information in Congress, see Keith Krehbiel, *Information and Legislative Organization* (Ann Arbor: University of Michigan Press, 1992).

19. Kenneth Shepsle, *The Giant Jigsaw Puzzle: Democratic Committee Assignments in the Modern House* (Chicago: University of Chicago Press, 1978).

20. Gary Cox and Mathew McCubbins, *Setting the Agenda: Responsible Party Government in the U.S. House of Representatives* (New York: Cambridge University Press, 2005).

21. See, for example, Keith Krehbiel, "Where's the Party?" *British Journal of Political Science* 23 (1993): 235–266.

22. Since the Civil War, southern politicians retained strong loyalties to the Democratic Party. Ideologically, however, they had more in common with northern Republicans. Beginning in the 1970s, over a century after the Civil War's end, southern Democrats began to abandon their former partisan commitments in order to join the ranks of the Republican Party.

23. Nolan McCarty, Keith Poole, and Howard Rosenthal, *Polarized America: The Dance of Ideology and Unequal Riches* (Cambridge, MA: MIT Press, 2005).

24. William A. Galston, "The GOP's Grassroots Obstructionists," *Washington Post*, May 16, 2010.

25. For a profile of congressional staffers in 2007, see "The Hill People 2007: A Special Report," *National Journal*, June 23, 2007.

26. William Howell and Douglas Kriner, "Political Elites and Public Support for War," University of Chicago typescript, 2007.

27. Figures are available at people-press.org/reports/pdf/693.pdf.

28. William Howell and Jon Pevehouse, *While Dangers Gather: Congressional Checks on Presidential War Power* (Princeton, NJ: Princeton University Press, 2007). See also William Howell and Jon Pevehouse, "When Congress Stops Wars," *Foreign Affairs* 86, no. 5 (2007): 95–108.

29. Barbara Sinclair, *Unorthodox Lawmaking: New Legislative Processes in the U.S. Congress* (Washington, DC: CQ Press, 1997).

30. It is possible to bypass the Rules Committee. With a two-thirds vote, members can send a bill directly to the floor, where only 40 minutes of debate are allowed and all amendments are forbidden. To enact the bill under this fast-track

procedure, though, supporters must garner the support of two-thirds of the House. Typically, only those bills that are either trivial in importance or that enjoy widespread support are thus considered.

31. The Senate also offers its members several other ways of prolonging the legislative process. For instance, senators can place anonymous holds on bills, which prevent them from moving forward. Additionally, senators have more opportunities to introduce amendments to bills than do representatives in the House, where the party leadership exercises more control over deliberations.

32. It is worth noting, though, that floors have some powers to check such tendencies—for example, the discharge petition allows a majority of floor members to force a committee to release a bill for a floor vote.

33. Norman Ornstein, Thomas Mann, and Michael Malbin, *Vital Statistics on Congress, 1995–1996* (Washington, DC: CQ Press, 1996): 169. For more on the filibuster, see Gregory Wawro and Eric Schickler, Filibuster: Obstruction and Lawmaking in the U.S. Senate (Princeton, NJ: Princeton University Press, 2006).

34. Information on the 111th Congress available at: www.rollcall.com/news/-201997-1.html.

35. The two exceptions: Franklin Pierce, who ranks near the bottom of most ratings of presidential greatness; and Andrew Johnson, who ranks no higher and whom the House went on to impeach. See Lyn Ragsdale, *Vital Statistics on the Presidency* (Washington, DC: CQ Press, 1998): 27–28.

36. Harold Stanley and Richard Niemi, *Vital Statistics on American Politics 2009–2010* (Washington, DC: Congressional Quarterly Press, 2010).

37. Walter J. Oleszek, "Self-Executing Rules Reported by the House Committee on Rules," December 21, 2006, usgovinfo.about.com/library/PDF/self_executing.pdf.

38. Don Wolfensberger, "Bimonthly Column on Procedural Politics," June 19, 2006, www.wilsoncenter.org/index.cfm?topic_id=1412&fuseaction=topics.publications&doc_id=190504&group_id=180829.

39. Rachel L. Swarns, "Split over Immigration Reflects Nation's Struggle," *New York Times*, March 29, 2006: A17; Robert Pear, "Bush Ties Drop in Illegal Immigration to His Policies," *New York Times*, April 10, 2007: A18; Robert Pear, "Many Employers See Flaws as Immigration Bill Evolves," New York Times, May 27, 2007: 1.23.

40. T. W. Farnam, "Obama Pitches Immigration Policy," *Wall Street Journal*, September 10, 2010.

41. "Remarks by the President at Cinco de Mayo Reception," President Barack Obama, May 5, 2010.

42. Julia Preston, "Grass Roots Roared, and an Immigration Plan Fell," *New York Times*, June 10, 2007: A1.

43. Jeff Zeleny, "Immigration Bill Prompts Some Menacing Responses," *New York Times*, June 28, 2007: A18.

44. June Kronholz and Sarah Lueck, "State of the Union: Immigration Proposals Reverse Party Loyalties," *Wall Street Journal*, January 24, 2007: A2.

45. Jonathan Weisman, "Immigration Bill Dies in Senate; Bipartisan Compromise Fails to Satisfy the Right or the Left," *Washington Post*, June 29, 2007: A1.

46. Peter Baker, "Bush May Be out Of Chances for a Lasting Domestic Victory," *Washington Post*, June 29, 2007: A1.

47. Sandy Streeter, CRS Report 97-684, *The Congressional Appropriations Process: An Introduction* (Washington, DC: Congressional Research Service, 2006): 4.

48. Allen Schick and Felix LoStracco, *The Federal Budget: Politics, Policy, and Progress* (Washington, DC: Brookings Institution, 2000): 235, 236, 238.

49. See appropriations.senate.gov/budgetprocess.cfm.

50. See Taxpayers for Common Sense, www.taxpayer.net.

Chapter 11

1. "Obama: Victory Speech," *New York Times*, November 5, 2008.

2. See Richard Pious, *The Presidency* (New York: Longman, 1995).

3. For an analysis of the president's place in the American political system, see Charles O. Jones, *The Presidency in a Separated System* (Washington, DC: Brookings Institution, 1994).

4. See, for example, John Yoo *Crisis and Command: A History of Executive Power from George Washington to George W. Bush* (New York: Kaplan, 2010); Steven Calabresi and Christopher Yoo, *The Unitary Executive: Presidential Power from Washington to Bush* (New Haven: Yale University Press, 2008).

5. See, for example, James Pfiffner, *Power Play: The Bush Presidency and the Constitution*. (Washington, DC: Brookings Institution, 2009).

6. The Twenty-second Amendment, a reaction to Franklin Roosevelt's four-term presidency, limited the president to two terms in office.

7. Technically, Lincoln suspended the writ of habeas corpus. A defendant can request a writ of habeas corpus, which is a court order that requires a government official to explain to a judge why an individual is incarcerated.

8. Roosevelt proposed that for every justice over the age of 70, the president could nominate one additional justice until the Supreme Court reached a maximum size of 15. The plan would have allowed Roosevelt to offset older, more conservative justices with those more likely to accommodate his proposals. For more on this "court packing" plan, see Jeff Shesol, *Supreme Power: Franklin Roosevelt vs. the Supreme Court* (New York: Norton, 2010).

9. The scandal was so named because of the break-in at the Democratic National Committee's headquarters at the Watergate Hotel in Washington, D.C., on June 17, 1972. The president's aides were responsible for arranging the break-in, and the president engineered a cover-up designed to keep the truth from coming out. The discovery of that break-in prompted investigations that revealed a wide range of White House abuses of power, ultimately leading to Nixon's resignation in August 1974.

10. Isaiah J. Poole, "Two Steps Up, One Step Down," *CQ Weekly*, January 9, 2006: 80.

11. On different leadership styles, see Fred I. Greenstein, *The Presidential Difference: Leadership Style from FDR to George W. Bush* (Princeton, NJ: Princeton University Press, 2004).

12. For a skeptical view of the president's ability to change public opinion, see George Edwards, *On Deaf Ears: The Limits of the Bully Pulpit* (New Haven: Yale University Press, 2003).

13. Whether the bill was originally one of interest to the president or not, to become law both Congress and the president must approve of the legislation.

14. Charles M. Cameron, *Veto Bargaining: Presidents and the Politics of Negative Power* (New York: Cambridge University Press, 2000).

15. William G. Howell, *Power Without Persuasion: The Politics of Direct Presidential Action* (Princeton, NJ: Princeton University Press, 2003).

16. Craig Crawford, "Stubborner than a Donkey," *CQ Weekly*, May 28, 2007: 1638.

17. See Richard Neustadt, *Presidential Power and the Modern Presidents: The Politics of Leadership from Roosevelt to Reagan* (New York: Free Press, 1991).

18. U.S. Government Accountability Office, "Presidential Signing Statements Accompanying the Fiscal Year 2006 Appropriations Acts," June 18, 2007, www.gao.gov/decisions/appro/308603.pdf. The investigation looked at appropriations bills only. Of the 12 bills, the president questioned a total of 160 provisions in 11 of the bills. The investigation tracked 19 of these and found noncompliance on 6 of those 19.

19. *Rasul v. Bush* (2004); *al Odah v. United States* (2004); *Hamdi v. Rumsfeld* (2004).

20. Congress can also impeach other executive branch officials or members of the judiciary.

21. George Edwards, *At the Margins: Presidential Leadership of Congress* (New Haven: Yale University Press, 1990).

22. The exact figures are available at: www.gallup.com/poll/113980/Gallup-Daily-Obama-Job-Approval.aspx.

23. Gary Jacobson, *A Divider, Not a Uniter: George W. Bush and the American People* (New York: Longman, 2006).

24. Samuel Kernell, *Going Public: New Strategies of Presidential Leadership*, 3rd ed. (Washington, DC: CQ Press, 1997).

25. Patricia Heidotting Conley, *Presidential Mandates: How Elections Shape the National Agenda* (Chicago: University of Chicago Press, 2001).

26. Chris Cillizza, "The White House Cheat Sheet: The Obama Mandate," *Washington Post*, January 27, 2009. Available online at: voices.washingtonpost.com/thefix/cheat-sheet/white-house-cheat-sheet-pollin.html.

27. See John J. Coleman, "Unified Government, Divided Government, and Party Responsiveness," *American Political Science Review* 93, no. 4 (1999): 821–835, for an overview of literature on lawmaking during unified and divided government.

28. For a useful historical timeline on U.S. health care reform, see the health timeline available online at: www.nytimes.com/interactive/2009/07/19/us/politics/20090717_HEALTH_TIMELINE.html.

29. For a complete discussion of these programs, see Chapter 14.

30. "Remarks by the President to a Joint Session of Congress on Health Care," White House, Office of the Press Secretary, September 9, 2009. Available online at: www.whitehouse.gov/the_press_office/remarks-by-the-president-to-a-joint-session-of-congress-on-health-care/.

31. "House Passes Health Care Reform Bill," CNN, November 8, 2009. Available online at: www.cnn.com/2009/POLITICS/11/07/health.care/index.html.

32. David M. Herszenhorn and Sheryl G. Stolberg, "Obama Rallies House Democrats," *New York Times*, November 7, 2009. Available online at: prescriptions.blogs.nytimes.com/2009/11/07/obamas-in-the-house/?scp=5&sq=obama%20health%20care%20personal%20appeal%20house%20of%20representatives&st=cse.

33. Representative Tammy Baldwin of Wisconsin expresses this sentiment in these remarks: "I think one of the challenges I've had as I've moved from working on domestic issues to now having a vote and a say on international issues is, I would say, a frustration with the limits to your information sources. If I look at almost any domestic issues imaginable, I can easily obtain information from a variety of perspectives and weigh the pros and cons of most policy decisions. It's much more difficult on a wide range of international issues, be they trade issues, global environmental issues, issues of war and peace. The information that's easiest to obtain is usually through the filter of the State Department, the military, or an agency of the United States government. It has been a real challenge for me to try to get information from a broader array of resources." *Badger Herald*, July 8, 1999, University of Wisconsin.

34. John P. Burke, *The Institutional Presidency: Organizing and Managing the White House from FDR to Clinton* (Baltimore: Johns Hopkins University Press, 2000).

35. Charles O. Jones, "Clinton's Cabinet: Stability in Disorder," *PRG Report* 24, no. 1 (2001): 13–16.

36. One such list is available online at: www.glennbeck.com/content/articles/article/198/29391/.

37. Fletcher and Dennis, "Obama's Many Policy 'Czars' Draw Ire from Conservatives," 19. See also Mimi Hall, "Number, Role of Obama's Policy 'Czars' Spark Debate," *USA Today*, September 30, 2009.

38. Like the secretaries of Cabinet departments, the president's appointments of the heads of the various EOP offices must be confirmed by the Senate.

Chapter 12

1. *Citizens United v. Federal Election Commission*, 558 U.S. — (2010).

2. Jess Bravin, "Court Kills Limits on Corporate Politicking," *Wall Street Journal*, January 22, 2010. Web online.wsj.com/article/SB10001424052748703699204575016942930090152.html.

3. Barack Obama, "Remarks of President Barack Obama—As Prepared for Delivery," Address to Joint Session of Congress, February 24, 2009.

4. Robert A. Dahl, "Decision-Making in a Democracy: The Supreme Court as a National Policy-Maker," *Journal of Public Law* 6, no. 2 (1957): 279–95. Quote on p. 293.

5. These are the last available data on public approval ratings for the judiciary. Approval ratings for Congress and the president remained reasonably constant through June 2010. See www.realclearpolitics.com/polls.

6. When it comes to the judicial branch as a whole, Americans hold similarly positive views. Over the past 25 years, a majority of Americans have reported a "great deal" or "fair amount" of confidence in the courts. From 1973 to 2005, levels of public trust ranged from a low of 63 percent in 1976 to a high of 80 percent in 1999. Confidence in the judiciary was consistently higher than trust in either the executive branch or the legislative branch during the same period. See Joseph Carroll, "Slim Majority of Americans Approve of the Supreme Court: Approval Rating Still Lower Following Partial-Birth Abortion Ban Earlier This Year," *Gallup News Service*, September 26, 2007, www.gallup.com/poll/28798/Slim-Majority-Americans-Approve-Supreme-Court.aspx.

7. See Judicial Facts and Figures, www.uscourts.gov/uscourts/Statistics/JudicialFactsAndFigures/2008/Table101.pdf.

8. "Workload of the Courts," *Third Branch* 39, no. 1 (January 2007), www.uscourts.gov/ttb/2007-01/workload/index.html. Figure for 2009 available at otd.oyez.org/cases/2009.

9. Most recent data available at www.supremecourt.gov/publicinfo/year-end/2009year-endreport.pdf.

10. Strictly speaking, appellate court rulings in one circuit are not binding for appellate courts in other circuits. As a result, different circuits can produce different appellate rulings on similar cases.

11. If the chief justice is part of the minority, then the justice in the majority who has the most seniority makes the assignment.

12. If a justice recuses himself or herself from a case, a majority can be achieved with less than five supporters.

13. Timothy L. Hall, ed., *The U.S. Legal System* (Pasadena, CA: Salem, 2004).

14. For a sampling of the arguments made for and against jury trials, see Jeffrey Abramson, *We, the Jury: The Jury System and the Ideal of Democracy* (Cambridge, MA: Harvard University Press, 2000); William Dwyer, *In the Hands of the People: The Trial Jury's Origins, Triumphs, Troubles, and Future in American Democracy* (New York: St. Martin's Griffin, 2004); Stephen Adler, *The Jury: Trial and Error in the American Courtroom* (New York: Times Books, 1994).

15. *Abbott Laboratories v. Gardner*, 387 U.S. 136 (1967), at 148.

16. George Fisher, *Plea Bargaining's Triumph: A History of Plea Bargaining in America.* (Stanford, CA: Stanford University Press, 2003): 222.

17. See Judicial Facts and Figures, www.uscourts.gov/uscourts/Statistics/JudicialFactsAndFigures/2008/Table501.pdf.

18. Richard A. Posner, *The Federal Courts: Challenge and Reform* (Cambridge, MA: Harvard University Press, 1996): 59–61.

19. Robert A. Kagan, "American Lawyers, Legal Cultures, and Adversarial Legalism," in Lawrence M. Friedman and Harry N. Scheiber, *Legal Culture and the Legal Profession* (Boulder: Westview, 1996): 13–14; Office of Management and Budget, "Historical Tables, Budget of the United States Government, FY 2011," 77, 83, available online at www.gpoaccess.gov/usbudget/fy11/pdf/hist.pdf.

20. David M. O'Brien, "The Dynamics of the Judicial Process," in David M. O'Brien, ed., *Judges on Judging: Views from the Bench* (Chatham, NJ: Chatham House, 1997): 34.

21. Quoted in O'Brien, "The Dynamics of the Judicial Process," 34.

22. Quoted in Jethro K. Lieberman, *The Litigious Society* (New York: Basic Books, 1981): xi.

23. John Ferejohn and Barry Weingast, "A Positive Theory of Statutory Interpretation," *International Review of Law and Economics* 12 (1992): 265.

24. Averages calculated from data found in Sheldon Goldman, Elliot Slotnick, Gerard Gryski, and Sara Schiavoni, "W. Bush's Judiciary: The First Term Record," *Judicature* 88, no. 6 (May–June 2005): 269, 274.

25. Jeffrey Segal, Lee Epstein, Charles Cameron, and Harold Spaeth, "Ideological Values and the Votes of U.S. Supreme Court Justices Revisited," *Journal of Politics* 57, no. 3 (1995): 812–23.

26. See Lee Epstein and Jack Knight, *The Choices Justices Make* (Washington, DC: CQ Press, 1998); Forrest Maltzman, James Spriggs, and Paul Wahlbeck, "Strategy and Judicial Choice: New Institutionalist Approaches to Supreme Court Decision Making," in Cornell W. Clayton and Howard Gillman, eds., *Supreme Court Decision-Making: New Institutional Approaches* (Chicago: University of Chicago Press, 1999).

27. For more on the solicitor general, see Rebecca Mae Salokar, *The Solicitor General: The Politics of Law* (Philadelphia: Temple University Press, 1992).

28. Lincoln Caplan, *The Tenth Justice: The Solicitor General and the Rule of Law* (New York: Knopf, 1987): 295; William Howell and Faisal Ahmed, "Voting for the President: The Supreme Court During War" (Chicago: University of Chicago, 2010), Typescript.

29. Abner Greene, *Understanding the 2000 Election* (New York: New York University Press, 2001).

30. Greene, *Understanding the 2000 Election*.

31. Greene, *Understanding the 2000 Election*.

32. Jeffrey A. Segal and Harold J. Spaeth, "The Influence of Stare Decisis on the Votes of United States Supreme Court Justices," *American Journal of Political Science* 40, no. 4 (1996): 971–1003.

33. Jeffrey A. Segal and Harold J. Spaeth, *The Supreme Court and the Attitudinal Model Revisited* (New York: Cambridge University Press, 2002): 171.

34. Segal and Spaeth, *The Supreme Court and the Attitudinal Model Revisited*, 172–74.

35. See, for example, Richard Z. Chesnoff, "Europe Worries as U.S. Re-Counts," *Daily News*, November 12, 2000; "The Nation's Mood: Get It Resolved, but Get It Right; Americans Express Faith in the Electoral System, but Many Say, 'We Need to Move On,'" *Grand Rapids Press*, November 12, 2000.

36. Terrence Hunt, "Election Impasse 'Nothing to Worry About,' Clinton Tells Putin," *Star-Ledger*, November 15, 2000, 11.

37. Decades later, the U.S. government would officially apologize for the internment of Japanese Americans and pay upward of $1 billion in reparations to their families. In 1998, President Bill Clinton selected Fred Korematsu as a recipient of the Presidential Medal of Freedom.

38. Timothy Johnson and Andrew Martin, "The Public's Conditional Response to Supreme Court Decisions," *American Political Science Review* 92 (1998): 299–309; Jennifer Hochschild, *The New American Dilemma: Liberal Democracy and School Desegregation* (New Haven: Yale University Press, 1984).

39. Data available at Judges and Judgeships, www.uscourts.gov/ JudgesAndJudgeships/Viewer.aspx?doc=/uscourts/Judges-Judgeships/docs/apptsbypres.pdf.

40. Goldman et al., "W. Bush's Judiciary," 269.

41. Goldman et al., "W. Bush's Judiciary." See also Harold Stanley and Richard Niemi, *Vital Statistics on American Politics 2009–2010* (Washington, DC: CQ Press, 2009): 270. As of this writing, information on Barack Obama's appointments are not yet available.

42. The ABA refused to give Thomas a "well-qualified" rating.

43. "Hearing of the Senate Judiciary Committee on the Nomination of Clarence Thomas to the Supreme Court," Electronic Text Center, University of Virginia Library, October 11, 1991, etext.lib.virginia.edu.

44. Seven justices who were confirmed nonetheless declined to serve, the most recent being Roscoe Conkling in 1882. Data available online at www.senate.gov/pagelayout/reference/ nominations/Nominations.htm.

45. Karen O'Connor, Alixandra Yanus, and Linda Mancillas Patterson, "Where Have All the Interest Groups Gone? An Analysis of Interest Group Participation in Presidential Nominations to the Supreme Court of the United States," in Allan Cigler and Burdett Loomis, eds., *Interest Group Politics*, 7th ed. (Washington, DC: CQ Press, 2007).

46. Transcript of Obama-Sotomayor announcement, May 26, 2009. Available online at www.cnn.com/2009/POLITICS/05/26/obama.sotomayor.transcript/index.html.

47. Sonia Sotomayor, "A Latina Judge's Voice," University of California, Berkeley, School of Law, 26 Oct. 2001. Available online at: berkeley.edu/news/media/releases/2009/05/26_ sotomayor.shtml.

48. Seth Stern and Keith Perine, "Sotomayor a Steady Hand at Hearings," *CQ Weekly* (2009): 1712–1713; *CQ Weekly*, Web. 7 Feb., 2010. Available online at library.cqpress.com/cqweekly/ weeklyreport111-000003170512..

49. Manuel Miranda, "The Original Borking: Lessons from a Supreme Court Nominee's Defeat," *Wall Street Journal*, August 24, 2005, www.opinionjournal.com/ nextjustice/?id=110007149.

Chapter 13

1. Elizabeth Becker and Elaine Sciolino, "A Nation Challenged: Homeland Security; A New Federal Office Opens Amid Concern That Its Head Won't Have Enough Power," *New York Times*, October 9, 2001: B11.

2. Binyamin Appelbaum, "On Finance Reform Bill, Lobbying Shifts to Regulations," *New York Times*, June 26, 2010.

3. Cornelius Kerwin, *Rulemaking: How Government Agencies Write Law and Make Policy* (Washington, DC: CQ Press, 2003).

4. Some of the increase in the length of the *Federal Register* can be explained by the introduction of stricter requirements for publication of final rules. In 1973, the Administrative Committee of the Federal Register decided that every rule must include a summary of its subject matter in its preamble. As of 1977, the preamble of a rule must also include a summary of public comments about the rule as well as the agency's answers to questions raised by the public.

5. James Fesler, "The Higher Public Service in Western Europe," in Ralph Clark Chandler, ed., *A Centennial History of the American Administrative State* (New York: Free Press, 1987).

6. Stephen Skowronek, *Building a New American State: The Expansion of National Administrative Capabilities, 1877–1920* (New York: Cambridge University Press, 1982).

7. The number of bureaucrats working for state and local government, however, has increased dramatically. At the local level, there were approximately 3 million bureaucrats in 1946. By 2003, that number climbed to upward of 14 million. During the same period, state bureaucrats grew from less than 1 million to over 5 million. U.S. Bureau of the

Census, *Historical Statistics of the United States: Colonial Times to 1970* (Washington, DC: Government Printing Office, 1975); *Statistical Abstract of the United States, 2006* (Washington, DC: GPO, 2006).

8. "About the Commission," Financial Crisis Inquiry Commission, www.fcic.gov/about/

9. All in all, the 2006–2007 edition of the *U.S. Government Manual* lists 110 independent agencies and government corporations. However, the actual number may be larger than 110. It is particularly difficult to determine the number of government corporations in operation; actual counts vary significantly. National Archives and Records Administration, Office of the Federal Register, *U.S. Government Manual 2006–2007* (Washington, DC: Government Printing Office, 2006): 361–554, available online at www.gpoaccess.gov/gmanual/browse-gm-06.html. See also General Accountability Office, *Government Corporations: Profiles of Existing Government Corporations*, GAO/GGD-96-14 (Washington, DC: General Accounting Office, 1995), available online at www.gao.gov/archive/1996/gg96014.pdf.

10. For a classic treatment of this topic, see Max Weber, "Bureaucracy," in H. H. Gerth and C. Wright Mills, eds., *From Max Weber: Essays in Sociology* (New York: Oxford University Press, 1946).

11. This idea was developed most fully by the Nobel Prize–winning economist George Stigler. See, for example, *Citizen and the State: Essays on Regulation* (Chicago: University of Chicago Press, 1975).

12. John Carey, "A Shot at Making Drugs Safer: Congress Could Revamp the Cozy Ties Between Drugmakers and the FDA. Will It?" *Business Week*, May 21, 2007: 71.

13. Michael Powell, "Boston's Big Dig Awash in Troubles: Leaks, Cost Overruns Plague Project," *Washington Post*, November 19, 2004: A3; Elizabeth Taurasi, "Boston's Big Dig: One of Engineering's Biggest Mistakes?" *Design News*, July 28, 2006, www.designnews.com/index.asp?layout=article&articleid=CA6357443.

14. See www.mountainstateslegal.org/mission.cfm.

15. Thomas Weko, *The Politicizing Presidency: The White House Personnel Office, 1948–1994* (Lawrence: University Press of Kansas, 1995); Terry Moe, "The Politicized Presidency," in John Chubb and Paul Peterson, eds., *New Directions in American Politics* (Washington, DC: Brookings Institution, 1985); David Lewis, *The Politics of Presidential Appointments: Political Control and Bureaucratic Performance* (Princeton, NJ: Princeton University Press, 2008).

16. Lewis, *The Politics of Presidential Appointments*.

17. Randall Mikkelsen, "Clinton Shuns the GOP in Naming Lee as Civil Rights Enforcer," *Star-Ledger*, August 4, 2000: 15; Christopher Marquis, "Clinton Sidesteps Senate to Fill Civil Rights Enforcement Job," *New York Times*, August 4, 2000: A14.

18. Address to the Nation, President Bush, New Orleans, Louisiana, September 15, 2005.

19. Mike Ahlers, "Criticism of FEMA's Katrina Response Deserved," CNN, April 14, 2006.

20. Dan Eggen, "Justice Department Fires 8th U.S. Attorney: Dispute over Death Penalty Cited," *Washington Post*, February 24, 2007: A2; Richard Schmitt, "Gonzales Gets Rare Rebuke from Bush," *Los Angeles Times*, March 15, 2007: A14.

21. Richard Serrano, "Gonzales to Admit Mistakes in Firings," *Los Angeles Times*, April 16, 2007: A1.

22. See Lewis, *The Politics of Presidential Appointments*.

23. U.S. Office of Personnel Management, *Federal Civilian Workforce Statistics: The Fact Book, 2005 Edition*, www.opm.gov/FedData/factbook/index.asp; Government of Canada Privy Council Office, *Fifteenth Annual Report to the Prime Minister on the Public Service of Canada*, March 31, 2008, www.pco-bcp.gc.ca/index.asp?lang=eng&Page=information&Sub=publications&Doc=ar-ra/15-2008/table_e.htm.

24. See Donald J. Savoie, *Breaking the Bargain: Public Servants, Ministers, and Parliament* (Toronto: University of Toronto Press, 2003): 28, 136.

25. Lewis, *The Politics of Presidential Appointments*: 98.

26. Lewis, *The Politics of Presidential Appointments*: 20–21.

27. Lewis, *The Politics of Presidential Appointments*: 218.

28. "NASA's Greedy Overseers," *New York Times*, April 30, 2006.

29. In 2007, the House passed the Whistleblower Protection Enhancement Act of 2007. It would have amended the original Whistleblower Protection Act by providing protections for national security, government contractor, and science-based agency whistleblowers and by enhancing the existing whistleblower protections for all federal employees. The bill, however, never passed the Senate. For more on the legislative history of this bill, see L. Paige Whitaker, "The Whistleblower Protection Act: An Overview," *Congressional Research Service*, March 12, 2007.

30. John Hart, *The Presidential Branch: Executive Office of the President from Washington to Clinton*, 2nd ed. (Chatham, NJ: Chatham House, 1995); Matthew Dickinson, *Bitter Harvest: FDR, Presidential Power, and the Growth of the Presidential Branch* (New York: Cambridge University Press, 1997).

31. Andrew Rudalevige, *Managing the President's Program: Presidential Leadership and Legislative Policy Formation* (Princeton, NJ: Princeton University Press, 2002).

32. Paul Light, *Thickening Government: Federal Hierarchy and the Diffusion of Accountability* (Washington, DC: Brookings Institution, 1995): 1.

33. Norman J. Vig and Michael E. Kraft, "Environmental Policy from the Seventies to the Eighties," in Norman J. Vig and Michael E. Kraft, eds., *Environmental Policy in the 1980s: Reagan's New Agenda* (Washington, DC: CQ Press, 1984): 3–26.

34. Vig and Kraft, "Environmental Policy from the Seventies to the Eighties."

35. Michael E. Kraft, "A New Environmental Policy Agenda: The 1980 Presidential Campaign and Its Aftermath," in Vig and Kraft, *Environmental Policy in the 1980s*: 29–50.

36. Norman J. Vig, "The President or the Environment: Revolution or Retreat?" in Vig and Kraft, *Environmental Policy in the 1980s*: 77–95.

37. J. Clarence Davies, "Environmental Institutions and the Reagan Administration," in Vig and Kraft, *Environmental Policy in the 1980s*: 143–160.

38. Richard J. Tobin, "Revising the Clean Air Act: Legislative Failure and Administrative Success," in Vig and Kraft, *Environmental Policy in the 1980s*: 227–249.

39. Davies, "Environmental Institutions and the Reagan Administration."

40. B. Dan Wood, "Principals, Bureaucrats, and Responsiveness in Clean Air Enforcements," *American Political Science Review* 82, no. 1 (1988): 213–234; Kenski and Kenski, "Congress Against the President."

41. Wood, "Principals, Bureaucrats, and Responsiveness in Clean Air Enforcements."

42. Tobin, "Revising the Clean Air Act: Legislative Failure and Administrative Success."

43. Davies, "Environmental Institutions and the Reagan Administration."

44. See Joel A. Mintz, "'Treading Water': A Preliminary Assessment of EPA Enforcement During the Bush II Administration," *Environmental Law Institute*, 2004, www.eli.org.

45. See, for example, Edward Felker, "EPA Rapidly Reversing Bush Policies," *Washington Times*, May 1, 2009; Charles Duhigg, "E.P.A. Vows Better Effort on Water," *New York Times*, October 15, 2009.

Chapter 14

1. Statement by Secretary Henry M. Paulson, Jr., on Treasury and Federal Housing Finance Agency Action to Protect Financial Markets and Taxpayers, Department of the Treasury, September 7, 2008, available online at: www.treas.gov/press/releases/hp1129.htm; "Lehman folds with record $613 billion debt," *MarketWatch*, September 15, 2008, available online at: www.marketwatch.com/story/lehman-folds-with-record-613-billion-debt; "WaMu Is Seized, Sold Off to J.P. Morgan, In Largest Failure in U.S. Banking History," *Wall Street Journal*, September 26, 2008: A1; "Misery math: Great Recession by the numbers," MSNBC/Associated Press, October 11, 2009, available online at: www.msnbc.msn.com/id/33266915/ns/business-eye_on_the_economy/t/misery-math-great-recession-numbers/.

2. City of Philadelphia, *Response to the Financial Crisis*, November 6, 2008, available online at: www.transformgov.org/assets/0/72/1412/723e5502-c3ac-4ee4-b3ce-0acc5a2fc8e4.pdf; New York State Governor's Office, *Governor Paterson Proposes Two-Year, $5.0 Billion Deficit Reduction Plan to Address Current-Year Budget Gap, Improve New York's Long-Term Fiscal Stability*, October 15, 2009, available online at: www.state.ny.us/governor/press/press_1015091.html;

Rich Connell, "Metrolink Cuts 10 Trains but Fares Stay Put," *Los Angeles Times*, January 9, 2010, available online at: articles.latimes.com/2010/jan/09/local/la-me-metrolink9-2010jan09

3. Vikas Bajaj, "Home Prices Fall for 10th Straight Month." *New York Times*, December 26, 2007, available online at: www.nytimes.com/2007/12/26/business/27home-web.html.

4. The list of 2010 bank failures is available online at www.fdic.gov/bank/individual/failed/banklist.html.

5. Jonathan D. Glater, "Credit Crisis Cuts Bankruptcy Lifeline," *New York Times*, October 19, 2008, available online at: www.nytimes.com/2008/11/19/business/worldbusiness/19iht-bankruptcy.4.17967473.html sec.

6. Obama's Speech on the Economy, as recorded by Federal News Service, January 8, 2009, transcript available online at: www.nytimes.com/2009/01/08/us/politics/08text-obama.html?pagewanted=1. See also David Cho, "Summers Comes Out Swinging on Economic Policy," *Washington Post*, October 13, 2009, available online at: www.washingtonpost.com/wp-dyn/content/article/2009/10/12/AR2009101203019.html?hpid=topnews.

7. These figures come from the U.S. Department of Labor, www.bls.gov/fls/intl_unemployment_rates_monthly.pdf.

8. Figures available at www.bls.gov/cpi/cpid1012.pdf.

9. More specifically, GDP is the sum of all domestic consumption spending, investment spending, government spending, and the differences between export and import spending.

10. Information on the gross domestic product available at the Bureau of Economic Analysis: www.bea.gov/national/nipaweb/TableView.asp?SelectedTable=5&ViewSeries=NO&Java=no&Request3Place=N&3Place=N&FromView=YES&Freq=Year&FirstYear=2010&LastYear=2010&3Place=N&Update=Update&JavaBox=no#Mid.

11. For the latest figures, see www.treasurydirect.gov/NP/BPDLogin?application=np.

12. For the latest figures, see www.treasury.gov/resource-center/data-chart-center/tic/Documents/mfh.txt.

13. For a longer discussion of these latter issues, see www.cfr.org/publication/20758/confronting_the_chinaus_economic_imbalance.html.

14. For more on this debate, see ricks.foreignpolicy.com/posts/2010/03/02/debt_s_life_debt_s_what_all_the_people_say_big_squeeze_coming_from_china.

15. In the 1940s and 1950s, there persisted a lively debate among two of the century's greatest economists, Milton Friedman and John Maynard Keynes, about the relative benefits of fiscal and monetary policy.

16. "Bush Calls for $145 Billion Stimulus Package," Associated Press, January 18, 2008, www.msnbc.msn.com/id/22725498/.

17. The Social Security Act also provided grants-in-aid and health and welfare services to states. The most important elements

of the act, though, concern the establishment of a retirement account, which we focus on here.

18. Individuals born after 1938 qualify for full benefits at the age of 67.

19. Figures available at www.ssa.gov/OACT/STATS/OASDIbenies.html.

20. Figures available at www.ssa.gov/cgi-bin/awards.cgi.

21. Figures available at www.ssa.gov/cgi-bin/awards.cgi.

22. Figures available at www.ssa.gov/OACT/STATS/table4a1.html.

23. In addition to the elderly, Medicare also provides some assistance to the disabled.

24. Figures available at www.cms.gov/DataCompendium/14_2010_Data_Compendium.asp#TopOfPage.

25. Alan Weil, "There's Something About Medicaid," *Health Affairs* 22, no. 1 (2003), content.healthaffairs.org/cgi/reprint/22/1/13.pdf. See also: familiesusa.org/issues/medicaid/.

26. Figures available at www.hhs.gov/budget/09budget/2009BudgetInBrief.pdf.

27. Longer description of the legislation's main provisions can be found at energycommerce.house.gov/Press_111/20090714/hr3200_summary.pdf and www.cbsnews.com/8301-503544_162-20000846-503544.html. The legislation itself is available at democrats.senate.gov/reform/patient-protection-affordable-care-act-as-passed.pdf.

28. Shailagh Murray, "Congress Approves Fixes to Health Care Bill," *Washington Post*, March 26, 2010, available online at www.washingtonpost.com/wp-dyn/content/article/2010/03/25/AR2010032500006.html.

29. Consulates can be thought of as "subembassies," usually located in large noncapital cities abroad to help American citizens or support the main embassy. Many employees of foreign embassies and consulates are foreign nationals providing support for American personnel.

30. This number excludes U.S. Postal Service employees, as well as those working for the CIA, NSA, Defense Intelligence Agency, and National Imagery and Mapping Agency. These latter four agencies do not make their employment figures public for national security reasons. See U.S. Department of Labor, Bureau of Labor Statistics, *Career Guide to Industries: Federal Government, Excluding the Postal Service*, available online at: www.bls.gov/oco/cg/cgs041.htm.

31. Gary Hufbauer, Jeffrey Schott, and Kimberly Elliot, *Economic Sanctions Reconsidered: History and Current Policy* (Peterson Institute, 1990).

32. Daniel Drezner, *The Sanctions Paradox: Economic Statecraft and International Relations* (New York: Cambridge University Press, 1999).

33. Dean Lacy and Emerson M. S. Niou, "Theory of Economic Sanctions and Issue Linkage: The Roles of Preferences, Information, and Threats," *Journal of Politics* 66, no. 1 (2004): 25–42.

34. For additional reading, see David Baldwin, *Economic Statecraft* (Princeton, NJ: Princeton University Press, 1985); Robert Pape, "Why Economic Sanctions Do Not Work," *International Security* 22, no. 2 (1997): 90–136; A. Cooper Drury, "Sanctions as Coercive Diplomacy: The U. S. President's Decision to Initiate Economic Sanctions," *Political Research Quarterly* 54, no. 3 (2001): 485–508.

35. The National Reconnaissance Office (NRO) is also in charge of data monitoring, but its tools are spy aircraft and reconnaissance satellites. Also unacknowledged for many years, the NRO operates under the cover of the U.S. Air Force.

36. I. M. Destler, *American Trade Politics*, 3rd ed. (Washington, DC: Institute for International Economics, 1995).

37. Brian Knowlton, "House Panel Says Armenian Deaths Were Genocide," *New York Times*, March 4, 2010, available online at: www.nytimes.com/2010/03/05/world/europe/05armenia.html?_r=1&scp=2&sq=armenian%20genocide&st=cse.

38. See, for example, Louis Fisher, *Presidential War Power*, 2nd ed. (Lawrence: University Press of Kansas, 2004).

39. This 60-day clock can be extended for another 30 days if the president certifies that the time is necessary for the troops' safety.

40. Louis Fisher, *Congressional Abdication on War and Spending* (College Station: Texas A&M University Press, 2000): 65. See also David Auerswald and Peter Cowhey, "Ballotbox Diplomacy: The War Powers Resolution and the Use of Force," *International Studies Quarterly* 41, no. 3 (1997): 505–28.

41. Figures available online at: www.senate.gov/artandhistory/history/common/briefing/Treaties.htm.

42. Donald G. McNeil, "Audit Finds Bush's AIDS Effort Limited by Restrictions," *New York Times*, March 31, 2007: A12.

43. Sheryl Gay Stolberg, "Getting Religion on AIDS," *New York Times*, February 2, 2003: 4.1.

44. Stolberg, "Getting Religion on AIDS."

45. Marc Sandalow, "Jesse Helms, Global AIDS Activist," *San Francisco Chronicle*, April 1, 2002: B7.

46. Elizabeth Becker, "With Record Rise in Foreign Aid Comes Change in How It Is Monitored," *New York Times*, December 7, 2003: A10.

47. Holly Burkhalter, "The Politics of AIDS: Engaging Conservative Activists," *Foreign Affairs* 83, no. 1 (2004): 10.

48. Stolberg, "In Global Battle on AIDS, Bush Creates Legacy," *New York Times*, January 5, 2008, available online at www.nytimes.com/2008/01/05/washington/05aids.html.

49. Joseph Kahn, "A Star Close to the Heart of Aid Policy," *New York Times*, March 15, 2002: A8.

50. Stolberg, "Getting Religion on AIDS."

51. Becker, "With Record Rise in Foreign Aid Comes Change in How It Is Monitored."

52. Stevenson, "Middle Path Emerges in Debate on Africa Aid."

53. McNeil, "Audit Finds Bush's AIDS Effort Limited by Restrictions."

54. Stolberg, "In Global Battle on AIDS, Bush Creates Legacy."

55. Social Security Administration, *The 2007 Annual Report of the Board of Trustees of the Federal Old-Age and Survivors Insurance and Federal Disability Insurance Trust Funds*, available online at www.ssa.gov/OACT/TR/TR07/.

56. White House Press Release, "Vice President and Chairman Thomas' Remarks at a Town Hall Meeting on Social Security," March 21, 2005, www.whitehouse.gov/news/releases/2005/03/20050321-14.html.

57. Tax rates and maximum taxable earnings available at ssa-custhelp.ssa.gov/app/answers/detail/a_id/240.

58. United Nations, "NPT Treaty Status," available online at: disarmament.un.org/TreatyStatus.nsf/NPT%20(in%20alphabetical%20order)?OpenView&Start=1.

59. American Presidency Project, "George W. Bush: Address Before a Joint Session of the Congress on the State of the Union, January 29, 2002," available online at www.presidency.ucsb.edu.

60. "Timeline: North Korea's Nuclear Weapons Development," CNN, January 6, 2004, available online at: www.cnn.com/2003/WORLD/asiapcf/east/08/20/nkorea.timeline.nuclear/.

61. "Path of peace available to North Korea, Obama says," CNN, June 16, 2009, available online at www.cnn.com/2009/POLITICS/06/16/south.korea.meeting/index.html.

62. Stephen Brooks, *Producing Security: Multinational Corporations, Globalization, and the Changing Calculus of Conflict* (Princeton, NJ: Princeton University Press, 2005).

63. The lobbyists themselves disagreed about which remedy they desired under U.S. trade law. Some called for anti-dumping measures, which required minimal evidence of injury but could be applied only against specific products and countries. Others wanted to pursue a "Section 201" complaint, which would offer more comprehensive protection to the sector, but only if a much higher burden of proof was met.

64. Richard W. Stevenson, "Big Steel: An Invalid That Can Roar in Washington," *New York Times*, December 11, 2001: C1.

65. Paul Blustein, "Bush to Seek Protection for U.S. Steel Firms; President Yields to Industry Pressure," *Washington Post*, June 6, 2001: E1.

66. Steven Perlstein and Mike Allen, "Bush Faces Tough Choices on Steel Imports; Under Lobbying Pressure, President Must Decide by Wednesday Whether to Act to Aid U.S. Industry," *Washington Post*, February 28, 2002: A4.

67. Mike Allen and Steven Perlstein, "Bush Settles on Tariff for Steel Imports," *Washington Post*, March 5, 2002: A1.

68. Paul Blustein, "U.S. Indignant over EU Threat; Retaliatory Tariffs Would Be 'Hypocritical,' Official Says," *Washington Post*, April 18, 2002: E2.

69. Jonathan Weisman, "Bush Rescinds Tariffs on Steel; Trade War Averted; Industry Angry," *Washington Post*, December 5, 2003: A1.

70. Blustein, "Bush to Seek Protection for U.S. Steel Firms."

Appendix 2

1. Modified by the Sixteenth Amendment.

2. Replaced by Section 2, Fourteenth Amendment.

3. Repealed by the Seventeenth Amendment.

4. Modified by the Seventeenth Amendment.

5. Changed by the Twentieth Amendment.

6. Modified by the Sixteenth Amendment.

7. Changed by the Twelfth and Twentieth Amendments.

8. Modified by the Twenty-fifth Amendment.

9. Modified by the Twelfth Amendment.

10. Repealed by the Thirteenth Amendment.

11. Changed by the Twentieth Amendment.

12. Changed by the Twenty-sixth Amendment.

13. Repealed by the Twenty-first Amendment.

Credits

Text Credits

Page 30: American National Election Studies (www.electionstudies.org). Page 32: "Distrust, Discontent, Anger and Partisan Rancor: The People and Their Government," April 18, 2010, The Pew Research Center For The People & The Press, a project of the Pew Research Center. By permission. Page 40: Based on data from OECD Health Data 2010: Statistics and Indicators www.oecd.org/health/healthdata. Reprinted by permission. Page 210: American National Election Studies (www.electionstudies.org). Page 212: "Party Identification Over the Last Six Years." April 23, 2010, http://www.gallup.com/poll/127499/party-affiliation-gap-u.s.-narrowest-2005.aspx. Courtesy of Gallup, Inc. Page 229: Collet, Christian and Martin P. Wattenberg. 1999, from "Strategically Unambitious: Minor Party and Independent Candidates in the 1996 Congressional Elections." In Shea, Daniel and John C. Green, eds. THE STATE OF THE PARTIES, 3rd Edition. Lanham: Rowman and Littlefield. Reprinted by permission. Page 252: American National Election Studies (www.electionstudies.org). Page 295: Harold W. Stanley and Richard G. Niemi, VITAL STATISTICS ON AMERICAN POLITICS, 2009-2010. Copyright © 2010 CQ Press, a division of SAGE Publications, Inc. Reprinted by permission of CQ Press. Page 323: Harold W. Stanley and Richard G. Niemi, VITAL STATISTICS ON AMERICAN POLITICS, 2009-2010. Copyright © 2010 CQ Press, a division of SAGE Publications, Inc. Reprinted by permission of CQ Press. Page 326: Harold W. Stanley and Richard G. Niemi, VITAL STATISTICS ON AMERICAN POLITICS, 2009-2010. Copyright © 2010 CQ Press, a division of SAGE Publications, Inc. Reprinted by permission of CQ Press. Page 333: Harold W. Stanley and Richard G. Niemi, VITAL STATISTICS ON AMERICAN POLITICS, 2009-2010. Copyright © 2010 CQ Press, a division of SAGE Publications, Inc. Reprinted by permission of CQ Press.

Photo Credits

Page 1: © CBS/Landov; Page 9 (left): © AP Images/Dario Lopez-Mills; Page 9 (right): © AP Images/Las Cruces Sun-News, Norm Dettlaff; Page 10: © Time Life Pictures/Mansell/Time Life Pictures/Getty Images; Page 12: © Larry Downing/Reuters /Landov; Page 19: © E. Jason Wambsgans/MCT /Landov; Page 23: © Immigrant rights rally and march in Chicago, Illinois, USA; Page 26: © United States Army; Page 27: © Larry Downing/Reuters/Corbis; Page 29: © Scott Speakes/Corbis RF/Almay; Page 30: © Bettmann/Corbis; Page 33: © Mark Wilson/Getty Images; Page 43: © AP Images; Page 45: © AFP/Getty Images; Page 49: © PSL Images/Alamy; Page 55: © ClassicStock/Alamy; Page 60: © The Granger Collection, NYC; Page 70: © Picture History/Newscom; Page 75: © Larry Burrows/Time Magazine/Time & Life Pictures/Getty Images; Page 82: © Robert Galbraith/Reuters/Corbis; Page 84: © Official White House Photo by Pete Souza; Page 89: © Marice Cohn Band/MCT/Newscom; Page 96: © Image Source/Getty RF; Page 101: © Lon C. Diehl/PhotoEdit; Page 104: © AP Images/Rich Pedroncelli; Page 107: © AP Images/Matt York; Page 110: © Erich Schlegel/Corbis; Page 114: © Saul Loeb/AFP/Getty Images/Newscom; Page 124: © Clay Good/Zuma Press; Page 127: © AP Photo/Liberty Legal Institute, Henry and Wanda Sandoz; Page 135: © Library of Congress, Prints & Photographs Division, FSA/OWI Collection[LC-DIG-ppmsc-00199]; Page 136: © Bettmann/Corbis; Page 140: © Bruce Davidson/Magnum Photos; Page 144: © AP Images/Demotix Images, B. Carter; Page 145: © Jeff Greenberg/The Image Works; Page 149: © s70/s70/ZUMA Press/Newscom; Page 150: © AP Images/Pablo Martinez Monsivais; Page 155: © Library of Congress, Prints & Photographs Division, FSA/OWI Collection[LC-USF34-045815-D]; Page 161: © Roger Malloch/Magnum Photos; Page 162: © Official White House Photo by Pete Souza); Page 171: © Doug Mills/The New York Times/Redux; Page 174: © Alex Wong/Getty Images for Meet the Press; Page 175: © Axel Koester/The New York Times/Redux; Page 176 (left): © dbimages/Alamy; Page 176 (right): © Win McNamee/Getty Images; Page 179: © Hulton Archive/Archive Photos/Getty Images; Page 188: © CNN; Page 194: © Grant Faint/Photographer's Choice RF/Getty RF; Page 196 (left): © Kevork Djansezian/Getty Images; Page 196 (right): © Chip Somodevilla/Getty Images; Page 200: William B. Plowman/William B. Plowman/NBC NewsWire via AP Photo; Page 202: © Roger L. Wollenburg/UPI/Landov; Page 205: © Rolls Press/Popperfoto/Getty Images; Page 206: © Steve Sack/Star Tribune; Page 211: © Courtesy Ronald Reagan Library; Page 225: © Monica Almeida/The New York Times/Redux; Page 235: © Lucas Jackson/Reuters /Landov; Page 239: © Bettmann/Corbis; Page 242 (left): © AP Images/Pablo Martinez Monsivais; Page 242 (right): © Kurt Fehlhauer/Alamy; Page 243: © Emmanuel Parisse/AFP/Getty Images/Newscom; Page 245: © AP Images/Cliff Owen; Page 249: © AP Images/Charles Dharapak; Page 257: © Bettmann/Corbis; Page 262: © Peter Tobia KRT/Newscom; Page 266: © Scott Houston/Sygma/Corbis; Page 275: Stephen Crowley/The New York Times/Redux; Page 283: © AP Images/Matt Rourke; Page 287: © AP Images/Leslie E. Kossoff; Page 291: © Rachel Epstein / PhotoEdit; Page 293: © AP Images/Pablo Martinez Monsivais; Page 297: © Corbis; Page 304: © Jim Ruymen/UPI /Landov; Page 312: © Stephen Crowley/The New York Times/Redux; Page 317: © Jim Watson/AFP/Getty Images/Newscom; Page 320:© Bettmann/Corbis; Page 325: © Diana Walker/Time Life Pictures/Getty Images; Page 334: © Aristide Economopoulos/Star Ledger/Corbis; Page 343: Evan Vucci/AP Photo; Page 349: © Chip Somodevilla/Getty Images; Page 353: © Jim Sugar/Corbis; Page 358: © Tom Williams/Roll Call/Getty Images; Page 359: © Bettmann/Corbis; Page 362: © Mike Theiler/Reuters/Corbis; Page 364: © AP Images/J. Scott Applewhite; Page 369: © Cary Horowitz/Reuters/Corbis; © 372: © Irwin Thompson/Dallas Morning News/Corbis; Page 386: © Mario Tama/Getty Images News/Getty Images; Page 389: © Doug Mills/The New York Times/Redux; Page 398: © John Moore/Getty Images; Page 403: © AP Images; Page 406: © AP Images/J. Scott Applewhite; Page 409: © Bettmann/Corbis; Page 414: © Mike Hutchings/Reuters/Corbis; Page 418: © AP Images/Xinhua/Gao Haorong

Index

Page numbers followed by *f* or *t* indicate material in figures or tables, respectively.